America's Top Medical, Education & Human Services Jobs

Detailed Information on 88 Major Jobs at All Levels of Education and Training

FIFTH EDITION

J. Michael Farr

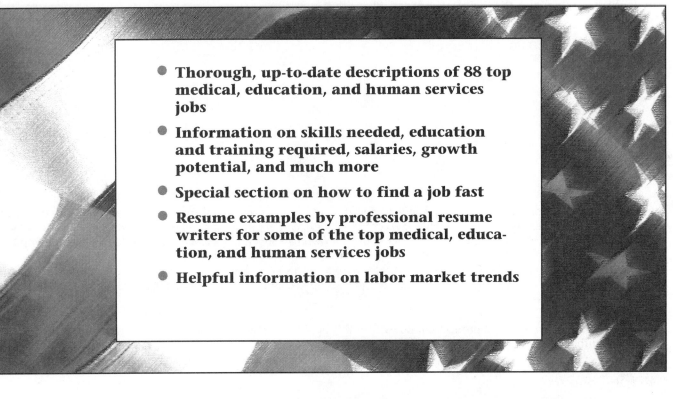

- **Thorough, up-to-date descriptions of 88 top medical, education, and human services jobs**

- **Information on skills needed, education and training required, salaries, growth potential, and much more**

- **Special section on how to find a job fast**

- **Resume examples by professional resume writers for some of the top medical, education, and human services jobs**

- **Helpful information on labor market trends**

jist Works

America's Top Medical, Education & Human Services Jobs, *Fifth Edition*
Detailed Information on 88 Major Jobs at All Levels of Education and Training

© 2001 by J. Michael Farr

Published by JIST Works, an imprint of JIST Publishing, Inc.
8902 Otis Avenue
Indianapolis, IN 46216-1033
Phone: 800-648-JIST   Fax: 800-JIST-FAX   E-mail: editorial@jist.com
Visit our Web site at **www.jist.com** for more details on JIST, free job search information and book chapters, and ordering information on our many products!

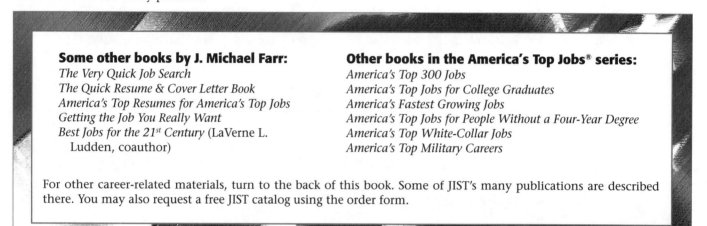

Some other books by J. Michael Farr:
The Very Quick Job Search
The Quick Resume & Cover Letter Book
America's Top Resumes for America's Top Jobs
Getting the Job You Really Want
Best Jobs for the 21ˢᵗ Century (LaVerne L.
    Ludden, coauthor)

Other books in the America's Top Jobs® series:
America's Top 300 Jobs
America's Top Jobs for College Graduates
America's Fastest Growing Jobs
America's Top Jobs for People Without a Four-Year Degree
America's Top White-Collar Jobs
America's Top Military Careers

For other career-related materials, turn to the back of this book. Some of JIST's many publications are described there. You may also request a free JIST catalog using the order form.

Quantity discounts are available for JIST books. Please call our Sales Department at 1-800-648-5478 for more information and a free catalog.

Editors: Susan Pines, Audra McFarland, Veda Dickerson
Cover and Interior Designer: Aleata Howard
Interior Layout: Carolyn J. Newland
Proofreader: Rebecca York

Printed in the United States of America

03 02 01 00   9 8 7 6 5 4 3 2 1

ISBN 1-56370-721-7

Relax—You Don't Have to Read This Whole Book!

This is a big book, but you don't need to read it all. I've organized it into easy-to-use sections so you can browse just the information you want. To get started, simply scan the table of contents, where you'll find brief explanations of the major sections plus a list of the jobs described in Section One. Really, this book is easy to use, and I hope that it helps you.

Some of the Best Opportunities Are in the Medical, Education, and Human Services Fields

The medical, education, and human services fields are large, rapidly growing, and provide many job opportunities at all levels of education and training. Many of these jobs require advanced education or substantial experience, while others offer entry-level and part-time opportunities that can lead to more responsibility later. This book features 88 descriptions of the diverse pursuits found in three fast-growing fields.

Who Should Use This Book?

Although job descriptions cover the largest part of this book, it contains other helpful information as well. I've spent quite a bit of time thinking about how to make this book's contents useful for a variety of situations, including the following:

- **For exploring career options.** The descriptions give a wealth of information on many of the most desirable jobs in the labor market.

- **For considering more education or training.** The information here can help you avoid costly mistakes in choosing a career or deciding on additional training or education—and increase your chances of planning a bright future.

- **For job seeking.** This book will help you identify new job targets, prepare for interviews, and write targeted resumes. The advice in Section Two has been proven to cut job search time in half!

- **For counseling.** This is a valuable source of information on jobs and trends. Section One provides thorough job descriptions, and Section Three gives data on trends in jobs and industries.

Credits: The occupational descriptions in this book come from the good people at the U.S. Department of Labor, as published in the most recent edition of the *Occupational Outlook Handbook*. The *OOH* is the best source of career information available, and the descriptions include the latest data on earnings and other details. The information in Section Three on labor market trends is also from various sources at the U.S. Department of Labor. Thank you to all the people at the Labor Department who toil on gathering, compiling, analyzing, and making sense of this information. It's good stuff, and I hope you can make good use of it.

Mike Farr

Mike Farr

Table of Contents

Summary of Major Sections

Introduction. The introduction explains each job description element, gives tips on using the book for career exploration and job seeking, and provides other details. *The introduction begins on page 1.*

Section One: Descriptions of 88 Major Medical, Education & Human Services Jobs. This is the book's major section, with thorough descriptions of 88 jobs in the medical, education, and human services areas. Each description gives information on working conditions, skills required, growth projections, training or education needed, typical earnings, and much more. The jobs are presented in alphabetic order. They are listed with their page numbers beginning at right. *Section One begins on page 9.*

Section Two: The Quick Job Search—Advice on Planning Your Career and Getting a Good Job in Less Time. This brief but important section offers results-oriented career planning and job search techniques, including tips on exploring career options, defining your ideal job, writing resumes, getting interviews, answering problem questions, and surviving unemployment. The second part of this section features professionally written and designed resumes for some of America's top medical, education, and human services jobs. *Section Two begins on page 225.*

Section Three: Important Trends in Jobs and Industries. This section includes two well-written articles on labor market trends, plus tables with information on hundreds of major jobs. The articles are short and worth your time. *Section Three begins on page 269.*

Titles of the articles and tables are as follows:

The 88 Jobs Described in Section One

The titles for the 88 jobs described in Section One are listed below in alphabetic order, with the page number where each description begins. Find jobs that seem interesting to you and read those descriptions. The descriptions are easy to understand, but the introduction provides additional information to help you interpret them.

INTRODUCTION

This book is about improving your life, not just about selecting a job. The right job will have an enormous impact on how you live your life.

According to information provided by the U.S. Department of Labor, overall employment is projected to grow 14 percent through the year 2008. But the growth rates for employment in the industries covered in this book are projected to be even higher:

- Health services up 25.7 percent

- Educational services up 15.3 percent

- Social services up 41 percent

Also, many of the specific occupations within these industries are projected to grow rapidly. For example, of the 20 fastest growing occupations, more than half are in the medical, education, and human services areas.

In selecting jobs for this book, I included ones that require special training or experience, such as counselor, dentist, occupational therapist, physician assistant, and special education teacher. But you will also find jobs such as janitor, busdriver, and secretary. I included these more general jobs to help you understand that any complex organization, such as a hospital or school, needs people with a wide range of skills.

A certain type of work or workplace may interest you as much as a particular job. For example, if you are interested in public relations, you can do this in a variety of work environments, industries, and jobs—including ones in the medical, education, and human services areas.

While a huge amount of information is available on occupations, most people don't know where to find accurate, reliable facts to help them make good career decisions—or they don't take the time to look. Important choices such as what to do with your career or whether to get additional training or education deserve your time.

If you are considering a job change, this book will likely help you identify one or more interesting possibilities. If you are considering more training or education, this book will help with solid information. More training and education is typically required to get better jobs now, but some jobs that have high pay do not require advanced education. The education, training, skills, and experience needed for the jobs described in this book vary enormously. This book is designed to give you facts to help you explore your options.

Also remember that money is not everything. The time you spend in career planning can pay off in more than higher earnings. Being satisfied with your work—and your life—is often more important than how much you earn. This book can help you find the work that suits you best.

Keep in Mind That Your Situation Is *Not* "Average"

While the employment growth and earnings trends for many occupations and industries are quite positive, the averages in this book will not be true for many individuals. Within any field, some earn much more and some much less.

My point is, your situation is probably not average. Some people do better than others, and others are willing to accept less pay for a more desirable work environment. Earnings vary enormously in different parts of the country, in different occupations, and in different industries. But this book's solid information is a great place to start. Good information will give you a strong foundation for good decisions.

Four Important Labor Market Trends That Will Affect Your Career

Our economy has changed in dramatic ways over the past 10 years, with profound effects on how we work and live. Section Three provides more information on labor market trends but, in case you don't read it, here are four trends that you simply *must* consider.

I. Education and Earnings Are Related

It should come as no surprise that people with higher education and training levels have higher average earnings. The data that follows comes from the Department of Labor's Internet site. The site presents the median earnings for people with various levels of education (median is the point where half earn more and half less) as well as the average percentage unemployed. Based on this information, I computed the earnings advantage at various levels of education compared to those with a high school diploma.

Earnings and Unemployment Rate for Year-Round, Full-Time Workers Age 25 and Over, by Educational Attainment			
Level of Education	**Median Annual Earnings**	**Premium Over High School Grads**	**Unemployment Rate**
Professional degree	$72,700	180%	1.3%
Doctoral degree	$62,400	140%	1.4%
Master's degree	$50,000	92%	1.6%
Bachelor's degree	$40,100	54%	1.9%
Associate degree	$31,700	22%	2.5%
Some college, no degree	$30,400	17%	3.2%
High school graduate	$26,000	—	4.0%
Less than a high school diploma	$19,700	–24%	7.1%

Source: Unemployment rate—Bureau of Labor Statistics, 1998 data; Earnings—Bureau of the Census, 1997 data

The earnings difference between a college graduate and someone with a high school education is $14,100 a year—enough to buy a nice car, make a down payment on a house, or even take a month's vacation for two to Europe. As you see, over a lifetime, this earnings difference will make an enormous difference in lifestyle.

And there is more. Jobs that require a four-year college degree are projected to grow about twice as fast as jobs that do not. People with higher levels of education also tend to be unemployed at lower rates and for shorter periods. Overall, the data on earnings and other criteria indicate that those with more education and training do better than those with less. There are exceptions, of course, but the facts are quite clear.

Many jobs can be obtained without a college degree, but most better paying jobs require training beyond high school or substantial work experience. Still, some workers without college degrees earn more than those with degrees. According to the U.S. Department of Labor, two out of five workers without

college degrees earned more than the average for all workers. One in six earned as much—or more—than the average for those with four-year college degrees.

2. Knowledge of Computer and Other Technologies Is Increasingly Important

As you looked over the list of jobs on the contents page, you may have noticed that many require computer or technical skills. Even jobs that do not appear to be technical often call for computer literacy. Bookkeepers without basic computer skills will have limited job options, since most bookkeeping jobs now require such skills. Maintenance mechanics and many others often need technical training to handle increasingly technical jobs.

In all fields, those without job-related technical and computer skills will have a more difficult time finding good opportunities since they are competing with those who have these skills. Older workers, by the way, often do not have the computer skills that younger workers do. Employers tend to hire the skills they need, and people without these abilities won't get the best jobs.

3. Ongoing Education and Training Are Essential

School and work once were separate activities, and most people did not go back to school when they began working. But with rapid changes in technology, most people will be or are required to learn throughout their work lives. Jobs are constantly upgraded, and today's jobs often cannot be handled with the knowledge and skills that workers had just a few years ago. To remain competitive, those without technical or computer skills must get them. Those who do not will face increasingly limited job options.

What this means is that you should plan to upgrade your job skills throughout your working life. This can include taking formal courses—or it could mean reading work-related magazines at home, signing up for on-the-job training, and participating in other forms of education. Continuing to upgrade your work-related skills is no longer optional for most jobs, and you ignore doing so at your peril.

4. Good Career Planning Has Increased in Importance

Most people spend more time watching TV during a week than they spend on career planning during an entire year. Yet most people will change their jobs many times and make major career changes five to seven times. It just makes sense to spend more time on career planning.

While you probably picked up this book for its information on jobs, it also provides a great deal of information on career planning. For example, Section Two gives career and job search

advice, and Section Three has good information on labor market trends and other important topics. I urge you to read these and related materials because career planning and job-seeking skills are survival skills for this new economy.

Information on the Major Sections of This Book

It should be easy to understand how to use this book. I offered some brief comments on each section in the table of contents, and that may be all you need. If you want more, here are some additional details that you may find useful.

Section One: Descriptions of 88 Major Medical, Education & Human Services Jobs

Section One is the main part of the book and probably the reason you picked it up. It contains brief, well-written descriptions for 88 major jobs in the medical, education, and human services areas. These jobs are presented in alphabetic order. To make the job descriptions easy to find, I created a table of contents that shows where each one begins.

Together, the jobs in Section One provide enormous variety at all levels of earnings and training. One way to explore career options is to go to the table of contents and identify those jobs that seem interesting. You can quickly spot jobs you want to learn more about, and you may see other jobs that you had not considered before.

Your next step would be to read the descriptions for the jobs that interest you and, based on what you learn, identify those that *most* interest you. These are the jobs you should consider, and Sections Two and Three will give you additional information on how you might best do so.

Each occupational description in this book follows a standard format, making it easier for you to compare jobs. This overview explains how the occupational descriptions are organized. It highlights information presented in each part of a description, gives examples of specific occupations in some cases, and offers some hints on how to interpret the information provided.

Job Title

This is the title used for the job in the *Occupational Outlook Handbook*, published by the U.S. Department of Labor.

Those Numbers at the Beginning of Each Description

The numbers in parentheses that appear just below the title of most occupational descriptions are from the new Occupational Information Network (O*NET). The O*NET was developed by the U.S. Department of Labor to replace the older *Dictionary of Occupational Titles (DOT)*. Like the *DOT* in the past, the O*NET is used by state employment service offices to classify applicants and job openings, and by some career information centers and libraries to file occupational information.

Significant Points

The bullet points under "Significant Points" highlight key characteristics for each job.

Nature of the Work

This segment discusses what workers do. Individual job duties may vary by industry or employer. For instance, workers in larger firms tend to be more specialized, whereas those in smaller firms often have a wider variety of duties. Most occupations have several levels of skills and responsibilities through which workers may progress. Beginners may start as trainees performing routine tasks under close supervision. Experienced workers usually undertake more difficult tasks and are expected to perform with less supervision.

The influence of technological advancements on the way work is done is mentioned. For example, the Internet allows cleaning supervisors to acquire supplies with a click of the mouse, saving time and money. This part also discusses emerging specialties within occupations.

Working Conditions

This part identifies the typical hours worked, the workplace environment, susceptibility to injury, special equipment, physical activities, and the extent of travel required. In many occupations people work regular business hours—40 hours a week, Monday through Friday—but many do not. For example, people in food and beverage service occupations often work evenings and weekends.

The work setting can range from a hospital, to a high school, to a private home. Police and detectives might be susceptible to injury, while paralegals have high job-related stress. Nuclear medicine technologists may wear protective clothing or equipment; veterinary assistants do physically demanding work; and registered nurses frequently work at night.

Employment

This part reports the number of jobs the occupation provided in 1998 and the key industries where these jobs are found. When significant, the geographic distribution of jobs and the proportion of part-time (less than 35 hours a week) and self-employed workers in the occupation are mentioned.

Self-employed workers accounted for nearly 9 percent of the workforce in 1998; however, they were concentrated in a small number of occupations.

Training, Other Qualifications, and Advancement

After knowing what a job is all about, a person must understand how to train for it. This part describes the most significant sources of training, including the training preferred by employers, the typical length of training, and advancement possibilities. In addition to training requirements, the descriptions also mention desirable skills, aptitudes, and personal characteristics.

Some occupations require certification or licensing to enter the field, to advance, or to practice independently. Certification or licensing generally involves completing courses and passing examinations. Many occupations increasingly have continuing education or skill improvement requirements to keep up with the changing economy or to improve advancement opportunities.

Key Phrases Used in the Descriptions

This box explains how to interpret the key phrases used to describe projected changes in employment. It also explains the terms used to describe the relationship between the number of job openings and the number of job seekers. The descriptions of this relationship in a particular occupation reflect the knowledge and judgment of economists in the Bureau's Office of Employment Projections.

Changing Employment Between 1998 and 2008

If the statement reads:	Employment is projected to:
Grow much faster than average	Increase 36 percent or more
Grow faster than average	Increase 21 to 35 percent
Grow about as fast as average	Increase 10 to 20 percent
Grow more slowly than average or little or no change	Increase 0 to 9 percent
Decline	Decrease 1 percent or more

Opportunities and Competition for Jobs

If the statement reads:	Job openings compared to job seekers may be:
Very good to excellent opportunities	More numerous
Good or favorable opportunities	In rough balance
May face keen competition or can expect keen competition	Fewer

---

Job Outlook

In planning for the future, an individual should consider potential job opportunities. This part describes the factors that

will result in growth or decline in the number of jobs. In some cases, this book mentions the relative number of job openings an occupation is likely to provide. Occupations that are large and have high turnover rates generally provide the most job openings—reflecting the need to replace workers who transfer to other occupations or stop working.

Some descriptions discuss the relationship between the number of job seekers and job openings. In some occupations, there is a rough balance between job seekers and openings, whereas other occupations are characterized by shortages or surpluses. Limited training facilities, salary regulations, or undesirable aspects of the work can cause shortages of entrants. On the other hand, glamorous or potentially high-paying occupations generally have surpluses of job seekers. Variation in job opportunities by industry, size of firm, or geographic location also may be discussed. Even in crowded fields, job openings do exist. Good students or well-qualified individuals should not be deterred from undertaking training or seeking entry.

Susceptibility to layoffs due to imports, slowdowns in economic activity, technological advancements, or budget cuts are also addressed in this part.

Earnings

This part discusses typical earnings and how workers are compensated—annual salaries, hourly wages, commissions, piece rates, tips, or bonuses. Within every occupation, earnings vary by experience, responsibility, performance, tenure, and geographic area. Earnings data from the Bureau of Labor Statistics and, in some cases, from outside sources are included. Data may cover the entire occupation or a specific group within the occupation.

Benefits account for more than a quarter of total compensation costs to employers. Benefits such as paid vacation, health insurance, and sick leave generally are not mentioned because they are so widespread. Less common benefits include child care, tuition for dependents, housing assistance, summers off, and free or discounted merchandise or services. Employers increasingly offer flexible hours and profit-sharing plans to attract and retain highly qualified workers.

Related Occupations

Occupations involving similar aptitudes, interests, education, and training are listed.

Sources of Additional Information

No single publication can completely describe all aspects of an occupation. Thus, this book lists mailing addresses for associations, government agencies, unions, and other organizations that can provide occupational information. In some cases, toll-free phone numbers and Internet addresses are listed. Free or relatively inexpensive publications offering more information may be mentioned; some of these may also be available in libraries, school career centers, guidance offices, or on the Internet.

Section Two: The Quick Job Search—Advice on Planning Your Career and Getting a Good Job in Less Time

For the past 20 years, I've been interested in helping people find better jobs in less time. If you have ever experienced unemployment, you know it is not pleasant. Unemployment is something most people want to get over quickly, and the quicker the better. Section Two will give you some techniques to help.

I know that most people who read this book want to improve themselves. You want to look at career and training options that lead to a better job and life in whatever way you define this—better pay, more flexibility, more enjoyable or more meaningful work, to prove to your mom that you really can do anything you set your mind to, and so on. That is why I included advice on career planning and job search in Section Two. It's a short section, but it includes the basics that are most important in planning your career and in reducing the time it takes to get a job. I hope it will get you thinking about what is important to you in the long run.

I know you will resist completing the activities in Section Two, but consider this: It is often not the best person who gets the job, it is the best job seeker. Those who do their career planning and job search homework often get jobs over those with better credentials.

The reason is that those who have spent time planning their careers and who know how to conduct an effective job search have distinct advantages over those who do not:

1. They get more interviews, including many for jobs that will never be advertised.

2. They do better in interviews.

People who understand what they want and what they have to offer employers will present their skills more convincingly and are much better at answering problem questions. And, because they have learned more about job search techniques, they are likely to get more interviews with employers who need the skills they have.

Doing better in interviews will often make the difference between getting a job offer or sitting at home. And spending some time on planning your career can make an enormous difference to your happiness and lifestyle over time. So please consider reading Section Two and completing its activities. Go ahead and schedule a time right now to at least read Section Two. An hour or so spent there can help you do just enough better in your career planning, job seeking, or interviewing to make the difference. Go ahead—get out your schedule book and get it over with (nag, nag, nag).

The second part of Section Two showcases professionally written resumes for some of America's top medical, education, and human services jobs. Use these examples when creating your resume.

One other thing: If you work through Section Two, and it helps you in some significant way, I'd like to hear from you. Please write or e-mail me via the publisher, whose contact information appears elsewhere in this book.

Section Three: Important Trends in Jobs and Industries

This section is made up of two very good articles on labor market trends and additional data on hundreds of major jobs. The information comes directly from various U.S. Department of Labor sources. The articles are interesting, well written, and short. I know this section sounds boring, but the articles are quick reads and will give you a good idea of the trends that will impact your career in the years to come.

The first article is titled "Tomorrow's Jobs: Important Labor Market Trends Through the Year 2008." It highlights the many important trends in employment and includes information on the fastest growing jobs, jobs with high pay at various levels of education, and other details.

The second article is titled "Employment Trends in Major Industries." I included this information because you can often use your skills or training in industries you may not have considered. It provides a good review of major trends with an emphasis on helping you make good employment decisions. This information can help you seek jobs in industries with higher pay or that are more likely to interest you. Also, the industry you work in, while often overlooked, is often as important as the occupation you choose.

At the end of "Employment Trends in Major Industries," I also included brief reviews of the three industries that are the focus of this book: health, education, and social services. Like the article itself, these reviews are based on U.S. Department of Labor information.

After the two articles comes a table titled "Details on 500 Major Jobs." Tables on various jobs are, I admit, boring. This one provides growth projections and other information on 500 jobs that employ over 90 percent of the labor force. This table covers many more jobs than described in this book, and reviewing it can help you identify possibilities you might not otherwise consider.

The final part of Section Three includes a list I created that arranges a group of major jobs in order of percentage growth

projected through 2008. This is an interesting list, and it includes all the jobs described in Section One as well as many others. Use the details to be the life of the next party you attend.

Tips on Using This Book

This book is based on information provided by government sources, so it includes the most up-to-date and accurate data available anywhere. The entries are well written and pack a lot of information into short descriptions. The information in *America's Top Medical, Education & Human Services Jobs* is used in many ways, but this discussion will provide tips on the four most frequent uses:

- For exploring career, education, or training alternatives
- For job seekers
- For employers and business people
- For counselors, instructors, and other career specialists

Tips for Exploring Career, Education, or Training Alternatives

America's Top Medical, Education & Human Services Jobs is an excellent resource for anyone exploring career, education, or training alternatives. While many people take career interest tests to identify career options, using this book can perform a similar function.

Many people do not have a good idea of what they want to do in their careers. They may be considering additional training or education—but don't know what sort they should get. If you are one of these people, *America's Top Medical, Education & Human Services Jobs* can help in several ways. Here are a few pointers.

Review the list of jobs. Trust yourself. Many research studies indicate that most people have a good sense of their interests. Your interests can be used to guide you to career options to consider in more detail.

Begin by looking over the occupations listed in the table of contents. If others will be using this book, please don't mark in it. Instead, on a separate sheet of paper, list the jobs that interest you. Or make a photocopy of the table of contents and mark the jobs that interest you. Look at all the jobs, because you may identify previously overlooked possibilities.

The next step is to read the job descriptions that most interest you. A quick review will often eliminate one or more of these jobs based on pay, working conditions, education required, or other considerations. Once you have identified the three or four jobs that seem most interesting, research each one more thoroughly before making any important decisions.

Study the jobs and their training and education requirements. Too many people decide to obtain additional training or education without knowing much about the jobs the training will lead to. Reviewing the descriptions in *America's Top Medical, Education & Human Services Jobs* is one way to learn more about an occupation before you enroll in an education or training program. If you are currently a student, the job descriptions in this book can also help you decide on a major course of study or learn more about the jobs for which your studies are preparing you.

Do not too quickly eliminate a job that interests you. If a job requires more education or training than you currently have, you can obtain this training in many ways.

Don't abandon your past experience and education too quickly. If you have significant work experience, training, or education, these should not be abandoned too quickly. Many skills you have learned and used in previous jobs or other settings can apply to related jobs. Many people have changed careers after carefully considering what they wanted to do and found that the skills they have can still be used.

America's Top Medical, Education & Human Services Jobs can help you explore career options in several ways. First, carefully review descriptions for jobs you have held in the past. On a separate sheet of paper, write the words used to describe the skills needed in those jobs. Then do the same with jobs that interest you now. You will be able to identify skills used in previous jobs that are needed in the jobs that interest you for the future. These "transferable" skills form the basis for transferring to a new career.

You can also identify skills you have developed or used in nonwork activities, such as hobbies, family responsibilities, volunteer work, school, military, and extracurricular activities.

The descriptions in *America's Top Medical, Education & Human Services Jobs* can even be used if you want to stay with the same employer. For example, you may identify jobs within your organization that offer more rewarding work, higher pay, or other advantages over your present job. Read the descriptions related to these jobs, and you may be able to transfer into another job rather than leave the organization.

Tips for Job Seekers

You can use the descriptions in this book to give you an edge in finding job openings and in getting job offers over those with better credentials. Here are some ways *America's Top Medical, Education & Human Services Jobs* can help you in the job search.

Identify related job targets. You are probably limiting your job search to a small number of jobs that you feel qualified for. But this approach eliminates many jobs that you could do and could enjoy. Your search for a new job should be broadened to include more possibilities.

Go through the entire list of jobs in the table of contents and check any that require skills similar to those you have. Look over all jobs, since doing so will sometimes help you identify targets that you would have otherwise overlooked.

Many people are also not aware of the many specialized jobs related to their training or experience. The descriptions in *America's Top Medical, Education & Human Services Jobs* are for major job titles, but a variety of more specialized jobs may require similar skills. Reference books that list more specialized job titles include the *Enhanced Occupational Outlook Handbook* and *The O*NET Dictionary of Occupational Titles*. Both are published by JIST. Similar information is available in software form.

The descriptions can also point out job prospects related to the jobs that interest you but that have higher responsibility or compensation levels. While you may not consider yourself qualified for such jobs now, you should think about seeking jobs that are above your previous levels but within your ability to handle.

Prepare for interviews. This book's job descriptions are an essential source of information to help you prepare for interviews. Before an interview, carefully review the description for the job, and you will be much better prepared to emphasize your key skills. You should also review descriptions for past jobs and identify skills needed in the new job.

Negotiate pay. The job descriptions in this book will help you know what pay range to expect. Note that local pay and other details can differ substantially from the national averages in the descriptions.

Tips for Employers and Business People

Employers, human resource personnel, and other business people can use this book's information in a variety of ways. The material can help you write job descriptions, study pay ranges, and set criteria for new employees. The information can also help you conduct more effective interviews by providing a list of key skills needed by new hires.

Tips for Counselors, Instructors, and Other Career Specialists

Suggestions for using this book to help people explore career options or find jobs are mostly self-explanatory or contained in the previous tips. My best suggestion to professionals is to get this book off the bookshelf and into the hands of those who need it. Leave it on a table or desk and show people how the information can help them. Wear this book out! Its real value is as a tool used often and well.

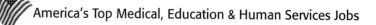

Additional Information About the Projections

Readers interested in more information about projections and details on the labor force, economic growth, industry and occupational employment, or the methods and assumptions used in this book's projections should consult the November 1999 edition of the *Monthly Labor Review,* published by the Bureau of Labor Statistics, or the Winter 1999–2000 *Occupational Outlook Quarterly,* also published by BLS. Information on the limitations inherent in economic projections also can be found in these publications.

For more information about employment change, job openings, earnings, unemployment rates, and training requirements by occupation, consult *Occupational Projections and Training Data,* 2000–01 Edition, published by the BLS.

For occupational information from an industry perspective, including some occupations and career paths that *America's Top Medical, Education & Human Services Jobs* does not cover, consult another BLS publication—the *Career Guide to Industries,* 2000–2001 Edition. This book is also available from JIST.

Section One

Descriptions of 88 Major Medical, Education & Human Services Jobs

This is the book's major section. It contains descriptions for 88 major occupations arranged in alphabetic order. Refer to the table of contents for a list of the jobs and the page numbers where their descriptions begin.

A good way to identify job descriptions you want to explore is to use the table of contents as a checklist. If you are interested in technical jobs, for example, you can go through the list and quickly identify those you want to learn more about. If you look at all the titles, you may spot other jobs that might be interesting, and you should consider these as well.

While the descriptions are easy to understand, the introduction provides additional information that will help you interpret them. If you are not the sort of person to read introductions, feel free to jump right in and begin reading the descriptions that interest you. When reading the descriptions, keep in mind that they present information that is the average for the country. Conditions in your area and with specific employers may be quite different. For example, pay may be higher or lower than stated in the descriptions, and the same jobs are often in great demand in one location and hard to obtain in another. People just entering a job will typically earn less than the average pay for more experienced workers. These are just several examples of how the typical situation may not fit your own.

Of course, there is more to learning about and selecting career options than simply reading job descriptions. For this reason, I suggest you read Section Two, which provides advice on planning your career and on getting a good job. Section Three also offers information to help you weigh your options and make good decisions. For example, the article titled "Tomorrow's Jobs: Important Labor Market Trends Through the Year 2008" discusses rapidly growing jobs and trends in all major occupational groups.

Adult and Vocational Education Teachers

(O*NET 31314 and 31317)

Significant Points

- More than one-third work part time; many also hold other jobs—often involving work related to the subject they teach.

- Practical experience is often all that is needed to teach vocational courses, but a graduate degree may be required to teach nonvocational courses.

- Opportunities should be best for part-time positions.

Nature of the Work

Adult and vocational education teachers work in four main areas: adult vocational-technical education, adult remedial education, adult continuing education, and prebaccalaureate training. *Adult vocational-technical education teachers* provide instruction for occupations that do not require a college degree, such as welder, dental hygienist, x-ray technician, auto mechanic, and cosmetologist. Other instructors help people update their job skills or adapt to technological advances. For example, an *adult education teacher* may train students how to use new computer software programs. *Adult remedial education teachers* provide instruction in basic education courses for school dropouts or others who need to upgrade their skills to find a job. *Adult continuing education teachers* teach courses that students take for personal enrichment, such as cooking, dancing, writing, exercise and physical fitness, photography, and personal finance.

Adult and vocational education teachers may lecture in classrooms or work in an industry or laboratory setting to give students hands-on experience. Increasingly, adult vocational-technical education teachers integrate academic and vocational curriculums so students obtain a variety of skills that can be applied to the "real world." For example, an electronics student may be required to take courses in principles of mathematics and science in conjunction with hands-on electronics skills. Generally, teachers demonstrate techniques, have students apply them, and critique the students' work. For example, welding instructors show students various welding techniques, watch them use tools and equipment, and have them repeat procedures until they meet the specific standards required by the trade.

Increasingly, minimum standards of proficiency are being established for students in various vocational-technical fields. Adult and vocational education teachers must be aware of new standards and develop lesson plans to ensure that students meet basic criteria. Also, adult and vocational education teachers and community colleges are assuming a greater role in students' transition from school to work by helping establish internships and providing information about prospective employers.

Businesses also are increasingly providing their employees with work-related training to keep up with changing technology. Training is often provided through contractors, professional associations, or community colleges.

Adult education teachers who instruct in adult basic education programs may work with students who do not speak English; teach adults reading, writing, and mathematics up to the 8th-grade level; or teach adults through the 12th-grade level in preparation for the General Educational Development tests (GED). The GED offers the equivalent of a high school diploma. These teachers may refer students for counseling or job placement. Because many people who need adult basic education are reluctant to seek it, teachers also may recruit participants.

Adult and vocational education teachers also prepare lessons and assignments, grade papers and do related paperwork, attend faculty and professional meetings, and stay abreast of developments in their field.

Working Conditions

Since adult and vocational education teachers work with adult students, they do not encounter some of the behavioral or social problems sometimes found with younger students. The adults attend by choice, are highly motivated, and bring years of experience to the classroom—attributes that can make teaching these students rewarding and satisfying. However, teachers in adult basic education deal with students at different levels of development who may lack effective study skills and self-confidence and who may require more attention and patience than other students.

More than 1 in 3 adult and vocational education teachers work part time. To accommodate students who may have job or family responsibilities, many institutions offer courses at night or on weekends, which range from two- to four-hour workshops and from one-day mini-sessions to semester-long courses. Some adult and vocational education teachers have several part-time teaching assignments or work a full-time job in addition to their part-time teaching job, leading to long hours and a hectic schedule.

Although most adult and vocational education teachers work in classroom settings, some are consultants to businesses and teach classes at job sites.

Employment

Adult and vocational education teachers held about 588,000 jobs in 1998. About one-fifth were self-employed.

A variety of establishments employed adult and vocational education teachers in 1998: public school systems; community and junior colleges; universities; businesses that provide formal education and training for their employees; schools and institutes that teach automotive repair, bartending, business, computer skills, electronics, medical technology, and other subjects; dance studios; job training centers; community organizations; labor unions; and religious organizations.

Training, Other Qualifications, and Advancement

Training requirements vary by State and by subject. In general, teachers need work or other experiences in their field, and a license or certificate in fields where these usually are required for full professional status. In some cases, particularly at educational institutions, a master's or doctoral degree is required to teach nonvocational courses, which can be applied towards a 4-year degree program. Many vocational teachers in junior or community colleges do not have a master's or doctoral degree but draw on their work experience and knowledge, bringing practical experience to the classroom. For general adult education classes, an acceptable portfolio of work is required. For example, to secure a job teaching a photography course, an applicant would need to show examples of previous work.

Most States and the District of Columbia require adult basic education teachers and adult literacy instructors to have a bachelor's degree from an approved teacher training program, and some States require teacher certification.

Adult and vocational education teachers update their skills through continuing education to maintain certification—requirements vary among institutions. Teachers may take part in seminars, conferences, or graduate courses in adult education or training and development, or may return to work in business or industry for a limited time. Businesses are playing a growing role in adult education, forming consortiums with training institutions and junior colleges and providing input to curriculum development. Adult and vocational education teachers maintain an ongoing dialogue with businesses to determine the most current skills needed in the workplace.

Adult and vocational education teachers should communicate and relate well with students, enjoy working with them, and be able to motivate them. Adult basic education instructors, in particular, must be patient, understanding, and supportive in order to make students comfortable, develop trust, and help them better understand concepts.

Some teachers advance to administrative positions in departments of education, colleges and universities, and corporate training departments. These positions often require advanced degrees, such as a doctorate in adult and continuing education.

Job Outlook

Employment of adult and vocational education teachers is expected to grow about as fast as the average for all occupations through 2008 as the demand for adult education programs continues to rise. Opportunities should be best for part-time positions, especially in fields such as computer technology, automotive mechanics, and medical technology, which offer attractive—and often higher-paying—job opportunities outside of teaching.

According to the National Center for Education Statistics, an estimated 4 out of 10 adults participated in some form of adult education in 1997. Participation in continuing education grows as the educational attainment of the population increases. To keep abreast of changes in their fields and advances in technology, an increasing number of adults are taking courses—often subsidized or funded entirely by employers—for career advancement or to upgrade their skills. In addition, an increasing number of adults are participating in classes for personal enrichment and enjoyment. Enrollment in adult basic education and literacy programs is increasing because of changes in immigration policy that require basic competency in English and civics. And, more employers are demanding higher levels of basic academic skills—reading, writing, and arithmetic—which is increasing enrollment in remedial education and GED preparation classes.

Employment growth of adult vocational-technical education teachers will result from the need to train young adults for entry-level jobs. Experienced workers who want to switch fields or whose jobs have been eliminated due to changing technology or business reorganization also require training. Businesses are finding it essential to provide training to their workers to remain productive and globally competitive. Cooperation between businesses and educational institutions continues to increase to ensure that students are taught the skills employers desire. This should result in greater demand for adult and vocational education teachers, particularly at community and junior colleges. Since adult education programs receive State and Federal funding, employment growth may be affected by government budgets.

Additional job openings for adult and vocational education teachers will stem from the need to replace persons who leave the occupation. Many teach part time and move into and out of the occupation for other jobs, family responsibilities, or retirement.

Earnings

Median annual earnings of adult education teachers were $24,800 in 1998. The middle 50 percent earned between $18,170 and $34,140. The lowest 10 percent earned less than $13,080, and the highest 10 percent earned more than $47,430. Median annual earnings in the industries employing the largest numbers of adult education teachers in 1997 were:

Elementary and secondary schools	$29,900
Colleges and universities	25,900
Schools and educational services, not elsewhere classified	24,600
Dance studios, schools, and halls	23,600
Individual and family services	19,400

Median annual earnings of vocational education teachers were $34,430 in 1998. The middle 50 percent earned between $24,890 and $45,230. The lowest 10 percent earned less than $18,010, and the highest 10 percent earned more than $63,850. Median annual earnings in the industries employing the largest numbers of vocational education teachers in 1997 were:

State government, except education and hospitals	$37,200
Elementary and secondary schools	37,000
Colleges and universities	34,800
Vocational schools	32,600
Schools and educational services, not elsewhere classified	24,700

Earnings varied widely by subject, academic credentials, experience, and region of the country. Part-time instructors usually are paid hourly wages and do not receive benefits or pay for preparation time outside of class.

Related Occupations

Adult and vocational education teaching requires a wide variety of skills and aptitudes, including the ability to influence, motivate, train, and teach; organizational, administrative, and communication skills; and creativity. Workers in other occupations that require these aptitudes include other teachers, counselors, school administrators, public relations specialists, employee development specialists, and social workers.

Sources of Additional Information

Information on adult basic education programs and teacher certification requirements is available from State departments of education and local school districts.

For information about adult vocational-technical education teaching positions, contact State departments of vocational-technical education.

For information on adult continuing education teaching positions, contact departments of local government, State adult education departments, schools, colleges and universities, religious organizations, or a wide range of businesses that provide formal training for their employees.

General information on adult and vocational education is available from:

- Association for Career and Technical Education, 1410 King St., Alexandria, VA 22314. Internet: http://www.acteonline.org
- ERIC Clearinghouse on Adult, Career, and Vocational Education, 1900 Kenny Rd., Columbus, OH 43210-1090. Internet: http://www.ericacve.org

Agricultural and Food Scientists

(O*NET 24305A, 24305B, 24305C, and 24305D)

Significant Points

- A large proportion, about 40 percent, of salaried agricultural and food scientists works for Federal, State, and local governments.
- A bachelor's degree in agricultural science is sufficient for some jobs in applied research; a master's or doctoral degree is required for basic research.

- Those with advanced degrees have the best prospects; however, competition may be keen for some basic research jobs if Federal and State funding for these positions is cut.

Nature of the Work

The work of agricultural and food scientists plays an important part in maintaining the Nation's food supply through ensuring agricultural productivity and the safety of the food supply. Agricultural scientists study farm crops and animals and develop ways of improving their quantity and quality. They look for ways to improve crop yield and quality with less labor, control pests and weeds more safely and effectively, and conserve soil and water. They research methods of converting raw agricultural commodities into attractive and healthy food products for consumers.

Agricultural science is closely related to biological science, and agricultural scientists use the principles of biology, chemistry, physics, mathematics, and other sciences to solve problems in agriculture. They often work with biological scientists on basic biological research and in applying to agriculture the advances in knowledge brought about by biotechnology.

Many agricultural scientists work in basic or applied research and development. Others manage or administer research and development programs or manage marketing or production operations in companies that produce food products or agricultural chemicals, supplies, and machinery. Some agricultural scientists are consultants to business firms, private clients, or the government.

Depending on the agricultural or food scientist's area of specialization, the nature of the work performed varies.

Food science. Food scientists and technologists usually work in the food processing industry, universities, or the Federal government and help meet consumer demand for food products that are healthful, safe, palatable, and convenient. To do this, they use their knowledge of chemistry, microbiology, and other sciences to develop new or better ways of preserving, processing, packaging, storing, and delivering foods. Some food scientists engage in basic research, discovering new food sources; analyzing food content to determine levels of vitamins, fat, sugar, or protein; or searching for substitutes for harmful or undesirable additives, such as nitrites. They also develop ways to process, preserve, package, or store food according to industry and government regulations. Others enforce government regulations, inspecting food processing areas and ensuring that sanitation, safety, quality, and waste management standards are met. Food technologists generally work in product development, applying the findings from food science research to the selection, preservation, processing, packaging, distribution, and use of safe, nutritious, and wholesome food.

Plant science. Agronomy, crop science, entomology, and plant breeding are included in plant science. Scientists in these disciplines study plants and their growth in soils, helping producers of food, feed, and fiber crops to continue to feed a growing population while conserving natural resources and maintaining the environment. Agronomists and crop scientists not only help increase productivity, but also study ways to improve the nutritional value of crops and the quality of seed. Some crop scientists study the breeding, physiology, and management of crops and use genetic engineering to develop crops resistant to pests and drought. Entomologists conduct research to develop new technologies to control or eliminate pests in infested areas and prevent the spread of harmful pests to new areas, as well as technologies that are compatible with the environment. They also conduct research or engage in oversight activities aimed at halting the spread of insect-borne disease.

Soil science. Soil scientists study the chemical, physical, biological, and mineralogical composition of soils as they relate to plant or crop growth. They also study the responses of various soil types to fertilizers, tillage practices, and crop rotation. Many soil scientists who work for the Federal Government conduct soil surveys, classifying and mapping soils. They provide information and recommendations to farmers and other landowners regarding the best use of land and plant growth, and how to avoid or correct problems such as erosion. They may also consult with engineers and other technical personnel working on construction projects about the effects of, and solutions to, soil problems. Because soil science is closely related to environmental science, persons trained in soil science also apply their knowledge to ensure environmental quality and effective land use.

Animal science. Animal scientists work to develop better, more efficient ways of producing and processing meat, poultry, eggs, and milk. Dairy scientists, poultry scientists, animal breeders, and other related scientists study the genetics, nutrition, reproduction, growth, and development of domestic farm animals. Some animal scientists inspect and grade livestock food products, purchase livestock, or work in technical sales or marketing. As extension agents or consultants, animal scientists advise agricultural producers on how to upgrade animal housing facilities properly, lower mortality rates, handle waste matter, or increase production of animal products, such as milk and eggs.

Working Conditions

Agricultural scientists involved in management or basic research tend to work regular hours in offices and laboratories. The working environment for those engaged in applied research or product development varies, depending on the discipline of agricultural science and the type of employer. For example, food scientists in private industry may work in test kitchens while investigating new processing techniques. Animal scientists working for Federal, State, or university research stations may spend part of their time at dairies, farrowing houses, feedlots, or farm animal facilities or outdoors conducting research associated with livestock. Soil and crop scientists also spend time outdoors conducting research on farms and agricultural research stations. Entomologists work in laboratories, insectories, or agricultural research stations, and they may also spend time outdoors studying or collecting insects in their natural habitat.

Employment

Agricultural scientists held about 21,000 jobs in 1998. In addition, several thousand persons held agricultural science faculty positions in colleges and universities.

About 40 percent of all nonfaculty salaried agricultural and food scientists work for Federal, State, or local governments. Nearly 1 out of 4 worked for the Federal government in 1998, mostly in the Department of Agriculture. In addition, large numbers worked for State governments at State agricultural colleges or agricultural research stations. Some worked for agricultural service companies; others worked for commercial research and development laboratories, seed companies, pharmaceutical companies, wholesale distributors, and food products companies. About 3,700 agricultural scientists were self-employed in 1998, mainly as consultants.

Training, Other Qualifications, and Advancement

Training requirements for agricultural scientists depend on their specialty and the type of work they perform. A bachelor's degree in agricultural science is sufficient for working some jobs in applied research or for assisting in basic research, but a master's or doctoral degree is required for basic research. A Ph.D. in agricultural science is usually needed for college teaching and for advancement to administrative research positions. Degrees in related sciences such as biology, chemistry, or physics or in related engineering specialties also may qualify persons for some agricultural science jobs.

All States have a land-grant college that offers agricultural science degrees. Many other colleges and universities also offer agricultural science degrees or some agricultural science courses. However, not every school offers all specialties. A typical undergraduate agricultural science curriculum includes communications, economics, business, and physical and life sciences courses, in addition to a wide variety of technical agricultural science courses. For prospective animal scientists, these technical agricultural science courses might include animal breeding, reproductive physiology, nutrition, and meats and muscle biology.

Students preparing as food scientists take courses such as food chemistry, food analysis, food microbiology, and food processing operations. Those preparing as crop or soil scientists take courses in plant pathology, soil chemistry, entomology, plant physiology, and biochemistry, among others. Advanced degree programs include classroom and fieldwork, laboratory research, and a thesis or dissertation based on independent research.

Agricultural and food scientists should be able to work independently or as part of a team and be able to communicate clearly and concisely, both in speaking and in writing. Most agricultural scientists also need an understanding of basic business principles.

The American Society of Agronomy offers certification programs in crops, agronomy, crop advising, soils, horticulture, plant pathology, and weed science. To become certified, applicants must meet certain standards for examination, education, and professional work experience.

Agricultural scientists who have advanced degrees usually begin in research or teaching. With experience, they may advance to jobs such as supervisors of research programs or managers of other agriculture-related activities.

Job Outlook

Employment of agricultural scientists is expected to grow about as fast as the average for all occupations through 2008. Additionally, the need to replace agricultural and food scientists who retire or otherwise leave the occupation permanently will account for many more job openings than projected growth.

Past agricultural research has resulted in the development of higher-yielding crops, crops with better resistance to pests and plant pathogens, and chemically based fertilizers and pesticides. Further research is necessary as insects and diseases continue to adapt to pesticides, and as soil fertility and water quality deteriorate. Agricultural scientists are using new avenues of research in biotechnology to develop plants and food crops that require less fertilizer, fewer pesticides and herbicides, and even less rain.

Agricultural scientists will be needed to balance increased agricultural output with protection and preservation of soil, water, and ecosystems. They will increasingly encourage the practice "sustainable agriculture" by developing and implementing plans to manage pests, crops, soil fertility and erosion, and animal waste in ways that reduce the use of harmful chemicals and do little damage to the natural environment. Also, an expanding population and an increasing public focus on diet, health, and food safety will result in job opportunities for food scientists and technologists.

Graduates with advanced degrees will be in the best position to enter jobs as agricultural scientists. However, competition may be keen for teaching positions in colleges or universities and for some basic research jobs, even for doctoral holders. Federal and State budget cuts may limit funding for these positions through 2008.

Bachelor's degree holders can work in some applied research and product development positions, but usually only in certain subfields, such as food science and technology. Also, the Federal government hires bachelor's degree holders to work as soil scientists. Despite the more limited opportunities for those with only a bachelor's degree to obtain jobs as agricultural scientists, a bachelor's degree in agricultural science is useful for managerial jobs in businesses that deal with ranchers and farmers, such as feed, fertilizer, seed, and farm equipment manufacturers; retailers or wholesalers; and farm credit institutions. Four-year degrees may also help persons enter occupations such as farmer or farm or ranch manager, cooperative extension service agent, agricultural products inspector, or purchasing or sales agent for agricultural commodity or farm supply companies.

Earnings

Median annual earnings of agricultural and food scientists were $42,340 in 1998. The middle 50 percent earned between $32,370 and $59,240. The lowest 10 percent earned less than $24,200, and the highest 10 percent earned more than $79,820.

Average Federal salaries for employees in nonsupervisory, supervisory, and managerial positions in certain agricultural science specialties in 1999 were as follows: Animal science, $69,400; agronomy, $57,200; soil science, $53,600; horticulture, $53,800; and entomology, $65,600.

According to the National Association of Colleges and Employers, beginning salary offers in 1999 for graduates with a bachelor's degree in animal science averaged about $27,600 a year.

Related Occupations

The work of agricultural scientists is closely related to that of biologists and other natural scientists such as chemists, foresters, and conservation scientists. It is also related to agricultural production occupations such as farmer and farm manager and cooperative extension service agent. Certain specialties of agricultural science are also related to other occupations. For example, the work of animal scientists is related to that of veterinarians; horticulturists, to landscape architects; and soil scientists, to soil conservationists.

Sources of Additional Information

Information on careers in agricultural science is available from:

- American Society of Agronomy, Crop Science Society of America, Soil Science Society of America, 677 S. Segoe Rd., Madison, WI 53711-1086.
- Food and Agricultural Careers for Tomorrow, Purdue University, 1140 Agricultural Administration Bldg., West Lafayette, IN 47907-1140.

For information on careers in food technology, write to:

- Institute of Food Technologists, Suite 300, 221 N. LaSalle St., Chicago IL 60601-1291.

For information on education in food safety, contact:

- National Alliance for Food Safety, Office of the Secretariat, 205 Agriculture Building, University of Arkansas, Fayetteville, AR 72701.

For information on careers in entomology, contact:

- Entomological Society of America, 9301 Annapolis Rd., Lanham, MD 20706, Attn: Public Relations Coordinator.

Information on acquiring a job as an agricultural scientist with the Federal government may be obtained from the Office of Personnel Management through a telephone-based system. Consult your telephone directory under U.S. Government for a local number, or call (912) 757-3000 (TDD 912-744-2299). That number is not toll free, and charges may result. Information also is available from their Internet site: http://www.usajobs.opm.gov.

Architects, Except Landscape and Naval

(O*NET 22302)

Significant Points

- About 30 percent were self-employed; that's more than three times the proportion for all professionals.

- Licensing requirements include a professional degree in architecture, a period of practical training or internship, and passing all divisions of the Architect Registration Examination.

- Beginners may face competition, especially for jobs in the most prestigious firms; summer internship experience and knowledge of computer-aided design and drafting technology are advantages.

Nature of the Work

Architects design buildings and other structures. The design of a building involves far more than its appearance. Buildings must also be functional, safe, and economical, and must suit the needs of the people who use them. Architects take all these things into consideration when they design buildings and other structures.

Architects provide professional services to individuals and organizations planning a construction project. They may be involved in all phases of development, from the initial discussion with the client through the entire construction process. Their duties require specific skills: designing, engineering, managing, supervising, and communicating with clients and builders.

The architect and client discuss the objectives, requirements, and budget of a project. In some cases, architects provide various predesign services, such as conducting feasibility and environmental impact studies, selecting a site, or specifying the requirements the design must meet. For example, they may determine space requirements by researching the number and type of potential users of a building. The architect then prepares drawings and a report presenting ideas for the client to review.

After the initial proposals are discussed and accepted, architects develop final construction plans. These plans show the building's appearance and details for its construction. Accompanying these are drawings of the structural system; air-conditioning, heating, and ventilating systems; electrical systems; plumbing; and possibly site and landscape plans. They also specify the building materials and, in some cases, the interior furnishings. In developing designs, architects follow building codes, zoning laws, fire regulations, and other ordinances, such as those requiring easy access by disabled persons. Throughout the planning stage, they make necessary changes. Although they have traditionally used pencil and paper to produce design and construction drawings, architects are increasingly turning to computer-aided design and drafting (CADD) technology for these important tasks.

Architects may also assist the client in obtaining construction bids, selecting a contractor, and negotiating the construction contract. As construction proceeds, they may visit the building site to ensure the contractor is following the design, adhering to the schedule, using the specified materials, and meeting quality work standards. The job is not complete until all construction is finished, required tests are performed, and construction costs are paid. Sometimes, architects also provide post-construction services, such as facilities management. They advise on energy efficiency measures, evaluate how well the building design adapts to the needs of occupants, and make necessary improvements.

Architects design a wide variety of buildings, such as office and apartment buildings, schools, churches, factories, hospitals, houses, and airport terminals. They also design complexes such as urban centers, college campuses, industrial parks, and entire communities. They may also advise on the selection of building sites, prepare cost analysis and land-use studies, and do long-range planning for land development.

Architects sometimes specialize in one phase of work. Some specialize in the design of one type of building—for example, hospitals, schools, or housing. Others focus on planning and predesign services or construction management, and do little design work. They often work with engineers, urban planners, interior designers, landscape architects, and others. In fact, architects spend a great deal of their time coordinating information from, and the work of, other professionals engaged in the same project. Consequently, architects are now using the Internet to update designs and communicate changes for the sake of speed and cost savings.

During a training period leading up to licensing as architects, entry-level workers are called intern-architects. This training period, which generally lasts three years, gives them practical work experience while they prepare for the Architect Registration Examination (ARE). Typical duties may include preparing construction drawings on CADD or assisting in the design of one part of a project.

Working Conditions

Architects usually work in a comfortable environment. Most of their time is spent in offices consulting with clients, developing reports and drawings, and working with other architects and engineers. However, they often visit construction sites to review the progress of projects.

Architects may occasionally be under stress, working nights and weekends to meet deadlines. In 1998, almost 2 out of 5 architects worked more than 40 hours a week, in contrast to 1 in 4 workers in all occupations combined.

Employment

Architects held about 99,000 jobs in 1998. The majority of jobs were in architectural firms—most of which employ fewer than 5 workers. A few worked for general building contractors, and for government agencies responsible for housing, planning, or community development, such as the U.S. Departments of Defense and Interior, and the General Services Administration. About 3 in 10 architects were self-employed.

Training, Other Qualifications, and Advancement

All States and the District of Columbia require individuals to be licensed (registered) before they may call themselves architects or contract to provide architectural services. Many architecture school graduates work in the field even though they are not licensed. However, a licensed architect is required to take legal responsibility for all work. Licensing requirements include a professional degree in architecture, a period of practical training or internship, and passage of all sections of the ARE.

In many States, the professional degree in architecture must be from one of the 105 schools of architecture with programs accredited by the National Architectural Accrediting Board (NAAB). However, State architectural registration boards set their own standards, so graduation from a non NAAB-accredited program may meet the educational requirement for licensing in some States. Several types of professional degrees in architecture are available through colleges and universities. The majority of all architectural degrees are from five-year Bachelor of Architecture programs, intended for students entering from high school or with no previous architectural training. Some schools offer a two-year Master of Architecture program for students with a preprofessional undergraduate degree in architecture or a related area or a three- or four-year Master of Architecture program for students with a degree in another discipline. In addition, there are many combinations and variations of these programs.

The choice of degree type depends upon each individual's preference and educational background. Prospective architecture students should consider the available options before committing to a program. For example, although the 5-year Bachelor of Architecture program offers the fastest route to the professional degree, courses are specialized and, if the student does not complete the program, moving to a nonarchitectural program may be difficult. A typical program includes courses in architectural history and theory, building design, professional practice, math, physical sciences, and liberal arts. Central to most architectural programs is the design studio, where students put into practice the skills and concepts learned in the classroom. During the final semester of many programs, students devote their studio time to creating an architectural project from beginning to end, culminating in a three-dimensional model of their design.

Many schools of architecture also offer graduate education for those who already have a bachelor's or master's degree in architecture or other areas. Although graduate education beyond the professional degree is not required for practicing architects, it is for research, teaching, and certain specialties.

Architects must be able to visually communicate their ideas to clients. Artistic and drawing ability is very helpful in doing this, but not essential. More important are a visual orientation and the ability to conceptualize and understand spatial relationships. Good communication skills, the ability to work independently or as part of a team, and creativity are important qualities for anyone interested in becoming an architect. Computer literacy is also required as most firms use computers for writing specifications, two- and three-dimensional drafting, and financial management. A knowledge of computer-aided design and drafting (CADD) is helpful and will become essential as architectural firms continue to adopt this technology. Recently, the profession recognized National CAD Standards (NCS); architecture students who master NCS will have an advantage in the job market.

All State architectural registration boards require a training period before candidates may sit for the ARE and become licensed. Many States have adopted the training standards established by the Intern Development Program, a branch of the American Institute of Architects and the National Council of Architectural Registration Boards. These standards stipulate broad and diversified training under the supervision of a licensed architect over a three-year period. New graduates usually begin as intern-architects in architec-tural firms, where they assist in preparing architectural documents or drawings. They may also do research on building codes and materials or write specifications for building materials, installation criteria, the quality of finishes, and other related details. Graduates with degrees in architecture also enter related fields such as graphic, interior, or industrial design; urban planning; real estate development; civil engineering; or construction management. In such cases, an architectural license (and thus the internship period) is not required.

After completing the internship period, intern-architects are eligible to sit for the ARE. The examination tests candidates on architectural knowledge, and is given in sections throughout the year. Candidates who pass the ARE and meet all standards established by their State board are licensed to practice in that State.

After becoming licensed and gaining experience, architects take on increasingly responsible duties, eventually managing entire projects. In large firms, architects may advance to supervisory or managerial positions. Some architects become partners in established firms; others set up their own practice.

Several States require continuing education to maintain a license, and many more States are expected to adopt mandatory continuing education. Requirements vary by State, but they usually involve the completion of a certain number of credits every year or two through seminars, workshops, formal university classes, conferences, self-study courses, or other sources.

Job Outlook

Prospective architects may face competition for entry-level jobs, especially if the number of architectural degrees awarded remains at current levels or increases. Employment of architects is projected to grow about as fast as the average for all occupations through 2008, and additional job openings will stem from the need to replace architects who retire or leave the labor force for other reasons. However, many individuals are attracted to this occupation, and the number of applicants often exceeds the number of available jobs, especially in the most prestigious firms. Prospective architects who complete at least one summer internship—either paid or unpaid—while in school and who know CADD technology (especially that which conforms to the new national standards) will have a distinct advantage in obtaining an intern-architect position after graduation.

Employment of architects is strongly tied to the level of local construction, particularly nonresidential structures such as office buildings, shopping centers, schools, and healthcare facilities. After a boom in non-residential construction during the 1980s, building slowed significantly during the first half of the 1990s. Despite slower labor force growth and increases in telecommuting and flexiplace work, however, non-residential construction is expected to grow more quickly between 1998 and 2008 than during the previous decade, driving demand for more architects.

As the stock of buildings ages, demand for remodeling and repair work should grow considerably. The needed renovation and rehabilitation of old buildings, particularly in urban areas where space for new buildings is becoming limited, is expected to provide many job opportunities for architects. In addition, demographic trends and changes in health care delivery are influencing the demand for certain institutional structures, and should also provide more jobs for architects in the future. For example, increases in the school-age population have resulted in new school construction. Additions to existing schools (especially colleges and universities), as well as overall modernization, will continue to add to demand for architects through 2008. Growth is expected in the number of adult care centers, assisted-living facilities, and community health clinics, all of which are preferable, less costly alternatives to hospitals and nursing homes.

Because construction—particularly office and retail—is sensitive to cyclical changes in the economy, architects will face particularly strong competition for jobs or clients during recessions, and layoffs may occur. Those involved in the design of institutional buildings such as schools, hospitals, nursing homes, and correctional facilities, will be less affected by fluctuations in the economy.

Even in times of overall good job opportunities, however, there may be areas of the country with poor opportunities. Architects who are licensed to practice in one State must meet the licensing requirements of other States before practicing elsewhere. These requirements are becoming more standardized, however, facilitating movement to other States.

Earnings

Median annual earnings of architects were $47,710 in 1998. The middle 50 percent earned between $37,380 and $68,920. The lowest 10 percent earned less than $30,030, and the highest 10 percent earned more than $87,460.

According to the American Institute of Architects, the median compensation, including bonuses, for intern-architects in architectural firms was $35,200 in 1999. Licensed architects with 3 to 5 of years experience had median earnings of $41,100; licensed architects with 8 to 10 years of experience, but who were not managers or principals of a firm, earned $54,700. Principals or partners of firms had median earnings of $132,500 in 1999, although partners in some large practices earned considerably more. Similar to other industries, small architectural firms (fewer than five employees) are less likely than larger firms to provide employee benefits.

Earnings of partners in established architectural firms may fluctuate because of changing business conditions. Some architects may have difficulty establishing their own practices and may go through a period when their expenses are greater than their income, requiring substantial financial resources.

Related Occupations

Architects design and construct buildings and related structures. Others who engage in similar work are landscape architects, building contractors, civil engineers, urban planners, interior designers, industrial designers, and graphic designers.

Sources of Additional Information

Information about education and careers in architecture can be obtained from:

- Careers in Architecture Program, The American Institute of Architects, 1735 New York Ave. NW., Washington, DC 20006. Internet: http://www.aiaonline.com

Archivists, Curators, Museum Technicians, and Conservators

(O*NET 31511A, 31511B, 31511C, and 31511D)

Significant Points

- Employment usually requires graduate education and related work experience.

- Keen competition is expected because qualified applicants outnumber the most desirable job openings.

Nature of the Work

Archivists, curators, museum and archives technicians, and conservators search for, acquire, appraise, analyze, describe, arrange, catalogue, restore, preserve, exhibit, maintain, and store valuable items that can be used by researchers or for exhibitions, publications, broadcasting, and other educational programs. Depending on the occupation, these items include historical documents, audiovisual materials, institutional records, works of art, coins, stamps, minerals, clothing, maps, living and preserved plants and animals, buildings, computer records, or historic sites.

Archivists and curators plan and oversee the arrangement, cataloguing, and exhibition of collections and, along with technicians and conservators, maintain collections. Archivists and curators may coordinate educational and public outreach programs, such as tours, workshops, lectures, and classes, and may work with the boards of institutions to administer plans and policies. They also may research topics or items relevant to their collections. Although some duties of archivists and curators are similar, the types of items they deal with differ. Curators usually handle objects found in cultural, biological, or historical collections, such as sculptures, textiles, and paintings, while archivists mainly handle valuable records, documents, or objects that are retained because they originally accompanied and relate specifically to the document.

Archivists determine what portion of the vast amount of records maintained by various organizations, such as government agencies, corporations, or educational institutions, or by families and individuals, should be made part of permanent historical holdings, and which of these records should be put on exhibit. They maintain records in their original arrangement according to the creator's organizational scheme and describe records to facilitate retrieval. Records may be saved on any medium, including paper, film, video tape, audio tape, electronic disk, or computer. They also may be copied onto some other format in order to protect the original and to make them more accessible to researchers who use the records. As computers and various storage media evolve, archivists must keep abreast of technological advances in electronic information storage.

Archives may be part of a library, museum, or historical society, or they may exist as a distinct unit within an organization or company. Archivists consider any medium containing recorded information as documents, including letters, books, and other paper documents, photographs, blueprints, audiovisual materials, and computer records. Any document that reflects organizational transactions, hierarchy, or procedures can be considered a record. Archivists often specialize in an area of history or technology so they can better determine what records in that area qualify for retention and should become part of the archives. Archivists also may work with specialized forms of records, such as manuscripts, electronic records, photographs, cartographic records, motion pictures, and sound recordings.

Computers are increasingly used to generate and maintain archival records. Professional standards for use of computers in handling archival records are still evolving. However, computers are expected to transform many aspects of archival collections as computer capabilities, including multimedia and World Wide Web use, expand and allow more records to be stored and exhibited electronically.

Curators oversee collections in museums, zoos, aquariums, botanical gardens, nature centers, and historic sites. They acquire items through purchases, gifts, field exploration, inter-museum exchanges, or (in the case of some plants and animals) reproduction. Curators also plan and prepare exhibits. In natural history museums, curators collect and observe specimens in their natural habitat. Their work involves describing and classifying species, while specially trained collection managers and technicians provide hands-on care of natural history collections. Most curators use computer databases to catalogue and organize their collections. Many also use the Internet to make information available to other curators and the public. Increasingly, curators are expected to participate in grant writing and fundraising to support their projects.

Most curators specialize in a field, such as botany, art, paleontology, or history. Those working in large institutions may be highly specialized. A large natural history museum, for example, would employ specialists in birds, fishes, insects, and mollusks. Some curators maintain the collection, others do research, and others perform administrative tasks. Registrars, for example, keep track of and move objects in the collection. In small institutions with only one or a few curators, one curator may be responsible for multiple tasks, from maintaining collections to directing the affairs of the museum.

Conservators manage, care for, preserve, treat, and document works of art, artifacts, and specimens. This may require substantial historical, scientific, and archaeological research. They use x-rays, chemical testing, microscopes, special lights, and other laboratory equipment and techniques to examine objects and determine their condition, the need for treatment or restoration, and the appropriate method for preservation. They then document their findings and treat items to minimize deterioration or restore items to their original state. Conservators usually specialize in a particular material or group of objects, such as documents and books, paintings, decorative arts, textiles, metals, or architectural material.

Museum directors formulate policies, plan budgets, and raise funds for their museums. They coordinate activities of their staff to establish and maintain collections. As their role has evolved, museum directors increasingly need business backgrounds in addition to an understanding of the subject matter of their collections.

Museum technicians assist curators and conservators by performing various preparatory and maintenance tasks on museum items. Some museum technicians may also assist curators with research. Archives technicians help archivists organize, maintain, and provide access to historical documentary materials.

Working Conditions

The working conditions of archivists and curators vary. Some spend most of their time working with the public, providing reference assistance and educational services. Others perform research or process records, which often means working alone or in offices with only a few people. Those who restore and install exhibits or work with bulky, heavy record containers may climb, stretch, or lift. Those in zoos, botanical gardens, and other outdoor museums or historic sites frequently walk great distances.

Curators who work in large institutions may travel extensively to evaluate potential additions to the collection, organize exhibitions, and conduct research in their area of expertise. However, travel is rare for curators employed in small institutions.

Employment

Archivists, curators, museum technicians, and conservators held about 23,000 jobs in 1998. About a quarter were employed in museums, botanical gardens, and zoos, and approximately 2 in 10 worked in educational services, mainly in college and university libraries. More than one-third worked in Federal, State, and local government. Most Federal archivists work for the National Archives and Records Administration; others manage military archives in the Department of Defense. Most Federal government curators work at the Smithsonian Institute, in the military museums of the Department of Defense, and in archaeological and other museums managed by the Department of Interior. All State governments have archival or historical records sections employing archivists. State and local governments have numerous historical museums, parks, libraries, and zoos employing curators.

Some large corporations have archives or records centers, employing archivists to manage the growing volume of records created or maintained as required by law or necessary to the firms' operations. Religious and fraternal organizations, professional associations, conservation organizations, major private collectors, and research firms also employ archivists and curators.

Conservators may work under contract to treat particular items, rather than as a regular employee of a museum or other institution. These conservators may work on their own as private contractors, or as employees of conservation laboratories or regional conservation centers that contract their services to museums.

Training, Other Qualifications, and Advancement

Employment as an archivist, conservator, or curator usually requires graduate education and related work experience. Many archivists and curators work in archives or museums while completing their formal education, to gain the "hands-on" experience that many employers seek when hiring.

Employers usually look for archivists with undergraduate and graduate degrees in history or library science who have courses in archival science. Some positions may require knowledge of the discipline related to the collection, such as business or medicine. An increasing number of archivists have a double master's degree in history and library science. Currently no programs offer bachelor's or master's degrees in archival science. However, approximately 65 colleges and universities offer courses or practical training in archival science as part of history, library science, or another discipline. The Academy of Certified Archivists offers voluntary certification for archivists. Certification requires the applicant to have experience in the field and to pass an examination offered by the Academy.

Archivists need research and analytical ability to understand the content of documents and the context in which they were created and to decipher deteriorated or poor quality printed matter, handwritten manuscripts, or photographs and films. A background in preservation management is often required of archivists because they are responsible for taking proper care of their records. Archivists also must be able to organize large amounts of information and write clear instructions for its retrieval and use. In addition, computer skills and the ability to work with electronic records and databases are increasingly important.

Many archives are very small, including one-person shops, with limited promotion opportunities. Archivists typically advance by transferring to a larger unit with supervisory positions. A doctorate in history, library science, or a related field may be needed for some advanced positions, such as director of a State archive.

For employment as a curator, most museums require a master's degree in an appropriate discipline of the museum's specialty—art, history, or archaeology—or museum studies. Many employers prefer a doctoral degree, particularly for curators in natural history or science museums. Earning two graduate degrees—in museum studies (museology) and a specialized subject—gives a candidate a distinct advantage in this competitive job market. In small museums, curatorial positions may be available to individuals with a bachelor's degree. For some positions, an internship of full-time museum work supplemented by courses in museum practices is needed.

Curatorial positions often require knowledge in a number of fields. For historic and artistic conservation, courses in chemistry, physics, and art are desirable. Because curators—particularly those in small museums—may have administrative and managerial responsibilities, courses in business administration, public relations, marketing, and fundraising also are recommended. Similar to archivists, curators need computer skills and the ability to work with electronic databases. Curators also need to be familiar with digital imaging, scanning technology, and copyright infringement, because many are responsible for posting information on the Internet.

Curators must be flexible because of their wide variety of duties. They need to design and present exhibits and, in small museums, they need the manual dexterity to build exhibits or restore objects. Leadership ability and business skills are important for museum directors, and marketing skills are valuable for increasing museum attendance and fundraising.

In large museums, curators may advance through several levels of responsibility, eventually to museum director. Curators in smaller museums often advance to larger ones. Individual research and publications are important for advancement in larger institutions.

Museum technicians usually need a bachelor's degree in an appropriate discipline of the museum's specialty, museum studies training, or previous museum work experience, particularly in exhibit design. Similarly, archives technicians usually need a bachelor's degree in library science or history, or relevant work experience. Technician positions often serve as a stepping stone for individuals interested in archival and curatorial work. With the exception of small museums, a master's degree is needed for advancement.

When hiring conservators, employers look for a master's degree in conservation or a closely related field, as well as substantial experience. There are only a few graduate programs in museum conservation techniques in the United States. Competition for entry to these programs is keen; to qualify, a student must have a background in chemistry, archaeology or studio art, and art history, as well as work experience. For some programs, knowledge of a foreign language is also helpful. Conservation apprenticeships or internships as an undergraduate can also enhance one's admission prospects. Graduate programs last two to four years; the latter years include internship training. A few individuals enter conservation through apprenticeships with museums, nonprofit organizations, and conservators in private practice. Apprenticeships should be supplemented with courses in chemistry, studio art, and history. Apprenticeship training, although accepted, usually is a more difficult route into the conservation profession.

Relatively few schools grant a bachelor's degree in museum studies. More common are undergraduate minors or tracks of study that are part of an undergraduate degree in a related field, such as art history, history, or archaeology. Students interested in further study may obtain a master's degree in museum studies. Colleges and universities throughout the country offer master's degrees in museum studies. However, many employers feel that, while museum studies are helpful, a thorough knowledge of the museum's specialty and museum work experience are more important.

Continuing education, which enables archivists, curators, conservators, and museum technicians to keep up with developments in the field, is available through meetings, conferences, and workshops sponsored by archival, historical, and museum associations. Some larger organizations, such as the National Archives, offer such training in-house.

Job Outlook

Competition for jobs as archivists, curators, museum technicians, and conservators is expected to be keen because qualified applicants outnumber job openings. Graduates with highly specialized training, such as master's degrees in both library science and history, with a concentration in archives or records management, and extensive computer skills should have the best opportunities for jobs as archivists. A curator job is attractive to many people, and many applicants have the necessary training and subject knowledge; but there are only a few openings. Consequently, candidates may have to work part time, as an intern, or even as a volunteer assistant curator or research associate after completing their formal education. Substantial work experience in collection management, exhibit design, or restoration, as well as database management skills, will be necessary for permanent status. Job opportunities for curators should be best in art and history museums, which are the largest employers in the museum industry.

The job outlook for conservators may be more favorable, particularly for graduates of conservation programs. However, competition is stiff for the limited number of openings in these programs, and applicants need a technical background. Students who qualify and successfully complete the program, have knowledge of a foreign language, and are willing to relocate, will have an advantage over less qualified candidates.

Employment of archivists, curators, museum technicians, and conservators is expected to increase about as fast as the average for all occupations through 2008. Jobs are expected to grow as public and private organizations emphasize establishing archives and organizing records and information, and as public interest in science, art, history, and technology increases. However, museums and other cultural institutions are often subject to funding cuts during recessions or periods of budget tightening, reducing demand for archivists and curators during these times. Although the rate of turnover among archivists and curators is relatively low, the need to replace workers who leave the occupation or stop working will create some additional job openings.

Earnings

Median annual earnings of archivists, curators, museum technicians, and conservators in 1998 were $31,750. The middle 50 percent earned between $23,090 and $43,840. The lowest 10 percent earned less than $16,340, and the highest 10 percent earned more than $63,580. Median annual earnings of archivists, curators, museum technicians, and conservators in 1997 were $28,400 in museums and art galleries.

Earnings of archivists and curators vary considerably by type and size of employer, and often by specialty. Average salaries in the Federal government, for example, are usually higher than those in religious organizations. Salaries of curators in large, well-funded museums can be several times higher than those in small ones.

The average annual salary for all museum curators in the Federal government in nonsupervisory, supervisory, and managerial positions was about $59,200 in 1999. Archivists averaged $57,500; museum specialists and technicians, $40,400; and archives technicians, $40,000.

Related Occupations

The skills that archivists, curators, museum technicians, and conservators use to preserve, organize, and display objects or information of historical interest are shared by anthropologists, arborists, archaeologists, botanists, ethnologists, folklorists, genealogists, historians, horticulturists, information specialists, librarians, paintings restorers, records managers, and zoologists.

Sources of Additional Information

For information on archivists and on schools offering courses in archival studies, contact:

- Society of American Archivists, 527 South Wells St., 5th floor, Chicago, IL 60607-3922. Internet: http://www.archivists.org

For general information about careers as a curator and schools offering courses in museum studies, contact:

- American Association of Museums, 1575 I St. NW., Suite 400, Washington, DC 20005. Internet: http://www.aam-us.org

For information about conservation and preservation careers and education programs, contact:

- American Institute for Conservation of Historic and Artistic Works, 1717 K St. NW., Suite 301, Washington, DC 20006. Internet: http://palimpsest.stanford.edu/aic

Armed Forces

(O*NET 99003)

Significant Points

- Opportunities should be good in all branches of the Armed Forces for applicants who meet designated standards.

- Enlisted personnel need at least a high school diploma; officers need a bachelor's or advanced degree.

- Hours and working conditions can be arduous and vary substantially.

- Some training and duty assignments are hazardous, even in peacetime.

Nature of the Work

Maintaining a strong national defense encompasses such diverse activities as running a hospital, commanding a tank, programming computers, operating a nuclear reactor, and repairing and maintaining a helicopter. The military provides training and work experience in these fields and many others for more than 1.2 million people who serve in the active Army, Navy, Marine Corps, Air Force, and Coast Guard, their Reserve components, and the Air and Army National Guard.

The military distinguishes between enlisted and officer careers. Enlisted personnel comprise about 85 percent of the Armed Forces and carry out the fundamental operations of the military in areas such as combat, administration, construction, engineering, health care, and human resources. Officers, who make up the remaining 15 percent of the Armed Forces, are the leaders of the military. They supervise and manage activities in every occupational specialty in the military.

The following sections discuss the major occupational groups for enlisted personnel and officers.

Enlisted occupational groups:

Administrative careers include a wide variety of positions. The military must keep accurate information for planning and managing its operations. Paper and electronic records are kept on equipment, funds, personnel, supplies, and other property of the military. Enlisted administrative personnel record information, type reports, and maintain files to assist military offices. Personnel may work in a specialized area such as finance, accounting, legal, maintenance, or supply.

Combat specialty occupations refer to those enlisted specialties, such as infantry, artillery, and special forces, that operate weapons or execute special missions during combat situations. They normally specialize by the type of weapon system or combat operation. These personnel maneuver against enemy forces, and they position and fire artillery, guns, and missiles to destroy enemy positions. They may also operate tanks and amphibious assault vehicles in combat or scouting missions. When the military has difficult and dangerous missions to perform, they call upon special operations teams. These elite combat forces stay in a constant state of readiness to strike anywhere in the world on a moment's notice. Special operations forces team members conduct offensive raids, demolitions, intelligence, search and rescue, and other missions from aboard aircraft, helicopters, ships, or submarines.

Construction occupations in the military include personnel who build or repair buildings, airfields, bridges, foundations, dams, bunkers, and the electrical and plumbing components of these structures. Enlisted personnel in construction occupations operate bulldozers, cranes, graders, and other heavy equipment. Construction specialists may also work with engineers and other building specialists as part of military construction teams. Some personnel specialize in areas such as plumbing or electrical wiring. Plumbers and pipe fitters install and repair the plumbing and pipe systems needed in buildings, on aircraft, and on ships. Building electricians install and repair electrical wiring systems in offices, airplane hangars, and other buildings on military bases.

Electronic and electrical equipment repair personnel repair and maintain electronic and electrical equipment used in the military today. Repairers normally specialize by type of equipment being repaired, such as avionics, computer, communications, or weapons systems. For example, avionics technicians install, test, maintain, and repair a wide variety of electronic systems including navigational and communications equipment on aircraft. Weapons maintenance technicians maintain and repair weapons used by combat forces, most of which have electronic components and systems that assist in locating targets, aiming weapons, and firing them.

The military has many *engineering, science, and technical* occupations that require specific knowledge to operate technical equipment, solve complex problems or to provide and interpret information. Enlisted personnel normally specialize in an area such as information technology, space operations, environmental health and safety, or intelligence. Information technology specialists, for example, develop software programs and operate computer systems. Space operations specialists use and repair spacecraft ground control command equipment, including electronic systems that track spacecraft location and operation. Environmental health and safety specialists inspect military facilities and food supplies for the presence of disease, germs, or other conditions hazardous to health and the environment. Intelligence specialists gather and study information using aerial photographs and various types of radar and surveillance systems.

Health care personnel assist medical professionals in treating and providing services for patients. They may work as part of a patient service team in close contact with doctors, dentists, nurses, and physical therapists to provide the necessary support functions within a hospital or clinic. Health care specialists normally specialize in a particular area. They may provide emergency medical treatment, operate diagnostic equipment such as x-ray and ultrasound equipment, conduct laboratory tests on tissue and blood samples, maintain pharmacy supplies, or maintain patient records.

Human resource development specialists recruit and place qualified personnel and provide the training programs necessary to help people perform their jobs effectively. Personnel in this career area normally specialize by activity. Recruiting specialists, for example, provide information about military careers to young people, parents, schools, and local communities. They explain service employment and training opportunities, pay and benefits, and the nature of service life. Personnel specialists collect and store information about people's careers in the military, including training, job assignment, promotion, and health information. Training specialists and instructors provide military personnel with the knowledge needed to perform their jobs.

Machine operator and production careers include occupations that require the operation of industrial equipment, machinery, and tools to fabricate and repair parts for a variety of items and structures. They may operate boilers, turbines, nuclear reactors, and portable generators aboard ships and submarines. Personnel often specialize by type of work performed. Welders, for instance, work with various types of metals to repair or form the structural parts of ships, submarines, buildings, or other equipment. Other specialists inspect, maintain, and repair survival equipment such as parachutes and aircraft life support equipment.

Media and public affairs careers include those occupations that are involved in the public presentation and interpretation of military information and events. Enlisted media and public affairs personnel take and develop photographs; film, record, and edit audio and video programs; present news and music programs; and produce graphic artwork, drawings, and other visual displays. Other public affairs specialists act as interpreters and translators to convert written or spoken foreign languages into English or other languages.

Protective service personnel enforce military laws and regulations and provide emergency response to natural and man-made disasters. Personnel normally specialize by function. Specialists in emergency management implement response procedures for all types of disasters, such as floods, earthquakes, hurricanes, or enemy attack. Military police control traffic, prevent crime, and respond to emergencies. Other law enforcement and security specialists investigate crimes committed on military property and guard inmates in military correctional facilities. Firefighters put out, control, and help prevent fires in buildings, aircraft, and aboard ships.

Support services occupations include subsistence services and occupations that support the morale and well-being of military personnel and their families. Food service specialists prepare all types of food in dining halls, hospitals, and ships. Counselors help military personnel and their families to overcome social problems. They work as part of a team that may include social workers, psychologists, medical officers, chaplains, personnel specialists, and commanders. The military also provides chaplains and religious program specialists to help meet the spiritual needs of its personnel. Religious program specialists assist chaplains with religious services, religious education programs, and administrative duties.

Transportation and material handling specialists ensure the safe transport of people and cargo. Most personnel within this occupational group are classified according to mode of transportation (i.e. aircraft, automotive vehicle, or ship). Air crew members operate equipment on board aircraft during operations. Vehicle drivers operate all types of heavy military vehicles including fuel or water tank trucks, semi-tractor trailers, heavy troop transports, and passenger buses. Boat operators navigate and pilot many types of small water craft, including tugboats, gunboats, and barges. Cargo specialists load and unload military supplies and material using equipment such as forklifts and cranes.

Vehicle and machinery mechanics conduct preventive and corrective maintenance on aircraft, automotive and heavy equipment, heating and cooling systems, marine engines, and powerhouse station equipment. They typically specialize by the type of equipment they maintain. Aircraft mechanics inspect, service, and repair helicopters and airplanes. Automotive and heavy equipment mechanics maintain and repair vehicles such as jeeps, cars, trucks, tanks, self-propelled missile launchers, and other combat vehicles. They also repair bulldozers, power shovels, and other construction equipment. Heating and cooling mechanics install and repair air conditioning, refrigeration, and heating equipment. Marine engine mechanics repair and maintain gasoline and diesel engines on ships, boats, and other water craft. They also repair shipboard mechanical and electrical equipment. Powerhouse mechanics install, maintain, and repair electrical and mechanical equipment in power-generating stations.

Officer occupational groups:

Combat specialty officers plan and direct military operations, oversee combat activities, and serve as combat leaders. This category includes officers in charge of tanks and other armored assault vehicles, artillery systems, special forces, and infantry. They normally specialize by type of unit that they lead. Within the unit, they may specialize by the type of weapon system. Artillery and missile system officers, for example, direct personnel as they target, launch, test, and maintain various types of missiles and artillery. Special forces officers lead their units in offensive raids, demolitions, intelligence gathering, and search and rescue missions.

Engineering, science, and technical officers have a wide range of responsibilities based on their area of expertise. They lead or perform activities in areas such as information technology, environmental health and safety, and engineering. These officers may direct the operations of communications centers or the development of complex computer systems. Environmental health and safety officers study the air, ground, and water to identify and analyze sources of pollution and its effects. They also direct programs to control safety and health hazards in the workplace. Other personnel work as aerospace engineers to design and direct the development of military aircraft, missiles, and spacecraft.

Executive, administrative, and managerial officers oversee and direct military activities in key functional areas such as finance, accounting, health administration, logistics, and supply. Health services administrators, for instance, are responsible for the overall quality of care provided at the hospitals and clinics they operate. They

must ensure that each department works together to provide the highest quality of care. As another example, the military buys billions of dollars worth of equipment, supplies, and services from private industry each year. Purchasing and contracting managers negotiate and monitor contracts for purchasing equipment, materials, and services.

Health care officers provide health services at military facilities based on their area of specialization. Officers who examine, diagnose, and treat patients with illness, injury, or disease include physicians, registered nurses, and dentists. Other health care officers provide therapy, rehabilitative treatment, and other services for patients. Physical and occupational therapists plan and administer therapy to help patients adjust to disabilities, regain independence, and return to work. Speech therapists evaluate and treat patients with hearing and speech problems. Dietitians manage food service facilities and plan meals for hospital patients and outpatients who need special diets. Pharmacists manage the purchasing, storing, and dispensing of drugs and medicines.

Human resource development officers manage recruitment, placement, and training strategies and programs in the military. Personnel in this area normally specialize by activity. Recruiting managers direct recruiting efforts and provide information about military careers to young people, parents, schools, and local communities. Personnel managers direct military personnel functions such as job assignment, staff promotion, and career counseling. Training and education directors identify training needs and develop and manage educational programs designed to keep military personnel current in the skills they need to perform their jobs.

Support services officers include personnel who manage food service activities and perform services in support of the morale and well being of military personnel and their families. Food service managers oversee the preparation and delivery of food services within dining facilities located on military installations and vessels. Social workers focus on improving conditions that cause social problems, such as drug and alcohol abuse, racism, and sexism. Chaplains conduct worship services for military personnel and perform other spiritual duties covering beliefs and practices of all religious faiths.

Media and public affairs officers oversee the development, production, and presentation of information or events for the public. These officers may produce and direct motion pictures, videotapes, and TV and radio broadcasts that are used for training, news, and entertainment. Some plan, develop, and direct the activities of military bands. Public affairs officers respond to inquiries about military activities and prepare news releases and reports to keep the public informed.

Protective service officers are responsible for the safety and protection of individuals and property on military bases and vessels. Emergency management officers plan and prepare for all types of natural and man-made disasters. They develop warning, control, and evacuation plans to be used in the event of a disaster. Law enforcement and security officers enforce applicable laws on military bases and investigate crimes when the law has been transgressed.

Officers in *transportation* occupations manage and perform activities related to the safe transport of military personnel and material by air, road, rail, and water. Officers normally specialize by mode of transportation or area of expertise because, in many cases, there are licensing and certification requirements. Pilots in the military fly various types of specialized airplanes and helicopters to carry troops and equipment and execute combat missions. Navigators use radar, radio, and other navigation equipment to determine their positions and plan their routes of travel. Officers on ships and submarines work as a team to manage the various departments aboard their vessels. Transportation officers must also direct the maintenance of transportation equipment.

Employment

In 1999, more than 1.2 million individuals were on active duty in the Armed Forces—about 445,000 in the Army, 272,000 in the Navy, 343,000 in the Air Force, 143,000 in the Marine Corps, and 26,000 in the Coast Guard. Table 1 shows the occupational composition of enlisted personnel in 1999; table 2 presents similar information for officer personnel.

TABLE 1
Military enlisted personnel by broad occupational category and branch of military service, 1999

Occupational Group—Enlisted	Army	Air Force	Coast Guard	Marine Corps	Navy	Total, all services
Administrative occupations	17,124	16,599	1,834	11,078	13,569	60,204
Combat specialty occupations	105,811	214	—	30,009	1,926	137,960
Construction occupations	4,214	5,732	2,181	3,972	2,775	18,874
Electronic and electrical repair occupations	25,431	51,900	3,075	12,876	43,879	137,161
Engineering, science, and technical occupations	39,362	47,091	2,193	15,705	34,726	139,077
Health care occupations	28,933	21,770	688	0[1]	23,090	74,481
Support services occupations	12,994	7,210	1,158	3,109	8,654	33,125
Machine operator and precision work occupations	2,295	7,066	1,501	1,940	18,807	31,609
Media and public affairs occupations	8,001	6,393	125	1,831	2,985	19,335
Protective service occupations	24,562	18,602	180	6,315	7,038	56,697
Transportation and material handling occupations	53,556	31,582	4,244	27,876	28,524	145,782
Vehicle machinery mechanic occupations	46,783	47,807	2,392	15,796	39,541	152,319
Human resource development occupations	14,504	10,376	348	1,672	12,459	39,359
Total, by service[2]	383,570	272,342	19,919	132,179	237,973	1,045,983

[1] The Marine Corps employs no medical personnel. Their medical services are provided by the Navy.
[2] Sum of individual items may not equal totals because personnel on temporary assignment are not included in these occupational classifications.
SOURCE: U.S. Department of Defense, Defense Manpower Data Center East

TABLE 2
Military officer personnel by broad occupational category and branch of service, 1999

Occupational Group—Officer	Army	Air Force	Coast Guard	Marine Corps	Navy	Total, all services
Combat specialty occupations	19,470	5,951	42	1,102	2,232	28,797
Engineering, science, and technical occupations	16,106	15,840	1,392	1,706	7,924	42,968
Executive, administrative, and managerial occupations	8,259	8,905	349	1,290	6,321	25,124
Health care occupations	11,055	11,073	8	0[1]	7,332	29,468
Support services occupations	1,211	1,636	—	45	1,155	4,047
Media and public affairs occupations	50	1,570	18	142	335	2,115
Protective service occupations	1,671	1,446	374	330	786	4,607
Transportation occupations	1,851	19,890	3,341	5,017	13,140	43,239
Human resource development occupations	1,256	4,093	265	1,673	4,136	11,423
Total, by service[2]	60,929	70,404	5,789	11,305	43,361	191,788
Total (Enlisted and Officer)[2]	444,499	342,746	25,708	143,484	281,334	1,237,771

[1] The Marine Corps employs no medical personnel. Their medical services are provided by the Navy.
[2] Sum of individual items may not equal totals because personnel on temporary assignment are not included in these occupational classifications.
SOURCE: U.S. Department of Defense, Defense Manpower Data Center East

Military personnel are stationed throughout the United States and in many countries around the world. More than one-third of military jobs are located in California, Texas, North Carolina, and Virginia. About 258,000 individuals were stationed outside the United States in 1998, including those assigned to ships at sea. More than 116,000 of these were stationed in Europe, mainly in Germany, and another 96,000 were assigned to East Asia and the Pacific area, mostly in Japan and the Republic of Korea.

Training, Other Qualifications, and Advancement

Enlisted personnel. In order to join the services, enlisted personnel must sign a legal agreement called an enlistment contract, which usually involves a commitment to eight years of service. Depending on the terms of the contract, two to six years are spent on active duty, and the balance are spent in the reserves. The enlistment contract obligates the service to provide the agreed-upon job, rating, pay, cash bonuses for enlistment in certain occupations, medical and other benefits, occupational training, and continuing education. In return, enlisted personnel must serve satisfactorily for the specified period of time.

Requirements for each service vary, but certain qualifications for enlistment are common to all branches. In order to enlist, one must be between the ages of 17 and 35, be a U.S. citizen or immigrant alien holding permanent resident status, not have a felony record, and possess a birth certificate. Applicants who are 17 must have the consent of a parent or legal guardian before entering the service. Air Force enlisted personnel must enter active duty before their 28th birthday. Applicants must pass both a written examination—the Armed Services Vocational Aptitude Battery—and meet certain minimum physical standards such as height, weight, vision, and overall health. All branches require high school gradua-

tion or its equivalent for certain enlistment options. In 1999, more than 9 out of 10 volunteers were high school graduates. Single parents are generally not eligible to enlist.

People thinking about enlisting in the military should learn as much as they can about military life before making a decision. This is especially important if you are thinking about making the military a career. Speaking to friends and relatives with military experience is a good idea. Determine what the military can offer you and what it will expect in return. Then talk to a recruiter, who can determine if you qualify for enlistment, explain the various enlistment options, and tell you which military occupational specialties currently have openings. Bear in mind that the recruiter's job is to recruit promising applicants into their branch of military service, so the information he or she gives you is likely to stress the positive aspects of military life in the branch in which the recruiter serves.

Ask the recruiter for the branch you have chosen to assess your chances of being accepted for training in the occupation or occupations of your choice, or, better still, take the aptitude exam to see how well you score. The military uses the aptitude exam as a placement exam, and test scores largely determine an individual's chances of being accepted into a particular training program. Selection for a particular type of training depends on the needs of the service, your general and technical aptitudes, and your personal preference. Because all prospective recruits are required to take the exam, those who do so before committing themselves to enlist have the advantage of knowing in advance whether they stand a good chance of being accepted for training in a particular specialty. The recruiter can schedule you for the Armed Services Vocational Aptitude Battery without any obligation. Many high schools offer the exam as an easy way for students to explore the possibility of a military career, and the test also provides insight into career areas where the student has demonstrated aptitudes and interests.

If you decide to join the military, the next step is to pass the physical examination and sign an enlistment contract. This involves choosing, qualifying, and agreeing on a number of enlistment options such as length of active duty time, which may vary according to the enlistment option. Most active duty programs have enlistment options ranging from three to six years, although there are some two-year programs. The contract will also state the date of enlistment and other options such as bonuses and types of training to be received. If the service is unable to fulfill its part of the contract, such as providing a certain kind of training, the contract may become null and void.

All services offer a "delayed entry program" by which an individual can delay entry into active duty for up to one year after enlisting. High school students can enlist during their senior year and enter a service after graduation. Others choose this program because the job training they desire is not currently available but will be within the coming year or because they need time to arrange personal affairs.

Women are eligible to enter most military specialties. Although many women serve in medical and administrative support positions, women also work as mechanics, missile maintenance technicians, heavy equipment operators, fighter pilots, and intelligence officers. Only occupations involving direct exposure to combat are excluded.

People planning to apply the skills gained through military training to a civilian career should first determine how good the prospects are for civilian employment in jobs related to the military specialty that interests them. Second, they should know the prerequisites for the related civilian job. Many occupations require a license, certification, or minimum level of education. In such cases, it is important to determine whether military training is sufficient to enter the civilian equivalent and, if not, what additional training will be required. Such information often can be obtained from school counselors.

Following enlistment, new members of the Armed Forces undergo recruit training, which is better known as "basic" training. Recruit training provides a 6- to 11-week introduction to military life with courses in military skills and protocol. Days and nights are carefully structured and include rigorous physical exercises designed to improve strength and endurance and build unit cohesion.

Following basic training, most recruits take additional training at technical schools that prepare them for a particular military occupational specialty. The formal training period generally lasts from 10 to 20 weeks, although training for certain occupations—nuclear power plant operator, for example—may take as long as a year. Recruits not assigned to classroom instruction receive on-the-job training at their first duty assignment.

Many service people get college credit for the technical training they receive on duty, which, combined with off-duty courses, can lead to an associate's degree through community college programs such as the Community College of the Air Force. In addition to on-duty training, military personnel may choose from a variety of educational programs. Most military installations have tuition assistance programs for people wishing to take courses during off-duty hours. These may be correspondence courses or degree programs offered by local colleges or universities. Tuition assistance pays up to 75 percent of college costs. Also available are courses designed to help service personnel earn high school equivalency diplomas. Each service branch provides opportunities for full-time study to a limited number of exceptional applicants. Military personnel accepted into these highly competitive programs receive full pay, allowances, tuition, and related fees. In return, they must agree to serve an additional amount of time in the service. Other very selective programs enable enlisted personnel to qualify as commissioned officers through additional military training.

Warrant officers. Warrant officers are technical and tactical leaders who specialize in a specific technical area; for example, one group of warrant officers is Army aviators. The Army Warrant Officer Corps comprises less than 3 percent of the total Army. Although small in size, their level of responsibility is high. They receive extended career opportunities, worldwide leadership assignments, and increased pay and retirement benefits. Selection to attend the Warrant Officer Candidate School is highly competitive and restricted to those with the rank of E5 or higher (see table 3).

Officers. Officer training in the Armed Forces is provided through the Federal service academies (Military, Naval, Air Force, and Coast Guard); the Reserve Officers Training Corps (ROTC) offered at many colleges and universities; Officer Candidate School (OCS) or Officer Training School (OTS); the National Guard (State Officer Candidate School programs); the Uniformed Services University of Health Sciences; and other programs. All are very selective and are good options for those wishing to make the military a career.

Federal service academies provide a four-year college program leading to a Bachelor of Science degree. Midshipmen or cadets are provided free room and board, tuition, medical care, and a monthly allowance. Graduates receive regular or reserve commissions and have a five-year active duty obligation, or longer if entering flight training.

To become a candidate for appointment as a cadet or midshipman in one of the service academies, most applicants obtain a nomination from an authorized source (usually a member of Congress). Candidates do not need to know a member of Congress personally to request a nomination. Nominees must have an academic record of the requisite quality, college aptitude test scores above an established minimum, and recommendations from teachers or school officials; they must also pass a medical examination. Appointments are made from the list of eligible nominees. Appointments to the Coast Guard Academy, however, are made strictly on a competitive basis. A nomination is not required.

ROTC programs train students in about 950 Army, 60 Navy and Marine Corps, and 550 Air Force units at participating colleges and universities. Trainees take two to five hours of military instruction a week in addition to regular college courses. After graduation, they may serve as officers on active duty for a stipulated period of time. Some may serve their obligation in the Reserves or Guard. In the last two years of a ROTC program, students receive a monthly allowance while attending school and additional pay for summer training. ROTC scholarships for two, three, and four years are available on a competitive basis. All scholarships pay for tuition and have allowances for subsistence, textbooks, supplies, and other fees.

College graduates can earn a commission in the Armed Forces through OCS or OTS programs in the Army, Navy, Air Force, Marine Corps, Coast Guard, and National Guard. These officers generally must serve their obligation on active duty. Those with training in certain health professions may qualify for direct appointment as officers. In the case of health professions students, financial assistance and internship opportunities are available from the military in return for specified periods of military service. Prospective medical students can apply to the Uniformed Services University of Health Sciences, which offers free tuition in a program leading to a Doctor of Medicine (M.D.) degree. In return, graduates must serve for seven years in either the military or the Public Health Service. Direct appointments also are available for those qualified to serve in other special duties, such as the judge advocate general (legal) or chaplain corps. Flight training is available to commissioned officers in each branch of the Armed Forces. In addition, the Army has a direct enlistment option to become a warrant officer aviator.

Each service has different criteria for promoting personnel. Generally, the first few promotions for both enlisted and officer personnel come easily; subsequent promotions are much more competitive. Criteria for promotion may include time in service and grade, job performance, a fitness report (supervisor's recommendation), and written examinations. People who are passed over for promotion several times generally must leave the military. The following table shows the officer, warrant officer, and enlisted ranks by service.

Table 3
Military rank and employment for active duty personnel, March 1999

Grade	Rank and title				
	Army	**Navy and Coast Guard**	**Air Force**	**Marine Corps**	**Total DOD Employment**
Commissioned officers:					
O-10	General	Admiral	General	General	38
O-9	Lieutenant General	Vice Admiral	Lieutenant General	Lieutenant General	114
O-8	Major General	Rear Admiral Upper	Major General	Major General	287
O-7	Brigadier General	Rear Admiral Lower	Brigadier General	Brigadier General	446
O-6	Colonel	Captain	Colonel	Colonel	11,423
O-5	Lieutenant Colonel	Commander	Lieutenant Colonel	Lieutenant Colonel	28,428
O-4	Major	Lieutenant Commander	Major	Major	43,027
O-3	Captain	Lieutenant	Captain	Captain	69,358
O-2	1st Lieutenant	Lieutenant (JG)	1st Lieutenant	1st Lieutenant	28,096
O-1	2nd Lieutenant	Ensign	2nd Lieutenant	2nd Lieutenant	22,038
Warrant officers:					
W-5	Chief Warrant Officer	Chief Warrant Officer	—	Chief Warrant Officer	459
W-4	Chief Warrant Officer	Chief Warrant Officer	—	Chief Warrant Officer	2,123
W-3	Chief Warrant Officer	Chief Warrant Officer	—	Chief Warrant Officer	4,019
W-2	Chief Warrant Officer	Chief Warrant Officer	—	Chief Warrant Officer	6,455
W-1	Warrant Officer	Warrant Officer	—	Warrant Officer	2,402
Enlisted personnel:					
E-9	Sergeant Major	Master Chief Petty Officer	Chief Master Sergeant	Sergeant Major	10,241
E-8	1st Sergeant/Master Sergeant	Sr. Chief Petty Officer	Senior Master Sergeant	Master Sergeant/1st Sergeant	26,014
E-7	Sergeant First Class	Chief Petty Officer	Master Sergeant	Gunnery Sergeant	99,201
E-6	Staff Sergeant	Petty Officer 1st Class	Technical Sergeant	Staff Sergeant	163,075
E-5	Sergeant	Petty Officer 2nd Class	Staff Sergeant	Sergeant	232,854
E-4	Corporal/Specialist	Petty Officer 3rd Class	Senior Airman	Corporal	264,757
E-3	Private First Class	Seaman	Airman 1st Class	Lance Corporal	186,647
E-2	Private	Seaman Apprentice	Airman	Private 1st Class	98,115
E-1	Private	Seaman Recruit	Airman Basic	Private	57,961

SOURCE: U.S. Department of Defense

Job Outlook

Opportunities should be good for qualified individuals in all branches of the Armed Forces through 2008. Many military personnel retire after 20 years of service with a pension while still young enough to start a new career. About 365,000 enlisted personnel and officers must be recruited each year to replace those who complete their commitment or retire. Since the end of the draft in 1973, the military has met its personnel requirements through volunteers. When the economy is good, it is more difficult for all the services to meet their quotas; it is much easier to do so in times of recession.

America's strategic position is stronger than it has been in decades. Although there were reductions in personnel due to the reduction in the threat from Eastern Europe and Russia, the number of active duty personnel is now expected to remain about constant through 2008. The Armed Forces' goal is to maintain a sufficient force to fight and win two major regional conflicts occurring at the same time. Political events, however, could cause these plans to change.

Educational requirements will continue to rise as military jobs become more technical and complex. High school graduates and applicants with a college background will be sought to fill the ranks of enlisted personnel, while virtually all officers will need at least a bachelor's degree and, in some cases, an advanced degree as well.

Earnings

The earnings structure for military personnel are shown in table 4. Most enlisted personnel started as recruits at Grade E-1 in 1999; however, those with special skills or above-average education started as high as Grade E-4. Most warrant officers started at Grade W-1 or W-2, depending upon their occupational and academic qualifications and the branch of service, but these individuals all had previous military service, and this is not an entry-level occupation. Most commissioned officers started at Grade O-1, while some highly trained officers (for example, physicians, engineers, and scientists) started as high as Grade O-3 or O-4.

In addition to basic pay, military personnel receive free room and board (or a tax-free housing and subsistence allowance), medical and dental care, a military clothing allowance, military supermarket and department store shopping privileges, 30 days of paid vacation a year (referred to as leave), and travel opportunities. Other allowances are paid for foreign duty, hazardous duty, submarine and flight duty, and employment as a medical officer. Athletic and other recreational facilities such as libraries, gymnasiums, tennis courts, golf courses, bowling centers, and movies are available on many military installations. Military personnel are eligible for retirement benefits after 20 years of service.

The Veterans Administration (VA) provides numerous benefits to those who have served at least two years in the Armed Forces. Veterans are eligible for free care in VA hospitals for all service-related disabilities regardless of time served; those with other medical problems are eligible for free VA care if they are unable to pay the cost of hospitalization elsewhere. Admission to a VA medical center depends on the availability of beds, however. Veterans are also eligible for certain loans, including home loans. Veterans, regardless of health, can convert a military life insurance policy to an individual policy with any participating company in the veteran's State of residence. In addition, job counseling, testing, and placement services are available.

Veterans who participate in the New Montgomery GI Bill Program receive educational benefits. Under this program, Armed Forces personnel may elect to deduct from their pay up to $100 a month to put toward their future education for the first 12 months of active duty. Veterans who serve on active duty for three years or more, or two years active duty plus four years in the Selected Reserve or National Guard, will receive $427.87 a month in basic benefits for 36 months. Those who enlist and serve for less than three years will receive $347.65 a month. In addition, each service provides its own additional contributions for future education. This sum becomes the service member's educational fund. Upon separation from active duty, the fund can be used to finance educational costs at any VA-approved institution. VA-approved schools include many vocational, correspondence, business, technical, and flight training schools; community and junior colleges; and colleges and universities.

TABLE 4
Military basic monthly pay by grade for active duty personnel, January 1, 1999

Grade	Years of service					
	Less than 2	Over 4	Over 8	Over 12	Over 16	Over 20
O-9	6,947.10	7,281.00	7,466.10	7,776.90	8,425.80	8,892.60
O-8	6,292.20	6,634.50	7,129.20	7,466.10	7,776.90	8,425.80
O-7	5,228.40	5,583.90	5,834.40	6,172.50	7,129.20	7,619.70
O-6	3,875.10	4,536.60	4,536.60	4,536.60	5,432.40	5,834.40
O-5	3,099.60	3,891.00	3,891.00	4,224.30	4,845.00	5,277.90
O-4	2,612.40	3,393.30	3,608.70	4,071.90	4,444.80	4,566.60
O-3	2,427.60	3,210.60	3,484.80	3,855.30	3,949.50	3,949.50
O-2	2,117.10	2,871.30	2,930.40	2,930.40	2,930.40	2,930.40
O-1	1,838.10	2,312.10	2,312.10	2,312.10	2,312.10	2,312.10

| | Years of service | | | | | |
Grade	Less than 2	Over 4	Over 8	Over 12	Over 16	Over 20
W-5	—	—	—	—	—	4,221.30
W-4	2,473.20	2,714.10	2,962.80	3,303.00	3,577.80	3,792.00
W-3	2,247.90	2,469.90	2,681.70	2,930.40	3,114.00	3,335.70
W-2	1,968.90	2,192.10	2,438.40	2,623.80	2,809.50	2,993.10
W-1	1,640.40	2,037.90	2,221.50	2,407.20	2,591.70	2,777.70
E-8	—	—	2,412.60	2,547.30	2,682.90	2,811.30
E-7	1,684.80	1,952.10	2,082.90	2,216.70	2,382.60	2,480.40
E-6	1,449.30	1,715.40	1,844.10	2,010.00	2,140.20	2,172.60
E-5	1,271.70	1,514.70	1,680.30	1,811.10	1,844.10	1,844.10
E-4	1,185.90	1,428.60	1,485.30	1,485.30	1,485.30	1,485.30
E-3	1,179.80	1,274.70	1,274.70	1,274.70	1,274.70	1,274.70
E-2	1,075.80	1,075.80	1,075.80	1,075.80	1,075.80	1,075.80
E-1 >4mos	959.40	959.40	959.40	959.40	959.40	959.40

SOURCE: U.S. Department of Defense—Defense Finance and Accounting Service

Sources of Additional Information

Each of the military services publishes handbooks, fact sheets, and pamphlets describing entrance requirements, training and advancement opportunities, and other aspects of military careers. These publications are widely available at all recruiting stations, at most State employment service offices, and in high schools, colleges, and public libraries. Information on educational and other veterans' benefits is available from VA offices located throughout the country.

In addition, the *Military Career Guide Online* is a compendium of military occupational, training, and career information presented by the Defense Manpower Data Center, a Department of Defense agency which is designed for use by students and jobseekers. This information is available on the Internet at http://www.militarycareers.com.

Biological and Medical Scientists

(O*NET 24308A, 24308B, 24308C, 24308D, 24308E, 24308F, 24308G, 24308H, 24308J, and 24311)

Significant Points

- Biological scientists usually require a Ph.D. degree for independent research, but a master's degree is sufficient for some jobs in applied research or product development; a bachelor's degree is adequate for some non-research jobs.

- Medical scientist jobs require a Ph.D. degree in a biological science, but some jobs need a medical degree.

- Doctoral degree holders face considerable competition for independent research positions; holders of bachelor's or master's degrees in biological science can expect better opportunities in non-research positions.

Nature of the Work

Biological and medical scientists study living organisms and their relationship to their environment. Most specialize in some area of biology such as zoology (the study of animals) or microbiology (the study of microscopic organisms).

Many biological scientists and virtually all medical scientists work in research and development. Some conduct basic research to advance knowledge of living organisms, including viruses, bacteria, and other infectious agents. Past research has resulted in the development of vaccines, medicines, and treatments for cancer and other diseases. Basic biological and medical research continues to provide the building blocks necessary to develop solutions to human health problems and to preserve and repair the natural environment. Many biological and medical scientists work independently in private industry, university, or government laboratories, often exploring new areas of research or expanding on specialized research started in graduate school. Those who are not wage and salary workers in private industry typically submit grant proposals to obtain funding for their projects. Colleges and universities, private industry, and Federal government agencies, such as the National Institutes of Health and the National Science Foundation, contribute to the support of scientists whose research proposals are determined to be financially feasible and have the potential to advance new ideas or processes.

Biological and medical scientists who work in applied research or product development use knowledge provided by basic research to develop new drugs and medical treatments, increase crop yields, and protect and clean up the environment. They usually have less autonomy than basic researchers to choose the emphasis of their research, relying instead on market-driven directions based on the firm's products and goals. Biological and medical scientists doing applied research and product development in private industry may be required to express their research plans or results to nonscientists who are in a position to veto or approve their ideas, and they must understand the business impact of their work. Scientists are increasingly working as part of teams, interacting with engineers, scientists of other disciplines, business managers, and technicians. Some biological and medical scientists also work with customers or suppliers and manage budgets.

Biological and medical scientists who conduct research usually work in laboratories and use electron microscopes, computers, thermal cyclers, or a wide variety of other equipment. Some conduct experiments using laboratory animals or greenhouse plants. For some biological scientists, a good deal of research is performed outside of laboratories. For example, a botanist may do research in tropical rain forests to see what plants grow there, or an ecologist may study how a forest area recovers after a fire.

Some biological and medical scientists work in managerial or administrative positions, usually after spending some time doing research and learning about the firm, agency, or project. They may plan and administer programs for testing foods and drugs, for example, or direct activities at zoos or botanical gardens. Some biological scientists work as consultants to business firms or to government, while others test and inspect foods, drugs, and other products.

In the 1980s, swift advances in basic biological knowledge related to genetics and molecules spurred growth in the field of biotechnology. Biological and medical scientists using this technology manipulate the genetic material of animals or plants, attempting to make organisms more productive or resistant to disease. Research using biotechnology techniques, such as recombining DNA, has led to the discovery of important drugs, including human insulin and growth hormone. Many other substances not previously available in large quantities are starting to be produced by biotechnological means; some may be useful in treating cancer and other diseases. Today, many biological and medical scientists are involved in biotechnology, including those who work on the Human Genome project, isolating, identifying, and sequencing human genes. This work continues to lead to the discovery of the genes associated with specific diseases and inherited traits, such as certain types of cancer or obesity. These advances in biotechnology have opened up research opportunities in almost all areas of biology, including commercial applications in agriculture, environmental remediation, and the food and chemical industries.

Most biological scientists who come under the category of *biologist* are further classified by the type of organism they study or by the specific activity they perform, although recent advances in the understanding of basic life processes at the molecular and cellular levels have blurred some traditional classifications.

Aquatic biologists study plants and animals living in water. *Marine biologists* study salt water organisms, and *limnologists* study fresh water organisms. Marine biologists are sometimes mistakenly called oceanographers, but oceanography is the study of the physical characteristics of oceans and the ocean floor.

Biochemists study the chemical composition of living things. They analyze the complex chemical combinations and reactions involved in metabolism, reproduction, growth, and heredity. Biochemists and molecular biologists do most of their work in biotechnology, which involves understanding the complex chemistry of life.

Botanists study plants and their environment. Some study all aspects of plant life; others specialize in areas such as identification and classification of plants, the structure and function of plant parts, the biochemistry of plant processes, the causes and cures of plant diseases, and the geological record of plants.

Microbiologists investigate the growth and characteristics of microscopic organisms such as bacteria, algae, or fungi. *Medical microbiologists* study the relationship between organisms and disease or the effect of antibiotics on microorganisms. Other microbiologists specialize in environmental, food, agricultural, or industrial microbiology, virology (the study of viruses), or immunology (the study of mechanisms that fight infections). Many microbiologists use biotechnology to advance knowledge of cell reproduction and human disease.

Physiologists study life functions of plants and animals, both in the whole organism and at the cellular or molecular level, under normal and abnormal conditions. Physiologists often specialize in functions such as growth, reproduction, photosynthesis, respiration, or movement, or in the physiology of a certain area or system of the organism.

Zoologists study animals—their origin, behavior, diseases, and life processes. Some experiment with live animals in controlled or natural surroundings while others dissect dead animals to study their structure. Zoologists are usually identified by the animal group studied—ornithologists (birds), mammalogists (mammals), herpetologists (reptiles), and ichthyologists (fish).

Ecologists study the relationship among organisms and between organisms and their environments and the effects of influences such as population size, pollutants, rainfall, temperature, and altitude.

Biological scientists who do biomedical research are usually called *medical scientists*. Medical scientists work on basic research into normal biological systems to understand the causes of and to discover treatment for disease and other health problems. Medical scientists try to identify changes in a cell, chromosome, or even gene that signal the development of medical problems, such as different types of cancer. After identifying structures of or changes in organisms that provide clues to health problems, medical scientists work on the treatment of problems. For example, a medical scientist involved in cancer research may formulate a combination of drugs that will lessen the effects of the disease. Medical scientists with a medical degree can administer these drugs to patients in clinical trials, monitor their reactions, and observe the results. (Medical scientists without a medical degree normally collaborate with a medical doctor who deals directly with patients.) The medical scientist will return to the laboratory to examine the results and, if necessary, adjust the dosage levels to reduce negative side effects or to try to induce even better results. In addition to using basic research to develop treatments for health problems, medical scientists attempt to discover ways to prevent health problems from developing, such as affirming the link between smoking and increased risk of lung cancer or between alcoholism and liver disease.

Working Conditions

Biological and medical scientists usually work regular hours in offices or laboratories and usually are not exposed to unsafe or unhealthy conditions. Those who work with dangerous organisms or toxic substances in the laboratory must follow strict safety procedures to avoid contamination. Medical scientists also spend time working in clinics and hospitals administering drugs and treatments to patients in clinical trials. Many biological scientists such as botanists, ecologists, and zoologists take field trips that involve strenuous physical activity and primitive living conditions.

Some biological and medical scientists depend on grant money to support their research. They may be under pressure to meet deadlines and conform to rigid grant-writing specifications when preparing proposals to seek new or extended funding.

Employment

Biological and medical scientists held about 112,000 jobs in 1998. Almost 4 in 10 biological scientists were employed by Federal, State, and local governments. Federal biological scientists worked mainly in the U.S. Departments of Agriculture, the Interior, and Defense, and in the National Institutes of Health. Most of the rest worked in the drug industry, which includes pharmaceutical and biotechnology establishments, hospitals, and research and testing laboratories. About 2 in 10 medical scientists worked in State government; most of the remainder worked in research and testing laboratories, educational institutions, the drug industry, and hospitals.

In addition, many biological and medical scientists held biology faculty positions in colleges and universities.

Training, Other Qualifications, and Advancement

For biological scientists, the Ph.D. degree usually is necessary for independent research and for advancement to administrative positions. A master's degree is sufficient for some jobs in applied research or product development and for jobs in management, inspection, sales, and service. The bachelor's degree is adequate for some non-research jobs. Some graduates with a bachelor's degree start as biological scientists in testing and inspection or get jobs related to biological science such as technical sales or service representatives. In some cases, graduates with a bachelor's degree are able to work in a laboratory environment on their own projects, but this is unusual. Some may work as research assistants. Others become biological technicians, medical laboratory technologists, or with courses in education, high school biology teachers. Many with a bachelor's degree in biology enter medical, dental, veterinary, or other health profession schools.

Most colleges and universities offer bachelor's degrees in biological science and many offer advanced degrees. Curriculums for advanced degrees often emphasize a subfield such as microbiology or

botany, but not all universities offer all curriculums. Advanced degree programs include classroom and field work, laboratory research, and a thesis or dissertation. Biological scientists who have advanced degrees often take temporary postdoctoral research positions that provide specialized research experience. In private industry, some may become managers or administrators within biology; others leave biology for nontechnical managerial, administrative, or sales jobs.

Biological scientists should be able to work independently or as part of a team and be able to communicate clearly and concisely, both orally and in writing. Those in private industry, especially those who aspire to management or administrative positions, should possess strong business and communication skills and be familiar with regulatory issues and marketing and management techniques. Those doing field research in remote areas must have physical stamina.

The Ph.D. degree in a biological science is the minimum education required for prospective medical scientists because the work of medical scientists is almost entirely research oriented. A Ph.D. degree qualifies one to do research on basic life processes or on particular medical problems or diseases and to analyze and interpret the results of experiments on patients. Medical scientists who administer drug or gene therapy to human patients or who otherwise interact medically with patients—such as drawing blood, excising tissue, or performing other invasive procedures—must have a medical degree. It is particularly helpful for medical scientists to earn both Ph.D. and medical degrees.

In addition to formal education, medical scientists usually spend several years in postdoctoral positions before they apply for permanent jobs. Postdoctoral work provides valuable laboratory experience, including experience in specific processes and techniques, such as gene splicing, which are transferable to other research projects. In some institutions, the postdoctoral position can lead to a permanent position.

Job Outlook

Despite prospects of faster-than-average job growth over the 1998-2008 period, biological and medical scientists can expect to face considerable competition for basic research positions. The Federal government funds much basic research and development, including many areas of medical research. Recent budget tightening has led to smaller increases in Federal basic research and development expenditures, further limiting the dollar amount of each grant and slowing the growth of the number of grants awarded to researchers. At the same time, the number of newly trained scientists has continued to increase at a steady rate, so both new and established scientists have experienced greater difficulty winning and renewing research grants. If the number of advanced degrees awarded continues to grow unabated, this competitive scenario is likely to persist. Additionally, applied research positions in private industry may become more difficult to obtain if more scientists seek jobs in private industry than in the past due to the competitive job market for college and university faculty.

Opportunities for those with a bachelor's or master's degree in biological science are expected to be better. The number of science-related jobs in sales, marketing, and research management, for which non-Ph.D.s usually qualify, are expected to be more plentiful than independent research positions. Non-Ph.Ds may also fill positions as science or engineering technicians or health technologists and technicians. Some become high school biology teachers, while those with a doctorate in biological science may become college and university faculty.

Biological and medical scientists enjoyed very rapid gains in employment between the mid-1980s and mid-1990s, in part reflecting increased staffing requirements in new biotechnology companies. Employment growth should slow somewhat as increases in the number of new biotechnology firms slows and existing firms merge or are absorbed into larger ones. However, much of the basic biological research done in recent years has resulted in new knowledge, including the isolation and identification of new genes. Biological and medical scientists will be needed to take this knowledge to the next stage, which is the understanding of how certain genes function within an entire organism so that gene therapies can be developed to treat diseases. Even pharmaceutical and other firms not solely engaged in biotechnology are expected to increasingly use biotechnology techniques, spurring employment increases for biological and medical scientists. In addition, efforts to discover new and improved ways to clean up and preserve the environment will continue to add to growth. More biological scientists will be needed to determine the environmental impact of industry and government actions and to prevent or correct environmental problems. Expected expansion in research related to health issues, such as AIDS, cancer, and Alzheimer's disease, should also result in employment growth.

Biological and medical scientists are less likely to lose their jobs during recessions than those in many other occupations because many are employed on long-term research projects. However, a recession could further influence the amount of money allocated to new research and development efforts, particularly in areas of risky or innovative research. A recession could also limit the possibility of extension or renewal of existing projects.

Earnings

Median annual earnings of biological scientists were $46,140 in 1998. The middle 50 percent earned between $35,200 and $67,850. The lowest 10 percent earned less than $27,930, and the highest 10 percent earned more than $86,020. Median annual earnings in the industries employing the largest numbers of biological scientists in 1997 were:

Federal government	$48,600
Drugs	46,300
Research and testing services	40,800
State government, except education and hospitals	38,000

Median annual earnings of medical scientists were $50,410 in 1998. The middle 50 percent earned between $37,740 and $79,370. The lowest 10 percent earned less than $29,550, and the highest 10 percent earned more than $109,050. Median annual earnings of medical scientists in 1997 were $52,200 in research and testing services.

According to the National Association of Colleges and Employers, beginning salary offers in 1999 averaged $29,000 a year for bachelor's degree recipients in biological science, about $34,450 for master's degree recipients, and about $45,700 for doctoral degree recipients.

In the Federal government in 1999, general biological scientists in nonsupervisory, supervisory, and managerial positions earned an average salary of $56,000, microbiologists earned $62,600, ecologists earned $57,100, physiologists earned $71,300, and geneticists earned $68,200.

Related Occupations

Many other occupations deal with living organisms and require a level of training similar to that of biological and medical scientists. These include agricultural scientists, such as animal breeders, horticulturists, and entomologists, and the conservation occupations of forester, range manager, and soil conservationist. Many health occupations, such as medical doctors, dentists, and veterinarians, are also related to those in the biological sciences.

Sources of Additional Information

For information on careers in the biological sciences, contact:

- American Institute of Biological Sciences, Suite 200, 1444 I St. NW., Washington, DC 20005. Internet: http://www.aibs.org

For information on careers in physiology, contact:

- American Physiological Society, Education Office, 9650 Rockville Pike, Bethesda, MD 20814. Internet: http://www.faseb.org/aps

For information on careers in biotechnology, contact:

- Biotechnology Industry Organization, 1625 K St. NW., Suite 1100, Washington, DC 20006. Internet: http://www.bio.org

For information on careers in biochemistry, contact:

- American Society for Biochemistry and Molecular Biology, 9650 Rockville Pike, Bethesda, MD 20814. Internet: http://www.faseb.org/asbmb

For a brochure titled *Is a Career in the Pharmaceutical Sciences Right for Me?* contact:

- American Association of Pharmaceutical Scientists, 1650 King Street, Suite 200, Alexandria, VA 22314. Internet: http://www.aaps.org/sciaffairs/careerinps.htm

For information on careers in botany, contact:

- Botanical Society of America, Business Office, 1735 Neil Ave., Columbus, OH 43210-1293. Internet: http://www.botany.org

For information on careers in microbiology, contact:

- American Society for Microbiology, Office of Education and Training—Career Information, 1325 Massachusetts Ave. NW., Washington, DC 20005. Internet: http://www.asmusa.org

For a free copy of "Sources of Career Information on Careers in Biology, Conservation, and Oceanography," visit the Smithsonian Institute website at http://www.si.edu/resource/faq/nmnh/careers.htm or call (202) 782-4612. That number is not toll-free and charges may result.

Information on acquiring a job as a biological or medical scientist with the Federal government may be obtained from the Office of Personnel Management through a telephone-based system. Consult your telephone directory under U.S. government for a local number or call (912) 757-3000; TDD (912) 744-2299. That number is not toll-free and charges may result. Information also is available from their Internet site: http://www.usajobs.opm.gov.

Bookkeeping, Accounting, and Auditing Clerks

(O*NET 49023B, 55338A, and 55338B)

Significant Points

- Most jobs require only a high school diploma.
- Numerous job opportunities should arise due to high turnover in this occupation.

Nature of the Work

Bookkeeping, accounting, and auditing clerks are an organization's financial record keepers. They compute, classify, record, and verify numerical data to develop and maintain financial records.

In small establishments, *bookkeeping clerks* handle all aspects of financial transactions. They record debits and credits, compare current and past balance sheets, summarize details of separate ledgers, and prepare reports for supervisors and managers. They may also prepare bank deposits by compiling data from cashiers, verifying and balancing receipts, and sending cash, checks, or other forms of payment to the bank.

In large offices and accounting departments, *accounting clerks* have more specialized tasks. Their titles often reflect the type of accounting they do, such as accounts payable clerk or accounts receivable clerk. In addition, responsibilities vary by level of experience. Entry-level accounting clerks post details of transactions, total accounts, and compute interest charges. They may also monitor loans and accounts to ensure that payments are up to date.

More advanced accounting clerks may total, balance, and reconcile billing vouchers; ensure completeness and accuracy of data on accounts; and code documents according to company procedures. They post transactions in journals and on computer files and update these files when needed. Senior clerks also review computer printouts against manually maintained journals and make necessary corrections. They may also review invoices and statements to ensure that all information is accurate and complete, and reconcile computer reports with operating reports.

Auditing clerks verify records of transactions posted by other workers. They check figures, postings, and documents for correct entry, mathematical accuracy, and proper codes. They also correct or note errors for accountants or other workers to adjust.

As organizations continue to computerize their financial records, many bookkeeping, accounting, and auditing clerks use specialized accounting software on personal computers. They increasingly post charges to accounts on computer spreadsheets and databases, as manual posting to general ledgers is becoming obsolete. These workers now enter information from receipts or bills into computers, which is then stored either electronically, as computer printouts, or both. Widespread use of computers has also enabled bookkeeping, accounting, and auditing clerks to take on additional responsibilities, such as payroll, timekeeping, and billing.

Working Conditions

Most clerks typically are employed in an office environment. Most work alongside other clerical workers, but some clerks work in centralized units away from the front office.

Because the majority of clerks use computers on a daily basis, these workers may experience eye and muscle strain, backaches, headaches, and repetitive motion injuries. Also, clerks who review detailed data may have to sit for extended periods of time.

Most clerks work regular business hours. Accounting clerks may work longer hours to meet deadlines at the end of the fiscal year, during tax time, or when monthly and yearly accounting audits are performed. Billing, bookkeeping, and accounting clerks in hotels, restaurants, and stores may work overtime during peak holiday and vacation seasons.

Employment

Bookkeeping, accounting, and auditing clerks held about 2.1 million jobs in 1998. About 25 percent worked in wholesale and retail trade, and 16 percent were in organizations providing business, health, and social services. Approximately 1 out of 3 of bookkeeping, accounting, and auditing clerks worked part time in 1998.

Training, Other Qualifications, and Advancement

Employers typically require applicants to have at least a high school diploma or its equivalent, although many employers prefer to hire clerks with a higher level of education. Most employers prefer clerks who are computer-literate. Knowledge of word processing and spreadsheet software is especially valuable, as are experience working in an office and good interpersonal skills.

Clerks often learn the skills they need in high schools, business schools, and community colleges. Business education programs offered by these institutions typically include courses in typing, word processing, shorthand, business communications, records management, and office systems and procedures.

Some entrants into the occupation are college graduates with degrees in business, finance, or liberal arts. Although a degree is rarely required, many graduates accept entry-level clerical positions to get into a particular company or to enter the finance or accounting field with the hope of being promoted to professional or managerial positions. Some companies, such as accounting firms, have a set plan of advancement that tracks college graduates from entry-level clerical jobs into managerial positions. Workers with college degrees are likely to start at higher salaries and advance more easily than those without degrees.

Once hired, clerks usually receive on-the-job training. Under the guidance of a supervisor or other senior worker, new employees learn company procedures. Some formal classroom training may also be necessary, such as training in specific computer software.

Clerks must be careful, orderly, and detail-oriented to avoid making errors and to recognize errors made by others. These workers should also be discreet and trustworthy because they frequently come in contact with confidential material. Additionally, bookkeeping, accounting, and auditing clerks should have a strong aptitude for numbers.

Clerks usually advance by taking on more duties in the same occupation for higher pay or transferring to a closely related occupation. Most companies fill office and administrative support supervisory and managerial positions by promoting individuals from within their organizations, so clerks who acquire additional skills, experience, and training improve their advancement opportunities. With appropriate experience and education, some clerks may become accountants.

Job Outlook

Virtually all job openings for bookkeeping, accounting, and auditing clerks through 2008 will stem from replacement needs. Each year, numerous jobs will become available, as these clerks transfer to other occupations or leave the labor force. Although turnover is lower than among other record clerks, the large size of the occupation ensures plentiful job openings, including many opportunities for temporary and part-time work.

Employment of bookkeeping, accounting, and auditing clerks is expected to decline through 2008. Although a growing economy will result in more financial transactions and other activities that require these clerical workers, the continuing spread of office automation will lift worker productivity and contribute to employment decline. In addition, organizations of all sizes will continue to consolidate various record keeping functions, thus reducing the demand for these clerks.

Earnings

Salaries of clerks vary. The region of the country, size of city, and type and size of establishment all influence salary levels. The level of industry or technical expertise required and the complexity and uniqueness of a clerk's responsibilities may also affect earnings. Median annual earnings of full-time bookkeeping, accounting, and auditing clerks in 1998 were $23,190.

Related Occupations

Today, most clerks enter data into a computer system and perform basic analysis of the data. Other clerical workers who enter and manipulate data include bank tellers, statistical clerks, receiving clerks, medical record clerks, hotel and motel clerks, credit clerks, and reservation and transportation ticket agents.

Sources of Additional Information

State employment service offices can provide information about job openings for this occupation.

Busdrivers

(O*NET 97108 and 97111)

Significant Points

- Opportunities should be good, particularly for school busdriver jobs.

- A commercial driver's license is required to operate on interstate bus routes.

- Busdrivers must posses strong customer service skills, including communication skills and the ability to manage large groups of people.

Nature of the Work

Millions of Americans every day leave the driving to busdrivers. Busdrivers are essential in providing passengers with an alternative to their automobiles or other forms of transportation. Intercity busdrivers transport people between regions of a State or of the country; local transit busdrivers transport people within a metropolitan area or county; motorcoach drivers transport people on charter excursions and tours; and school busdrivers transport people to and from schools and related events.

Drivers pick up and drop off passengers at bus stops, stations, or (in the case of students) at regularly scheduled neighborhood locations based on strict time schedules. Drivers must operate vehicles safely, especially when traffic is heavier than normal. However, they cannot let light traffic put them ahead of schedule so that they miss passengers.

Intercity and *local transit busdrivers* report to their assigned terminal or garage, where they stock up on tickets or transfers and prepare trip report forms. In some firms, maintenance departments are responsible for keeping vehicles in good condition. In others, drivers may check their vehicle's tires, brakes, windshield wipers, lights, oil, fuel, and water supply before beginning their routes. Drivers usually verify that the bus has safety equipment, such as fire extinguishers, first aid kits, and emergency reflectors in case of an emergency.

During the course of their shift, intercity and local transit busdrivers collect fares; answer questions about schedules, routes, and transfer points; and sometimes announce stops. Intercity busdrivers may make only a single one-way trip to a distant city or a round trip each day. They may stop at towns just a few miles apart or only at large cities hundreds of miles apart. Local transit busdrivers may make several trips each day over the same city and suburban streets, stopping as frequently as every few blocks.

Local transit busdrivers submit daily trip reports with a record of trips made, significant schedule delays, and mechanical problems. Intercity drivers who drive across State or national boundaries must comply with U.S. Department of Transportation regulations. These include completing vehicle inspection reports and recording distances traveled and the periods of time they spend driving, performing other duties, and off duty.

Motorcoach drivers transport passengers on charter trips and sightseeing tours. Drivers routinely interact with customers and tour guides to make the trip as comfortable and informative as possible. They are directly responsible for keeping to strict schedules, adhering to the guidelines of the tour's itinerary, and the overall success of the trip. Trips frequently last more than one day, and if they are assigned to an extended tour, they may be away for a week or more. As with all drivers who drive across State or national boundaries, motorcoach drivers must comply with U.S. Department of Transportation regulations.

School busdrivers usually drive the same routes each day, stopping to pick up pupils in the morning and return them to their homes in the afternoon. Some school busdrivers also transport students and teachers on field trips or to sporting events.

Busdrivers must be alert to prevent accidents, especially in heavy traffic or in bad weather, and to avoid sudden stops or swerves that jar passengers. School busdrivers must exercise particular caution when children are getting on or off the bus. They must maintain order on their bus and enforce school safety standards by allowing only students to board. In addition, they must know and enforce rules regarding student conduct used throughout the school system.

School busdrivers do not always have to report to an assigned terminal or garage. In some cases, school busdrivers often have the choice of taking their bus home or parking it in a more convenient area. School busdrivers do not collect fares. Instead, they prepare weekly reports on the number of students, trips or runs, work hours, miles, and the amount of fuel consumption. Their supervisors set time schedules and routes for the day or week.

Working Conditions

Driving a bus through heavy traffic while dealing with passengers is not physically strenuous, but it can be stressful and fatiguing. On the other hand, many drivers enjoy the opportunity to work without direct supervision, with full responsibility for their bus and passengers.

Intercity busdrivers may work nights, weekends, and holidays and often spend nights away from home, where they stay in hotels at company expense. Senior drivers with regular routes have regular weekly work schedules, but others do not have regular schedules and must be prepared to report for work on short notice. They report for work only when called for a charter assignment or to drive extra buses on a regular route. Intercity bus travel and charter work tends to be seasonal. From May through August, drivers may work the maximum number of hours per week that regulations allow. During winter, junior drivers may work infrequently, except for busy holiday travel periods, and may be furloughed for periods of time.

School busdrivers work only when school is in session. Many work 20 hours a week or less, driving one or two routes in the morning and afternoon. Drivers taking field or athletic trips or who also have midday kindergarten routes may work more hours a week.

Regular local transit busdrivers usually have a five-day workweek; Saturdays and Sundays are considered regular workdays. Some drivers work evenings and after midnight. To accommodate commuters, many work "split shifts," such as 6 a.m. to 10 a.m. and 3 p.m. to 7 p.m., with time off in between.

Tour and charter bus drivers may work any day and all hours of the day, including weekends and holidays. Their hours are dictated by the charter trips booked and the schedule and prearranged itinerary of tours. However, like all busdrivers, their weekly hours must be consistent with the Department of Transportation's rules and regulations concerning hours of service. For example, a long-distance driver may not work more than 60 hours in any seven-day period, and drivers must rest 8 hours for every 10 hours of driving.

Employment

Busdrivers held about 638,000 jobs in 1998. More than a third worked part time. About two-thirds of all drivers worked for school systems or companies providing school bus services under contract. Most of the remainder worked for private and local government transit systems; some also worked for intercity and charter bus lines.

Training, Other Qualifications, and Advancement

Busdriver qualifications and standards are established by State and Federal regulations. All drivers must comply with Federal regulations and any State regulations that exceed Federal requirements. Federal regulations require drivers who operate vehicles designed to transport 16 or more passengers to hold a commercial driver's license (CDL) from the State in which they live.

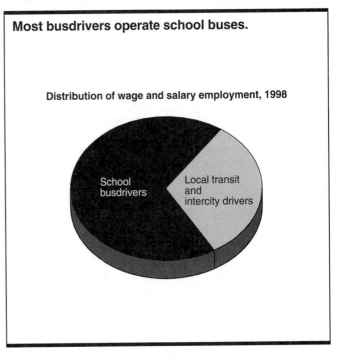

Most busdrivers operate school buses.

Distribution of wage and salary employment, 1998

School busdrivers

Local transit and intercity drivers

To qualify for a commercial driver's license, applicants must pass a written test on rules and regulations and then demonstrate they can operate a bus safely. A national data bank permanently records all driving violations incurred by persons who hold commercial licenses.

A State may not issue a commercial driver's license to a driver who already has a license suspended or revoked in another State. A driver with a CDL must accompany trainees until the trainees get their own CDLs. Information on how to apply for a commercial driver's license may be obtained from State motor vehicle administrations.

While many States allow those who are 18 years and older to drive buses within State borders, the U.S. Department of Transportation establishes minimum qualifications for busdrivers engaged in interstate commerce. Federal Motor Carrier Safety Regulations require drivers to be at least 21 years old and pass a physical examination once every two years. The main physical requirements include good hearing, 20/40 vision with or without glasses or corrective lenses, and a 70-degree field of vision in each eye. Drivers must not be color blind. Drivers must be able to hear a forced whisper in one ear at not less than five feet, with or without a hearing aid. Drivers must have normal use of arms and legs and normal blood pressure. Drivers may not use any controlled substances, unless prescribed by a licensed physician. Persons with epilepsy or diabetes controlled by insulin are not permitted to be interstate busdrivers. Federal regulations also require employers to test their drivers for alcohol and drug use as a condition of employment, and require periodic random tests while on duty. In addition, a driver must not have been convicted of a felony involving the use of a motor vehicle, a crime involving drugs, driving under the influence of drugs or alcohol, or hit-and-run driving that resulted in injury or death. All drivers must be able to read and speak English well enough to read road signs, prepare reports, and communicate with law enforcement officers and the public. In addition, drivers must take a written examination on the Motor Carrier Safety Regulations of the U.S. Department of Transportation.

Many employers prefer high school graduates and require a written test of ability to follow complex bus schedules. Many intercity and public transit bus companies prefer applicants who are at least 24 years of age; some require several years of bus or truck driving experience. In some States, school busdrivers must pass a background investigation to uncover any criminal record or history of mental problems.

Because busdrivers deal with passengers, they must be courteous. They need an even temperament and emotional stability because driving in heavy, fast-moving, or stop-and-go traffic and dealing with passengers can be stressful. Drivers must have strong customer service skills, including communication skills and the ability to coordinate and manage large groups of people.

Most intercity bus companies and local transit systems give driver trainees 2 to 8 weeks of classroom and "behind-the-wheel" instruction. In the classroom, trainees learn U.S. Department of Transportation and company work rules, safety regulations, State and municipal driving regulations, and safe driving practices. They also learn to read schedules, determine fares, keep records, and deal courteously with passengers.

School busdrivers are also required to obtain a commercial driver's license from the State in which they live. Many persons who enter school busdriving have never driven any vehicle larger than an automobile. They receive between one and four weeks of driving instruction plus classroom training on State and local laws, regulations, and policies of operating school buses; safe driving practices; driver-pupil relations; first aid; disabled student special needs; and emergency evacuation procedures. School busdrivers must also be aware of school systems rules for discipline and conduct for busdrivers and the students they transport.

During training, busdrivers practice driving on set courses. They practice turns and zigzag maneuvers, backing up, and driving in narrow lanes. Then they drive in light traffic and, eventually, on congested highways and city streets. They also make trial runs, without passengers, to improve their driving skills and learn the routes. Local transit trainees memorize and drive each of the runs operating out of their assigned garage. New drivers begin with a "break-in" period. They make regularly scheduled trips with passengers, accompanied by an experienced driver who gives helpful tips, answers questions, and evaluates the new driver's performance.

New intercity and local transit drivers are usually placed on an "extra" list to drive charter runs, extra buses on regular runs, and special runs (for example, during morning and evening rush hours and to sports events). They also substitute for regular drivers who are ill or on vacation. New drivers remain on the extra list, and may work only part time, perhaps for several years, until they have enough seniority to receive a regular run.

Senior drivers may bid for runs they prefer, such as those with more work hours, lighter traffic, weekends off, or in the case of intercity busdrivers, higher earnings or fewer workdays per week.

Opportunities for promotion are generally limited. However, experienced drivers may become supervisors or dispatchers, assigning buses to drivers, checking whether drivers are on schedule, rerouting buses to avoid blocked streets or other problems, and dispatching extra vehicles and service crews to scenes of accidents and breakdowns. In transit agencies with rail systems, drivers may become train operators or station attendants. A few drivers become managers. Promotion in publicly owned bus systems is often by competitive civil service examination. Some motorcoach drivers purchase their own equipment and go in to business for themselves.

Job Outlook

Persons seeking jobs as busdrivers over the 1998-2008 period should encounter good opportunities. Many employers have recently had difficulty finding qualified candidates to fill vacancies left by departing employees. Opportunities should be best for individuals with good driving records who are willing to start on a part-time or irregular schedule, as well as for those seeking jobs as school busdrivers in rapidly growing metropolitan areas. Those seeking higher paying intercity and public transit busdriver positions may encounter competition.

Employment of busdrivers is expected to increase about as fast as average for all occupations through the year 2008, primarily to meet the transportation needs of a growing school-age population and local environmental concerns. Thousands of additional job openings are expected to occur each year because of the need to replace workers who take jobs in other occupations, retire, or leave the occupation for other reasons.

School busdriver jobs should be easiest to acquire because most are part-time positions with high turnover and minimal training requirements. The number of school busdrivers is expected to increase as a result of growth in elementary and secondary school enrollments. In addition, as more of the Nation's population is concentrated in suburban areas (where students generally ride school buses) and less in the central cities (where transportation is not provided for most pupils) more school busdrivers will be needed.

Employment of local transit and intercity drivers will grow as bus ridership increases. Local and intercity bus travel is expected to increase as the population and labor force grows. However, more individual travelers will opt to travel by airplane or automobile rather than by bus. Most growth in intercity drivers will probably be in group charter travel, rather than scheduled intercity bus services. There may continue to be competition for local transit and intercity busdriver jobs in some areas because many of these positions offer relatively high wages and attractive benefits. The most competitive positions will be those offering regular hours and steady driving routes.

Full-time busdrivers are rarely laid off during recessions. However, hours of part-time local transit and intercity busdrivers may be reduced if bus ridership decreases because fewer extra buses would be needed. Seasonal layoffs are common. Many intercity busdrivers with little seniority, for example, are furloughed during the winter when regular schedule and charter business falls off; school busdrivers seldom work during the summer or school holidays.

Earnings

Median hourly earnings of transit and intercity busdrivers were $11.72 in 1998. The middle 50 percent earned between $8.58 and $16.04 an hour. The lowest 10 percent earned less than $6.66, and the highest 10 percent earned more than $19.18 an hour. Median hourly earnings in the industries employing the largest numbers of transit and intercity busdrivers in 1997 were as follows:

Local government, except education and hospitals	$14.20
Intercity and rural bus transportation	10.50
Local and suburban transportation	10.20
School buses, contract	10.20
Bus charter service	8.80

Median hourly earnings of school busdrivers were $9.05 in 1998. The middle 50 percent earned between $6.33 and $11.44 an hour. The lowest 10 percent earned less than $5.59, and the highest 10 percent earned more than $14.00 an hour. Median hourly earnings of school busdrivers in 1997 were $9.20 in contract school buses and $8.60 in elementary and secondary schools.

According to the American Public Transit Association, in early 1999 local transit busdrivers in metropolitan areas with more than two million inhabitants were paid an average top hourly wage rate of about $17.90 by companies with over 1,000 employees and about $16.00 by those with fewer than 1,000 employees. In smaller metropolitan areas, they had an average top hourly wage rate of about $14.70 in areas with between 250,000 and 500,000 residents and about $12.60 in areas with resident populations below 50,000. Generally, drivers can reach the top rate in three or four years.

The benefits busdrivers receive from their employers vary greatly. Most intercity and local transit busdrivers receive paid health and life insurance, sick leave, and free bus rides on any of the regular routes of their line or system. Drivers who work full time also get as much as four weeks of vacation annually. Most local transit

busdrivers are also covered by dental insurance and pension plans. School busdrivers receive sick leave, and many are covered by health and life insurance and pension plans. Because they generally do not work when school is not in session, they do not get vacation leave. In a number of States, local transit and school busdrivers employed by local governments are covered by a Statewide public employee pension system.

Most intercity and many local transit busdrivers are members of the Amalgamated Transit Union. Local transit busdrivers in New York and several other large cities belong to the Transport Workers Union of America. Some drivers belong to the United Transportation Union and the International Brotherhood of Teamsters.

Related Occupations

Other workers who drive vehicles on highways and city streets are taxi drivers, truck drivers, and chauffeurs.

Sources of Additional Information

For further information on employment opportunities, contact local transit systems, intercity buslines, school systems, or the local offices of the State employment service.

General information on busdriving is available from:

- American Bus Association, 1100 New York Avenue NW., Suite 1050, Washington, DC 20005. Internet: http://www.buses.org

General information on school busdriving is available from:

- National School Transportation Association, P.O. Box 2639, Springfield, VA 22152. Internet: http://www.schooltrans.com

General information on local transit busdriving is available from:

- American Public Transit Association, 1201 New York Ave. NW., Suite 400, Washington, DC 20005. Internet: http://www.apta.com

General information on motorcoach driving is available from:

- United Motorcoach Association, 113 S. West St., 4th Floor, Alexandria, VA 22314. Telephone (toll free): 1-800-424-8262. Internet: http://www.uma.org

Cardiovascular Technologists and Technicians

(O*NET 32925 and 32926)

Significant Points

- Employment will grow as fast as the average, but the number of job openings created will be low, because the occupation is small.

- About 8 out of 10 jobs are in hospitals, in both inpatient and outpatient settings.

Nature of the Work

Cardiovascular technologists and technicians assist physicians in diagnosing and treating cardiac (heart) and peripheral vascular (blood vessel) ailments.

Cardiovascular technologists specializing in cardiac catheterization procedures are called *cardiology technologists*. They assist physicians with invasive procedures in which a small tube, or catheter, is wound through a patient's blood vessel from a spot on the patient's leg into the heart. This is done to determine if a blockage exists and for other diagnostic purposes. In balloon angioplasty, a procedure used to treat blockages of blood vessels, technologists assist physicians who insert a catheter with a balloon on the end to the point of the obstruction.

Technologists prepare patients for these procedures by first positioning them on an examining table and then shaving, cleaning, and administering anesthesia to the top of the patient's leg near the groin. During the procedures, they monitor patients' blood pressure and heart rate using electrocardiogram (EKG) equipment and notify the physician if something appears wrong. Technologists may also prepare and monitor patients during open-heart surgery and the implantation of pacemakers.

Cardiovascular technologists and technicians may specialize in noninvasive peripheral vascular tests. Those who assist physicians in the diagnosis of disorders affecting circulation are known as *vascular technologists*. Vascular technologists use ultrasound instrumentation, such as doppler ultrasound, to noninvasively record vascular information, such as blood pressure, limb volume changes, oxygen saturation, cerebral circulation, peripheral circulation, and abdominal circulation. Many of these tests are performed during or immediately after surgery. Technologists and technicians who use ultrasound on the heart are referred to as *echocardiographers*. They use ultrasound equipment that transmits sound waves and then collects the echoes to form an image on a screen.

Cardiovascular technicians who obtain electrocardiograms are known as *electrocardiograph (*abbreviated *EKG* or *ECG) technicians*. To take a basic EKG, which traces electrical impulses transmitted by the heart, technicians attach electrodes to the patient's chest, arms, and legs, and then manipulate switches on an electrocardiograph machine to obtain a reading. This test is done before most kinds of surgery and as part of a routine physical examination, especially for persons who have reached middle age or have a history of cardiovascular problems.

EKG technicians with advanced training perform Holter monitor and stress testing. For a Holter monitoring, technicians place electrodes on the patient's chest and attach a portable EKG monitor to the patient's belt. Following 24 to 48 hours of normal routine for the patient, the technician removes a cassette tape from the monitor and places it in a scanner. After checking the quality of the recorded impulses on an electronic screen, the technician prints the information from the tape, so a physician can interpret it later. The printed output from the scanner is eventually used by a physician to diagnose heart ailments.

For a treadmill stress test, EKG technicians document the patient's medical history, explain the procedure, connect the patient to an EKG monitor, and obtain a baseline reading and resting blood pressure. Next, they monitor the heart's performance, while the patient is walking on a treadmill, gradually increasing the treadmill's speed to observe the effect of increased exertion. Those cardiovascular technicians who perform EKG and stress tests are known as "noninvasive" technicians, because the techniques they use do not require the insertion of probes or other instruments into the patient's body.

Some cardiovascular technologists and technicians schedule appointments, type doctor interpretations, maintain patient files, and care for equipment.

Working Conditions

Technologists and technicians generally work a 5-day, 40-hour week that may include weekends. Those in catheterization labs tend to work longer hours and may work evenings. They may also be on call during the night and on weekends.

Cardiovascular technologists and technicians spend a lot of time walking and standing. Those who work in catheterization labs may face stressful working conditions because they are in close contact with patients who have serious heart ailments. Some patients, for example, may encounter complications from time to time that have life or death implications.

Employment

Cardiovascular technologists and technicians held about 33,000 jobs in 1998. Most worked in hospital cardiology departments, whereas some worked in cardiologists' offices, cardiac rehabilitation centers, or ambulatory surgery centers. About one-third were EKG technicians.

Training, Other Qualifications, and Advancement

Although some cardiovascular technologists, vascular technologists, and echocardiographers are currently trained on the job, an increasing number receive training in two- to four-year programs. Cardiology technologists normally complete a two-year junior or community college program. One year is dedicated to core courses, followed by a year of specialized instruction in either invasive, noninvasive, or noninvasive peripheral cardiology. Those who are qualified in a related allied health profession only need to complete the year of specialized instruction. Graduates from programs accredited by the Joint Review Committee on Education in Cardiovascular Technology are eligible to register as professional technologists with the American Registry of Diagnostic Medical Sonographers or Cardiovascular Credentialing International.

For basic EKGs, Holter monitoring, and stress testing, one-year certificate programs exist; but most EKG technicians are still trained on the job by an EKG supervisor or a cardiologist. On-the-job training usually lasts about 8 to 16 weeks. Most employers prefer to train people already in the health care field, nursing aides, for example. Some EKG technicians are students enrolled in two-year programs to become technologists, who are working part time to gain experience and make contact with employers.

Cardiovascular technologists and technicians must be reliable, have mechanical aptitude, and be able to follow detailed instructions. A pleasant, relaxed manner for putting patients at ease is an asset.

Job Outlook

Employment of cardiovascular technologists and technicians is expected to grow as fast as the average for all occupations through the year 2008, with technologists and technicians experiencing different patterns of employment change.

Employment of *cardiology technologists* is expected to grow much faster than the average for all occupations. Growth will occur as the population ages, because older people have a higher incidence of heart problems. Likewise, employment of vascular technologists will grow faster than the average, as advances in vascular technology reduce the need for more costly and invasive procedures.

In contrast, employment of *EKG technicians* is expected to decline, as hospitals train nursing aides and others to perform basic EKG procedures. Individuals trained in Holter monitoring and stress testing are expected to have more favorable job prospects than those who can only perform a basic EKG.

Some job openings for cardiovascular technologists and technicians will arise from replacement needs, as individuals transfer to other jobs or leave the labor force. However, relatively few job openings are expected to come about due to growth and replacement needs because the occupation is small.

Earnings

Median annual earnings of cardiology technologists were $35,770 in 1998. The middle 50 percent earned between $29,060 and $42,350 a year. The lowest 10 percent earned less than $23,010, and the highest 10 percent earned more than $49,780 a year. Median annual earnings of cardiology technologists in 1997 were $34,500 in hospitals.

Median annual earnings of EKG technicians were $24,360 in 1998. The middle 50 percent earned between $19,660 and $30,860 a year. The lowest 10 percent earned less than $16,130, and the highest 10 percent earned more than $39,060 a year. Median annual earnings of EKG technicians in 1997 were $23,200 in hospitals.

Related Occupations

Cardiovascular technologists and technicians operate sophisticated equipment that helps physicians and other health practitioners diagnose and treat patients. So do nuclear medicine technologists, radiologic technologists, diagnostic medical sonographers, electroneurodiagnostic technologists, perfusionists, radiation therapists, and respiratory therapists.

Sources of Additional Information

For general information about a career in cardiovascular technology contact:

- Alliance of Cardiovascular Professionals, 910 Charles St., Fredericksburg, VA 22401.

For a list of accredited programs in cardiovascular technology, contact:

- Joint Review Committee on Education in Cardiovascular Technology, 3525 Elliott Mills Dr., Suite N, Elliott City, MD 21043-4547.

For information on vascular technology, contact:

- The Society of Vascular Technology, 4601 Presidents Dr., Suite 260, Lanham, MD 20706-4365.

For information on echocardiography, contact:

- American Society of Echocardiography, 4101 Lake Boone Trail, Suite 201, Raleigh, NC 27607.

For information regarding registration and certification contact:

- Cardiovascular Credentialing International, 4456 Corporation Lane, Suite 110, Virginia Beach, VA 23462.
- American Registry of Diagnostic Medical Sonographers, 600 Jefferson Plaza, Suite 360, Rockville, MD 20852-1150.

Chefs, Cooks, and Other Kitchen Workers

(O*NET 65021, 65026, 65028, 65032, 65035, 65038A, 65038B, and 69999E)

Significant Points

- Many young people work as chefs, cooks, and other kitchen workers; over 20 percent are between 16 and 19 years old.

- About 35 percent of these workers work part-time.

- Job openings are expected to be plentiful through 2008, reflecting average growth and substantial turnover in this large occupation.

Nature of the Work

A reputation for serving good food is essential to the success of any restaurant or hotel, whether it offers exotic cuisine or hamburgers. Chefs, cooks, and other kitchen workers are largely responsible for establishing and maintaining this reputation. Chefs and cooks do this by preparing meals, while other kitchen workers assist them by cleaning surfaces, peeling vegetable, and performing other duties.

In general, *chefs* and *cooks* measure, mix, and cook ingredients according to recipes. In the course of their work they use a variety of pots, pans, cutlery, and other equipment, including ovens, broilers, grills, slicers, grinders, and blenders. Chefs and cooks are often responsible for directing the work of other kitchen workers, estimating food requirements, and ordering food supplies. Some chefs and cooks also help plan meals and develop menus. Although the terms chef and cook are still used interchangeably, chefs tend to be more highly skilled and better trained than most cooks. Due to their skillful preparation of traditional dishes and refreshing twists in creating new ones, many chefs have earned fame for both themselves and the establishments where they work.

The specific responsibilities of chefs and cooks are determined by a number of factors, including the type of restaurant in which they work. *Institutional chefs* and *cooks*, for example, work in the kitchens of schools, cafeterias, businesses, hospitals, and other institutions. For each meal, they prepare a large quantity of a limited number of entrees, vegetables, and desserts. *Restaurant chefs* and *cooks* usually prepare a wider selection of dishes, cooking most orders individually. *Short-order cooks* prepare foods in restaurants and coffee shops that emphasize fast service. They grill and garnish hamburgers, prepare sandwiches, fry eggs, and cook French fries, often working on several orders at the same time. *Specialty fast-food cooks* prepare a limited selection of menu items in fast-food restaurants. They cook and package batches of food, such as hamburgers and fried chicken, which are prepared to order or kept warm until sold.

Bread and *pastry bakers*, called pastry chefs in some kitchens, produce baked goods for restaurants, institutions, and retail bakery shops. Unlike bakers who work in large, automated industrial bakeries, bread and pastry bakers need only to supply the customers who visit their establishment. They bake small quantities of breads, rolls, pastries, pies, and cakes, doing most of the work by hand. These bakers measure and mix ingredients, shape and bake the dough, and apply fillings and decorations. Some related workers are employed in coffee houses, which may also serve pastries or other snacks. These workers operate specialized equipment such as cappuccino and espresso machines. Some food products are made on the premises, while others are delivered daily.

Other kitchen workers, under the direction of chefs and cooks, perform tasks requiring less skill. They weigh and measure ingredients, go after pots and pans, and stir and strain soups and sauces. These workers also clean, peel, and slice vegetables and fruits and make salads. They may cut and grind meats, poultry, and seafood in preparation for cooking. Their responsibilities also include cleaning work areas, equipment, utensils, dishes, and silverware.

The number and types of workers employed in kitchens depends on the type of establishment. For example, fast-food outlets offer only a few items, which are prepared by fast-food cooks. Small, full-service restaurants offering casual dining often feature a limited number of easy-to-prepare items supplemented by short-order specialties and ready-made desserts. Typically, one cook prepares all the food with the help of a short-order cook and one or two other kitchen workers.

Large eating places tend to have varied menus and employ kitchen workers who prepare much more of the food they serve from scratch. Kitchen staffs often include several chefs and cooks, sometimes called assistant or apprentice chefs and cooks; a bread and pastry baker; and many less-skilled kitchen workers. Each chef or cook usually has a special assignment and often a special job title—vegetable, fry, or sauce cook, for example. Executive chefs coordinate the work of the kitchen staff and often direct the preparation of certain foods. They decide the size of servings, plan menus, and buy food supplies.

Working Conditions

Many restaurant and institutional kitchens have modern equipment, convenient work areas, and air-conditioning, but many kitchens in older and smaller eating places are not as well equipped. Working conditions depend on the type and quantity of food being prepared and the local laws governing food service operations.

Workers usually must withstand the pressure and strain of working in close quarters, standing for hours at a time, lifting heavy pots and kettles, and working near hot ovens and grills. Job hazards include slips and falls, cuts, and burns, but injuries are seldom serious.

Work hours in restaurants may include early mornings, late evenings, holidays, and weekends. Work schedules of chefs, cooks, and other kitchen workers in factory and school cafeterias may be more regular. Nearly 1 in 3 cooks and 2 out of 5 other kitchen and food preparation workers work part time, compared to 1 out of 6 workers throughout the economy.

The wide range in dining hours creates work opportunities attractive to homemakers, students, and other individuals seeking supplemental income. For example, over 20 percent of kitchen and food preparation workers are 16-19 years old. Kitchen workers employed by public and private schools may work during the school year only, usually for 9 or 10 months. Similarly, establishments at vacation resorts usually only offer seasonal employment.

Employment

Chefs, cooks, and other kitchen workers held more than 3.3 million jobs in 1998. Restaurant cooks held 783,000 of these jobs; short-order and fast-food cooks, 677,000; institutional cooks, 418,000; bread and pastry bakers, 171,000; and other kitchen workers, 1,256,000.

About three-fifths of all chefs, cooks, and other kitchen workers were employed in restaurants and other retail eating and drinking places. One-fifth worked in institutions such as schools, universities, hospitals, and nursing homes. Grocery stores, hotels, and other organizations employed the remainder.

Training, Other Qualifications, and Advancement

Most chefs, cooks, and other kitchen workers start as fast-food or short-order cooks or in another lower-skilled kitchen position. These positions require little education or training, and most skills are learned on the job. After acquiring some basic food handling, preparation, and cooking skills, these workers may be able to advance to an assistant cook or short-order cook position.

Although a high school diploma is not required for beginning jobs, it is recommended for those planning a career as a cook or chef. High school or vocational school courses in business arithmetic and business administration are particularly helpful. Many school districts, in cooperation with State departments of education, provide on-the-job training and summer workshops for cafeteria kitchen workers with aspirations of becoming cooks. Large corporations in the food service and entertainment industries also offer paid internships and summer jobs, which can provide valuable experience.

To achieve the level of skill required of an executive chef or cook in a fine restaurant, many years of training and experience are necessary. An increasing number of chefs and cooks obtain their training through high school, post-high school vocational programs, or two- or four-year colleges. Chefs and cooks also may be trained in apprenticeship programs offered by professional culinary institutes, industry associations, and trade unions. An example is the three-year apprenticeship program administered by local chapters of the American Culinary Federation in cooperation with local employers and junior colleges or vocational education institutions. In addition, some large hotels and restaurants operate their own training programs for cooks and chefs.

People who have had courses in commercial food preparation may be able to start in a cook or chef job without having to spend time in a lower-skilled kitchen job. Their education may give them an advantage when looking for jobs in better restaurants and hotels, where hiring standards often are high. Although some vocational programs in high schools offer training, employers usually prefer training given by trade schools, vocational centers, colleges, professional associations, or trade unions. Post-secondary courses range from a few months to two years or more and are open in some cases only to high school graduates. The Armed Forces are also a good source of training and experience.

Although curricula may vary, students in these programs usually spend most of their time learning to prepare food through actual practice. They learn to bake, broil, and otherwise prepare food, and to use and care for kitchen equipment. Training programs often include courses in menu planning, determination of portion size, food cost control, purchasing food supplies in quantity, selection and storage of food, and use of leftover food to minimize waste. Students also learn hotel and restaurant sanitation and public health rules for handling food. Training in supervisory and management skills sometimes is emphasized in courses offered by private vocational schools, professional associations, and university programs.

About 700 schools offer culinary courses across the Nation. The American Culinary Federation accredited about 100 training programs and a number of apprenticeship programs in 1998. Typical apprenticeships last three years and combine classroom and work experience. Accreditation is an indication that a culinary program meets recognized standards regarding course content, facilities, and quality of instruction. The American Culinary Federation also certifies pastry professionals, culinary educators, and chefs and cooks at the levels of cook, working chef, executive chef, and master chef. Certification standards are based primarily on experience and formal training.

Important characteristics for chefs, cooks, and other kitchen workers include the ability to work as part of a team, a keen sense of taste and smell, and personal cleanliness. Most States require health certificates indicating workers are free from communicable diseases.

Advancement opportunities for chefs and cooks are better than for most other food and beverage preparation and service occupations. Many chefs and cooks acquire high-paying positions and new cooking skills by moving from one job to another. Besides culinary skills, advancement also depends on ability to supervise less-skilled workers and limit food costs by minimizing waste and accurately anticipating the amount of perishable supplies needed. Some chefs and cooks go into business as caterers or restaurant owners, while others become instructors in vocational programs in high schools, community colleges, or other academic institutions. A number of cooks and chefs advance to executive chef positions or supervisory or management positions, particularly in hotels, clubs, and larger, more elegant restaurants.

Job Outlook

Job openings for chefs, cooks, and other kitchen workers are expected to be plentiful through 2008. While job growth will create new positions, the overwhelming majority of job openings will stem from the need to replace workers who leave their jobs. Minimal educational and training requirements, combined with a large number of part-time positions, make employment as chefs, cooks, and other kitchen workers attractive to people seeking a short-term source of income and a flexible schedule. In coming years, these workers will continue to transfer to other occupations or stop working to assume household responsibilities or to attend school full time, creating numerous openings for those entering the field.

These openings will be supplemented by new openings resulting from employment growth, as overall employment of chefs, cooks, and other kitchen workers is expected to increase about as fast as the average for all occupations through 2008. Employment growth will be spurred by increases in population, household income, and leisure time that will allow people to dine out and take vacations more often. In addition, growth in the number of two-income households will lead more families to opt for the convenience of dining out.

Projected employment growth varies by specialty. Increases in the number of families and the more affluent 55-and-older population will lead to a growing number of restaurants that offer table service and more varied menus, which require higher-skilled cooks and chefs. Also, the popularity of fresh baked breads and pastries should ensure continued rapid growth in the employment of bakers. Employment of short-order and specialty fast-food cooks, most of whom work in fast-food restaurants, also is expected to increase in response to growth of the 16-24 year-old population and the continuing fast-paced lifestyle of many Americans.

Employment of institutional and cafeteria chefs and cooks, on the other hand, will grow more slowly than other types of cooks. Their employment will not keep pace with the rapid growth in the educational and health services industries, where their employment is concentrated. As many high schools and hospitals try to make "institutional food" more attractive to students, staff, visitors, and patients, they increasingly contract out their food services. Many of the contracted companies emphasize fast food and employ short-order and fast-food cooks, instead of institutional and cafeteria cooks, reducing the demand for these workers.

Earnings

Wages of chefs, cooks, and other kitchen workers depend greatly on the part of the country and the type of establishment in which they are employed. Wages usually are highest in elegant restaurants and hotels, where many executive chefs are employed.

Median hourly earnings of restaurant cooks were $7.81 in 1998, with most earning between $6.38 and $9.53. Cooks in fast-food restaurants and short-order cooks had median hourly earnings of $6.12, with most earning between $5.69 and $7.38. Median hourly earnings of bread and pastry bakers were $8.17; most earned between $6.57 and $10.36. Median hourly earnings in the industries employing the largest number of food preparation workers in 1997 were:

Hospitals	$7.55
Grocery stores	7.21
Elementary and secondary schools	7.16
Nursing and personal care facilities	6.92
Eating and drinking places	5.87

Some employers provide employees with uniforms and free meals, but Federal law permits employers to deduct from their employees' wages the cost or fair value of any meals or lodging provided, and some employers do so. Chefs, cooks, and other kitchen workers who work full time often receive typical benefits, but part-time workers usually do not.

In some large hotels and restaurants, kitchen workers belong to unions. The principal unions are the Hotel Employees and Restaurant Employees International Union and the Service Employees International Union.

Related Occupations

Workers who perform tasks similar to those of chefs, cooks, and other kitchen workers include butchers and meat cutters, cannery workers, and industrial bakers.

Sources of Additional Information

Information about job opportunities may be obtained from local employers and local offices of the State employment service.

Career information about chefs, cooks, and other kitchen workers, as well as a directory of two- and four-year colleges that offer courses or programs that prepare persons for food service careers, is available from:

● The National Restaurant Association, 1200 17th St. NW., Washington, DC 20036-3097.

For information on the American Culinary Federation's apprenticeship and certification programs for cooks, as well as a list of accredited culinary programs, send a self addressed, stamped envelope to:

● American Culinary Federation, P.O. Box 3466, St. Augustine, FL 32085.

For general information on hospitality careers, write to:

● Council on Hotel, Restaurant, and Institutional Education, 1200 17th St. NW., Washington, DC 20036-3097.

Chemists

(O*NET 24105)

Significant Points

● A bachelor's degree in chemistry or a related discipline is usually the minimum educational requirement; however, many research jobs require a Ph.D.

● Job growth will be concentrated in drug manufacturing and research and testing services firms.

Nature of the Work

Everything in the environment, whether it occurs naturally or is of human design, is composed of chemicals. Chemists search for and put to use new knowledge about chemicals. Chemical research has led to the discovery and development of new and improved synthetic fibers, paints, adhesives, drugs, cosmetics, electronic components, lubricants, and thousands of other products. Chemists also develop processes that save energy and reduce pollution, such as improved oil refining and petrochemical processing methods. Research on the chemistry of living things spurs advances in medicine, agriculture, food processing, and other fields.

Chemists apply their knowledge of chemistry in various ways. Many work in research and development (R&D). In basic research, chemists investigate properties, composition, and structure of matter and the laws that govern the combination of elements and reactions of substances. In applied research and development, they create new products and processes or improve existing ones, often using knowledge gained from basic research. For example, synthetic rubber and plastics resulted from research on small molecules uniting to form large ones, a process called polymerization. R&D chemists use computers and a wide variety of sophisticated laboratory instrumentation. The use of computers to analyze complex data allows chemists to practice combinatorial chemistry. This technique makes and tests large quantities of chemical compounds simultaneously in order to find compounds with desired properties. Combinatorial chemistry makes chemists more productive by saving time and materials and could result in more products being developed in the future. They also spend time documenting and analyzing the results of their work and writing formal reports.

Chemists also work in production and quality control in chemical manufacturing plants. They prepare instructions for plant workers that specify ingredients, mixing times, and temperatures for each stage in the process. They also monitor automated processes to ensure proper product yield, and they test samples of raw materials or finished products to ensure they meet industry and government standards, including the regulations governing pollution. Chemists record and report on test results and improve existing or develop new test methods.

Chemists often specialize in a subfield. *Analytical chemists* determine the structure, composition, and nature of substances by examining and identifying the various elements or compounds that make up a substance. They study the relations and interactions of the parts and develop analytical techniques. They also identify the presence and concentration of chemical pollutants in air, water, and soil. *Organic chemists* study the chemistry of the vast number of carbon compounds that make up all living things. Organic chemists who synthesize elements or simple compounds to create new compounds or substances that have different properties and applications have developed many commercial products, such as drugs, plastics, and elastomers (elastic substances similar to rubber). *Inorganic chemists* study compounds consisting mainly of elements other than carbon, such as those in electronic components. *Physical chemists* study the physical characteristics of atoms and molecules and investigate how chemical reactions work. Their research may result in new and better energy sources.

Working Conditions

Chemists usually work regular hours in offices and laboratories. Research chemists spend much time in laboratories, but also work in offices when they do theoretical research or plan, record, and report on their lab research. Although some laboratories are small, others are large enough to incorporate prototype chemical manufacturing facilities as well as advanced equipment. Chemists do some of their work in a chemical plant or outdoors—while gathering water samples to test for pollutants, for example. Some chemists are exposed to health or safety hazards when handling certain chemicals, but there is little risk if proper procedures are followed.

Employment

Chemists held about 96,000 jobs in 1998. Nearly half of chemists are employed in manufacturing firms—mostly in the chemical manufacturing industry, which includes firms that produce plastics and synthetic materials, drugs, soaps and cleaners, paints, industrial organic chemicals, and other miscellaneous chemical products. Chemists also work for State and local governments and for Federal agencies. Health and Human Services (which includes the Food and Drug Administration, the National Institutes of Health, and the Center for Disease Control) is the major Federal employer of chemists. The Departments of Defense and Agriculture and the Environmental Protection Agency also employ chemists. Other chemists work for research, development, and testing services. In addition, thousands of persons held chemistry faculty positions in colleges and universities.

Chemists are employed in all parts of the country, but they are mainly concentrated in large industrial areas.

Training, Other Qualifications, and Advancement

A bachelor's degree in chemistry or a related discipline is usually the minimum educational requirement for entry-level chemist jobs. However, many research jobs require a Ph.D.

Many colleges and universities offer a bachelor's degree program in chemistry, about 620 of which are approved by the American Chemical Society (ACS). Several hundred colleges and universities also offer advanced degree programs in chemistry; around 320 master's programs and about 190 doctoral programs are ACS-approved.

Students planning careers as chemists should take courses in science and mathematics and should like working with their hands building scientific apparatus and performing experiments. Perseverance, curiosity, and the ability to concentrate on detail and to work independently are essential. In addition to required courses in analytical, inorganic, organic, and physical chemistry, undergraduate chemistry majors usually study biological sciences, mathematics, and physics. Those interested in the environmental field should also take courses in environmental studies and become familiar with current legislation and regulations. Computer courses are essential, as employers increasingly prefer job applicants who are able to apply computer skills to modeling and simulation tasks and operate computerized laboratory equipment.

Because research and development chemists are increasingly expected to work on interdisciplinary teams, some understanding of other disciplines, including business and marketing or economics, is desirable, along with leadership ability and good oral and written communication skills. Experience, either in academic laboratories or through internships or co-op programs in industry, also is useful. Some employers of research chemists, particularly in the pharmaceutical industry, prefer to hire individuals with several years of postdoctoral experience.

Graduate students typically specialize in a subfield of chemistry, such as analytical chemistry or polymer chemistry, depending on their interests and the kind of work they wish to do. For example, those interested in doing drug research in the pharmaceutical industry usually develop a strong background in synthetic organic chemistry. However, students normally need not specialize at the undergraduate level. In fact, undergraduates who are broadly trained have more flexibility when job hunting or changing jobs than if they narrowly define their interests. Most employers provide new graduates additional training or education.

In government or industry, beginning chemists with a bachelor's degree work in quality control or analytical testing or assist senior chemists in research and development laboratories. Many employers prefer chemists with a Ph.D. or at least a master's degree to lead basic and applied research. A Ph.D. is also often preferred for advancement to many administrative positions.

Job Outlook

Employment of chemists is expected to grow about as fast as the average for all occupations through 2008. Job growth will be concentrated in drug manufacturing and research, development, and testing services firms. The chemical industry, the major employer of chemists, should face continued demand for goods such as new and better pharmaceuticals and personal care products, as well as more specialty chemicals designed to address specific problems or applications. To meet these demands, chemical firms will continue to devote money to research and development—through in-house teams or outside contractors—spurring employment growth for chemists.

Within the chemical industry, job opportunities are expected to be most plentiful in pharmaceutical and biotechnology firms. Stronger competition among drug companies and an aging population are contributing to the need for innovative and improved drugs discovered through scientific research. Chemical firms that develop and manufacture personal products such as toiletries and cosmetics must continually innovate and develop new and better products to remain competitive. Additionally, as the population grows and becomes better informed, the demand for different or improved grooming products (including vegetable-based products, products with milder formulas, treatments for aging skin, and products that have been developed using more benign chemical processes than in the past) will remain strong, spurring the need for chemists.

In most of the remaining segments of the chemical industry, employment growth is expected to decline as companies downsize and turn to outside contractors to provide specialized services. Nevertheless, some job openings will result from the need to replace chemists who retire or otherwise leave the labor force. Quality control will continue to be an important issue in the chemical and other industries that use chemicals in their manufacturing processes. Chemists will also be needed to develop and improve the technologies and processes used to produce chemicals for all purposes, and to monitor and measure air and water pollutants to ensure compliance with local, State, and Federal environmental regulations.

Outside the chemical industry, firms that provide research, development, and testing services are expected to be the source of numerous job opportunities between 1998 and 2008. Chemical companies, including drug manufacturers, are increasingly turning to these services to perform specialized research and other work formerly done by in-house chemists. Chemists will also be needed to work in research and testing firms that focus on environmental testing and cleanup.

During periods of economic recession, layoffs of chemists may occur—especially in the industrial chemicals industry. This industry provides many of the raw materials to the auto manufacturing and construction industries, both of which are vulnerable to temporary slowdowns during recessions.

Earnings

Median annual earnings of chemists in 1998 were $46,220. The middle 50 percent earned between $34,580 and $68,360. The lowest 10 percent earned less than $27,240, and the highest 10 percent earned more than $86,260. Median annual earnings in the industries employing the largest numbers of chemists in 1997 were:

Federal government $62,800

Drugs 43,300

Research and testing services 34,500

A survey by the American Chemical Society reports that the median salary of all their members with a bachelor's degree was $50,100 a year in 1999; with a master's degree, $61,000; and with a Ph.D., $76,000. Median salaries were highest for those working in private industry; those in academia earned the least. According to an ACS survey of recent graduates, inexperienced chemistry graduates with a bachelor's degree earned a median starting salary of $29,500 in 1998; with a master's degree, $38,500; and with a Ph.D., $59,300. Among bachelor's degree graduates, those who had completed internships or had other work experience while in school commanded the highest starting salaries.

In 1999, chemists in nonsupervisory, supervisory, and managerial positions in the Federal government earned an average salary of $64,200.

Related Occupations

The work of chemical engineers, agricultural scientists, biological scientists, and chemical technicians is closely related to the work done by chemists. The work of other physical and life science occupations, such as physicists and medical scientists, may also be similar to that of chemists.

Sources of Additional Information

General information on career opportunities and earnings for chemists is available from:

● American Chemical Society, Education Division, 1155 16th St. NW., Washington, DC 20036. Internet: http://www.acs.org

Information on acquiring a job as a chemist with the Federal government may be obtained from the Office of Personnel Management through a telephone-based system. Consult your telephone directory under U.S. government for a local number or call (912) 757-3000; TDD (912) 744-2299. That number is not toll free and charges may result. Information also is available from their Internet site: http://www.usajobs.opm.gov.

Chiropractors

(O*NET 32113)

Significant Points

● Employment of chiropractors is expected to increase rapidly, and job prospects should be good.

● Chiropractic care of back, neck, extremities, and other joint damage has become more accepted as a result of recent research and changing attitudes.

● In chiropractic, as in other types of independent practice, earnings are relatively low in the beginning, but they increase as the practice grows.

Nature of the Work

Chiropractors, also known as doctors of chiropractic or chiropractic physicians, diagnose and treat patients whose health problems are associated with the body's muscular, nervous, and skeletal systems, especially the spine. Chiropractors believe interference with these systems impairs normal functions and lowers resistance to disease. They also hold that spinal or vertebral dysfunction alters many important body functions by affecting the nervous system, and that skeletal imbalance through joint or articular dysfunction, especially in the spine, can cause pain.

The chiropractic approach to health care is holistic, stressing the patient's overall health and wellness. It recognizes that many factors affect health, including exercise, diet, rest, environment, and heredity. Chiropractors use natural, drugless, nonsurgical health treatments, and rely on the body's inherent recuperative abilities. They also recommend lifestyle changes—in eating, exercise, and sleeping habits, for example—to their patients. When appropriate, chiropractors consult with and refer patients to other health practitioners.

Like other health practitioners, chiropractors follow a standard routine to secure the information needed for diagnosis and treatment. They take the patient's medical history; conduct physical, neurological, and orthopedic examinations; and may order laboratory tests. X-rays and other diagnostic images are important tools because of the emphasis on the spine and its proper function. Chiropractors also employ a postural and spinal analysis common to chiropractic diagnosis.

In cases in which difficulties can be traced to involvement of musculoskeletal structures, chiropractors manually adjust the spinal column. Many chiropractors use water, light, massage, ultrasound, electric, and heat therapy. They may also apply supports such as straps, tapes, and braces. Chiropractors counsel patients about wellness concepts such as nutrition, exercise, lifestyle changes, and stress management, but do not prescribe drugs or perform surgery.

Some chiropractors specialize in sports injuries, neurology, orthopedics, nutrition, internal disorders, or diagnostic imaging.

Many chiropractors are solo or group practitioners who also have the administrative responsibilities of running a practice. In larger offices, chiropractors delegate these tasks to office managers and chiropractic assistants. Chiropractors in private practice are responsible for developing a patient base, hiring employees, and keeping records.

Working Conditions

Chiropractors work in clean, comfortable offices. The average workweek is about 40 hours, although longer hours are not uncommon. Solo practitioners set their own hours, but may work evenings or weekends to accommodate patients.

Chiropractors, like other health practitioners, are sometimes on their feet for long periods of time. Chiropractors who take x-rays employ appropriate precautions against the dangers of repeated exposure to radiation.

Employment

Chiropractors held about 46,000 jobs in 1998. Most chiropractors are in solo practice, although some are in group practice or work for other chiropractors. A small number teach, conduct research at chiropractic institutions, or work in hospitals and clinics.

Many chiropractors are located in small communities. There are geographic imbalances in the distribution of chiropractors, in part because many establish practices close to chiropractic institutions.

Training, Other Qualifications, and Advancement

All States and the District of Columbia regulate the practice of chiropractic and grant licenses to chiropractors who meet educational and examination requirements established by the State. Chiropractors can only practice in States where they are licensed. Some States have agreements permitting chiropractors licensed in one State to obtain a license in another without further examination, provided that educational, examination, and practice credentials meet State specifications.

Most State boards require at least two years of undergraduate education, and an increasing number require a four-year bachelor's degree. All boards require completion of a four-year chiropractic college course at an accredited program leading to the Doctor of Chiropractic degree.

For licensure, most State boards recognize either all or part of the four-part test administered by the National Board of Chiropractic Examiners. State examinations may supplement the National Board tests, depending on State requirements.

To maintain licensure, almost all States require completion of a specified number of hours of continuing education each year. Continuing education programs are offered by accredited chiropractic programs and institutions and chiropractic associations. Special councils within some chiropractic associations also offer programs leading to clinical specialty certification, called "diplomate" certification, in areas such as orthopedics, neurology, sports injuries, occupational and industrial health, nutrition, diagnostic imaging, thermography, and internal disorders.

In 1998, there were 16 chiropractic programs and institutions in the United States accredited by the Council on Chiropractic Education. All required applicants to have at least 60 semester hours of undergraduate study leading toward a bachelor's degree, including courses in English, the social sciences or humanities, organic and inorganic chemistry, biology, physics, and psychology. Many applicants have a bachelor's degree, which may eventually become the minimum entry requirement. Several chiropractic colleges offer prechiropractic study, as well as a bachelor's degree program. Recognition of prechiropractic education offered by chiropractic colleges varies among the State boards.

During the first two years, most chiropractic programs emphasize classroom and laboratory work in basic science subjects such as anatomy, physiology, public health, microbiology, pathology, and biochemistry. The last two years stress courses in manipulation and spinal adjustments and provide clinical experience in physical and laboratory diagnosis, neurology, orthopedics, geriatrics, physiotherapy, and nutrition. Chiropractic programs and institutions grant the degree of Doctor of Chiropractic (D.C.).

Chiropractic requires keen observation to detect physical abnormalities. It also takes considerable hand dexterity to perform adjustments, but not unusual strength or endurance. Chiropractors should be able to work independently and handle responsibility. As in other health-related occupations, empathy, understanding, and the desire to help others are good qualities for dealing effectively with patients.

Newly licensed chiropractors can set up a new practice, purchase an established one, or enter into partnership with an established practitioner. They may also take a salaried position with an established chiropractor, a group practice, or a health care facility.

Job Outlook

Job prospects are expected to be good for persons who enter the practice of chiropractic. Employment of chiropractors is expected to grow faster than the average for all occupations through the year 2008 as consumer demand for alternative medicine grows. Chiropractors emphasize the importance of healthy lifestyles and do not prescribe drugs or perform surgery. As a result, chiropractic care is appealing to many health-conscious Americans. Chiropractic treatment of back, neck, extremities, and other joint damage has become more accepted as a result of recent research and changing attitudes about alternative health care practices. The rapidly expanding older population, with their increased likelihood of mechanical and structural problems, will also increase demand.

Demand for chiropractic treatment is also related to the ability of patients to pay, either directly or through health insurance. Although more insurance plans now cover chiropractic services, the extent of such coverage varies among plans. Increasingly, chiropractors must educate communities about the benefits of chiropractic care in order to establish a successful practice.

In this occupation, replacement needs arise almost entirely from retirements. Chiropractors usually remain in the occupation until they retire; few transfer to other occupations. Establishing a new practice will be easiest in areas with a low concentration of chiropractors.

Earnings

Median annual earnings of salaried chiropractors were $63,930 in 1998. The middle 50 percent earned between $36,820 and $110,820 a year.

Self-employed chiropractors usually earn more than salaried chiropractors. According to the American Chiropractic Association, average income for all chiropractors, including the self-employed, was about $86,500 (after expenses) in 1997. In chiropractic, as in other types of independent practice, earnings are relatively low in the beginning and increase as the practice grows. Earnings are also influenced by the characteristics and qualifications of the practitioner and geographic location. Self-employed chiropractors must provide for their own health insurance and retirement.

Related Occupations

Chiropractors treat and work to prevent bodily disorders and injuries. So do physicians, dentists, optometrists, podiatrists, veterinarians, occupational therapists, and physical therapists.

Sources of Additional Information

General information on chiropractic as a career is available from:

- American Chiropractic Association, 1701 Clarendon Blvd., Arlington, VA 22209. Internet: http://www.amerchiro.org
- International Chiropractors Association, 1110 North Glebe Rd., Suite 1000, Arlington, VA 22201. Internet: http://www.chiropractic.org
- World Chiropractic Alliance, 2950 N. Dobson Rd., Suite 1, Chandler, AZ 85224-1802.
- Dynamic Chiropractic, P.O. Box 6100, Huntington, CA 92615. Internet: http://www.chiroweb.com

For a list of chiropractic programs and institutions, as well as general information on chiropractic education, contact:

- Council on Chiropractic Education, 7975 North Hayden Rd., Suite A-210, Scottsdale, AZ 85258.

For information on State education and licensure requirements, contact:

- Federation of Chiropractic Licensing Boards, 901 54th Ave., Suite 101, Greeley, CO 80634. Internet: http://www.fclb.org/fclb

For information on requirements for admission to a specific chiropractic college, as well as scholarship and loan information, contact the admissions office of the individual college.

Clergy

Nature of the Work

Religious beliefs—such as Buddhist, Christian, Jewish, or Moslem—are significant influences in the lives of millions of Americans, and they prompt many believers to participate in organizations that reinforce their faith. Even within a religion, many denominations may exist, with each group having unique traditions and responsibilities assigned to its clergy. For example, Christianity has more than 70 denominations, while Judaism has four major branches, as well as groups within each branch, with diverse customs.

Clergy are religious and spiritual leaders and teachers and interpreters of their traditions and faith. Most members of the clergy serve in a pulpit. They organize and lead regular religious services and officiate at special ceremonies, including confirmations, weddings, and funerals. They may lead worshipers in prayer, administer the sacraments, deliver sermons, and read from sacred texts such as the Bible, Torah, or Koran. When not conducting worship services, clergy organize, supervise, and lead religious education programs for their congregations. Clergy visit the sick or bereaved to provide comfort, and they counsel persons who are seeking religious or moral guidance or who are troubled by family or personal problems. They also may work to expand the membership of their congregations and solicit donations to support their activities and facilities.

Clergy who serve large congregations often share their duties with associates or more junior clergy. Senior clergy may spend considerable time on administrative duties. They oversee the management of buildings, order supplies, contract for services and repairs, and supervise the work of staff and volunteers. Associate or assistant members of the clergy sometimes specialize in an area of religious service, such as music, education, or youth counseling. Clergy also work with committees and officials, elected by the congregation, who guide the management of the congregation's finances and real estate.

Some members of the clergy serve their religious communities in ways that do not call for them to hold positions in congregations. Some serve as chaplains in the Armed Forces and in hospitals, while others help to carry out the missions of religious community and social services agencies. A few members of the clergy serve in administrative or teaching posts in schools at all grade levels, including seminaries.

Working Conditions

Members of the clergy typically work long and irregular hours. Those who do not work in congregational settings may have more routine schedules. In 1998, almost one-fifth of full-time clergy worked 60 or more hours a week, three times that of all workers in professional specialty occupations. Although many of their activities are sedentary and intellectual in nature, clergy frequently are called upon on short notice to visit the sick, comfort the dying and their families, and provide counseling to those in need. Involvement in community, administrative, and educational activities sometimes requires clergy to work evenings, early mornings, holidays, and weekends.

Because of their roles as leaders regarding spiritual and moral issues, some members of the clergy often feel obligated to address and resolve both societal problems and the personal problems of their congregations' members, which can lead to stress.

Training and Other Qualifications

Educational requirements for entry into the clergy vary greatly. Similar to other professional occupations, about 3 out of 4 members of the clergy have completed at least a bachelor's degree. Many denominations require that clergy complete a bachelor's degree and a graduate-level program of theological study; others will admit anyone who has been "called" to the vocation. Some faiths do not allow women to become clergy; however, those that do are experiencing increases in the numbers of women seeking ordination. Men and women considering careers in the clergy should consult their religious leaders to verify specific entrance requirements.

Individuals considering a career in the clergy should realize they are choosing not only a career but also a way of life. In fact, most members of the clergy remain in their chosen vocation throughout their lives; in 1998, 12 percent of clergy were 65 or older, compared to only 3 percent of workers in all professional specialty occupations.

Religious leaders must exude confidence and motivation, yet remain tolerant and able to listen to the needs of others. They should be capable of making difficult decisions, working under pressure, and living up to the moral standards set by their faith and community.

The following statements provide more detailed information on Protestant ministers, rabbis, and Roman Catholic priests.

Protestant Ministers

(O*NET 27502)

Significant Points

- Entry requirements vary greatly; many denominations require a bachelor's degree followed by study at a theological seminary, whereas others have no formal educational requirements.

- Competition for positions is generally expected because of the large number of qualified candidates, but it will vary among denominations and geographic regions.

Nature of the Work

Protestant ministers lead their congregations in worship services and administer the various rites of the church, such as baptism, confirmation, and Holy Communion. The services that ministers conduct differ among the numerous Protestant denominations and even among congregations within a denomination. In many de-

nominations, ministers follow a traditional order of worship; in others, they adapt the services to the needs of youth and other groups within the congregation. Most services include Bible readings, hymn singing, prayers, and a sermon. In some denominations, Bible readings by members of the congregation and individual testimonials constitute a large part of the service. In addition to these duties, ministers officiate at weddings, funerals, and other occasions.

Each Protestant denomination has its own hierarchical structure. Some ministers are responsible only to the congregation they serve, whereas others are assigned duties by elder ministers or by the bishops of the diocese they serve. In some denominations, ministers are reassigned to a new pastorate by a central governing body or diocese every few years.

Ministers who serve small congregations usually work personally with parishioners. Those who serve large congregations may share specific aspects of the ministry with one or more associates or assistants, such as a minister of education or a minister of music.

Employment

According to the National Council of Churches, there were more than 400,000 Protestant ministers in 1998, including those who served without a regular congregation or those who worked in closely related fields, such as chaplains working in hospitals, the Armed Forces, universities, and correctional institutions. Although there are many denominations, most ministers are employed by the five largest Protestant bodies: Baptist, Episcopalian, Lutheran, Methodist, and Presbyterian.

Although most ministers are located in urban areas, many serve two or more smaller congregations in less densely populated areas. Some small churches increasingly employ part-time ministers who are seminary students, retired ministers, or holders of secular jobs. Unpaid pastors serve other churches with meager funds. In addition, some churches employ specially trained members of the laity to conduct nonliturgical functions.

Training and Other Qualifications

Educational requirements for entry into the Protestant ministry vary greatly. Many denominations require, or at least strongly prefer, a bachelor's degree followed by study at a theological seminary. However, some denominations have no formal educational requirements, and others ordain persons having various types of training from Bible colleges or liberal arts colleges. Many denominations now allow women to be ordained, but others do not. Persons considering a career in the ministry should first verify the ministerial requirements with their particular denomination.

In general, each large denomination has its own schools of theology that reflect its particular doctrine, interests, and needs. However, many of these schools are open to students from other denominations. Several interdenominational schools associated with universities give both undergraduate and graduate training covering a wide range of theological points of view.

In 1998-99, the Association of Theological Schools in the United States and Canada accredited 135 Protestant denominational theological schools. These schools admit only students who have received a bachelor's degree or its equivalent from an accredited college. After college graduation, many denominations require a three-year course of professional study in one of these accredited schools, or seminaries, for the degree of Master of Divinity.

The standard curriculum for accredited theological schools consists of four major categories: Biblical studies, history, theology, and practical theology. Courses of a practical nature include pastoral care, preaching, religious education, and administration. Many accredited schools require that students work under the supervision of a faculty member or experienced minister. Some institutions offer Doctor of Ministry degrees to students who have completed additional study—usually two or more years—and served at least two years as a minister. Scholarships and loans often are available for students of theological institutions.

Persons who have denominational qualifications for the ministry usually are ordained after graduation from a seminary or after serving a probationary pastoral period. Denominations that do not require seminary training ordain clergy at various appointed times. Some churches ordain ministers with only a high school education.

Women and men entering the clergy often begin their careers as pastors of small congregations or as assistant pastors in large churches. Pastor positions in large metropolitan areas or in large congregations often require many years of experience.

Job Outlook

Competition is expected to continue for paid Protestant ministers through the year 2008, reflecting slow growth of church membership and the large number of qualified candidates. Graduates of theological schools should have the best prospects. The degree of competition for paid positions will vary among denominations and geographic regions. For example, relatively favorable prospects are expected for ministers in evangelical churches. Competition, however, will be keen for responsible positions serving large urban congregations. Ministers willing to work part time or for small, rural congregations should have better opportunities. Most job openings will stem from the need to replace ministers who retire, die, or leave the ministry.

For newly ordained Protestant ministers who are unable to find parish positions, employment alternatives include working in youth counseling, family relations, and social welfare organizations; teaching in religious educational institutions; or serving as chaplains in the Armed Forces, hospitals, universities, and correctional institutions.

Earnings

Salaries of Protestant clergy vary substantially, depending on experience, denomination, size and wealth of the congregation, and geographic location. For example, some denominations tie a minister's pay to the average pay of the congregation or the community. As a result, ministers serving larger, wealthier congregations often earned significantly higher salaries than those in smaller, less affluent areas or congregations. Ministers with modest salaries sometimes earn additional income from employment in secular occupations.

Sources of Additional Information

Persons who are interested in entering the Protestant ministry should seek the counsel of a minister or church guidance worker. Theological schools can supply information on admission requirements. Prospective ministers also should contact the ordination supervision body of their particular denomination for information on special requirements for ordination.

Rabbis

(O*NET 27502)

Significant Points

- Ordination usually requires completion of a college degree followed by a four- or five-year program at a Jewish seminary.

- Graduates of Jewish seminaries have excellent job prospects, reflecting current unmet needs for rabbis and the need to replace the many rabbis approaching retirement age.

Nature of the Work

Rabbis serve Orthodox, Conservative, Reform, and Reconstructionist Jewish congregations. Regardless of the branch of Judaism they serve or their individual points of view, all rabbis preserve the substance of Jewish religious worship. Congregations differ in the extent to which they follow the traditional form of worship—for example, in the wearing of head coverings, in the use of Hebrew as the language of prayer, and in the use of instrumental music or a choir. Additionally, the format of the worship service and, therefore, the ritual that the rabbi uses may vary even among congregations belonging to the same branch of Judaism.

Rabbis have greater independence in religious expression than other clergy, because of the absence of a formal religious hierarchy in Judaism. Instead, rabbis are responsible directly to the board of trustees of the congregation they serve. Those serving large congregations may spend considerable time in administrative duties, working with their staffs and committees. Large congregations frequently have associate or assistant rabbis, who often serve as educational directors. All rabbis play a role in community relations. For example, many rabbis serve on committees, alongside business and civic leaders in their communities to help find solutions to local problems.

Rabbis also may write for religious and lay publications and teach in theological seminaries, colleges, and universities.

Employment

Based on information from organizations representing the four major branches of Judaism, there were approximately 1,800 Reform, 1,175 Conservative, 1,800 Orthodox, and 250 Reconstructionist rabbis in 1999. Although the majority served congregations, many rabbis functioned in other settings. Some taught in Jewish studies programs at colleges and universities, and others served as chaplains in hospitals, colleges, or the military. Additionally, some rabbis held positions in one of the many social service or Jewish community agencies.

Although rabbis serve Jewish communities throughout the Nation, they are concentrated in major metropolitan areas with large Jewish populations.

Training and Other Qualifications

To become eligible for ordination as a rabbi, a student must complete a course of study in a seminary. Entrance requirements and the curriculum depend upon the branch of Judaism with which the seminary is associated. Most seminaries require applicants to be college graduates.

Jewish seminaries typically take five years for completion of studies, with an additional preparatory year required for students without sufficient grounding in Hebrew and Jewish studies. In addition to the core academic program, training generally includes fieldwork and internships providing hands-on experience and, in some cases, study in Jerusalem. Seminary graduates are awarded the title Rabbi and earn the Master of Arts in Hebrew Letters degree. After more advanced study, some earn the Doctor of Hebrew Letters degree.

In general, the curricula of Jewish theological seminaries provide students with a comprehensive knowledge of the Bible, the Torah, rabbinic literature, Jewish history, Hebrew, theology, and courses in education, pastoral psychology, and public speaking. Students receive extensive practical training in dealing with social problems in the community. Training for alternatives to the pulpit, such as leadership in community services and religious education, is increasingly stressed. Some seminaries grant advanced academic degrees in such fields as biblical and Talmudic research. All Jewish theological seminaries make scholarships and loans available.

Major rabbinical seminaries include the Jewish Theological Seminary of America, which educates rabbis for the Conservative branch; the Hebrew Union College—Jewish Institute of Religion, which educates rabbis for the Reform branch; and the Reconstructionist Rabbinical College, which educates rabbis in the newest branch of Judaism. About 35 seminaries educate and ordain Orthodox rabbis. Although the number of Orthodox seminaries is relatively high, the number of students attending each seminary is low. The Orthodox movement, as a whole, constitutes only about 10 percent of the American Jewish community. The Rabbi Isaac Elchanan Theological Seminary and the Beth Medrash Govoha Seminary are representative Orthodox seminaries. In all cases, rabbinic training is rigorous. When students have become sufficiently learned in the Torah, the Bible, and other religious texts, they may be ordained with the approval of an authorized rabbi, acting either independently or as a representative of a rabbinical seminary.

Newly ordained rabbis usually begin as spiritual leaders of small congregations, assistants to experienced rabbis, directors of Hillel Foundations on college campuses, teachers in educational institutions, or chaplains in the Armed Forces. As a rule, experienced rabbis fill the pulpits of large well-established Jewish congregations.

Job Outlook

Job opportunities for rabbis are expected to be excellent in all four of the major branches of Judaism through the year 2008, reflecting current unmet needs for rabbis, together with the need to replace the many rabbis approaching retirement age. Rabbis willing to work in small, underserved communities should have particularly good prospects.

Graduates of Orthodox seminaries who seek pulpits should have good opportunities as growth in enrollments slows and as many graduates seek alternatives to the pulpit. Reconstructionist rabbis are expected to have very good employment opportunities as membership expands rapidly. Conservative and Reform rabbis are expected to have excellent job opportunities serving congregations or in other settings because job prospects will be numerous in these two largest Jewish movements.

Earnings

Based on limited information, annual average earnings of rabbis generally ranged from $50,000 to $100,000 in 1998, including benefits. Benefits may include housing, health insurance, and a retirement plan. Income varies widely, depending on the size and financial status of the congregation, as well as denominational branch and geographic location. Rabbis may earn additional income from gifts or fees for officiating at ceremonies such as bar or bat mitzvahs and weddings.

Sources of Additional Information

Persons who are interested in becoming rabbis should discuss with a practicing rabbi their plans for this vocation. Information on the work of rabbis and allied occupations can be obtained from:

- Rabbinical Council of America, 305 7th Ave., New York, NY 10001. (Orthodox) Internet: http://www.rabbis.org

- The Jewish Theological Seminary of America, 3080 Broadway, New York, NY 10027. (Conservative) Internet: http://www.jtsa.edu

- Hebrew Union College-Jewish Institute of Religion, One West 4th St., New York, NY 10012. (Reform) Internet: http://www.huc.edu

- Reconstructionist Rabbinical College, 1299 Church Rd., Wyncote, PA 19095. (Reconstructionist) Internet: http://www.rrc.edu

Roman Catholic Priests

(O*NET 27502)

Significant Points

- Preparation generally requires eight years of study beyond high school, usually including a college degree followed by four or more years of theology study at a seminary.

- The shortage of Roman Catholic priests is expected to continue, resulting in a very favorable outlook.

Nature of the Work

Priests in the Catholic Church belong to one of two groups: diocesan or religious. Both types of priests have the same powers, acquired through ordination by a bishop. Differences lie in their way of life, type of work, and the Church authority to which they are responsible. *Diocesan priests* commit their lives to serving the people of a diocese, a church administrative region, and generally work in parishes assigned by the bishop of their diocese. Diocesan priests take oaths of celibacy and obedience. *Religious priests* belong to a religious order, such as the Jesuits, Dominicans, or Franciscans. In addition to the vows taken by diocesan priests, religious priests take a vow of poverty.

Diocesan priests attend to the spiritual, pastoral, moral, and educational needs of the members of their church. A priest's day usually begins with morning meditation and mass and may end with an individual counseling session or an evening visit to a hospital or home. Many priests direct and serve on church committees, work in civic and charitable organizations, and assist in community projects. Some counsel parishioners preparing for marriage or the birth of a child.

Religious priests receive duty assignments from their superiors in their respective religious orders. Some religious priests specialize in teaching, whereas others serve as missionaries in foreign countries, where they may live under difficult and primitive conditions. Other religious priests live a communal life in monasteries, where they devote their lives to prayer, study, and assigned work.

Both religious and diocesan priests hold teaching and administrative posts in Catholic seminaries, colleges and universities, and high schools. Priests attached to religious orders staff many of the Church's institutions of higher education and many high schools, whereas diocesan priests usually are concerned with the parochial schools attached to parish churches and with diocesan high schools. Members of religious orders do much of the missionary work conducted by the Catholic Church in this country and abroad.

Employment

According to *The Official Catholic Directory*, there were approximately 47,000 priests in 1998; about two-thirds were diocesan priests. There are priests in nearly every city and town and in many rural communities; however, the most work in metropolitan areas, where most Catholics reside.

Training and Other Qualifications

Men exclusively are ordained as priests. Women may serve in church positions that do not require priestly ordination. Preparation for the priesthood generally requires eight years of study beyond high school, usually including a college degree followed by four or more years of theology study at a seminary.

Preparatory study for the priesthood may begin in the first year of high school, at the college level, or in theological seminaries after college graduation. Nine high-school seminaries provided a college preparatory program in 1998. Programs emphasize English grammar, speech, literature, and social studies, as well as religious formation. Latin may be required, and modern languages are encouraged.

In Hispanic communities, knowledge of Spanish is mandatory.

Those who begin training for the priesthood in college do so in one of 87 priesthood formation programs offered either through Catholic colleges or universities or in freestanding college seminaries. Preparatory studies usually include training in philosophy, religious studies, and prayer.

Today, most candidates for the priesthood have a four-year degree from an accredited college or university and then attend one of 47 theological seminaries (also called theologates) and earn either the Master of Divinity or the Master of Arts degree. Thirty-five theologates primarily train diocesan priests; the other 12 theologates mostly educate priests for religious orders. (Slight variations in training reflect the differences in their expected duties.) Theology coursework includes sacred scripture; dogmatic, moral, and pastoral theology; homiletics (art of preaching); Church history; liturgy (sacraments); and canon (church) law. Fieldwork experience usually is required.

Young men are never denied entry into seminaries because of lack of funds. In seminaries for diocesan priests, scholarships or loans are available, and contributions of benefactors and the Catholic Church finance those in religious seminaries—who have taken a vow of poverty and are not expected to have personal resources.

Graduate work in theology beyond that required for ordination is also offered at a number of American Catholic universities or at ecclesiastical universities around the world, particularly in Rome. Also, many priests do graduate work in fields unrelated to theology. Priests are encouraged by the Catholic Church to continue their studies, at least informally, after ordination. In recent years, the Church has stressed continuing education for ordained priests in the social sciences, such as sociology and psychology.

A newly ordained diocesan priest usually works as an assistant pastor. Newly ordained priests of religious orders are assigned to the specialized duties for which they have been trained. Depending on the talents, interests, and experience of the individual, many opportunities for additional responsibility exist within the Church.

Job Outlook

The shortage of Roman Catholic priests is expected to continue, resulting in a very favorable job outlook through the year 2008. Many priests will be needed in the years ahead to provide for the spiritual, educational, and social needs of the increasing number of Catholics. In recent years, the number of ordained priests has been insufficient to fill the needs of newly established parishes and other Catholic institutions and to replace priests who retire, die, or leave the priesthood. This situation is likely to continue, as seminary enrollments remain below the levels needed to overcome the current shortfall of priests.

In response to the shortage of priests, permanent deacons and teams of clergy and laity increasingly are performing certain traditional functions within the Catholic Church. The number of ordained deacons has increased five-fold over the past 20 years, and this trend should continue. Throughout most of the country, permanent deacons have been ordained to preach and perform liturgical functions, such as baptisms, marriages, and funerals, and to provide service to the community. Deacons are not authorized to celebrate Mass, nor are they allowed to administer the Sacraments of

Reconciliation and the Anointing of the Sick. Teams of clergy and laity undertake some liturgical and nonliturgical functions, such as hospital visits and religious teaching.

Earnings

Diocesan priests' salaries vary from diocese to diocese. According to the National Federation of Priests' Council, low-end cash only salaries averaged $12,936 per year in 1998; high-end salaries averaged $15,483 per year. Average salaries, including in-kind earnings, were $30,713 per year in 1998. In addition to a salary, diocesan priests receive a package of benefits that may include a car allowance, room and board in the parish rectory, health insurance, and a retirement plan.

Diocesan priests who do special work related to the church, such as teaching, usually receive a salary which is less than a lay person in the same position would receive. The difference between the usual salary for these jobs and the salary the priest receives is called "contributed service." In some situations, housing and related expenses may be provided; in other cases, the priest must make his own arrangements. Some priests doing special work receive the same compensation a lay person would receive.

Religious priests take a vow of poverty and are supported by their religious order. Any personal earnings are given to the order. Their vow of poverty is recognized by the Internal Revenue Service, which exempts them from paying Federal income tax.

Sources of Additional Information

Young men interested in entering the priesthood should seek the guidance and counsel of their parish priests and diocesan vocational office. For information regarding the different religious orders and the diocesan priesthood, as well as a list of the seminaries that prepare students for the priesthood, contact the diocesan director of vocations through the office of the local pastor or bishop.

Individuals seeking additional information about careers in the Catholic Ministry should contact their local diocese.

For information on training programs for the Catholic ministry, contact:

- Center for Applied Research in the Apostolate (CARA), Georgetown University, Washington, DC 20057.

Clinical Laboratory Technologists and Technicians

(O*NET 32902, 32905, and 66099D)

Significant Points

- Medical and clinical laboratory technologists usually have a bachelor's degree with a major in medical technology

or in one of the life sciences; medical and clinical laboratory technicians need either an associate's degree or a certificate.

- Competition for jobs has increased, and individuals may now have to spend more time seeking employment than in the past.

Nature of the Work

Clinical laboratory testing plays a crucial role in the detection, diagnosis, and treatment of disease. Clinical laboratory technologists and technicians, also known as medical technologists and technicians, perform most of these tests.

Clinical laboratory personnel examine and analyze body fluids, tissues, and cells. They look for bacteria, parasites, and other microorganisms; analyze the chemical content of fluids; match blood for transfusions; and test for drug levels in the blood to show how a patient is responding to treatment. These technologists also prepare specimens for examination, count cells, and look for abnormal cells. They use automated equipment and instruments capable of performing a number of tests simultaneously, as well as microscopes, cell counters, and other sophisticated laboratory equipment. Then they analyze the results and relay them to physicians. With increasing automation and the use of computer technology, the work of technologists and technicians has become less hands-on and more analytical.

The complexity of tests performed, the level of judgment needed, and the amount of responsibility workers assume depend largely on the amount of education and experience they have.

Medical and clinical laboratory technologists generally have a bachelor's degree in medical technology or in one of the life sciences, or they have a combination of formal training and work experience. They perform complex chemical, biological, hematological, immunologic, microscopic, and bacteriological tests. Technologists microscopically examine blood, tissue, and other body substances. They make cultures of body fluid and tissue samples to determine the presence of bacteria, fungi, parasites, or other microorganisms. They analyze samples for chemical content or reaction and determine blood glucose and cholesterol levels. They also type and cross match blood samples for transfusions.

Medical and clinical laboratory technologists evaluate test results, develop and modify procedures, and establish and monitor programs to ensure the accuracy of tests. Some medical and clinical laboratory technologists supervise medical and clinical laboratory technicians.

Technologists in small laboratories perform many types of tests, whereas those in large laboratories generally specialize. Technologists who prepare specimens and analyze the chemical and hormonal contents of body fluids are *clinical chemistry technologists*. Those who examine and identify bacteria and other microorganisms are *microbiology technologists*. *Blood bank technologists* collect, type, and prepare blood and its components for transfusions. *Immunology technologists* examine elements and responses of the human immune system to foreign bodies. *Cytotechnologists* prepare slides of body cells and microscopically examine these cells for abnormalities that may signal the beginning of a cancerous growth.

Medical and clinical laboratory technicians perform less complex tests and laboratory procedures than technologists. Technicians may prepare specimens and operate automatic analyzers, for example, or they may perform manual tests following detailed instructions. Like technologists, they may work in several areas of the clinical laboratory or specialize in just one. *Histology technicians* cut and stain tissue specimens for microscopic examination by pathologists, and *phlebotomists* collect blood samples. They usually work under the supervision of medical and clinical laboratory technologists or laboratory managers.

Working Conditions

Hours and other working conditions vary according to the size and type of employment setting. In large hospitals or in independent laboratories that operate continuously, personnel usually work the day, evening, or night shift and may work weekends and holidays. Laboratory personnel in small facilities may work on rotating shifts, rather than on a regular shift. In some facilities, laboratory personnel are on call several nights a week or on weekends, available in case of emergency.

Clinical laboratory personnel are trained to work with infectious specimens. When proper methods of infection control and sterilization are followed, few hazards exist.

Laboratories usually are well-lighted and clean; however, specimens, solutions, and reagents used in the laboratory sometimes produce odors. Laboratory workers may spend a great deal of time on their feet.

Employment

Clinical laboratory technologists and technicians held about 313,000 jobs in 1998. About half worked in hospitals. Most of the remaining jobs were found in medical laboratories or offices and clinics of physicians. A small number were in blood banks, research and testing laboratories, and in the Federal government (at Department of Veterans Affairs hospitals and U.S. Public Health Service facilities). About 1 laboratory worker in 5 worked part time.

Training, Other Qualifications, and Advancement

The usual requirement for an entry-level position as a medical or clinical laboratory technologist is a bachelor's degree with a major in medical technology or in one of the life sciences. Universities and hospitals offer medical technology programs. It is also possible to qualify through a combination of on-the-job and specialized training.

Bachelor's degree programs in medical technology include courses in chemistry, biological sciences, microbiology, mathematics, and specialized courses devoted to knowledge and skills used in the clinical laboratory. Many programs also offer or require courses in management, business, and computer applications. The Clinical Laboratory Improvement Act (CLIA) requires technologists who perform certain highly complex tests to have at least an associate's degree.

Medical and clinical laboratory technicians generally have either an associate's degree from a community or junior college or a certificate from a hospital, vocational or technical school, or from one of the Armed Forces. A few technicians learn their skills on the job.

Nationally recognized accrediting agencies in clinical laboratory science include the National Accrediting Agency for Clinical Laboratory Sciences (NAACLS), the Commission on Accreditation of Allied Health Education Programs (CAAHEP), and the Accrediting Bureau of Health Education Schools (ABHES). The NAACLS fully accredits 288 and approves 249 programs providing education for medical and clinical laboratory technologists, histologic technicians, and medical and clinical laboratory technicians. ABHES accredits training programs for medical and clinical laboratory technicians.

Some States require laboratory personnel to be licensed or registered. Information on licensure is available from State departments of health or boards of occupational licensing. Certification is a voluntary process by which a nongovernmental organization, such as a professional society or certifying agency, grants recognition to an individual whose professional competence meets prescribed standards. Widely accepted by employers in the health industry, certification is a prerequisite for most jobs and often is necessary for advancement. Agencies certifying medical and clinical laboratory technologists and technicians include the Board of Registry of the American Society of Clinical Pathologists, the American Medical Technologists, and the Credentialing Commission of the International Society for Clinical Laboratory Technology. These agencies have different requirements for certification and different organizational sponsors.

Clinical laboratory personnel need good analytical judgment and the ability to work under pressure. Close attention to detail is essential, because small differences or changes in test substances or numerical readouts can be crucial for patient care. Manual dexterity and normal color vision are highly desirable. With the widespread use of automated laboratory equipment, computer skills are important. In addition, technologists in particular are expected to be good at problem solving.

Technologists may advance to supervisory positions in laboratory work or become chief medical or clinical laboratory technologists or laboratory managers in hospitals. Manufacturers of home diagnostic testing kits and laboratory equipment and supplies seek experienced technologists to work in product development, marketing, and sales. Graduate education in medical technology, one of the biological sciences, chemistry, management, or education usually speeds advancement. A doctorate is needed to become a laboratory director. However, federal regulation allows directors of moderate complexity laboratories to have either a master's degree or a bachelor's degree combined with the appropriate amount of training and experience. Technicians can become technologists through additional education and experience.

Job Outlook

Employment of clinical laboratory workers is expected to grow about as fast as the average for all occupations through the year 2008, as the volume of laboratory tests increases with population growth and the development of new types of tests. Hospitals and independent laboratories have recently undergone considerable consolidation and restructuring, which boosts productivity and allows the same number of personnel to perform more tests than previously possible. Consequently, competition for jobs has increased; and individuals may now have to spend more time seeking employment than in the past.

Technological advances will continue to have two opposing effects on employment through 2008. New, increasingly powerful diagnostic tests will encourage additional testing and spur employment. However, advances in laboratory automation and simple tests, which make it possible for each worker to perform more tests, should slow growth. Research and development efforts are targeted at simplifying routine testing procedures, so nonlaboratory personnel, physicians and patients, in particular, can perform tests now done in laboratories. In addition, automation may be used to prepare specimens, a job traditionally done by technologists and technicians.

Although significant, growth will not be the only source of opportunities. As in most occupations, many openings will result from the need to replace workers who transfer to other occupations, retire, or stop working for some other reason.

Earnings

Median annual earnings of clinical laboratory technologists and technicians were $32,440 in 1998. The middle 50 percent earned between $24,970 and $39,810 a year. The lowest 10 percent earned less than $19,380, and the highest 10 percent earned more than $48,290 a year. Median annual earnings in the industries employing the largest numbers of medical and clinical laboratory technologists in 1997 were:

Offices and clinics of medical doctors	$40,300
Federal government	39,600
Hospitals	36,500
Medical and dental laboratories	35,600

Median annual earnings in the industries employing the largest numbers of medical and clinical laboratory technicians in 1997 were:

Hospitals	$26,600
Offices and clinics of medical doctors	25,500
Medical and dental laboratories	24,800
Health and allied services, not elsewhere classified	22,400

Related Occupations

Clinical laboratory technologists and technicians analyze body fluids, tissue, and other substances using a variety of tests. Similar or related procedures are performed by analytical, water purification, and other chemists; science technicians; crime laboratory analysts; food testers; and veterinary laboratory technicians.

Sources of Additional Information

Career and certification information is available from:

- American Society of Clinical Pathologists, Board of Registry, P.O. Box 12277, Chicago, IL 60612. Internet: http://www.ascp.org/bor
- American Medical Technologists, 710 Higgins Rd., Park Ridge, IL 60068. Internet: http://www.amt1.com
- American Society of Cytopathology, 400 West 9th St., Suite 201, Wilmington, DE 19801.
- International Society for Clinical Laboratory Technology, 917 Locust St., Suite 1100, St. Louis, MO 63101-1413.

For more career information, write to:

- American Society for Clinical Laboratory Science, 7910 Woodmont Ave., Suite 530, Bethesda, MD 20814.
- American Association of Blood Banks, 8101 Glenbrook Rd., Bethesda, MD 20814-2749.

For a list of accredited and approved educational programs for clinical laboratory personnel, write to:

- National Accrediting Agency for Clinical Laboratory Sciences, 8410 W. Bryn Mawr Ave., Suite 670, Chicago, IL 60631.

For a list of training programs for medical and clinical laboratory technicians accredited by the Accrediting Bureau of Health Education Schools, write to:

- Accrediting Bureau of Health Education Schools, 803 West Broad St., Suite 730, Falls Church, VA 22046. Internet: http://www.abhes.org

For information about a career as a medical and clinical laboratory technician and schools offering training, contact:

- National Association of Health Career Schools, 2301 Academy Dr., Harrisburg, PA 17112.

College and University Faculty

(O*NET 31202, 31204, 31206, 31209, 31210, 31212, 31114, 31216, 31218, 31222, 31224, 31226, and 31299)

Significant Points

- A Ph.D. is usually required for full-time, tenure-track positions in four-year colleges and universities.

- Applicants for full-time college faculty positions should expect to face keen competition.

- Job prospects will continue to be better in certain fields—computer science, engineering, and business, for example—that offer attractive nonacademic job opportunities and attract fewer applicants for academic positions.

Nature of the Work

College and university faculty teach and advise nearly 15 million full- and part-time college students and perform a significant part of our Nation's research. Faculty also keep up with developments in their fields and consult with government, business, nonprofit, and community organizations.

Faculty usually are organized into departments or divisions based on subject or field. They usually teach several different courses—algebra, calculus, and statistics, for example. They may instruct undergraduate or graduate students or both. College and university faculty may give lectures to several hundred students in large halls, lead small seminars, or supervise students in laboratories. They prepare lectures, exercises, and laboratory experiments; grade exams and papers; and advise and work with students individually. In universities, they also supervise graduate students' teaching and research. College faculty work with an increasingly varied student population made up of growing shares of part-time, older, and culturally and racially diverse students.

Faculty keep abreast of developments in their field by reading current literature, talking with colleagues, and participating in professional conferences. They also do their own research to expand knowledge in their field. They perform experiments; collect and analyze data; and examine original documents, literature, and other source material. From this process, they arrive at conclusions and publish their findings in scholarly journals, books, and electronic media.

College and university faculty increasingly use technology in all areas of their work. In the classroom, they may use computers—including the Internet, electronic mail, software programs such as statistical packages, and CD-ROMs—as teaching aids. Some faculty use closed-circuit and cable television, satellite broadcasts, and video, audio, and Internet teleconferencing to teach courses to students at remote sites. Faculty post course content, class notes, class schedules, and other information on the Internet. They also use computers to do research, participate in discussion groups, or publicize professional research papers. Faculty will use these technologies more as quality and affordability improve.

Most faculty members serve on academic or administrative committees that deal with the policies of their institution, departmental matters, academic issues, curricula, budgets, equipment purchases, and hiring. Some work with student and community organizations. Department chairpersons are faculty members who usually teach some courses but usually have heavier administrative responsibilities.

The proportion of time spent on research, teaching, administrative, and other duties varies by individual circumstance and type of institution. Faculty members at universities normally spend a significant part of their time doing research; those in four-year colleges, somewhat less; and those in two-year colleges, relatively little. The teaching load, however, often is heavier in two-year colleges and somewhat lower at four-year institutions. Full professors at all types of institutions usually spend a larger portion of their time conducting research than do assistant professors, instructors, and lecturers.

Working Conditions

College faculty usually have flexible schedules. They must be present for classes, usually 12 to 16 hours per week, and for faculty and committee meetings. Most establish regular office hours for student consultations, usually 3 to 6 hours per week. Otherwise,

faculty are free to decide when and where they will work and how much time to devote to course preparation, grading, study, research, graduate student supervision, and other activities.

Initial adjustment to these responsibilities can be challenging as new faculty adapt to switching roles from student to teacher. This adjustment may be even more difficult should class sizes grow in response to faculty and budget cutbacks, increasing an instructor's workload. Also, many institutions are increasing their reliance on part-time faculty, who usually have limited administrative and student advising duties, which leaves the declining number of full-time faculty with a heavier workload. To ease the transition from student to teacher, some institutions offer career development programs.

Some faculty members work staggered hours and teach night and weekend classes. This is particularly true for faculty who teach at two-year community colleges or institutions with large enrollments of older students with full-time jobs or family responsibilities. Most colleges and universities require faculty to work nine months of the year, which allows them the time to teach additional courses, do research, travel, or pursue nonacademic interests during the summer and school holidays. Colleges and universities usually have funds to support faculty research or other professional development needs, including travel to conferences and research sites.

Faculty may experience a conflict between their responsibilities to teach students and the pressure to do research and to publish their findings. This may be a particular problem for young faculty seeking advancement in four-year research universities. However, increasing emphasis on undergraduate teaching performance in tenure decisions may alleviate some of this pressure.

Part-time faculty usually spend little time on campus because they do not have offices. In addition, they may teach at more than one college, requiring travel between places of employment, earning the name "gypsy faculty." Part-time faculty are usually not eligible for tenure. For those seeking full-time employment in academia, dealing with this lack of job security can be stressful.

Employment

College and university faculty held about 865,000 jobs in 1998, mostly in public institutions.

About 3 out of 10 college and university faculty worked part time in 1998. Some part-timers, known as "adjunct faculty," have primary jobs outside of academia—in government, private industry, or in nonprofit research—and teach "on the side." Others prefer to work part-time hours or seek full-time jobs but are unable to obtain them due to intense competition for available openings. Some work part time in more than one institution. Many adjunct faculty are not qualified for tenure-track positions because they lack a doctoral degree.

Training, Other Qualifications, and Advancement

Most college and university faculty are in four academic ranks: professor, associate professor, assistant professor, and instructor. These positions are usually considered to be tenure-track positions. A small number of faculty, called lecturers, usually are not on the tenure track.

Most faculty members are hired as instructors or assistant professors. Four-year colleges and universities usually consider doctoral degree holders for full-time tenure-track positions, but may hire master's degree holders or doctoral candidates for certain disciplines, such as the arts, or for part-time and temporary jobs. In two-year colleges, master's degree holders fill most full-time positions. However, with increasing competition for available jobs, institutions can be more selective in their hiring practices. Master's degree holders may find it increasingly difficult to obtain employment as they are passed over in favor of candidates holding a Ph.D.

Doctoral programs, including time spent completing a master's degree and a dissertation, take an average of six to eight years of full-time study beyond the bachelor's degree. Some programs, such as the humanities, take longer to complete; others, such as engineering, usually are shorter. Candidates specialize in a subfield of a discipline—for example, organic chemistry, counseling psychology, or European history—but also take courses covering the entire discipline. Programs include 20 or more increasingly specialized courses and seminars plus comprehensive examinations on all major areas of the field. Candidates also must complete a dissertation—a written report on original research in the candidate's major field of study. The dissertation sets forth an original hypothesis or proposes a model and tests it. Students in the natural sciences and engineering usually do laboratory work; in the humanities, they study original documents and other published material. The dissertation, done under the guidance of one or more faculty advisors, usually takes one or two years of full-time work.

In some fields, particularly the natural sciences, some students spend an additional two years on postdoctoral research and study before taking a faculty position. Some Ph.D.s extend or take new postdoctoral appointments if they are unable to find a faculty job. Most of these appointments offer a nominal salary.

A major step in the traditional academic career is attaining tenure. New tenure-track faculty are usually hired as instructors or assistant professors and must serve a certain period (usually seven years) under term contracts. At the end of the contract period, their record of teaching, research, and overall contribution to the institution is reviewed; tenure is granted if the review is favorable. According to the American Association of University Professors, in 1998-99 about 65 percent of all full-time faculty held tenure, and about 86 percent were in tenure-track positions. Those denied tenure usually must leave the institution. Tenured professors cannot be fired without just cause and due process. Tenure protects the faculty's academic freedom—the ability to teach and conduct research without fear of being fired for advocating unpopular ideas. It also gives both faculty and institutions the stability needed for effective research and teaching and provides financial security for faculty. Some institutions have adopted post-tenure review policies to encourage ongoing evaluation of tenured faculty.

The number of tenure-track positions is expected to decline as institutions seek flexibility in dealing with financial matters and changing student interests. Institutions will rely more heavily on limited term contracts and part-time faculty, shrinking the total pool of tenured faculty. Some institutions offer limited term contracts to prospective faculty—typically two-, three-, or five-year, full-time contracts. These contracts may be terminated or extended at the end of the period. Institutions are not obligated to grant tenure to these contract holders. In addition, some institutions have limited the percentage of faculty who can be tenured.

Some faculty—based on teaching experience, research, publication, and service on campus committees and task forces—move into administrative and managerial positions, such as departmental chairperson, dean, and president. At four-year institutions, such advancement requires a doctoral degree. At two-year colleges, a doctorate is helpful but not usually required, except for advancement to some top administrative positions.

College faculty should have inquiring and analytical minds and a strong desire to pursue and disseminate knowledge. They must be able to communicate clearly and logically, both orally and in writing. They should be able to establish rapport with students and, as models for them, be dedicated to the principles of academic integrity and intellectual honesty. Additionally, they must be self-motivated and able to work in an environment where they receive little direct supervision.

Job Outlook

Employment of college and university faculty is expected to increase faster than the average for all occupations through 2008 as enrollments in higher education increase. Many additional openings will arise as faculty members retire. Nevertheless, prospective job applicants should expect to face competition, particularly for full-time tenure-track positions at four-year institutions.

Between 1998 and 2008, the traditional college-age (18-24) population will grow again after several years of decline. This population increase, along with a higher proportion of 18- to 24-year-olds attending college and a growing number of part-time, female, minority, and older students, will spur college enrollments. Enrollment is projected to rise from 14.6 million in 1998 to 16.1 million in 2008, an increase of about 10 percent.

Growing numbers of students will necessitate hiring more faculty to teach. At the same time, many faculty will be retiring, opening up even more positions. Also, the number of doctoral degrees is expected to grow more slowly than in the past, somewhat easing the competition for some faculty positions.

Despite expected job growth and the need to replace retiring faculty, many in the academic community are concerned that institutions will increasingly favor the hiring of adjunct faculty over full-time, tenure-track faculty. For many years, keen competition for faculty jobs forced some applicants to accept part-time academic appointments that offered little hope of tenure and forced others to seek nonacademic positions. Many colleges, faced with reduced State funding for higher education and growing numbers of part-time and older students, increased the hiring of part-time faculty to save money on pay and benefits and to accommodate the needs of nontraditional-age students. If funding remains tight over the projection period, this trend of hiring adjunct or part-time faculty is likely to continue. Because of uncertainty about future funding sources, some colleges and universities are also controlling costs by changing the mix of academic programs offered, eliminating some programs altogether, and increasing class size.

Even if the proportion of full-time positions does not shrink, job competition will remain keen for coveted tenure-track jobs. Some institutions are expected to increasingly hire full-time faculty on limited-term contracts, reducing the number of tenure-track positions available. Overall, job prospects will continue to be better in

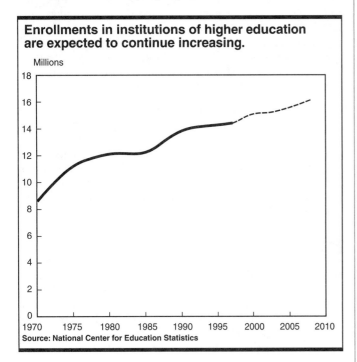

Enrollments in institutions of higher education are expected to continue increasing.

Millions

Source: National Center for Education Statistics

certain fields—business, engineering, health science, and computer science, for example—that offer attractive nonacademic job opportunities and attract fewer applicants for academic positions. Also, excellent job prospects in a field—for example, computer science—result in higher student enrollments, increasing faculty needs in that field. On the other hand, poor job prospects in a field, such as history in recent years, discourages students and reduces demand for faculty.

Earnings

Median annual earnings of college and university faculty in 1998 were $46,630. The middle 50 percent earned between $33,390 and $71,360. The lowest 10 percent earned less than $23,100; the highest 10 percent earned more than $90,360.

Earnings vary according to faculty rank and type of institution, geographic area, and field. According to a 1998-99 survey by the American Association of University Professors, salaries for full-time faculty averaged $56,300. By rank, the average for professors was $72,700; associate professors, $53,200; assistant professors, $43,800; instructors, $33,400; and lecturers, $37,200. Faculty in four-year institutions earn higher salaries, on the average, than those in two-year schools. Average salaries for faculty in public institutions ($55,900) were lower in 1998-99 than those for private independent institutions ($63,500) but higher than those for religiously affiliated private colleges and universities ($49,400). In fields with high-paying nonacademic alternatives (notably medicine and law but also engineering and business, among others) earnings exceed these averages. In others, such as the humanities and education, they are lower.

Most faculty members have significant earnings in addition to their base salary, from consulting, teaching additional courses, researching, writing for publication, or other employment.

Most college and university faculty enjoy some unique benefits, including access to campus facilities, tuition waivers for dependents, housing and travel allowances, and paid sabbatical leaves. Part-time faculty usually have fewer benefits (including health insurance, retirement benefits, and sabbatical leave) than full-time faculty do.

Related Occupations

College and university faculty function both as teachers and as researchers. They communicate information and ideas. Related occupations include elementary and secondary school teachers, librarians, writers, consultants, lobbyists, trainers and employee development specialists, and policy analysts. Faculty research activities often are similar to those of scientists, as well as managers and administrators in industry, government, and nonprofit research organizations.

Sources of Additional Information

Professional societies generally provide information on academic and nonacademic employment opportunities in their fields.

Special publications on higher education, such as *The Chronicle of Higher Education*, are available in libraries and list specific employment opportunities for faculty.

Counselors

(O*NET 31514)

Significant Points

- About 6 out of 10 counselors have a master's degree.

- Most States require some form of counselor credentialing, licensure, certification, or registry for practice outside schools; all States require school counselors to hold a State school counseling certification.

Nature of the Work

Counselors assist people with personal, family, educational, mental health, and career decisions and problems. Their duties depend on the individuals they serve and the settings in which they work.

School and college counselors in elementary, secondary, and postsecondary schools help students evaluate their abilities, interests, talents, and personality characteristics to develop realistic academic and career goals. Counselors use interviews, counseling sessions, tests, or other methods when evaluating and advising students. They operate career information centers and career education programs. High school counselors advise on college majors, admission requirements, entrance exams, and financial aid and on trade, technical school, and apprenticeship programs. They help students develop job search skills such as resume writing and interviewing techniques. College career planning and placement counselors assist alumni or students with career development and job hunting techniques.

Elementary school counselors observe younger children during classroom and play activities and confer with their teachers and parents to evaluate their strengths, problems, or special needs. They also help students develop good study habits. They do less vocational and academic counseling than secondary school counselors.

School counselors at all levels help students understand and deal with their social, behavioral, and personal problems. They emphasize preventive and developmental counseling to provide students with the life skills needed to deal with problems before they occur, and to enhance personal, social, and academic growth. Counselors provide special services, including alcohol and drug prevention programs, and classes that teach students to handle conflicts without resorting to violence. Counselors also try to identify cases involving domestic abuse and other family problems that can affect a student's development. Counselors work with students individually, in small groups, or with entire classes. They consult and work with parents, teachers, school administrators, school psychologists, school nurses, and social workers.

Rehabilitation counselors help people deal with the personal, social, and vocational effects of disabilities. They counsel people with disabilities resulting from birth defects, illness or disease, accidents, or the stress of daily life. They evaluate the strengths and limitations of individuals, provide personal and vocational counseling, and arrange for medical care, vocational training, and job placement. Rehabilitation counselors interview individuals with disabilities and their families, evaluate school and medical reports, and confer and plan with physicians, psychologists, occupational therapists, and employers to determine the capabilities and skills of the individual. Conferring with the client, they develop a rehabilitation program, which often includes training to help the person develop job skills. They also work toward increasing the client's capacity to live independently.

Employment, or *vocational*, *counselors* help individuals make career decisions. They explore and evaluate the client's education, training, work history, interests, skills, and personal traits and arrange for aptitude and achievement tests. They also work with individuals to develop job search skills and assist clients in locating and applying for jobs.

Mental health counselors emphasize prevention and work with individuals and groups to promote optimum mental health. They help individuals deal with addictions and substance abuse; suicide; stress management; problems with self-esteem; issues associated with aging; job and career concerns; educational decisions; issues of mental and emotional health; and family, parenting, and marital problems. Mental health counselors work closely with other mental health specialists, including psychiatrists, psychologists, clinical social workers, psychiatric nurses, and school counselors.

Other counseling specialties include marriage and family, multicultural, and gerontological counseling. A gerontological counselor provides services to elderly persons who face changing lifestyles because of health problems and helps families cope with these changes. A multicultural counselor helps employers adjust to an increasingly diverse workforce.

Working Conditions

Most school counselors work the traditional 9- to 10-month school year with a 2- to 3-month vacation, although an increasing number are employed on 10 1/2- or 11-month contracts. They usually have the same hours as teachers. College career planning and placement counselors work long and irregular hours during recruiting periods.

Rehabilitation and employment counselors usually work a standard 40-hour week. Self-employed counselors and those working in mental health and community agencies often work evenings to counsel clients who work during the day.

Counselors must possess high physical and emotional energy to handle the array of problems they address. Dealing with these problems daily can cause stress.

Since privacy is essential for confidential and frank discussions with clients, counselors usually have private offices.

Employment

Counselors held about 182,000 jobs in 1998. (This employment estimate only includes vocational and educational counselors; employment data are not available for other counselors discussed in this statement, such as rehabilitation and mental health counselors.)

In addition to elementary and secondary schools and colleges and universities, counselors work in a wide variety of public and private establishments. These include health care facilities; job training, career development, and vocational rehabilitation centers; social agencies; correctional institutions; and residential care facilities, such as halfway houses for criminal offenders and group homes for children, the aged, and the disabled. Counselors also work in organizations engaged in community improvement and social change, as well as drug and alcohol rehabilitation programs and State and local government agencies. A growing number of counselors work in health maintenance organizations, insurance companies, group practice, and private practice. This growth has been spurred by laws allowing counselors to receive payments from insurance companies and requiring employers to provide rehabilitation and counseling services to employees.

Training, Other Qualifications, and Advancement

Formal education is necessary to gain employment as a counselor. About 6 out of 10 counselors have a master's degree; fields of study include college student affairs, elementary or secondary school counseling, education, gerontological counseling, marriage and family counseling, substance abuse counseling, rehabilitation counseling, agency or community counseling, clinical mental health counseling, counseling psychology, career counseling, and related fields.

Graduate-level counselor education programs in colleges and universities usually are in departments of education or psychology. Courses are grouped into eight core areas: Human growth and development; social and cultural foundations; helping relationships; group work; career and lifestyle development; appraisal; research and program evaluation; and professional orientation. In an accredited program, 48 to 60 semester hours of graduate study, including a period of supervised clinical experience in counseling, are required for a master's degree. In 1999, 133 institutions offered programs in counselor education, including career, community, gerontological, mental health, school, student affairs, and marriage and family counseling that were accredited by the Council for Accreditation of Counseling and Related Educational Programs (CACREP). Another organization, the Council on Rehabilitation Education (CORE), accredits graduate programs in rehabilitation counseling. Accredited master's degree programs include a minimum of two years of full-time study, including 600 hours of supervised clinical internship experience.

In 1999, 45 States and the District of Columbia had some form of counselor credentialing, licensure, certification, or registry legislation governing practice outside schools. Requirements vary from State to State. In some States, credentialing is mandatory; in others, it is voluntary.

All States require school counselors to hold State school counseling certification; however, certification requirements vary from State to State. Some States require public school counselors to have both counseling and teaching certificates. Depending on the State, a master's degree in counseling and two to five years of teaching experience could be required for a school counseling certificate.

Counselors must be aware of educational and training requirements that are often very detailed and that vary by area and by counseling specialty. Prospective counselors should check with State and local governments, employers, and national voluntary certification organizations in order to determine which requirements apply.

Many counselors elect to be nationally certified by the National Board for Certified Counselors (NBCC), which grants the general practice credential, "National Certified Counselor." To be certified, a counselor must hold a graduate degree in counseling from a regionally accredited institution, have at least two years of supervised field experience in a counseling setting (graduates from counselor education programs accredited by the above-mentioned CACREP are exempted), and pass NBCC's National Counselor Examination for Licensure and Certification (NCE). This national certification is voluntary and distinct from State certification. However, in some States those who pass the national exam are exempt from taking a State certification exam. NBCC also offers specialty certification in school, clinical mental health, and addictions counseling. To maintain their certification, counselors must repeat and pass the NCE or complete 100 hours of acceptable continuing education credit every five years.

Another organization, the Commission on Rehabilitation Counselor Certification, offers voluntary national certification for rehabilitation counselors. Many employers require rehabilitation counselors to be nationally certified. To become certified, rehabilitation counselors usually must graduate from an accredited educa-

tional program, complete an internship, and pass a written examination. (Certification requirements vary according to an applicant's educational history. Employment experience, for instance, is required for those without a counseling degree other than the rehabilitation specialty.) They are then designated as "Certified Rehabilitation Counselors." To maintain their certification, counselors must re-take the certification exam or complete 100 hours of acceptable continuing education credit every five years.

Vocational and related rehabilitation agencies usually require a master's degree in rehabilitation counseling, counseling and guidance, or counseling psychology for rehabilitation counselor jobs. Some, however, accept applicants with a bachelor's degree in rehabilitation services, counseling, psychology, sociology, or related fields. A bachelor's degree often qualifies a person to work as a counseling aide, rehabilitation aide, or social service worker. Experience in employment counseling, job development, psychology, education, or social work is helpful.

Some States require counselors in public employment offices to have a master's degree; others accept a bachelor's degree with appropriate counseling courses.

Clinical mental health counselors usually have a master's degree in mental health counseling, another area of counseling, or psychology or social work. Voluntary certification is available through the National Board for Certified Counselors, Inc. Generally, to receive certification as a clinical mental health counselor, a counselor must have a master's degree in counseling, two years of post-master's experience, a period of supervised clinical experience, a taped sample of clinical work, and a passing grade on a written examination.

Some employers provide training for newly hired counselors. Many have work-study programs so those employed counselors can earn graduate degrees. Counselors must participate in graduate studies, workshops, and personal studies to maintain their certificates and licenses.

Persons interested in counseling should have a strong interest in helping others and the ability to inspire respect, trust, and confidence. They should be able to work independently or as part of a team. Counselors follow the code of ethics associated with their respective certifications and licenses.

Prospects for advancement vary by counseling field. School counselors can move to a larger school; become directors or supervisors of counseling, guidance, or pupil personnel services; or, usually with further graduate education, become counselor educators, counseling psychologists, or school administrators. Some counselors choose to work at the State department of education.

Rehabilitation, mental health, and employment counselors can become supervisors or administrators in their agencies. Some counselors move into research, consulting, or college teaching or go into private or group practice.

Job Outlook

Overall employment of counselors is expected to grow faster than the average for all occupations through 2008. In addition, numerous job openings will occur as many counselors reach retirement age. (This employment projection applies only to vocational and educational counselors. Future job market conditions for rehabilitation and mental health counselors are discussed later in this section.)

Employment of school and vocational counselors is expected to grow as a result of increasing enrollments, particularly in secondary and post-secondary schools, State legislation requiring counselors in elementary schools, and the expanded responsibilities of counselors. Counselors are becoming more involved in crisis and preventive counseling, helping students deal with issues ranging from drug and alcohol abuse to death and suicide. Also, the growing diversity of student populations is presenting challenges to counselors in dealing with multicultural issues. Budgetary constraints, however, can dampen job growth of school counselors. When funding is tight, schools usually prefer to hire new teachers before adding counselors in an effort to keep classroom sizes at acceptable levels. If this happens, student-to-counselor ratios in many schools could increase as student enrollments grow.

As with other government jobs, the number of employment counselors who work primarily for State and local government could be limited by budgetary constraints. However, demand for government employment counseling could grow as new welfare laws require welfare recipients to find jobs. Opportunities for employment counselors working in private job training services should grow as counselors provide training and other services to laid-off workers, experienced workers seeking new or second careers, full-time homemakers seeking to enter or reenter the work force, and workers who want to upgrade their skills.

Demand is expected to be strong for rehabilitation and mental health counselors. Under managed care systems, insurance companies increasingly provide for reimbursement of counselors, enabling many counselors to move from schools and government agencies to private practice. Counselors are also forming group practices to receive expanded insurance coverage. The number of people who need rehabilitation services will rise as advances in medical technology continue to save lives that only a few years ago would have been lost. In addition, legislation requiring equal employment rights for people with disabilities will spur demand for counselors. Counselors not only will help individuals with disabilities with their transition into the work force, but also will help companies comply with the law. Employers are also increasingly offering employee assistance programs that provide mental health and alcohol and drug abuse services. A growing number of people are expected to use these services as the elderly population grows, and as society focuses on ways of developing mental well-being, such as controlling stress associated with job and family responsibilities.

Earnings

Median annual earnings of vocational and educational counselors in 1998 were $38,650. The middle 50 percent earned between $28,400 and $49,960. The lowest 10 percent earned less than $21,230, and the highest 10 percent earned more than $73,920. Median annual earnings in the industries employing the largest numbers of vocational and educational counselors in 1997 were as follows:

Elementary and secondary schools	$42,100
State government, except education and hospitals	35,800
Colleges and universities	34,700
Job training and related services	24,100
Individual and family services	22,300

School counselors can earn additional income working summers in the school system or in other jobs.

Self-employed counselors who have well-established practices, as well as counselors employed in group practices, usually have the highest earnings, as do some counselors working for private firms, such as insurance companies and private rehabilitation companies.

Related Occupations

Counselors help people evaluate their interests, abilities, and disabilities and deal with personal, social, academic, and career problems. Others who help people in similar ways include college and student affairs workers, teachers, personnel workers and managers, human services workers, social workers, psychologists, psychiatrists, psychiatric nurses, members of the clergy, occupational therapists, training and employee development specialists, and equal employment opportunity/affirmative action specialists.

Sources of Additional Information

For general information about counseling, as well as information on specialties such as school, college, mental health, rehabilitation, multicultural, career, marriage and family, and gerontological counseling, contact:

- American Counseling Association, 5999 Stevenson Ave., Alexandria, VA 22304-3300. Internet: http://www.counseling.org

For information on accredited counseling and related training programs, contact:

- Council for Accreditation of Counseling and Related Educational Programs, American Counseling Association, 5999 Stevenson Ave., 4th floor, Alexandria, VA 22304. Internet: http://www.counseling.org/cacrep

For information on national certification requirements for counselors, contact:

- National Board for Certified Counselors, Inc., 3 Terrace Way, Suite D, Greensboro, NC 27403-3660. Internet: http://www.nbcc.org

For information on certification requirements for rehabilitation counselors and a list of accredited rehabilitation education programs, contact:

- Commission on Rehabilitation Counselor Certification, 1835 Rohlwing Rd., Suite E, Rolling Meadows, IL 60008.

State departments of education can supply information on colleges and universities that offer approved guidance and counseling training for State certification and licensure requirements.

State employment service offices have information about job opportunities and entrance requirements for counselors.

Court Reporters, Medical Transcriptionists, and Stenographers

(O*NET 55302A and 55302B)

Significant Points

- A high school diploma is sufficient for stenographers; employers prefer medical transcriptionists who have completed a vocational school or community college program; and court reporters usually need a two- or four-year post-secondary school degree.

- Overall employment is projected to grow about as fast as the average, as rapid growth among medical transcriptionists is offset by the decline among stenographers.

- Because of their relatively high salaries, keen competition should exist for court reporter positions; certified court reporters and medical transcriptionists should enjoy the best job prospects.

Nature of the Work

Although court reporters, medical transcriptionists, and stenographers all transcribe spoken words, the specific responsibilities of each of these workers differ markedly. Court reporters and stenographers typically take verbatim reports of speeches, conversations, legal proceedings, meetings, and other events when written accounts of spoken words are necessary for correspondence, records, or legal proof. Medical transcriptionists, on the other hand, translate and edit recorded dictation by physicians and other health care providers regarding patient assessment and treatment.

Court reporters document all statements made in official proceedings using a stenotype machine, which allows them to press multiple keys at a time to record combinations of letters representing sounds, words, or phrases. These symbols are then recorded on computer disks or CD-ROM, which are then translated and displayed as text in a process called computer-aided transcription. Stenotype machines used for real-time captioning are linked directly to the computer. As the reporter keys in the symbols, they instantly appear as text on the screen. This is used for closed captioning for the hearing-impaired on television or in courts, classrooms, or meetings. In all of these cases, accuracy is crucial because only one person is creating an official transcript.

Although many court reporters record official proceedings in the courtroom, the majority of court reporters work outside the courtroom. Freelance reporters, for example, take depositions for attorneys in offices and document proceedings of meetings, conventions, and other private activities. Others capture the proceedings in government agencies of all levels, from the U.S. Congress to State and local governing bodies. Court reporters who specialize in captioning live television programming, commonly known as *stenocaptioners*,

work for television networks or cable stations captioning news, emergency broadcasts, sporting events, and other programming.

Medical transcriptionists use headsets and transcribing machines to listen to recordings by physicians and other health care professionals. These workers transcribe a variety of medical reports about emergency room visits, diagnostic imaging studies, operations, chart reviews, and final summaries. To understand and accurately transcribe dictated reports into a format that is clear and comprehensible for the reader, the medical transcriptionist must understand the language of medicine, anatomy and physiology, diagnostic procedures, and treatment. They also must be able to translate medical jargon and abbreviations into their expanded forms. After reviewing and editing for grammar and clarity, the medical transcriptionist transcribes the dictated reports and returns them in either printed or electronic form to the dictator for review and signature, or correction. These reports eventually become a part of the patient's permanent file.

Stenographers take dictation and then transcribe their notes on a word processor or onto a computer diskette. They may take dictation using either shorthand or a stenotype machine, which prints shorthand symbols. General stenographers, including most beginners, take routine dictation and perform other office tasks such as typing, filing, answering telephones, and operating office machines. Experienced and highly skilled stenographers often supervise other stenographers, typists, and clerical workers and take more difficult dictation. For example, skilled stenographers may attend staff meetings and provide word-for-word records or summary reports of the proceedings to the participants. Some experienced stenographers take dictation in foreign languages; others work as public stenographers serving traveling business people and others. Technical stenographers must know the medical, legal, engineering, or scientific terminology used in a particular profession.

Working Conditions

The majority of these workers are employed in comfortable settings. Court reporters, for example, work in the offices of attorneys, courtrooms, legislatures, and conventions. Medical transcriptionists are found in hospitals, doctors' offices, or medical transcription services. Stenographers usually work in clean, well-lighted offices. An increasing number of court reporters and medical transcriptionists work from home-based offices as subcontractors for law firms, hospitals, and transcription services.

Work in these occupations presents few hazards, although sitting in the same position for long periods can be tiring, and workers can suffer wrist, back, neck, or eye problems due to strain and risk repetitive motion injuries such as carpal tunnel syndrome. Also, the pressure to be accurate and fast can also be stressful.

Many court reporters, medical transcriptionists, and stenographers work a standard 40-hour week, although about 1 in 4 works part time. A substantial number of court reporters and medical transcriptionists are self-employed, which may result in irregular working hours.

Employment

Court reporters, medical transcriptionists, and stenographers held about 110,000 jobs in 1998. More than 1 in 4 were self-employed.

Of those who worked for a wage or salary, about one-third worked for State and local governments, a reflection of the large number of court reporters working in courts, legislatures, and various agencies. About 1 in 4 worked for hospitals and physicians' offices, reflecting the concentration of medical transcriptionists in health services. Other transcriptionists, stenographers, and court reporters worked for colleges and universities, secretarial and court reporting services, temporary help supply services, and law firms.

Training, Other Qualifications, and Advancement

The training for each of the three occupations varies significantly. Court reporters usually complete a two- or four-year training program offered by about 300 post-secondary vocational and technical schools and colleges. Currently, the National Court Reporters Association (NCRA) has approved about 110 programs, all of which offer courses in computer-aided transcription and real-time reporting. NCRA-approved programs require students to capture 225 words per minute. Court reporters in the Federal government usually must capture at least 205 words a minute.

Some States require court reporters to be Notary Publics or to be a Certified Court Reporter (CCR); reporters must pass a State certification test administered by a board of examiners to earn this designation. The National Court Reporters Association confers the designation Registered Professional Reporter (RPR) upon those who pass a two-part examination and participate in continuing education programs. Although voluntary, the RPR designation is recognized as a mark of distinction in this field.

For medical transcriptionist positions, understanding medical terminology is essential. Good English grammar and punctuation skills are required, as well as familiarity with personal computers and word processing software. Good listening skills are also necessary, because some doctors and health care professionals speak English as a second language.

Employers prefer to hire transcriptionists who have completed post-secondary training in medical transcription, which is offered by many vocational schools and community colleges. Completion of a two-year associate's degree program—including coursework in anatomy, medical terminology, medicolegal issues, and English grammar and punctuation—is highly recommended. Many of these programs include supervised on-the-job experience. The American Association for Medical Transcription awards the voluntary designation Certified Medical Transcriptionist (CMT) to those who earn passing scores on written and practical examinations. As in many other fields, certification is recognized as a sign of competence in medical transcription.

Stenographic skills are taught in high schools, vocational schools, community colleges, and proprietary business schools. For stenographer jobs, employers prefer to hire high school graduates and seldom have a preference among the many different shorthand methods. Although requirements vary in private firms, applicants with the best speed and accuracy usually receive first consideration in hiring. To qualify for jobs in the Federal government, stenographers must be able to take dictation at a minimum of 80 words per minute and type at least 40 words per minute. Workers must achieve higher rates to advance to more responsible positions.

Stenographers, especially those with strong interpersonal and communication skills may advance to secretarial positions with more responsibilities. In addition, some stenographers complete the necessary education to become court reporters or medical transcriptionists.

Job Outlook

Overall employment of court reporters, medical transcriptionists, and stenographers is projected to grow about as fast as the average for all occupations through 2008. Employment growth among medical transcriptionists should be offset by the decline among stenographers; the number of court reporters should remain fairly constant.

Demand for medical transcriptionists is expected to increase due to rapid growth in health care industries spurred by a growing and aging population. Advancements in voice recognition technology are not projected to reduce the need for medical transcriptionists because these workers will continue to be needed to review and edit drafts for accuracy. Moreover, growing numbers of medical transcriptionists will be needed to amend patients' records, edit for grammar, and discover discrepancies in medical records. Job opportunities should be the best for those who earn an associate's degree or certification from the American Association for Medical Transcription.

There should be little or no change in employment of court reporters. Despite increasing numbers of civil and criminal cases, budget constraints limit the ability of Federal, State, and local courts to expand. The growing number of conventions, conferences, depositions, seminars, and similar meetings in which proceedings are recorded should create limited demand for court reporters. Although many of these events are videotaped, a written transcript must still be created for legal purposes or if the proceedings are to be published. In addition, the trend to provide instantaneous written captions for the deaf and hearing-impaired should strengthen demand for stenocaptioners. Because of their relatively high salaries, keen competition should exist for court reporter positions; those with certification should enjoy the best job prospects.

The widespread use of dictation machines has greatly reduced the need for office stenographers. Audio recording equipment and the use of personal computers by managers and other professionals should continue to further decrease the demand for these workers.

Earnings

Court reporters, medical transcriptionists, and stenographers had median annual earnings of $25,430 in 1998. The middle 50 percent earned between $21,060 and $31,470; the lowest paid 10 percent earned less than $17,060; and the highest paid 10 percent earned more than $39,070. Median 1997 annual salaries in the industries employing the largest number of these workers were as follows:

Local government, except education and hospitals $29,300

State government, except education and hospitals 29,000

Mailing, reproduction, and stenographic services 28,600

Hospitals 23,500

Offices and clinics of medical doctors 22,600

Court reporters usually earn higher salaries than stenographers or medical transcriptionists, and many supplement their income by doing additional freelance work. According to a National Court Reporters Association survey of its members, average annual earnings for court reporters were about $54,000 in 1999. According to the 1999 HayGroup survey, about three-quarters of health care institutions paid their medical transcriptionists for time worked, with average salaries ranging from $20,000 to $30,000 annually. About a fifth of those respondents used a combination of payment methods (time worked plus incentive for production), with average salaries ranging from $28,000 to $36,000 annually. Regardless of specialty, earnings depend on education, experience, and geographic location.

Related Occupations

A number of other workers type, record information, and process paperwork. Among these are administrative assistants, bookkeepers, receptionists, secretaries, and human resource clerks. Other workers who provide medical and legal support include paralegals, medical assistants, and medical record technicians.

Sources of Additional Information

For information about careers, training, and certification in court reporting, contact:

- National Court Reporters Association, 8224 Old Courthouse Rd., Vienna, VA 22182. Internet: http://www.verbatimreporters.com

For information on a career as a medical transcriptionist, contact:

- American Association for Medical Transcription, P.O. Box 576187, Modesto, CA 95357. Internet: http://www.aamt.org/aamt

For information on a career as a federal court reporter, contact:

- United States Court Reporters Association, 1904 Marvel Lane, Liberty, MO 64068. Internet: http://www.uscra.org

State employment service offices can provide information about job openings for court reporters, medical transcriptionists, and stenographers.

Dental Assistants

(O*NET 66002)

Significant Points

- Rapid employment growth and above average job turnover should result in good job opportunities.

- Population growth and greater retention of natural teeth by middle-aged and older people will fuel demand for dental services and create opportunities for dental assistants.

- Dentists are expected to hire more assistants to perform routine tasks so they may devote their own time to more profitable procedures.

Nature of the Work

Dental assistants perform a variety of patient care, office, and laboratory duties. They work at chair-side as dentists examine and treat patients. They make patients as comfortable as possible in the dental chair, prepare them for treatment, and obtain dental records. Assistants hand instruments and materials to dentists, and keep patients' mouths dry and clear by using suction or other devices. Assistants also sterilize and disinfect instruments and equipment, prepare tray setups for dental procedures, and instruct patients on postoperative and general oral health care.

Some dental assistants prepare materials for making impressions and restorations, expose radiographs, and process dental x-ray film as directed by a dentist. They may also remove sutures, apply anesthetics and cavity preventive agents to teeth and gums, remove excess cement used in the filling process, and place rubber dams on the teeth to isolate them for individual treatment.

Those with laboratory duties make casts of the teeth and mouth from impressions taken by dentists, clean and polish removable appliances, and make temporary crowns. Dental assistants with office duties schedule and confirm appointments, receive patients, keep treatment records, send bills, receive payments, and order dental supplies and materials.

Dental assistants should not be confused with dental hygienists, who are licensed to perform different clinical tasks.

Working Conditions

Dental assistants work in a well-lighted, clean environment. Their work area is usually near the dental chair, so they can arrange instruments, materials, and medication, and hand them to the dentist when needed. Dental assistants wear gloves and masks to protect themselves from infectious diseases. Following safety procedures minimizes the risks of handling radiographic equipment.

Most dental assistants have a 32- to 40-hour workweek, which may include work on Saturdays or evenings.

Employment

Dental assistants held about 229,000 jobs in 1998. More than 3 out of 10 worked part time, sometimes in more than one dental office.

Virtually all dental assistants work in private dental offices. A small number work in dental schools, private and government hospitals, State and local public health departments, or clinics.

Training, Other Qualifications, and Advancement

Most assistants learn their skills on the job, though some are trained in dental assisting programs offered by community and junior colleges, trade schools, technical institutes, or the Armed Forces. Assistants must be a dentist's "third hand"; therefore, dentists look for people who are reliable, can work well with others, and have good manual dexterity. High school students interested in a career as a dental assistant should take courses in biology, chemistry, health, and office practices.

The American Dental Association's Commission on Dental Accreditation approved 251 dental assisting training programs in 1999. Programs include classroom, laboratory, and preclinical instruction in dental assisting skills and related theory. In addition, students gain practical experience in dental schools, clinics, or dental offices. Most programs take one year or less to complete and lead to a certificate or diploma. Two-year programs offered in community and junior colleges lead to an associate degree. All programs require a high school diploma or its equivalent, and some require a typing or science course for admission. Some private vocational schools offer four- to six-month courses in dental assisting, but the Commission on Dental Accreditation does not accredit these.

Certification is available through the Dental Assisting National Board. Certification is an acknowledgment of an assistant's qualifications and professional competence and may be an asset when seeking employment. In several States that have adopted standards for dental assistants who perform radiological procedures, completion of the certification examination meets those standards. Candidates may qualify to take the certification examination by graduating from an accredited training program or by having two years of full-time experience as a dental assistant. In addition, applicants must have current certification in cardiopulmonary resuscitation.

Without further education, advancement opportunities are limited. Some dental assistants working the front office become office managers. Others, working chair-side, go back to school to become dental hygienists.

Job Outlook

Job prospects for dental assistants should be good. Employment is expected to grow much faster than the average for all occupations through the year 2008. Also, the proportion of workers leaving the occupation and who must be replaced is above average. Many opportunities are for entry-level positions offering on-the-job training.

Population growth and greater retention of natural teeth by middle-aged and older people will fuel demand for dental services. Older dentists, who are less likely to employ assistants, will leave and be replaced by recent graduates, who are more likely to use one, or even two. In addition, as dentists' workloads increase, they are expected to hire more assistants to perform routine tasks so they may devote their own time to more profitable procedures.

Numerous job openings for dental assistants will arise from the need to replace assistants who leave the occupation. For many, this entry-level occupation provides basic training and experience and serves as a stepping stone to more highly skilled and higher paying jobs. Other assistants leave the job to take on family responsibilities, return to school, retire, or for other reasons.

Earnings

Median hourly earnings of dental assistants were $10.88 in 1998. The middle 50 percent earned between $8.94 and $13.11 an hour. The lowest 10 percent earned less than $7.06, and the highest 10 percent earned more than $15.71 an hour.

Related Occupations

Workers in other occupations supporting health practitioners include medical assistants, physical therapist assistants, occupational therapy assistants, pharmacy technicians and assistants, and veterinary assistants.

Sources of Additional Information

Information about career opportunities, scholarships, accredited dental assistant programs, and requirements for certification is available from:

- Commission on Dental Accreditation, American Dental Association, 211 E. Chicago Ave., Suite 1814, Chicago, IL 60611. Internet: http://www.ada.org
- Dental Assisting National Board, Inc., 676 North Saint Clair, Suite 1880, Chicago, IL 60611. Internet: http://www.dentalassisting.com

For general information about a career as a dental assistant, including training and continuing education, contact:

- American Dental Assistants Association, 203 North LaSalle St., Suite 1320, Chicago, IL 60601.

For information about a career as a dental assistant and schools offering training, contact:

- National Association of Health Career Schools, 2301 Academy Dr., Harrisburg, PA 17112.

Information about certification as a dental assistant is available from:

- American Medical Technologists, 710 Higgins Rd., Park Ridge, IL 60068-5765. Internet: http://www.amt1.com

Dental Hygienists

(O*NET 32908)

Significant Points

- Dental hygienists are projected to be one of the 30 fastest growing occupations.
- Population growth and greater retention of natural teeth will stimulate demand for dental hygienists.
- Opportunities for part-time work and flexible schedules are common.

Nature of the Work

Dental hygienists clean teeth and provide other preventive dental care, as well as teach patients how to practice good oral hygiene. Hygienists examine patients' teeth and gums, recording the presence of diseases or abnormalities. They remove calculus, stains, and plaque from teeth; take and develop dental x-rays; and apply cavity preventive agents such as fluorides and pit and fissure sealants. In some States, hygienists administer local anesthetics and anesthetic gas; place and carve filling materials, temporary fillings, and periodontal dressings; remove sutures; and smooth and polish metal restorations.

Dental hygienists also help patients develop and maintain good oral health. For example, they may explain the relationship between diet and oral health, inform patients how to select toothbrushes, and show patients how to brush and floss their teeth.

Dental hygienists use hand and rotary instruments, lasers, and ultrasonics to clean teeth; x-ray machines to take dental pictures; syringes with needles to administer local anesthetics; and models of teeth to explain oral hygiene.

Working Conditions

Flexible scheduling is a distinctive feature of this job. Full-time, part-time, evening, and weekend work is widely available. Dentists frequently hire hygienists to work only two or three days a week, so hygienists may hold jobs in more than one dental office.

Dental hygienists work in clean, well-lighted offices. Important health safeguards include strict adherence to proper radiological procedures, and use of appropriate protective devices when administering anesthetic gas. Dental hygienists also wear safety glasses, surgical masks, and gloves to protect themselves from infectious diseases.

Employment

Dental hygienists held about 143,000 jobs in 1998. Because multiple job holding is common in this field, the number of jobs exceeds the number of hygienists. About 3 out of 5 dental hygienists worked part time (less than 35 hours a week).

Almost all dental hygienists work in private dental offices. Some work in public health agencies, hospitals, and clinics.

Training, Other Qualifications, and Advancement

Dental hygienists must be licensed by the State in which they practice. To qualify for licensure, a candidate must graduate from an accredited dental hygiene school and pass both a written and clinical examination. The American Dental Association Joint Commission on National Dental Examinations administers the written examination accepted by all States and the District of Columbia. State or regional testing agencies administer the clinical examination. In addition, most States require an examination on legal aspects of dental hygiene practice. Alabama allows candidates to take its examinations if they have been trained through a State-regulated on-the-job program in a dentist's office.

In 1999, the Commission on Dental Accreditation accredited about 250 programs in dental hygiene. Although some programs lead to a bachelor's degree, most grant an associate degree. Thirteen universities offer master's degree programs in dental hygiene or a related area.

An associate degree is sufficient for practice in a private dental office. A bachelor's or master's degree is usually required for research, teaching, or clinical practice in public or school health programs.

About half of the dental hygiene programs prefer applicants who have completed at least one year of college. However, requirements vary from school to school. Schools offer laboratory, clinical, and classroom instruction in subjects such as anatomy, physiology, chemistry, microbiology, pharmacology, nutrition, radiography, histology (the study of tissue structure), periodontology (the study of gum diseases), pathology, dental materials, clinical dental hygiene, and social and behavioral sciences.

Dental hygienists should work well with others and must have good manual dexterity because they use dental instruments within a patient's mouth with little room for error. High school students interested in becoming dental hygienists should take courses in biology, chemistry, and mathematics.

Job Outlook

Employment of dental hygienists is expected to grow much faster than the average for all occupations through 2008, in response to increasing demand for dental care and the greater substitution of hygienists for services previously performed by dentists. Job prospects are expected to remain very good unless the number of dental hygienist program graduates grows much faster than during the last decade and results in a much larger pool of qualified applicants.

Population growth and greater retention of natural teeth will stimulate demand for dental hygienists. Older dentists, who are less likely to employ dental hygienists, will leave and be replaced by recent graduates, who are more likely to do so. In addition, as dentists' workloads increase, they are expected to hire more hygienists to perform preventive dental care such as cleaning so they may devote their own time to more profitable procedures.

Earnings

Median hourly earnings of dental hygienists were $22.06 in 1998. The middle 50 percent earned between $17.28 and $29.28 an hour. The lowest 10 percent earned less than $12.37, and the highest 10 percent earned more than $38.81 an hour.

Earnings vary by geographic location, employment setting, and years of experience. Dental hygienists who work in private dental offices may be paid on an hourly, daily, salary, or commission basis.

Benefits vary substantially by practice setting and may be contingent upon full-time employment. Dental hygienists who work for school systems, public health agencies, the Federal Government, or State agencies usually have substantial benefits.

Related Occupations

Workers in other occupations supporting health practitioners in an office setting include dental assistants, ophthalmic medical assistants, podiatric medical assistants, office nurses, medical assistants, physician assistants, physical therapist assistants, and occupational therapy assistants.

Sources of Additional Information

For information on a career in dental hygiene and the educational requirements to enter this occupation, contact:

● Division of Professional Development, American Dental Hygienists' Association, 444 N. Michigan Ave., Suite 3400, Chicago, IL 60611. Internet: http://www.adha.org

For information about accredited programs and educational requirements, contact:

● Commission on Dental Accreditation, American Dental Association, 211 E. Chicago Ave., Suite 1814, Chicago, IL 60611. Internet: http://www.ada.org

The State Board of Dental Examiners in each State can supply information on licensing requirements.

Dental Laboratory Technicians

(O*NET 89921)

Significant Points

● Employment should increase slowly, as the public's improving dental health requires fewer dentures but more bridges and crowns.

● Dental laboratory technicians need artistic aptitude for detailed and precise work, a high degree of manual dexterity, and good vision.

Nature of the Work

Dental laboratory technicians fill prescriptions from dentists for crowns, bridges, dentures, and other dental prosthetics. First, dentists send a specification of the item to be fabricated, along with an impression (mold) of the patient's mouth or teeth. Then dental laboratory technicians, also called dental technicians, create a model of the patient's mouth by pouring plaster into the impression and allowing it to set. Next, they place the model on an apparatus that mimics the bite and movement of the patient's jaw. The model serves as the basis of the prosthetic device. Technicians examine the model, noting the size and shape of the adjacent teeth, as well as gaps within the gum line. Based upon these observations and the dentist's specifications, technicians build and shape a wax tooth or teeth model, using small hand instruments called wax spatulas and wax carvers. They use this wax model to cast the metal framework for the prosthetic device.

Once the wax tooth has been formed, dental technicians pour the cast and form the metal, and using small hand-held tools, they prepare the surface to allow the metal and porcelain to bond. They then apply porcelain in layers to arrive at the precise shape and color of a tooth. Technicians place the tooth in a porcelain furnace to bake the porcelain onto the metal framework, and then they adjust the shape and color with subsequent grinding and addition of porcelain to achieve a sealed finish. The final product is a near exact replica of the lost tooth or teeth.

In some laboratories, technicians perform all stages of the work, whereas in other labs, each technician does only a few. Dental laboratory technicians can specialize in one of five areas: orthodontic appliances, crowns and bridges, complete dentures, partial dentures, or ceramics. Job titles can reflect specialization in these areas. For example, technicians who make porcelain and acrylic restorations are called *dental ceramists*.

Working Conditions

Dental laboratory technicians generally work in clean, well lighted, and well-ventilated areas. Technicians usually have their own workbenches, which can be equipped with Bunsen burners, grinding and polishing equipment, and hand instruments, such as wax spatulas and wax carvers. The work is extremely delicate and time consuming. Salaried technicians usually work 40 hours a week, but self-employed technicians frequently work longer hours.

Employment

Dental laboratory technicians held about 44,000 jobs in 1998. Most jobs were in commercial dental laboratories, which usually are small privately owned businesses with fewer than five employees. However, some laboratories are large; a few employ more than 50 technicians.

Some dental laboratory technicians worked in dentists' offices. Others worked for hospitals providing dental services, including Department of Veterans Affairs' hospitals. Some technicians work in dental laboratories in their homes, in addition to their regular job. Approximately 1 technician in 5 is self-employed, a higher proportion than in most other occupations.

Training, Other Qualifications, and Advancement

Most dental laboratory technicians learn their craft on the job. They begin with simple tasks, such as pouring plaster into an impression, and progress to more complex procedures, such as making porcelain crowns and bridges. Becoming a fully trained technician requires an average of three to four years, depending upon the individual's aptitude and ambition; but it may take a few years more to become an accomplished technician. Training in dental laboratory technology is also available through community and junior colleges, vocational-technical institutes, and the Armed Forces. Formal training programs vary greatly both in length and the level of skill they impart.

In 1998, 34 programs in dental laboratory technology were approved (accredited) by the Commission on Dental Accreditation in conjunction with the American Dental Association (ADA). These programs provide classroom instruction in dental materials science, oral anatomy, fabrication procedures, ethics, and related subjects. In addition, each student is given supervised practical experience in a school or an associated dental laboratory. Accredited programs normally take two years to complete and lead to an associate's degree.

Graduates of two-year training programs need additional hands-on experience to become fully qualified. Each dental laboratory owner operates in a different way, and classroom instruction does not necessarily expose students to techniques and procedures favored by individual laboratory owners. Students who have taken enough courses to learn the basics of the craft are usually considered good candidates for training, regardless of whether they have completed a formal program. Many employers will train someone without any classroom experience.

The National Board offers certification, which is voluntary, in five specialty areas: crowns and bridges, ceramics, partial dentures, complete dentures, and orthodontic appliances.

In large dental laboratories, technicians may become supervisors or managers. Experienced technicians may teach or take jobs with dental suppliers in such areas as product development, marketing, and sales. Still, for most technicians, opening one's own laboratory is the way toward advancement and higher earnings.

A high degree of manual dexterity, good vision, and the ability to recognize very fine color shadings and variations in shape are necessary. An artistic aptitude for detailed and precise work is also important. High school students interested in becoming dental laboratory technicians should take courses in art, metal and wood shop, drafting, and sciences. Courses in management and business may help those wishing to operate their own laboratories.

Job Outlook

Job opportunities for dental laboratory technicians should be favorable, despite very slow growth in the occupation. Employers have difficulty filling trainee positions, probably because of relatively low entry-level salaries and lack of familiarity with the occupation.

Although job opportunities are favorable, little or no change in the employment of dental laboratory technicians is expected through the year 2008, due to changes in dental care. The overall dental health of the population has improved because of fluoridation of drinking water, which has reduced the incidence of dental cavities, and greater emphasis on preventive dental care since the early 1960s. As a result, full dentures will be less common, as most people will need only a bridge or crown. However, during the last few years, demand has arisen from an aging public that is growing increasingly interested in cosmetic prosthesis. For example, many dental laboratories are filling orders for composite fillings that are white and look like a natural tooth to replace older, less attractive fillings.

Earnings

Median annual earnings of salaried precision dental laboratory technicians were $25,660 in 1998. The middle 50 percent earned between $19,410 and $34,600 a year. The lowest 10 percent earned less than $14,720, and the highest 10 percent earned more than $45,980 a year. Median annual earnings of dental laboratory technicians in 1997 were $24,100 in medical and dental laboratories and $25,500 in offices and clinics of dentists. In general, earnings of self-employed technicians exceed those of salaried workers. Technicians in large laboratories tend to specialize in a few procedures and, therefore, tend to be paid a lower wage than those employed in small laboratories that perform a variety of tasks.

Related Occupations

Dental laboratory technicians fabricate artificial teeth, crowns and bridges, and orthodontic appliances, following specifications and instructions provided by dentists. Other workers who make medical devices include arch-support technicians, orthotics technicians (braces and surgical supports), prosthetics technicians (artificial limbs and appliances), opticians, and ophthalmic laboratory technicians.

Sources of Additional Information

For a list of accredited programs in dental laboratory technology, contact:

- Commission on Dental Accreditation, American Dental Association, 211 E. Chicago Ave., Chicago, IL 60611. Internet: http://www.ada.org

General information on grants and scholarships is available from dental technology schools.

For information on requirements for certification, contact:

- National Board for Certification in Dental Technology, 8201 Greensboro Dr., Suite 300, McLean, VA 22101.

For information on career opportunities in commercial laboratories, contact:

- National Association of Dental Laboratories, 8201 Greensboro Dr., Suite 300, McLean, VA 22101. Internet: http://www.nadl.org

Dentists

(O*NET 32105A, 32105B, 32105D, 32105F, and 32105G)

Significant Points

- Most dentists have at least eight years of education beyond high school.

- Employment of dentists is expected to grow slower than the average as young people are troubled less by tooth decay.

- Dental care will focus more on prevention, including teaching people how to better care for their teeth.

Nature of the Work

Dentists diagnose, prevent, and treat teeth and tissue problems. They remove decay, fill cavities, examine x-rays, place protective plastic sealants on children's teeth, straighten teeth, and repair fractured teeth. They also perform corrective surgery on gums and supporting bones to treat gum diseases. Dentists extract teeth and make models and measurements for dentures to replace missing teeth. They provide instruction on diet, brushing, flossing, the use of fluorides, and other aspects of dental care. They also administer anesthetics and write prescriptions for antibiotics and other medications.

Dentists use a variety of equipment, including x-ray machines, drills, and instruments such as mouth mirrors, probes, forceps, brushes, and scalpels. They wear masks, gloves, and safety glasses to protect themselves and their patients from infectious diseases.

Dentists in private practice oversee a variety of administrative tasks, including bookkeeping, and buying equipment and supplies. They may employ and supervise dental hygienists, dental assistants, dental laboratory technicians, and receptionists.

Most dentists are general practitioners, handling a variety of dental needs. Other dentists practice in one of eight specialty areas. *Orthodontists*, the largest group of specialists, straighten teeth. The next largest group, *oral and maxillofacial surgeons*, operate on the mouth and jaws. The remainder may specialize as *pediatric dentists* (dentistry for children); *periodontists* (treating gums and bone supporting the teeth); *prosthodontists* (making artificial teeth or dentures); *endodontists* (root canal therapy); *public health dentists*; and *oral pathologists* (studying oral diseases).

Working Conditions

Most dentists work four or five days a week. Some work evenings and weekends to meet their patients' needs. Most full-time dentists work about 40 hours a week, but others work more. Initially, dentists may work more hours as they establish their practice. Experienced dentists often work fewer hours. A considerable number continue in part-time practice well beyond the usual retirement age.

Most dentists are "solo practitioners," meaning they own their own businesses and work alone or with a small staff. Some dentists have partners, and a few work for other dentists as associate dentists.

Employment

Dentists held about 160,000 jobs in 1998. About 9 out of 10 dentists are in private practice. Others work in private and public hospitals and clinics, for the Federal government, and in dental research.

Training, Other Qualifications, and Advancement

All 50 States and the District of Columbia require dentists to be licensed. In most States, a candidate must graduate from a dental school accredited by the American Dental Association's Commission on Dental Accreditation and pass written and practical examinations to qualify for a license. Candidates may fulfill the written part of the State licensing by passing the National Board Dental Examinations. Individual States or regional testing agencies give the written or practical examinations.

Currently, about 17 States require dentists to obtain a specialty license before practicing as a specialist. Requirements include two to four years of postgraduate education and, in some cases, completion of a special State examination. Most State licenses permit dentists to engage in both general and specialized practice. Dentists who want to teach or do research usually spend an additional two to five years in advanced dental training, in programs operated by dental schools or hospitals.

Dental schools require a minimum of two years of college-level predental education. However, most dental students have at least a bachelor's degree. Predental education emphasizes course work in the sciences.

All dental schools require applicants to take the Dental Admissions Test (DAT). When selecting students, schools consider scores earned on the DAT, the applicant's grade point average, and information gathered through recommendations and interviews.

Dental school usually lasts four academic years. Studies begin with classroom instruction and laboratory work in basic sciences including anatomy, microbiology, biochemistry, and physiology. Beginning courses in clinical sciences, including laboratory techniques, are also provided at this time. During the last two years, students treat patients, usually in dental clinics, under the supervision of licensed dentists.

Most dental schools award the degree of Doctor of Dental Surgery (D.D.S.). The rest award an equivalent degree, Doctor of Dental Medicine (D.M.D.).

Dentistry requires diagnostic ability and manual skills. Dentists should have good visual memory, excellent judgment of space and shape, a high degree of manual dexterity, and scientific ability. Good business sense, self-discipline, and communication skills are helpful for success in private practice. High school and college students who want to become dentists should take courses in biology, chemistry, physics, health, and mathematics.

Some dental school graduates work for established dentists as associates for a year or two in order to gain experience and save money to equip an office of their own. Most dental school graduates, however, purchase an established practice or open a new practice immediately after graduation. Each year about one-fourth to one-third of new graduates enroll in postgraduate training programs to prepare for a dental specialty.

Job Outlook

Employment of dentists is expected to grow slower than the average for all occupations through 2008. Although employment growth will provide some job opportunities, most jobs will result from the need to replace the large number of dentists projected to retire. Job prospects should be good if the number of dental school graduates does not grow significantly, keeping the supply of newly qualified dentists near current levels.

Demand for dental care should grow substantially through 2008. As members of the baby-boom generation advance into middle age, a large number will need maintenance on complicated dental work, such as bridges. In addition, elderly people are more likely to retain their teeth than were their predecessors, so they will require much more care than in the past. The younger generation will continue to need preventive check-ups despite treatments such as fluoridation of the water supply, which decreases the incidence of tooth decay.

Dental care will focus more on prevention, including teaching people how to better care for their teeth. Dentists will increasingly provide care that is aimed at preventing tooth loss (rather than just providing treatments, such as fillings). Improvements in dental technology will also allow dentists to provide more effective and less painful treatment to their patients.

However, the employment of dentists is not expected to grow as rapidly as the demand for dental services. As their practices expand, dentists are likely to hire more dental hygienists and dental assistants to handle routine services.

Earnings

Median annual earnings of salaried dentists were $110,160 in 1998. Earnings vary according to number of years in practice, location, hours worked, and specialty.

Self-employed dentists in private practice tend to earn more than salaried dentists. A relatively large proportion of dentists is self-employed. Like other business owners, these dentists must provide their own health insurance, life insurance, and retirement benefits.

Related Occupations

Dentists examine, diagnose, prevent, and treat diseases and abnormalities. So do clinical psychologists, optometrists, physicians, chiropractors, veterinarians, and podiatrists.

Sources of Additional Information

For information on dentistry as a career and a list of accredited dental schools, contact:

- American Dental Association, Commission on Dental Accreditation, 211 E. Chicago Ave., Chicago, IL 60611. Internet: http://www.ada.org
- American Association of Dental Schools, 1625 Massachusetts Ave. NW., Washington, DC 20036. Internet: http://www.aads.jhu.edu

The American Dental Association will also furnish a list of State boards of dental examiners. Persons interested in practicing dentistry should obtain the requirements for licensure from the board of dental examiners of the State in which they plan to work.

Prospective dental students should contact the office of student financial aid at the schools to which they apply, for information on scholarships, grants, and loans, including Federal financial aid.

Dietitians and Nutritionists

(O*NET 32521)

Significant Points

- Employment of dietitians is expected to grow about as fast as the average for all occupations through the year 2008 due to increased emphasis on disease prevention by improved health habits.

- Dietitians and nutritionists need at least a bachelor's degree in dietetics, foods and nutrition, food service systems management, or a related area.

Nature of the Work

Dietitians and nutritionists plan food and nutrition programs and supervise the preparation and serving of meals. They help prevent and treat illnesses by promoting healthy eating habits, scientifically evaluating clients' diets, and suggesting diet modifications, such as less salt for those with high blood pressure or reduced fat and sugar intake for those who are overweight.

Dietitians run food service systems for institutions such as hospitals and schools, promote sound eating habits through education, and conduct research. Major areas of practice are clinical, community, management, research, business and industry, and consultant dietetics.

Clinical dietitians provide nutritional services for patients in institutions such as hospitals and nursing homes. They assess patients' nutritional needs, develop and implement nutrition programs, and evaluate and report the results. They also confer with doctors and other health care professionals in order to coordinate medical and nutritional needs. Some clinical dietitians specialize in the management of overweight patients, care of the critically ill, or care of renal (kidney) and diabetic patients. In addition, clinical dietitians in nursing homes, small hospitals, or correctional facilities may also manage the food service department.

Community dietitians counsel individuals and groups on nutritional practices designed to prevent disease and promote good health. Working in places such as public health clinics, home health agencies, and health maintenance organizations, they evaluate individual needs, develop nutritional care plans, and instruct individuals and their families. Dietitians working in home health agencies provide instruction on grocery shopping and food preparation to the elderly, individuals with special needs, and children.

Increased interest in nutrition has led to opportunities in food manufacturing, advertising, and marketing, in which dietitians analyze foods, prepare literature for distribution, or report on issues such as the nutritional content of recipes, dietary fiber, or vitamin supplements.

Management dietitians oversee large-scale meal planning and preparation in health care facilities, company cafeterias, prisons, and schools. They hire, train, and direct other dietitians and food service workers; budget for and purchase food, equipment, and supplies; enforce sanitary and safety regulations; and prepare records and reports.

Consultant dietitians work under contract with health care facilities or in their own private practice. They perform nutrition screenings for their clients and offer advice on diet-related concerns such as weight loss or cholesterol reduction. Some work for wellness programs, sports teams, supermarkets, and other nutrition-related businesses. They may consult with food service managers, providing expertise in sanitation, safety procedures, menu development, budgeting, and planning.

Working Conditions

Most dietitians work a regular 40-hour week, although some work weekends. Many dietitians work part time.

Dietitians and nutritionists usually work in clean, well-lighted, and well-ventilated areas. However, some dietitians work in warm, congested kitchens. Many dietitians and nutritionists are on their feet for most of the workday.

Employment

Dietitians and nutritionists held about 54,000 jobs in 1998. Over half were in hospitals, nursing homes, or offices and clinics of physicians.

State and local governments provided about 1 job in 6—mostly in health departments and other public health related areas. Other jobs were in restaurants, social service agencies, residential care facilities, diet workshops, physical fitness facilities, school systems, colleges and universities, and the Federal government (mostly in the Department of Veterans Affairs). Some were employed by firms that provide food services on contract to such facilities as colleges and universities, airlines, correctional facilities, and company cafeterias.

Some dietitians were self-employed, working as consultants to facilities such as hospitals and nursing homes and seeing individual clients.

Training, Other Qualifications, and Advancement

High school students interested in becoming a dietitian or nutritionist should take courses in biology, chemistry, mathematics, health, and communications. Dietitians and nutritionists need at least a bachelor's degree in dietetics, foods and nutrition, food service systems management, or a related area. College students in these majors take courses in foods, nutrition, institution management, chemistry, biochemistry, biology, microbiology, and physiology. Other suggested courses include business, mathematics, statistics, computer science, psychology, sociology, and economics.

Twenty-seven of the 41 States with laws governing dietetics require licensure, 13 require certification, and 1 requires registration. The Commission on Dietetic Registration of the American Dietetic Association (ADA) awards the Registered Dietitian credential to those who pass a certification exam after completing their academic coursework and supervised experience. Since practice requirements vary by State, interested candidates should determine the requirements of the State in which they want to work before sitting for any exam.

As of 1999, there were 235 bachelor's and master's degree programs approved by the ADA's Commission on Accreditation/Approval for Dietetics Education (CAADE). Supervised practice experience can be acquired in two ways. There are 51 ADA-accredited coordinated programs combining academic and supervised practice experience in a four- to five-year program. The second option requires completion of 900 hours of supervised practice experience, either in one of the 225 CAADE-accredited internships or in one of the 25 CAADE-approved preprofessional practice programs. Internships and preprofessional practice programs may be full-time programs lasting nine months to a year or part-time programs lasting two years. Students interested in research, advanced clinical positions, or public health may need a graduate degree.

Experienced dietitians may advance to assistant, associate, or director of a dietetic department or might become self-employed. Some dietitians specialize in areas such as renal or pediatric dietetics. Others may leave the occupation to become sales representatives for equipment, pharmaceutical, or food manufacturers.

Job Outlook

Employment of dietitians is expected to grow about as fast as the average for all occupations through 2008 due to increased emphasis on disease prevention by improved dietary habits. A growing and aging population will increase the demand for meals and nutritional counseling in nursing homes, schools, prisons, community health programs, and home health care agencies. Public interest in nutrition and the emphasis on health education and prudent lifestyles will also spur demand, especially in management. Besides employment growth, job openings will also result from the need to replace experienced workers who leave the occupation.

The number of dietitian positions in hospitals is expected to grow slowly as hospitals continue to contract out food service operations. On the other hand, employment is expected to grow fast in contract providers of food services, social services agencies, and offices and clinics of physicians.

Employment growth for dietitians and nutritionists may be somewhat constrained by some employers substituting other workers such as health educators, food service managers, and dietetic technicians. Growth also is constrained by limitations on insurance reimbursement for dietetic services.

Earnings

Median annual earnings of dietitians and nutritionists were $35,020 in 1998. The middle 50 percent earned between $28,010 and $42,720 a year. The lowest 10 percent earned less than $20,350, and the highest 10 percent earned more than $51,320 a year. Median annual earnings in the industries employing the largest number of dietitians and nutritionists in 1997 were as follows:

Hospitals $34,900

Local government, except education and hospitals 31,200

Nursing and personal care facilities 28,400

According to the American Dietetic Association, median annual income for registered dietitians in 1997 varied by practice area as follows: clinical nutrition, $35,500; food and nutrition management, $44,900; community nutrition, $34,900; consultation and business, $46,000; and education and research, $45,200. Salaries also vary by years in practice, educational level, geographic region, and size of community.

Related Occupations

Dietitians and nutritionists apply the principles of food and nutrition in a variety of situations. Jobs similar to management dietitians' include home economists and food service managers. Nurses and health educators often provide services related to those of community dietitians.

Sources of Additional Information

For a list of academic programs, scholarships, and other information about dietetics, contact:

- The American Dietetic Association, 216 West Jackson Blvd., Suite 800, Chicago, IL 60606-6995. Internet: http://www.eatright.org

Education Administrators

(O*NET 15005A and 15005B)

Significant Points

- Most jobs require experience in a related occupation, such as teacher or admissions counselor, and a master's or doctoral degree.

- Many jobs offer high earnings, considerable community prestige, and the satisfaction of working with young people.

- Competition will be keen for jobs in higher education, but opportunities should be better at the elementary and secondary school level.

Nature of the Work

Smooth operation of an educational institution requires competent administrators. Education administrators provide direction, leadership, and day-to-day management of educational activities in schools, colleges and universities, businesses, correctional institutions, museums, and job training and community service organizations. *Education administrators* set educational standards and goals and establish the policies and procedures to carry them out. They develop academic programs; monitor students' educational progress; train and motivate teachers and other staff; manage guidance and other student services; administer record keeping; prepare budgets; handle relations with parents, prospective and current students, employers, and the community; and perform many other duties.

Education administrators also supervise managers, support staff, teachers, counselors, librarians, coaches, and others. In an organization such as a small daycare center, one administrator may handle all these functions. In universities or large school systems, responsibilities are divided among many administrators, each with a specific function.

Those who manage elementary and secondary schools are called *principals*. They set the academic tone and hire, evaluate, and help improve the skills of teachers and other staff. Principals confer with staff to advise, explain, or answer procedural questions. They visit classrooms, observe teaching methods, review instructional objectives, and examine learning materials. They actively work with teachers to develop and maintain high curriculum standards, develop mission statements, and set performance goals and objectives. Principals must use clear, objective guidelines for teacher appraisals, since pay is often based on performance ratings.

Principals also meet and interact with other administrators, students, parents, and representatives of community organizations. Decision-making authority has increasingly shifted from school district central offices to individual schools. Thus, parents, teachers, and other members of the community play an important role in setting school policies and goals. Principals must pay attention to the concerns of these groups when making administrative decisions.

Principals prepare budgets and reports on various subjects, including finances and attendance, and oversee the requisitioning and allocation of supplies. As school budgets become tighter, many principals are more involved in public relations and fund raising to secure financial support for their schools from local businesses and the community.

Principals must take an active role to ensure that students meet national academic standards. Many principals develop school/business partnerships and school-to-work transition programs for students. Increasingly, principals must be sensitive to the needs of the rising number of non-English speaking and culturally diverse students. Growing enrollments, which are leading to overcrowding at many existing schools, are also a cause for concern. When addressing problems of inadequate resources, administrators serve as advocates to build new schools or repair existing ones.

Schools continue to be involved with students' emotional welfare as well as their academic achievement. As a result, principals face responsibilities outside the academic realm. For example, in response to the growing number of dual-income and single-parent families and teenage parents, schools have established before- and after-school child-care programs or family resource centers, which also may offer parenting classes and social service referrals. With the help of community organizations, some principals have established programs to combat increases in crime, drug and alcohol abuse, and sexually transmitted disease among students.

Assistant principals aid the principal in the overall administration of the school. Some assistant principals hold this position for several years to prepare for advancement to principal; others are career assistant principals. They are responsible for scheduling student classes, ordering textbooks and supplies, and coordinating transportation, custodial, cafeteria, and other support services. They usually handle discipline, attendance, social and recreational programs, and health and safety. They also may counsel students on personal, educational, or vocational matters. With site-based management, assistant principals play a greater role in developing curriculum, evaluating teachers, and building school-community relations—responsibilities previously assumed solely by the principal. The number of assistant principals a school employs may vary depending on the number of students.

Administrators in school district central offices manage public schools under their jurisdiction. This group includes those who direct subject area programs such as English, music, vocational education, special education, and mathematics. They plan, evaluate, standardize, and improve curriculums and teaching techniques and help teachers improve their skills and learn about new methods and materials. They oversee career counseling programs and testing that measures students' abilities and helps place them in appropriate classes. Central office administrators also include directors of programs such as guidance, school psychology, athletics, curriculum and instruction, and professional development. With site-based management, administrators have transferred primary responsibility for many of these programs to the principals, assistant principals, teachers, and other staff.

In colleges and universities, *academic deans, deans of faculty, provosts,* and *university deans* assist presidents and develop budgets and academic policies and programs. They also direct and coordinate the activities of deans of individual colleges and chairpersons of academic departments.

College or university department heads or *chairpersons* are in charge of departments such as English, biological science, and mathematics. In addition to teaching, they coordinate schedules of classes and teaching assignments; propose budgets; recruit, interview, and hire applicants for teaching positions; evaluate faculty members; encourage faculty development; and perform other administrative duties. In overseeing their departments, chairpersons must consider and balance the concerns of faculty, administrators, and students.

Higher education administrators provide student services. *Vice presidents of student affairs or student life, deans of students,* and *directors of student services* may direct and coordinate admissions, foreign student services, health and counseling services, career services, financial aid, and housing and residential life, as well as social, recreational, and related programs. In small colleges, they may counsel students. *Registrars* are custodians of students' records. They register students, prepare student transcripts, evaluate academic records, assess and collect tuition and fees, plan and implement commencement, oversee the preparation of college catalogs and schedules of classes, and analyze enrollment and demographic statistics. *Directors of admissions* manage the process of recruiting, evaluating, and admitting students and work closely with financial aid directors, who oversee scholarship, fellowship, and loan programs. Registrars and admissions officers must adapt to technological innovations in student information systems. For example, for those whose institutions present information—such as college catalogs and schedules—on the Internet, knowledge of on-line resources, imaging, and other computer skills is important. *Directors of student* activities plan and arrange social, cultural, and recreational activities, assist student-run organizations, and may conduct new student orientation. *Athletic directors* plan and direct intramural and intercollegiate athletic activities, including publicity for athletic events, preparation of budgets, and supervision of coaches.

Working Conditions

Education administrators hold management positions with significant responsibility. Coordinating and interacting with faculty, parents, and students can be fast-paced and stimulating, but also stressful and demanding. Some jobs include travel. Principals and assistant principals whose main duty often is discipline may find working with difficult students challenging and frustrating. The number of school-age children is rising, and some school systems have hired assistant principals because a school's population increased significantly. However, in other school systems, principals may manage larger student bodies, which can be stressful.

Many education administrators work more than 40 hours a week, including some nights and weekends when they oversee school activities. Most administrators work 10 or 11 months a year, but some work year round.

Employment

Education administrators held about 447,000 jobs in 1998. About 9 out of 10 were in educational services, which includes elementary, secondary, and technical schools, and colleges and universities. The rest worked in child day care centers, religious organizations, job training centers, State departments of education, and businesses and other organizations that provided training for their employees.

Training, Other Qualifications, and Advancement

Most education administrators begin their careers in related occupations and prepare for jobs in education administration by completing their master's or doctoral degrees. Because of the diversity of duties and levels of responsibility, their educational backgrounds and experience vary considerably. Principals, assistant principals, central office administrators, and academic deans usually held teaching positions before moving into administration. Some teachers move directly into principal positions; others first become assistant principals or gain experience in other central office administrative jobs at either the school or district level in positions such as department head, curriculum specialist, or subject matter advisor. In some cases, administrators move up from related staff jobs such as recruiter, guidance counselor, librarian, residence hall director, or financial aid or admissions counselor.

To be considered for education administrator positions, workers must first prove themselves in their current jobs. In evaluating candidates, supervisors look for determination, confidence, innovativeness, motivation, and leadership. The ability to make sound decisions and organize and coordinate work efficiently is essential. Since much of an administrator's job involves interacting with others—such as students, parents, and teachers—they must have strong interpersonal skills and be effective communicators and motivators. Knowledge of management principles and practices, gained through work experience and formal education, is important. A familiarity with computer technology is a plus for principals, who are becoming increasingly involved in gathering information and coordinating technical resources for their students and classrooms.

In most public schools, principals, assistant principals, and school administrators in central offices need a master's degree in education administration or educational supervision. Some principals and central office administrators have a doctorate or specialized degree in education administration. In private schools, which are not subject to State certification requirements, some principals and assistant principals hold only a bachelor's degree; however, the majority have a master's or doctoral degree. Most States require principals to be licensed as school administrators. License requirements vary by State. National standards for school leaders, including principals and supervisors, were recently developed by the Interstate School Leaders Licensure Consortium. Several States currently use these national standards as guidelines to assess beginning principals for licensure, and many more States are expected to adopt the standards for this purpose. Some States require administrators to take continuing education courses to keep their certification, thus ensuring that administrators have the most up-to-date skills. The number and type of courses required to maintain certification vary by State.

Academic deans and chairpersons usually have a doctorate in their specialty. Most have held a professorship in their department before advancing. Admissions, student affairs, and financial aid directors and registrars sometimes start in related staff jobs with bachelor's degrees (any field usually is acceptable) and obtain advanced degrees in college student affairs or higher education administration. A Ph.D. or Ed.D. usually is necessary for top student affairs positions. Computer literacy and a background in mathematics or statistics may be assets in admissions, records, and financial work.

Advanced degrees in higher education administration, educational supervision, and college student affairs are offered in many colleges and universities. The National Council for Accreditation of Teacher Education accredits these programs. Education administration degree programs include courses in school management, school law, school finance and budgeting, curriculum development and evaluation, research design and data analysis, community relations, politics in education, counseling, and leadership. Educational supervision degree programs include courses in supervision of instruction and curriculum, human relations, curriculum development, research, and advanced pedagogy courses.

Education administrators advance by moving up an administrative ladder or transferring to larger schools or systems. They also may become superintendent of a school system or president of an educational institution.

Job Outlook

Expect substantial competition for prestigious jobs as higher education administrators. Many faculty and other staff meet the education and experience requirements for these jobs and seek promotion. However, the number of openings is relatively small; only the most highly qualified are selected. Candidates who have the most formal education and who are willing to relocate should have the best job prospects.

On the other hand, it is becoming more difficult to attract candidates for some principal, vice principal, and administration jobs at the elementary and secondary school level, particularly in districts where crowded conditions and smaller budgets make the work more stressful. Many teachers no longer have a strong incentive to move into these positions. The pay is not significantly higher and does not compensate for the added workload, responsibilities, and pressures of the position. Also, site-based management has given teachers more decision-making responsibility in recent years, possibly satisfying their desire to move into administration.

Employment of education administrators is expected to grow about as fast as the average for all occupations over the 1998-2008 period. Additional openings will result from the need to replace administrators who retire or transfer to other occupations.

School enrollments at the elementary, secondary, and post-secondary level are all expected to grow over the projection period. Rather than opening new schools, many schools will enlarge to accommodate more students, increasing the need for additional assistant principals to help with the larger workload. Employment of education administrators will also grow as more services are provided to students and as efforts to improve the quality of education continue.

However, budget constraints are expected to moderate growth in this profession. At the post-secondary level, some institutions have been reducing administrative staffs to contain costs. Some colleges are consolidating administrative jobs and contracting with other providers for some administrative functions.

Earnings

Salaries of education administrators depend on several factors, including the location and enrollment size of the school or school district. Median annual earnings of education administrators in 1998 were $60,400 a year. The middle 50 percent earned between $43,870 and $80,030 a year. The lowest 10 percent earned less than $30,480; the highest 10 percent earned more than $92,680. Median annual earnings in the industries employing the largest numbers of education administrators in 1997 were as follows:

Elementary and secondary schools	$61,800
Colleges and universities	60,000
Vocational schools	43,700
Miscellaneous schools and educational services	33,800
Child day care services	25,000

According to a survey of public schools, conducted by the Educational Research Service, average salaries for principals and assistant principals in the 1997-98 school year were as follows:

Directors, managers, coordinators, and supervisors of instructional services	$73,058
Principals:	
Elementary school	$64,653
Junior high/middle school	68,740
Senior high school	74,380
Assistant principals:	
Elementary school	$53,206
Junior high/middle school	57,768
Senior high school	60,999

In 1997-98, according to the College and University Personnel Association, median annual salaries for selected administrators in higher education were as follows:

Academic deans:	
Medicine	$235,000
Law	160,400
Engineering	121,841
Business	90,745
Arts and sciences	87,293
Education	85,013
Social sciences	64,022
Mathematics	60,626

Student services directors:

Admissions and registrar $52,500

Student financial aid 48,448

Student activities 36,050

Related Occupations

Education administrators apply organizational and leadership skills to provide services to individuals. Workers in related occupations include medical and health services managers, social service agency administrators, recreation and park managers, museum directors, library directors, and professional and membership organization executives. Since principals and assistant principals usually have extensive teaching experience, their backgrounds are similar to those of teachers and many school counselors.

Sources of Additional Information

For information on elementary and secondary school principals, assistant principals, and central office administrators, contact:

- American Federation of School Administrators, 1729 21st St. NW., Washington, DC 20009.
- American Association of School Administrators, 1801 North Moore St., Arlington, VA 22209.

For information on elementary school principals and assistant principals, contact:

- The National Association of Elementary School Principals, 1615 Duke St., Alexandria, VA 22314-3483.

For information on collegiate registrars and admissions officers, contact:

- American Association of Collegiate Registrars and Admissions Officers, One Dupont Circle NW., Suite 520, Washington, DC 20036-1171.

For information on college and university personnel, contact:

- The College and University Personnel Association, 1233 20th St. NW., Washington, DC 20036-1250.

For information on professional development and graduate programs for college student affairs administrators, visit the National Association of Student Personnel Administrators Internet site: http://www.naspa.org.

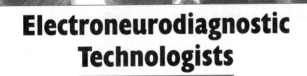

Electroneurodiagnostic Technologists

(O*NET 32923)

Significant Points

- The number of job openings created will be limited by slower-than-average employment growth and low replacement needs.

- Most technologists learn on the job, but opportunities should be best for technologists with formal post-secondary training.

Nature of the Work

Electroneurodiagnostic technologists use instruments such as an electroencephalograph (EEG) machine to record electrical impulses transmitted by the brain and the nervous system. They help physicians diagnose brain tumors, strokes, epilepsy, and sleep disorders. They also measure the effects of infectious diseases on the brain and determine whether individuals with mental or behavioral problems have an organic impairment, such as Alzheimer's disease. Furthermore, they determine *cerebral death*, the absence of brain activity, and assess the probability of recovery from a coma.

Electroneurodiagnostic technologists who specialize in basic or *resting* EEGs are called *EEG technologists*. The range of tests performed by electroneurodiagnostic technologists is broader than, but includes, those conducted by EEG technologists. Because it provides a more accurate description of work typically performed in the field, the title electroneurodiagnostic technologist generally has replaced that of EEG technologist.

Electroneurodiagnostic technologists take patients' medical histories, help patients relax, and then apply electrodes to designated spots on the patients' heads. They must choose the most appropriate combination of instrument controls and electrodes to correct for mechanical and electrical interference from somewhere other than the brain, such as eye movement or radiation from electrical sources.

Increasingly, technologists perform EEGs in the operating room, which requires that they understand anesthesia's effect on brain waves. For special procedure EEGs, technologists may secure electrodes to the chest, arm, leg, or spinal column to record activity from both the central and peripheral nervous systems.

In ambulatory monitoring, technologists attach small recorders to patients to monitor the brain, and sometimes the heart, while patients carry out normal activities over a 24-hour period. They then remove the recorder and obtain a readout. Technologists review the readouts, selecting sections for the physician to examine.

Using *evoked potential* testing, technologists measure sensory and physical responses to specific stimuli. After attaching electrodes to the patient, they set the instrument for the type and intensity of the stimulus, increase the intensity until the patient reacts, and note the sensation level.

For nerve conduction tests, which are used to diagnose muscle and nerve problems, technologists place electrodes on the patient's skin over a nerve and over a muscle. Then they stimulate the nerve with an electrical current and record how long it takes the nerve impulse to reach the muscle.

Technologists who specialize in and administer sleep disorder studies are called *polysomnographic technologists*. Sleep disorder studies are usually conducted in a clinic called a sleep center. During the procedure, these technologists monitor the patient's respiration and heart and brain wave activity. These workers must know the dynamics of the cardiopulmonary systems during each stage of sleep.

They coordinate readings from several organ systems, separate the readings according to the stages of sleep, and relay results to the physician. Polysomnographic technologists may also write technical reports summarizing test results.

Additionally, technologists look for changes in a patient's neurologic, cardiac, and respiratory status, which may indicate an emergency, such as a heart attack, and provide emergency care until help arrives.

Electroneurodiagnostic technologists may have supervisory or administrative responsibilities. They may manage an electroneurodiagnostic laboratory, arrange work schedules, keep records, schedule appointments, order supplies, provide instruction to less-experienced technologists, and maintain equipment.

Working Conditions

Electroneurodiagnostic technologists usually work in clean, well-lighted surroundings and spend about half of their time on their feet. They often work with patients who are very ill and require assistance. Technologists employed in hospitals may do all their work in a single room or may push equipment to a patient's bedside and obtain recordings there. Most technologists work a standard workweek, although those in hospitals may be on call evenings, weekends, and holidays. Those performing sleep studies usually work evenings and nights.

Employment

Electroneurodiagnostic technologists held about 5,400 jobs in 1998. Most worked in neurology laboratories of hospitals; others worked in offices and clinics of neurologists and neurosurgeons, sleep centers, or psychiatric facilities.

Training, Other Qualifications, and Advancement

Although most electroneurodiagnostic technologists currently employed learned their skills on the job, employers are beginning to favor those who have completed formal training. Some hospitals require applicants for trainee positions to have post-secondary training, whereas others expect only a high school diploma. Recommended high school and college subjects for prospective technologists include health, biology, anatomy, and mathematics. Often, on-the-job trainees are transfers from other hospital jobs, such as licensed practical nurses.

Formal post-secondary training is offered in hospitals and community colleges. In 1998, the Joint Review Committee on Education in Electroneurodiagnostic Technology approved 12 formal programs. Programs usually last from one to two years and include laboratory experience, as well as classroom instruction in human anatomy and physiology, neurology, neuroanatomy, neurophysiology, medical terminology, computer technology, electronics, and instrumentation. Graduates receive associate's degrees or certificates.

The American Board of Registration of Electroencephalographic and Evoked Potential Technologists awards the credentials Registered EEG Technologist, Registered Evoked Potential Technologist, and

Certificate in Neurophysiologic Intraoperative Monitoring to qualified applicants. The Association of Polysomnographic Technologists registers polysomnographic technologists. Applicants interested in taking the registration exam must have worked in a sleep center for at least one year. Although not generally required for staff-level jobs, registration indicates professional competence and is usually necessary for supervisory or teaching jobs. In addition, the American Association of Electrodiagnostic Technologists provides certification in the field of nerve conduction studies for electroneurodiagnostic technologists. These technologists should have manual dexterity, good vision, good writing skills, an aptitude for working with electronic equipment, and the ability to work with patients as well as with other health personnel.

Experienced electroneurodiagnostic technologists can advance to chief or manager of an electroneurodiagnostic laboratory. Chief technologists are generally supervised by a physician—an electroencephalographer, neurologist, or neurosurgeon. Technologists may also teach or go into research.

Job Outlook

Employment of electroneurodiagnostic technologists is expected to grow more slowly than the average for all occupations through the year 2008. Although employment will increase as new procedures and technologies are developed and as the size of the population grows, productivity gains caused by increasingly sophisticated equipment and cross-trained employees will limit employment growth. Only a small number of openings are expected each year, due primarily to the need to replace technologists who transfer to other occupations or retire. Most jobs will be found in hospitals, but growth will be fastest in offices and clinics of neurologists.

Earnings

Median annual earnings of electroneurodiagnostic technologists were $32,070 in 1998. The middle 50 percent earned between $26,610 and $38,500 a year. The lowest 10 percent earned less than $22,200, and the highest 10 percent earned more than $46,620 a year.

Related Occupations

Other health personnel who operate medical equipment to diagnose and treat patients include radiologic technologists, nuclear medicine technologists, sonographers, perfusionists, and cardiovascular technologists.

Sources of Additional Information

For general information about a career in electroneurodiagnostics and a list of accredited training programs, contact:

- Executive Office, American Society of Electroneurodiagnostic Technologists, Inc., 204 W. 7th St., Carroll, IA 51401. Internet: http://www.aset.org

For information on opportunities in sleep studies, contact:

- Association of Polysomnographic Technology, 2025 South Washington, Suite 300, Lansing, MI 48910-0817.

Information about specific accredited training programs is also available from:

- Joint Review Committee on Electroneurodiagnostic Technology, Route 1, Box 63A, Genoa, WI 54632.

Information on becoming a registered electroneurodiagnostic technologist is available from:

- American Board of Registration of Electroencephalgraphic and Evoked Potential Technologists, P.O. Box 916633, Longwood, FL 32791-6633.

Information on certification in the field of nerve conduction studies is available from:

- American Association of Electrodiagnostic Technologists, 35 Hallett Lane, Chatham, MA 02633-2408.

Emergency Medical Technicians and Paramedics

(O*NET 32508)

Significant Points

- Irregular hours and treating patients in life-or-death situations lead to job stress in this occupation.

- State requirements vary, but formal training and certification are required.

- Employment is projected to grow rapidly as paid emergency medical technician positions replace unpaid volunteers.

Nature of the Work

People's lives often depend on the quick reaction and competent care of emergency medical technicians (EMTs) and paramedics. Incidents as varied as automobile accidents, heart attacks, drownings, childbirth, and gunshot wounds all require immediate medical attention. EMTs and paramedics provide this vital attention as they care for and transport the sick or injured to a medical facility.

Depending on the nature of the emergency, EMTs and paramedics typically are dispatched to the scene by a 911 operator and often work with police and fire department personnel. Once they arrive, they determine the nature and extent of the patient's condition while trying to ascertain whether the patient has preexisting medical problems. Following strict procedures, they give appropriate emergency care and transport the patient. Some conditions can be handled following general rules and guidelines, while more complicated problems are carried out under the direction of medical doctors by radio.

EMTs and paramedics may use special equipment such as backboards to immobilize patients before placing them on stretchers and securing them in the ambulance for transport to a medical facility. Usually, one EMT or paramedic drives, while the other monitors the patient's vital signs and gives additional care as needed. Some who work for hospital trauma centers, which use helicopters to transport critically ill or injured patients, are part of the flight crew.

At the medical facility, EMTs and paramedics help transfer patients to the emergency department, report their observations and actions to staff, and may provide additional emergency treatment. Some paramedics are trained to treat patients with minor injuries on the scene of an accident or at their home without transporting them to a medical facility. After each run, EMTs replace used supplies and check equipment. If a transported patient had a contagious disease, EMTs decontaminate the interior of the ambulance and report cases to the proper authorities.

Beyond these general duties, the specific responsibilities of EMTs and paramedics depend on their level of qualification and training. To determine this, the National Registry of Emergency Medical Technicians (NREMT) registers emergency medical service (EMS) providers at four levels: First Responder, EMT-Basic, EMT-Intermediate, and EMT-Paramedic. Some States, however, do their own certification and use numeric ratings from 1 to 4 to distinguish levels of proficiency.

The lowest level—First Responders—are trained to provide basic emergency medical care because they tend to be the first persons to arrive at the scene of an incident. Many firefighters, police officers, and other emergency workers have this level of training. The EMT-Basic, also known as EMT-1, represents the first component of the emergency medical technician system. An EMT-1 is trained to care for patients on accident scenes and on transport by ambulance to the hospital under medical direction. The EMT-1 has the emergency skills to assess a patient's condition and manage respiratory, cardiac, and trauma emergencies.

The EMT-Intermediate (EMT-2 and EMT-3) has more advanced training that allows administration of intravenous fluids, use of manual defibrillators to give lifesaving shocks to a stopped heart, and use of advanced airway techniques and equipment to assist patients experiencing respiratory emergencies. EMT-Paramedics (EMT-4) provide the most extensive pre-hospital care. In addition to the procedures already described, paramedics may administer drugs orally and intravenously, interpret electrocardiograms (EKGs), perform endotracheal intubations, and use monitors and other complex equipment.

Working Conditions

EMTs and paramedics work both indoors and outdoors, in all types of weather. They are required to do considerable kneeling, bending, and heavy lifting. These workers risk noise-induced hearing loss from sirens and back injuries from lifting patients. In addition, EMTs and paramedics may be exposed to diseases such as Hepatitis-B and AIDS, as well as violence from drug overdose victims or psychologically disturbed patients. The work is not only physically strenuous, but also stressful, involving life-or-death situations and suffering patients. Nonetheless, many people find the work exciting and challenging and enjoy the opportunity to help others.

EMTs and paramedics employed by fire departments work about 50 hours a week. Those employed by hospitals frequently work between 45 and 60 hours a week, and those in private ambulance services work between 45 and 50 hours. Some of these workers, especially those in police and fire departments, are on call for extended periods. Because emergency services function 24 hours a day, EMTs and paramedics have irregular working hours that add to job stress.

Employment

EMTs and paramedics held about 150,000 jobs in 1998. In addition, there are many more volunteer EMTs, especially in smaller cities, towns, and rural areas, who work for departments where they may respond to only a few calls for service per month. Most career EMTs and paramedics work in metropolitan areas.

EMTs and paramedics are employed in a number of industries. Nearly half work in local and suburban transportation for private ambulance firms that transport and treat individuals on an emergency or non-emergency basis. About a third of EMTs and paramedics work in local government for fire departments and third-service providers, in which emergency medical services are provided by an independent agency. Another fifth are found in hospitals, where they may work full-time within the medical facility or respond to calls in ambulances or helicopters to transport critically ill or injured patients.

Training, Other Qualifications, and Advancement

Formal training and certification is needed to become an EMT or paramedic. All 50 States possess a certification procedure. In 38 States and the District of Columbia, registration with the National Registry is required at some or all levels of certification. Other States administer their own certification examination or provide the option of taking the National Registry examination. To maintain certification, EMTs and paramedics must re-register, usually every two years. In order to re-register, an individual must be working as an EMT and meet a continuing education requirement.

Training is offered at progressive levels: EMT-Basic, also known as EMT-1; EMT-Intermediate, or EMT-2 and EMT-3; and EMT-paramedic, or EMT-4. The EMT-Basic represents the first level of skills required to work in the emergency medical system. Coursework typically emphasizes emergency skills such as managing respiratory, trauma, and cardiac emergencies and patient assessment. Formal courses are often combined with time in an emergency room or ambulance. The program also provides instruction and practice in dealing with bleeding, fractures, airway obstruction, cardiac arrest, and emergency childbirth. Students learn to use and maintain care for common emergency equipment, such as backboards, suction devices, splints, oxygen delivery systems, and stretchers. Graduates of approved EMT basic training programs who pass a written and practical examination administered by the State certifying agency or the National Registry of Emergency Medical Technicians earn the title of Registered EMT-Basic. The course is also a prerequisite for EMT-Intermediate and EMT-Paramedic training.

EMT-Intermediate training requirements vary from State to State. Applicants can opt to receive training in EMT-Shock Trauma, where the caregiver learns to start intravenous fluids and give certain medications, or in EMT-Cardiac, which includes learning heart rhythms and administering advanced medications. Training commonly includes 35-55 hours of additional instruction beyond EMT-Basic coursework and covers patient assessment as well as the use of advanced airway devices and intravenous fluids. Prerequisites for taking the EMT-Intermediate examination include registration as an EMT-Basic, required classroom work, and a specified amount of clinical experience.

The most advanced level of training for this occupation is EMT-Paramedic. At this level, the caregiver receives additional training in body function and more advanced skills. The Paramedic Technology program usually lasts up to two years and results in an associate degree in applied science. Such education prepares the graduate to take the National Registry of Emergency Medical Technicians examination and become certified as an EMT-Paramedic. Extensive related coursework and clinical and field experience is required. Due to the longer training requirement, almost all EMT-Paramedics are in paid positions. Refresher courses and continuing education are available for EMTs and paramedics at all levels.

EMTs and paramedics should be emotionally stable, have good dexterity, agility, and physical coordination, and be able to lift and carry heavy loads. They also need good eyesight (corrective lenses may be used) with accurate color vision.

Advancement beyond the EMT-Paramedic level usually means leaving fieldwork. An EMT-Paramedic can become a supervisor, operations manager, administrative director, or executive director of emergency services. Some EMTs and paramedics become instructors, dispatchers, or physician assistants, while others move into sales or marketing of emergency medical equipment. A number of people become EMTs and paramedics to assess their interest in health care and then decide to return to school and become registered nurses, physicians, or other health workers.

Job Outlook

Employment of EMTs is expected to grow much faster than the average for all occupations through 2008. Much of this growth will occur as positions change from volunteer to paid and as the population grows, particularly older age groups that are the greatest users of emergency medical services. In addition to job growth, openings will occur because of replacement needs; some workers leave because of stressful working conditions, limited advancement potential, and the modest pay and benefits in the private sector.

Most opportunities for EMTs and paramedics are expected to arise in hospitals and private ambulance services. Competition will be greater for jobs in local government, including fire, police, and third-service rescue squad departments, where job growth for these workers is expected to be slower.

Earnings

Earnings of EMTs depend on the employment setting and geographic location as well as the individual's training and experience. Median annual earnings of EMTs were $20,290 in 1998. The middle 50 percent earned between $15,660 and $26,240. The lowest 10 percent earned less than $12,700, and the highest 10 percent earned more than $34,480. In local and suburban transportation, where private ambulance firms are located, the median salary was $18,300 in 1997. In local government, except education and hospitals, the median salary was $21,900. In hospitals, the median salary was $19,900.

Those in emergency medical services who are part of fire or police departments receive the same benefits as firefighters or police officers. For example, many are covered by pension plans that provide retirement at half pay after 20 or 25 years of service or if a worker becomes disabled in the line of duty.

Related Occupations

Other workers in occupations that require quick and level-headed reactions to life-or-death situations are police officers, firefighters, air traffic controllers, and workers in other health occupations.

Sources of Additional Information

General information about EMTs and paramedics is available from:

- National Association of Emergency Medical Technicians, 408 Monroe St., Clinton, MS 39056. Internet: http://www.naemt.org
- National Registry of Emergency Medical Technicians, P.O. Box 29233, Columbus, OH 43229. Internet: http://www.nremt.org
- National Highway Transportation Safety Administration, EMS Division, 400 7th St. SW., NTS-14, Washington DC. Internet: http://www.nhtsa.dot.gov/people/injury/ems/

Employment Interviewers, Private or Public Employment Service

(O*NET 21508)

Significant Points

- Although employers prefer applicants with a college degree, educational requirements range from a high school diploma to a master's or doctoral degree.
- Most new jobs will arise in personnel supply firms, especially those specializing in temporary help.

Nature of the Work

Whether you are looking for a job or trying to fill one, you might need the help of an employment interviewer. These workers, sometimes called personnel consultants, human resources coordinators, personnel development specialists, or employment brokers, help jobseekers find employment and employers find qualified employees. Employment interviewers obtain information from employers as well as jobseekers and put together the best combination of applicant and job.

The majority of employment interviewers are employed in private personnel supply firms or State employment security offices. Those in personnel supply firms who place permanent employees are usually called counselors. These workers offer tips on personal appearance, suggest ways to present a positive image, provide background information on the company with which an interview is scheduled, and recommend interviewing techniques. Employment interviewers in some firms specialize in placing applicants in particular kinds of jobs—for example, secretarial, word processing, computer programming and computer systems analysis, engineering, accounting, law, or health. Counselors in such firms usually have three to five years of work experience in their field.

Some employment interviewers work in temporary help services companies, placing the company's employees in firms that need temporary help. Employment interviewers take job orders from client firms and match their requests against a list of available workers. They select the most qualified workers available and assign them to the firms requiring assistance.

Regular evaluation of employee job skills is an important part of the job for interviewers working in temporary help services companies. Initially, interviewers evaluate or test new employees' skills to determine their abilities and weaknesses. The results are kept on file and referred to when filling job orders. In some cases, the company trains employees to improve their skills, so interviewers periodically reevaluate or retest employees to identify any new skills they may have developed.

Traditionally, firms that placed permanent employees dealt with highly skilled applicants, such as lawyers or accountants, and those placing temporary employees dealt with less skilled workers, such as secretaries or data entry operators. However, temporary help services increasingly place workers with a wide range of educational backgrounds and work experience. Businesses are now turning to temporary employees to fill all types of positions—from clerical to managerial, professional, and technical—to reduce the wage and benefit costs associated with hiring permanent employees.

The duties of employment interviewers in job service centers differ somewhat from those in personnel supply firms because applicants may lack marketable skills. In these centers, jobseekers present resumes and fill out forms regarding education, job history, skills, awards, certificates, and licenses. An employment interviewer reviews these forms and asks the applicant about the type of job sought and salary range desired.

Because an applicant in these centers may have unrealistic expectations, employment interviewers must be tactful but persuasive. Some applicants are high school dropouts or have poor English skills, a history of drug or alcohol dependency, or a prison record. The amount and nature of special help for such applicants vary from State to State. In some States, it is the employment interviewer's responsibility to counsel hard-to-place applicants and refer them elsewhere for literacy or language instruction, vocational training, transportation assistance, child care, and other services. In other States, specially trained counselors perform this task.

Applicants may also need help identifying the kind of work for which they are best suited. The employment interviewer evaluates the applicant's qualifications and either chooses an appropriate occupation or class of occupations or refers the applicant for vocational testing. After identifying an appropriate job type, the employment interviewer searches the file of job orders seeking a possible job match and refers the applicant to the employer if a match is found. If no match is found, the interviewer shows the applicant how to use listings of available jobs.

Besides helping individuals find jobs, employment interviewers help firms fill job openings. The services they provide depend on the company or type of agency they work for and the clientele it serves. In most of these agencies, employers usually pay private agencies to recruit workers. The employer places a "job order" with the agency describing the opening and listing requirements including education, licenses or credentials, and experience. Employment interviewers often contact the employer to determine their exact personnel needs. The employment interviewer then reviews the job requirements and the jobseeker qualifications to determine the best possible match of position and applicant. Although computers are increasingly used to keep records and match employers with jobseekers, personal contact with an employment interviewer remains an essential part of an applicant's job search.

A private industry employment interviewer must also be a salesperson. Counselors pool together a group of qualified applicants and try to sell them to many different companies. Often a consultant will call a company that has never been a client with the aim of filling their employment needs. Maintaining good relations with employers is an important part of the employment interviewer's job because this helps assure a steady flow of job orders. Being prepared to fill an opening quickly with a qualified applicant impresses employers most and keeps them as clients.

Working Conditions

Employment interviewers usually work in comfortable, well-lit offices, often using a computer to match information about employers and jobseekers. Some interviewers, however, may spend much of their time out of the office conducting interviews. The work can be hectic, especially in temporary help service companies that supply clients with immediate help for short periods of time. The private placement industry is competitive, and some overtime may be required.

Employment

Employment interviewers held about 66,000 jobs in 1998. Over half worked in the private sector for personnel supply services, typically for employment placement firms or temporary help services companies. About 2 out of 10 worked for State or local government. Others were employed by organizations that provide various services, such as job training and vocational rehabilitation.

Employees of career consulting or outplacement firms are not included in these estimates. Workers in these firms help clients market themselves; they do not act as job brokers, nor do they match individuals with particular vacancies.

Training, Other Qualifications, and Advancement

Although most public and private agencies prefer to hire college graduates for interviewer jobs, a degree is not always necessary.

Hiring requirements in the private sector reflect a firm's management approach as well as the placements in which its interviewers specialize. Those who place highly trained individuals such as accountants, lawyers, engineers, physicians, or managers usually have some training or experience in the field in which they are placing workers. Thus, a bachelor's, master's, or even a doctoral degree may be a prerequisite for some interviewers. Even with the right education, however, sales ability is still required to succeed in the private sector.

Educational requirements play a lesser role for interviewers placing clerks or laborers; a high school diploma may be sufficient. In these positions, qualities such as energy level, telephone voice, and sales ability take precedence over educational attainment. Other desirable qualifications for employment interviewers include good communications skills, a desire to help people, office skills, and adaptability. A friendly, confidence-winning manner is an asset because personal interaction plays a large role in this occupation. Increasingly, employment interviewers use computers as a tool; thus, basic knowledge of computers is helpful.

Entry-level employment interviewer positions in the public sector are usually filled by college graduates, even though the positions do not always require a bachelor's degree. Some States allow substitution of suitable work experience for college education. Suitable experience is usually defined as working in close contact with the public or spending time in other jobs, including clerical jobs, in a job service office. In States that permit employment interviewers to engage in counseling, course work in counseling may be required.

Most States and many large city and county governments use some form of merit system for hiring interviewers. Applicants may take a written exam, undergo a preliminary interview, or submit records of their education and experience for evaluation. Those who meet the standards are placed on a list from which the top-ranked candidates are selected for later interviews and possible hiring.

Advancement as an employment interviewer in the public sector is often based on a system providing regular promotions and salary increases for those meeting established standards. Advancement to supervisory positions is highly competitive. In personnel supply firms, advancement often depends on one's success in placing workers and usually takes the form of greater responsibility and higher income. Successful individuals occasionally establish their own businesses.

Job Outlook

Employment in this occupation is expected to grow about as fast as the average for all occupations through the year 2008. The majority of new jobs will arise in personnel supply firms, especially those specializing in temporary help. Job growth is not anticipated in State job service offices because of budgetary limitations, the growing use of computerized job matching and information systems, and increased contracting out of employment services to private firms. In addition to openings resulting from growth, a small number of openings will stem from the need to replace experienced interviewers who transfer to other occupations, retire, or stop working for other reasons.

Economic expansion and new business formation should mean growing demand for the services of personnel supply firms and employment interviewers. Firms that lack the time or resources to develop their own screening procedures will continue to turn to personnel firms. Rapid expansion of firms supplying temporary help in particular will be responsible for much of the growth in this occupation. Businesses of all types are turning to temporary help services companies for additional workers to handle short-term assignments, staff one-time projects, launch new programs, and reduce wage and benefit costs associated with hiring permanent employees.

Entry into this occupation is relatively easy for college graduates and for people who have had some college courses, except in those positions specializing in placement of workers with highly specialized training, such as lawyers, doctors, and engineers.

Employment interviewers who place permanent workers may lose their jobs during recessions because employers reduce or eliminate hiring for permanent positions during downturns in the economy. State job service employment interviewers are less susceptible to layoffs than those who place permanent or temporary personnel in the private sector.

Earnings

Median annual earnings of employment interviewers in 1998 were $29,800. The middle 50 percent earned between $23,520 and $39,600. The lowest 10 percent earned less than $18,420, and the highest 10 percent earned more than $73,180. Employment interviewers earn slightly more in urban areas.

Earnings in private firms vary, in part because the basis for compensation varies. Workers in personnel supply firms tend to be paid on a commission basis; those in temporary help service companies receive a salary. When workers are paid on a commission basis, total earnings depend on the type and number of placements. In general, those who place more highly skilled or hard-to-find employees earn more. An interviewer or counselor working strictly on a commission basis often makes around 30 percent of what he or she bills the client, although this varies widely from firm to firm.

Some employment interviewers work on a salary-plus-commission basis because they fill difficult or highly specialized positions requiring long periods of search. The salary is usually small by normal standards; however, it guarantees these individuals security through slow times. The commission provides the incentive and opportunity for higher earnings.

Some personnel supply firms employ new workers for a two- to three-month probationary period during which they draw a regular salary. This gives new workers time to develop their skills and acquire clients while simultaneously giving employers an opportunity to evaluate them. If they are hired, their earnings are then usually based on commission.

Related Occupations

Employment interviewers serve as intermediaries for jobseekers and employers. Workers in several other occupations do similar jobs. Personnel officers, for example, screen and help hire new employees, but they concern themselves mainly with the hiring needs of the firm; they never represent individual jobseekers. Personnel officers may also have additional duties in areas such as payroll or benefits management.

Career counselors help students and alumni find jobs, but they primarily emphasize career counseling and decision making, not placement. Counselors in community organizations and vocational rehabilitation facilities help clients find jobs, but they also assist with drug or alcohol dependencies, housing, transportation, child care, and other problems that stand in the way of finding and keeping a job.

Sources of Additional Information

For information on a career as an employment interviewer/counselor, contact:

- National Association of Personnel Services, 3133 Mt. Vernon Ave., Alexandria, VA 22305. Internet: http://www.napsweb.org
- American Staffing Association, 277 South Washington St., Suite 200, Alexandria, VA 22314. Internet: http://www.natss.org

For information on a career as an employment interviewer in State employment security offices, contact:

- Interstate Conference of Employment Security Agencies, 444 North Capitol St. NW., Suite 142, Washington, DC 20001. Internet: http://www.icesa.org

File Clerks

(O*NET 55321)

Significant Points

- Most jobs required only a high school diploma.
- Numerous job opportunities should arise due to high turnover in this occupation.

Nature of the Work

The amount of information generated by organizations continues to grow rapidly. File clerks classify, store, retrieve, and update this information. In many small offices, they often have additional responsibilities, such as data entry, word processing, sorting mail, and operating copying or fax machines. They are employed across the Nation by organizations of all types.

File clerks, also called records, information, or record center clerks, examine incoming material and code it numerically, alphabetically, or by subject matter. They then store forms, letters, receipts, or reports in paper form or enter necessary information into other storage devices. Some clerks operate mechanized files that rotate to bring the needed records to them; others convert documents to films that are then stored on microforms, such as microfilm or microfiche. A growing number of file clerks use imaging systems that scan paper files or film and store the material on optical disks.

In order for records to be useful, they must be up-to-date and accurate. File clerks ensure that new information is added to the files in a timely manner and may get rid of outdated file materials or transfer them to inactive storage. They also check files at regular intervals to make sure that all items are correctly sequenced and placed. Whenever records cannot be found, the file clerk attempts to locate the missing material. As an organization's needs for information change, file clerks also implement changes to the filing system established by supervisory personnel.

When records are requested, file clerks locate them and give them to the borrower. The record may be a sheet of paper stored in a file cabinet or an image on microform. In the first example, the clerk manually retrieves the document and hands or forwards it to the borrower. In the latter example, the clerk retrieves the microform and displays it on a microform reader. If necessary, file clerks make copies of records and distribute them. In addition, they keep track of materials removed from the files to ensure that borrowed files are returned.

Increasingly, file clerks use computerized filing and retrieval systems. These systems use a variety of storage devices, such as a mainframe computer, magnetic tape, CD-ROM, or floppy disk. To retrieve a document in these systems, the clerk enters the document's identification code, obtains the location, and pulls the document. Accessing files in a computer database is much quicker than locating and physically retrieving paper files. Even when files are stored electronically, however, backup paper or electronic copies usually are also kept.

Working Conditions

Most file clerks typically are employed in an office environment. Most work alongside other clerical workers, but some work in centralized units away from the front office.

Because the majority of clerks use computers on a daily basis, these workers may experience eye and muscle strain, backaches, headaches, and repetitive motion injuries. Also, clerks who review detailed data may have to sit for extended periods of time. Although the work does not require heavy lifting, file clerks spend a lot of time on their feet and frequently stoop, bend, and reach. Most clerks work regular business hours.

Employment

File clerks held about 272,000 jobs in 1998. Although file clerk jobs are found in nearly every sector of the economy, about 90 percent of these workers are employed in services, government, finance, insurance, and real estate. More than 1 out of every 4 is employed in temporary services firms, and about 1 out of 3 worked part time in 1998.

Training, Other Qualifications, and Advancement

Employers typically require applicants to have at least a high school diploma or its equivalent, although many employers prefer to hire clerks with a higher level of education. Most employers prefer workers who are computer-literate. Knowledge of word processing and spreadsheet software is especially valuable, as are experience working in an office and good interpersonal skills.

File clerks often learn the skills they need in high schools, business schools, and community colleges. Business education programs offered by these institutions typically include courses in typing, word processing, shorthand, business communications, records management, and office systems and procedures.

Some entrants are college graduates with degrees in business, finance, or liberal arts. Although a degree is rarely required, many graduates accept entry-level clerical positions to get into a particular company with the hope of being promoted to professional or managerial positions. Once hired, clerks usually receive on-the-job training. Under the guidance of a supervisor or other senior worker, new employees learn company procedures. Some formal classroom training may also be necessary, such as training in specific computer software.

Clerks must be careful, orderly, and detail-oriented in order to avoid making errors and to recognize errors made by others. These workers should also be discreet and trustworthy because they frequently come in contact with confidential material.

Clerks usually advance by taking on more duties in the same occupation for higher pay or transferring to a closely related occupation. Most companies fill office and administrative support supervisory and managerial positions by promoting individuals from within their organizations, so clerks who acquire additional skills, experience, and training improve their advancement opportunities.

Job Outlook

Employment of file clerks is expected to grow about as fast as the average for all occupations through 2008. Projected job growth stems from rising demand for file clerks to record and retrieve information in organizations across the economy. This growth will be moderated, however, by productivity gains stemming from office automation and the consolidation of clerical jobs. Nonetheless, job opportunities for file clerks should be plentiful because a large number of workers will be needed to replace workers who leave the occupation each year. High turnover among file clerks reflects the lack of formal training requirements, limited advancement potential, and relatively low pay.

Jobseekers who have typing and other secretarial skills and are familiar with a wide range of office machines, especially personal computers, should have the best job opportunities. File clerks should find many opportunities for temporary or part-time work, especially during peak business periods.

Earnings

Salaries of file clerks vary. The region of the country, size of city, and type and size of establishment all influence salary levels. The level of industry or technical expertise required and the complexity and uniqueness of a clerk's responsibilities may also affect earnings. Median annual earnings of full-time file clerks in 1998 were $16,830.

Related Occupations

Other clerical workers who classify, update, and retrieve information include bank tellers, statistical clerks, receiving clerks, medical record clerks, hotel and motel clerks, credit clerks, and reservation and transportation ticket agents.

Sources of Additional Information

State employment service offices can provide information about job openings for records processing occupations.

Food and Beverage Service Occupations

(O*NET 65002, 65005, 65008A, 65008B, 65011, 65014, 65017, 65041, 65099A, and 65099B)

Significant Points

- Most jobs are part time, and many opportunities exist for young people. Nearly 2 out of 3 food counter and fountain workers are 16-19 years old.

- Job openings are expected to be abundant through 2008, reflecting substantial turnover.

- Tips comprise a major portion of earnings; consequently, keen competition is expected for bartender, waiter and waitress, and other jobs in popular restaurants and fine dining establishments where potential earnings from tips are greatest.

Nature of the Work

Whether they work in small, informal diners or large, elegant restaurants, all food and beverage service workers aim to help customers have a positive dining experience in their establishments. These workers are responsible for greeting customers, taking food and drink orders, serving food, cleaning up after patrons, and preparing tables and dining areas. All of these duties require a high quality of services customers will return.

The largest group of these workers, *waiters* and *waitresses*, take customers' orders, serve food and beverages, prepare itemized checks, and sometimes accept payments. Their specific duties vary considerably, depending on the establishment where they work. In coffee shops, they are expected to provide fast and efficient, yet courteous service. In fine restaurants, where gourmet meals are accompanied by attentive formal service, waiters and waitresses serve meals at a more leisurely pace and offer more personal service to patrons. For example, servers may recommend a certain wine as a complement to a particular entree, explain how various items on the menu are prepared, or complete preparations on a salad or other special dishes at table side. Additionally, waiters and waitresses may check the identification of patrons to ensure they meet the minimum age requirement for the purchase of alcohol and tobacco products.

Depending on the type of restaurant, waiters and waitresses may perform additional duties usually associated with other food and beverage service occupations. These tasks may include escorting guests to tables, serving customers seated at counters, setting up and clearing tables, or operating a cash register. However, formal restaurants frequently hire other staff to perform these duties, allowing their waiters and waitresses to concentrate on customer service.

Bartenders fill drink orders that waiters and waitresses take from customers. They prepare standard mixed drinks and, occasionally, are asked to mix drinks to suit a customer's taste. Most bartenders know dozens of drink recipes and are able to mix drinks accurately, quickly, and without waste, even during the busiest periods. Besides mixing and serving drinks, bartenders collect payment, operate the cash register, clean up after customers leave, and often serve food to customers seated at the bar. Bartenders also check identification of customers seated at the bar to ensure they meet the minimum age requirement for the purchase of alcohol and tobacco products. Bartenders usually are responsible for ordering and maintaining an inventory of liquor, mixes, and other bar supplies. They often form attractive displays out of bottles and glassware and wash the glassware and utensils after each use.

The majority of bartenders who work in eating and drinking establishments directly serve and interact with patrons. Because customers typically frequent drinking establishments for the friendly atmosphere, most bartenders must be friendly and helpful with customers. Bartenders at service bars, on the other hand, have little contact with customers because they work in small bars in restaurants, hotels, and clubs where only waiters and waitresses serve drinks. Some establishments, especially larger ones, use automatic equipment to mix drinks of varying complexity at the push of a button. Even in these establishments, however, bartenders still must be efficient and knowledgeable in case the device malfunctions or a customer requests a drink not handled by the equipment.

Hosts and *hostesses* try to create a good impression of a restaurant by warmly welcoming guests. Because hosts and hostesses are restaurants' personal representatives, they try to ensure that service is prompt and courteous and that the meal meets expectations. They may courteously direct patrons to where coats and other personal items may be left and indicate where patrons can wait until their table is ready. Hosts and hostesses assign guests to tables suitable for the size of their group, escort patrons to their seats, and provide menus. They also schedule dining reservations, arrange parties, and organize any special services that are required. In some restaurants, they also act as cashiers.

Dining room attendants and *bartender helpers* assist waiters, waitresses, and bartenders by cleaning tables, removing dirty dishes, and keeping serving areas stocked with supplies. They replenish the supply of clean linens, dishes, silverware, and glasses in the dining room and keep the bar stocked with glasses, liquor, ice, and drink garnishes. Bartender helpers also keep bar equipment clean and wash glasses. Dining room attendants set tables with clean tablecloths, napkins, silverware, glasses, and dishes and serve ice water, rolls, and butter. At the conclusion of meals, they remove dirty dishes and soiled linens from tables. Cafeteria attendants stock serving tables with food, trays, dishes, and silverware and may carry trays to dining tables for patrons.

Counter attendants take orders and serve food at counters. In cafeterias, they serve food displayed on counters and steam tables, carve meat, dish out vegetables, ladle sauces and soups, and fill beverage glasses. In lunchrooms and coffee shops, counter attendants take orders from customers seated at the counter, transmit orders to the kitchen, and pick up and serve food. They also fill cups with coffee, soda, and other beverages and prepare fountain specialties, such as milkshakes and ice cream sundaes. Counter attendants prepare some short-order items, such as sandwiches and salads, and wrap or place orders in containers for carry out. They also clean counters, write itemized checks, and sometimes accept payment.

Fast-food workers take orders from customers at counters or drive-through windows at fast-food restaurants. They pick up the ordered beverage and food items, serve them to a customer, and accept payment. Many fast-food workers also cook and package food, make coffee, and fill beverage cups using drink-dispensing machines.

Working Conditions

Food and beverage service workers are on their feet most of the time and often carry heavy trays of food, dishes, and glassware. During busy dining periods, they are under pressure to serve customers quickly and efficiently. The work is relatively safe, but care must be taken to avoid slips, falls, and burns.

Part-time work is more common among food and beverage service workers than among workers in almost any other occupation. Those on part-time schedules include half of all waiters and waitresses, and 6 out of 10 food counter and fountain workers, compared to 1 out of 6 workers throughout the economy. Slightly more than half of all bartenders work full time, with 35 percent working part time and the remainder working a variable schedule.

The wide range in dining hours creates work opportunities attractive to homemakers, students, and other individuals seeking supplemental income. In fact, nearly 2 out of 3 food counter and fountain workers are between 16 and 19 years old. Many food and beverage service workers work evenings, weekends, and holidays. Some work split shifts—that is, they work for several hours during the middle of the day, take a few hours off in the afternoon, and then return to their jobs for evening hours.

Employment

Food and beverage service workers held over 5.4 million jobs in 1998. Waiters and waitresses held about 2,019,000 of these jobs; counter attendants and fast-food workers, 2,025,000; dining room and cafeteria attendants and bartender helpers, 405,000; bartenders, 404,000; hosts and hostesses, 297,000; and all other food preparation and service workers, 280,000.

Restaurants, coffee shops, bars, and other retail eating and drinking places employed the overwhelming majority of food and beverage service workers. Others worked in hotels and other lodging places, bowling alleys, casinos, country clubs, and other membership organizations.

Jobs are located throughout the country but are typically plentiful in large cities and tourist areas. Vacation resorts offer seasonal employment, and some workers alternate between summer and winter resorts, instead of remaining in one area the entire year.

Training, Other Qualifications, and Advancement

There are no specific educational requirements for food and beverage service jobs. Although many employers prefer to hire high school graduates for waiter and waitress, bartender, and host and hostess positions, completion of high school is usually not required for fast-food workers, counter attendants, and dining room attendants and bartender helpers. For many people, a job as a food and beverage service worker serves as a source of immediate income, rather than a career. Many entrants to these jobs are in their late teens or early twenties and have a high school education or less. Usually, they have little or no work experience. Many are full-time students or homemakers. Food and beverage service jobs are a major source of part-time employment for high school and college students.

Because maintaining a restaurant's image is important to its success, employers emphasize personal qualities. Food and beverage service workers are in close contact with the public, so these workers should be well-spoken and have a neat, clean appearance. They should enjoy dealing with all kinds of people and possess a pleasant disposition.

Waiters and waitresses need a good memory to avoid confusing customers' orders and to recall faces, names, and preferences of frequent patrons. These workers should also be good at arithmetic so they can total bills without the assistance of a calculator or cash register if necessary. In restaurants specializing in foreign foods, knowledge of a foreign language is helpful. Prior experience waiting on tables is preferred by restaurants and hotels that have rigid table service standards. Jobs at these establishments often have higher earnings, but they may also have higher educational requirements than less demanding establishments.

Usually, bartenders must be at least 21 years of age, but employers prefer to hire people who are 25 or older. Bartenders should be familiar with State and local laws concerning the sale of alcoholic beverages.

Most food and beverage service workers pick up their skills on the job by observing and working with more experienced workers. Some employers, particularly those in fast-food restaurants, use self-instruction programs with audiovisual presentations and instructional booklets to teach new employees food preparation and service skills. Some public and private vocational schools, restaurant associations, and large restaurant chains provide classroom training in a generalized food service curriculum.

Some bartenders acquire their skills by attending a bartending or vocational and technical school. These programs often include instruction on State and local laws and regulations, cocktail recipes, attire and conduct, and stocking a bar. Some of these schools help their graduates find jobs.

Due to the relatively small size of most food-serving establishments, opportunities for promotion are limited. After gaining some experience, some dining room and cafeteria attendants and bartender helpers are able to advance to waiter, waitress, or bartender jobs. For waiters, waitresses, and bartenders, advancement usually is limited to finding a job in a more expensive restaurant or bar where prospects for tip earnings are better. A few bartenders open their own businesses. Some hosts and hostesses and waiters and waitresses advance to supervisory jobs, such as maitre d'hotel, dining room supervisor, or restaurant manager. In larger restaurant chains, food and beverage service workers who excel at their work are often invited to enter the company's formal management training program.

Job Outlook

Job openings are expected to be abundant for food and beverage service workers. Employment of food and beverage service occupations is expected to grow about as fast as the average for all occupations through 2008, stemming from increases in population, personal incomes, and leisure time. While employment growth will produce many new jobs, the overwhelming majority of openings will arise from the need to replace the high proportion of workers who leave this occupation each year. There is substantial movement into and out of the occupation because education and training requirements are minimal, and the predominance of part-time jobs is attractive to people seeking a short-term source of income rather than a career. However, keen competition is expected for bartender, waiter and waitress, and other food and beverage service jobs in popular restaurants and fine dining establishments, where potential earnings from tips are greatest.

Projected employment growth will vary by type of food and beverage service job. Growth in the number of families and the more affluent, 55-and-older population will result in more restaurants that offer table service and more varied menus—requiring waiters and waitresses and hosts and hostesses. Employment of fast-food workers also is expected to increase in response to the continuing fast-paced lifestyle of many Americans and the addition of healthier foods at many of these restaurants. However, little change is expected in the employment of dining room attendants, as waiters and waitresses increasingly assume their duties. Employment of bartenders is expected to decline as drinking of alcoholic beverages outside the home—particularly cocktails—continues to drop.

Earnings

Food and beverage service workers derive their earnings from a combination of hourly wages and customer tips. Earnings vary greatly, depending on the type of job and establishment. For example, fast-food workers and hosts and hostesses usually do not receive tips, so their wage rates may be higher than those of waiters and waitresses and bartenders, who may earn more from tips than from wages. In some restaurants, these workers contribute a portion of their tips to a tip pool, which is distributed among the establishment's other food and beverage service workers and kitchen staff. Tip pools allow workers who normally do not receive tips, such as dining room attendants, to share in the rewards of a well-served meal.

In 1998, median hourly earnings (not including tips) of full-time waiters and waitresses were $5.85. The middle 50 percent earned between $5.58 and $6.32; the top 10 percent earned at least $7.83. For most waiters and waitresses, higher earnings are primarily the result of receiving more in tips rather than higher hourly wages. Tips usually average between 10 and 20 percent of guests' checks, so waiters and waitresses working in busy, expensive restaurants earn the most.

Full-time bartenders had median hourly earnings (not including tips) of $6.25 in 1998. The middle 50 percent earned from $5.72 and $7.71; the top 10 percent earned at least $9.19 an hour. Like waiters and waitresses, bartenders employed in public bars may receive more than half of their earnings as tips. Service bartenders are often paid higher hourly wages to offset their lower tip earnings.

Median weekly hourly earnings (not including tips) of full-time dining room attendants and bartender helpers were $6.03 in 1998. The middle 50 percent earned between $5.67 and $7.11; the top 10 percent earned over $8.49 an hour. Most received over half of their earnings as wages; the rest of their income was a share of the proceeds from tip pools.

Full-time counter attendants and fast-food workers, except cooks, had median hourly earnings (not including tips) of $6.06 in 1998. The middle 50 percent earned between $5.67 and $7.14, while the highest 10 percent earned over $8.45 a hour. Although some counter attendants receive part of their earnings as tips, fast-food workers usually do not.

In establishments covered by Federal law, most workers beginning at the minimum wage earned $5.15 an hour in 1998. However, various minimum wage exceptions apply under specific circumstances to disabled workers, full-time students, youth under age 20 in their first 90 days of employment, tipped employees, and student-learners. Employers are also permitted to deduct from wages the cost, or fair value, of any meals or lodging provided. However, many employers provide free meals and furnish uniforms. Food and beverage service workers who work full time often receive typical benefits, while part-time workers usually do not.

In some large restaurants and hotels, food and beverage service workers belong to unions—principally the Hotel Employees and Restaurant Employees International Union and the Service Employees International Union.

Related Occupations

Other workers whose jobs involve serving customers and helping them enjoy themselves include flight attendants, butlers, and tour bus drivers.

Sources of Additional Information

Information about job opportunities may be obtained from local employers and local offices of the State employment service.

A guide to careers in restaurants, a list of two- and four-year colleges that have food service programs, and information on scholarships to those programs is available from:

- National Restaurant Association, 1200 17th St. NW., Washington, DC 20036-3097.

For general information on hospitality careers, write to:

- Council on Hotel, Restaurant, and Institutional Education, 1200 17th St. NW., Washington, DC 20036-3097.

Funeral Directors and Morticians

(O*NET 39011 and 39014)

Significant Points

- Job opportunities should be good, but mortuary science graduates may have to relocate to find jobs as funeral directors.

- Funeral directors must be licensed by their State.

Nature of the Work

Funeral practices and rites vary greatly among various cultures and religions. Among the many diverse groups in the United States, funeral practices usually share some common elements: removal of the deceased to a mortuary, preparation of the remains, performance of a ceremony that honors the deceased and addresses the spiritual needs of the family, and the burial or destruction of the remains. Funeral directors arrange and direct these tasks for grieving families.

Funeral directors also are called morticians or undertakers. This career may not appeal to everyone, but those who work as funeral directors take great pride in their ability to provide efficient and appropriate services. They also comfort the family and friends of the deceased.

Funeral directors arrange the details and handle the logistics of funerals. They interview the family to learn what they desire with regard to the nature of the funeral, the clergy members or other persons who will officiate, and the final disposition of the remains. Sometimes the deceased leaves detailed instructions for his or her own funeral. Together with the family, funeral directors establish the location, date, and time of the wake, memorial service, and burial. They arrange for a hearse to carry the body to the funeral home or mortuary.

Funeral directors also prepare obituary notices and have them placed in newspapers, arrange for pallbearers and clergy, schedule the opening and closing of a grave with the cemetery, decorate and prepare the sites of all services, and provide transportation for the remains, mourners, and flowers between sites. They also direct preparation and shipment of remains for out-of-State burial.

Most funeral directors also are trained, licensed, and practicing *embalmers*. Embalming is a sanitary, cosmetic, and preservative process through which the body is prepared for interment. If more than 24 hours elapse between death and interment, State laws usually require that the remains be refrigerated or embalmed.

The embalmer washes the body with germicidal soap and replaces the blood with embalming fluid to preserve the body. Embalmers may reshape and reconstruct disfigured or maimed bodies using materials such as clay, cotton, plaster of Paris, and wax. They also

may apply cosmetics to provide a natural appearance, and then dress the body and place it in a casket. Embalmers maintain records such as embalming reports and itemized lists of clothing or valuables delivered with the body. In large funeral homes, an embalming staff of two or more embalmers, plus several apprentices, may be employed.

Funeral services may take place in a home, house of worship, funeral home, or at the gravesite or crematory. Services may be non-religious, but often they reflect the religion of the family, so funeral directors must be familiar with the funeral and burial customs of many faiths, ethnic groups, and fraternal organizations. For example, members of some religions seldom have the bodies of the deceased embalmed or cremated.

Burial in a casket is the most common method of disposing of remains in this country, although entombment also occurs. Cremation, which is the burning of the body in a special furnace, is increasingly selected because it can be more convenient and less costly. Cremations are appealing because the remains can be shipped easily, kept at home, buried, or scattered. Memorial services can be held anywhere, and at any time, sometimes months later when all relatives and friends can get together. Even when the remains are cremated, many people still want a funeral service.

A funeral service followed by cremation need not be any different from a funeral service followed by a burial. Usually cremated remains are placed in some type of permanent receptacle, or urn, before being committed to a final resting place. The urn may be buried, placed in an indoor or outdoor mausoleum or columbarium, or interred in a special urn garden that many cemeteries provide for cremated remains.

Funeral directors handle the paper work involved with the person's death, such as submitting papers to State authorities so that a formal certificate of death may be issued and copies distributed to the heirs. They may help family members apply for veterans' burial benefits and notify the Social Security Administration of the death. Also, funeral directors may apply for the transfer of any pensions, insurance policies, or annuities on behalf of survivors.

Funeral directors also prearrange funerals. Increasingly, they arrange funerals in advance of need to provide peace of mind by ensuring that the client's wishes will be taken care of in a way that is satisfying to the person and to those who will survive.

Most funeral homes are small, family-run businesses, and the funeral directors either are owner-operators or employees of the operation. Funeral directors, therefore, are responsible for the success and the profitability of their businesses. Directors keep records of expenses, purchases, and services rendered; prepare and send invoices for services; prepare and submit reports for unemployment insurance; prepare Federal, State, and local tax forms; and prepare itemized bills for customers. Funeral directors increasingly are using computers for billing, bookkeeping, and marketing. Some are beginning to use the Internet to communicate with clients who are pre-planning their funerals and to assist clients by developing electronic obituaries and guest books. Directors strive to foster a cooperative spirit and friendly attitude among employees and a compassionate demeanor towards the families. A growing number of funeral directors also are involved in helping individuals adapt to changes in their lives following a death through post-death support group activities.

Most funeral homes have a chapel, one or more viewing rooms, a casket-selection room, and a preparation room. An increasing number also have a crematory on the premises. Equipment may include a hearse, a flower car, limousines, and sometimes an ambulance. They usually stock a selection of caskets and urns for families to purchase or rent.

Working Conditions

Funeral directors often work long, irregular hours. Many work on an on-call basis, because they may be needed to remove remains in the middle of the night. Shift work sometimes is necessary because funeral home hours include evenings and weekends. In smaller funeral homes, working hours vary, but in larger homes, employees usually work eight hours a day, five or six days a week.

Funeral directors occasionally come into contact with the remains of persons who had contagious diseases, but the possibility of infection is remote if strict health regulations are followed.

To show proper respect and consideration for the families and the dead, funeral directors must dress appropriately. The profession usually requires short, neat haircuts and trim beards, if any, for men. Suits, ties, and dresses are customary for a conservative look.

Employment

Funeral directors held about 28,000 jobs in 1998. Almost 1 in 10 were self-employed. Nearly all worked in the funeral service and crematory industry.

Training, Other Qualifications, and Advancement

Funeral directors must be licensed in all but one State (Colorado). Licensing laws vary from State to State, but most require applicants to be 21 years old, have two years of formal education that includes studies in mortuary science, serve a one-year apprenticeship, and pass a qualifying examination. After becoming licensed, new funeral directors may join the staff of a funeral home. Embalmers must be licensed in all States, and some States issue a single license for both funeral directors and embalmers. In States that have separate licensing requirements for the two positions, most people in the field obtain both licenses. Persons interested in a career as a funeral director should contact their State licensing board for specific requirements.

College programs in mortuary science usually last from two to four years; the American Board of Funeral Service Education accredits 49 mortuary science programs. Two-year programs are offered by a small number of community and junior colleges, and a few colleges and universities offer both two- and four-year programs. Mortuary science programs include courses in anatomy, physiology, pathology, embalming techniques, restorative art, business management, accounting and use of computers in funeral home management, and client services. They also include courses in the social sciences and legal, ethical, and regulatory subjects, such as psychology, grief counseling, oral and written communication, funeral service law, business law, and ethics.

The Funeral Service Educational Foundation and many State associations offer continuing education programs designed for licensed funeral directors. These programs address issues in communications, counseling, and management. Thirty-two States require funeral directors to receive continuing education credits in order to maintain their licenses.

Apprenticeships must be completed under an experienced and licensed funeral director or embalmer. Depending on State regulations, apprenticeships last from one to three years and may be served before, during, or after mortuary school. Apprenticeships provide practical experience in all facets of the funeral service, from embalming to transporting remains.

State board licensing examinations vary, but they usually consist of written and oral parts and include a demonstration of practical skills. Persons who want to work in another State may have to pass the examination for that State; however, some States have reciprocity arrangements and will grant licenses to funeral directors from another State without further examination.

High school students can start preparing for a career as a funeral director by taking courses in biology and chemistry and participating in public speaking or debate clubs. Part-time or summer jobs in funeral homes consist mostly of maintenance and clean-up tasks, such as washing and polishing limousines and hearses, but these tasks can help students become familiar with the operation of funeral homes.

Important personal traits for funeral directors are composure, tact, and the ability to communicate easily with the public. They also should have the desire and ability to comfort people in their time of sorrow.

Advancement opportunities are best in larger funeral homes: Funeral directors may earn promotions to higher paying positions, such as branch manager or general manager. Some directors eventually acquire enough money and experience to establish their own funeral home businesses.

Job Outlook

Employment of funeral directors is expected to increase about as fast as the average for all occupations through 2008. Not only is the population expanding, but also the proportion of people over the age of 55 is projected to grow during the coming decade. Consequently, the number of deaths is expected to increase, spurring demand for funeral services.

The need to replace funeral directors and morticians who retire or leave the occupation for other reasons will account for even more job openings than employment growth. Typically, a number of mortuary science graduates leave the profession shortly after becoming licensed funeral directors to pursue other career interests, and this trend is expected to continue. Also, more funeral directors are 55 years old and over compared to workers in other occupations, and they will be retiring in greater numbers between 1998 and 2008. Although employment opportunities for funeral directors are expected to be good, mortuary science graduates may have to relocate to find jobs in funeral service.

Earnings

Median annual earnings for funeral directors were $35,040 in 1998. The middle 50 percent earned between $25,510 and $48,260. The lowest 10 percent earned less than $17,040, and the top 10 percent more than $78,550.

Salaries of funeral directors depend on the number of years of experience in funeral service, the number of services performed, the number of facilities operated, the area of the country, the size of the community, and the level of formal education. Funeral directors in large cities earned more than their counterparts in small towns and rural areas.

Related Occupations

The job of a funeral director requires tact, discretion, and compassion when dealing with grieving people. Others who need these qualities include members of the clergy, social workers, psychologists, psychiatrists, and other health care professionals.

Sources of Additional Information

For a list of accredited mortuary science programs and information on the funeral service profession, write to:

- The National Funeral Directors Association, 13625 Bishop's Drive, Brookfield, WI 53005.

For information about college programs in mortuary science, scholarships, and funeral service as a career, contact:

- The American Board of Funeral Service Education, 38 Florida Avenue, Portland, ME 04103.

For information on continuing education programs in funeral service, contact:

- The Funeral Service Educational Foundation, 13625 Bishop's Drive, Brookfield, WI 53005.

General Managers and Top Executives

(O*NET 19005B)

Significant Points

- General managers and top executives are among the highest paid workers; however, long hours and considerable travel are often required.

- Competition for top managerial jobs should remain intense due to the large number of qualified applicants and relatively low turnover.

Nature of the Work

All organizations have specific goals and objectives that they strive to meet. General managers and top executives devise strategies and formulate policies to ensure that these objectives are met. Although they have a wide range of titles—such as chief executive officer, president, executive vice president, owner, partner, brokerage office manager, school superintendent, and police chief—all formulate policies and direct the operations of businesses and corporations, nonprofit institutions, and other organizations.

A corporation's goals and policies are established by the chief executive officer in collaboration with other top executives, who are overseen by a board of directors. In a large corporation, the chief executive officer meets frequently with subordinate executives to ensure that operations are implemented in accordance with these policies. The chief executive officer of a corporation retains overall accountability; however, a chief operating officer may be delegated several responsibilities, including the authority to oversee executives who direct the activities of various departments and implement the organization's policies on a day-to-day basis. In publicly held and nonprofit corporations, the board of directors is ultimately accountable for the success or failure of the enterprise, and the chief executive officer reports to the board.

The nature of other high-level executives' responsibilities depends upon the size of the organization. In large organizations, their duties are highly specialized. Managers of cost and profit centers, for instance, are responsible for the overall performance of one aspect of the organization, such as manufacturing, marketing, sales, purchasing, finance, personnel, training, administrative services, electronic data processing, property management, transportation, or the legal services department.

In smaller organizations, such as independent retail stores or small manufacturers, a partner, owner, or general manager is often also responsible for purchasing, hiring, training, quality control, and day-to-day supervisory duties.

Working Conditions

Top executives are usually provided with spacious offices and support staff. General managers in large firms or nonprofit organizations usually have comfortable offices close to the top executives to whom they report. Long hours, including evenings and weekends, are standard for most top executives and general managers, though their schedules may be flexible.

Substantial travel between international, national, regional, and local offices to monitor operations and meet with customers, staff, and other executives often is required of managers and executives. Many managers and executives also attend meetings and conferences sponsored by various associations. The conferences provide an opportunity to meet with prospective donors, customers, contractors, or government officials and allow managers and executives to keep abreast of technological and managerial innovations.

In large organizations, frequent job transfers between local offices or subsidiaries are common. General managers and top executives are under intense pressure to earn higher profits, provide better service, or attain fundraising and charitable goals. Executives in charge of poorly performing organizations or departments usually find their jobs in jeopardy.

Employment

General managers and top executives held over 3.3 million jobs in 1998. They are found in every industry, but wholesale, retail, and services industries employ more than 6 out of 10.

Training, Other Qualifications, and Advancement

The educational background of managers and top executives varies as widely as the nature of their responsibilities. Many general managers and top executives have a bachelor's degree or higher in liberal arts or business administration. Their major often is related to the departments they direct; for example, a manager of finance may have a degree in accounting, and a manager of information systems might have a degree in computer science. Graduate and professional degrees are common. Many managers in administrative, marketing, financial, and manufacturing activities have a master's degree in business administration. Managers in highly technical manufacturing and research activities often have a master's degree in engineering or a doctoral degree in a scientific discipline. A law degree is mandatory for managers of legal departments; hospital administrators generally have a master's degree in health services administration or business administration.

In the public sector, many managers have liberal arts degrees in public administration or one of the social sciences. Park superintendents, for example, often have liberal arts degrees, whereas police chiefs are usually graduates of law enforcement academies and hold degrees in criminal justice or a related field. College presidents typically have a doctorate in the field they originally taught, and school superintendents often have a masters degree in education administration.

Since many general manager and top executive positions are filled by promoting experienced lower level managers when an opening occurs, many are promoted from within the organization. In industries such as retail trade or transportation, for instance, it is possible for individuals without a college degree to work their way up within the company and become managers. Many companies prefer, however, that their top executives have specialized backgrounds, and they hire individuals who are managers in other organizations.

General managers and top executives must have highly developed personal skills. An analytical mind able to quickly assess large amounts of information and data is very important, as is the ability to consider and evaluate the interrelationships of numerous factors. General managers and top executives must also be able to communicate clearly and persuasively. Other qualities critical for managerial success include leadership, self-confidence, motivation, decisiveness, flexibility, sound business judgment, and determination.

Advancement may be accelerated by participation in company training programs that impart a broader knowledge of company policy and operations. Managers can also help their careers by becoming familiar with the latest developments in management techniques at national or local training programs sponsored by various industry and trade associations. Senior managers who often have experience in a particular field, such as accounting or engineering, also attend executive development programs to facilitate their promotion to general managers. Participation in conferences and seminars can expand knowledge of national and international issues influencing the organization and can help develop a network of useful contacts.

General managers may advance to top executive positions (such as executive vice president) in their own firms, or they may take corresponding positions in other firms. They may even advance to peak corporate positions such as chief operating officer or chief executive officer. Chief executive officers often become members of the board of directors of one or more firms, typically as a director of their own firm and often as chair of its board of directors. Some general managers and top executives establish their own firms or become independent consultants.

Job Outlook

Employment of general managers and top executives is expected to grow about as fast as the average for all occupations through 2008. These high-level managers are essential employees because they plan, organize, direct, control, and coordinate the operations of an organization and its major departments or programs. Therefore, top managers should be more immune to automation and corporate restructuring—factors which are expected to adversely affect employment of lower level managers. Because this is a large occupation, many openings will occur each year as executives transfer to other positions, start their own businesses, or retire. Because many executives who leave their jobs transfer to other executive or managerial positions, however, openings for new entrants are limited, and intense competition is expected for top managerial jobs.

Projected employment growth of general managers and top executives varies widely among industries, largely reflecting overall industry growth. Overall employment growth is expected to be faster than average in services industries, but only about as fast as average in finance, insurance, and real estate industries. Employment of general managers and top executives is projected to decline along with overall employment in most manufacturing industries.

Experienced managers whose accomplishments reflect strong leadership qualities and the ability to improve the efficiency or competitive position of an organization will have the best opportunities. In an increasingly global economy, experience in international economics, marketing, information systems, and knowledge of several languages may also be beneficial.

Earnings

General managers and top executives are among the highest paid workers. However, salary levels vary substantially depending upon the level of managerial responsibility, length of service, and type, size, and location of the firm. For example, a top manager in a very large corporation can earn significantly more than a counterpart in a small firm.

Median annual earnings of general managers and top executives in 1998 were $55,890. The middle 50 percent earned between $34,970 and $94,650. Because the specific responsibilities of general managers vary significantly within industries, earnings also tend to vary considerably. Median annual earnings in the industries employing the largest numbers of general managers and top executives in 1997 were:

Management and public relations	$91,400
Computer and data processing services	90,600
Wholesale trade machinery, equipment, and supplies	65,900
Gasoline service stations	36,800
Eating and drinking places	33,000

Salaries vary substantially by type and level of responsibilities and by industry. According to a salary survey done by Executive Compensation Reports (a division of Harcourt Brace & Company), the median salary for CEOs of public companies from the fiscal year 1998 *Fortune 500* list was approximately $800,000. Three quarters of CEOs in the nonprofit sector made under $100,000 in 1998, according to a survey by Abbott, Langer, & Associates.

In addition to salaries, total compensation often includes stock options, dividends, and other performance bonuses. The use of executive dining rooms and company cars, expense allowances, and company-paid insurance premiums and physical examinations also are among benefits commonly enjoyed by general managers and top executives in private industry. A number of CEOs also are provided with company-paid club memberships, a limousine with driver, and other amenities.

Related Occupations

General managers and top executives plan, organize, direct, control, and coordinate the operations of an organization and its major departments or programs. The members of the board of directors and lower level managers are also involved in these activities. Other managerial occupations have similar responsibilities; however, they are concentrated in specific industries or are responsible for a specific department within an organization. They include administrative services managers, education administrators, financial managers, and restaurant and food service managers. Government occupations with similar functions are President, governor, mayor, commissioner, and legislator.

Sources of Additional Information

For a variety of information on general managers and top executives, including educational programs and job listings, contact:

- American Management Association, 1601 Broadway, New York, NY 10019-7420. Internet: http://www.amanet.org
- National Management Association, 2210 Arbor Blvd., Dayton, OH 45439. Internet: http://www.nma1.org

Health Information Technicians

(O*NET 32911)

Significant Points

- Health information technicians are projected to be one of the 20 fastest growing occupations.

- High school students can improve chances of acceptance into a health information education program by taking courses in biology, chemistry, health, and especially computer training.

- Most technicians will be employed by hospitals, but job growth will be greater in offices and clinics of physicians, nursing homes, and home health agencies.

Nature of the Work

Every time health care personnel treat a patient, they record what they observed and how the patient was treated medically. This record includes information the patient provides concerning his symptoms and medical history, the results of examinations, reports of x-rays and laboratory tests, diagnoses, and treatment plans. Health information technicians organize and evaluate these records for completeness and accuracy.

Health information technicians, who may also be called medical record technicians, begin to assemble patients' health information by first making sure their initial medical charts are complete. They make sure that all forms are completed and properly identified and signed and that all necessary information is in the computer. Sometimes they talk to physicians or others to clarify diagnoses or get additional information.

Technicians assign a code to each diagnosis and procedure. They consult classification manuals and rely on their knowledge of disease processes. Technicians then use a software program to assign the patient to one of several hundred "diagnosis-related groups," or DRGs. The DRG determines the amount the hospital will be reimbursed if the patient is covered by Medicare or other insurance programs using the DRG system. Technicians who specialize in coding are called health information coders, medical record coders, coder/abstractors, or coding specialists. In addition to the DRG system, coders use other coding systems, such as those geared toward ambulatory settings.

Technicians also use computer programs to tabulate and analyze data to help improve patient care or control costs, for use in legal actions, or in response to surveys. *Tumor registrars* compile and maintain records of patients who have cancer to provide information to physicians and for research studies.

Health information technicians' duties vary with the size of the facility. In large to medium facilities, technicians may specialize in one aspect of health information or supervise health information clerks and transcribers, while a *health information administrator* manages the department. In small facilities, an accredited health information technician sometimes manages the department.

Working Conditions

Health information technicians usually work a 40-hour week. Some overtime may be required. In hospitals where health information departments are open 18-24 hours a day 7 days a week, they may work day, evening, and night shifts.

Health information technicians work in pleasant and comfortable offices. This is one of the few health occupations in which there is little or no physical contact with patients. Because accuracy is essential, technicians must pay close attention to detail. Health information technicians who work at computer monitors for prolonged periods must guard against eyestrain and muscle pain.

Employment

Health information technicians held about 92,000 jobs in 1998. About 2 out of 5 jobs were in hospitals. The rest were mostly in nursing homes, medical group practices, clinics, and home health agencies. Insurance firms that deal in health matters employ a small number of health information technicians to tabulate and analyze health information. Public health departments also hire technicians to supervise data collection from health care institutions and to assist in research.

Training, Other Qualifications, and Advancement

Health information technicians entering the field usually have an associate degree from a community or junior college. In addition to general education, coursework includes medical terminology, anatomy and physiology, legal aspects of health information, coding and abstraction of data, statistics, database management, quality improvement methods, and computer training. Applicants can improve their chances of admission into a program by taking biology, chemistry, health, and computer courses in high school.

Hospitals sometimes advance promising health information clerks to jobs as health information technicians, although this practice may be less common in the future. Advancement usually requires two-four years of job experience and completion of a hospital's in-house training program.

Most employers prefer to hire Accredited Record Technicians (ART), who must pass a written examination offered by AHIMA. To take the examination, a person must graduate from a two-year associate degree program accredited by the Commission on Accreditation of Allied Health Education Programs (CAAHEP) of the American Medical Association. Technicians trained in non-CAAHEP accredited programs or on the job are not eligible to take the examination. In 1998, CAAHEP accredited 168 programs for health information technicians. Technicians who specialize in coding may also obtain voluntary certification.

Experienced health information technicians usually advance in one of two ways: by specializing or managing. Many senior health information technicians specialize in coding, particularly Medicare coding, or in tumor registry.

In large health information departments, experienced technicians may advance to section supervisor, overseeing the work of the coding, correspondence, or discharge sections, for example. Senior technicians with ART credentials may become director or assistant director of a health information department in a small facility. However, in larger institutions, the director is a health information administrator with a bachelor's degree in health information administration.

Job Outlook

Job prospects for formally trained technicians should be very good. Employment of health information technicians is expected to grow much faster than the average for all occupations through 2008, due to rapid growth in the number of medical tests, treatments, and procedures that will be increasingly scrutinized by third-party payers, regulators, courts, and consumers.

Hospitals will continue to employ a large percentage of health information technicians, but growth will not be as fast as in other areas. Increasing demand for detailed records in offices and clinics of physicians should result in fast employment growth, especially in large group practices. Rapid growth is also expected in nursing homes and home health agencies.

Earnings

Median annual earnings of health information technicians were $20,590 in 1998. The middle 50 percent earned between $16,670 and $25,440 a year. The lowest 10 percent earned less than $14,150, and the highest 10 percent earned more than $31,570 a year. Median annual earnings in the industries employing the largest number of health information technicians in 1997 were as follows:

Hospitals $20,900

Nursing and personal care facilities 20,100

Offices and clinics of medical doctors 18,100

According to a 1997 survey by the American Health Information Management Association, the median annual salary for accredited health information technicians was $30,500. The average annual salary for health information technicians employed by the Federal government was $27,500 in early 1999.

Related Occupations

Health information technicians need a strong clinical background to analyze the contents of medical records. Other occupations that require knowledge of medical terminology, anatomy, and physiology but do not require workers to directly touch the patient are medical secretaries, medical transcriptionists, medical writers, and medical illustrators.

Sources of Additional Information

Information on careers in health information technology, including a list of CAAHEP-accredited programs, is available from:

- American Health Information Management Association, 233 N. Michigan Ave., Suite 2150, Chicago, IL 60601. Internet: http://www.ahima.org

Health Services Managers

(O*NET 15008A and 15008B)

Significant Points

- Earnings of health services managers are high, but long work hours are common.

- Employment will grow fastest in home health agencies, residential care facilities, and practitioners' offices and clinics.

Nature of the Work

Health care is a business, and like every other business, it needs good management to keep it running smoothly, especially during times of change. The term "health services manager" encompasses individuals who plan, direct, coordinate, and supervise the delivery of health care. Health services managers include generalists and specialists. Generalists manage or help to manage an entire facility or system, while specialists are in charge of specific clinical departments or services.

The structure and financing of health care is changing rapidly. Future health services managers must be prepared to deal with evolving integrated health care delivery systems, restructuring of work, technological innovations, and an increased focus on preventive care. They will be called upon to improve efficiency in health care facilities and the quality of the health care provided. Increasingly, health services managers work in organizations in which they must optimize efficiency of a variety of interrelated services, ranging from inpatient care to outpatient follow-up care, for example.

Large facilities usually have several assistant administrators to aid the top administrator and to handle daily decisions. They may direct activities in clinical areas (such as nursing, surgery, therapy, medical records or health information) or in nonhealth areas (such as finance, housekeeping, human resources, and information management). Because the nonhealth departments are not directly related to health care, these managers are not included in this job description.

In smaller facilities, top administrators handle more of the details of daily operations. For example, many nursing home administrators manage personnel, finance, facility operations, and admissions and have a larger role in resident care.

Clinical managers have more specific responsibilities than generalists do, and they have training and/or experience in a specific clinical area. For example, directors of physical therapy are experienced physical therapists, and most health information and medical record administrators have a bachelor's degree in health information or medical record administration. These managers establish and implement policies, objectives, and procedures for their departments; evaluate personnel and work; develop reports and budgets; and coordinate activities with other managers.

In group practices, managers work closely with physicians. Whereas an office manager may handle business affairs in small medical groups and leave policy decisions to the physicians themselves, larger groups usually employ a full-time administrator to advise on business strategies and coordinate day-to-day business.

A small group of 10 or 15 physicians might employ one administrator to oversee personnel matters, billing and collection, budgeting, planning, equipment outlays, and patient flow. A large practice of 40 or 50 physicians may have a chief administrator and several assistants, each of which is responsible for different areas.

Health services managers in health maintenance organizations (HMOs) and other managed care settings perform functions similar to those in large group practices, except their staffs may be larger. In addition, they may do more work in the areas of community outreach and preventive care than managers of a group practice. The size of the administrative staff in HMOs varies according to the size and type of HMO.

Some health services managers oversee the activities of a number of facilities in health systems. Such systems may contain both inpatient and outpatient facilities and offer a wide range of patient services.

Working Conditions

Most health services managers work long hours. Facilities such as nursing homes and hospitals operate around the clock, and administrators and managers may be called at all hours to deal with problems. They may also travel to attend meetings or inspect satellite facilities.

Employment

Health services managers held about 222,000 jobs in 1998. Almost one-half of all jobs were in hospitals. About 1 in 4 were in nursing and personal care facilities or offices and clinics of physicians. The remainder worked mostly in home health agencies, ambulatory facilities run by State and local governments, offices of dentists and other health practitioners, medical and dental laboratories, residential care facilities, and other social service agencies.

Training, Other Qualifications, and Advancement

Health services managers must be familiar with management principles and practices. A master's degree in health services administration, long-term care administration, health sciences, public health, public administration, or business administration is the standard credential for most generalist positions in this field. However, a bachelor's degree is adequate for some entry-level positions in smaller facilities and for some entry-level positions at the departmental level within health care organizations. Physicians' offices and some other facilities may substitute on-the-job experience for formal education.

For clinical department heads, a degree in the appropriate field and work experience may be sufficient for entry, but a master's degree in health services administration or a related field may be required to advance. For example, nursing service administrators are usually chosen from among supervisory registered nurses with administrative abilities and a graduate degree in nursing or health services administration.

Bachelor's, master's, and doctoral degree programs in health administration are offered by colleges, universities, and schools of public health, medicine, allied health, public administration, and business administration. In 1999, 67 schools had accredited programs leading to the master's degree in health services administration, according to the Accrediting Commission on Education for Health Services Administration.

Some graduate programs seek students with undergraduate degrees in business or health administration; however, many graduate programs prefer students with a liberal arts or health profession background. Candidates with previous work experience in health care may also have an advantage. Competition for entry to these programs is keen, and applicants need above-average grades to gain admission.

These programs usually last between two and three years. They may include up to one year of supervised administrative experience and course work in areas such as hospital organization and management, marketing, accounting and budgeting, human resources administration, strategic planning, health economics, and health information systems. Some programs allow students to specialize in one type of facility: hospitals, nursing homes, mental health facilities, HMOs, or medical groups. Other programs encourage a generalist approach to health administration education.

New graduates with master's degrees in health services administration may start as department managers or in staff positions. The level of the starting position varies with the experience of the applicant and size of the organization. Hospitals and other health facilities offer postgraduate residencies and fellowships, which usually are staff positions. Graduates from master's degree programs also take jobs in HMOs, large group medical practices, clinics, mental health facilities, multifacility nursing home corporations, and consulting firms.

Graduates with bachelor's degrees in health administration usually begin as administrative assistants or assistant department heads in larger hospitals or as department heads or assistant administrators in small hospitals or nursing homes.

All States and the District of Columbia require nursing home administrators to have a bachelor's degree, pass a licensing examination, complete a State-approved training program, and pursue continuing education. A license is not required in other areas of health services management.

Health services managers are often responsible for millions of dollars of facilities and equipment and hundreds of employees. To make effective decisions, they need to be open to different opinions and good at analyzing contradictory information. They must understand finance and information systems and be able to interpret data. Motivating others to implement their decisions requires strong leadership abilities. Tact, diplomacy, flexibility, and communication skills are essential because health services managers spend most of their time interacting with others.

Health services managers advance by moving into more responsible and higher paying positions, such as assistant or associate administrator, or by moving to larger facilities.

Job Outlook

Employment of health services managers is expected to grow faster than the average for all occupations through 2008 as health services continue to expand and diversify. Opportunities for health services managers should be closely related to growth in the industry in which they are employed. Opportunities will be especially good in home health care, long-term care, and nontraditional health organizations (such as managed care operations and consulting firms), particularly for health services managers with work experience in the health care field and strong business and management skills.

Hospitals will continue to employ the most managers, although the number of jobs will grow slowly compared to other areas. As hospitals continue to consolidate, centralize, and diversify functions, competition will increase at all job levels.

Employment will grow the fastest in home health agencies, residential care facilities, and practitioners' offices and clinics. Many services previously provided in hospitals will be shifted to these sectors, especially as medical technologies improve. Demand in medical group practice management will grow as medical group practices become larger and more complex. Health services managers will need to deal with the pressures of cost containment and financial accountability, as well as the increased focus on preventive care. They will also become more involved in trying to improve the health of their communities.

Health services managers will also be employed by health care management companies who provide management services to hospitals and other organizations, as well as specific departments such as emergency, information management systems, managed care contract negotiations, and physician recruiting.

Earnings

Median annual earnings of medical and health service managers were $48,870 in 1998. The middle 50 percent earned between $37,900 and $71,580 a year. The lowest 10 percent earned less than $28,600, and the highest 10 percent earned more than $88,730 a year. Median annual earnings in the industries employing the largest number of medical and health service managers in 1997 were as follows:

Hospitals	$52,600
Home health care services	45,800
Health and allied services, not elsewhere classified	44,700
Nursing and personal care facilities	43,600
Offices and clinics of medical doctors	39,600

Earnings of health services managers vary by type and size of the facility, as well as by level of responsibility. For example, the Medical Group Management Association reported the following median salaries in 1998 for administrators by group practice size: fewer than 7 physicians, $60,000; 7 to 25 physicians, $76,700; and more than 26 physicians, $124,500.

A survey by *Modern Healthcare* magazine reported the following median annual compensations in 1998 for managers of specific clinical departments: Respiratory therapy, $57,700; home health care, $62,400; ambulatory and outpatient services, $66,200; radiology, $66,800; clinical laboratory, $66,900; physical therapy, $68,100; rehabilitation services, $73,400; and nursing services, $100,200. Salaries also varied according to size of facility and geographic region.

According to the Buck Survey conducted by the American Health Care Association in 1997, nursing home administrators' median annual earnings were $52,800. The middle 50 percent earned between $44,300 and $60,300 a year. Assistant administrators had median annual earnings of about $35,000, with the middle 50 percent earning between $28,700 and $41,200.

Related Occupations

Health services managers have training or experience in both health and management. Other occupations requiring knowledge of both fields are public health directors, social welfare administrators, directors of voluntary health agencies and health professional associations, and underwriters in health insurance companies.

Sources of Additional Information

General information about health administration is available from:

- American College of Healthcare Executives, One North Franklin St., Suite 1700, Chicago, IL 60606. Internet: http://www.ache.org

Information about undergraduate and graduate academic programs in this field is available from:

- Association of University Programs in Health Administration, 730 11th St., NW., Washington, DC 20001-4510. Internet: http://www.aupha.org

For a list of accredited graduate programs in health services administration, contact:

- Accrediting Commission on Education for Health Services Administration, 730 11th St., NW., Washington, DC 20001-4510.

For information about career opportunities in long-term care administration, contact:

- American College of Health Care Administrators, 325 S. Patrick St., Alexandria, VA 22314.

For information about career opportunities in medical group practices and ambulatory care management, contact:

- Medical Group Management Association, 104 Inverness Terrace East, Englewood, CO 80112.

For information about health care office managers, contact:

- Professional Association of Health Care Office Managers, 461 East Ten Mile Rd., Pensacola, FL 32534-9712. Internet: http://www.pahcom.com

Home Health and Personal Care Aides

(O*NET 66011 and 68035)

Significant Points

- Numerous job openings will result due to very fast employment growth and very high turnover.

- Education required for entry-level jobs is generally minimal, but earnings are low.

Nature of the Work

Home health and personal care aides help elderly, disabled, and ill persons live in their own homes instead of in a health facility. Most work with elderly or disabled clients who need more extensive care than family or friends can provide. Some home health and personal care aides work with families in which a parent is incapacitated and small children need care. Others help discharged hospital patients who have relatively short-term needs.

In general, *home health aides* provide health-related services, such as administering oral medications under physicians' orders or direction of a nurse. In contrast, *personal care* and *home care aides* provide mainly housekeeping and routine personal care services. However, there can be substantial variation in job titles and overlap of duties.

Most home health and personal care aides provide some housekeeping services, as well as personal care to their clients. They clean clients' houses, do laundry, and change bed linens. Some aides plan meals (including special diets), shop for food, and cook. Home health and personal care aides may also help clients move from bed, bathe, dress, and groom. Some accompany clients outside the home, serving as guide, companion, and aide.

Home health and personal care aides also provide instruction and psychological support. For example, they may assist in toilet training a severely mentally handicapped child, or just listen to clients talk about their problems.

Home health aides may check pulse, temperature, and respiration; help with simple prescribed exercises; and assist with medication routines. Occasionally, they change nonsterile dressings, use special equipment such as a hydraulic lift, give massages and alcohol rubs, or assist with braces and artificial limbs.

In home care agencies, it is usually a registered nurse, a physical therapist, or a social worker who assigns specific duties and supervises home health and personal care aides. Aides keep records of services performed and of clients' condition and progress. They report changes in the client's condition to the supervisor or case manager. Home health and personal care aides also participate in case reviews, consulting with the team caring for the client, which might include registered nurses, therapists, and other health professionals.

Working Conditions

The home health and personal care aide's daily routine may vary. Aides may go to the same home every day for months or even years. However, most aides work with a number of different clients, each job lasting a few hours, days, or weeks. Aides often visit four or five clients on the same day.

Surroundings differ from case to case. Some homes are neat and pleasant, while others are untidy or depressing. Some clients are angry, abusive, depressed, or otherwise difficult; others are pleasant and cooperative.

Home health and personal care aides generally work on their own, with periodic visits by their supervisor. They receive detailed instructions explaining when to visit clients and what services to perform. Many aides work part time, and weekend hours are common.

Aides are individually responsible for getting to the client's home. They may spend a good portion of the work day traveling from one client to another; motor vehicle accidents are always a danger. They are particularly susceptible to injuries resulting from all types of overexertion when assisting patients and to falls inside and outside their patients' homes. Mechanical lifting devices that are available in institutional settings are seldom available in patients' homes.

Employment

Home health and personal care aides held about 746,000 jobs in 1998. Most aides are employed by home health and personal care agencies, visiting nurse associations, residential care facilities with home health departments, hospitals, public health and welfare departments, community volunteer agencies, nursing and personal care facilities, and temporary help firms. Self-employed aides have no agency affiliation or supervision; they accept clients, set fees, and arrange work schedules on their own.

Training, Other Qualifications, and Advancement

In some States, this occupation is open to individuals with no formal training. On-the-job training is generally provided. Other States may require formal training, depending on Federal or State law.

The Federal government has enacted guidelines for home health aides whose employers receive reimbursement from Medicare. Federal law requires home health aides to pass a competency test covering 12 areas: communication skills; observation, reporting, and documentation of patient status and the care or services furnished; reading and recording vital signs; basic infection control procedures; basic elements of body function and changes; maintenance of a clean, safe, and healthy environment; recognition of, and procedures for, emergencies; the physical, emotional, and developmental characteristics of the patients served; personal hygiene and grooming; safe transfer techniques; normal range of motion and positioning; and basic nutrition.

A home health aide may take training before taking the competency test. Federal law suggests at least 75 hours of classroom and practical training supervised by a registered nurse. Training and testing programs may be offered by the employing agency, but must meet the standards of the Health Care Financing Administration. Training programs vary depending upon State regulations.

The National Association for Home Care offers national certification for home health and personal care aides. The certification is a voluntary demonstration that the individual has met industry standards.

Successful home health and personal care aides like to help people and do not mind hard work. They should be responsible, compassionate, emotionally stable, and cheerful. Aides should also be tactful, honest, and discreet because they work in private homes.

Home health and personal care aides must be in good health. A physical examination including State regulated tests (such as those for tuberculosis) may be required.

Advancement is limited. In some agencies, workers start out performing homemaker duties, such as cleaning. With experience and training, they may take on personal care duties. The most experienced home health aides assist with medical equipment such as ventilators, which help patients breathe.

Job Outlook

A large number of job openings are expected for home health and personal care aides, due to substantial growth and very high turnover. Home health and personal care aides is expected to be one of the fastest growing occupations through the year 2008.

The number of people in their seventies and older is projected to rise substantially. This age group is characterized by mounting health problems requiring some assistance. Also, there will be an increasing reliance on home care for patients of all ages. This trend reflects several developments: efforts to contain costs by moving patients out of hospitals and nursing facilities as quickly as possible, the realization that treatment can be more effective in familiar surroundings than in clinical surroundings, and the development and improvement of medical technologies for in-home treatment.

In addition to jobs created by the increase in demand for these workers, replacement needs are expected to produce numerous openings. Turnover is high, a reflection of the relatively low skill requirements, low pay, and high emotional demands of the work. For these same reasons, many people are unwilling to perform this kind of work. Therefore, persons who are interested in this work and suited for it should have excellent job opportunities, particularly those with experience or training as home health, personal care, or nursing aides.

Earnings

Median hourly earnings of home health and personal care aides were $7.58 in 1998. The middle 50 percent earned between $6.41 and $8.81 an hour. The lowest 10 percent earned less than $5.73, and the highest 10 percent earned more than $10.51 an hour. Median hourly earnings in the industries employing the largest number of home health aides in 1997 were as follows:

Home health care services	$8.00
Hospitals	7.90
Personnel supply services	7.70
Residential care	7.20
Individual and family services	7.20

Median hourly earnings in the industries employing the largest number of personal and home care aides in 1997 are shown below:

Local government, except education and hospitals $8.00

Job training and related services 7.30

Residential care 7.20

Individual and family services 7.00

Home health care services 6.00

Most employers give slight pay increases with experience and added responsibility. Aides are usually paid only for the time worked in the home. They normally are not paid for travel time between jobs. Most employers hire only "on-call" hourly workers and provide no benefits.

Related Occupations

Home health and personal care aide is a service occupation combining duties of health workers and social service workers. Workers in related occupations that involve personal contact to help or instruct others include attendants in children's institutions, child care attendants in schools, child monitors, companions, nursing aides, nursery school attendants, occupational therapy aides, nursing aides, physical therapy aides, playroom attendants, and psychiatric aides.

Sources of Additional Information

General information about training and referrals to State and local agencies about opportunities for home health and personal care aides, a list of relevant publications, and information on national certification are available from:

- National Association for Home Care, 228 7th St. SE., Washington, DC 20003. Internet: http://www.nahc.org

For information about a career as a home health aide and schools offering training, contact:

- National Association of Health Career Schools, 2301 Academy Dr., Harrisburg, PA 17112.

Human Resources Clerks, Except Payroll and Timekeeping

(O*NET 55314)

Significant Points

- Most jobs require only a high school diploma.
- Replacement needs will account for most job openings for human resources clerks.

Nature of the Work

Human resources clerks maintain the personnel records of an organization's employees. These records include information such as name, address, job title, and earnings, benefits such as health and life insurance, and tax withholding. On a daily basis, these clerks record and answer questions about employee absences and supervisory reports on job performance. When an employee receives a promotion or switches health insurance plans, the human resources clerk updates the appropriate form. Human resources clerks may also prepare reports for managers elsewhere within the organization. For example, they might compile a list of employees eligible for an award.

In smaller organizations, some human resources clerks perform a variety of other clerical duties. They answer telephone or letter inquiries from the public, send out announcements of job openings or job examinations, and issue application forms. When credit bureaus and finance companies request confirmation of a person's employment, the human resources clerk provides authorized information from the employee's personnel records. Payroll departments and insurance companies may also be contacted to verify changes to records.

Some human resources clerks are also involved in hiring. They screen job applicants to obtain information such as education and work experience; administer aptitude, personality, and interest tests; explain the organization's employment policies and refer qualified applicants to the employing official; and request references from present or past employers. Also, human resources clerks inform job applicants, by telephone or letter, of their acceptance or rejection for employment.

Other human resources clerks are known as assignment clerks. Their role is to notify a firm's existing employees of position vacancies and to identify and assign qualified applicants. They keep track of vacancies throughout the organization and complete and distribute vacancy advertisement forms. These clerks review applications in response to advertisements and verify information using personnel records. After a selection is made, they notify all the applicants of their acceptance or rejection.

In some job settings, human resources clerks have specific job titles. Identification clerks are responsible for security matters at defense installations. They compile and record personal data about vendors, contractors, and civilian and military personnel and their dependents. Job duties include interviewing applicants; corresponding with law enforcement authorities; and preparing badges, passes, and identification cards.

Working Conditions

Most clerks typically are employed in an office environment. Because the majority of clerks uses computers on a daily basis, these workers may experience eye and muscle strain, backaches, headaches, and repetitive motion injuries. Also, clerks who review detailed data may have to sit for extended periods of time. Most clerks work regular business hours.

Employment

Human resources clerks held about 142,000 jobs in 1998. Although these workers are found in most industries, about 1 in every 5 works for a government agency. Colleges and universities, hospitals, department stores, and banks also employ large numbers of human resources clerks.

Training, Other Qualifications, and Advancement

Employers typically require applicants to have at least a high school diploma or its equivalent, although many employers prefer to hire clerks with a higher level of education. Regardless of the type of work, most employers prefer workers who are computer-literate. Knowledge of word processing and spreadsheet software is especially valuable, as are experience working in an office and good interpersonal skills.

Clerks often learn the skills they need in high schools, business schools, and community colleges. Business education programs offered by these institutions typically include courses in typing, word processing, shorthand, business communications, records management, and office systems and procedures. Some entrants are college graduates. Although a degree is rarely required, many graduates accept entry-level positions to get into a particular company or to enter the field with the hope of being promoted to professional or managerial positions.

Once hired, clerks usually receive on-the-job training. Under the guidance of a supervisor or other senior worker, new employees learn company procedures. Some formal classroom training may also be necessary, such as training in specific computer software.

Clerks must be careful, orderly, and detail-oriented in order to avoid making errors and to recognize errors made by others. These workers should also be discreet and trustworthy because they frequently come in contact with confidential material.

Clerks usually advance by taking on more duties in the same occupation for higher pay or transferring to a closely related occupation. Most companies fill office and administrative support supervisory and managerial positions by promoting individuals from within their organizations, so clerks who acquire additional skills, experience, and training improve their advancement opportunities. With appropriate experience and education, some clerks may become personnel specialists.

Job Outlook

Replacement needs will account for most job openings for human resources clerks. Jobs will open up as clerks advance within the personnel department, take jobs unrelated to personnel administration, or leave the labor force. Little or no change is expected in employment of human resources clerks through the year 2008, largely due to the increased use of computers. The growing use of computers in personnel or human resource departments means that a lot of data entry done by human resources clerks can be eliminated, as employees themselves enter the data and send it to the personnel office. This is most feasible in large organizations with multiple personnel offices. The increasing use of computers and other automated office equipment by managers and professionals in personnel offices also could mean less work for human resources clerks.

Earnings

Salaries of human resources clerks vary. The region of the country, size of city, and type and size of establishment all influence salary levels. The level of industry or technical expertise required and the complexity and uniqueness of a clerk's responsibilities may also affect earnings. Median annual earnings of full-time human resources clerks in 1998 were $24,360. The average salary for all human resources clerks employed by the Federal government was $29,500 in 1999.

Related Occupations

Today, most clerks enter data into a computer system and perform basic analysis of the information. Other clerical workers who enter and manipulate data include bank tellers, statistical clerks, receiving clerks, medical record clerks, hotel and motel clerks, credit clerks, and reservation and transportation ticket agents.

Sources of Additional Information

State employment service offices can provide information about job openings for this occupation.

Human Resources, Training, and Labor Relations Specialists and Managers

(O*NET 13005A, 13005B, 13005C, 13005E, 21511A, 21511B, 21511C, 21511D, 21511E, and 21511F)

Significant Points

- Employers usually seek college graduates for entry-level jobs.

- Depending on the job duties, a strong background in human resources, business, technical, or liberal arts subjects may be preferred.

- The job market is likely to remain competitive because of the abundant supply of qualified college graduates and experienced workers.

Nature of the Work

Attracting the most qualified employees and matching them to the jobs for which they are best suited is important for the success of any organization. However, many enterprises are too large to permit close contact between top management and employees. Human resources, training, and labor relations specialists and managers provide this link. These individuals recruit and interview employees and advise on hiring decisions in accordance with policies and requirements that have been established in conjunction with top management. In an effort to improve morale and productivity and limit job turnover, they also help their firms effectively use employee skills, provide training opportunities to enhance those skills, and boost employee satisfaction with their jobs and working conditions. Although some jobs in the human resources field require only limited contact with people outside the office, dealing with people is an essential part of the job.

In a small organization, a *human resources generalist* may handle all aspects of human resources work, requiring a broad range of knowledge. The responsibilities of human resources generalists can vary widely, depending on their employer's needs. In a large corporation, the top human resources executive usually develops and coordinates personnel programs and policies. These policies are usually implemented by a director or manager of human resources and, in some cases, a director of industrial relations.

The *director of human resources* may oversee several departments, each headed by an experienced manager, who most likely specializes in one personnel activity such as employment, compensation, benefits, training and development, or employee relations.

Employment and placement managers oversee the hiring and separation of employees and supervise various workers, including equal employment opportunity specialists and recruitment specialists.

Recruiters maintain contacts within the community and may travel extensively, often to college campuses, to search for promising job applicants. Recruiters screen, interview, and in some cases, test applicants. They may also check references and extend job offers. These workers must be thoroughly familiar with the organization and its personnel policies to discuss wages, working conditions, and promotional opportunities with prospective employees. They must also keep informed about equal employment opportunity (EEO) and affirmative action guidelines and laws, such as the Americans With Disabilities Act.

EEO officers, representatives, or *affirmative action coordinators* handle this area in large organizations. They investigate and resolve EEO grievances, examine corporate practices for possible violations, and compile and submit EEO statistical reports.

Employer relations representatives, who usually work in government agencies, maintain working relationships with local employers and promote the use of public employment programs and services. Similarly, *employment interviewers*—whose many job titles include *personnel consultants, personnel development specialists,* and *human resources coordinators*—help match jobseekers with employers.

Job analysts, sometimes called *position classifiers,* perform very exacting work. They collect and examine detailed information about job duties to prepare job descriptions. These descriptions explain the duties, training, and skills each job requires. Whenever a large organization introduces a new job or reviews existing jobs, it calls upon the expert knowledge of the job analyst.

Occupational analysts conduct research, usually in large firms. They are concerned with occupational classification systems and study the effects of industry and occupational trends upon worker relationships. They may serve as technical liaisons between the firm and industry, government, and labor unions.

Establishing and maintaining a firm's pay system is the principal job of the *compensation manager*. Assisted by staff specialists, compensation managers devise ways to ensure fair and equitable pay rates. They may conduct surveys to see how their rates compare with others and to see that the firm's pay scale complies with changing laws and regulations. In addition, compensation managers often oversee their firm's performance evaluation system, and they may design reward systems such as pay-for-performance plans.

Employee benefits managers handle the company's employee benefits program, notably its health insurance and pension plans. Expertise in designing and administering benefits programs continues to gain importance as employer-provided benefits account for a growing proportion of overall compensation costs, and as benefit plans increase in number and complexity. For example, pension benefits might include savings and thrift, profit sharing, and stock ownership plans; health benefits may include long-term catastrophic illness insurance and dental insurance. Familiarity with health benefits is a top priority, as more firms struggle to cope with the rising cost of health care for employees and retirees. In addition to health insurance and pension coverage, some firms offer employees life and accidental death and dismemberment insurance, disability insurance, and relatively new benefits designed to meet the needs of a changing work force, such as parental leave, child and elder care, long-term nursing home care insurance, employee assistance and wellness programs, and flexible benefits plans. Benefits managers must keep abreast of changing Federal and State regulations and legislation that may affect employee benefits.

Employee assistance plan managers, also called *employee welfare managers,* are responsible for a wide array of programs covering occupational safety and health standards and practices; health promotion and physical fitness, medical examinations, and minor health treatment, such as first aid; plant security; publications; food service and recreation activities; car pooling and transportation programs, such as transit subsidies; employee suggestion systems; child and elder care; and counseling services. Child care and elder care are increasingly important due to growth in the number of dual-income households and the elderly population. Counseling may help employees deal with emotional disorders, alcoholism, and marital, family, consumer, legal, and financial problems. Some employers offer career counseling as well. In large firms, certain programs, such as security and safety, may be in separate departments headed by other managers.

Training and development managers supervise training. Increasingly, management recognizes that training offers a way of developing skills, enhancing productivity and quality of work, and building loyalty to the firm. Training is widely accepted as a method of improving employee morale, but this is only one of the reasons for its growing importance. Other factors include the complexity of the work environment, the rapid pace of organizational and technological change, and the growing number of jobs in fields that constantly generate new knowledge. In addition, advances in learning theory have provided insights into how adults learn, and how training can be organized most effectively for them.

Training specialists plan, organize, and direct a wide range of training activities. Trainers conduct orientation sessions and arrange on-the-job training for new employees. They help rank-and-file workers maintain and improve their job skills and possibly prepare for jobs requiring greater skill. They help supervisors improve their interpersonal skills in order to deal effectively with employees. They may set up individualized training plans to strengthen an employee's existing skills or teach new ones. Training specialists in some companies set up programs to develop executive potential among employees in lower-level positions. In government-supported training programs, training specialists function as case managers. They first assess the training needs of clients and then guide them through the most appropriate training method. After training, clients may either be referred to employer relations representatives or receive job placement assistance.

Planning and program development is an important part of the training specialist's job. In order to identify and assess training needs within the firm, trainers may confer with managers and supervisors or conduct surveys. They also periodically evaluate training effectiveness.

Depending on the size, goals, and nature of the organization, trainers may differ considerably in their responsibilities and in the methods they use. Training methods include on-the-job training; schools in which shop conditions are duplicated for trainees prior to putting them on the shop floor; apprenticeship training; classroom training; programmed instruction, which may involve interactive videos and other computer-aided instructional technologies; simulators; conferences; and workshops.

The *director of industrial relations* forms labor policy, oversees industrial labor relations, negotiates collective bargaining agreements, and coordinates grievance procedures to handle complaints resulting from disputes with unionized employees. The director of industrial relations also advises and collaborates with the director of human resources, other managers, and members of their staff, because all aspects of personnel policy—such as wages, benefits, pensions, and work practices—may be involved in drawing up a new or revised contract.

Labor relations managers and their staff implement industrial labor relations programs. When a collective bargaining agreement is up for negotiation, labor relations specialists prepare information for management to use during negotiation, which requires familiarity with economic and wage data as well as extensive knowledge of labor law and collective bargaining trends. The labor relations staff interprets and administers the contract with respect to grievances, wages and salaries, employee welfare, health care, pensions, union and management practices, and other contractual stipulations. As union membership continues to decline in most industries, industrial relations personnel work more with employees who are not members of a labor union.

Dispute resolution—attaining tacit or contractual agreements—has become increasingly important as parties to a dispute attempt to avoid costly litigation, strikes, or other disruptions. Dispute resolution also has become more complex, involving employees, management, unions, other firms, and government agencies. Specialists involved in dispute resolution must be highly knowledgeable and experienced and often report to the director of industrial relations. *Conciliators*, or *mediators*, advise and counsel labor and management to prevent and, when necessary, resolve disputes over labor agreements or other labor relations issues. *Arbitrators*, sometimes called umpires or referees, decide disputes that bind both labor and management to specific terms and conditions of labor contracts. Labor relations specialists who work for unions perform many of the same functions on behalf of the union and its members.

Other emerging specialists include *international human resources managers*, who handle human resources issues related to a company's foreign operations, and *human resources information system specialists*, who develop and apply computer programs to process personnel information, match jobseekers with job openings, and handle other personnel matters.

Working Conditions

Personnel work usually takes place in clean, pleasant, and comfortable office settings. Arbitrators and mediators may work out of their homes. Many human resources, training, and labor relations specialists and managers work a standard 35- to 40-hour week. However, longer hours might be necessary for some workers—for example, labor relations specialists and managers, arbitrators, and mediators—when contract agreements are being prepared and negotiated.

Although most human resources, training, and labor relations specialists and managers work in the office, some travel extensively. For example, recruiters regularly attend professional meetings and visit college campuses to interview prospective employees; arbitrators and mediators often must travel to the site chosen for negotiations.

Employment

Human resources, training, and labor relations specialists and managers held about 597,000 jobs in 1998. They were employed in virtually every industry. Specialists accounted for 3 out of 5 positions and managers for 2 out of 5. About 14,000 specialists were self-employed, working as consultants to public and private employers.

The private sector accounted for about 80 percent of salaried jobs. Among these salaried jobs, services industries—including business, health, social, management, and educational services—accounted for about 40 percent of jobs. Labor organizations, the largest employer among specific services industries, accounted for more than 20 percent of those. Manufacturing industries accounted for 17 percent of salaried jobs, while finance, insurance, and real estate firms accounted for about 11 percent of jobs.

Federal, State, and local governments employed about 14 percent of human resources specialists and managers. They handled the recruitment, interviewing, job classification, training, salary administration, benefits, employee relations, and related matters of the Nation's public employees.

Training, Other Qualifications, and Advancement

Because of the diversity of duties and level of responsibility, the educational backgrounds of human resources, training, and labor relations specialists and managers vary considerably. When filling entry-level jobs, employers usually seek college graduates. Many employers prefer applicants who have majored in human resources, personnel administration, or industrial and labor relations. Others look for college graduates with a technical or business background or a well-rounded liberal arts education.

Many colleges and universities have programs leading to a degree in personnel, human resources, or labor relations. Some offer degree programs in personnel administration or human resources management, training and development, or compensation and benefits. Depending on the school, courses leading to a career in human resources management may be found in departments of business administration, education, instructional technology, organizational development, human services, communication, or public administration or within a separate human resources institution or department.

Because an interdisciplinary background is appropriate in this field, a combination of courses in the social sciences, business, and behavioral sciences is useful. Some jobs may require a more technical or specialized background in engineering, science, finance, or law, for example. Most prospective human resources specialists should take courses in compensation, recruitment, training and development, and performance appraisal, as well as courses in principles of management, organizational structure, and industrial psychology. Other relevant courses include business administration, public administration, psychology, sociology, political science, economics, and statistics. Courses in labor law, collective bargaining, labor economics, labor history, and industrial psychology also provide a valuable background for the prospective labor relations specialist. As in many other fields, knowledge of computers and information systems is also useful.

An advanced degree is increasingly important for some jobs. Many labor relations jobs require graduate study in industrial or labor relations. A strong background in industrial relations and law is highly desirable for contract negotiators, mediators, and arbitrators; in fact, many people in these specialties are lawyers. A background in law is also desirable for employee benefits managers and others who must interpret the growing number of laws and regulations. A master's degree in human resources, labor relations, or in business administration with a concentration in human resources management is highly recommended for those seeking general and top management positions.

For many specialized jobs in the human resources field, previous experience is an asset; for more advanced positions (including managers, as well as arbitrators and mediators), it is essential. Many employers prefer entry-level workers who have gained some experience through an internship or work-study program while in school. Personnel administration and human resources development require the ability to work with individuals as well as a commitment to organizational goals. This field also demands other skills people may develop elsewhere—using computers, selling, teaching, supervising, and volunteering, among others. This field offers clerical workers opportunities for advancement to professional positions. Responsible positions are sometimes filled by experienced individuals from other fields, including business, government, education., social services administration, and the military.

The human resources field demands a range of personal qualities and skills. Human resources, training, and labor relations specialists and managers must speak and write effectively. The growing diversity of the workforce requires that they work with or supervise people with various cultural backgrounds, levels of education, and experience. They must be able to cope with conflicting points of view, function under pressure, and demonstrate discretion, integrity, fair-mindedness, and a persuasive, congenial personality.

The duties given to entry-level workers will vary depending on whether they have a degree in human resource management, have completed an internship, or have some other type of human resources-related experience. Entry-level employees commonly learn the profession by performing administrative duties, such as helping to enter data into computer systems, compiling employee handbooks, researching information for a supervisor, or answering the phone and handling routine questions. Entry-level workers often enter formal or on-the-job training programs in which they learn how to classify jobs, interview applicants, or administer employee benefits. They then are assigned to specific areas in the personnel department to gain experience. Later, they may advance to a managerial position, overseeing a major element of the personnel program—compensation or training, for example.

Exceptional human resources workers may be promoted to director of personnel or industrial relations, which can eventually lead to a top managerial or executive position. Others may join a consulting firm or open their own business. A Ph.D. is an asset for teaching, writing, or consulting work.

Most organizations specializing in human resources offer classes intended to enhance the marketable skills of their members. Some organizations offer certification programs, which are signs of competence and can enhance one's advancement opportunities. For example, the International Foundation of Employee Benefit Plans confers the Certified Employee Benefit Specialist designation to persons who complete a series of college-level courses and pass exams covering employee benefit plans. The Society for Human Resources Management has two levels of certification: Professional in Human Resources, and Senior Professional in Human Resources. Both require experience and a comprehensive exam.

Job Outlook

The job market for human resources, training, and labor relations specialists and managers is likely to remain competitive given the abundant supply of qualified college graduates and experienced workers. In addition to openings due to growth, many job openings will result from the need to replace workers who transfer to other occupations or leave the labor force.

Employment of human resources, training, and labor relations specialists and managers is expected to grow about as fast as the average for all occupations through 2008. New jobs will stem from increasing efforts throughout industry to recruit and retain quality employees. Employers are expected to devote greater resources to job-specific training programs in response to the increasing complexity of many jobs, the aging of the work force, and technological advances that can leave employees with obsolete skills. In addition, legislation and court rulings setting standards in various areas—occupational safety and health, equal employment opportunity, wages, health, pension, and family leave, among others—will increase demand for human resources, training, and labor relations experts. Rising health care costs, in particular, should spur demand for specialists to develop creative compensation and benefits packages that firms can offer prospective employees. Employment of labor relations staff, including arbitrators and mediators, should grow as firms become more involved in labor relations and attempt to resolve potentially costly labor-management disputes out of court. Additional job growth may stem from increasing demand for specialists in international human resources management and human resources information systems.

Employment demand should be strong among firms involved in management, consulting, and personnel supply, as businesses increasingly contract out personnel functions or hire personnel specialists on a temporary basis to meet the increasing cost and complexity of training and development programs. Demand should also increase in firms that develop and administer complex employee benefits and compensation packages for other organizations.

Demand for human resources, training, and labor relations specialists and managers is also governed by the staffing needs of the firms for which they work. A rapidly expanding business is likely to hire additional human resources workers either as permanent employees or consultants, while a business that has experienced a merger or a reduction in its work force will require fewer human resources workers. Also, as human resources management becomes increasingly important to the success of an organization, some small and medium-size businesses that do not have a human resources department may assign employees various human resources duties together with other unrelated responsibilities. In any particular firm, the size and the job duties of the human resources staff are determined by the firm's organizational philosophy and goals, skills of its work force, pace of technological change, government regulations, collective bargaining agreements, standards of professional practice, and labor market conditions.

Job growth could be limited by the widespread use of computerized human resources information systems that make workers more productive. Similar to other workers, employment of human resources, training, and labor relations specialists and managers, particularly in larger firms, may be adversely affected by corporate downsizing and restructuring.

Earnings

Median annual earnings of human resources managers were $49,010 in 1998. The middle 50 percent earned between $35,400 and $73,830. The lowest 10 percent earned less than $25,750, and the highest 10 percent earned more than $91,040. Median annual earnings in the industries employing the largest numbers of human resources managers in 1997 were:

Local government, except education and hospitals	$50,800
Hospitals	48,200
Management and public relations	44,800
Labor organizations	36,700
Personnel supply services	35,900

Median annual earnings of human resources, training, and labor relations specialists were $37,710 in 1998. The middle 50 percent earned between $28,200 and $50,160. The lowest 10 percent earned less than $20,310, and the highest 10 percent earned more than $75,440. Median annual earnings in the industries employing the largest numbers of human resources, training, and labor relations specialists in 1997 were:

Federal government	$51,800
Local government, except education and hospitals	39,900
Hospitals	35,000
State government, except education and hospitals	34,100
Labor organizations	29,700

According to a 1999 salary survey conducted by the National Association of Colleges and Employers, bachelor's degree candidates majoring in human resources, including labor relations, received starting offers averaging $29,800 a year.

According to a November 1998 survey of compensation in the human resources field, conducted by Abbott, Langer, and Associates of Crete, Illinois, the median total cash compensation for selected personnel and labor relations occupations were:

Industrial and labor relations directors	$183,900
Compensation and benefits directors	88,000
Divisional human resources directors	84,100
Training directors	79,400
Recruitment and interviewing managers	75,100
Employee and community relations directors	73,500
Plant/location human resources managers	62,000
Compensation supervisors	53,300
Human resources information systems specialists	49,300
Employee assistance and employee counseling specialists	47,500
Employee services and employee recreation specialists	47,300
Employee and industrial plant nurses	46,000
EEO and affirmative action specialists	44,800
Safety specialists	43,700
Training material development specialists	43,500
Benefits specialists (managerial and professional jobs)	41,500
Training generalists (computer)	39,600
Classroom instructors	35,300
Employment interviewing specialists	35,100
Job evaluation specialists	34,100
Human resources records specialists	32,400

In the Federal government, persons with a bachelor's degree or three years' general experience in the personnel field generally started at $23,300 a year in 1999. Those with a superior academic record or an additional year of specialized experience started at $28,000 a year. Those with a master's degree may start at $33,400, and those with a doctorate in a personnel field may start at $44,500. Beginning salaries were slightly higher in areas where the prevailing local pay level was higher. There are no formal entry-level requirements for managerial positions. Applicants must possess a suitable combination of educational attainment, experience, and record of accomplishment.

Related Occupations

All human resources occupations are closely related. Other workers with skills and expertise in interpersonal relations include counselors, lawyers, psychologists, sociologists, social workers, public relations specialists, and teachers.

Sources of Additional Information

For information about careers in employee training and development, contact:

- American Society for Training and Development, 1640 King St., Box 1443, Alexandria, VA 22313. Internet: http://www.astd.org

For information about careers and certification in employee compensation and benefits, contact:

- American Compensation Association, 14040 Northsight Blvd., Scottsdale, AZ 85260. Internet: http://www.acaonline.org

Information about careers and certification in employee benefits is available from:

- International Foundation of Employee Benefit Plans, 18700 W. Bluemound Rd., P.O. Box 69, Brookfield, WI 53008-0069. Internet: http://www.ifebp.org

For information about academic programs in industrial relations, write to:

- Industrial Relations Research Association, University of Wisconsin, 7226 Social Science Bldg., 1180 Observatory Dr., Madison, WI 53706. Internet: http://www.irra.ssc.wisc.edu

Information about personnel careers in the health care industry is available from:

- American Society for Healthcare Human Resources Administration, One North Franklin, 31st Floor, Chicago, IL 60606. Internet: http://www.ashhra.org

Human Service Workers and Assistants

(O*NET 27308)

Significant Points

- Human service worker and assistant occupations are projected to be among the fastest growing.

- Job opportunities should be excellent, particularly for applicants with appropriate post-secondary education, but pay is low.

Nature of the Work

Human service workers and assistants is a generic term for people with various job titles, including social service assistant, case management aide, social work assistant, community support worker, alcohol or drug abuse counselor, mental health aide, community outreach worker, life skill counselor, and gerontology aide. They usually work under the direction of professionals from a variety of fields, such as nursing, psychiatry, psychology, rehabilitative or physical therapy, or social work. The amount of responsibility and supervision they are given varies a great deal. Some have little direct supervision; others work under close direction.

Human service workers and assistants provide direct and indirect client services. They assess clients' needs, establish their eligibility for benefits and services, and help clients obtain them. They examine financial documents such as rent receipts and tax returns to determine whether the client is eligible for food stamps, Medicaid, welfare, and other human service programs. They also arrange for transportation and escorts, if necessary, and provide emotional support. Human service workers and assistants monitor and keep case records on clients and report progress to supervisors and case managers. Human service workers and assistants also may transport or accompany clients to group meal sites, adult daycare centers, or doctors' offices. They may telephone or visit clients' homes to make sure services are being received or to help resolve disagreements, such as those between tenants and landlords. They also may help clients complete insurance or medical forms, as well as applications for financial assistance. Additionally, social and human service workers and assistants may assist others with daily living needs.

Human service workers and assistants play a variety of roles in a community. They may organize and lead group activities, assist clients in need of counseling or crisis intervention, or administer a food bank or emergency fuel program. In halfway houses, group homes, and government-supported housing programs, they assist adults who need supervision with personal hygiene and daily living skills. They review clients' records, ensure that they take correct doses of medication, talk with family members, and confer with medical personnel and other care givers to gain better insight into clients' backgrounds and needs. Human service workers and assistants also provide emotional support and help clients become involved in their own well being, in community recreation programs, and in other activities.

In psychiatric hospitals, rehabilitation programs, and outpatient clinics, human service workers and assistants work with professional care providers such as psychiatrists, psychologists, and social workers to help clients master everyday living skills and to teach them how to communicate more effectively and get along better with others. They support the client's participation in a treatment plan, such as individual or group counseling or occupational therapy.

Working Conditions

Working conditions of human service workers and assistants vary. Some work in offices, clinics, and hospitals, while others work in group homes, shelters, sheltered workshops, and day programs. Many spend their time in the field visiting clients. Most work a 40-hour week, although some work in the evening and on weekends.

The work, while satisfying, can be emotionally draining. Understaffing and relatively low pay may add to the pressure. Turnover is reported to be high, especially among workers without academic preparation for this field.

Employment

Human service workers and assistants held about 268,000 jobs in 1998. Almost half worked in private social or human services agencies, offering a variety of services, including adult daycare, group meals, crisis intervention, counseling, and job training. Many human service workers and assistants supervised residents of group homes and halfway houses. About one-third were employed by State and local governments, primarily in public welfare agencies and facilities for mentally disabled and developmentally challenged individuals. Human service workers and assistants also held jobs in clinics, detoxification units, community mental health centers, psychiatric hospitals, day treatment programs, and sheltered workshops.

Training, Other Qualifications, and Advancement

Although a bachelor's degree usually is not required for this occupation, employers increasingly are seeking individuals with relevant work experience or education beyond high school. Certificates or associate degrees in subjects such as social work, human services, or one of the social or behavioral sciences meet most employers' requirements.

Human services programs have a core curriculum that trains students to observe patients and record information, conduct patient interviews, implement treatment plans, employ problem-solving techniques, handle crisis intervention matters, and use proper case management and referral procedures. General education courses in liberal arts, sciences, and the humanities also are part of the curriculum. Many degree programs require completion of a supervised internship.

Educational attainment often influences the kind of work employees may be assigned and the degree of responsibility that may be entrusted to them. For example, workers with no more than a high school education are likely to receive extensive on-the-job training to work in direct-care services, while employees with a college degree might be assigned to do supportive counseling, coordinate program activities, or manage a group home. Human service workers and assistants with proven leadership ability, either from previous experience or as a volunteer in the field, often receive greater autonomy in their work. Regardless of the academic or work background of employees, most employers provide some form of in-service training, such as seminars and workshops, to their employees.

Hiring requirements in group homes tend to be more stringent than in other settings. For example, employers may require employees to have a valid driver's license or to submit to a criminal background investigation.

Employers try to select applicants who have effective communication skills, a strong sense of responsibility, and the ability to manage time effectively. Many human services jobs involve direct contact with people who are vulnerable to exploitation or mistreatment; therefore, patience, understanding, and a strong desire to help others, are highly valued characteristics.

Formal education almost always is necessary for advancement. In general, advancement requires a bachelor's or master's degree in counseling, rehabilitation, social work, human services management, or a related field.

Job Outlook

Opportunities for human service workers and assistants are expected to be excellent, particularly for applicants with appropriate post-secondary education. The number of human service workers and assistants is projected to grow much faster than the average for all occupations between 1998 and 2008—ranking among the most rapidly growing occupations. The need to replace workers who move into new positions due to advancement, retirement, or for other reasons will create many additional job opportunities. This occupation, however, is not attractive to everyone. It can be draining emotionally, and the pay is relatively low. Qualified applicants should have little difficulty finding employment.

Faced with rapid growth in the demand for social and human services, employers are developing new strategies for delivering and funding services. Many employers increasingly will rely on human service workers and assistants to undertake greater responsibility in delivering services to clients.

Opportunities are expected to be best in job training programs, residential care facilities, and private social service agencies, which include such services as adult daycare and meal delivery programs. Demand for these services will expand with the growing number of elderly, who are more likely to need services. In addition, social and human service workers and assistants will continue to be needed to provide services to pregnant teenagers, the homeless, the mentally disabled and developmentally challenged, and those with substance-abuse problems.

Job training programs are expected to require additional human service workers and assistants. As social welfare policies shift focus from benefit-based programs to work-based initiatives, there will be an increased demand for people to teach job skills to the people who are new to or re-entering the workforce. Additionally, streamlined and downsized businesses create increased demand for persons with job retraining expertise. Human service workers and assistants will help companies to cope with new modes of conducting business and employees to master new job skills.

Residential care establishments should face increased pressures to respond to the needs of the chronically and mentally ill. Many of these patients have been deinstitutionalized and lack the knowledge or the ability to care for themselves. Also, more community-based programs, supported independent living sites, and group residences are expected to be established to house and assist the homeless, and the chronically and mentally ill. As a result, demand for human service workers and assistants will increase.

The number of jobs for human service workers and assistants will grow more rapidly than overall employment in State and local governments. State and local governments employ many of their human service workers and assistants in corrections and public assistance departments. Although employment in corrections departments is growing, employment of social and human service workers and assistants is not expected to grow as rapidly as employment in other corrections jobs, such as guards or corrections officers. Public assistance programs have been employing more human service workers and assistants in an attempt to employ fewer social workers, who are more educated and, therefore, more highly paid.

Earnings

Median annual earnings of human service workers and assistants were $21,360 in 1998. The middle 50 percent earned between $16,620 and $27,070. The top 10 percent earned more than $33,840, while the lowest 10 percent earned less than $13,540.

Median hourly earnings in the industries employing the largest numbers of human service workers and assistants in 1997 were:

State government, except education and hospitals $25,600

Local government, except education and hospitals 23,500

Hospitals 21,200

Health and allied services, not elsewhere classified 20,600

Social services, not elsewhere classified 20,200

Related Occupations

Workers in other occupations that require skills similar to those of human service workers and assistants include social workers, religious workers, residential counselors, child-care workers, occupational therapy assistants, physical therapy assistants, psychiatric aides, and activity leaders.

Sources of Additional Information

Information on academic programs in human services may be found in most directories of two- and four-year colleges, available at libraries or career counseling centers.

For information on programs and careers in human services, contact:

- **National Organization for Human Service Education, Brookdale Community College, Lincroft, NJ 07738.**
- **Council for Standards in Human Services Education, Northern Essex Community College, Haverhill, MA 01830.**

Information on job openings may be available from State employment service offices or directly from city, county, or State departments of health, mental health and mental retardation, and human resources.

Instructors and Coaches, Sports and Physical Training

(O*NET 31321)

Significant Points

- Work hours are often irregular.
- For many positions, certification is required.

Nature of the Work

An increasing value is being placed upon physical fitness within our society. Consequently, Americans are engaging in more physical fitness programs, joining athletic clubs, and being encouraged to participate in physical education and activity at all ages. Sports and physical training instructors and coaches help participants improve their physical fitness and athletic skills.

Sports instructors and coaches teach non-professional individual and team sports to students. Sports instructors and coaches organize, lead, instruct, and referee outdoor and indoor games such as volleyball, football, and soccer. They instruct individuals or groups in beginning or advanced exercises. Using their knowledge of sports, physiology, and corrective techniques, they determine the type and level of difficulty of exercises, prescribe specific movements, and correct individuals' technique. Some instructors and coaches also teach and demonstrate use of training apparatus, such as trampolines or weights. Sports instructors and coaches may also select, store, issue, and inventory equipment, materials, and supplies.

Physical training instructors tend to focus more on physical fitness activities than on organized sports. They teach and lead exercise activities to individuals or groups ranging from beginning to advanced levels. These activities take place in a gym, health club, or other recreational facility. Because activities are as diverse as aerobics, calisthenics, weight lifting, gymnastics, scuba diving, yoga, and may include self-defense training such as karate, instructors tend to specialize in one or a few types of activities. *Personal trainers* work one-on-one in health clubs or clients' homes. They evaluate an individual's abilities, determine a suitable training program, demonstrate a variety of exercises, offer encouragement, and monitor their correct use of exercise equipment and other apparatus.

Depending on the sport or physical activity involved, instructors and coaches use different kinds of equipment. Many work with children or young adults, helping them to learn new physical and social skills, while also improving their physical condition.

Working Conditions

Irregular work hours are common: Many instructors and coaches work part-time, evenings, and weekends. Instructors and coaches in educational institutions may work additional hours during the sports season. Some coach more than one sport, and many work year round. Some work outdoors, depending on the sport or activity. Instructors and coaches may travel frequently to games and other sporting events. Their work is often strenuous, and they must guard against injury when participating in activities or instructing others.

Employment

Sports and physical training instructors and coaches held about 359,000 jobs in 1998. About 1 out of 6 was self-employed. Almost half of salaried workers were in public or private educational institutions. Amusement and recreation services, including health clubs, gymnasiums, and sports and recreation clubs provided almost as many jobs. Most of the remaining jobs were found in civic and social associations.

Training, Other Qualifications, and Advancement

Education and training requirements for instructors and coaches vary greatly by type of employer, area of expertise, and level of responsibilities. Some entry-level positions require only experience derived as a participant in the sport or activity, while others require substantial education or experience. For example, aerobics instructor jobs are usually filled by persons who develop an avid interest in the activity by taking aerobics classes and then become certified. On the other hand, some coaches must have qualifying experience such as past participation in the sport, or must work their way up through the coaching ranks.

School coaches and sports instructors at all levels usually have a bachelor's degree. Employers within the education industry often draw first from teachers and faculty when seeking to fill a position. If no one suitable is found, they hire someone from outside. Coaches may have to be certified in accordance with the school district's policies. Some districts require re-certification every two years. A master's degree may increase opportunities for employment and advancement. Degree programs are offered in exercise sports science, physiology, kinesiology, nutrition and fitness, physical education, and sports medicine.

Certification is highly desirable for those interested in becoming a fitness, aerobics, tennis, karate, golf, or any other kind of instructor. Often one must be at least 18 years old and CPR certified. There are many certifying organizations specific to the various types of sports or activities and their training requirements vary depending on their standards. Part-time workers and those in smaller facilities are less likely to need formal education or training.

Instructors and coaches must relate well to others. They also must be resourceful and flexible to successfully instruct and motivate individual students or groups. Good communication and leadership skills are essential.

Job Outlook

An increased need for instructors and coaches is expected to increase employment in this occupation faster than the average for all occupations through the year 2008. Additional job opportunities will be generated by the need to replace workers who leave the occupation. Job prospects should be best for those with bachelor's degrees and extensive experience within their specialization.

Demand for instructors and coaches will remain high as long as the public continues to participate in sports as a form of entertainment, recreation, and physical conditioning. Health and fitness clubs will continue to change to address the public's ever-changing tastes. In addition, as the more active baby-boomers replace their more sedentary parents in retirement, the demand for sports and recreation instructors and coaches will increase.

Earnings

Median hourly earnings of sports and physical training instructors and coaches were $10.69 in 1998. The middle 50 percent earned between $6.54 and $16.48 an hour. The lowest 10 percent earned less than $5.70, and the highest 10 percent earned more than $23.10 an hour. Median hourly earnings in the industries employing the largest number of sports and physical training instructors and coaches in 1997 were as follows:

Colleges and universities	$13.70
Elementary and secondary schools	11.00
Miscellaneous amusement and recreation services	9.70
Civic and social associations	7.80

Earnings vary by education level, certification, and geographic region. Some instructors and coaches are paid a salary, others may be paid by the hour, per session, or based on the number of participants.

Related Occupations

Coaches and instructors have extensive knowledge of physiology and sports, and they instruct, inform, and encourage participants. Other workers with similar duties include athletic directors, athletic trainers, dietitians and nutritionists, physical therapists, recreational therapists, school teachers, and umpires.

Sources of Additional Information

Information about a career as a fitness professional is available from:

- American Council on Exercise, 5820 Oberlin Dr., Suite 102, San Diego, CA 92121-3787. Internet: http://www.acefitness.org

For information on a career as a coach, contact:

- National High School Athletic Coaches Association, P.O. Box 4342, Hamden, CT 06514. Internet: http://www.hscoaches.org

Janitors and Cleaners and Institutional Cleaning Supervisors

(O*NET 61008, 67002, and 67005)

Significant Points

- Plentiful job openings should arise primarily from the need to replace those who leave this very large occupation each year; limited training requirements, low pay, and numerous part-time and temporary jobs should contribute to these replacement needs.

- Businesses providing janitorial and cleaning services on a contract basis are expected to be among the fastest growing employers of these workers.

Nature of the Work

Janitors and cleaners—also called building custodians, executive housekeepers, or maids—keep office buildings, hospitals, stores, apartment houses, hotels, and other types of buildings clean and in good condition. Some only do cleaning, while others have a wide range of duties. They may fix leaky faucets, empty trash cans, do painting and carpentry, replenish bathroom supplies, mow lawns, and see that heating and air-conditioning equipment works properly. On a typical day, janitors may wet- or dry-mop floors, clean bathrooms, vacuum carpets, dust furniture, make minor repairs, and exterminate insects and rodents. In hospitals, where they are mostly known as maids or housekeepers, they may also wash bed frames, brush mattresses, make beds, and disinfect and sterilize equipment and supplies using germicides and sterilizing equipment. In hotels, aside from cleaning and maintaining the premises, they may deliver ironing boards, cribs, and rollaway beds to guests' rooms.

Janitors and cleaners use various equipment, tools, and cleaning materials. For one job, they may need a mop and bucket; for another, an electric polishing machine and a special cleaning solution. Improved building materials, chemical cleaners, and power equipment have made many tasks easier and less time-consuming, but janitors must learn proper use of equipment and cleaners to avoid harming floors, fixtures, and themselves.

Cleaning supervisors coordinate, schedule, and supervise the activities of janitors and cleaners. They assign tasks and inspect building areas to see that work has been done properly, issue supplies and equipment, inventory stocks to ensure an adequate amount of supplies are present, screen and hire job applicants, and recommend promotions, transfers, or dismissals. They also train new and experienced employees. Supervisors may prepare reports concerning room occupancy, hours worked, and department expenses. Some also perform cleaning duties.

Working Conditions

Because most office buildings are cleaned while they are empty, many cleaners work evening hours. Some, however, such as school and hospital custodians, work in the daytime. When there is a need for 24-hour maintenance, janitors may be assigned to shifts. Most full-time janitors, cleaners, and cleaning supervisors work about 40 hours a week. Part-time cleaners usually work in the evenings and on weekends.

Janitors and cleaners and institutional cleaning supervisors in large office and residential buildings often work in teams. These teams consist of workers who specialize in vacuuming, trash pickup, and restroom cleaning, among other things. Supervisors conduct inspections to ensure the building is cleaned properly and the team is functioning efficiently.

Janitors and cleaners usually work inside heated, well-lighted buildings. However, they sometimes work outdoors sweeping walkways, mowing lawns, or shoveling snow. Working with machines can be noisy, and some tasks, such as cleaning bathrooms and trash rooms, can be dirty and unpleasant. Janitors may suffer cuts, bruises, and burns from machines, hand tools, and chemicals. They spend most of their time on their feet, sometimes lifting or pushing heavy furniture or equipment. Many tasks, such as dusting and sweeping, require constant bending, stooping, and stretching. As a result, janitors may also suffer back injuries and sprains.

Employment

Janitors and cleaners and institutional cleaning supervisors held nearly 3.3 million jobs in 1998. Less than 5 percent were self employed.

Janitors and cleaners work in nearly every type of establishment and held about 97 percent of all jobs. About 23 percent worked for firms supplying building maintenance services on a contract basis; 16 percent worked in educational institutions; and 14 percent worked in hotels. Other employers included hospitals, restaurants, religious institutions, manufacturing firms, government agencies, and operators of apartment buildings, office buildings, and other types of real estate.

Institutional cleaning supervisors held about 87,000 jobs. About 37 percent were employed in hotels; 23 percent in firms supplying building maintenance services on a contract basis; 12 percent in hospitals; and 12 percent in nursing and personal care facilities. Other employers included educational institutions, residential care establishments, and amusement and recreation facilities.

Although cleaning jobs can be found in all cities and towns, most are located in highly populated areas where there are many office buildings, schools, apartment houses, and hospitals.

Training, Other Qualifications, and Advancement

No special education is required for most janitorial or cleaning jobs, but beginners should know simple arithmetic and be able to follow instructions. High school shop courses are helpful for jobs involving repair work.

Most janitors and cleaners learn their skills on the job. Usually, beginners work with an experienced cleaner, doing routine cleaning. As they gain more experience, they are assigned more complicated tasks.

In some cities, programs run by unions, government agencies, or employers teach janitorial skills. Students learn how to clean buildings thoroughly and efficiently, how to select and safely use various cleansing agents, and how to operate and maintain machines, such as wet and dry vacuums, buffers, and polishers. Students learn to plan their work, to follow safety and health regulations, to interact positively with people in the buildings they clean, and to work without supervision. Instruction in minor electrical, plumbing, and other repairs may also be given. Those who come in contact with the public should have good communication skills. Employers usually look for dependable, hard-working individuals who are in good health, follow directions well, and get along with other people.

Janitors and cleaners usually find work by answering newspaper advertisements, applying directly to organizations where they would like to work, contacting local labor unions, or contacting State employment service offices.

Advancement opportunities for janitorial workers are usually limited in organizations where they are the only maintenance worker. Where there is a large maintenance staff, however, janitors can be promoted to supervisor and to area supervisor or manager. A high school diploma improves the chances for advancement. Some janitors set up their own maintenance business.

Supervisors usually move up through the ranks. In many establishments, they are required to take some in-service training to improve their housekeeping techniques and procedures and to enhance their supervisory skills.

A small number of cleaning supervisors and managers are members of the International Executive Housekeepers Association (IEHA). IEHA offers two kinds of certification programs to cleaning supervisors and managers: Certified Executive Housekeeper (CEH) and Registered Executive Housekeeper (REH). The CEH designation is offered to those with a high school education, while the REH designation is offered to those who have a four-year college degree. Both designations are earned by attending courses and passing exams and must be renewed every two years to ensure that workers keep abreast of new cleaning methods. Those with the REH designation usually oversee the cleaning services of hotels, hospitals, casinos, and other large institutions that rely on well-trained experts for their cleaning needs.

Job Outlook

Job openings should be plentiful for janitors and cleaners primarily because of the need to replace those who leave this very large occupation each year. Limited formal education and training requirements, low pay, and numerous part-time and temporary jobs should contribute to these replacement needs.

Many job opportunities will stem from job growth in addition to the need to replace workers who transfer to other occupations or leave the labor force. Employment of janitors and cleaners and institutional cleaning supervisors is expected to grow about as fast as average for all occupations through the year 2008. To clean the increasing number of office complexes, apartment houses, schools, factories, hospitals, and other buildings, more workers will be assigned to teams with more efficient cleaning equipment and supplies. As many firms reduce costs by hiring independent contractors, businesses providing janitorial and cleaning services on a contract basis are expected to be one of the faster growing employers of these workers.

Earnings

Median annual earnings of janitors and cleaners, including maids and housekeeping cleaners, were $15,340 in 1998. The middle 50 percent earned between $12,560 and $19,110. The lowest 10 percent earned less than $11,620, and the highest 10 percent earned more than $25,060. Median annual earnings in the industries employing the largest numbers of janitors and cleaners, including maids and housekeeping cleaners, in 1997 are shown here:

Federal government	$27,900
Hospitals	16,800
Hotels and motels	15,400
Nursing and personal care facilities	15,200
Services to buildings	13,900

Median annual earnings of institutional cleaning supervisors were $19,600 in 1998. The middle 50 percent earned between $15,580 and $24,850. The lowest 10 percent earned less than $13,150, and the highest 10 percent earned more than $31,930. Median annual earnings in the industries employing the largest numbers of institutional cleaning supervisors in 1997 are shown below:

Hospitals	$22,400
Nursing and personal care facilities	20,200
Services to buildings	18,500
Hotels and motels	17,200

Related Occupations

Workers who specialize in one of the many job functions of janitors and cleaners include refuse collectors, floor waxers, street sweepers, window cleaners, gardeners, boiler tenders, pest controllers, and general maintenance repairers. Private household workers also have job duties similar to janitors and cleaners.

Sources of Additional Information

Information about janitorial jobs may be obtained from State employment service offices.

For information on certification in executive housekeeping, contact:

● International Executive Housekeepers Association, Inc., 1001 Eastwind Dr., Suite 301, Westerville, OH 43081-3361. Internet: http://www.ieha.org

Landscaping, Groundskeeping, Nursery, Greenhouse, and Lawn Service Occupations

(O*NET 15017A, 15031, 15032, 72002D, 72002E, 79005, 79030B, 79033, 79036, and 79041)

Significant Points

● Seldom are there minimum educational requirements for entry-level jobs, and most workers learn through short-term on-the-job training.

- Opportunities should be excellent due to significant job turnover, but earnings for laborer jobs are low.

Nature of the Work

Attractively designed, healthy, and well-maintained lawns, gardens, and grounds create a positive first impression, establish a peaceful mood, and increase property values. Workers in landscaping, groundskeeping, nursery, greenhouse, and lawn service occupations are responsible for the variety of tasks necessary to achieve a pleasant and functional outdoor environment. They also care for indoor gardens and plantings in commercial and public facilities, such as malls, hotels, and botanical gardens.

Nursery and greenhouse workers help to cultivate the plants used to beautify landscapes. They prepare nursery acreage or greenhouse beds for planting; water, weed, and spray trees, shrubs, and plants; cut, roll, and stack sod; stake trees; tie, wrap, and pack flowers, plants, shrubs, and trees to fill orders; and dig up or move field-grown and containerized shrubs and trees. *Nursery and greenhouse managers* make decisions about the type and quantity of horticultural plants to be grown; select and purchase seed, fertilizers, and disease control chemicals; hire laborers and direct and coordinate their activities; manage record keeping, accounting, and marketing activities; and generally oversee operations.

Landscape contractors usually follow the designs developed by a landscape architect. They coordinate and oversee the installation of trees, flowers, shrubs, sod, benches, and other ornamental features. They also implement construction plans at the site, which may involve grading the property, installing lighting or sprinkler systems, and building walkways, terraces, patios, decks, and fountains. They must determine the type and amount of labor, equipment, and materials needed to complete a project, and they inspect work at various stages of completion. Some work exclusively on large properties, such as office buildings and shopping malls, whereas others also provide these services to residential customers.

Landscaping laborers physically install and maintain landscaped areas. In addition to initially transporting and planting new vegetation, they also transplant, mulch, fertilize, water, and prune flowering plants, trees, and shrubs, and mow and water lawns. *Supervisors* generally perform the same work but are also responsible for directing the landscaping crew's activities, adhering to schedules, and keeping track of labor costs. Some landscaping laborers, called *pruners*, specialize in pruning, trimming, and shaping ornamental trees and shrubs. Others, called *lawn service workers*, specialize in maintaining lawns and shrubs for a fee. A growing number of residential and commercial clients, such as managers of office buildings, shopping malls, multiunit residential buildings, and hotels and motels favor this full-service landscape maintenance. These workers perform a range of duties on a regular basis during the growing season, including mowing, edging, trimming, fertilizing, dethatching, and mulching. Those working for chemical lawn service firms are more specialized. They inspect lawns for problems and apply fertilizers, herbicides, pesticides, and other chemicals to stimulate growth and prevent or control weed, disease, or insect infestation, as well as practice integrated pest management techniques. *Lawn service managers* oversee operations, negotiate fees, schedule jobs, and hire and train new workers.

Groundskeeping laborers, also called groundskeepers or grounds maintenance personnel, maintain a variety of facilities including athletic fields, golf courses, cemeteries, university campuses, and parks. Many of their duties are similar to those of landscaping laborers. However, they also rake and mulch leaves, clear snow from walkways and parking lots, employ irrigation methods to adjust the amount of water consumption and prevent waste, and apply pesticides. They see to the proper upkeep and repair of sidewalks, parking lots, groundskeeping equipment, pools, fountains, fences, planters, and benches. *Grounds managers* may participate in many of the same tasks as maintenance personnel but typically have more extensive knowledge in horticulture, turf management, ornamental plants, landscape design and construction, pest management, irrigation, and erosion control. In addition, grounds managers have supervisory responsibilities and must manage and train personnel, draw up work contracts, efficiently allocate labor and financial resources, and engage in public relations activities.

Groundskeepers who care for athletic fields keep natural and artificial turf fields in top condition and mark out boundaries and paint turf with team logos and names before events. Groundskeepers must make sure the underlying soil on natural turf fields has the required composition to allow proper drainage and to support the appropriate grasses used on the field. They regularly mow, water, fertilize, and aerate the fields. In addition, groundskeepers apply chemicals and fungicides to control weeds, kill pests, and prevent diseases. Groundskeepers also vacuum and disinfect synthetic turf after use in order to prevent growth of harmful bacteria. They periodically remove the turf and replace the cushioning pad.

Workers who maintain golf courses work under the direction of *golf course superintendents* and are called *greenskeepers*. Greenskeepers do many of the same things other groundskeepers do. In addition, greenskeepers periodically relocate the holes on putting greens to eliminate uneven wear of the turf and to add interest and challenge to the game. Greenskeepers also keep canopies, benches, ball washers, and tee markers repaired and freshly painted.

Some groundskeepers specialize in caring for cemeteries and memorial gardens. They dig graves to specified depth, generally using a backhoe. They may place concrete slabs on the bottom and around the sides of the grave to line it for greater support. When readying a site for the burial ceremony, they position the casket-lowering device over the grave, cover the immediate area with an artificial grass carpet, erect a canopy, and arrange folding chairs to accommodate mourners. They regularly mow grass, apply fertilizers and other chemicals, prune shrubs and trees, plant flowers, and remove debris from graves. They also must periodically build the ground up around new gravesites to compensate for settling.

Groundskeepers in parks and recreation facilities care for lawns, trees, and shrubs, maintain athletic fields and playgrounds, clean buildings, and keep parking lots, picnic areas, and other public spaces free of litter. They may also remove snow and ice from roads and walkways, erect and dismantle snow fences, and maintain swimming pools. These workers inspect buildings and equipment, make needed repairs, and keep everything freshly painted.

Landscaping, groundskeeping, and lawn service workers use hand tools such as shovels, rakes, pruning saws, saws, hedge and brush trimmers, and axes, as well as power lawnmowers, chain saws, snow blowers, and electric clippers. Some use equipment such as tractors and twin-axle vehicles. Park, school, cemetery, and golf course groundskeepers may use sod cutters to harvest sod that will be replanted elsewhere. Athletic turf groundskeepers use vacuums and other devices to remove water from athletic fields. In addition, some workers in large operations use spraying and dusting equipment. Landscape contractors and those in managerial positions increasingly use computers to develop plans and blueprints, to estimate and track project costs, and to maintain payroll and personnel information.

Working Conditions

Many of the jobs for landscaping, groundskeeping, and nursery workers are seasonal, mainly in the spring, summer, and fall when most planting, mowing and trimming, and cleanup are necessary. The work, most of which is performed outdoors in all kinds of weather, can be physically demanding and repetitive, involving much bending, lifting, and shoveling. Landscaping and groundskeeping workers may be under pressure to get the job completed, especially when preparing for scheduled events, such as athletic competitions or burials.

Those who work with pesticides, fertilizers, and other chemicals, as well as potentially dangerous equipment and tools such as power lawnmowers, chain saws, and power clippers, must exercise safety precautions. Workers who use motorized equipment must take care to protect against hearing damage.

Employment

Landscaping, groundskeeping, nursery, greenhouse, and lawn service workers held about 1,285,000 jobs in 1998. Employment was distributed as follows:

Landscaping and groundskeeping laborers 1,130,000
Lawn service managers 86,000
Pruners 45,000
Sprayers and applicators 19,000
Nursery and greenhouse managers 5,000

About one-third of wage and salaried workers were employed in companies providing landscape and horticultural services. Others worked for firms operating and building real estate, amusement and recreation facilities such as golf courses and race tracks, and retail nurseries and garden stores. Some were employed by local governments, installing and maintaining landscaping for parks, schools, hospitals, and other public facilities.

Almost 2 out of every 10 landscaping, groundskeeping, nursery, greenhouse, and lawn service workers were self-employed, providing landscape maintenance directly to customers on a contract basis. About 1 of every 6 worked part time, many of whom were school age.

Training, Other Qualifications, and Advancement

There usually are no minimum educational requirements for entry-level laborer positions in landscaping, groundskeeping, nurs-

ery, greenhouse, and lawn service occupations. In 1998, more than 4 in 10 workers did not have a high school diploma, although this diploma is necessary for some jobs. Short-term on-the-job training usually is sufficient to teach new hires how to operate equipment such as mowers, trimmers, leaf blowers, and small tractors, and follow correct safety procedures. Entry-level workers must be able to follow directions and learn proper planting procedures. If driving is an essential part of a job, employers look for applicants with a good driving record and some experience driving a truck. Workers who deal directly with customers must get along well with people. Employers also look for responsible, self-motivated individuals, because many gardeners and groundskeepers work with little supervision.

Laborers who demonstrate a willingness to work hard and quickly, have good communication skills, and take an interest in the business may advance to crew leader or other supervisory positions. Advancement or entry into positions as grounds manager or landscape contractor usually requires some formal education beyond high school, and several years of progressively responsible experience.

Prospective grounds managers or landscape contractors should be knowledgeable about turf care, horticulture, ornamental plants, soils, and erosion prevention and irrigation techniques. They must be familiar with all landscaping and grounds maintenance equipment, and know how and when to mix and apply fertilizers and pesticides. Some are responsible for designing and developing installation and maintenance plans for landscapes and proper grounds management. They also estimate and track project costs and handle personnel issues. Those in managerial positions must also be aware of local or Federal environmental regulations and building codes. Several years of hands-on experience plus a four-year bachelor's degree, a two-year associate's degree, or a one-year vocational-technical degree in grounds management or landscape design or a closely related "green" discipline usually provide a good background for those who wish to deal with the full range of landscaping responsibilities. Some schools offer cooperative education programs in which students work alternate semesters or quarters for a lawn care or landscape contractor.

Most States require certification for workers who apply pesticides. Certification requirements vary, but usually include passing a test on the proper and safe use and disposal of insecticides, herbicides, and fungicides. Some States require that landscape contractors be licensed.

The Professional Grounds Management Society (PGMS) offers certification to grounds managers who have a combination of eight years of experience and formal education beyond high school and who pass an examination covering subjects such as equipment management, personnel management, environmental issues, turf care, ornamentals, and circulatory systems. The PGMS also offers certification to groundskeepers who have a high school diploma or equivalent, plus two years of experience in the grounds maintenance field.

The Associated Landscape Contractors of America (ALCA) offers the designations Certified Landscape Professional or Certified Landscape Technician to those who meet established education and experience standards and pass an ALCA examination. The hands-on test for technicians covers areas such as maintenance equipment operation and the installation of plants by reading a plan. A written safety test is also administered.

Some workers in landscaping, groundskeeping, nursery, greenhouse, and lawn service occupations open their own business after several years of experience.

Job Outlook

Those interested in landscaping, groundskeeping, nursery, greenhouse, and lawn service occupations should find excellent job opportunities in the future. Because of high turnover, a large number of job openings is expected to result from the need to replace workers who transfer to other occupations or leave the labor force. These occupations attract many part-time workers. Some take landscaping, groundskeeping, or nursery jobs to earn money for school or only until they find a better-paying job. Because wages for beginners are low and the work is physically demanding, many employers have difficulty attracting enough workers to fill all openings.

Employment of landscaping, groundskeeping, nursery, greenhouse, and lawn service workers is expected to grow about as fast as the average for all occupations through the year 2008 in response to increasing demand for landscaping, groundskeeping, and related services. Expected growth in the construction of commercial and industrial buildings, shopping malls, homes, highways, and recreational facilities should contribute to demand for these workers. Developers will continue to use landscaping services, both interior and exterior, to attract prospective buyers and tenants.

The upkeep and renovation of existing landscaping and grounds are growing sources of demand for landscaping, groundskeeping, and lawn service workers. Owners of many existing buildings and facilities, including colleges and universities, recognize the importance of curb appeal and are expected to use these services more extensively to maintain and upgrade their properties. In recent years, the large number of baby boomers, wishing to conserve leisure time by contracting out for basic yard services, spurred employment growth in landscaping and lawn service occupations. Homeowners are expected to continue using such services to maintain the beauty and value of their properties. As the "echo" boom generation (children of baby boomers) comes of age, the demand for parks, athletic fields, and recreational facilities also can be expected to add to the demand for landscaping, groundskeeping, and lawn service workers. The need for nursery and greenhouse laborers and managers will grow because of the continued popularity of home gardening, as well as the need to cultivate and provide the vegetation used by landscaping services.

Job opportunities for nonseasonal work are more numerous in regions with temperate climates where landscaping and lawn services are required all year. However, opportunities may vary depending on local economic conditions.

Earnings

Earnings vary widely depending on the particular landscaping position and experience, ranging from the minimum wage in some beginning laborer positions to more than $20.00 an hour in some manager jobs. The following table presents 1998 median hourly earnings for landscaping, groundskeeping, nursery, greenhouse, and lawn service occupations:

Lawn service managers $12.22
Nursery and greenhouse managers....................................12.19
Pruners 10.61
Sprayers and applicators 10.41
Landscaping and groundskeeping laborers 8.24

Median hourly earnings in the industries employing the largest numbers of landscaping and groundskeeping laborers in 1997 are shown below:

Concrete work $10.40
Local government, except education and hospitals 10.00
Real estate operators and lessors 7.70
Landscape and horticultural services 7.70
Miscellaneous amusement and recreation services 7.50

Related Occupations

Landscaping, groundskeeping, nursery, greenhouse, and lawn service workers perform most of their work outdoors and have some knowledge of plants and soils. Others whose jobs may be performed outdoors and are otherwise related are botanists, construction workers, landscape architects, farmers, horticultural workers, tree surgeon helpers, forest conservation workers, and soil conservation technicians.

Sources of Additional Information

For career and certification information, contact:

- Associated Landscape Contractors of America, Inc., 150 Elden Street, Suite 270, Herndon, VA 20170.
- Professional Grounds Management Society, 120 Cockeysville Rd., Suite 104, Hunt Valley, MD 21030.

Lawyers and Judicial Workers

(O*NET 28102, 28105, and 28108)

Significant Points

- Formal educational requirements for lawyers include a four-year college degree, three years in law school, and successful completion of a written bar examination.
- Competition for admission to most law schools is intense.
- Aspiring lawyers and judges should encounter significant competition for jobs.

Nature of the Work

The legal system affects nearly every aspect of our society, from buying a home to crossing the street. Lawyers and judicial workers form the backbone of this vital system, linking the legal system and society in myriad ways. For this reason, they hold positions of great responsibility and are obligated to adhere to a strict code of ethics.

Lawyers, also called *attorneys*, act both as advocates and advisors in our society. As advocates, they represent one of the parties in criminal and civil trials by presenting evidence and arguing in court to support their client. As advisors, lawyers counsel their clients concerning their legal rights and obligations and suggest particular courses of action in business and personal matters. Whether acting as advocate or advisor, all attorneys research the intent of laws and judicial decisions and apply the law to the specific circumstances faced by their client.

The more detailed aspects of a lawyer's job depend upon his or her field of specialization and position. While all lawyers are licensed to represent parties in court, some appear in court more frequently than others. Trial lawyers, who specialize in trial work, must be able to think quickly and speak with ease and authority. In addition, familiarity with courtroom rules and strategy are particularly important in trial work. Still, trial lawyers spend the majority of their time outside the courtroom conducting research, interviewing clients and witnesses, and handling other details in preparation for trial.

Lawyers may specialize in a number of different areas, such as bankruptcy, probate, international, or elder law. Those specializing in environmental law, for example, may represent public interest groups, waste disposal companies, or construction firms in their dealings with the Environmental Protection Agency (EPA) and other State and Federal agencies. They help clients prepare and file for licenses and applications for approval before certain activities may occur. In addition, they represent clients' interests in administrative adjudications.

Some lawyers concentrate in the growing field of intellectual property. These lawyers help protect clients' claims to copyrights, art work under contract, product designs, and computer programs. Still other lawyers advise insurance companies about the legality of insurance transactions. They write insurance policies to conform with the law and to protect companies from unwarranted claims. When claims are filed against insurance companies, they review the claims and represent the companies in court.

The majority of lawyers are found in private practice, where they concentrate on criminal or civil law. In criminal law, lawyers represent individuals who have been charged with crimes and argue their cases in courts of law. Attorneys dealing with civil law assist clients with litigation, wills, trusts, contracts, mortgages, titles, and leases. Other lawyers handle only public interest cases—civil or criminal—which may have an impact extending well beyond the individual client.

Lawyers are sometimes employed full time by a single client. If the client is a corporation, the lawyer is known as "house counsel," and he or she usually advises the company concerning legal issues related to its business activities. These issues might involve patents, government regulations, contracts with other companies, property interests, or collective bargaining agreements with unions.

A significant number of attorneys are employed at the various levels of government. Lawyers who work for State attorneys general, prosecutors, public defenders, and courts play a key role in the criminal justice system. At the Federal level, attorneys investigate cases for the Department of Justice and other agencies. Government lawyers also help develop programs, draft and interpret laws and legislation, establish enforcement procedures, and argue civil and criminal cases on behalf of the government.

Other lawyers work for legal aid societies—private, nonprofit organizations established to serve disadvantaged people. These lawyers generally handle civil, rather than criminal cases. A relatively small number of trained attorneys work in law schools. Most are faculty members who specialize in one or more subjects; however, some serve as administrators. Others work full time in nonacademic settings and teach part time.

To perform the varied tasks described above more efficiently, lawyers increasingly utilize various forms of technology. While all lawyers continue to use law libraries to prepare cases, some supplement their search of conventional printed sources with computer sources, such as the Internet and legal databases. Software is used to search this legal literature automatically and to identify legal texts relevant to a specific case. In litigation involving many supporting documents, lawyers may use computers to organize and index material. Lawyers also use electronic filing, videoconferencing, and voice-recognition technology to more effectively share information with other parties involved in a case.

Many attorneys advance to become *judges* and other *judicial workers*. Judges apply the law and oversee the legal process in courts according to local, State, and Federal statutes. They preside over cases concerning every aspect of society, from traffic offenses to disputes over management of professional sports, or from the rights of huge corporations to questions of disconnecting life support equipment for terminally ill persons. They must ensure that trials and hearings are conducted fairly and that the court administers justice in a manner that safeguards the legal rights of all parties involved.

The most visible responsibility of judges is presiding over trials or hearings and listening as attorneys represent the parties present. Judges rule on the admissibility of evidence and the methods of conducting testimony, and they may be called upon to settle disputes between opposing attorneys. They ensure that rules and procedures are followed, and if unusual circumstances arise for which standard procedures have not been established, judges determine the manner in which the trial will proceed based on their interpretation of the law.

Judges often hold pretrial hearings for cases. They listen to allegations and determine whether the evidence presented merits a trial. In criminal cases, judges may decide that persons charged with crimes should be held in jail pending their trial, or they may set conditions for release. In civil cases, judges occasionally impose restrictions upon the parties until a trial is held.

In many trials, juries are selected to decide guilt or innocence in criminal cases or liability and compensation in civil cases. Judges instruct juries on applicable laws, direct them to deduce the facts from the evidence presented, and hear their verdict. When the law does not require a jury trial or when the parties waive their right to a jury, judges decide the cases. In such cases, the judge determines guilt and imposes sentences in a criminal case; in civil cases, the judge rewards relief—such as compensation for damages—to the parties in the lawsuit (also called litigants).

Judges also work outside the courtroom "in chambers." In their private offices, judges read documents on pleadings and motions, research legal issues, write opinions, and oversee the court's operations. In some jurisdictions, judges also manage the courts' administrative and clerical staff.

Judges' duties vary according to the extent of their jurisdictions and powers. *General trial court judges* of the Federal and State court systems have jurisdiction over any case in their system. They usually try civil cases transcending the jurisdiction of lower courts and all cases involving felony offenses. Federal and State *appellate court judges*, although few in number, have the power to overrule decisions made by trial court or administrative law judges if they determine that legal errors were made in a case or if legal precedent does not support the judgment of the lower court. They rule on a small number of cases and rarely have direct contacts with litigants. Instead, they usually base their decisions on lower court records and lawyers' written and oral arguments.

Many State court judges preside in courts in which jurisdiction is limited by law to certain types of cases. A variety of titles are assigned to these judges, but among the most common are *municipal court judge, county court judge, magistrate,* or *justice of the peace.* Traffic violations, misdemeanors, small claims cases, and pretrial hearings constitute the bulk of the work of these judges, but some States allow them to handle cases involving domestic relations, probate, contracts, and other selected areas of the law.

Administrative law judges, sometimes called *hearing officers* or *adjudicators,* are employed by government agencies to make determinations for administrative agencies. They make decisions on a person's eligibility for various Social Security benefits or worker's compensation, protection of the environment, enforcement of health and safety regulations, employment discrimination, and compliance with economic regulatory requirements.

Working Conditions

Lawyers and judicial workers do most of their work in offices, law libraries, and courtrooms. Lawyers sometimes meet in clients' homes or places of business and, when necessary, in hospitals or prisons. They may travel to attend meetings, gather evidence, and appear before courts, legislative bodies, and other authorities.

Salaried lawyers usually have structured work schedules. Lawyers in private practice may work irregular hours while conducting research, conferring with clients, or preparing briefs during nonoffice hours. Lawyers often work long hours; about half regularly work 50 hours or more per week. They may face particularly heavy pressure, especially when a case is being tried. Preparation for court includes keeping abreast of the latest laws and judicial decisions.

Although work is not generally seasonal, the work of tax lawyers and other specialists may be an exception. Because lawyers in private practice can often determine their own workload and when they will retire, many stay in practice well beyond the usual retirement age.

Many judges work a standard 40-hour week, but a third of all judges work over 50 hours per week. Some judges with limited jurisdiction are employed part time and divide their time between their judicial responsibilities and other careers.

Employment

Lawyers held about 681,000 jobs in 1998; judges, magistrates and other judicial workers about 71,000. About 7 out of 10 lawyers practiced privately, either in law firms or in solo practices. Most of the remaining lawyers held positions in government, the greatest number at the local level. In the Federal Government, lawyers work for many different agencies but are concentrated in the Departments of Justice, Treasury, and Defense. A small number of lawyers are employed as house counsel by public utilities, banks, insurance companies, real estate agencies, manufacturing firms, welfare and religious organizations, and other business firms and nonprofit organizations. Some salaried lawyers also have part-time independent practices; others work as lawyers part time while working full time in another occupation.

All judges, magistrates, and other judicial workers were employed by Federal, State, or local governments; about 4 out of 10 held positions in the Federal government.

Training, Other Qualifications, and Advancement

To practice law in the courts of any State or other jurisdiction, a person must be licensed, or admitted to its bar, under rules established by the jurisdiction's highest court. All States require that applicants for admission to the bar pass a written bar examination; most jurisdictions also require applicants to pass a separate written ethics examination. Lawyers who have been admitted to the bar in one jurisdiction may occasionally be admitted to the bar in another without taking an examination if they meet that jurisdiction's standards of good moral character and have a specified period of legal experience. Federal courts and agencies set their own qualifications for those practicing before them.

To qualify for the bar examination in most States, an applicant must usually obtain a college degree and graduate from a law school accredited by the American Bar Association (ABA) or the proper State authorities. ABA accreditation signifies that the law school—particularly its library and faculty—meets certain standards developed to promote quality legal education. ABA currently accredits 183 law schools; others are approved by State authorities only. With certain exceptions, graduates of schools not approved by the ABA are restricted to taking the bar examination and practicing in the State or other jurisdiction in which the school is located; most of these schools are in California. In 1997, seven States accepted the study of law in a law office or in combination with study in a law school; only California accepts the study of law by correspondence as qualifying for taking the bar examination. Several States require registration and approval of students by the State Board of Law Examiners either before they enter law school or during the early years of legal study.

Although there is no nationwide bar examination, 47 States, the District of Columbia, Guam, the Northern Mariana Islands, Puerto

Rico and the Virgin Islands require the six-hour Multistate Bar Examination (MBE) as part of the bar examination; the MBE is not required in Indiana, Louisiana, and Washington. The MBE covers issues of broad interest and is sometimes given in addition to a locally prepared State bar examination. The three-hour Multistate Essay Examination (MEE) is used as part of the State bar examination in several States. States vary in their use of MBE and MEE scores.

Many states have begun to require Multistate Performance Testing (MPT) to test the practical skills of beginning lawyers. This program has been well received, and many more States are expected to require performance testing in the future. Requirements vary by State, although the test usually is taken at the same time as the bar exam and is a one-time requirement.

The required college and law school education usually takes seven years of full-time study after high school: four years of undergraduate study followed by three years in law school. Although some law schools accept a very small number of students after three years of college, most require applicants to have a bachelor's degree. To meet the needs of students who can attend only part time, a number of law schools have night or part-time divisions that usually require four years of study; about 1 in 10 graduates from ABA approved schools attends part time.

Although there is no recommended "prelaw" major, prospective lawyers should develop proficiency in writing and speaking, reading, researching, analyzing, and thinking logically—skills needed to succeed both in law school and in the profession. Regardless of major, a multidisciplinary background is recommended. Courses in English, foreign languages, public speaking, government, philosophy, history, economics, mathematics, and computer science, among others, are useful. Students interested in a particular aspect of law may find related courses helpful. For example, prospective patent lawyers need a strong background in engineering or science, and future tax lawyers must have extensive knowledge of accounting.

Acceptance by most law schools depends on the applicant's ability to demonstrate an aptitude for the study of law, usually through good undergraduate grades, the Law School Admission Test (LSAT), the quality of the applicant's undergraduate school, any prior work experience, and sometimes a personal interview. However, law schools vary in the weight they place on each of these and other factors.

All law schools approved by the ABA, except for those in Puerto Rico, require applicants to take the LSAT. Nearly all law schools require applicants to have certified transcripts sent to the Law School Data Assembly Service, which then sends applicants' LSAT scores and their standardized records of college grades to the law schools of their choice. Both this service and the LSAT are administered by the Law School Admission Council.

Competition for admission to many law schools is intense, especially for the most prestigious schools. Enrollments in these schools rose very rapidly during the 1970s, as applicants far outnumbered available seats. Although the number of applicants decreased markedly in the 1990s, the number of applicants to most law schools still greatly exceeds the number that can be admitted.

During the first year or year and a half of law school, students usually study core courses such as constitutional law, contracts, property law, torts, civil procedure, and legal writing. In the remaining time, they may elect specialized courses in fields such as tax, labor, or corporate law. Law students often acquire practical experience by participation in school-sponsored legal clinic activities, in the school's moot court competitions in which students conduct appellate arguments, in practice trials under the supervision of experienced lawyers and judges, and through research and writing on legal issues for the school's law journal.

A number of law schools have clinical programs in which students gain legal experience through practice trials and law school projects under the supervision of practicing lawyers and law school faculty. Law school clinical programs might include work in legal aid clinics, for example, or on the staff of legislative committees. Part-time or summer clerkships in law firms, government agencies, and corporate legal departments also provide valuable experience. Such training can lead directly to a job after graduation and help students decide what kind of practice best suits them. Clerkships may also be an important source of financial aid.

In 1997, law students in 52 jurisdictions were required to pass the Multistate Professional Responsibility Examination (MPRE), which tests their knowledge of the ABA codes on professional responsibility and judicial conduct. In some States, the MPRE may be taken during law school, usually after completing a course on legal ethics.

Law school graduates receive the degree of *juris doctor* (J.D.) as the first professional degree. Advanced law degrees may be desirable for those planning to specialize, research, or teach. Some law students pursue joint degree programs, which usually require an additional semester or year. Joint degree programs are offered in a number of areas, including law and business administration or public administration.

After graduation, lawyers must keep informed about legal and non-legal developments that affect their practice. Currently, 39 States and jurisdictions mandate Continuing Legal Education (CLE). Many law schools and State and local bar associations provide continuing education courses that help lawyers stay abreast of recent developments. Some States allow CLE credits to be obtained through participation in seminars on the Internet.

The practice of law involves a great deal of responsibility. Individuals planning careers in law should like to work with people and be able to win the respect and confidence of their clients, associates, and the public. Perseverance, creativity, and reasoning ability are also essential to lawyers, who often analyze complex cases and handle new and unique legal problems.

Most beginning lawyers start in salaried positions. Newly hired, salaried attorneys usually start as associates and work with more experienced lawyers or judges. After several years of gaining more responsibilities, some lawyers are admitted to partnership in their firm or go into practice for themselves. Others become full-time law school faculty or administrators; a growing number of these lawyers have advanced degrees in other fields as well.

Some attorneys use their legal training in administrative or managerial positions in various departments of large corporations. A transfer from a corporation's legal department to another department often is viewed as a way to gain administrative experience and rise in the ranks of management.

A number of lawyers become judges, and most judges have first been lawyers. In fact, Federal and State judges are usually required to be lawyers. About 40 States allow nonlawyers to hold limited jurisdiction judgeships, but opportunities are better for those with law experience. Federal administrative law judges must be lawyers and pass a competitive examination administered by the U.S. Office of Personnel Management. Some State administrative law judges and other hearing officials are not required to be lawyers, but law degrees are preferred for most positions.

Federal judges are appointed for life by the President and are confirmed by the Senate. Federal administrative law judges are appointed by the various Federal agencies with virtually lifetime tenure. Some State judges are appointed, and the remainder are elected in partisan or nonpartisan State elections. Many State and local judges serve fixed renewable terms, which range from four or six years for some trial court judgeships to as long as 14 years or life for other trial or appellate court judges. Judicial nominating commissions, composed of members of the bar and the public, are used to screen candidates for judgeships in many States and for some Federal judgeships.

All States have some type of orientation for newly elected or appointed judges. The Federal Judicial Center, ABA, National Judicial College, and National Center for State Courts provide judicial education and training for judges and other judicial branch personnel. General and continuing education courses usually last from a couple of days to three weeks in length. Over half of all States and Puerto Rico require judges to enroll in continuing education courses while serving on the bench.

Job Outlook

Individuals interested in pursuing careers as lawyers or judicial workers should encounter stiff competition through 2008. The number of law school graduates is expected to continue to strain the economy's capacity to absorb them. As for judges, the prestige associated with serving on the bench should ensure continued, intense competition for openings.

Employment of lawyers grew very rapidly from the early 1970s through the early 1990s but has started to level off recently. Through 2008, employment is expected to grow about as fast as the average for all occupations. Continuing demand for lawyers will result primarily from growth in the population and the general level of business activities. Demand will also be spurred by growth of legal action in such areas as health care, intellectual property, international law, elder law, environmental law, and sexual harassment. In addition, the wider availability and affordability of legal clinics and prepaid legal service programs should result in increased use of legal services by middle-income people.

However, employment growth is expected to be slower than in the past. In an effort to reduce the money spent on legal fees, many businesses are increasingly utilizing large accounting firms and paralegals to perform some of the same functions as lawyers. For example, accounting firms may provide employee benefit counseling, process documents, or handle various other services previously performed by the law firm. Also, mediation and dispute resolution are increasingly used as alternatives to litigation.

Competition for job openings should continue to be keen because of the large numbers graduating from law school each year. During the 1970s, the annual number of law school graduates more than doubled, outpacing the rapid growth of jobs. Growth in the yearly number of law school graduates slowed during the early to mid-1980s, but increased again to current levels in the late 1980s to early 1990s. Although graduates with superior academic records from well-regarded law schools will have more job opportunities, most graduates should encounter stiff competition for jobs.

Perhaps as a result of this fierce competition, lawyers are increasingly finding work in nontraditional areas for which legal training is an asset but not normally a requirement—for example, administrative, managerial, and business positions in banks, insurance firms, real estate companies, government agencies, and other organizations. Employment opportunities are expected to continue to arise in these organizations at a growing rate.

As in the past, some graduates may have to accept positions in areas outside their field of interest or for which they feel overqualified. Some recent law school graduates who are unable to find permanent positions are turning to the growing number of temporary staffing firms that place attorneys in short-term jobs until they are able to secure full-time positions. This service allows companies to hire lawyers on an "as needed" basis and allows beginning lawyers to develop practical skills while looking for permanent positions.

Due to the competition for jobs, a law graduate's geographic mobility and work experience assume greater importance. The willingness to relocate may be an advantage in getting a job, but to be licensed in another State, a lawyer may have to take an additional State bar examination. In addition, employers increasingly seek graduates who have advanced law degrees and experience in a specialty such as tax, patent, or admiralty law.

Employment growth for lawyers will continue to be concentrated in salaried jobs, as businesses and all levels of government employ a growing number of staff attorneys, and as employment in the legal services industry grows in larger law firms. Most salaried positions are in urban areas where government agencies, law firms, and big corporations are concentrated. The number of self-employed lawyers is expected to increase slowly, reflecting the difficulty of establishing a profitable new practice in the face of competition from larger, established law firms. Moreover, the growing complexity of law, which encourages specialization, along with the cost of maintaining up-to-date legal research materials, favors larger firms.

For lawyers who wish to work independently, establishing a new practice will probably be easiest in small towns and expanding suburban areas. In such communities, competition from larger established law firms is likely to be less than in big cities, and new lawyers may find it easier to become known to potential clients.

Some lawyers are adversely affected by cyclical swings in the economy. During recessions, the demand declines for some discretionary legal services, such as planning estates, drafting wills, and handling real estate transactions. Also, corporations are less likely to litigate cases when declining sales and profits result in budgetary restrictions. Some corporations and law firms will not hire new attorneys until business improves or may cut staff to contain costs. Several factors, however, mitigate the overall impact of recessions on lawyers. During recessions, for example, individuals and corporations face other legal problems, such as bankruptcies, foreclosures, and divorces requiring legal action.

Employment of judges is expected to grow more slowly than the average for all occupations. Contradictory social forces affect the demand for judges. Growing public concerns about crime, safety, and efficient administration of justice should spur demand, while public budgetary pressures will limit job growth.

Competition for judgeships should remain intense. As in the past, most job openings will arise as judges retire. Although judges traditionally have held their positions until late in life, early retirement is becoming more common, a factor which should increase job openings. Nevertheless, becoming a judge will still be difficult; not only must judicial candidates compete with other qualified people, they often must also gain political support in order to be elected or appointed.

Earnings

In 1998, the median annual earnings of all lawyers was $78,170. The middle half of the occupation earned between $51,450 and $114,520. The bottom decile earned less than $37,310. Median annual earnings in the industries employing the largest numbers of lawyers in 1997 are shown below.

Legal services	$78,700
Federal government	78,200
Fire, marine, and casualty insurance	74,400
State government	59,400
Local government	49,200

Median salaries of lawyers six months after graduation from law school in 1998 varied by type of work, as indicated by Table 1.

TABLE 1

Median salaries of lawyers six months after graduation, 1998

All graduates	$45,000

Type of work	
Private practice	60,000
Business/industry	50,000
Academe	38,000
Judicial clerkship	37,500
Government	36,000
Public interest	31,000

SOURCE: National Association for Law Placement

Salaries of experienced attorneys vary widely according to the type, size, and location of their employer. Lawyers who own their own practices usually earn less than those who are partners in law firms. Lawyers starting their own practice may need to work part time in

other occupations to supplement their income until their practice is well established.

Earnings among judicial workers also vary significantly. According to the Administrative Office of the U.S. Courts, the Chief Justice of the United States Supreme Court earned $175,400, and the Associate Justices earned $167,900. Federal district court judges had salaries of $136,700 in 1998, as did judges in the Court of Federal Claims and the Court of International Trade; circuit court judges earned $145,000 a year. Federal judges with limited jurisdiction, such as magistrates and bankruptcy court judges, had salaries of $125,800.

According to a survey by the National Center for State Courts, annual salaries of associate justices of States' highest courts averaged $105,100 in 1997, and ranged from about $77,100 to $137,300. Salaries of State intermediate appellate court judges averaged $103,700, and ranged from $79,400 to $124,200. Salaries of State judges of general jurisdiction trial courts averaged $94,000, and ranged from $72,000 to $115,300.

Most salaried lawyers and judges are provided health and life insurance, and contributions are made on their behalf to retirement plans. Lawyers who practice independently are covered only if they arrange and pay for such benefits themselves.

Related Occupations

Legal training is useful in many other occupations. Some of these are arbitrator, mediator, journalist, patent agent, title examiner, legislative assistant, lobbyist, FBI special agent, political office holder, and corporate executive.

Sources of Additional Information

Information on law schools and a career in law may be obtained from:

- American Bar Association, 750 North Lake Shore Dr., Chicago, IL 60611. Internet: http://www.abanet.org

Information on the LSAT, the Law School Data Assembly Service, applying to law school, and financial aid for law students may be obtained from:

- Law School Admission Council, P.O. Box 40, Newtown, PA 18940. Internet: http://www.lsac.org

Information on acquiring a job as a lawyer with the Federal government may be obtained from the Office of Personnel Management through a telephone-based system. Consult your telephone directory under U.S. Government for a local number or call (912) 757-3000; TDD (912) 744-2299. This number is not toll-free, and charges may result. Information also is available from their Internet site: http://www.usajobs.opm.gov.

The requirements for admission to the bar in a particular State or other jurisdiction may also be obtained at the State capital from the clerk of the Supreme Court or the administrator of the State Board of Bar Examiners.

Librarians

(O*NET 31502A and 31502B)

Significant Points

- A master's degree in library science is usually required; special librarians often need an additional graduate or professional degree.

- Applicants for librarian jobs in large cities or suburban areas will face competition, while those willing to work in rural areas should have better job prospects.

Nature of the Work

The traditional concept of a library is being redefined, from a place to access paper records or books, to one which also houses the most advanced mediums, including CD-ROM, the Internet, virtual libraries, and remote access to a wide range of resources. Consequently, librarians are increasingly combining traditional duties with tasks involving quickly changing technology. Librarians assist people in finding information and using it effectively in their personal and professional lives. They must have knowledge of a wide variety of scholarly and public information sources, and follow trends related to publishing, computers, and the media to effectively oversee the selection and organization of library materials. Librarians manage staff and develop and direct information programs and systems for the public to ensure information is organized to meet users' needs.

Most librarian positions incorporate three aspects of library work: user services, technical services, and administrative services. Even librarians specializing in one of these areas perform other responsibilities. Librarians in user services, such as reference and children's librarians, work with the public to help them find the information they need. This involves analyzing users' needs to determine what information is appropriate and searching for, acquiring, and providing information. It also includes an instructional role, such as showing users how to access information. For example, librarians commonly help users navigate the Internet, showing them how to most efficiently search for relevant information. Librarians in technical services, such as acquisitions and cataloguing, acquire and prepare materials for use and often do not deal directly with the public. Librarians in administrative services oversee the management and planning of libraries; negotiate contracts for services, materials, and equipment; supervise library employees; perform public relations and fundraising duties; prepare budgets; and direct activities to ensure that everything functions properly.

In small libraries or information centers, librarians usually handle all aspects of the work. They read book reviews, publishers' announcements, and catalogues to keep up with current literature and other available resources, and they select and purchase materials from publishers, wholesalers, and distributors. Librarians prepare new materials by classifying them by subject matter, and describe books and other library materials so they are easy to find.

They supervise assistants who prepare cards, computer records, or other access tools that direct users to resources. In large libraries, librarians often specialize in a single area, such as acquisitions, cataloguing, bibliography, reference, special collections, or administration. Teamwork is increasingly important to ensure quality service to the public.

Librarians also compile lists of books, periodicals, articles, and audiovisual materials on particular subjects, analyze collections, and recommend materials. They collect and organize books, pamphlets, manuscripts, and other materials in a specific field, such as rare books, genealogy, or music. In addition, they coordinate programs such as storytelling for children and literacy skills and book talks for adults; conduct classes; publicize services; provide reference help; write grants; and oversee other administrative matters.

Librarians are classified according to the type of library in which they work—public libraries, school library media centers, academic libraries, and special libraries. Some librarians work with specific groups, such as children, young adults, adults, or the disadvantaged. In school library media centers, librarians help teachers develop curricula, acquire materials for classroom instruction, and sometimes team-teach.

Librarians also work in information centers or libraries maintained by government agencies, corporations, law firms, advertising agencies, museums, professional associations, medical centers, hospitals, religious organizations, and research laboratories. They build and arrange an organization's information resources, which are usually limited to subjects of special interest to the organization. These special librarians can provide vital information services by preparing abstracts and indexes of current periodicals, organizing bibliographies, or analyzing background information and preparing reports on areas of particular interest. For instance, a special librarian working for a corporation could provide the sales department with information on competitors or new developments affecting their field.

Many libraries have access to remote databases and maintain their own computerized databases. The widespread use of automation in libraries makes database searching skills important to librarians. Librarians develop and index databases and help train users to develop searching skills for the information they need. Some libraries are forming consortiums with other libraries through electronic mail. This allows patrons to simultaneously submit information requests to several libraries. The Internet is also expanding the amount of available reference information. Librarians must be aware of how to use these resources in order to locate information.

Librarians with computer and information systems skills can work as automated systems librarians, planning and operating computer systems, and information science librarians, designing information storage and retrieval systems and developing procedures for collecting, organizing, interpreting, and classifying information. These librarians analyze and plan for future information needs. The increased use of automated information systems enables librarians to focus on administrative and budgeting responsibilities, grant writing, and specialized research requests, while delegating more technical and user services responsibilities to technicians.

Increasingly, librarians apply their information management and research skills to arenas outside of libraries—for example, database development, reference tool development, information systems, publishing, Internet coordination, marketing, and training of database users. Entrepreneurial librarians sometimes start their own consulting practices, acting as freelance librarians or information brokers and providing services to other libraries, businesses, or government agencies.

Working Conditions

Librarians spend a significant portion of time at their desks or in front of computer terminals; extended work at video display terminals can cause eyestrain and headaches. Assisting users in obtaining information for their jobs, recreational purposes, and other uses can be challenging and satisfying; at the same time, working with users under deadlines can be demanding and stressful.

More than 2 out of 10 librarians work part time. Public and college librarians often work weekends and evenings and have to work some holidays. School librarians usually have the same workday schedule as classroom teachers and similar vacation schedules. Special librarians usually work normal business hours, but in fast-paced industries, such as advertising or legal services, they can work longer hours during peak times.

Employment

Librarians held about 152,000 jobs in 1998. Most were in school and academic libraries; others were in public and special libraries. A small number of librarians worked for hospitals and religious organizations. Others worked for governments.

Training, Other Qualifications, and Advancement

A master's degree in library science (MLS) is necessary for librarian positions in most public, academic, and special libraries, and in some school libraries. The Federal government requires an MLS or the equivalent in education and experience. Many colleges and universities offer MLS programs, but employers often prefer graduates of the approximately 50 schools accredited by the American Library Association. Most MLS programs require a bachelor's degree; any liberal arts major is appropriate.

Most MLS programs take one year to complete; others take two. A typical graduate program includes courses in the foundations of library and information science, including the history of books and printing, intellectual freedom and censorship, and the role of libraries and information in society. Other basic courses cover material selection and processing, the organization of information, reference tools and strategies, and user services. Courses are adapted to educate librarians to use new resources brought about by advancing technology such as on-line reference systems, Internet search methods, and automated circulation systems. Course options can include resources for children or young adults; classification, cataloguing, indexing, and abstracting; library administration; and library automation. Computer-related course work is an increasingly important part of an MLS degree.

An MLS provides general preparation for library work, but some individuals specialize in a particular area such as reference, technical services, or children's services. A Ph.D. degree in library and

information science is advantageous for a college teaching position or a top administrative job in a college or university library or large library system.

In special libraries, an MLS is also usually required. In addition, most special librarians supplement their education with knowledge of the subject specialization, sometimes earning a master's, doctoral, or professional degree in the subject. Subject specializations include medicine, law, business, engineering, and the natural and social sciences. For example, a librarian working for a law firm may also be a licensed attorney, holding both library science and law degrees. In some jobs, knowledge of a foreign language is needed.

State certification requirements for public school librarians vary widely. Most States require school librarians, often called library media specialists, to be certified as teachers and have courses in library science. In some cases, an MLS, perhaps with a library media specialization, or a master's in education with a specialty in school library media or educational media, is needed. Some States require certification of public librarians employed in municipal, county, or regional library systems.

Librarians participate in continuing training once they are on the job to keep abreast of new information systems brought about by changing technology.

Experienced librarians can advance to administrative positions, such as department head, library director, or chief information officer.

Job Outlook

Slower than average employment growth, coupled with an increasing number of MLS graduates, will result in more applicants competing for fewer jobs. However, because MLS programs increasingly focus on computer skills, graduates will be qualified for other, computer-related occupations. Applicants for librarian jobs in large metropolitan areas, where most graduates prefer to work, will face competition; those willing to work in rural areas should have better job prospects.

Some job openings for librarians will stem from projected slower-than-average employment growth through 2008. Replacement needs will account for more job openings over the next decade, as some librarians reach retirement age.

The increasing use of computerized information storage and retrieval systems could contribute to slow growth in the demand for librarians. Computerized systems make cataloguing easier, which library technicians now handle. In addition, many libraries are equipped for users to access library computers directly from their homes or offices. These systems allow users to bypass librarians and conduct research on their own. However, librarians are needed to manage staff, help users develop database searching techniques, address complicated reference requests, and define users' needs.

Opportunities will be best for librarians outside traditional settings. Nontraditional library settings include information brokers, private corporations, and consulting firms. Many companies are turning to librarians because of their research and organizational skills and knowledge of computer databases and library automation systems. Librarians can review vast amounts of information and analyze, evaluate, and organize it according to a company's specific needs. Librarians are also hired by organizations to set up information on the Internet. Librarians working in these settings may be classified as systems analysts, database specialists and trainers, webmasters or web developers, or LAN (local area network) coordinators.

Earnings

Salaries of librarians vary according to the individual's qualifications and the type, size, and location of the library. Librarians with primarily administrative duties often have greater earnings. Median annual earnings of librarians in 1998 were $38,470. The middle 50 percent earned between $30,440 and $48,130. The lowest 10 percent earned less than $22,970, and the highest 10 percent earned more than $67,810. Median annual earnings in the industries employing the largest numbers of librarians in 1997 were as follows:

Elementary and secondary schools $38,900

Colleges and universities 38,600

Local government, except education and hospitals 32,600

The average annual salary for all librarians in the Federal government in nonsupervisory, supervisory, and managerial positions was $56,400 in 1999.

Related Occupations

Librarians play an important role in the transfer of knowledge and ideas by providing people with access to the information they need and want. Jobs requiring similar analytical, organizational, and communicative skills include archivists, information scientists, museum curators, publishers' representatives, research analysts, information brokers, and records managers. The management aspect of a librarian's work is similar to the work of managers in a variety of business and government settings. School librarians have many duties similar to those of school teachers. Other jobs requiring the computer skills of some librarians include webmasters or web developers, database specialists, and systems analysts.

Sources of Additional Information

Information on librarianship, including information on scholarships or loans, is available from the American Library Association. For a listing of accredited library education programs, check their homepage:

● American Library Association, Office for Human Resource Development and Recruitment, 50 East Huron St., Chicago, IL 60611. Internet: http://www.ala.org

For information on a career as a special librarian, write to:

● Special Libraries Association, 1700 18th St. NW., Washington, DC 20009.

Information on graduate schools of library and information science can be obtained from:

● Association for Library and Information Science Education, P.O. Box 7640, Arlington, VA 22207. Internet: http://www.sils.umich.edu/ALISE

For information on a career as a law librarian, scholarship information, and a list of ALA-accredited schools offering programs in law librarianship, contact:

● American Association of Law Libraries, 53 West Jackson Blvd., Suite 940, Chicago, IL 60604. Internet: http://www.ala.org

For information on employment opportunities as a health sciences librarian, scholarship information, credentialing information, and a list of MLA-accredited schools offering programs in health sciences librarianship, contact:

● Medical Library Association, 6 N. Michigan Ave., Suite 300, Chicago, IL 60602. Internet: http://www.mlanet.org

Information on acquiring a job as a librarian with the Federal government may be obtained from the Office of Personnel Management through a telephone-based system. Consult your telephone directory under U.S. Government for a local number or call (912) 757-3000; TDD (912) 744-2299. That number is not toll free, and charges may result. Information also is available from their Internet site: http://www.usajobs.opm.gov.

Information concerning requirements and application procedures for positions in the Library of Congress can be obtained directly from:

● Human Resources Office, Library of Congress, 101 Independence Ave. SE., Washington, DC 20540-2231.

State library agencies can furnish information on scholarships available through their offices, requirements for certification, and general information about career prospects in the State. Several of these agencies maintain job hotlines reporting openings for librarians.

State departments of education can furnish information on certification requirements and job opportunities for school librarians.

Many library science schools offer career placement services to their alumni and current students. Some allow non-affiliated students and jobseekers to use their services.

Library Assistants and Bookmobile Drivers

(O*NET 53902)

Significant Points

● Most jobs require only a high school diploma.

● Numerous opportunities should arise due to high turnover.

Nature of the Work

Library assistants and bookmobile drivers organize library resources and make them available to users. They assist librarians and, in some cases, library technicians.

Library assistants—sometimes referred to as library media assistants, library aides, or circulation assistants—register patrons so they can borrow materials from the library. They record the borrower's name and address from an application and then issue a library card. Most library assistants enter and update patrons' records using computer databases.

At the circulation desk, assistants lend and collect books, periodicals, video tapes, and other materials. When an item is borrowed, assistants stamp the due date on the material and record the patron's identification from his or her library card. They inspect returned materials for damage, check due dates, and compute fines for overdue material. They review records to compile a list of overdue materials and send out notices. They also answer patrons' questions and refer those they cannot answer to a librarian.

Throughout the library, assistants sort returned books, periodicals, and other items and return them to their designated shelves, files, or storage areas. They locate materials to be loaned, either for a patron or another library. Many card catalogues are computerized, so library assistants must be familiar with the computer system. If any materials have been damaged, these workers try to repair them. For example, they use tape or paste to repair torn pages or book covers and other specialized processes to repair more valuable materials.

Some library assistants specialize in helping patrons who have vision problems. Sometimes referred to as library, talking-books, or Braille-and-talking-books clerks, they review the borrower's list of desired reading material. They locate those materials or closely related substitutes from the library collection of large type or Braille volumes, tape cassettes, and open-reel talking books. They complete the paperwork and give or mail the materials to the borrower.

To extend library services to more patrons, many libraries operate bookmobiles. Bookmobile drivers take trucks stocked with books to designated sites on a regular schedule. Bookmobiles serve community organizations such as shopping centers, apartment complexes, schools, and nursing homes. They may also be used to extend library service to patrons living in remote areas. Depending on local conditions, drivers may operate a bookmobile alone or may be accompanied by a library technician.

When working alone, the drivers perform many of the same functions as a library assistant in a main or branch library. They answer patrons' questions, receive and check out books, collect fines, maintain the book collection, shelve materials, and occasionally operate audiovisual equipment to show slides or films. They participate and may assist in planning programs sponsored by the library such as reader advisory programs, used book sales, or outreach programs. Bookmobile drivers keep track of their mileage, the materials lent out, and the amount of fines collected. In some areas, they are responsible for maintenance of the vehicle and any photocopiers or other equipment in it. They record statistics on circulation and the number of people visiting the bookmobile. Drivers may also record requests for special items from the main library and arrange for the materials to be mailed or delivered to a patron during the next scheduled visit. Many bookmobiles are equipped with personal computers and CD-ROM systems linked to the main library system; this allows bookmobile drivers to reserve or locate books immediately. Some bookmobiles now offer Internet access to users.

Because bookmobile drivers may be the only link some people have to the library, much of their work is helping the public. They may assist handicapped or elderly patrons to the bookmobile, or shovel snow to assure their safety. They may enter hospitals or nursing homes to deliver books to patrons who are bedridden.

Working Conditions

Because most library assistants use computers on a daily basis, these workers may experience eye and muscle strain, backaches, headaches, and repetitive motion injuries. Also, assistants who review detailed data may have to sit for extended periods of time. Although the work does not require heavy lifting, library assistants spend a lot of time on their feet and frequently stoop, bend, and reach. Library assistants may work evenings and weekends, but those employed in school libraries usually work only during the school year.

Bookmobile drivers must maneuver large vehicles in all kinds of traffic and weather conditions and may also be responsible for the maintenance of the bookmobile. The schedules of bookmobile drivers depend on the size of the area being served. Some of these workers go out on their routes every day, while others go only on certain days. On these other days, they work at the library. Some also work evenings and weekends to give patrons as much access to the library as possible.

Employment

Library assistants and bookmobile drivers held about 127,000 jobs in 1998. Over one-half of these workers were employed by local government in public libraries; most of the remaining worked in school libraries. Opportunities for flexible schedules are abundant; over one-half of these workers were on part-time schedules.

Training, Other Qualifications, and Advancement

Employers typically require applicants to have at least a high school diploma or its equivalent. Most employers prefer workers who are computer-literate. Knowledge of word processing and spreadsheet software is especially valuable, as are experience working in an office and good interpersonal skills.

Library assistants often learn the skills they need in high schools, business schools, and community colleges. Business education programs offered by these institutions typically include courses in typing, word processing, shorthand, business communications, records management, and office systems and procedures.

Some entrants are college graduates with degrees in liberal arts. Although a degree is rarely required, many graduates accept entry-level positions with the hope of being promoted. Workers with college degrees are likely to start at higher salaries and advance more easily than those without degrees.

Once hired, library assistants and bookmobile drivers usually receive on-the-job training. Under the guidance of a supervisor or other senior worker, new employees learn procedures. Some formal classroom training may also be necessary, such as training in specific computer software. Library assistants and bookmobile drivers must be careful, orderly, and detail-oriented in order to avoid making errors and to recognize errors made by others. Many bookmobile drivers are now required to have a commercial driver's license.

These employees usually advance by taking on more duties in the same occupation for higher pay or transferring to a closely related occupation. Most companies fill supervisory and managerial positions by promoting individuals from within their organizations, so those who acquire additional skills, experience, and training improve their advancement opportunities. With appropriate experience and education, some may become librarians.

Job Outlook

Opportunities should be good for persons interested in jobs as library assistants or bookmobile drivers through 2008. Turnover of these workers is quite high, reflecting the limited investment in training and subsequent weak attachment to this occupation. This work is attractive to retirees, students, and others who want a part-time schedule, and there is a lot of movement into and out of the occupation. Many openings will become available each year to replace workers who transfer to other occupations or leave the labor force. Some positions become available as library assistants move within the organization. Library assistants can be promoted to library technicians and eventually supervisory positions in public service or technical service areas. Advancement opportunities are greater in larger libraries and may be more limited in smaller ones.

Employment is expected to grow about as fast as the average for all occupations through 2008. The vast majority of library assistants and bookmobile drivers work in public or school libraries. Efforts to contain costs in local governments and academic institutions of all types may result in more hiring of library support staff than librarians. Because most are employed by public institutions, library assistants and bookmobile drivers are not directly affected by the ups and downs of the business cycle. Some of these workers may lose their jobs, however, if there are cuts in government budgets.

Earnings

Salaries of library assistants and bookmobile drivers vary. The region of the country, size of city, and type and size of establishment all influence salary levels. Median annual earnings of full-time library assistants and bookmobile drivers in 1998 were $16,980.

Related Occupations

Other clerical workers who enter and manipulate data include bank tellers, statistical clerks, receiving clerks, medical record clerks, hotel and motel clerks, credit clerks, and reservation and transportation ticket agents.

Sources of Additional Information

Information about a career as a library assistant can be obtained from:

- Council on Library/Media Technology, P.O. Box 951, Oxon Hill, MD 20750. Internet: http://library.ucr.edu/COLT

Public libraries and libraries in academic institutions can provide information about job openings for library assistants and bookmobile drivers.

Library Technicians

(O*NET 31505)

Significant Points

- Training ranges from on-the-job to a bachelor's degree.
- Experienced library technicians can advance by obtaining a Master of Library Science degree.

Nature of the Work

Library technicians help librarians acquire, prepare, and organize material, and assist users in finding information. Technicians in small libraries handle a range of duties; those in large libraries usually specialize. As libraries increasingly use new technologies (such as CD-ROM, the Internet, virtual libraries, and automated databases) the duties of library technicians will expand and evolve accordingly. Library technicians are assuming greater responsibilities, in some cases taking on tasks previously performed by librarians.

Depending on the employer, library technicians can have other titles, such as library technical assistants. Library technicians direct library users to standard references, organize and maintain periodicals, prepare volumes for binding, handle interlibrary loan requests, prepare invoices, perform routine cataloguing and coding of library materials, retrieve information from computer databases, and supervise support staff.

The widespread use of computerized information storage and retrieval systems has resulted in technicians handling more technical and user services (such as entering catalogue information into the library's computer) that were once performed by librarians. Technicians assist with customizing databases. In addition, technicians instruct patrons how to use computer systems to access data. The increased use of automation has reduced the amount of clerical work performed by library technicians. Many libraries now offer self-service registration and circulation with computers, decreasing the time library technicians spend manually recording and inputting records.

Some library technicians operate and maintain audiovisual equipment, such as projectors, tape recorders, and videocassette recorders, and assist users with microfilm or microfiche readers. They also design posters, bulletin boards, or displays.

Those in school libraries encourage and teach students to use the library and media center. They also help teachers obtain instructional materials and assist students with special assignments. Some work in special libraries maintained by government agencies, corporations, law firms, advertising agencies, museums, professional societies, medical centers, and research laboratories, where they conduct literature searches, compile bibliographies, and prepare abstracts, usually on subjects of particular interest to the organization.

Working Conditions

Technicians answer questions and provide assistance to library users. Those who prepare library materials sit at desks or computer terminals for long periods and can develop headaches or eyestrain from working with video display terminals. Some duties, like calculating circulation statistics, can be repetitive and boring. Others, such as performing computer searches using local and regional library networks and cooperatives, can be interesting and challenging.

Library technicians in school libraries work regular school hours. Those in public libraries and college and university (academic) libraries also work weekends, evenings, and some holidays. Library technicians in special libraries usually work normal business hours, although they often work overtime as well.

Library technicians usually work under the supervision of a librarian, although they work independently in certain situations.

Employment

Library technicians held about 72,000 jobs in 1998. Most worked in school, academic, or public libraries. Some worked in hospitals and religious organizations. The Federal government, primarily the Department of Defense and the Library of Congress, and State and local governments also employed library technicians.

Training, Other Qualifications, and Advancement

Training requirements for library technicians vary widely, ranging from a high school diploma to specialized post-secondary training. Some employers hire individuals with work experience or other training; others train inexperienced workers on the job. Other employers require that technicians have an associate or bachelor's degree. Given the rapid spread of automation in libraries, computer skills are needed for many jobs. Knowledge of databases, library automation systems, on-line library systems, on-line public access systems, and circulation systems is valuable.

Some two-year colleges offer an associate of arts degree in library technology. Programs include both liberal arts and library-related study. Students learn about library and media organization and operation and how to order, process, catalogue, locate, and circulate library materials and work with library automation. Libraries and associations offer continuing education courses to keep technicians abreast of new developments in the field.

Library technicians usually advance by assuming added responsibilities. For example, technicians often start at the circulation desk, checking books in and out. After gaining experience, they may become responsible for storing and verifying information. As they advance, they may become involved in budget and personnel matters in their department. Some library technicians advance to supervisory positions and are in charge of the day-to-day operation of their department.

Job Outlook

Employment of library technicians is expected to grow about as fast as the average for all occupations through 2008. Some job openings will result from the need to replace library technicians who transfer to other fields or leave the labor force. Similar to other fields, willingness to relocate enhances an aspiring library technician's job prospects.

The increasing use of library automation is expected to spur job growth among library technicians. Computerized information systems have simplified certain tasks, such as descriptive cataloguing, which can now be handled by technicians instead of librarians. For instance, technicians can now easily retrieve information from a central database and store it in the library's computer. Although budgetary constraints could dampen employment growth of library technicians in school, public, and college and university libraries, libraries sometimes use technicians to perform some librarian duties in an effort to stretch shrinking budgets. Growth in the number of professionals and other workers who use special libraries should result in relatively fast employment growth among library technicians in those settings.

Earnings

Median annual earnings of library technicians in 1998 were $21,730. The middle 50 percent earned between $16,500 and $27,340. The lowest 10 percent earned less than $12,610, and the highest 10 percent earned more than $33,370. Median annual earnings in the industries employing the largest numbers of library technicians in 1997 are shown below:

Local government, except education and hospitals $22,200
Colleges and universities 21,400
Elementary and secondary schools 18,300

Salaries of library technicians in the Federal government averaged $29,700 in 1999.

Related Occupations

Library technicians perform organizational and administrative duties. Workers in other occupations with similar duties include library assistants, information clerks, record clerks, medical record technicians, and title searchers.

Sources of Additional Information

Information about a career as a library technician can be obtained from:

- Council on Library/Media Technology, P.O. Box 951, Oxon Hill, MD 20750. Internet: http://library.ucr.edu/COLT

For information on training programs for library/media technical assistants, write to:

- American Library Association, Office for Human Resource Development and Recruitment, 50 East Huron St., Chicago, IL 60611. Internet: http://www.ala.org

Information on acquiring a job as a library technician with the Federal government may be obtained from the Office of Personnel Management through a telephone-based system. Consult your telephone directory under U.S. Government for a local number or call (912) 757-3000; TDD (912) 744-2299. That number is not toll free, and charges may result. Information also is available from their Internet site: http://www.usajobs.opm.gov.

Information concerning requirements and application procedures for positions in the Library of Congress can be obtained directly from:

- Human Resources Office, Library of Congress, 101 Independence Ave. SE., Washington, DC 20540-2231.

State library agencies can furnish information on requirements for technicians, as well as general information about career prospects in the State. Several of these agencies maintain job hotlines reporting openings for library technicians.

State departments of education can furnish information on requirements and job opportunities for school library technicians.

Licensed Practical Nurses

(O*NET 32505)

Significant Points

- Training lasting about one year is available in about 1,100 State-approved programs, mostly in vocational or technical schools.

- Nursing homes will offer the most new jobs. Jobseekers in hospitals may face competition.

Nature of the Work

Licensed practical nurses (L.P.N.s), or licensed vocational nurses as they are called in Texas and California, care for the sick, injured, convalescent, and disabled under the direction of physicians and registered nurses.

Most L.P.N.s provide basic bedside care. They take vital signs such as temperature, blood pressure, pulse, and respiration. They also treat bedsores, prepare and give injections and enemas, apply dressings, give alcohol rubs and massages, apply ice packs and hot water bottles, and insert catheters. L.P.Ns observe patients and report adverse reactions to medications or treatments. They collect samples from patients for testing, perform routine laboratory tests, feed them, and record food and liquid intake and output. They help patients with bathing, dressing, and personal hygiene, keep them comfortable, and care for their emotional needs. In States where the law allows, they may administer prescribed medicines or start intravenous fluids. Some L.P.N.s help deliver, care for, and feed infants. Some experienced L.P.N.s supervise nursing assistants and aides.

In addition to providing routine bedside care, L.P.N.s in nursing homes may also help evaluate residents' needs, develop care plans, and supervise the care provided by nursing aides. In doctors' offices and clinics, they may also make appointments, keep records, and perform other clerical duties. L.P.N.s who work in private homes may also prepare meals and teach family members simple nursing tasks.

Working Conditions

Most licensed practical nurses in hospitals and nursing homes work a 40-hour week, but because patients need round-the-clock care, some work nights, weekends, and holidays. They often stand for long periods and help patients move in bed, stand, or walk.

L.P.N.s may face hazards from caustic chemicals, radiation, and infectious diseases such as hepatitis. They are subject to back injuries when moving patients and shock from electrical equipment. They often must deal with the stress of heavy workloads. In addition, the patients they care for may be confused, irrational, agitated, or uncooperative.

Employment

Licensed practical nurses held about 692,000 jobs in 1998. Thirty-two percent of L.P.N.s worked in hospitals, 28 percent worked in nursing homes, and 14 percent in doctors' offices and clinics. Others worked for temporary help agencies, home health care services, residential care facilities, schools, or government agencies. About 1 in 4 worked part time.

Training, Other Qualifications, and Advancement

All States require L.P.N.s to pass a licensing examination after completing a State-approved practical nursing program. A high school diploma is usually required for entry, but some programs accept people without a diploma.

In 1998, approximately 1,100 State-approved programs provided practical nursing training. Almost 6 out of 10 students were enrolled in technical or vocational schools, while 3 out of 10 were in community and junior colleges. Others were in high schools, hospitals, and colleges and universities.

Most practical nursing programs last about one year and include both classroom study and supervised clinical practice (patient care). Classroom study covers basic nursing concepts and patient-care related subjects, including anatomy, physiology, medical-surgical nursing, pediatrics, obstetrics, psychiatric nursing, administration of drugs, nutrition, and first aid. Clinical practice is usually in a hospital, but sometimes includes other settings.

L.P.N.s should have a caring, sympathetic nature. They should be emotionally stable because work with the sick and injured can be stressful. As part of a health care team, they must be able to follow orders and work under close supervision.

Job Outlook

Employment of L.P.N.s is expected to grow as fast as the average for all occupations through 2008 in response to the long-term care needs of a rapidly growing population of very old people and to the general growth of health care. However, L.P.N.s seeking positions in hospitals may face competition, as the number of hospital jobs for L.P.N.s declines; the number of inpatients, with whom most L.P.N.s work, is not expected to increase much. As in most other occupations, replacement needs will be a major source of job openings.

Employment in nursing homes is expected to grow faster than the average. Nursing homes will offer the most new jobs for L.P.N.s as the number of aged and disabled persons in need of long-term care rises. In addition to caring for the aged, nursing homes will be called on to care for the increasing number of patients who have been released from the hospital and have not recovered enough to return home.

Much faster than average growth is expected in home health care services. This is in response to a growing number of older persons with functional disabilities, consumer preference for care in the home, and technological advances that make it possible to bring increasingly complex treatments into the home.

An increasing proportion of sophisticated procedures that once were performed only in hospitals are being performed in physicians' offices and clinics, including ambulatory surgicenters and emergency medical centers, thanks largely to advances in technology. As a result, employment is projected to grow much faster than average in these places as health care in general expands.

Earnings

Median annual earnings of licensed practical nurses were $26,940 in 1998. The middle 50 percent earned between $23,160 and $31,870 a year. The lowest 10 percent earned less than $20,210, and the highest 10 percent earned more than $37,540 a year. Median annual earnings in the industries employing the largest numbers of licensed practical nurses in 1997 were as follows:

Personnel supply services	$30,200
Home health care services	27,600
Hospitals	25,300
Nursing and personal care facilities	26,200
Offices and clinics of medical doctors	24,500

Related Occupations

L.P.N.s work closely with people while helping them. So do emergency medical technicians, social and human service assistants, surgical technologists, and teacher assistants.

Sources of Additional Information

For information about practical nursing, contact:

- National League for Nursing, 61 Broadway, New York, NY 10006. Internet: http://www.nln.org
- National Association for Practical Nurse Education and Service, Inc., 1400 Spring St., Suite 330, Silver Spring, MD 20910.

Maintenance Mechanics, General Utility

(O*NET 85119C and 85132)

Significant Points

- Most general maintenance mechanics are trained on the job; others learn by working as helpers to other repairers or construction workers such as carpenters, electricians, or machinery repairers.

- Despite slower-than-average employment growth resulting from advancements in machinery, job openings should be plentiful due to significant turnover in this large occupation.

Nature of the Work

Most craft workers specialize in one kind of work such as plumbing or carpentry. General maintenance mechanics, however, have skills in many different crafts. They repair and maintain machines, mechanical equipment, and buildings, and work on plumbing, electrical, and air-conditioning and heating systems. They build partitions, make plaster or drywall repairs, and fix or paint roofs, windows, doors, floors, woodwork, and other parts of building structures. They also maintain and repair specialized equipment and machinery found in cafeterias, laundries, hospitals, stores, offices, and factories. Typical duties include troubleshooting and fixing faulty electrical switches, repairing air-conditioning motors, and unclogging drains. New buildings sometimes have computer-controlled systems, requiring mechanics to acquire basic computer skills. For example, new air conditioning systems often can be controlled from a central computer terminal. Additionally, light sensors can be electronically controlled to automatically turn off lights after a set amount of time.

General maintenance mechanics inspect and diagnose problems and determine the best way to correct them, often checking blueprints, repair manuals, and parts catalogs. They obtain supplies and repair parts from distributors or storerooms. They use common hand and power tools such as screwdrivers, saws, drills, wrenches, and hammers, as well as specialized equipment and electronic testing devices. They replace or fix worn or broken parts, where necessary, or make adjustments.

These mechanics also do routine preventive maintenance and ensure that machines continue to run smoothly, building systems operate efficiently, and the physical condition of buildings does not deteriorate. Following a checklist, they may inspect drives, motors, and belts, check fluid levels, replace filters, and perform other maintenance actions. Maintenance mechanics keep records of maintenance and repair work.

Mechanics in small establishments, where they are often the only maintenance worker, do all repairs except for very large or difficult jobs. In larger establishments, their duties may be limited to the general maintenance of everything in a workshop or a particular area.

Working Conditions

General maintenance mechanics often do several different tasks in a single day, at any number of locations. They may work inside of a single building or in several different buildings. They may have to stand for long periods, lift heavy objects, and work in uncomfortably hot or cold environments, in awkward and cramped positions, or on ladders. They are subject to electrical shock, burns, falls, cuts, and bruises. Most general maintenance workers work a 40-hour week. Some work evening, night, or weekend shifts, or are on call for emergency repairs.

Those employed in small establishments, where they may be the only maintenance worker, often operate with only limited supervision. Those working in larger establishments often are under the direct supervision of an experienced worker.

Employment

General maintenance mechanics held over 1.2 million jobs in 1998. They were employed in almost every industry. Around 35 percent worked in service industries, mainly in elementary and secondary schools, colleges and universities, hotels, and hospitals and nursing homes. About 16 percent worked in manufacturing industries. Others worked for wholesale and retail firms, government agencies, and real estate firms that operate office and apartment buildings.

Training, Other Qualifications, and Advancement

Most general maintenance mechanics learn their skills informally on the job. They start as helpers, watching and learning from skilled maintenance workers. Helpers begin by doing simple jobs such as fixing leaky faucets and replacing light bulbs, and progress to more difficult tasks such as overhauling machinery or building walls.

Others learn their skills by working as helpers to other repair or construction workers such as carpenters, electricians, or machinery repairers. Necessary skills can also be learned in high school shop classes and post-secondary trade or vocational schools. It generally takes one to four years of on-the-job training or school, or a combination of both, to become fully qualified, depending on the skill level required. Because a growing proportion of new buildings rely on computers to control building systems, general maintenance mechanics may need basic computer skills (such as knowing how to log on to a central computer system and navigate through a series of menus). Usually companies that install computer-controlled equipment provide on-site training for general maintenance mechanics.

Graduation from high school is preferred for entry into this occupation. High school courses in mechanical drawing, electricity, woodworking, blueprint reading, science, mathematics, and computers are useful. Mechanical aptitude, ability to use shop math,

and manual dexterity are important. Good health is necessary because the job involves much walking, standing, reaching, and heavy lifting. Difficult jobs require problem-solving ability, and many positions require the ability to work without direct supervision.

Many general maintenance mechanics in large organizations advance to maintenance supervisor or to one of the crafts such as electrician, heating and air-conditioning mechanic, or plumber. Within small organizations, promotion opportunities are limited.

Job Outlook

Job openings should be plentiful. General maintenance mechanics is a large occupation with significant turnover, and many job openings should result from the need to replace workers who transfer to other occupations or stop working for other reasons.

Employment of general maintenance mechanics is expected to grow more slowly than the average for all occupations through 2008. Employment is related to the number of buildings—for example, office and apartment buildings, stores, schools, hospitals, hotels, and factories—and the amount of equipment needing maintenance and repair. As machinery becomes more advanced, however, the need for general mechanics diminishes.

Earnings

Median hourly earnings of general maintenance mechanics were $11.20 in 1998. The middle 50 percent earned between $8.43 and $14.99. The lowest 10 percent earned less than $6.56, and the highest 10 percent earned more than $18.83. Median hourly earnings in the industries employing the largest numbers of general maintenance mechanics in 1997 are shown below:

Local government, except education and hospitals	$11.90
Hospitals	11.30
Real estate agents and managers	9.80
Real estate operators and lessors	9.40
Hotels and motels	8.20

Some general maintenance mechanics are members of unions, including the American Federation of State, County, and Municipal Employees and the United Automobile Workers.

Related Occupations

Some duties of general maintenance mechanics are similar to those of carpenters, plumbers, industrial machinery repairers, electricians, and heating, air-conditioning, and refrigeration mechanics.

Sources of Additional Information

Information about job opportunities may be obtained from local employers and local offices of the State Employment Service.

Medical Assistants

(O*NET 66005 and 66099A)

Significant Points

- The job of medical assistant is expected to be one of the 10 fastest growing occupations through the year 2008.

- Job prospects should be best for medical assistants with formal training or experience.

Nature of the Work

Medical assistants perform routine administrative and clinical tasks to keep the offices and clinics of physicians, podiatrists, chiropractors, and optometrists running smoothly. They should not be confused with physician assistants, who examine, diagnose, and treat patients under the direct supervision of a physician.

The duties of medical assistants vary from office to office, depending on office location, size, and specialty. In small practices, medical assistants are usually "generalists," handling both administrative and clinical duties and reporting directly to an office manager, physician, or other health practitioner. Those in large practices tend to specialize in a particular area under the supervision of department administrators.

Medical assistants perform many administrative duties. They answer telephones, greet patients, update and file patient medical records, fill out insurance forms, handle correspondence, schedule appointments, arrange for hospital admission and laboratory services, and handle billing and bookkeeping.

Clinical duties vary according to State law and include taking medical histories and recording vital signs, explaining treatment procedures to patients, preparing patients for examination, and assisting the physician during the examination. Medical assistants collect and prepare laboratory specimens or perform basic laboratory tests on the premises, dispose of contaminated supplies, and sterilize medical instruments. They instruct patients about medication and special diets, prepare and administer medications as directed by a physician, authorize drug refills as directed, telephone prescriptions to a pharmacy, draw blood, prepare patients for x rays, take electrocardiograms, remove sutures, and change dressings.

Medical assistants may also arrange examining room instruments and equipment, purchase and maintain supplies and equipment, and keep waiting and examining rooms neat and clean.

Assistants who specialize have additional duties. *Podiatric medical assistants* make castings of feet, expose and develop x-rays, and assist podiatrists in surgery. *Ophthalmic medical assistants* help ophthalmologists provide medical eye care. They administer diagnostic tests, measure and record vision, and test the functioning of eyes and eye muscles. They also show patients how to use eye dressings, protective shields, and safety glasses, and how to insert, remove, and care for contact lenses. Under the direction of the physician, they may administer medications, including eye drops. They also maintain optical and surgical instruments and assist the ophthalmologist in surgery.

Working Conditions

Medical assistants work in well-lighted, clean environments. They constantly interact with other people and may have to handle several responsibilities at once.

Most full-time medical assistants work a regular 40-hour week. Some work part-time, evenings, or weekends.

Employment

Medical assistants held about 252,000 jobs in 1998. Sixty-five percent were in physicians' offices, and 14 percent were in offices of other health practitioners such as chiropractors, optometrists, and podiatrists. The rest were in hospitals, nursing homes, and other health care facilities.

Training, Other Qualifications, and Advancement

Most employers prefer to hire graduates of formal programs in medical assisting. Such programs are offered in vocational-technical high schools, post-secondary vocational schools, community and junior colleges, and in colleges and universities. Post-secondary programs usually last either one year, resulting in a certificate or diploma, or two years, resulting in an associate degree. Courses cover anatomy, physiology, and medical terminology as well as typing, transcription, record keeping, accounting, and insurance processing. Students learn laboratory techniques, clinical and diagnostic procedures, pharmaceutical principles, medication administration, and first aid. They study office practices, patient relations, medical law, and ethics. Accredited programs include an internship that provides practical experience in physicians' offices, hospitals, or other health care facilities.

Although formal training in medical assisting is available, such training—while generally preferred—is not always required. Some medical assistants are trained on the job, although this is less common than in the past. Applicants usually need a high school diploma or the equivalent. Recommended high school courses include mathematics, health, biology, typing, bookkeeping, computers, and office skills. Volunteer experience in the health care field is also helpful.

Two agencies recognized by the U.S. Department of Education accredit programs in medical assisting: the Commission on Accreditation of Allied Health Education Programs (CAAHEP) and the Accrediting Bureau of Health Education Schools (ABHES). In 1999, there were about 450 medical assisting programs accredited by CAAHEP and over 140 accredited by ABHES. The Committee on Accreditation for Ophthalmic Medical Personnel accredited 14 programs in ophthalmic medical assisting.

Although there is no licensing for medical assistants, some States require them to take a test or a short course before they can take x-rays or perform other specific clinical tasks. Employers prefer to hire experienced workers or certified applicants who have passed a national examination, indicating that the medical assistant meets certain standards of competence. The American Association of Medical Assistants awards the Certified Medical Assistant credential; the American Medical Technologists awards the Registered Medical Assistant credential; the American Society of Podiatric Medical Assistants awards the Podiatric Medical Assistant Certified credential; and the Joint Commission on Allied Health Personnel in Ophthalmology awards the Ophthalmic Medical Assistant credential at three levels—Certified Ophthalmic Assistant, Certified Ophthalmic Technician, and Certified Ophthalmic Medical Technologist.

Because medical assistants deal with the public, they must be neat and well-groomed and have a courteous, pleasant manner. Medical assistants must be able to put patients at ease and explain physicians' instructions. They must respect the confidential nature of medical information. Clinical duties require a reasonable level of manual dexterity and visual acuity.

Medical assistants may be able to advance to office manager. They may qualify for a variety of administrative support occupations or may teach medical assisting. With additional education, some enter other health occupations such as nursing and medical technology.

Job Outlook

Employment of medical assistants is expected to grow much faster than the average for all occupations through the year 2008 as the health services industry expands due to technological advances in medicine and a growing and aging population. It is one of the fastest growing occupations.

Employment growth will be driven by the increase in the number of group practices, clinics, and other health care facilities that need a high proportion of support personnel, particularly the flexible medical assistant who can handle both administrative and clinical duties. Medical assistants primarily work in outpatient settings, where much faster-than-average growth is expected.

In view of the preference of many health care employers for trained personnel, job prospects should be best for medical assistants with formal training or experience, particularly those with certification.

Earnings

The earnings of medical assistants vary, depending on experience, skill level, and location. Median annual earnings of medical assistants were $20,680 in 1998. The middle 50 percent earned between $17,020 and $24,340 a year. The lowest 10 percent earned less than $14,020, and the highest 10 percent earned more than $28,640 a year. Median annual earnings in the industries employing the largest number of medical assistants in 1997 were as follows:

Offices and clinics of medical doctors	$20,800
Hospitals	20,400
Offices of osteopathic physicians	19,600
Health and allied services, not elsewhere classified	19,300
Offices of other health practitioners	18,500

Related Occupations

Workers in other medical support occupations include medical secretaries, hospital admitting clerks, pharmacy helpers, medical record clerks, dental assistants, occupational therapy aides, and physical therapy aides.

Sources of Additional Information

Information about career opportunities, CAAHEP-accredited educational programs in medical assisting, and the Certified Medical Assistant exam is available from:

- The American Association of Medical Assistants, 20 North Wacker Dr., Suite 1575, Chicago, IL 60606-2903. Internet: http://www.aama-ntl.org

Information about career opportunities and the Registered Medical Assistant certification exam is available from:

- Registered Medical Assistants of American Medical Technologists, 710 Higgins Rd., Park Ridge, IL 60068-5765. Internet: http://www.amt1.com

For a list of ABHES-accredited educational programs in medical assisting, write:

- Accrediting Bureau of Health Education Schools, 803 West Broad St., Suite 730, Falls Church, VA 22046. Internet: http://www.abhes.org

For information about a career as a medical assistant and schools offering training, contact:

- National Association of Health Career Schools, 2301 Academy Dr., Harrisburg, PA 17112.

Information about career opportunities, training programs, and the Certified Ophthalmic Assistant exam is available from:

- Joint Commission on Allied Health Personnel in Ophthalmology, 2025 Woodlane Dr., St. Paul, MN 55125-2995. Internet: http://www.jcahpo.org

Information about careers for podiatric assistants is available from:

- American Society of Podiatric Medical Assistants, 2124 S. Austin Blvd., Cicero, IL 60650.

Nuclear Medicine Technologists

(O*NET 32914)

Significant Points

- Relatively few job openings will occur because the occupation is small.
- Technologists trained in both nuclear medicine and radiologic technology or other modalities will have the best prospects.

Nature of the Work

In nuclear medicine, radionuclides—unstable atoms that emit radiation spontaneously—are used to diagnose and treat disease. Radionuclides are purified and compounded like other drugs to form radiopharmaceuticals. Nuclear medicine technologists administer these radiopharmaceuticals to patients and then monitor the characteristics and functions of tissues or organs in which they localize. Abnormal areas show higher or lower concentrations of radioactivity than normal.

Nuclear medicine technologists operate cameras that detect and map the radioactive drug in the patient's body to create an image on photographic film or a computer monitor. Radiologic technologists also operate diagnostic imaging equipment, but their equipment creates an image by projecting an x-ray through the patient.

Nuclear medicine technologists explain test procedures to patients. They prepare a dosage of the radiopharmaceutical and administer it by mouth, injection, or other means. When preparing radiopharmaceuticals, technologists adhere to safety standards that keep the radiation dose to workers and patients as low as possible.

Technologists position patients and start a gamma scintillation camera, or "scanner," which creates images of the distribution of a radiopharmaceutical as it localizes in and emits signals from the patient's body. Technologists produce the images on a computer screen or on film for a physician to interpret. Some nuclear medicine studies, such as cardiac function studies, are processed with the aid of a computer.

Nuclear medicine technologists also perform radioimmunoassay studies that assess the behavior of a radioactive substance inside the body. For example, technologists may add radioactive substances to blood or serum to determine levels of hormones or therapeutic drug content.

Technologists keep patient records and record the amount and type of radionuclides received, used, and disposed of.

Working Conditions

Nuclear medicine technologists generally work a 40-hour week. This may include evening or weekend hours in departments that operate on an extended schedule. Opportunities for part-time and shift work are also available. In addition, technologists in hospitals may have on-call duty on a rotational basis.

Because technologists are on their feet much of the day and may lift or turn disabled patients, physical stamina is important.

Although there is potential for radiation exposure in this field, it is kept to a minimum by the use of shielded syringes, gloves, and other protective devices and adherence to strict radiation safety guidelines. Technologists also wear badges that measure radiation levels. Because of safety programs, however, badge measurements rarely exceed established safety levels.

Employment

Nuclear medicine technologists held about 14,000 jobs in 1998. About 8 out of 10 jobs were in hospitals. The rest were in physicians' offices and clinics, including imaging centers.

Training, Other Qualifications, and Advancement

Nuclear medicine technology programs range in length from one to four years and lead to a certificate, associate's degree, or bachelor's degree. Generally, certificate programs are offered in hospitals, associate programs in community colleges, and bachelor's programs in four-year colleges and in universities. Courses cover physical sciences, the biological effects of radiation exposure, radiation protection and procedures, the use of radiopharmaceuticals, imaging techniques, and computer applications.

One-year certificate programs are for health professionals, especially radiologic technologists and ultrasound technologists, who wish to specialize in nuclear medicine. They also attract medical technologists, registered nurses, and others who wish to change fields or specialize. Others interested in the nuclear medicine technology field have three options: a two-year certificate program, a two-year associate's degree program, or a four-year bachelor's degree program.

The Joint Review Committee on Education Programs in Nuclear Medicine Technology accredits most formal training programs in nuclear medicine technology. In 1999, 96 programs were accredited.

All nuclear medicine technologists must meet the minimum Federal standards on the administration of radioactive drugs and the operation of radiation detection equipment. In addition, about half of all States require technologists to be licensed. Technologists also may obtain voluntary professional certification or registration. Registration or certification is available from the American Registry of Radiologic Technologists and from the Nuclear Medicine Technology Certification Board. Most employers prefer to hire certified or registered technologists.

Technologists may advance to supervisor, then to chief technologist, and to department administrator or director. Some technologists specialize in a clinical area such as nuclear cardiology or computer analysis or leave patient care to take positions in research laboratories. Some become instructors or directors in nuclear medicine technology programs, a step that usually requires a bachelor's degree or a master's in nuclear medicine technology. Others leave the occupation to work as sales or training representatives for medical equipment and radiopharmaceutical manufacturing firms, or as radiation safety officers in regulatory agencies or hospitals.

Job Outlook

Employment of nuclear medicine technologists is expected to grow about as fast as the average for all occupations through the year 2008. The number of openings each year will be very low because the occupation is small. Growth will arise from an increase in the number of middle-aged and older persons who are the primary users of diagnostic procedures, including nuclear medicine tests. Nonetheless, jobseekers will face more competition for jobs than in the recent past. In an attempt to employ fewer technologists and lower labor costs, hospitals continue to merge nuclear medicine and radiologic technology departments. Consequently, opportunities will be best for technologists who can perform both nuclear medicine and radiologic procedures.

Technological innovations may increase the diagnostic uses of nuclear medicine. One example is the use of radiopharmaceuticals in combination with monoclonal antibodies to detect cancer at far earlier stages than is customary today, and without resorting to surgery. Another is the use of radionuclides to examine the heart's ability to pump blood. Wider use of nuclear medical imaging to observe metabolic and biochemical changes for neurology, cardiology, and oncology procedures will also spur some demand for nuclear medicine technologists.

On the other hand, cost considerations will affect the speed with which new applications of nuclear medicine grow. Some promising nuclear medicine procedures, such as positron emission tomography, are extremely costly, and hospitals contemplating them will have to consider equipment costs, reimbursement policies, and the number of potential users.

Earnings

Median annual earnings of nuclear medicine technologists were $39,610 in 1998. The middle 50 percent earned between $34,910 and $46,570 a year. The lowest 10 percent earned less than $30,590, and the highest 10 percent earned more than $52,770 a year.

Related Occupations

Nuclear medical technologists operate sophisticated equipment to help physicians and other health practitioners diagnose and treat patients. Radiologic technologists, diagnostic medical sonographers, cardiovascular technologists, electroneurodiagnostic technologists, clinical laboratory technologists, perfusionists, radiation therapists, and respiratory therapists also perform similar functions.

Sources of Additional Information

Additional information on a career as a nuclear medicine technologist is available from:

- The Society of Nuclear Medicine-Technologist Section, 1850 Samuel Morse Dr., Reston, VA 22090.

For information on a career as a nuclear medicine technologist, enclose a stamped, self-addressed business size envelope with your request to:

- American Society of Radiologic Technologists, Customer Service Department, 15000 Central Ave. SE., Albuquerque, NM 87123-3917, or call (800) 444-2778.

For a list of accredited programs in nuclear medicine technology, write to:

- Joint Review Committee on Educational Programs in Nuclear Medicine Technology, PMB 418, 1 2nd Avenue East, Suite C, Polson, MT 59860-2107.

Information on certification is available from:

- Nuclear Medicine Technology Certification Board, 2970 Clairmont Rd., Suite 610, Atlanta, GA 30329.

Nursing and Psychiatric Aides

(O*NET 66008 and 66014)

Significant Points

- Job prospects for nursing aides will be good because of fast growth and high turnover in this large occupation.

- Minimum education or training is generally required for entry-level jobs, but earnings are low.

Nature of the Work

Nursing and psychiatric aides help care for physically or mentally ill, injured, disabled, or infirm individuals confined to hospitals, nursing or residential care facilities, and mental health settings.

Nursing aides, also known as nursing assistants, geriatric aides, unlicensed assistive personnel, or hospital attendants, perform routine tasks under the supervision of nursing and medical staff. They answer patients' call bells, deliver messages, serve meals, make beds, and help patients eat, dress, and bathe. Aides may also provide skin care to patients; take temperatures, pulse, respiration, and blood pressure; and help patients get in and out of bed and walk. They may also escort patients to operating and examining rooms, keep patients' rooms neat, set up equipment, or store and move supplies. Aides observe patients' physical, mental, and emotional conditions and report any change to the nursing or medical staff.

Nursing aides employed in nursing homes are often the principal caregivers, having far more contact with residents than other members of the staff. Because some residents may stay in a nursing home for months or even years, aides develop ongoing relationships with them and interact with them in a positive, caring way.

Psychiatric aides are also known as mental health assistants and psychiatric nursing assistants. They care for mentally impaired or emotionally disturbed individuals. They work under a team that may include psychiatrists, psychologists, psychiatric nurses, social workers, and therapists. In addition to helping patients dress, bathe, groom, and eat, psychiatric aides socialize with them and lead them in educational and recreational activities. Psychiatric aides may play games such as cards with the patients, watch television with them, or participate in group activities such as sports or field trips. They observe patients and report any physical or behavioral signs which might be important for the professional staff to know. They accompany patients to and from wards for examination and treatment. Because they have the closest contact with patients, psychiatric aides have a great deal of influence on their outlook and treatment.

Working Conditions

Most full-time aides work about 40 hours a week, but because patients need care 24 hours a day, some aides work evenings, nights, weekends, and holidays. Many work part-time. Aides spend many hours standing and walking, and they often face heavy workloads. Because they may have to move patients in and out of bed or help them stand or walk, aides must guard against back injury. Nursing aides may also face hazards from minor infections and major diseases such as hepatitis, but can avoid infections by following proper procedures.

Nursing aides often have unpleasant duties; they empty bed pans and change soiled bed linens. The patients they care for may be disoriented, irritable, or uncooperative. Psychiatric aides must be prepared to care for patients whose illness may cause violent behavior. While their work can be emotionally demanding, many aides gain satisfaction from assisting those in need.

Employment

Nursing aides held about 1.4 million jobs in 1998, and psychiatric aides held about 95,000 jobs. About one-half of all nursing aides worked in nursing homes, and about one-fourth worked in hospitals. Others worked in residential care facilities, such as halfway houses and homes for the aged or disabled, or in private households. Most psychiatric aides worked in psychiatric units of general hospitals, psychiatric hospitals, State and county mental institutions, homes for mentally retarded and psychiatric patients, and community mental health centers.

Training, Other Qualifications, and Advancement

In many cases, neither a high school diploma nor previous work experience is necessary for a job as a nursing or psychiatric aide. A few employers, however, require some training or experience. Hospitals may require experience as a nursing aide or home health aide. Nursing homes often hire inexperienced workers who must complete a minimum of 75 hours of mandatory training and pass a competency evaluation program within four months of employment. Aides who complete the program are placed on the State registry of nursing aides. Some States require psychiatric aides to complete a formal training program.

These occupations can offer individuals an entry into the world of work. The flexibility of night and weekend hours also provides high school and college students a chance to work during the school year.

Nursing aide training is offered in high schools, vocational-technical centers, some nursing homes, and community colleges. Courses cover body mechanics, nutrition, anatomy and physiology, infection control, communication skills, and resident rights. Personal care skills such as how to help patients bathe, eat, and groom are also taught.

Some facilities, other than nursing homes, provide classroom instruction for newly hired aides, while others rely exclusively on informal on-the-job instruction from a licensed nurse or an experienced aide. Such training may last several days to a few months. From time to time, aides may also attend lectures, workshops, and in-service training.

Applicants should be healthy, tactful, patient, understanding, emotionally stable, dependable, and have a desire to help people. They should also be able to work as part of a team, have good communication skills, and be willing to perform repetitive, routine tasks.

Opportunities for advancement within these occupations are limited. To enter other health occupations, aides generally need additional formal training. Some employers and unions provide opportunities by simplifying the educational paths to advancement. Experience as an aide can also help individuals decide whether to pursue a career in the health care field.

Job Outlook

Job prospects for nursing aides should be good through the year 2008. Numerous openings will arise from a combination of fast growth and high turnover for this large occupation. Employment of nursing aides is expected to grow faster than the average for all occupations in response to an emphasis on rehabilitation and the long-term care needs of a rapidly growing elderly population. Employment will increase as a result of the expansion of nursing homes and other long-term care facilities for people with chronic illnesses and disabling conditions, many of whom are elderly. Financial pressure on hospitals to release patients as soon as possible should produce more nursing home admissions. Modern medical technology will also increase the employment of nursing aides. This technology, while saving and extending more lives, increases the need for long-term care provided by aides. As a result, nursing and personal care facilities are expected to grow rapidly and to provide most of the new jobs for nursing aides.

Employment of psychiatric aides is expected to grow slower than the average for all occupations. Employment will rise in response to the sharp increase in the number of older persons—many of whom will require mental health services. Employment of aides in outpatient community mental health centers is likely to grow because of increasing public acceptance of formal treatment for drug abuse and alcoholism and a lessening of the stigma attached to those receiving mental health care. However, employment in hospitals—where one-half of psychiatric aides work—is likely to decline due to attempts to contain costs by limiting inpatient psychiatric treatment.

Replacement needs will constitute the major source of openings for aides. Turnover is high, which is a reflection of modest entry requirements, low pay, and lack of advancement opportunities.

Earnings

Median hourly earnings of nursing aides, orderlies, and attendants were $7.99 in 1998. The middle 50 percent earned between $6.72 and $9.54 an hour. The lowest 10 percent earned less than $5.87, and the highest 10 percent earned more than $11.33 an hour. Median hourly earnings in the industries employing the largest number of nursing aides, orderlies, and attendants in 1997 were as follows:

Local government, except education and hospitals	$9.20
Hospitals	8.10
Personnel supply services	8.10
Nursing and personal care facilities	7.50
Residential care	7.20

Median hourly earnings of psychiatric aides were $10.66 in 1998. The middle 50 percent earned between $8.33 and $13.36 an hour. The lowest 10 percent earned less than $6.87, and the highest 10 percent earned more than $15.28 an hour. Median hourly earnings of psychiatric aides in 1997 were $11.20 in State government and $9.80 in hospitals.

Aides in hospitals generally receive at least one week of paid vacation after one year of service. Paid holidays and sick leave, hospital and medical benefits, extra pay for late-shift work, and pension plans also are available to many hospital and some nursing home employees.

Related Occupations

Nursing and psychiatric aides help people who need routine care or treatment. So do home health and personal care aides, child-care workers, companions, occupational therapy aides, and physical therapy aides.

Sources of Additional Information

Information about employment opportunities may be obtained from local hospitals, nursing homes, psychiatric facilities, State boards of nursing and local offices of the State employment service.

For information about a career as a nursing aide and schools offering training, contact:

- National Association of Health Career Schools, 2301 Academy Dr., Harrisburg, PA 17112.

Occupational Therapists

(O*NET 32305)

Significant Points

- Employment is projected to increase over the 1998-2008 period, but due to the effects of Federal limits on reimbursement for therapy services, the majority of expected employment growth is expected to occur during the second half of the projection period.

- Occupational therapists are increasingly taking on supervisory roles.

- More than one-fourth of occupational therapists work part time.

Nature of the Work

Occupational therapists help people improve their ability to perform tasks in their daily living and working environments. They work with individuals who have conditions that are mentally, physically, developmentally, or emotionally disabling. They also help them to develop, recover, or maintain daily living and work skills. Occupational therapists not only help clients improve basic motor functions and reasoning abilities, but also compensate for permanent loss of function. Their goal is to help clients have independent, productive, and satisfying lives.

Occupational therapists assist clients in performing activities of all types, ranging from using a computer, to caring for daily needs such as dressing, cooking, and eating. Physical exercises may be used to increase strength and dexterity, while paper and pencil exercises may be chosen to improve visual acuity and the ability to discern patterns. A client with short-term memory loss, for instance, might be encouraged to make lists to aid recall. A person with co-ordination problems might be assigned exercises to improve hand-eye coordination. Occupational therapists also use computer programs to help clients improve decision making, abstract reasoning, problem solving, and perceptual skills, as well as memory, sequencing, and coordination—all of which are important for independent living.

For those with permanent functional disabilities, such as spinal cord injuries, cerebral palsy, or muscular dystrophy, therapists instruct in the use of adaptive equipment such as wheelchairs, splints, and aids for eating and dressing. They also design or make special equipment needed at home or at work. Therapists develop computer-aided adaptive equipment and teach clients with severe limitations how to use it. This equipment enables clients to communicate better and to control other aspects of their environment.

Some occupational therapists, called industrial therapists, treat individuals whose ability to function in a work environment has been impaired. They arrange employment, plan work activities, and evaluate the client's progress.

Occupational therapists may work exclusively with individuals in a particular age group or with particular disabilities. In schools, for example, they evaluate children's abilities, recommend and provide therapy, modify classroom equipment, and in general, help children participate as fully as possible in school programs and activities. Occupational therapy is also beneficial to the elderly population. Therapists help senior citizens lead more productive, active, and independent lives through a variety of methods, including the use of adaptive equipment.

Occupational therapists in mental health settings treat individuals who are mentally ill, mentally retarded, or emotionally disturbed. To treat these problems, therapists choose activities that help people learn to cope with daily life. Activities include time management skills, budgeting, shopping, homemaking, and use of public transportation. They may also work with individuals who are dealing with alcoholism, drug abuse, depression, eating disorders, or stress-related disorders.

Recording a client's activities and progress is an important part of an occupational therapist's job. Accurate records are essential for evaluating clients, billing, and reporting to physicians and others.

Working Conditions

Occupational therapists in hospitals and other health care and community settings usually work a 40-hour week. Those in schools may also participate in meetings and other activities, during and after the school day. More than one-fourth of occupational therapists work part-time.

In large rehabilitation centers, therapists may work in spacious rooms equipped with machines, tools, and other devices generating noise. The job can be tiring, because therapists are on their feet much of the time. Those providing home health care may spend time driving from appointment to appointment. Therapists also face hazards such as back strain from lifting and moving clients and equipment.

Therapists are increasingly taking on supervisory roles. Due to rising health care costs, third-party payers are beginning to encourage occupational therapy assistants and aides to take more hands-on responsibility. By having assistants and aides work more closely with clients under the guidance of a therapist, the cost of therapy should be more modest.

Employment

Occupational therapists held about 73,000 jobs in 1998; about 1 in 4 worked part time. About 1 in 10 occupational therapists held more than one job in 1998. The largest number of jobs was in hospitals, including many in rehabilitation and psychiatric hospitals. Other major employers include offices and clinics of occupational therapists and other health practitioners, school systems, home health agencies, nursing homes, community mental health centers, adult daycare programs, job training services, and residential care facilities.

Some occupational therapists are self-employed in private practice. They see clients referred by physicians or other health professionals, or they provide contract or consulting services to nursing homes, schools, adult daycare programs, and home health agencies.

Training, Other Qualifications, and Advancement

A bachelor's degree in occupational therapy is the minimum requirement for entry into this field. All States, Puerto Rico, and the District of Columbia regulate occupational therapy. To obtain a license, applicants must graduate from an accredited educational program and pass a national certification examination. Those who pass the test are awarded the title of registered occupational therapist.

In 1999, entry-level education was offered in 88 bachelor's degree programs, 11 post-bachelor's certificate programs for students with a degree other than occupational therapy, and 53 entry-level master's degree programs. Nineteen programs offered a combined bachelor's and master's degree, and two offered an entry-level doctoral degree. Most schools have full-time programs, although a growing number also offer weekend or part-time programs.

Occupational therapy coursework includes physical, biological, and behavioral sciences, and the application of occupational therapy theory and skills. Completion of six months of supervised fieldwork is also required.

Persons considering this profession should take high school courses in biology, chemistry, physics, health, art, and the social sciences. College admissions offices also look favorably at paid or volunteer experience in the health care field.

Occupational therapists need patience and strong interpersonal skills to inspire trust and respect in their clients. Ingenuity and imagination in adapting activities to individual needs are assets. Those working in home health care must be able to successfully adapt to a variety of settings.

Job Outlook

Employment of occupational therapists is expected to increase faster than the average for all occupations through 2008. However, federal legislation imposing limits on reimbursement for therapy services may continue to adversely affect the job market for occupational therapists in the near term. Because of the effects of these provisions, the majority of expected employment growth for occupational therapists is expected to occur in the second half of the projection period.

Over the long run, the demand for occupational therapists should continue to rise as a result of growth in the number of individuals with disabilities or limited function requiring therapy services. The baby-boom generation's movement into middle age, a period when the incidence of heart attack and stroke increases, will increase the demand for therapeutic services. The rapidly growing population 75 years of age and above (an age that suffers from a high incidence of disabling conditions) will also demand additional services. Medical advances now enable more patients with critical problems to survive. These patients may need extensive therapy.

Hospitals will continue to employ a large number of occupational therapists to provide therapy services to acutely ill inpatients. Hospitals will also need occupational therapists to staff their outpatient rehabilitation programs.

Employment growth in schools will result from expansion of the school-age population and extended services for disabled students. Therapists will be needed to help children with disabilities prepare to enter special education programs.

Earnings

Median annual earnings of occupational therapists were $48,230 in 1998. The middle 50 percent earned between $39,140 and $68,570 a year. The lowest 10 percent earned less than $30,850, and the highest 10 percent earned more than $86,540 a year. Median annual earnings in the industries employing the largest number of occupational therapists in 1997 were as follows:

Nursing and personal care facilities $57,000

Offices of other health care practitioners 51,800

Hospitals 46,200

Elementary and secondary schools 38,200

Related Occupations

Occupational therapists use specialized knowledge to help individuals perform daily living skills and achieve maximum independence. Other workers performing similar duties include orthotists, prosthetists, physical therapists, chiropractors, speech pathologists, audiologists, rehabilitation counselors, and recreational therapists.

Sources of Additional Information

For more information on occupational therapy as a career and a list of education programs, send a self-addressed label and $5.00 to:

- The American Occupational Therapy Association, 4720 Montgomery Ln., P.O. Box 31220, Bethesda, MD 20824-1220. Internet: http://www.aota.org

Occupational Therapy Assistants and Aides

(O*NET 66021)

Significant Points

- Qualifications of occupational therapy assistants are regulated by the States, and these workers must complete an associate's degree or certificate program. In contrast, occupational therapy aides usually receive most of their training on the job.

- Aides are not licensed, so by law, they are not allowed to perform as wide a range of tasks as occupational therapy assistants do.

- Employment is projected to increase over the 1998-2008 period, but due to the effects of federal limits on reimbursement for therapy services, the majority of expected employment growth is expected to occur during the second half of the projection period.

Nature of the Work

Occupational therapy assistants and aides work under the direction of occupational therapists to provide rehabilitative services to persons with mental, physical, emotional, or developmental impairments. The ultimate goal is to improve clients' quality of life by helping them compensate for limitations. For example, occupational therapy assistants help injured workers re-enter the labor force by helping them improve their motor skills or help persons with learning disabilities increase their independence by teaching them to prepare meals or use public transportation.

Occupational therapy assistants help clients with rehabilitative activities and exercises outlined in a treatment plan developed in collaboration with an occupational therapist. Activities range from teaching the proper method of moving from a bed into a wheelchair to the best way to stretch and limber the muscles of the hand. Assistants monitor an individual's activities to make sure they are performed correctly and to provide encouragement. They also record their client's progress for use by the occupational therapist. If the treatment is not having the intended effect or the client is not improving as expected, the therapist may alter the treatment program in hopes of obtaining better results. In addition, occupational therapy assistants document billing of the client's health

insurance provider.

Occupational therapy aides typically prepare materials and assemble equipment used during treatment and are responsible for a range of clerical tasks. Duties can include scheduling appointments, answering the telephone, restocking or ordering depleted supplies, and filling out insurance forms or other paperwork. Aides are not licensed, so by law, they are not allowed to perform as wide a range of tasks as occupational therapy assistants do.

Working Conditions

Occupational therapy assistants and aides usually work during the day, but some may occasionally work evenings or weekends to accommodate a client's schedule. These workers should be in good physical condition, because they are on their feet for long periods of time and may be asked to help lift and move clients or equipment.

Employment

Occupational therapy assistants and aides held 19,000 jobs in 1998. About 4 out of 10 assistants and aides worked in offices of occupational therapists, and about 3 out of 10 worked in hospitals. The remainder worked primarily in nursing and personal care facilities, offices and clinics of physicians, social services agencies, outpatient rehabilitation centers, and home health agencies.

Training, Other Qualifications, and Advancement

Persons must complete an associate's degree or certificate program from an accredited community college or technical school to qualify for occupational therapy assistant jobs. In contrast, occupational therapy aides usually receive most of their training on the job.

There were 165 accredited occupational therapy assistant programs in the United States in 1999. The first year of study typically involves an introduction to health care, basic medical terminology, anatomy, and physiology. In the second year, courses are more rigorous and usually include occupational therapy courses in areas such as mental health, gerontology, and pediatrics. Students must also complete supervised fieldwork in a clinic or community setting. Applicants to occupational therapy assistant programs can improve their chances of admission by taking high school courses in biology and health and by performing volunteer work in nursing homes, occupational or physical therapist's offices, or elsewhere in the health care field.

Occupational therapy assistants are regulated in most States and must pass a national certification examination after they graduate. Those who pass the test are awarded the title of certified occupational therapy assistant.

Occupational therapy aides usually receive most of their training on the job. Qualified applicants must have a high school diploma, strong interpersonal skills, and a desire to help people in need. Applicants may increase their chances of getting a job by volunteering their services, thus displaying initiative and aptitude to the employer.

Assistants and aides must be responsible, patient, and willing to take directions and work as part of a team. Furthermore, they should be caring and want to help people who are not able to help themselves.

Job Outlook

Employment of occupational therapy assistants and aides is expected to grow much faster than the average for all occupations through 2008. Growth will result from an aging population, including the baby-boom cohort, which will probably need substantial occupational therapy services. Demand will also result from advances in medicine that allow more people with critical problems to survive and then need rehabilitative therapy.

Employment growth would be even faster, except for federal legislation imposing limits on reimbursement for therapy services. However, at the same time, third-party payers, concerned with rising health care costs, are beginning to encourage occupational therapists to delegate more of the hands-on therapy work to occupational therapy assistants and aides. By having assistants and aides work more closely with clients under the guidance of a therapist, the cost of therapy should be more modest than otherwise.

Earnings

Median annual earnings of occupational therapy assistants and aides were $28,690 in 1998. The middle 50 percent earned between $20,050 and $36,900 a year. The lowest 10 percent earned less than $15,000, and the highest 10 percent earned more than $45,740 a year. Median annual earnings of occupational therapy assistants and aides in 1997 were $32,200 in offices of other health care practitioners and $27,000 in hospitals.

Related Occupations

Occupational therapy assistants and aides work under the direction of occupational therapists. Other occupations in the health care field that work under the supervision of professionals include dental assistants, medical assistants, optometric assistants, pharmacy assistants, and physical therapy assistants and aides.

Sources of Additional Information

Information on a career as an occupational therapy assistant and a list of accredited programs can be obtained by sending a self-addressed label and $5.00 to:

- The American Occupational Therapy Association, 4720 Montgomery Ln., P.O. Box 31220, Bethesda, MD 20824-1220. Internet: http://www.aota.org

Office Clerks, General

(O*NET 55347)

Significant Points

- Although most jobs are entry level, previous office or business experience may be required for some positions.

- Plentiful job opportunities should stem from employment growth, the large size of the occupation, and turnover.

Nature of the Work

As opposed to a single specialized task, the daily responsibilities of a general office clerk change with the needs of the specific jobs and the employer. Whereas some clerks spend their days filing or typing, others enter data at a computer terminal. They can also be called upon to operate photocopiers, fax machines, and other office equipment; prepare mailings; proofread copies; and answer telephones and deliver messages.

The specific duties assigned to a clerk vary significantly depending upon the type of office in which a clerk works. An office clerk in a doctor's office, for example, would not perform the same tasks as a clerk in a large financial institution or in the office of an auto parts wholesaler. Although they may sort checks, keep payroll records, take inventory, and access information, clerks also perform duties unique to their employer, such as organizing medications, making transparencies for a presentation, or filling orders received by fax machine.

The specific duties assigned to a clerk also vary by level of experience. Whereas inexperienced employees make photocopies, stuff envelopes, or record inquiries, experienced clerks are usually given additional responsibilities. For example, they may maintain financial or other records, verify statistical reports for accuracy and completeness, handle and adjust customer complaints, make travel arrangements, take inventory of equipment and supplies, answer questions on departmental services and functions, or help prepare invoices or budgetary requests. Senior office clerks may be expected to monitor and direct the work of lower level clerks.

Working Conditions

For the most part, working conditions for office clerks are the same as those for other office employees within the same company. Those on a full-time schedule usually work a standard 40-hour week; however, some work shifts or overtime during busy periods. About 1 in 3 works part time, whereas many other office clerks work as temporary workers.

Employment

Office clerks held about 3,021,000 jobs in 1998. Most are employed in relatively small businesses. Although they work in every sector of the economy, almost 60 percent worked in the services or wholesale and retail trade industries.

Training, Other Qualifications, and Advancement

Although most office clerk jobs are entry-level administrative support positions, some previous office or business experience may be needed. Employers usually require a high school diploma, and some require typing, basic computer skills, and other general office skills. Familiarity with computer word processing software and applications is becoming increasingly important.

Training for this occupation is available through business education programs offered in high schools, community and junior colleges, and post-secondary vocational schools. Courses in word processing, other computer applications, and office practices are particularly helpful.

Because office clerks usually work with other office staff, they should be cooperative and able to work as part of a team. In addition, they should have good communication skills, be detail-oriented, and adaptable.

General office clerks who exhibit strong communication, interpersonal, and analytical skills may be promoted to supervisory positions. Others may move into different, more senior clerical or administrative jobs, such as receptionist, secretary, and administrative assistant. After gaining some work experience or specialized skills, many workers transfer to jobs with higher pay or greater advancement potential. Advancement to professional occupations within an establishment normally requires additional formal education, such as a college degree.

Job Outlook

Plentiful job opportunities are expected for general office clerks due to employment growth, the large size of the occupation, and turnover. Furthermore, growth in part-time and temporary clerical positions will lead to a large number of job openings. Prospects should be brightest for those who have knowledge of basic computer applications and office machinery, such as fax machines and copiers.

Employment of general office clerks is expected to grow about as fast as the average for all occupations through 2008. The employment outlook for office clerks will be affected by the increasing use of computers, expanding office automation, and the consolidation of clerical tasks. Automation has led to productivity gains, allowing a wide variety of duties to be performed by few office workers. However, automation also has led to a consolidation of clerical staffs and a diversification of job responsibilities. This consolidation increases the demand for general office clerks, because they perform a variety of clerical tasks. It will become increasingly common within small businesses to find a single general office clerk in charge of all clerical work.

Earnings

Median annual earnings of full-time office clerks were $19,580 in 1998; the middle 50 percent earned between $15,210 and $24,370 annually. Ten percent earned less than $12,570, and 10 percent earned more than $30,740. Median annual salaries in the indus-

tries employing the largest number of office clerks in 1997 are shown below:

Local government, except education and hospitals	$20,300
State government, except education and hospitals	20,100
Hospitals	19,400
Colleges and universities	18,600
Personnel supply services	16,700

In early 1999, the Federal government paid office clerks a starting salary of between $13,400 and $18,400 a year, depending on education and experience. Office clerks employed by the Federal government earned an average annual salary of about $28,100 in 1999.

Related Occupations

The duties of office clerks can include a combination of bookkeeping, typing, office machine operation, and filing; other administrative support workers who perform similar duties include information clerks and records processing clerks. Nonclerical entry-level jobs include cashier, medical assistant, teacher aide, and food and beverage service worker.

Sources of Additional Information

State employment service offices and agencies can provide information about job openings for general office clerks.

Ophthalmic Laboratory Technicians

(O*NET 89917A and 89917D)

Significant Points

- Although some lenses are still produced by hand, technicians increasingly use automated equipment to make lenses.

- Nearly all ophthalmic laboratory technicians learn their skills on the job.

- The number of job openings will be low because the occupation is small, and slow growth in employment is expected.

Nature of the Work

Ophthalmic laboratory technicians—also known as manufacturing opticians, optical mechanics, or optical goods workers—make prescription eyeglass lenses. Prescription lenses are curved in such a way that light is correctly focused onto the retina of the patient's eye, improving vision. Some ophthalmic laboratory technicians manufacture lenses for other optical instruments, such as telescopes and binoculars. Ophthalmic laboratory technicians cut, grind, edge, and finish lenses according to specifications provided by dispensing opticians, optometrists, or ophthalmologists, and they may insert lenses into frames to produce finished glasses. Although some lenses are still produced by hand, technicians increasingly use automated equipment to make lenses.

Ophthalmic laboratory technicians should not be confused with workers in other vision care occupations. Ophthalmologists and optometrists are "eye doctors" who examine eyes, diagnose and treat vision problems, and prescribe corrective lenses. Ophthalmologists are physicians who perform eye surgery. Dispensing opticians, who may also do work described here, help patients select frames and lenses and adjust finished eyeglasses.

Ophthalmic laboratory technicians read prescription specifications and then select standard glass or plastic lens blanks and mark them to indicate where the curves specified on the prescription should be ground. They place the lens into the lens grinder, set the dials for the prescribed curvature, and start the machine. After a minute or so, the lens is ready to be "finished" by a machine that rotates it against a fine abrasive to grind it and smooth out rough edges. The lens is then placed in a polishing machine with an even finer abrasive, to polish it to a smooth, bright finish.

Next, the technician examines the lens through a lensometer, an instrument similar in shape to a microscope, to make sure the degree and placement of the curve is correct. The technician then cuts the lenses and bevels the edges to fit the frame, dips each lens into dye if the prescription calls for tinted or coated lenses, polishes the edges, and assembles the lenses and frame parts into a finished pair of glasses.

In small laboratories, technicians usually handle every phase of the operation. In large ones, technicians may be responsible for operating computerized equipment where virtually every phase of operation is automated. Technicians also inspect the final product for quality and accuracy.

Working Conditions

Ophthalmic laboratory technicians work in relatively clean and well-lighted laboratories and have limited contact with the public. Surroundings are relatively quiet despite the humming of machines. At times, technicians wear goggles to protect their eyes, and they may spend a great deal of time standing. Most ophthalmic laboratory technicians work a 5-day, 40-hour week, which may include weekends, evenings, or occasionally, some overtime. Some work part time. Ophthalmic laboratory technicians need to take precautions against the hazards associated with cutting glass, handling chemicals, and working near machinery.

Employment

Ophthalmic laboratory technicians held about 23,000 jobs in 1998. Thirty-three percent were in retail optical stores that manufacture and sell prescription glasses. Slightly more than 31 percent were in optical laboratories. These laboratories manufacture eyewear for sale by retail stores that fabricate prescription glasses and by ophthalmologists and optometrists. Most of the rest were in wholesalers or in optical laboratories that manufacture lenses for other optical instruments, such as telescopes and binoculars.

Training, Other Qualifications, and Advancement

Nearly all ophthalmic laboratory technicians learn their skills on the job. Employers filling trainee jobs prefer applicants who are high school graduates. Courses in science, mathematics, and computers are valuable; manual dexterity and the ability to do precision work are essential.

Technician trainees producing lenses by hand start on simple tasks such as marking or blocking lenses for grinding, and then they progress to lens grinding, lens cutting, edging, beveling, and eyeglass assembly. Depending on individual aptitude, it may take up to six months to become proficient in all phases of the work.

Technicians using automated systems will find computer skills valuable. Training is completed on the job and varies in duration depending on the type of machinery and individual aptitude.

Some ophthalmic laboratory technicians learn their trade in the Armed Forces. Others attend the few programs in optical technology offered by vocational-technical institutes or trade schools. These programs have classes in optical theory, surfacing and lens finishing, and the reading and applying of prescriptions. Programs vary in length from six months to a year, and most award certificates or diplomas.

Ophthalmic laboratory technicians can become supervisors and managers. Some technicians become dispensing opticians, although further education or training is generally required.

Job Outlook

Overall employment of ophthalmic laboratory technicians is expected to grow more slowly than average through the year 2008. Employment is expected to increase slowly in manufacturing as firms invest in automated machinery. In retail trade, employment is expected to decline.

Demographic trends make it likely that many more Americans will need vision care in the years ahead. Not only will the population grow, but also the proportion of middle-aged and older adults is projected to increase rapidly. Middle age is a time when many people use corrective lenses for the first time, and elderly persons require more vision care, on the whole, than others.

Fashion, too, influences demand. Frames come in a variety of styles and colors—encouraging people to buy more than one pair. Demand is also expected to grow in response to the availability of new technologies that improve the quality and look of corrective lenses, such as anti-reflective coatings and bifocal lenses without the line that's visible in traditional bifocals.

Most job openings will arise from the need to replace technicians who transfer to other occupations or leave the labor force. Only a small number of total job openings will occur each year because the occupation is small.

Earnings

Median hourly earnings of ophthalmic laboratory technicians were $9.39 in 1998. The middle 50 percent earned between $7.56 and $11.58 an hour. The lowest 10 percent earned less than $6.48, and the highest 10 percent earned more than $15.74 an hour. Median hourly earnings of ophthalmic laboratory technicians in 1997 were $8.60 in ophthalmic goods and $8.30 in retail stores, not elsewhere classified.

Related Occupations

Workers in other precision production occupations include bio-medical equipment technicians, dental laboratory technicians, orthodontic technicians, orthotics technicians, prosthetics technicians, and instrument repairers.

Sources of Additional Information

For general information about a career as an ophthalmic laboratory technician and a list of accredited programs in ophthalmic laboratory technology, contact:

- Commission on Opticianry Accreditation, 10111 Martin Luther King, Jr. Hwy., Suite 100, Bowie, MD 20720-4299. Internet: http://www.coaccreditation.com

Opticians, Dispensing

(O*NET 32514)

Significant Points

- Although training requirements vary by State, most dispensing opticians receive training on the job or through apprenticeships lasting two to four years.

- Employment of dispensing opticians is expected to increase as fast as the average for all occupations through 2008 as demand grows for corrective lenses.

Nature of Work

Dispensing opticians fit eyeglasses and contact lenses, following prescriptions written by ophthalmologists or optometrists.

Dispensing opticians examine written prescriptions to determine lens specifications. They recommend eyeglass frames, lenses, and lens coatings after considering the prescription and the customer's occupation, habits, and facial features. Dispensing opticians measure clients' eyes, including the distance between the centers of the pupils and the distance between the eye surface and the lens. For customers without prescriptions, dispensing opticians may use a lensometer to record the present eyeglass prescription. They also may obtain a customer's previous record or verify a prescription with the examining optometrist or ophthalmologist.

Dispensing opticians prepare work orders that give ophthalmic laboratory technicians information needed to grind and insert lenses into a frame. The work order includes lens prescriptions and information on lens size, material, color, and style. Some dispensing opticians grind and insert lenses themselves. After the glasses are made, dispensing opticians verify that the lenses have been ground to specifications. Then they may reshape or bend the frame, by hand or using pliers, so that the eyeglasses fit the customer properly and comfortably. Some also fix, adjust, and refit broken frames. They instruct clients about adapting to, wearing, or caring for eyeglasses.

Some dispensing opticians specialize in fitting contacts, artificial eyes, or cosmetic shells to cover blemished eyes. To fit contact lenses, dispensing opticians measure eye shape and size, select the type of contact lens material, and prepare work orders specifying the prescription and lens size. Fitting contact lenses requires considerable skill, care, and patience. Dispensing opticians observe customers' eyes, corneas, lids, and contact lenses with special instruments and microscopes. During several visits, opticians show customers how to insert, remove, and care for their contacts and ensure the fit is correct.

Dispensing opticians keep records on customer prescriptions, work orders, and payments; track inventory and sales; and perform other administrative duties.

Working Conditions

Dispensing opticians work indoors in attractive, well-lighted, and well-ventilated surroundings. They may work in medical offices or small stores where customers are served one at a time, or in large stores where several dispensing opticians serve a number of customers at once. Opticians spend a lot of time on their feet. If they prepare lenses, they need to take precautions against the hazards associated with glass cutting, chemicals, and machinery.

Most dispensing opticians work a 40-hour week, although some work longer hours. Those in retail stores may work evenings and weekends. Some work part time.

Employment

Dispensing opticians held about 71,000 jobs in 1998. About 50 percent worked for ophthalmologists or optometrists who sell glasses directly to patients. Many also work in retail optical stores that offer one-stop shopping. Customers may have their eyes examined, choose frames, and have glasses made on the spot. Some work in optical departments of drug and department stores.

Training, Other Qualifications, and Advancement

Employers usually hire individuals with no background in opticianry or those who have worked as ophthalmic laboratory technicians and then provide the required training. Training may be informal, on-the-job, or formal apprenticeship. Some employers, however, seek people with post-secondary training in opticianry.

Knowledge of physics, basic anatomy, algebra, geometry, and mechanical drawing is particularly valuable because training usually includes instruction in optical mathematics, optical physics, and the use of precision measuring instruments and other machinery and tools. Dispensing opticians deal directly with the public so they should be tactful, pleasant, and communicate well. Manual dexterity and the ability to do precision work are essential.

Large employers usually offer structured apprenticeship programs, and small employers provide more informal on-the-job training. In the 21 States that offer a license to dispensing opticians, individuals without post-secondary training work from two to four years as apprentices. Apprenticeship or formal training is offered in most States as well.

Apprentices receive technical training and learn office management and sales. Under the supervision of an experienced optician, optometrist, or ophthalmologist, apprentices work directly with patients, fitting eyeglasses and contact lenses. In the 21 States requiring licensure, information about apprenticeships and licensing procedures is available from the State board of occupational licensing.

Formal opticianry training is offered in community colleges and a few colleges and universities. In 1999, there were 25 programs accredited by the Commission on Opticianry Accreditation that awarded two-year associate degrees in ophthalmic dispensing or optometric technology. There are also shorter programs of one year or less. Some States that offer a license to dispensing opticians allow graduates to take the licensure exam immediately upon graduation; others require a few months to a year of experience.

Dispensing opticians may apply to the American Board of Opticianry and the National Contact Lens Examiners for certification of their skills. Certification must be renewed every three years through continuing education.

Many experienced dispensing opticians open their own optical stores. Others become managers of optical stores or sales representatives for wholesalers or manufacturers of eyeglasses or lenses.

Job Outlook

Employment in this occupation is expected to increase as fast as the average for all occupations through 2008 as demand grows for corrective lenses. The number of middle-aged and elderly persons is projected to increase rapidly. Middle age is a time when many individuals use corrective lenses for the first time, and elderly persons require more vision care, on the whole, than others.

Fashion, too, influences demand. Frames come in a growing variety of styles and colors—encouraging people to buy more than one pair. Demand is also expected to grow in response to the availability of new technologies that improve the quality and look of corrective lenses, such as anti-reflective coatings and bifocal lenses without the line that was visible in old-style bifocals. Improvements in bifocal, extended wear, and disposable contact lenses will also spur demand.

The need to replace those who leave the occupation will result in job openings. Nevertheless, the total number of job openings will be relatively small because the occupation is small. This occupation is vulnerable to changes in the business cycle because eyewear purchases can often be deferred for a time. Employment of opticians can fall somewhat during economic downturns.

Earnings

Median annual earnings of dispensing opticians were $22,440 in 1998. The middle 50 percent earned between $17,680 and $28,560 a year. The lowest 10 percent earned less than $14,240, and the highest 10 percent earned more than $37,080 a year. Median annual earnings in the industries employing the largest number of dispensing opticians in 1997 were as follows:

Offices and clinics of medical doctors $25,900
Retail stores, not elsewhere classified 21,500
Offices of other health care practitioners 20,100

Related Occupations

Other workers who deal with customers and perform delicate work include jewelers, locksmiths, ophthalmic laboratory technicians, orthodontic technicians, dental laboratory technicians, prosthetics technicians, camera repairers, and watch repairers.

Sources of Additional Information

For general information about a career as a dispensing optician, contact:

- Opticians Association of America, 10341 Democracy Lane, Fairfax, VA 22030-2521. Internet: http://www.opticians.org

For general information about a career as a dispensing optician and a list of accredited training programs, contact:

- Commission on Opticianry Accreditation, 10341 Democracy Lane, Fairfax, VA 22030-2521. Internet: http://www.coaccreditation.com

For general information on opticianry and a list of home-study programs, seminars, and review materials, contact:

- National Academy of Opticianry, 8401 Corporate Drive, Suite 605, Landover, MD 20785. Internet: http://www.nao.org

Optometrists

(O*NET 32108)

Significant Points

- All States and the District of Columbia require that optometrists be licensed, which requires a Doctor of Optometry degree from an accredited optometry school and passing both a written and a clinical State board examination.

- Employment growth will be fastest in retail optical stores and outpatient clinics.

- Optometrists usually remain in practice until they retire, so job openings arising from replacement needs are low.

Nature of the Work

Over half of the people in the United States wear glasses or contact lenses. Optometrists (doctors of optometry, also known as O.D.'s) provide most primary vision care.

Optometrists examine people's eyes to diagnose vision problems and eye diseases. They use instruments and observation to examine eye health and to test patients' visual acuity, depth and color perception, and their ability to focus and coordinate the eyes. They analyze test results and develop a treatment plan. Optometrists prescribe eyeglasses and contact lenses and provide vision therapy and low vision rehabilitation. They administer drugs to patients to aid in the diagnosis of eye vision problems and prescribe drugs to treat some eye diseases. Optometrists often provide pre- and post-operative care to cataract, laser vision correction, and other eye surgery patients. They also diagnose conditions due to systemic diseases such as diabetes and high blood pressure, and they refer patients to other health practitioners as needed.

Optometrists should not be confused with ophthalmologists or dispensing opticians. Ophthalmologists are physicians who perform eye surgery and who diagnose and treat eye diseases and injuries. Like optometrists, they also examine eyes and prescribe eyeglasses and contact lenses. Dispensing opticians fit and adjust eyeglasses and in some States may fit contact lenses according to prescriptions written by ophthalmologists or optometrists.

Most optometrists are in general practice. Some specialize in work with the elderly, children, or partially sighted persons who need specialized visual devices. Others develop and implement ways to protect workers' eyes from on-the-job strain or injury. Some specialize in contact lenses, sports vision, or vision therapy. A few teach optometry, perform research, or consult.

Most optometrists are private practitioners who also handle the business aspects of running an office, such as developing a patient base, hiring employees, keeping records, and ordering equipment and supplies. Optometrists who operate franchise optical stores may also have some of these duties.

Working Conditions

Optometrists work in places—usually their own offices—which are clean, well lighted, and comfortable. Most full-time optometrists work about 40 hours a week. Many work Saturdays and evenings to suit the needs of patients. Emergency calls, once uncommon, have increased with the passage of therapeutic drug laws expanding optometrists' ability to prescribe medications.

Employment

Optometrists held about 38,000 jobs in 1998. The number of jobs is greater than the number of practicing optometrists because some optometrists hold two or more jobs. For example, an optometrist may have a private practice but also work in another practice, clinic, or vision care center. According to the American Optometric Association, about two-thirds of practicing optometrists are in private practice.

Although many optometrists practice alone, a growing number are in a partnership or group practice. Some optometrists work as salaried employees of other optometrists or of ophthalmologists, hospitals, health maintenance organizations (HMOs), or retail optical stores. A small number of optometrists are consultants for industrial safety programs, insurance companies, manufacturers of ophthalmic products, HMOs, and others.

Training, Other Qualifications, and Advancement

All States and the District of Columbia require that optometrists be licensed. Applicants for a license must have a Doctor of Optometry degree from an accredited optometry school and pass both a written and a clinical State board examination. In many States, applicants can substitute the examinations of the National Board of Examiners in Optometry, usually taken during the student's academic career, for part or all of the written examination. Licenses are renewed every one to three years and in all States, continuing education credits are needed for renewal.

The Doctor of Optometry degree requires completion of a four-year program at an accredited optometry school preceded by at least three years of preoptometric study at an accredited college or university (most optometry students hold a bachelor's degree or higher). In 1999, 17 U.S. schools and colleges of optometry held an accredited status with the Council on Optometric Education of the American Optometric Association.

Requirements for admission to schools of optometry include courses in English, mathematics, physics, chemistry, and biology. A few schools require or recommend courses in psychology, history, sociology, speech, or business. Applicants must take the Optometry Admissions Test, which measures academic ability and scientific comprehension. Most applicants take the test after their sophomore or junior year. Competition for admission is keen.

Optometry programs include classroom and laboratory study of health and visual sciences, as well as clinical training in the diagnosis and treatment of eye disorders. Included are courses in pharmacology, optics, vision science, biochemistry, and systemic disease.

Business ability, self-discipline, and the ability to deal tactfully with patients are important for success. The work of optometrists requires attention to detail and good manual dexterity.

Optometrists wishing to teach or do research may study for a master's degree or Ph.D. in visual science, physiological optics, neurophysiology, public health, health administration, health information and communication, or health education. One-year postgraduate clinical residency programs are available for optometrists who wish to specialize in any of the following areas: family practice optometry, pediatric optometry, geriatric optometry, vision therapy, contact lenses, hospital based optometry, primary care optometry, or ocular disease.

Job Outlook

Employment of optometrists is expected to grow about as fast as the average for all occupations through 2008 in response to the vision care needs of a growing and aging population. As baby boomers age, they will be more likely to visit optometrists and ophthalmologists because of the onset of vision problems in middle age, including computer-related vision problems. The demand for optometric services will also increase because of growth in the oldest age group, with their increased likelihood of cataracts, glaucoma, diabetes, and hypertension. Employment of optometrists will also grow due to greater recognition of the importance of vision care, rising personal incomes, and growth in employee vision care plans. Employment growth will be fastest in retail optical stores and outpatient clinics.

Employment of optometrists would grow more rapidly were it not for anticipated productivity gains that will allow each optometrist to see more patients. These gains will result from greater use of optometric assistants and other support personnel and the introduction of new equipment and procedures. New surgical procedures using lasers are available that can correct some vision problems, but they remain expensive.

In addition to growth, the need to replace optometrists who leave the occupation will create employment opportunities. Relatively few opportunities from this source are expected, however, because most optometrists continue to practice until they retire; few transfer to other occupations.

Earnings

Median annual earnings of salaried optometrists were $68,500 in 1998. The middle 50 percent earned between $43,750 and $93,700 a year. The lowest 10 percent earned less than $24,820, and the highest 10 percent earned more than $123,770 a year. Salaried optometrists tend to earn more initially than optometrists who set up independent practices. In the long run, however, those in private practice usually earn more.

According to the American Optometric Association, new optometry graduates in their first year of practice earned median net incomes of $55,000 in 1998. Overall, optometrists earned median net incomes of $92,000.

Related Occupations

Workers in other occupations who apply scientific knowledge to prevent, diagnose, and treat disorders and injuries are chiropractors, dentists, physicians, podiatrists, veterinarians, speech-language pathologists, and audiologists.

Sources of Additional Information

For information on optometry as a career and a listing of accredited optometric educational institutions, as well as required preoptometry courses, contact:

- American Optometric Association, Educational Services, 243 North Lindbergh Blvd., St. Louis, MO 63141-7881. Internet: http://www.aoanet.org
- Association of Schools and Colleges of Optometry, 6110 Executive Blvd., Suite 510, Rockville, MD 20852. Internet: http://www.opted.org

The Board of Optometry in each State can supply information on licensing requirements.

For information on specific admission requirements and sources of financial aid, contact the admissions officer of individual optometry schools.

Paralegals

(O*NET 28305)

Significant Points

- While some paralegals train on the job, employers increasingly prefer graduates of post-secondary paralegal training programs.
- Paralegals are projected to rank among the fastest growing occupations in the economy as they increasingly perform many legal tasks formerly carried out by lawyers.
- Stiff competition is expected as the number of graduates of paralegal training programs and others seeking to enter the profession outpaces job growth.

Nature of the Work

While lawyers assume ultimate responsibility for legal work, they often delegate many of their tasks to paralegals. In fact, paralegals continue to assume a growing range of tasks in the Nation's legal offices and perform many of the same tasks as lawyers. Nevertheless, they are still explicitly prohibited from carrying out duties that are considered to be the practice of law, such as setting legal fees, giving legal advice, and presenting cases in court.

One of a paralegal's most important tasks is helping lawyers prepare for closings, hearings, trials, and corporate meetings. Paralegals investigate the facts of cases and ensure all relevant information is considered. They also identify appropriate laws, judicial decisions, legal articles, and other materials that are relevant to assigned cases. After they analyze and organize the information, paralegals may prepare written reports that attorneys use in determining how cases should be handled. Should attorneys decide to file lawsuits on behalf of clients, paralegals may help prepare the legal arguments, draft pleadings and motions to be filed with the court, obtain affidavits, and assist attorneys during trials. Paralegals also organize and track files of all important case documents and make them available and easily accessible to attorneys.

In addition to this preparatory work, paralegals also perform a number of other vital functions. For example, they help draft contracts, mortgages, separation agreements, and trust instruments. They may also assist in preparing tax returns and planning estates. Some paralegals coordinate the activities of other law office employees and maintain financial records for the office. Various additional tasks may differ depending on the employer.

Paralegals are found in all types of organizations, but most are employed by law firms, corporate legal departments, and various levels of government. In these organizations, they may work in all areas of the law, including litigation, personal injury, corporate law, criminal law, employee benefits, intellectual property, labor law, and real estate. Within specialties, functions often are broken down further so paralegals may deal with a specific area. For example, paralegals specializing in labor law may deal exclusively with employee benefits.

The duties of paralegals also differ widely based on the type of organization in which they are employed. Paralegals who work for corporations often assist attorneys with employee contracts, shareholder agreements, stock option plans, and employee benefit plans. They may also help prepare and file annual financial reports, maintain corporate minute books and resolutions, and secure loans for the corporation. Paralegals also occasionally review government regulations to ensure the corporation operates within the law.

The duties of paralegals who work in the public sector usually vary in each agency. In general, they analyze legal material for internal use, maintain reference files, conduct research for attorneys, and collect and analyze evidence for agency hearings. They may then prepare informative or explanatory material on laws, agency regulations, and agency policy for general use by the agency and the public. Paralegals employed in community legal service projects help the poor, the aged, and others in need of legal assistance. They file forms, conduct research, and prepare documents, and when authorized by law, they may represent clients at administrative hearings.

Paralegals in small and medium-sized law firms usually perform a variety of duties that require a general knowledge of the law. For example, they may research judicial decisions on improper police arrests or help prepare a mortgage contract. Paralegals employed by large law firms, government agencies, and corporations, however, are more likely to specialize in one aspect of the law.

A growing number of paralegals use computers in their work. Computer software packages and the Internet are increasingly used to search legal literature stored in computer databases and on CD-ROM. In litigation involving many supporting documents, paralegals may use computer databases to retrieve, organize, and index various materials. Imaging software allows paralegals to scan documents directly into a database, while billing programs help them to track hours billed to clients. Computer software packages may also be used to perform tax computations and explore the consequences of possible tax strategies for clients.

Working Conditions

Paralegals employed by corporations and government usually work a standard 40-hour week. Although most paralegals work year round, some are temporarily employed during busy times of the year and then released when the workload diminishes. Paralegals who work for law firms sometimes work very long hours when they are under pressure to meet deadlines. Some law firms reward such loyalty with bonuses and additional time off.

These workers handle many routine assignments, particularly when they are inexperienced. As they gain experience, paralegals usually assume more varied tasks with additional responsibility. Paralegals do most of their work at desks in offices and law libraries. Occasionally, they travel to gather information and perform other duties.

Employment

Paralegals held about 136,000 jobs in 1998. Private law firms employed the vast majority; most of the remainder worked for corporate legal departments and the various levels of government. Within the Federal government, the Department of Justice is the largest employer, followed by the Departments of Treasury and Defense and the Federal Deposit Insurance Corporation. Other employers include State and local governments, publicly funded legal service centers, banks, real estate development companies, and insurance companies. A small number of paralegals own their own businesses and work as freelance legal assistants, contracting their services to attorneys or corporate legal departments.

Training, Other Qualifications, and Advancement

There are several ways to become a paralegal. Employers usually require formal paralegal training obtained through associate or bachelor's degree programs or through a certification program. Increasingly, employers prefer graduates of four-year paralegal programs or college graduates who have completed paralegal certificate programs. Some employers prefer to train paralegals on the job, hiring college graduates with no legal experience or promoting experienced legal secretaries. Other entrants have experience in a technical field that is useful to law firms, such as a background in tax preparation for tax and estate practice or nursing or health administration for personal injury practice.

More than 800 formal paralegal training programs are offered by four-year colleges and universities, law schools, community and junior colleges, business schools, and proprietary schools. There are currently 232 programs approved by the American Bar Association (ABA). Although this approval is neither required nor sought by many programs, graduation from an ABA-approved program can enhance one's employment opportunities. The requirements for admission to these programs vary. Some require certain college courses or a bachelor's degree; others accept high school graduates or those with legal experience; and a few schools require standardized tests and personal interviews.

Paralegal programs include two-year associate's degree programs, four-year bachelor's degree programs, and certificate programs that take only a few months to complete. Many certificate programs require only a high school diploma or GED for admission. Programs typically include courses on law and legal research techniques, in addition to courses covering specialized areas of law, such as real estate, estate planning and probate, litigation, family law, contracts, and criminal law. Many employers prefer applicants with specialized training.

The quality of paralegal training programs varies; the better programs usually include job placement. Programs increasingly include courses introducing students to the legal applications of computers. Many paralegal training programs include an internship in which students gain practical experience by working for several months in a law office, corporate legal department, or government agency. Experience gained in internships is an asset when seeking a job after graduation. Prospective students should examine the experiences of recent graduates before enrolling in those programs.

Although most employers do not require certification, earning a voluntary certificate from a professional society may offer advantages in the labor market. The National Association of Legal Assistants, for example, has established standards for certification requiring various combinations of education and experience. Paralegals who meet these standards are eligible to take a two-day examination, which is given three times each year at several regional testing centers. Those who pass this examination may use the designation Certified Legal Assistant (CLA). In addition, the Paralegal Advanced Competency Exam, established in 1996 and administered through the National Federation of Paralegal Associations, offers professional recognition to paralegals with a bachelor's degree and at least two years of experience. Those who pass this examination may use the designation Registered Paralegal (RP).

Paralegals must be able to document and present their findings and opinions to their supervising attorney. They need to understand legal terminology and have good research and investigative skills. Familiarity with the operation and applications of computers in legal research and litigation support is also increasingly important. Paralegals should stay informed of new developments in the laws that affect their area of practice. Participation in continuing legal education seminars allows paralegals to maintain and expand their legal knowledge.

Because paralegals frequently deal with the public, they should be courteous and uphold the ethical standards of the legal profession. The National Association of Legal Assistants, the National Federation of Paralegal Associations, and a few States have established ethical guidelines for paralegals to follow.

Paralegals are usually given more responsibilities and less supervision as they gain work experience. Experienced paralegals who work in large law firms, corporate legal departments, and government agencies may supervise and delegate assignments to other paralegals and clerical staff. Advancement opportunities also include promotion to managerial and other law-related positions within the firm or corporate legal department. However, some paralegals find it easier to move to another law firm when seeking increased responsibility or advancement.

Job Outlook

Paralegals are projected to rank among the fastest growing occupations in the economy through 2008. However, stiff competition for jobs should continue as the number of graduates of paralegal training programs and others seeking to enter the profession outpaces job growth. Employment growth stems from law firms and other employers with legal staffs increasingly hiring paralegals in order to lower the cost and increase the availability and efficiency of legal services. The majority of job openings for paralegals in the future will be new jobs created by rapid employment growth; other job openings will arise as people leave the occupation.

Private law firms will continue to be the largest employers of paralegals, but a growing array of other organizations, such as corporate legal departments, insurance companies, real estate and title insurance firms, and banks will also continue to hire paralegals. These organizations are expected to grow as an increasing population requires additional legal services, especially in areas such as intellectual property, health care, international, elder, sexual harassment, and environmental law. The growth of prepaid legal plans should also contribute to the demand for legal services. Paralegal employment in these organizations is expected to increase as paralegals are assigned a growing range of tasks and are increasingly employed in small and medium-sized establishments.

Job opportunities for paralegals will expand in the public sector as well. Community legal service programs, which provide assistance to poor, aged, minorities, and middle-income families, will employ additional paralegals to minimize expenses and serve the most people. Federal, State, and local government agencies, consumer organizations, and the courts should also continue to hire paralegals in increasing numbers.

To a limited extent, paralegal jobs are affected by the business cycle. During recessions, demand declines for some discretionary legal services, such as planning estates, drafting wills, and handling real estate transactions. Corporations are less inclined to initiate litigation when falling sales and profits lead to fiscal belt tightening. As a result, full-time paralegals employed in offices adversely affected by a recession may be laid off or have their work hours reduced. On the other hand, during recessions, corporations and individuals are more likely to face other problems that require legal assistance, such as bankruptcies, foreclosures, and divorces. Paralegals, who provide many of the same legal services as lawyers at a lower cost, tend to fare relatively better in difficult economic conditions.

Earnings

Earnings of paralegals vary greatly. Salaries depend on education, training, experience, type and size of employer, and the geographic location of the job. In general, paralegals who work for large law firms or in large metropolitan areas earn more than those who work for smaller firms or in less populated regions. In 1998, full-time, wage and salary paralegals had median annual earnings of $32,760. The middle 50 percent earned between $26,240 and 40,960. The top 10 percent earned more than $50,290, while the bottom 10 percent earned less than $21,770. Median annual earnings in the industries employing the largest numbers of paralegals in 1997 are shown below:

Federal government	$43,900
Local government	32,200
Legal services	30,300

According to the National Association of Legal Assistants, paralegals had an average salary of $34,000 in 1997. In addition to a salary, many paralegals received a bonus, which averaged about $2,100. According to the National Federation of Paralegal Associations, starting salaries of paralegals with one year or less experience averaged $30,700 in 1997.

Related Occupations

Several other occupations call for a specialized understanding of the law and the legal system but do not require the extensive training of a lawyer. These include abstractors, claim examiners, compliance and enforcement inspectors, occupational safety and health workers, patent agents, and title examiners.

Sources of Additional Information

General information on a career as a paralegal can be obtained from:

● Standing Committee on Legal Assistants, American Bar Association, 750 North Lake Shore Dr., Chicago, IL 60611. Internet: http://www.abanet.org/legalassts

For information on the Certified Legal Assistant exam, schools that offer training programs in a specific State, and standards and guidelines for paralegals, contact:

● National Association of Legal Assistants, Inc., 1516 South Boston St., Suite 200, Tulsa, OK 74119. Internet: http://www.nala.org

Information on a career as a paralegal, schools that offer training programs, job postings for paralegals, the Paralegal Advanced Competency Exam, and local paralegal associations can be obtained from:

● National Federation of Paralegal Associations, P.O. Box 33108, Kansas City, MO 64114. Internet: http://www.paralegals.org

Information on paralegal training programs, including the pamphlet "How to Choose a Paralegal Education Program," may be obtained from:

● American Association for Paralegal Education, P.O. Box 40244, Overland Park, KS 66204. Internet: http://www.aafpe.org

Information on acquiring a job as a paralegal specialist with the Federal government may be obtained from the Office of Personnel Management through a telephone-based system. Consult your telephone directory under U.S. Government for a local number or call (912) 757-3000; TDD (912) 744-2299. This call is not toll-free, and charges may result. Information also is available from their Internet site: http://www.usajobs.opm.gov.

Pharmacists

(O*NET 32517)

Significant Points

● Pharmacists are becoming more involved in drug therapy decision-making and patient counseling.

● Earnings are very high, but some pharmacists work long hours, nights, weekends, and holidays.

Nature of the Work

Pharmacists dispense drugs prescribed by physicians and other health practitioners and provide information to patients about medications and their use. They advise physicians and other health practitioners on the selection, dosages, interactions, and side effects of medications. Pharmacists must understand the use, composition, and clinical effects of drugs. Compounding—the actual mixing of ingredients to form powders, tablets, capsules, ointments, and solutions—is only a small part of a pharmacist's practice, because most medicines are produced by pharmaceutical companies in a standard dosage and drug delivery form.

Pharmacists in community or retail pharmacies counsel patients, as well as answer questions about prescription drugs, such as possible adverse reactions or interactions. They provide information about over-the-counter drugs and make recommendations after asking a series of health questions, such as whether the customer is taking any other medications. They also give advice about durable medical equipment and home health care supplies. Those who own or manage community pharmacies may sell nonhealth-related merchandise, hire and supervise personnel, and oversee the general operation of the pharmacy. Some community pharmacists provide specialized services to help patients manage conditions such as diabetes, asthma, smoking cessation, or high blood pressure.

Pharmacists in hospitals and clinics dispense medications and advise the medical staff on the selection and effects of drugs. They may make sterile solutions and buy medical supplies. They also assess, plan, and monitor drug regimens. They counsel patients on the use of drugs while in the hospital and on their use at home when they are discharged. Pharmacists may also evaluate drug use patterns and outcomes for patients in hospitals or managed care organizations.

Pharmacists who work in home health care monitor drug therapy and prepare infusions—solutions that are injected into patients—and other medications for use in the home.

Most pharmacists keep confidential computerized records of patients' drug therapies to ensure that harmful drug interactions do not occur. They frequently teach pharmacy students serving as interns in preparation for graduation and licensure.

Some pharmacists specialize in specific drug therapy areas, such as psychiatric disorders, intravenous nutrition support, oncology, nuclear pharmacy, and pharmacotherapy.

Working Conditions

Pharmacists usually work in clean, well-lighted, and well-ventilated areas. Many pharmacists spend most of their workday on their feet. When working with sterile or potentially dangerous pharmaceutical products, pharmacists wear gloves and masks and work with other special protective equipment. Many community and hospital pharmacies are open for extended hours or around the clock, so pharmacists may work evenings, nights, weekends, and holidays. Consultant pharmacists may travel to nursing homes or other facilities to monitor people's drug therapy.

About 1 out of 7 pharmacists worked part time in 1998. Most full-time salaried pharmacists worked about 40 hours a week. Some, including most self-employed pharmacists, worked more than 50 hours a week.

Employment

Pharmacists held about 185,000 jobs in 1998. About 3 out of 5 worked in community pharmacies that were either independently owned or part of a drug store chain, grocery store, department store, or mass merchandiser. Most community pharmacists were salaried employees, but some were self–employed owners. About one-quarter of salaried pharmacists worked in hospitals, and others worked in clinics, mail-order pharmacies, pharmaceutical wholesalers, home health care agencies, or the Federal government.

Some pharmacists hold more than one job. They may work a standard week in their primary work setting and work part time elsewhere.

Training, Other Qualifications, and Advancement

A license to practice pharmacy is required in all States, the District of Columbia, and U.S. territories. To obtain a license, one must serve an internship under a licensed pharmacist, graduate from an accredited college of pharmacy, and pass a State examination. Most States grant a license without extensive reexamination to qualified pharmacists already licensed by another State (check with State boards of pharmacy for details). Many pharmacists are licensed to practice in more than one State. States may require continuing education for license renewal.

In 1998, 81 colleges of pharmacy were accredited to confer degrees by the American Council on Pharmaceutical Education. Nearly all pharmacy programs grant the degree of Doctor of Pharmacy (Pharm.D.) which requires at least six years of post-secondary study. A small number of pharmacy schools continue to award the five-year Bachelor of Science (B.S.) in pharmacy degree. However, all accredited pharmacy schools are expected to graduate their last B.S. class by the year 2005. Either a Pharm.D. or B.S. degree currently fulfills the requirements to take the licensure examination of a state board of pharmacy.

Requirements for admission to colleges of pharmacy vary. A few colleges admit students directly from high school. However, most colleges of pharmacy, require one or two years of college-level prepharmacy education. Entry requirements usually include mathematics and basic sciences, such as chemistry, biology, and physics, as well as courses in the humanities and social sciences. Some colleges require the applicant to take the Pharmacy College Admissions Test.

All colleges of pharmacy offer courses in pharmacy practice, designed to teach students to dispense prescriptions, to communicate with patients and other health professionals, and to strengthen their understanding of professional ethics and practice management responsibilities. Pharmacists' training increasingly emphasizes direct patient care, as well as consultative services to other health professionals.

In the 1997-1998 academic year, 60 colleges of pharmacy awarded the Master of Science degree or the Ph.D. degree. Although a number of pharmacy graduates interested in further training pursue an advanced degree in pharmacy, there are other options. Some complete one- or two-year residency programs or fellowships. Pharmacy residencies are postgraduate training programs in pharmacy practice. Pharmacy fellowships are highly individualized programs designed to prepare participants to work in research laboratories.

Areas of graduate study include pharmaceutics and pharmaceutical chemistry (physical and chemical properties of drugs and dosage forms), pharmacology (effects of drugs on the body), and pharmacy administration, including pharmacoeconomics and social-behavioral aspects of patient care.

Prospective pharmacists should have scientific aptitude, good communication skills, and a desire to help others. They must also be conscientious and pay close attention to detail, because the decisions they make affect human lives.

In community pharmacies, pharmacists usually begin at the staff level. After they gain experience and secure the necessary capital, some become owners or part owners of pharmacies. Pharmacists in chain drug stores may be promoted to pharmacy supervisor or manager at the store level, then to the district or regional level, and later to an executive position within the chain's headquarters.

Hospital pharmacists may advance to supervisory or administrative positions. Pharmacists in the pharmaceutical industry may advance in marketing, sales, research, quality control, production, packaging, and other areas.

Job Outlook

Employment of pharmacists is expected to grow slower than the average for all occupations through the year 2008, despite the increased pharmaceutical needs of a larger and older population and greater use of medication.

Retail pharmacies are taking steps to increase their prescription volume to make up for declining dispensing fees. Automation of drug dispensing and greater use of pharmacy technicians will help them to dispense more prescriptions. The number of community pharmacists needed in the future will depend on the expansion rate of chain drug stores and the willingness of insurers to reimburse pharmacists for providing clinical services to patients taking prescription medications. With its emphasis on cost control, managed care encourages growth of lower-cost prescription drug distributors such as mail-order firms for certain medications. Slower employment growth is expected in traditional chain and independent pharmacies.

Employment in hospitals is also expected to grow slowly, as hospitals reduce inpatient stays, downsize, and consolidate departments. Pharmacy services are shifting to long-term, ambulatory, and home care settings, where opportunities for pharmacists will be best. New opportunities for pharmacists are emerging in managed care organizations, where pharmacists analyze trends and patterns in medication use for their populations of patients. Fast growth is also expected for pharmacists trained in research, disease management, and pharmacoeconomics—determining the costs and benefits of different drug therapies.

Cost-conscious insurers and health systems may continue to emphasize the role of pharmacists in primary and preventive health services. They realize that the expense of using medication to treat diseases and conditions is often considerably less than the potential costs for patients whose conditions go untreated. Pharmacists can also reduce the expenses resulting from unexpected complications due to allergic reactions or medication interactions.

The increased number of middle aged and elderly people will spur demand for pharmacists in all practice settings. The number of prescriptions influences the demand for pharmacists, and the middle aged and elderly populations use more prescription drugs, on average, than younger people.

Other factors likely to increase the demand for pharmacists through the year 2008 include the likelihood of scientific advances that will make more drug products available, new developments in administering medication, and increasingly sophisticated consumers seeking more information about drugs.

Earnings

Median annual earnings of pharmacists in 1998 were $66,220. The middle 50 percent earned between $52,310 and $80,250 a year. The lowest 10 percent earned less than $42,550, and the highest 10 percent earned more than $88,670 a year. Median annual earnings in the industries employing the largest numbers of pharmacists in 1997 were as follows:

Grocery stores $67,000

Drug stores and proprietary stores 63,400

Hospitals 62,600

Federal government 61,700

According to a survey by *Drug Topics* magazine, published by Medical Economics Co., average base salaries of full-time, salaried pharmacists were about $59,700 a year in 1998. Pharmacists working in chain drug stores had an average base salary of about $62,300 a year, while pharmacists working in independent drug stores averaged about $56,300, and hospital pharmacists averaged about $59,500 a year. Overall, salaries for pharmacists were highest on the West coast. Many pharmacists also receive compensation in the form of bonuses, overtime, and profit-sharing.

Related Occupations

Persons in other professions who may work with pharmaceutical compounds are biological technicians, medical scientists, pharmaceutical chemists, and pharmacologists.

Sources of Additional Information

For information on pharmacy as a career, preprofessional and professional requirements, programs offered by all the colleges of pharmacy, and student financial aid, contact:

- American Association of Colleges of Pharmacy, 1426 Prince St., Alexandria, VA 22314. Internet: http://www.aacp.org

General information on careers in pharmacy is available from:

- American Society of Health-System Pharmacists, 7272 Wisconsin Ave., Bethesda, MD 20814. Internet: http://www.ashp.org
- American Pharmaceutical Association, 2215 Constitution Ave. NW., Washington, DC 20037-2985. Internet: http://www.aphanet.org
- National Association of Chain Drug Stores, 413 N. Lee St., P.O. Box 1417-D49, Alexandria, VA 22313-1480. Internet: www.nacds.org

State licensure requirements are available from each State's Board of Pharmacy.

Information on specific college entrance requirements, curriculums, and financial aid is available from any college of pharmacy.

Pharmacy Technicians and Assistants

(O*NET 32518)

Significant Points

- Opportunities for pharmacy technicians and assistants are expected to be good, especially for those with formal training or previous work experience.

- Many technicians and assistants work evenings, weekends, and some holidays.

- Seven out of 10 jobs were in retail pharmacies, either independently owned or part of a drug store chain, grocery store, department store, or mass merchandiser.

Nature of the Work

Pharmacy technicians and assistants help licensed pharmacists provide medication and other health care products to patients. *Pharmacy technicians* usually perform more complex tasks than assistants do, although in some States their duties and job titles overlap. Technicians usually perform routine tasks to help prepare prescribed medication for patients, such as counting and labeling. A pharmacist must check every prescription before it can be given to a patient. Technicians refer any questions regarding prescriptions, drug information, or health matters to a pharmacist. *Pharmacy assistants* usually have fewer, less complex responsibilities than technicians. Assistants are often clerks or cashiers who primarily answer telephones, handle money, stock shelves, and perform other clerical duties.

Pharmacy technicians who work in retail pharmacies have varying responsibilities depending on State rules and regulations. Technicians receive written prescriptions or requests for a prescription refill from patients or representatives. They must verify that the information on the prescription is complete and accurate. To prepare the prescription the technician must retrieve, count, pour, weigh, measure, and sometimes mix the medication. Then they prepare the prescription labels, select the type of prescription container, and affix the prescription and auxiliary labels to the container. Once the prescription is filled, technicians price and file the prescription, which must be checked by a pharmacist before it is given to a patient. Technicians may establish and maintain patient profiles, prepare insurance claim forms, and stock and take inventory of prescription and over-the-counter medications. Some also clean the pharmacy equipment, help with the maintenance of equipment and supplies, and manage the cash register.

In hospitals, technicians have added responsibilities. They read patient charts and prepare and deliver the medicine to patients. The pharmacist must check the order before it is delivered to the patient. The technician then copies the information about the prescribed medication onto the patient's profile. Technicians may also assemble a 24-hour supply of medicine for every patient. They package and label each dose separately. The package is then placed in the medicine cabinet of each patient, until the supervising pharmacist checks it. It is then given to the patient. Technicians are responsible for keeping a running inventory of medicines, chemicals, and other supplies used.

Working Conditions

Pharmacy technicians and assistants work in clean, organized, well-lighted, and well-ventilated areas. Most of their workday is spent on their feet. They may be required to lift heavy boxes or to use stepladders to retrieve supplies from high shelves.

Technicians and assistants work the same hours as pharmacists. This includes evenings, nights, weekends, and some holidays. Most technicians work 35-45 hours a week. Since some hospital and retail pharmacies are open 24 hours a day, technicians and assistants may work varying shifts. There are many opportunities for part-time work in both retail and hospital settings.

Employment

Pharmacy technicians and assistants held about 170,000 jobs in 1998. Seven out of 10 jobs were in retail pharmacies, either independently owned or part of a drug store chain, grocery store, department store, or mass merchandiser. Two out of 10 jobs were in hospitals, and a small number were in mail-order pharmacies, clinics, pharmaceutical wholesalers, and the Federal government.

Training, Other Qualifications, and Advancement

Although most pharmacy technicians receive informal on-the-job training, employers are beginning to favor those who have completed formal training. However, there are currently few State and no Federal requirements for formal training or education of pharmacy technicians. Employers who can neither afford, nor have the time to give on-the-job training, often seek formally educated pharmacy technicians. Formal education programs emphasize the technicians' interest and dedication to the work to potential employers. Some hospitals, proprietary schools, vocational or technical colleges, and community colleges offer formal education programs.

Formal pharmacy technician education programs require classroom and laboratory work in a variety of areas, including medical and pharmaceutical terminology, pharmaceutical calculations, pharmacy record keeping, pharmaceutical techniques, and pharmacy law and ethics. Technicians are also required to learn medication names, actions, uses, and doses. Many training programs include clerkship or internships, where students gain hands-on experience in actual pharmacies. Students receive a diploma, certificate, or an associate degree, depending on the program.

Prospective pharmacy technicians with experience working as an assistant in a community pharmacy or volunteering in a hospital may have an advantage. Employers also prefer applicants with strong customer service and communication skills and experience managing inventories, counting, measuring, and using a computer. Technicians entering the field need strong spelling and reading skills. A background in mathematics, chemistry, English, and health education may also be beneficial.

The Pharmacy Technician Certification Board administers the National Pharmacy Technician Certification Examination. This exam is voluntary and displays the competency of the individual to act as a pharmacy technician. Eligible exam candidates must have a high school diploma or GED, and those who pass the exam earn the title of Certified Pharmacy Technician. Certification helps technicians formalize their career and feel like part of a health care team. Employers know that individuals who pass the exam have a standardized body of knowledge and skills.

Certified technicians must be recertified every two years. Technicians must complete 20 contact hours of pharmacy related topics within the two-year certification period to become eligible for recertification. At least one contact hour must be in the area of pharmacy law. Contact hours can be earned from several different sources including pharmacy associations, pharmacy colleges, and pharmacy technician training programs. Up to 10 contact hours can be earned when the technician is employed under the direct supervision and instruction of the pharmacist.

Successful pharmacy technicians are alert, observant, organized, dedicated, and responsible. They should be willing and able to take directions. They must enjoy precise work; details are sometimes a matter of life and death. Although pharmacists must check and approve all their work, they should be able to work on their own without constant instruction from the pharmacist. Candidates interested in becoming pharmacy technicians cannot have prior records of drug or substance abuse.

Strong interpersonal and communication skills are needed because there is a lot of interaction with patients, coworkers, and health care professionals. Teamwork is very important because technicians are often required to work with other technicians.

Pharmacy assistants are almost always trained on the job. They may begin by observing a more experienced worker. After they become familiar with the store's equipment, policies, and procedures, they begin to work on their own. Once they become experienced workers, they are not likely to receive training, except when new equipment is introduced or when policies or procedures change. When necessary, on-the-job training is usually provided.

To become a pharmacy assistant, one should be able to perform repetitive work accurately. Assistants need good basic mathematics skills and good manual dexterity. Because they deal constantly with the public, pharmacy assistants should be neat in appearance and able to deal pleasantly and tactfully with customers. Some employers may prefer people with experience typing, handling money, or operating specialized equipment, including computers.

Advancement is usually limited, although some technicians enroll in pharmacy school and become pharmacists.

Job Outlook

Employment of pharmacy technicians and assistants is expected to grow as fast as average for all occupations through 2008 due to the increased pharmaceutical needs of a larger and older population and greater use of medication. The increased number of middle aged and elderly people will spur demand for technicians and assistants in all practice settings. The middle aged and elderly populations use more prescription drugs, on average, than younger people.

Job opportunities are expected to be good, especially for technicians and assistants with formal training or previous experience. Many jobs for pharmacy technicians and assistants will result from the need to replace workers who transfer to other occupations or leave the labor force. Opportunities for part-time work are also expected to be good.

Cost-conscious insurers, pharmacies, and health systems will continue to emphasize the role of technicians and assistants. As a result, pharmacy technicians and assistants will assume responsibility for more routine tasks previously performed by pharmacists. Pharmacy technicians will also need to learn and master new pharmacy technology as it surfaces. For example, robotic machines are used to dispense medicine into containers. Technicians oversee the machine, stock the bins, and label the containers. Although automation is becoming increasingly incorporated into the job, it will not necessarily reduce the need for technicians.

Many States have legislated the maximum number of technicians who can work under a pharmacist. In some States, increased demand for technicians has encouraged an expanded ratio of technicians to pharmacists.

Earnings

Median hourly earnings of pharmacy technicians in 1998 were $8.54. The middle 50 percent earned between $7.11 and $10.64; the lowest 10 percent earned less than $6.08 and the highest 10 percent more than $12.73. Median hourly earnings of pharmacy technicians were $8.00 in drug stores, $8.40 in grocery stores, and $8.50 in department stores in 1997.

Median hourly earnings of pharmacy aides, also called pharmacy technicians, were $8.88 in 1998. The middle 50 percent earned between $7.02 and $10.75; the lowest 10 percent earned less than $5.94 and the highest 10 percent more than $12.64. Median hourly earnings of pharmacy aides were $7.10 in drug stores and $9.60 in hospitals in 1997.

Certified technicians may earn more. Shift differentials for working evenings or weekends can also increase earnings. Some technicians belong to unions representing hospital or grocery store workers.

Related Occupations

Workers in other medical support occupations include dental assistants, health information technicians, licensed practical nurses, medical secretaries, medical transcriptionists, occupational therapy assistants and aides, physical therapist assistants and aides, and surgical technologists.

Sources of Additional Information

For information on certification and a National Pharmacy Technician Certification Examination Candidate Handbook contact:

- Pharmacy Technician Certification Board, 2215 Constitution Ave. NW., Washington DC 20037. Internet: http://www.ptcb.org

For information on a career as a pharmacy technician, contact:

- American Society of Health System Pharmacists, 7272 Wisconsin Ave., Bethesda, MD 20814. Internet: http://www.ashp.org
- National Association of Chain Drug Stores, 413 N. Lee St., P.O. Box 1417-D49, Alexandria, VA 22313-1480. Internet: www.nacds.org

Physical Therapist Assistants and Aides

(O*NET 66017)

Significant Points

- Employment is projected to increase over the 1998-2008 period, but due to the effects of Federal limits on reimbursement for therapy services, the majority of expected employment growth is expected to occur during the second half of the projection period.

- Most licensed physical therapist assistants have an associate's degree, but physical therapist aides usually learn skills on the job.

- Two-thirds of jobs for physical therapist assistants and aides were in hospitals or offices of physical therapists.

Nature of the Work

Physical therapist assistants and aides perform components of physical therapy procedures and related tasks selected and delegated by a supervising physical therapist. These workers assist physical therapists in providing services that help improve mobility, relieve pain, and prevent or limit permanent physical disabilities of patients suffering from injuries or disease. Patients include accident victims and individuals with disabling conditions, such as lower back pain, arthritis, heart disease, fractures, head injuries, and cerebral palsy.

Physical therapist assistants perform a variety of tasks. Treatment procedures delegated to these workers, under the direction of therapists, involve exercises, massages, electrical stimulation, paraffin baths, hot and cold packs, traction, and ultrasound. Physical therapist assistants record the patient's responses to treatment and report to the physical therapist the outcome of each treatment.

Physical therapist aides help make therapy sessions productive, under the direct supervision of a physical therapist or physical therapist assistant. They are usually responsible for keeping the treatment area clean and organized and preparing for each patient's therapy. When patients need assistance moving to or from a treatment area, aides push them in a wheelchair or provide them with a shoulder to lean on. Because they are not licensed, aides perform a more limited range of tasks than physical therapist assistants do.

The duties of aides include some clerical tasks, such as ordering depleted supplies, answering the phone, and filling out insurance forms and other paperwork. The extent to which an aide or an assistant performs clerical tasks depends on the size and location of the facility.

Working Conditions

The hours and days that physical therapist assistants and aides work vary depending on the facility and whether they are full or part-time employees. Many outpatient physical therapy offices and clinics have evening and weekend hours to help coincide with patients' personal schedules.

Physical therapist assistants and aides need to have a moderate degree of strength, due to the physical exertion required in assisting patients with their treatment. For example, in some cases, assistants and aides need to help lift patients. Additionally, kneeling, stooping, and standing for long periods are all part of the job.

Employment

Physical therapist assistants and aides held 82,000 jobs in 1998. They work alongside physical therapists in a variety of settings. Over two-thirds of all assistants and aides work in hospitals or offices of physical therapists. Others work in nursing and personal care facilities, outpatient rehabilitation centers, offices and clinics of physicians, and home health agencies.

Training, Other Qualifications, and Advancement

Physical therapist aides are trained on the job, but physical therapist assistants typically have earned an associate's degree from an accredited physical therapist assistant program. As of January 1997, 44 States and Puerto Rico regulated assistants. Additional requirements include certification in CPR and other first aid and a minimum number of hours of clinical experience.

According to the American Physical Therapy Association, there were 274 accredited physical therapist assistant programs in the United States as of 1999. Accredited physical therapist assistant programs are designed to last two years, or four semesters, and culminate in an associate's degree. Admission into physical therapist assistant programs is competitive, and it is not unusual for colleges to have long waiting lists of prospective candidates. Programs are divided into academic study and hands-on clinical experience. Academic coursework includes algebra, anatomy and physiology, biology, chemistry, and psychology. Before students begin their clinical field experience, many programs require that they complete a semester of anatomy and physiology and have certifications in CPR and other first aid. Both educators and prospective employers view clinical experience as an integral part of ensuring that students understand the responsibilities of a physical therapist assistant.

Employers typically require physical therapist aides to have a high school diploma, strong interpersonal skills, and a desire to assist people in need. Most employers provide clinical on-the-job training.

Job Outlook

Employment of physical therapist assistants and aides is expected to grow much faster than the average through the year 2008. However, Federal legislation imposing limits on reimbursement for therapy services may continue to adversely affect the job market for physical therapist assistants and aides in the near term. Because of the effects of these provisions, the majority of expected employment growth for physical therapist assistants and aides is expected to occur in the second half of the projection period.

Over the long run, demand for physical therapist assistants and aides will continue to rise, with growth in the number of individuals with disabilities or limited function. The rapidly growing elderly population is particularly vulnerable to chronic and debilitating conditions that require therapeutic services. These patients often need additional assistance in their treatment, making the roles of assistants and aides vital. The large baby-boom generation is entering the prime age for heart attacks and strokes, further increasing the demand for cardiac and physical rehabilitation. Additionally, future medical developments should permit an increased percentage of trauma victims to survive, creating added demand for therapy services.

Licensed physical therapist assistants can enhance the cost-effective provision of physical therapy services. Once a patient is evaluated, and a treatment plan is designed by the physical therapist, the physical therapist assistant can provide many aspects of treatment, as prescribed by the therapist.

Earnings

Median annual earnings of physical therapist assistants and aides were $21,870 in 1998. The middle 50 percent earned between $16,700 and $31,260 a year. The lowest 10 percent earned less than $13,760, and the highest 10 percent earned more than $39,730 a year. Median annual earnings in the industries employing the largest number of physical therapist assistants and aides in 1997 were as follows:

Hospitals $21,200
Offices of other health care practitioners 20,700
Nursing and personal care facilities 19,200

Related Occupations

Physical therapist assistants and aides work under the supervision of physical therapists. Other assistants and aides in the health care field that work under the supervision of professionals include dental, medical, occupational therapy, optometric, podiatric, recreational therapy, and pharmacy assistants.

Sources of Additional Information

Information on a career as a physical therapist assistant and a list of schools offering accredited programs can be obtained from:

- The American Physical Therapy Association, 1111 North Fairfax Street, Alexandria, VA 22314-1488. Internet: http://www.apta.org

Physical Therapists

(O*NET 32308)

Significant Points

- Although the effects of Federal limits on reimbursement for therapy services will cause keen competition for jobs during the first half of the projection period, employment is expected to increase over the 1998-2008 period.

- Competition for entrance into physical therapist educational programs is very intense.

- By 2002, all physical therapist programs seeking accreditation will be required to offer master's degrees and above.

Nature of the Work

Physical therapists provide services that help restore function, improve mobility, relieve pain, and prevent or limit permanent physical disabilities of patients suffering from injuries or disease. They restore, maintain, and promote overall fitness and health. Their patients include accident victims and individuals with disabling conditions such as lower back pain, arthritis, heart disease, fractures, head injuries, and cerebral palsy.

Therapists examine patients' medical histories, and then test and measure their strength, range of motion, balance and coordination, posture, muscle performance, respiration, and motor function. They also determine patients' ability to be independent and reintegrate into the community or workplace after injury or illness. Next, they develop treatment plans describing a treatment strategy, the purpose, and anticipated outcome. Physical therapist assistants, under the direction and supervision of a physical therapist, may be involved in the implementation of the treatment plan. Physical therapist aides perform routine support tasks, as directed by the therapist.

Treatment often includes exercise for patients who have been immobilized and lack flexibility, strength, or endurance. They encourage patients to use their own muscles to further increase flexibility and range of motion before finally advancing to other exercises improving strength, balance, coordination, and endurance. Their goal is to improve how an individual functions at work and home.

Physical therapists also use electrical stimulation, hot packs or cold compresses, and ultrasound to relieve pain and reduce swelling. They may use traction or deep-tissue massage to relieve pain. Therapists also teach patients to use assistive and adaptive devices such as crutches, prostheses, and wheelchairs. They may also show patients exercises to do at home to expedite their recovery.

As treatment continues, physical therapists document progress, conduct periodic examinations, and modify treatments when necessary. Such documentation is used to track the patient's progress and identify areas requiring more or less attention.

Physical therapists often consult and practice with a variety of other professionals, such as physicians, dentists, nurses, educators, social workers, occupational therapists, speech-language pathologists, and audiologists.

Some physical therapists treat a wide range of ailments; others specialize in areas such as pediatrics, geriatrics, orthopedics, sports medicine, neurology, and cardiopulmonary physical therapy.

Working Conditions

Physical therapists practice in hospitals, clinics, and private offices that have specially equipped facilities, or they treat patients in hospital rooms, homes, or schools.

Most physical therapists work a 40-hour week, which may include some evenings and weekends. The job can be physically demanding because therapists often have to stoop, kneel, crouch, lift, and stand for long periods of time. In addition, physical therapists move heavy equipment and lift patients or help them turn, stand, or walk.

Employment

Physical therapists held about 120,000 jobs in 1998; about 1 in 4 worked part time. The number of jobs is greater than the number of practicing physical therapists because some physical therapists hold two or more jobs. For example, some may have a private practice, but also work part time in another health facility. About 1 in 10 physical therapists held more than one job in 1998.

More than two-thirds of physical therapists were employed in either hospitals or offices of physical therapists. Other jobs were in home health agencies, outpatient rehabilitation centers, offices and clinics of physicians, and nursing homes. Some physical therapists are self-employed in private practices. They may provide services to individual patients or contract to provide services in hospitals, rehabilitation centers, nursing homes, home health agencies, adult daycare programs, and schools. They may be in solo practice or be part of a consulting group. Physical therapists also teach in academic institutions and conduct research.

Training, Other Qualifications, and Advancement

All States require physical therapists to pass a licensure exam after graduating from an accredited physical therapist educational program before they can practice.

According to the American Physical Therapy Association, there were 189 accredited physical therapist programs in 1999. Of the accredited programs, 24 offered bachelor's degrees, 157 offered master's degrees, and 8 offered doctoral degrees. By 2002, all physical therapist programs seeking accreditation will be required to offer degrees at the master's degree level and above, in accordance with the Commission on Accreditation in Physical Therapy Education.

Physical therapist programs start with basic science courses such as biology, chemistry, and physics, and then introduce specialized courses such as biomechanics, neuroanatomy, human growth and development, manifestations of disease, examination techniques, and therapeutic procedures. Besides classroom and laboratory instruction, students receive supervised clinical experience. Individuals who have a four-year degree in another field and want to be a physical therapist, should enroll in a master's or a doctoral level physical therapist educational program.

Competition for entrance into physical therapist educational programs is very intense, so interested students should attain superior grades in high school and college, especially in science courses. Courses useful when applying to physical therapist educational programs include anatomy, biology, chemistry, social science, mathematics, and physics. Before granting admission, many professional education programs require experience as a volunteer in a physical therapy department of a hospital or clinic.

Physical therapists should have strong interpersonal skills to successfully educate patients about their physical therapy treatments. They should also be compassionate and posses a desire to help patients. Similar traits are also needed to interact with the patient's family.

Physical therapists are expected to continue professional development by participating in continuing education courses and workshops. A number of States require continuing education to maintain licensure.

Job Outlook

Employment of physical therapists is expected to grow faster than the average for all occupations through 2008. However, Federal legislation imposing limits on reimbursement for therapy services may continue to adversely affect the job market for physical therapists in the near term. Because of the effects of these provisions, the majority of expected employment growth for physical therapists will occur in the second half of the projection period.

Over the long run, the demand for physical therapists should continue to rise as a result of growth in the number of individuals with disabilities or limited function requiring therapy services. The rapidly growing elderly population is particularly vulnerable to chronic and debilitating conditions that require therapeutic services. Also, the baby-boom generation is entering the prime age for heart attacks and strokes, increasing the demand for cardiac and physical rehabilitation. More young people will need physical therapy as technological advances save the lives of a larger proportion of newborns with severe birth defects.

Future medical developments should also permit a higher percentage of trauma victims to survive, creating additional demand for rehabilitative care. Growth may also result from advances in medical technology which permit treatment of more disabling conditions.

Widespread interest in health promotion should also increase demand for physical therapy services. A growing number of employers are using physical therapists to evaluate work sites, develop exercise programs, and teach safe work habits to employees in the hope of reducing injuries.

Earnings

Median annual earnings of physical therapists were $56,600 in 1998. The middle 50 percent earned between $44,460 and $77,810 a year.

The lowest 10 percent earned less than $35,700, and the highest 10 percent earned more than $90,870 a year. Median annual earnings in the industries employing the largest number of physical therapists in 1997 were as follows:

Home health care services	$65,600
Nursing and personal care facilities	60,400
Offices of other health care practitioners	56,600
Offices and clinics of medical doctors	55,100
Hospitals	50,100

Related Occupations

Physical therapists rehabilitate persons with physical disabilities. Others who work in the rehabilitation field include occupational therapists, speech pathologists, audiologists, orthotists, prosthetists, and respiratory therapists.

Sources of Additional Information

Additional information on a career as a physical therapist and a list of accredited educational programs in physical therapy are available from:

● American Physical Therapy Association, 1111 North Fairfax St., Alexandria, VA 22314-1488. Internet: http://www.apta.org

Physician Assistants

(O*NET 32511)

Significant Points

● The typical physician assistant program lasts about two years and usually requires at least two years of college and some health care experience for admission.

● Earnings are high, and job opportunities should be good.

Nature of the Work

Physician assistants (PAs) provide health care services with supervision by physicians. They should not be confused with medical assistants, who perform routine clinical and clerical tasks. PAs are formally trained to provide diagnostic, therapeutic, and preventive health care services, as delegated by a physician. Working as members of the health care team, they take medical histories, examine patients, order and interpret laboratory tests and x-rays, and make diagnoses. They also treat minor injuries by suturing, splinting, and casting. PAs record progress notes, instruct and counsel patients, and order or carry out therapy. In 46 States and the District of Columbia, physician assistants may prescribe medications. PAs may also have managerial duties. Some order medical and laboratory supplies and equipment and may supervise technicians and assistants.

Physician assistants always work with the supervision of a physician. However, PAs may provide care in rural or inner city clinics where a physician is present for only one or two days each week, conferring with the supervising physician and other medical professionals as needed or required by law. PAs may also make house calls or go to hospitals and nursing homes to check on patients and report back to the physician.

The duties of physician assistants are determined by the supervising physician and by State law. Aspiring PAs should investigate the laws and regulations in the States where they wish to practice.

Many PAs work in primary care areas such as general internal medicine, pediatrics, and family medicine. Others work in specialty areas, such as general and thoracic surgery, emergency medicine, orthopedics, and geriatrics. PAs specializing in surgery provide pre- and post-operative care and may work as first or second assistants during major surgery.

Working Conditions

Although PAs usually work in a comfortable, well-lighted environment, those in surgery often stand for long periods, and others do considerable walking. Schedules vary according to practice setting and often depend on the hours of the supervising physician. The workweek of PAs in physicians' offices may include weekends, night hours, or early morning hospital rounds to visit patients. They may also be on call. PAs in clinics usually work a 40-hour week.

Employment

Physician assistants held about 66,000 jobs in 1998. The number of jobs is greater than the number of practicing PAs because some hold two or more jobs. For example, some PAs work with a supervising physician but also work in another practice, clinic, or hospital. According to the American Academy of Physician Assistants, there were about 34,200 certified PAs in clinical practice as of January 1999.

Sixty-seven percent of jobs for PAs were in the offices and clinics of physicians, dentists, or other health practitioners. About 21 percent were in hospitals. The rest were mostly in public health clinics, nursing homes, prisons, home health care agencies, and the Department of Veterans Affairs.

According to the American Academy of Physician Assistants, about one-third of all PAs provide health care to communities having fewer than 50,000 residents, where physicians may be in limited supply.

Training, Other Qualifications, and Advancement

All States require that new PAs complete an accredited, formal education program. As of July 1999, there were 116 accredited or provisionally accredited educational programs for physician assistants; 64 of these programs offered a bachelor's degree or a degree option. The rest offered either a certificate, an associate degree, or a master's degree. Most PA graduates have at least a bachelor's degree.

Admission requirements vary, but many programs require two years of college and some work experience in the health care field. Students should take courses in biology, English, chemistry, math, psychology, and social sciences. More than half of all applicants hold a bachelor's or master's degree. Many applicants are former emergency medical technicians, other allied health professionals, or nurses.

PA programs usually last two years. Most programs are in schools of allied health, academic health centers, medical schools, or four-year colleges; a few are in community colleges, the military, or hospitals. Many accredited PA programs have clinical teaching affiliations with medical schools.

PA education includes classroom instruction in biochemistry, nutrition, human anatomy, physiology, microbiology, clinical pharmacology, clinical medicine, geriatric and home health care, disease prevention, and medical ethics. Students obtain supervised clinical training in several areas, including primary care medicine, inpatient medicine, surgery, obstetrics and gynecology, geriatrics, emergency medicine, psychiatry, and pediatrics. Sometimes, PA students serve one or more of these "rotations" under the supervision of a physician who is seeking to hire a PA. These rotations often lead to permanent employment.

As of 1999, 49 States and the District of Columbia had legislation governing the qualifications or practice of physician assistants; Mississippi did not. All jurisdictions required physician assistants to pass the Physician Assistants National Certifying Examination, administered by the National Commission on Certification of Physician Assistants (NCCPA)—open openly to graduates of accredited PA educational programs. Only those successfully completing the examination may use the credential "Physician Assistant-Certified (PA-C)." In order to remain certified, PAs must complete 100 hours of continuing medical education every two years. Every six years, they must pass a recertification examination or complete an alternate program combining learning experiences and a take-home examination.

Some PAs pursue additional education in order to practice in a specialty area such as surgery, neonatology, or emergency medicine. PA postgraduate residency training programs are available in areas such as internal medicine, rural primary care, emergency medicine, surgery, pediatrics, neonatology, and occupational medicine. Candidates must be graduates of an accredited program and be certified by the NCCPA.

Physician assistants need leadership skills, self-confidence, and emotional stability. They must be willing to continue studying throughout their career to keep up with medical advances.

As they attain greater clinical knowledge and experience, PAs can advance to added responsibilities and higher earnings. However, by the very nature of the profession, individual PAs are always supervised by physicians.

Job Outlook

Employment opportunities are expected to be good for physician assistants, particularly in areas or settings that have difficulty attracting physicians, such as rural and inner city clinics. Employment of PAs is expected to grow much faster than the average for all occupations through the year 2008 due to anticipated expansion of the health services industry and an emphasis on cost containment.

Physicians and institutions are expected to employ more PAs to provide primary care and assist with medical and surgical procedures because PAs are cost-effective and productive members of the health care team. Physician assistants can relieve physicians of routine duties and procedures. Telemedicine—using technology to facilitate interactive consultations between physicians and physician assistants—will also expand the use of physician assistants.

Besides the traditional office-based setting, PAs should find a growing number of jobs in institutional settings such as hospitals, academic medical centers, public clinics, and prisons. Additional PAs may be needed to augment medical staffing in inpatient teaching hospital settings if the number of physician residents is reduced. In addition, State-imposed legal limitations on the numbers of hours worked by physician residents are increasingly common and encourage hospitals to use PAs to supply some physician resident services. Opportunities will be best in States that allow PAs a wider scope of practice, such as the ability to prescribe medication.

Earnings

Median annual earnings of physician assistants were $47,090 in 1998. The middle 50 percent earned between $25,110 and $71,450 a year. The lowest 10 percent earned less than $18,600, and the highest 10 percent earned more than $86,760 a year. Median annual earnings of physician assistants in 1997 were $41,100 in offices and clinics of medical doctors and $57,100 in hospitals.

According to the American Academy of Physician Assistants, median income for physician assistants in full-time clinical practice in 1998 was about $62,200; median income for first-year graduates was about $54,000. Income varies by specialty, practice setting, geographical location, and years of experience.

Related Occupations

Other health workers who provide direct patient care that requires a similar level of skill and training include nurse practitioners, physical therapists, occupational therapists, clinical psychologists, nurse anesthetists, nurse midwives, clinical nurse specialists, speech-language pathologists, and audiologists.

Sources of Additional Information

For information on a career as a physician assistant, contact:

- American Academy of Physician Assistants Information Center, 950 North Washington St., Alexandria, VA 22314-1552. Internet: http://www.aapa.org

For a list of accredited programs and a catalog of individual PA training programs, contact:

- Association of Physician Assistant Programs, 950 North Washington St., Alexandria, VA 22314-1552. Internet: http://www.apap.org

For eligibility requirements and a description of the Physician Assistant National Certifying Examination, write to:

- National Commission on Certification of Physician Assistants, Inc., 157 Technology Pkwy., Suite 800, Norcross, GA 30092-2913. Internet: http://www.nccpa.net

Physicians

(O*NET 32102A, 32102B, 32102E, 32102F, 32102J, and 32102U)

Significant Points

- Physicians are much more likely to work as salaried employees of group medical practices, clinics, or health care networks than in the past.

- Formal education and training requirements are among the longest of any occupation, but earnings are among the highest.

Nature of the Work

Physicians serve a fundamental role in our society and have an effect upon all our lives. They diagnose illnesses and prescribe and administer treatment for people suffering from injury or disease. Physicians examine patients, obtain medical histories, and order, perform, and interpret diagnostic tests. They counsel patients on diet, hygiene, and preventive health care.

There are two types of physicians: The M.D.—Doctor of Medicine—and the D.O.—Doctor of Osteopathic Medicine. M.D.s are also known as allopathic physicians. While both M.D.s and D.O.s may use all accepted methods of treatment (including drugs and surgery), D.O.s place special emphasis on the body's musculoskeletal system, preventive medicine, and holistic patient care.

About a third of M.D.s—and more than half of D.O.s—are primary care physicians. They practice general and family medicine, general internal medicine, or general pediatrics and are usually the first health professionals patients consult. Primary care physicians tend to see the same patients on a regular basis for preventive care and to treat a variety of ailments. General and family practitioners emphasize comprehensive health care for patients of all ages and for the family as a group. Those in general internal medicine provide care mainly for adults who may have problems associated with the body's organs. General pediatricians focus on the whole range of children's health issues. When appropriate, primary care physicians refer patients to specialists, who are experts in medical fields such as obstetrics and gynecology, cardiology, psychiatry, or surgery (see Table 1).

TABLE 1

Percent distribution of M.D.s by specialty, 1997

	Percent
Total	100.0
Primary care	
Internal medicine	17.0
General and family practice	10.7
Pediatrics	7.3

(continues)

Medical specialties

Allergy 5

Cardiovascular diseases 2.5

Dermatology 1.2

Gastroenterology 1.3

Obstetrics and gynecology 5.2

Pediatric cardiology 2

Pulmonary diseases 9

Surgical specialties

Colon and rectal surgery 1

General surgery 5.4

Neurological surgery 6

Ophthalmology 2.3

Orthopedic surgery 3.0

Otolaryngology 1.2

Plastic surgery 8

Thoracic surgery 3

Urological surgery 1.3

Other specialties

Aerospace medicine 1

Anesthesiology 4.4

Child psychiatry 7

Diagnostic radiology 2.6

Emergency medicine 2.7

Forensic pathology 1

General preventive medicine 2

Neurology 1.6

Nuclear medicine 2

Occupational medicine 4

Pathology 2.4

Physical medicine and rehabilitation 8

Psychiatry 5.2

Public health 2

Radiology 1.1

Radiation oncology 5

Other specialty 8

Unspecified/unknown/inactive 14.1

SOURCE: American Medical Association

D.O.s are more likely to be primary care providers than M.D.s, although they can be found in all specialties. Over half of D.O.s practice general or family medicine, general internal medicine, or general pediatrics. Common specialties for D.O.s include emergency medicine, anesthesiology, obstetrics and gynecology, psychiatry, and surgery.

Working Conditions

Many physicians work long, irregular hours. More than one-third of all full-time physicians worked 60 hours or more a week in 1998. They must travel frequently between office and hospital to care for their patients. Increasingly, physicians practice in groups or health care organizations that provide back-up coverage and allow for more time off. These physicians often work as part of a team coordinating care for a population of patients; they are less independent than solo practitioners of the past. Physicians who are on call deal with many patients' concerns over the phone and may make emergency visits to hospitals or nursing homes.

Employment

Physicians (M.D.s and D.O.s) held about 577,000 jobs in 1998. About 7 out of 10 were in office-based practice, including clinics and Health Maintenance Organizations (HMOs); about 2 out of 10 were employed by hospitals. Others practiced in the Federal government, most in Department of Veterans Affairs hospitals and clinics or in the Public Health Service of the Department of Health and Human Services.

A growing number of physicians are partners or salaried employees of group practices. Organized as clinics or as groups of physicians, medical groups can afford expensive medical equipment and realize other business advantages. Also, hospitals are integrating physician practices into health care networks that provide a continuum of care both inside and outside the hospital setting.

The New England and Middle Atlantic States have the highest ratio of physicians to population; the South Central States, the lowest. D.O.s are more likely than M.D.s to practice in small cities and towns and in rural areas. M.D.s tend to locate in urban areas, close to hospital and educational centers.

Training, Other Qualifications, and Advancement

It takes many years of education and training to become a physician: four years of undergraduate school, four years of medical school, and three to eight years of internship and residency, depending on the specialty selected. A few medical schools offer a combined undergraduate and medical school program that lasts six years instead of the customary eight years.

Premedical students must complete undergraduate work in physics, biology, mathematics, English, and inorganic and organic chemistry. Students also take courses in the humanities and the social sciences. Some students also volunteer at local hospitals or clinics to gain practical experience in the health professions.

The minimum educational requirement for entry to a medical or osteopathic school is three years of college; most applicants, however, have at least a bachelor's degree, and many have advanced degrees. There are 144 medical schools in the United States—125 teach allopathic medicine and award a Doctor of Medicine (M.D.) degree; 19 teach osteopathic medicine and award the Doctor of Osteopathic Medicine (D.O.) degree. Acceptance to medical school is very competitive. Applicants must submit transcripts, scores from the Medical College Admission Test, and letters of recommendation. Schools also consider character, personality, leadership qualities, and participation in extracurricular activities. Most schools require an interview with members of the admissions committee.

Students spend most of the first two years of medical school in laboratories and classrooms taking courses such as anatomy, biochemistry, physiology, pharmacology, psychology, microbiology, pathology, medical ethics, and laws governing medicine. They also learn to take medical histories, examine patients, and diagnose illness. During the last two years, students work with patients under the supervision of experienced physicians in hospitals and clinics to learn acute, chronic, preventive, and rehabilitative care. Through rotations in internal medicine, family practice, obstetrics and gynecology, pediatrics, psychiatry, and surgery, they gain experience in the diagnosis and treatment of illness.

Following medical school, almost all M.D.s enter a residency—graduate medical education in a specialty that takes the form of paid on-the-job training, usually in a hospital. Most D.O.s serve a 12-month rotating internship after graduation before entering a residency, which may last two to six years. Physicians may benefit from residencies in managed care settings by gaining experience with this increasingly common type of medical practice.

All States, the District of Columbia, and U.S. territories license physicians. To be licensed, physicians must graduate from an accredited medical school, pass a licensing examination, and complete one to seven years of graduate medical education. Although physicians licensed in one State can usually get a license to practice in another without further examination, some States limit reciprocity. Graduates of foreign medical schools can usually qualify for licensure after passing an examination and completing a U.S. residency.

M.D.s and D.O.s seeking board certification in a specialty may spend up to seven years—depending on the specialty—in residency training. A final examination immediately after residency, or after one or two years of practice, is also necessary for board certification by the American Board of Medical Specialists (ABMS) or the American Osteopathic Association (AOA). There are 24 specialty boards, ranging from allergy and immunology to urology. For certification in a subspecialty, physicians usually need another one to two years of residency.

A physician's training is costly, and whereas education costs have increased, student financial assistance has not. More than 80 percent of medical students borrow money to cover their expenses.

People who wish to become physicians must have a desire to serve patients, be self-motivated, and be able to survive the pressures and long hours of medical education and practice. Physicians must also have a good bedside manner, emotional stability, and the ability to make decisions in emergencies. Prospective physicians must be willing to study throughout their career to keep up with medical advances. They will also need to be flexible to respond to the changing demands of a rapidly evolving health care system.

Job Outlook

Employment of physicians will grow faster than the average for all occupations through the year 2008 due to continued expansion of the health care industries. The growing and aging population will drive overall growth in the demand for physician services. In addition, new technologies permit more intensive care: Physicians can do more tests, perform more procedures, and treat conditions previously regarded as untreatable.

Although job prospects may be better for primary care physicians such as general and family practitioners, general pediatricians, and general internists, a substantial number of jobs for specialists will also be created in response to patient demand for access to specialty care.

The number of physicians in training has leveled off and is likely to decrease over the next few years, alleviating the effects of any physician oversupply. However, future physicians may be more likely to work fewer hours, retire earlier, have lower earnings, or have to practice in underserved areas. Opportunities should be good in some rural and low income areas, because some physicians find these areas unattractive due to lower earnings potential, isolation from medical colleagues, or other reasons.

Unlike their predecessors, newly trained physicians face radically different choices of where and how to practice. New physicians are much less likely to enter solo practice and more likely to take salaried jobs in group medical practices, clinics, and health care networks.

Earnings

Physicians have among the highest earnings of any occupation. According to the American Medical Association, median income, after expenses, for allopathic physicians was about $164,000 in 1997. The middle 50 percent earned between $120,000 and $250,000 a year. Self-employed physicians—those who own or are part owners of their medical practice—had higher median incomes than salaried physicians. Earnings vary according to number of years in practice; geographic region; hours worked; and skill, personality, and professional reputation. As shown in Table 2, median income of allopathic physicians, after expenses, also varies by specialty.

TABLE 2

Median net income of M.D.s after expenses, 1997

All physicians	$164,000
Radiology	260,000
Anesthesiology	220,000
Surgery	217,000
Obstetrics/gynecology	200,000
Emergency medicine	195,000
Pathology	175,000
General internal medicine	147,000
General/Family practice	132,000
Psychiatry	130,000
Pediatrics	120,000

SOURCE: American Medical Association

Average salaries of medical residents ranged from about $34,100 in 1998-99 for those in their first year of residency to about $42,100 for those in their sixth year, according to the Association of American Medical Colleges.

Related Occupations

Physicians work to prevent, diagnose, and treat diseases, disorders, and injuries. Professionals in other occupations requiring similar skills and critical judgment include acupuncturists, audiologists, chiropractors, dentists, nurse practitioners, optometrists, physician assistants, podiatrists, speech pathologists, and veterinarians.

Sources of Additional Information

For a list of allopathic medical schools and residency programs, as well as general information on premedical education, financial aid, and medicine as a career, contact:

- Association of American Medical Colleges, Section for Student Services, 2450 N St. NW., Washington, DC 20037-1131. Internet: http://www.aamc.org

For a list of osteopathic medical schools, as well as general information on premedical education, financial aid, and medicine as a career, contact:

- American Association of Colleges of Osteopathic Medicine, 5550 Friendship Blvd., Suite 310, Chevy Chase, MD 20815-7321. Internet: http://www.aacom.org

For general information on physicians, contact:

- American Medical Association, Department of Communications and Public Relations, 515 N. State St., Chicago, IL 60610. Internet: http://www.ama-assn.org

- American Osteopathic Association, Department of Public Relations, 142 East Ontario St., Chicago, IL 60611. Internet: http://www.aoanet.org

Information on Federal scholarships and loans is available from the directors of student financial aid at schools of allopathic and osteopathic medicine.

Information on licensing is available from State boards of examiners.

Physicists and Astronomers

(O*NET 24102A and 24102B)

Significant Points

- A doctoral degree is the usual educational requirement because most jobs are in basic research and development; a bachelor's or master's degree is sufficient for some jobs in applied research and development.

- Because funding for research grows slowly or not at all, new Ph.D. graduates will face competition for basic research jobs.

Nature of the Work

Physicists explore and identify basic principles governing the structure and behavior of matter, the generation and transfer of energy, and the interaction of matter and energy. Some physicists use these principles in theoretical areas, such as the nature of time and the origin of the universe; others apply their physics knowledge to practical areas, such as the development of advanced materials, electronic and optical devices, and medical equipment.

Physicists design and perform experiments with lasers, cyclotrons, telescopes, mass spectrometers, and other equipment. Based on observations and analysis, they attempt to discover and explain laws describing the forces of nature, such as gravity, electromagnetism, and nuclear interactions. Physicists also find ways to apply physical laws and theories to problems in nuclear energy, electronics, optics, materials, communications, aerospace technology, navigation equipment, and medical instrumentation.

Astronomy is sometimes considered a subfield of physics. *Astronomers* use the principles of physics and mathematics to learn about the fundamental nature of the universe, including the sun, moon, planets, stars, and galaxies. They also apply their knowledge to solve problems in navigation, space flight, and satellite communications and to develop the instrumentation and techniques used to observe and collect astronomical data.

Most physicists work in research and development. Some do basic research to increase scientific knowledge. Physicists who conduct applied research build upon the discoveries made through basic research and work to develop new devices, products, and processes. For instance, basic research in solid-state physics led to the development of transistors and then to the integrated circuits used in computers.

Physicists also design research equipment. This equipment often has additional unanticipated uses. For example, lasers are used in surgery; microwave devices are used for ovens; and measuring instruments can analyze blood or the chemical content of foods. A small number of physicists work in inspection, testing, quality control, and other production-related jobs in industry.

Much physics research is done in small or medium-size laboratories. However, experiments in plasma, nuclear, high energy, and some other areas of physics require extremely large, expensive equipment, such as particle accelerators. Physicists in these subfields often work in large teams. Although physics research may require extensive experimentation in laboratories, research physicists still spend time in offices planning, recording, analyzing, and reporting on research.

Almost all astronomers do research. Some are theoreticians, working on the laws governing the structure and evolution of astronomical objects. Others analyze large quantities of data gathered by observatories and satellites and write scientific papers or reports on their findings. Some astronomers actually operate, usually as part of a team, large space- or ground-based telescopes. However, astronomers may spend only a few weeks each year making observations with optical telescopes, radio telescopes, and other instruments. For many years, satellites and other space-based instruments have provided tremendous amounts of astronomical data. New technology resulting in improvements in analytical techniques and instruments, such as computers and optical telescopes and mounts, is leading to a resurgence in ground-based research. A small number of astronomers work in museums housing planetariums. These astronomers develop and revise programs presented to the public and may direct planetarium operations.

Physicists generally specialize in one of many subfields—elementary particle physics, nuclear physics, atomic and molecular physics, physics of condensed matter (solid-state physics), optics, acoustics, space physics, plasma physics, or the physics of fluids. Some specialize in a subdivision of one of these subfields. For example, within condensed matter physics, specialties include superconductivity, crystallography, and semiconductors. However, all physics involves the same fundamental principles, so specialties may overlap, and physicists may switch from one subfield to another. Also, growing numbers of physicists work in combined fields, such as biophysics, chemical physics, and geophysics.

Working Conditions

Physicists often work regular hours in laboratories and offices. At times, however, those who are deeply involved in research may work long or irregular hours. Most do not encounter unusual hazards in their work. Some physicists temporarily work away from home at national or international facilities with unique equipment, such as particle accelerators. Astronomers who make observations using ground-based telescopes may spend long periods of time in observatories; this work usually involves travel to remote locations. Long hours, including routine night work, may create temporarily stressful conditions.

Physicists and astronomers whose work is dependent on grant money are often under pressure to write grant proposals to keep their work funded.

Employment

Physicists and astronomers held nearly 18,000 jobs in 1998. About 2 in 10 nonfaculty physicists and astronomers worked for commercial or noncommercial research, development, and testing laboratories. The Federal government employed almost 2 in 10, mostly in the Department of Defense, but also in the National Aeronautics and Space Administration (NASA), and the Departments of Commerce, Health and Human Services, and Energy. Other physicists and astronomers worked in colleges and universities in nonfaculty positions or for State governments, drug companies, and electronic equipment manufacturers.

Besides the jobs described above, many physicists and astronomers held faculty positions in colleges and universities.

Although physicists and astronomers are employed in all parts of the country, most work in areas in which universities, large research and development laboratories, or observatories are located.

Training, Other Qualifications, and Advancement

A doctoral degree is the usual educational requirement for physicists and astronomers because most jobs are in basic research and development. Additional experience and training in a postdoctoral research appointment, although not required, is important for physicists and astronomers aspiring to permanent positions in basic research in universities and government laboratories. Many physics and astronomy Ph.D. holders ultimately teach at the college or university level.

Master's degree holders usually do not qualify for basic research positions but do qualify for many kinds of jobs requiring a physics background, including positions in manufacturing and applied research and development. Physics departments in some colleges and universities are creating professional master's degree programs to specifically prepare students for physics-related research and development in private industry that does not require a Ph.D. degree. A master's degree may suffice for teaching jobs in two-year colleges. Those with bachelor's degrees in physics are rarely qualified to fill positions as research or teaching physicists. They are, however, usually qualified to work in engineering-related areas, software development, and other scientific fields; to work as technicians; or to assist in setting up computer networks and sophisticated laboratory equipment. Some may qualify for applied research jobs in private industry or nonresearch positions in the Federal government. Some become science teachers in secondary schools. Astronomy bachelor's or master's degree holders often enter a field unrelated to astronomy, and they are qualified to work in planetariums running science shows, to assist astronomers doing research, and to operate space- and ground-based telescopes and other astronomical instrumentation.

About 760 colleges and universities offer a bachelor's degree in physics. Undergraduate programs provide a broad background in the natural sciences and mathematics. Typical physics courses include electromagnetism, optics, thermodynamics, atomic physics, and quantum mechanics.

In 1998, 183 colleges and universities had departments offering Ph.D. degrees in physics. Another 72 departments offered a master's as their highest degree. Graduate students usually concentrate in a subfield of physics, such as elementary particles or condensed matter. Many begin studying for their doctorate immediately after receiving their bachelor's degree.

About 70 universities grant degrees in astronomy, through either an astronomy or physics department or a combined physics/astronomy department. Applicants to astronomy doctoral programs face competition for available slots. Those planning a career in astronomy should have a very strong physics background. In fact, an undergraduate degree in either physics or astronomy is excellent preparation, followed by a Ph.D. in astronomy.

Mathematical ability, problem solving and analytical skills, an inquisitive mind, imagination, and initiative are important traits for anyone planning a career in physics or astronomy. Prospective physicists who hope to work in industrial laboratories applying physics knowledge to practical problems should broaden their educational background to include courses outside of physics, such as economics, computer technology, and business management. Good oral and written communication skills are also important because many physicists work as part of a team, write research papers or proposals, or have contact with clients or customers with non-physics backgrounds.

Many physics and astronomy Ph.D. holders begin their careers in postdoctoral research positions, where they may work with experienced physicists as they continue to learn about their specialty and develop ideas and results to be used in later work. Initial work may be under the close supervision of senior scientists. After some experience, physicists perform increasingly complex tasks and work more independently. Those who develop new products or processes sometimes form their own companies or join new firms to exploit their own ideas.

Job Outlook

Historically, many physicists and astronomers have been employed on research projects—often defense-related. Small or no increases in defense-related research and a continued slowdown in the growth of civilian physics-related basic research will result in little change in employment of physicists and astronomers through the year 2008. The need to replace physicists and astronomers who retire will account for almost all expected job openings. Budget tightening in the Federal government may also affect employment of physicists, especially those dependent on Federal research grants. The Federal government funds numerous noncommercial research facilities. The Federally Funded Research and Development Centers (FFRDCs), whose missions include a significant physics component, are largely funded by the Department of Energy (DOE) or the Department of Defense (DOD), and their R&D budgets have not kept pace with inflation in recent years. Continuing budget tightening may limit funding and, consequently, the scope of physics-related research in these facilities.

In recent years, many persons with a physics background have found employment in private industry in the areas of information technology, semiconductor technology, and other applied sciences. This trend is expected to continue; however, many of these positions will be under job titles such as computer software engineer, computer programmer, engineer, and systems developer, rather than physicist.

For several years, the number of doctorates granted in physics has been much greater than the number of openings for physicists, resulting in keen competition, particularly for research positions in colleges and universities and research and development centers. Competitive conditions are beginning to ease because the number of doctorate degrees awarded has begun dropping, following recent declines in enrollment in graduate physics programs. However, new doctoral graduates should still expect to face competition for research jobs, not only from fellow graduates, but also from an existing supply of postdoctoral workers seeking to leave low-paying, temporary positions and non-U.S. citizen applicants. Also, the competition for grant money for physics-related research projects is likely to remain intense during the projection period.

Although research and development budgets in private industry will continue to grow, many research laboratories in private industry are expected to reduce basic research, which includes much physics research, in favor of applied or manufacturing research and product and software development. Although many physicists and astronomers will be eligible for retirement over the next decade, it is probable not all of them will be replaced when they retire.

Opportunities may be more numerous for those with a master's degree, particularly graduates from programs preparing students for applied research and development, product design, and manufacturing positions in industry. Many of these positions, however, will have titles other than physicist, such as engineer or computer scientist.

Persons with only a bachelor's degree in physics or astronomy are not qualified to enter most physicist or astronomer research jobs but may qualify for a wide range of positions in engineering, technician, mathematics, and computer- and environment-related occupations. Those who meet State certification requirements can become high school physics teachers, an occupation reportedly in strong demand in many school districts. Despite competition for traditional physics and astronomy research jobs, individuals with a physics degree at any level will find their skills useful for entry to many other occupations.

Earnings

Median annual earnings of physicists and astronomers in 1998 were $73,240. The middle 50 percent earned between $56,230 and $90,440. The lowest 10 percent earned less than $41,830, and the highest 10 percent earned more than $113,800.

According to a 1999 National Association of Colleges and Employers survey, the average annual starting salary offer to physics doctoral degree candidates was $60,300.

The American Institute of Physics reported a median annual salary of $70,000 in 1998 for its members with Ph.D.s; with master's degrees, $57,000; and with bachelor's degrees, $54,000. Those working in temporary postdoctoral positions earned significantly less.

The average annual salary for physicists employed by the Federal government was $79,400 in early 1999, and for astronomy and space scientists, it was $81,300.

Related Occupations

The work of physicists and astronomers relates closely to that of engineers, chemists, atmospheric scientists, geophysicists, computer scientists, computer programmers, and mathematicians.

Sources of Additional Information

General information on career opportunities in physics is available from:

- American Institute of Physics, Career Services Division and Education and Employment Division, One Physics Ellipse, College Park, MD 20740-3843. Internet: http://www.aip.org
- The American Physical Society, One Physics Ellipse, College Park, MD 20740-3844. Internet: http://www.aps.org

For a brochure containing information on careers in astronomy, send your request to:

- American Astronomical Society, Education Office, University of Chicago, 5640 South Ellis Ave., Chicago IL 60637. Internet: http://www.aas.org

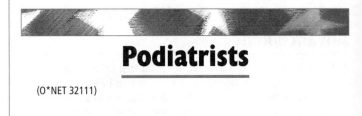

Podiatrists

(O*NET 32111)

Significant Points

- A limited number of job openings for podiatrists is expected because the occupation is small and most podiatrists remain in the occupation until they retire.

- Most podiatrists are solo practitioners, although more are entering partnerships and multi-specialty group practices.

- Podiatrists enjoy very high earnings.

Nature of the Work

Americans spend a great deal of time on their feet. As the Nation becomes more active across all age groups, the need for foot care will become increasingly important to maintaining a healthy lifestyle.

The human foot is a complex structure. It contains 26 bones—plus muscles, nerves, ligaments, and blood vessels—and is designed for balance and mobility. The 52 bones in your feet make up about one fourth of all the bones in your body. Podiatrists, also known as doctors of podiatric medicine (DPMs), diagnose and treat disorders, diseases, and injuries of the foot and lower leg to keep this part of the body working properly.

Podiatrists treat corns, calluses, ingrown toenails, bunions, heel spurs, and arch problems; ankle and foot injuries, deformities and infections; and foot complaints associated with diseases such as diabetes. To treat these problems, podiatrists prescribe drugs, order physical therapy, set fractures, and perform surgery. They also fit corrective inserts called orthotics, design plaster casts and strappings to correct deformities, and design custom-made shoes. Podiatrists may use a force plate to help design the orthotics. Patients walk across a plate connected to a computer that "reads" the patients' feet, picking up pressure points and weight distribution. From the computer readout, podiatrists order the correct design or recommend treatment.

To diagnose a foot problem, podiatrists also order x-rays and laboratory tests. The foot may be the first area to show signs of serious conditions such as arthritis, diabetes, and heart disease. For example, diabetics are prone to foot ulcers and infections due to poor circulation. Podiatrists consult with and refer patients to other health practitioners when they detect symptoms of these disorders.

Most podiatrists have a solo practice, although more are forming group practices with other podiatrists or health practitioners. Some specialize in surgery, orthopedics, primary care, or public health. Besides these board-certified specialties, podiatrists may practice a subspecialty such as sports medicine, pediatrics, dermatology, radiology, geriatrics, or diabetic foot care.

Podiatrists who are in private practice are responsible for running a small business. They may hire employees, order supplies, and keep records, among other tasks. In addition, some educate the community on the benefits of foot care through speaking engagements and advertising.

Working Conditions

Podiatrists usually work in their own offices. They may also spend time visiting patients in nursing homes or performing surgery at a hospital, but they usually have fewer after-hours emergencies than other doctors. Those with private practices set their own hours but may work evenings and weekends to meet the needs of their patients.

Employment

Podiatrists held about 14,000 jobs in 1998. Most podiatrists are solo practitioners, although more are entering partnerships and multi-specialty group practices. Others are employed in hospitals, nursing homes, the U.S. Public Health Service, and the Department of Veterans Affairs.

Training, Other Qualifications, and Advancement

All States and the District of Columbia require a license for the practice of podiatric medicine. Each defines its own licensing requirements. Generally, the applicant must be a graduate of an accredited college of podiatric medicine and pass written and oral examinations. Some States permit applicants to substitute the examination of the National Board of Podiatric Examiners, given in the second and fourth years of podiatric medical college, for part or all of the written State examination. Most States also require completion of a postdoctoral residency program. Many States grant reciprocity to podiatrists who are licensed in another State. Most States require continuing education for licensure renewal.

Prerequisites for admission to a college of podiatric medicine include the completion of at least 90 semester hours of undergraduate study, an acceptable grade point average, and suitable scores on the Medical College Admission Test (MCAT). All require eight semester hours each of biology, inorganic chemistry, organic chemistry, and physics, and six hours of English. The science courses should be those designed for premedical students. Potential podiatric medical students may also be evaluated on the basis of extracurricular and community activities, personal interviews, and letters of recommendation. More than 90 percent of podiatric students have at least a bachelor's degree.

Colleges of podiatric medicine offer a four-year program whose core curriculum is similar to that in other schools of medicine. During the first two years, students receive classroom instruction in basic sciences, including anatomy, chemistry, pathology, and pharmacology. Third- and fourth-year students have clinical rotations in private practices, hospitals, and clinics. During these rotations, they learn how to take general and podiatric histories, perform routine physical examinations, interpret tests and findings, make diagnoses, and perform therapeutic procedures. Graduates receive the doctor of podiatric medicine (DPM) degree.

Most graduates complete a hospital residency program after receiving a DPM. Residency programs last from one to three years. Residents receive advanced training in podiatric medicine and surgery and serve clinical rotations in anesthesiology, internal medicine, pathology, radiology, emergency medicine, and orthopedic and general surgery. Residencies lasting more than one year provide more extensive training in specialty areas.

There are a number of certifying boards for the podiatric specialties of orthopedics, primary medicine, or surgery. Certification means that the DPM meets higher standards than those required for licensure. Each board requires advanced training, completion of written and oral examinations, and experience as a practicing podiatrist. Most managed care organizations prefer board-certified podiatrists.

People planning a career in podiatry should have scientific aptitude, manual dexterity, interpersonal skills, and good business sense.

Podiatrists may advance to become professors at colleges of podiatric medicine, department chiefs of hospitals, or general health administrators.

Job Outlook

Employment of podiatrists is expected to grow about as fast as the average for all occupations through 2008. More people will turn to podiatrists for foot care as the elderly population grows. The elderly have more years of wear and tear on their feet and legs than most younger people, so they are more prone to foot ailments. Injuries sustained by an increasing number of men and women of all ages leading active lifestyles will also spur demand for podiatric care.

Medicare and most private health insurance programs cover acute medical and surgical foot services, as well as diagnostic x-rays and leg braces. Details of such coverage vary among plans. However, routine foot care—including the removal of corns and calluses—is ordinarily not covered unless the patient has a systemic condition that has resulted in severe circulatory problems or areas of desensitization in the legs or feet. Like dental services, podiatric care is more dependent on disposable income than other medical services.

Employment of podiatrists would grow even faster were it not for continued emphasis on controlling the costs of specialty health care. Insurers will balance the cost of sending patients to podiatrists against the cost and availability of substitute practitioners, such as physicians and physical therapists. Opportunities will be better for board-certified podiatrists, because many managed care organizations require board certification. Opportunities for newly trained podiatrists will be better in group medical practices, clinics, and health networks than in traditional solo practices. Establishing a practice will be most difficult in the areas surrounding colleges of podiatric medicine because podiatrists are concentrated in these locations.

Over the next 10 years, members of the "baby boom" generation will begin to retire, creating vacancies. Relatively few job openings from this source are expected, however, because the occupation is small.

Earnings

Median annual earnings of salaried podiatrists were $79,530 in 1998. However, only about one-half of podiatrists were salaried in 1998. Salaried podiatrists tend to earn less than self-employed podiatrists.

According to a survey by the American Podiatric Medical Association, average net income for podiatrists in private practice was about $116,000 in 1997. Those practicing for less than two years earned an average of about $61,000; those practicing 16 to 30 years earned an average of about $146,000.

Related Occupations

Workers in other occupations who apply scientific knowledge to prevent, diagnose, and treat disorders and injuries are chiropractors, dentists, optometrists, physicians, and veterinarians.

Sources of Additional Information

For information on podiatric medicine as a career, contact:

- American Podiatric Medical Association, 9312 Old Georgetown Rd., Bethesda, MD 20814-1621. Internet: http://www.apma.org

Information on colleges of podiatric medicine, entrance requirements, curriculums, and student financial aid is available from:

- American Association of Colleges of Podiatric Medicine, 1350 Piccard Dr., Suite 322, Rockville, MD 20850-4307. Internet: http://www.aacpm.org

Police and Detectives

(O*NET 21911C, 61005, 63011A, 63011B, 63014A, 63014B, 63021, 63023, 63026, 63028A, 63028B, 63032, 63038, and 63041)

Significant Points

- Police work can be dangerous and stressful.

- The number of qualified candidates exceeds the number of job openings in Federal and State law enforcement agencies but is inadequate to meet growth and replacement needs in many local and special police departments.

- The largest number of employment opportunities will arise in urban communities with relatively low salaries and high crime rates.

Nature of the Work

People depend on police officers and detectives to protect their lives and property. Law enforcement officers, some of whom are State or Federal special agents or inspectors, perform these duties in a variety of ways, depending on the size and type of their organization. In most jurisdictions, they are expected to exercise authority when necessary, whether on or off duty.

According to the Bureau of Justice Statistics, about 65 percent of State and local law enforcement officers are uniformed personnel, who regularly patrol and respond to calls for service. Police officers who work in small communities and rural areas have general law enforcement duties. They may direct traffic at the scene of a fire, investigate a burglary, or give first aid to an accident victim. In large police departments, officers usually are assigned to a specific type of duty. Many urban police agencies are becoming more involved in community policing—a practice in which an officer builds relationships with the citizens of local neighborhoods and mobilizes the public to help fight crime.

Police agencies are usually organized into geographic districts, with uniformed officers assigned to patrol a specific area, such as part of the business district or outlying residential neighborhoods. Officers may work alone, but in large agencies, they often patrol with a partner. While on patrol, officers attempt to become thoroughly familiar with their patrol area and remain alert for anything unusual. Suspicious circumstances and hazards to public safety are investigated or noted, and officers are dispatched to individual calls for assistance within their district. During their shift, they may identify, pursue, and arrest suspected criminals, resolve problems within the community, and enforce traffic laws.

Some police officers specialize in such diverse fields as chemical and microscopic analysis, training and firearms instruction, or handwriting and fingerprint identification. Others work with special units such as horseback, bicycle, motorcycle or harbor patrol, canine corps, or special weapons and tactics (SWAT) or emergency response teams. About 1 in 10 local and special law enforcement officers perform jail-related duties, and around 4 percent work in courts. Regardless of job duties or location, police officers and detectives at all levels must write reports and maintain meticulous records that will be needed if they testify in court.

Detectives are plainclothes investigators who gather facts and collect evidence for criminal cases. Some are assigned to interagency task forces to combat specific types of crime. They conduct interviews, examine records, observe the activities of suspects, and participate in raids or arrests. Detectives and State and Federal agents and inspectors usually specialize in one of a wide variety of violations such as homicide or fraud. They are assigned cases on a rotating basis and work on them until an arrest and conviction occurs or until the case is dropped.

Sheriffs and deputy sheriffs enforce the law on the county level. Sheriffs are usually elected to their posts and perform duties similar to those of a local or county police chief. Sheriffs' departments tend to be relatively small, most having fewer than 25 sworn officers. A deputy sheriff in a large agency will have similar specialized law enforcement duties as an officer in an urban police department. Nationwide, about 40 percent of full-time sworn deputies are uniformed officers assigned to patrol and respond to calls, 12 percent are investigators, 30 percent are assigned to jail-related duties, and 11 percent perform court-related duties, with the balance in administration. Police and sheriffs' deputies who provide security in city and county courts are sometimes called bailiffs.

State police officers (sometimes called State troopers or highway patrol officers) arrest criminals statewide and patrol highways to enforce motor vehicle laws and regulations. Uniformed officers are best known for issuing traffic citations to motorists who violate the law. At the scene of accidents, they may direct traffic, give first aid, and call for emergency equipment. They also write reports used to determine the cause of the accident. State police officers are frequently called upon to render assistance to other law enforcement agencies.

State law enforcement agencies operate in every State except Hawaii. Seventy percent of the full-time sworn personnel in the 49 State police agencies are uniformed officers who regularly patrol and respond to calls for service. Fifteen percent are investigators; 2 percent are assigned to court-related duties; and the remaining 13 percent work in administrative or other assignments.

Public college and university police forces, public school district police, and agencies serving transportation systems and facilities are examples of special police agencies. There are more than 1,300 of these agencies with special geographic jurisdictions or enforcement responsibilities in the United States. More than three-fourths of the sworn personnel in special agencies are uniformed officers, and about 15 percent are investigators.

The Federal government maintains a high profile in many areas of law enforcement. The Department of Justice is the largest employer of sworn Federal officers. *Federal Bureau of Investigation (FBI)* agents are the government's principal investigators, responsible for investigating violations of more than 260 statutes and conducting sensitive National security investigations. Agents may conduct surveillance, monitor court-authorized wiretaps, examine business records, investigate white-collar crime, track the interstate movement of stolen property, collect evidence of espionage activities, or participate in sensitive undercover assignments. The FBI investigates organized crime, public corruption, financial crime, fraud against the government, bribery, copyright infringement, civil rights violations, bank robbery, extortion, kidnapping, air piracy, terrorism, foreign counterintelligence, interstate criminal activity, drug trafficking, and other violations of Federal statutes.

Drug Enforcement Administration (DEA) agents enforce laws and regulations relating to illegal drugs. Not only is the DEA the lead agency for domestic enforcement of Federal drug laws, but it also has sole responsibility for coordinating and pursuing U.S. drug investigations abroad. Agents may conduct complex criminal investigations, carry out surveillance of criminals, and infiltrate illicit drug organizations using undercover techniques.

U.S. marshals and deputy marshals protect the Federal courts and ensure the effective operation of the judicial system. They provide protection for the Federal judiciary, transport Federal prisoners, protect Federal witnesses, and manage assets seized from criminal enterprises. In addition, the Marshals Service pursues and arrests 55 percent of all Federal fugitives, more than all other Federal agencies combined.

Immigration and Naturalization Service (INS) agents and inspectors facilitate the entry of legal visitors and immigrants to the United States and detain and deport those arriving illegally. They consist of border patrol agents, immigration inspectors, criminal investigators and immigration agents, and detention and deportation officers. Nearly half of sworn INS officers are border patrol agents. *U.S. Border Patrol agents* protect more than 8,000 miles of international land and water boundaries. Their missions are to detect and prevent the smuggling and unlawful entry of undocumented aliens into the United States, apprehend those persons found in violation of the immigration laws, and interdict contraband, such as narcotics. *Immigration* inspectors interview and examine people seeking entrance to the United States and its territories. They inspect passports to determine whether people are legally eligible to enter the United States. Immigration inspectors also prepare reports, maintain records, and process applications and petitions for immigration or temporary residence in the United States.

Special agents and inspectors employed by the U.S. Department of the Treasury work for the Bureau of Alcohol, Tobacco, and Firearms, the Customs Service, and the Secret Service. *Bureau of Alcohol, Tobacco, and Firearms* (ATF) agents regulate and investigate violations of Federal firearms and explosives laws, as well as Federal alcohol and tobacco tax regulations. *Customs agents* investigate violations of narcotics smuggling, money laundering, child pornography, customs fraud, and enforcement of the Arms Export Control Act. Domestic and foreign investigations involve the development and use of informants, physical and electronic surveillance, and examination of records from importers/exporters, banks, couriers, and manufacturers. They conduct interviews, serve on joint task forces with other agencies, and get and execute search warrants.

Customs inspectors inspect cargo, baggage, and articles worn or carried by people and carriers including vessels, vehicles, trains and aircraft entering or leaving the U.S. to enforce laws governing imports and exports. These inspectors examine, count, weigh, gauge, measure, and sample commercial and noncommercial cargoes entering and leaving the United States. Customs inspectors seize prohibited or smuggled articles, intercept contraband, and apprehend, search, detain, and arrest violators of U.S. laws. *U.S. Secret Service* special agents protect the President, Vice President, and their immediate families, Presidential candidates, ex-Presidents, and foreign dignitaries visiting the United States. Secret Service agents also investigate counterfeiting, forgery of government checks or bonds, and fraudulent use of credit cards.

The U.S. Department of State *Bureau of Diplomatic Security* special agents are engaged in the battle against terrorism, and their numbers are expected to grow rapidly as the threat of terrorism increases. Overseas, they advise ambassadors on all security matters and manage a complex range of security programs designed to protect personnel, facilities, and information. In the United States, they investigate passport and visa fraud, conduct personnel security investigations, issue security clearances, and protect the Secretary of State and a number of foreign dignitaries. They also train foreign civilian police and administer counter-terrorism and counter-narcotics reward programs.

Other Federal agencies employ police and special agents with sworn arrest powers and the authority to carry firearms. These agencies include the U.S. Postal Service, the Bureau of Indian Affairs Office of Law Enforcement under the Department of the Interior, the U.S. Forest Service under the Department of Agriculture, the National Park Service under the Department of the Interior, and Federal Air Marshals under the Department of Transportation. Other police agencies have evolved from the need for security for the agency's property and personnel. The largest such agency is the General Services Administration's Federal Protective Service, which provides security for Federal workers, buildings, and property.

Working Conditions

Police work can be very dangerous and stressful. In addition to the obvious dangers of confrontations with criminals, officers need to be constantly alert and ready to deal appropriately with a number of other threatening situations. Many law enforcement officers witness death and suffering resulting from accidents and criminal behavior. A career in law enforcement may take a toll on officers' private lives.

Uniformed officers, detectives, agents, and inspectors are usually scheduled to work 40-hour weeks, but paid overtime is common.

Shift work is necessary because protection must be provided around the clock. Junior officers frequently work weekends, holidays, and nights. Police officers and detectives are required to work at any time their services are needed and may work long hours during investigations. In most jurisdictions, whether on or off duty, officers are expected to be armed and to exercise their arrest authority whenever necessary.

The jobs of some Federal agents such as U.S. Secret Service and DEA special agents require extensive travel, often on very short notice. They may relocate a number of times over the course of their careers. Some special agents in agencies such as the U.S. Border Patrol work outdoors in rugged terrain for long periods and in all kinds of weather.

Employment

Police and detectives held about 764,000 jobs in 1998. About 64 percent of police detectives and investigators were employed by local governments, primarily in cities with more than 25,000 inhabitants. Some cities have very large police forces, while hundreds of small communities employ fewer than 25 officers each. State police agencies employed about 11 percent of all police, detectives, and investigators; and various Federal agencies employed the other 25 percent. Seventy local, special, and State agencies employed 1,000 or more full-time sworn officers, including 41 local police agencies, 15 State police agencies, 12 sheriffs' departments, and two special police agencies—the New York City public school system and the Port Authority of New York/New Jersey.

Training, Other Qualifications, and Advancement

Civil service regulations govern the appointment of police and detectives in practically all States, large municipalities, and special police agencies, as well as in many smaller ones. Candidates must be U.S. citizens, usually at least 20 years of age, and must meet rigorous physical and personal qualifications. Physical examinations for entrance into law enforcement often include tests of vision, hearing, strength, and agility. Eligibility for appointment usually depends on performance in competitive written examinations and previous education and experience. In larger departments, where the majority of law enforcement jobs are found, applicants usually must have at least a high school education. Federal and State agencies typically require a college degree.

Because personal characteristics such as honesty, judgment, integrity, and a sense of responsibility are especially important in law enforcement, candidates are interviewed by senior officers, and their character traits and backgrounds are investigated. In some agencies, candidates are interviewed by a psychiatrist or a psychologist or given a personality test. Most applicants are subjected to lie detector examinations or drug testing. Some agencies subject sworn personnel to random drug testing as a condition of continuing employment. Candidates for these positions should enjoy working with people and meeting the public.

The FBI has the largest number of special agents. To be considered for appointment as an FBI agent, an applicant must be either a graduate of an accredited law school or a college graduate with a major in accounting, fluency in a foreign language, or three years of full-time work experience. All new agents undergo 16 weeks of training at the FBI academy on the U.S. Marine Corps base in Quantico, Virginia.

Applicants for special agent jobs with the U.S. Department of Treasury's Secret Service and the Bureau of Alcohol, Tobacco, and Firearms must have a bachelor's degree or a minimum of three years' work experience. Prospective special agents undergo 10 weeks of initial criminal investigation training at the Federal Law Enforcement Training Center in Glynco, Georgia and another 17 weeks of specialized training with their particular agencies.

Applicants for special agent jobs with the U.S. Drug Enforcement Administration (DEA) must have a college degree and either one year of experience conducting criminal investigations, one year of graduate school, or have achieved at least a 2.95 grade point average while in college. DEA special agents undergo 14 weeks of specialized training at the FBI Academy in Quantico, Virginia.

Postal inspectors must have a bachelor's degree and one year of work experience. It is desirable that they have one of several professional certifications, such as that of certified public accountant. They also must pass a background suitability investigation, meet certain health requirements, undergo a drug screening test, possess a valid State driver's license, and be a U.S. citizen between 21 and 36 years of age when hired.

Law enforcement agencies are encouraging applicants to take post-secondary school training in law enforcement-related subjects. Many entry-level applicants for police jobs have completed some formal post-secondary education, and a significant number are college graduates. Many junior colleges, colleges, and universities offer programs in law enforcement or administration of justice. Other courses helpful in preparing for a career in law enforcement include accounting, finance, electrical engineering, computer science, and foreign languages. Physical education and sports are helpful in developing the competitiveness, stamina, and agility needed for many law enforcement positions. Knowledge of a foreign language is an asset in many Federal agencies and urban departments.

Before their first assignments, officers usually go through a period of training. In State and large local departments, recruits get training in their agency's police academy, often for 12 to 14 weeks. In small agencies, recruits often attend a regional or State academy. Training includes classroom instruction in constitutional law and civil rights, State laws and local ordinances, and accident investigation. Recruits also receive training and supervised experience in patrol, traffic control, use of firearms, self-defense, first aid, and emergency response. Police departments in some large cities hire high school graduates who are still in their teens as police cadets or trainees. They do clerical work and attend classes for usually one to two years, at which point they reach the minimum age requirement and may be appointed to the regular force.

Police officers usually become eligible for promotion after a probationary period ranging from six months to three years. In a large department, promotion may enable an officer to become a detective or specialize in one type of police work, such as working with juveniles. Promotions to corporal, sergeant, lieutenant, and captain usually are made according to a candidate's position on a promotion list, as determined by scores on a written examination and on-the-job performance.

Continuing training helps police officers, detectives, and special agents improve their job performance. Through police department academies, regional centers for public safety employees established by the States, and Federal agency training centers, instructors provide annual training in self-defense tactics, firearms, use-of-force policies, sensitivity and communications skills, crowd-control techniques, relevant legal developments, and advances in law enforcement equipment. Many agencies pay all or part of the tuition for officers to work toward degrees in criminal justice, police science, administration of justice, or public administration, and pay higher salaries to those who earn such a degree.

Job Outlook

The opportunity for public service through law enforcement work is attractive to many because the job is challenging and involves much personal responsibility. Furthermore, law enforcement officers in many agencies may retire with a pension after 20 or 25 years of service, allowing them to pursue a second career while still in their 40s. Because of relatively attractive salaries and benefits, the number of qualified candidates exceeds the number of job openings in Federal law enforcement agencies and in most State, local, and special police departments—resulting in increased hiring standards and selectivity by employers. Competition is expected to remain keen for the higher paying jobs with State and Federal agencies and police departments in more affluent areas. Applicants with college training in police science, military police experience, or both should have the best opportunities. Opportunities will be best in urban communities whose departments offer relatively low salaries and where the crime rate is relatively high.

Employment of police officers and detectives is expected to increase faster than the average for all occupations through 2008. A more security-conscious society and concern about drug-related crimes should contribute to the increasing demand for police services. At the local and State levels, growth is likely to continue as long as crime remains a serious concern. However, employment growth at the Federal level will be tempered by continuing budgetary constraints faced by law enforcement agencies. Turnover in police and detective positions is among the lowest of all occupations. Even so, the need to replace workers who retire, transfer to other occupations, or stop working for other reasons will be the source of many job openings.

The level of government spending determines the level of employment for police officers, detectives, and special agents. The number of job opportunities, therefore, can vary from year to year and from place to place. Layoffs, on the other hand, are rare because retirements enable most staffing cuts to be handled through attrition. Trained law enforcement officers who lose their jobs because of budget cuts usually have little difficulty finding jobs with other agencies.

Earnings

In 1998, the median salary of police and detective supervisors was $48,700 a year. The middle 50 percent earned between $37,130 and $69,440; the lowest 10 percent were paid less than $28,780, while the highest 10 percent earned more than $84,710 a year.

In 1998, the median salary of detectives and criminal investigators was $46,180 a year. The middle 50 percent earned between $35,540 and $62,520; the lowest 10 percent were paid less than $27,950, and the highest 10 percent earned more than $80,120 a year.

Police patrol officers had a median salary of $37,710 in 1998. The middle 50 percent earned between $28,840 and $47,890; the lowest 10 percent were paid less than $22,270, while the highest 10 percent earned more than $63,530 annually.

Sheriffs and deputy sheriffs had a median annual salary of $28,270 in 1998. The middle 50 percent earned between $23,310 and $36,090; the lowest 10 percent were paid less than $19,070, and the highest 10 percent earned more than $44,420.

Federal law provides special salary rates to Federal employees who serve in law enforcement. Additionally, Federal special agents and inspectors receive law enforcement availability pay (LEAP) or administratively uncontrolled overtime (AUO)—equal to 25 percent of the agent's grade and step—awarded because of the large amount of overtime that these agents are expected to work. For example, in 1999 FBI agents enter service as GS 10 employees on the government pay scale at a base salary of $34,400, yet they earned about $43,000 a year with availability pay. They can advance to the GS 13 grade level in field non-supervisory assignments at a base salary of $53,800, which is worth almost $67,300 with availability pay. Promotions to supervisory, management, and executive positions are available in grades GS 14 and GS 15, which pay a base salary of about $63,600 or $74,800 a year, respectively, and equaled $79,500 or $93,500 per year with availability pay. Salaries were slightly higher in selected areas where the prevailing local pay level was higher. Because Federal agents may be eligible for a special law enforcement benefits package, applicants should ask their recruiters for more information.

The International City-County Management Association's annual Police and Fire Personnel, Salaries, and Expenditures Survey revealed that 84 percent of the municipalities surveyed provided police services in 1997. The following pertains to sworn full-time positions in 1997.

Title	Minimum annual base salary	Maximum annual base salary
Police officer	$28,200	$38,500
Police Corporal	31,900	39,000
Police Sergeant	38,200	45,100
Police Lieutenant	42,900	51,200
Police Captain	46,500	56,600
Deputy Chief	48,400	59,800
Police Chief	56,300	69,600

Total earnings for local, State, and special police and detectives frequently exceed the stated salary because of payments for overtime, which can be significant. In addition to the common benefits—paid vacation, sick leave, and medical and life insurance—most police and sheriffs' departments provide officers with special allowances for uniforms. Because police officers usually are covered by liberal pension plans, many retire at half-pay after 20 or 25 years of service.

Related Occupations

Police and detectives maintain law and order. Workers in related occupations include correctional officers, guards, and fire marshals.

Sources of Additional Information

Information about entrance requirements may be obtained from Federal, State, and local law enforcement agencies.

Further information about qualifications for employment as an FBI Special Agent is available from the nearest State FBI office. The address and phone number are listed in the local telephone directory. Internet: http://www.fbi.gov

Information about qualifications for employment as a DEA Special Agent is available from the nearest DEA office, or call (800) DEA-4288. Internet: http://www.usdoj.gov/dea

Information about career opportunities, qualifications, and training to become a deputy marshal is available from:

- United States Marshals Service, Employment and Compensation Division, Field Staffing Branch, 600 Army Navy Dr., Arlington, VA 22202. Internet: http://www.usdoj.gov/marshals

Career opportunities, qualifications, and training for U.S. Secret Service Special Agents is available from:

- U.S. Secret Service, Personnel Division, Room 912, 1800 G St. NW., Washington, DC 20223. Internet: http://www.ustreas.gov/usss

Information on career opportunities and Bureau of Alcohol, Tobacco and Firearms operations by writing to:

- U.S. Bureau of Alcohol, Tobacco and Firearms, Personnel Division, 650 Massachusetts Avenue NW., Room 4170, Washington, DC 20226. Internet: http://www.atf.treas.gov

Information about careers in the United States Border Patrol is available from:

- U.S. Border Patrol, Chester A. Arthur Building, 425 I St. NW, Washington DC 20536. Internet: http://www.ins.usdoj.gov/bpmain/index.htm

Preschool Teachers and Child-Care Workers

(O*NET 31303 and 68038)

Significant Points

- About 40 percent of preschool teachers and child-care workers—more than four times the proportion for all workers—are self-employed; most of these are family child-care providers.

- A high school diploma and little or no experience are adequate for many jobs, but training requirements vary from a high school diploma to a college degree.

- Employment growth, high turnover, and relatively low training requirements will make it easy to enter this occupation.

Nature of the Work

Preschool teachers and child-care workers nurture and teach preschool children—age 5 or younger—in child-care centers, nursery schools, preschools, public schools, and family child-care homes. These workers play an important role in a child's development by caring for the child when parents are at work or away for other reasons. Some parents enroll their children in nursery schools or child-care centers primarily to provide them with the opportunity to interact with other children. In addition to attending to children's basic needs, these workers organize activities that stimulate the children's physical, emotional, intellectual, and social growth. They help children explore their interests, develop their talents and independence, build self-esteem, and learn how to behave with others.

Preschool teachers and child-care workers spend most of their day working with children. However, they do maintain contact with parents or guardians, through informal meetings or scheduled conferences, to discuss each child's progress and needs. Many preschool teachers and child-care workers keep records of each child's progress and suggest ways parents can increase their child's learning and development at home. Some preschools and child-care centers actively recruit parent volunteers to work with the children and participate in administrative decisions and program planning.

Most preschool teachers and child-care workers perform a combination of basic care and teaching duties. Through many basic care activities, preschool teachers and child-care workers provide opportunities for children to learn. For example, a worker who shows a child how to tie a shoe teaches the child and also provides for that child's basic care needs. Preschool and child-care programs help children learn about trust and gain a sense of security.

Children at this age learn mainly through play. Recognizing the importance of play, preschool teachers and child-care workers build their program around it. They capitalize on children's play to further language development (storytelling and acting games), improve social skills (working together to build a neighborhood in a sandbox), and introduce scientific and mathematical concepts (balancing and counting blocks when building a bridge or mixing colors when painting). Thus, a less structured approach is used to teach preschool children, including small group lessons, one-on-one instruction, and learning through creative activities, such as art, dance, and music.

Interaction with peers is an important part of a child's early development. Preschool children are given an opportunity to engage in conversation and discussions and learn to play and work cooperatively with their classmates. Preschool teachers and child-care workers play a vital role in preparing children to build the skills they will need in elementary school.

Preschool teachers and child-care workers greet children as they arrive, help them remove outer garments, and select an activity of interest. When caring for infants, they feed and change them. To ensure a well-balanced program, preschool teachers and child-care workers prepare daily and long-term schedules of activities. Each day's activities balance individual and group play and quiet and active time. Children are given some freedom to participate in activities in which they are interested.

Helping to keep children healthy is an important part of the job. Preschool teachers and child-care workers serve nutritious meals and snacks and teach good eating habits and personal hygiene. They ensure that children have proper rest periods. They spot children who may not feel well or show signs of emotional or developmental problems and discuss these matters with their supervisor and the child's parents. In some cases, preschool teachers and child-care workers help parents identify programs that will provide basic health services.

Early identification of children with special needs, such as those with behavioral, emotional, physical, or learning disabilities, is important to improve their future learning ability. Special education teachers often work with these preschool children to provide the individual attention they need.

Working Conditions

Preschool facilities include private homes, schools, religious institutions, workplaces where employers provide care for employees' children, and private buildings. Individuals who provide care in their own homes are generally called family child-care providers.

Watching children grow, enjoy learning, and gain new skills can be very rewarding. While working with children, preschool teachers and child-care workers often improve the child's communication, learning, and other personal skills. The work is never routine; new activities and challenges mark each day. However, child care can be physically and emotionally taxing, as workers constantly stand, walk, bend, stoop, and lift to attend to each child's interests and problems.

To ensure that children receive proper supervision, State or local regulations may require certain ratios of workers to children. The ratio varies with the age of the children. Child development experts generally recommend that a single caregiver be responsible for no more than 3 or 4 infants (less than 1 year old), 5 or 6 toddlers (1 to 2 years old), or 10 preschool-age children (between 2 and 5 years old).

The working hours of preschool teachers and child-care workers vary widely. Child care centers are usually open year round with long hours so that parents can drop off and pick up their children before and after work. Some centers employ full-time and part-time staff with staggered shifts to cover the entire day. Some workers are unable to take regular breaks during the day due to limited staffing. Public and many private preschool programs operate during the typical 9- or 10-month school year, employing both full-time and part-time workers. Preschool teachers may work extra unpaid hours each week on curriculum planning, parent meetings, and occasional fundraising activities. Family child-care providers have flexible hours and daily routines, but may work long or unusual hours to fit parents' work schedules.

Turnover in this occupation is high. Many preschool teachers and child-care workers leave the occupation temporarily to fulfill family responsibilities, study, or for other reasons. Some workers leave permanently because they are interested in pursuing other occupations or because of dissatisfaction with long hours, low pay and benefits, and stressful conditions.

Employment

Preschool teachers and child-care workers held about 1.3 million jobs in 1998. Many worked part time. About 4 out of 10 preschool teachers and child-care workers are self-employed, most of whom are family child-care providers.

More than 60 percent of all salaried preschool teachers and child-care workers are found in child-care centers and preschools, and about 14 percent work for religious institutions. The remainder work in other community organizations and in State and local government. Some child-care programs are for-profit centers; some of these are affiliated with a local or national chain. Religious institutions, community agencies, school systems, and State and local governments operate nonprofit programs. About 2 percent of private industry establishments operate on-site child-care centers for the children of their employees.

Training, Other Qualifications, and Advancement

The training and qualifications required of preschool teachers and child-care workers vary widely. Each State has its own licensing requirements that regulate caregiver training, ranging from a high school diploma, to community college courses, to a college degree in child development or early childhood education. Some States require continuing education for workers in this field. However, State requirements are often minimal. Often, child-care workers can obtain employment with a high school diploma and little or no experience. Local governments, private firms, and publicly funded programs may have more demanding training and education requirements.

Some employers prefer to hire preschool teachers and child-care workers with a nationally recognized child-care development credential, secondary or post-secondary courses in child development and early childhood education, or work experience in a child-care setting. Other schools require their own specialized training. Public schools typically require a bachelor's degree and State teacher certification. Teacher training programs include a variety of liberal arts courses, courses in child development, student teaching, and prescribed professional courses, including instruction in teaching gifted, disadvantaged, and other children with special needs.

Preschool teachers and child-care workers must be enthusiastic and constantly alert, anticipate and prevent problems, deal with disruptive children, and provide fair but firm discipline. They must communicate effectively with the children and their parents, as well as other teachers and child-care workers. Workers should be mature, patient, understanding, and articulate, and have energy and physical stamina. Skills in music, art, drama, and storytelling are also important. Those who work for themselves must have business sense and management abilities.

Opportunities for advancement are limited in this occupation. However, as preschool teachers and child-care workers gain experience, some may advance to supervisory or administrative positions in large child-care centers or preschools. Often these positions require additional training, such as a bachelor's or master's degree. Other workers move on to work in resource and referral agencies, consulting with parents on available child services. A few workers become involved in policy or advocacy work related to child care and early childhood education. With a bachelor's degree, preschool teachers may become certified to teach in public schools at the kindergarten, elementary, and secondary school levels. Some workers set up their own child-care businesses.

Job Outlook

Employment of preschool teachers and child-care workers is projected to increase faster than the average for all occupations through the year 2008. In addition, many preschool teachers and child-care workers leave the occupation each year for other jobs, family responsibilities, or other reasons. High turnover, combined with job growth, is expected to create many openings for preschool teachers and child-care workers. Qualified persons who are interested in this work should have little trouble finding and keeping a job.

Future employment growth of preschool teachers and child-care workers will be rapid, but nevertheless considerably slower than in the last two decades because demographic changes that fueled much of the past enrollment growth are projected to slow. Labor force participation of women of childbearing age will increase very little, and this group of women will decline as a percentage of the total labor force. Also, the number of children under 5 years of age is expected to rise very little by the year 2008. Nevertheless, the proportion of youngsters enrolled full- or part-time in child-care and preschool programs is likely to continue to increase, spurring demand for preschool teachers and child-care workers. Changes in perceptions of preprimary education may lead to increased public and private spending on child care. If more parents believe that some experience in center-based care and preschool is beneficial to children, enrollment will increase. Government policy often favors increased funding of early childhood education programs, and that trend should continue. The growing availability of government-funded programs may induce some parents to enroll their children in center-based care and preschool who otherwise would not. Some States also are increasing subsidization of the child-care services industry in response to welfare reform legislation. This reform may cause some mothers to enter the work force during the projection period as their welfare benefits are reduced or eliminated.

Earnings

Pay depends on the educational attainment of the worker and establishment type. Although the pay is generally very low, more education means higher earnings in some cases. Median annual earnings of preschool teachers were $17,310 in 1998. The middle 50 percent earned between $13,760 and $22,370. The lowest 10 percent earned less than $12,000, and the highest 10 percent earned more than $30,310. Median annual earnings in the industries employing the largest numbers of preschool teachers in 1997 were as follows:

Elementary and secondary schools $23,300

Individual and family services 18,800

Social services, not elsewhere classified 17,900

Civic and social associations 17,300

Child day care services 15,700

Median hourly earnings of child-care workers were $6.61 in 1998. The middle 50 percent earned between $5.82 and $8.13. The lowest 10 percent earned less than $5.49, and the highest 10 percent earned more than $9.65. Median hourly earnings in the industries employing the largest numbers of child-care workers in 1997 were as follows:

Residential care $7.60

Elementary and secondary schools 7.30

Civic and social associations 6.30

Child day care services 6.00

Miscellaneous amusement and recreation services 5.90

Earnings of self-employed child-care workers vary depending on the hours worked, number and ages of the children, and the location.

Benefits vary but are minimal for most preschool and child-care workers. Many employers offer free or discounted child care to employees. Some offer a full benefits package, including health insurance and paid vacations, but others offer no benefits at all. Some employers offer seminars and workshops to help workers improve upon or learn new skills. A few are willing to cover the cost of courses taken at community colleges or technical schools.

Related Occupations

Child-care work requires patience; creativity; an ability to nurture, motivate, teach, and influence children; and leadership, organizational, and administrative skills. Others who work with children and need these aptitudes include teacher assistants, children's tutors, kindergarten and elementary school teachers, early childhood program directors, and child psychologists.

Sources of Additional Information

For information on careers in educating children and issues affecting preschool teachers and child-care workers, contact:

- National Association for the Education of Young Children, 1509 16th St. NW., Washington, DC 20036. Internet: http://www.naeyc.org

- Association for Childhood Education International, 17904 Georgia Ave., Suite 215, Olney, MD 20832-2277.

For eligibility requirements and a description of the Child Development Associate credential, contact:

- Council for Early Childhood Professional Recognition, 2460 16th St. NW., Washington, DC 20009. Internet: http://www.cdacouncil.org

For information about family child care and accreditation, contact:

- National Association for Family Child Care, 525 SW 5th St., Suite A, Des Moines, Iowa 50309-4501. Internet: http://www.nafcc.org

For information on salaries and efforts to improve compensation in child care, contact:

- Center for the Child Care Workforce, 733 15th St. NW., Suite 1037, Washington, DC 20005. Internet: http://www.ccw.org

State Departments of Human Services or Social Services can supply State regulations and training requirements for child-care workers.

Protestant Ministers

(O*NET 27502)

Significant Points

- Entry requirements vary greatly; many denominations require a bachelor's degree followed by study at a theological seminary, whereas others have no formal educational requirements.

- Competition for positions is generally expected because of the large number of qualified candidates, but it will vary among denominations and geographic regions.

Nature of the Work

Protestant ministers lead their congregations in worship services and administer the various rites of the church, such as baptism, confirmation, and Holy Communion. The services that ministers conduct differ among the numerous Protestant denominations and even among congregations within a denomination. In many denominations, ministers follow a traditional order of worship; in others, they adapt the services to the needs of youth and other groups within the congregation. Most services include Bible readings, hymn singing, prayers, and a sermon. In some denominations, Bible readings by members of the congregation and individual testimonials constitute a large part of the service. In addition to these duties, ministers officiate at weddings, funerals, and other occasions.

Each Protestant denomination has its own hierarchical structure. Some ministers are responsible only to the congregation they serve, whereas others are assigned duties by elder ministers or by the bishops of the diocese they serve. In some denominations, ministers are reassigned to a new pastorate by a central governing body or diocese every few years.

Ministers who serve small congregations usually work personally with parishioners. Those who serve large congregations may share specific aspects of the ministry with one or more associates or assistants, such as a minister of education or a minister of music.

Working Conditions

For information on working conditions, see the earlier description for Clergy.

Employment

According to the National Council of Churches, there were more than 400,000 Protestant ministers in 1998, including those who served without a regular congregation or those who worked in closely related fields, such as chaplains working in hospitals, the Armed Forces, universities, and correctional institutions. Although there are many denominations, most ministers are employed by the five largest Protestant bodies: Baptist, Episcopalian, Lutheran, Methodist, and Presbyterian.

Although most ministers are located in urban areas, many serve two or more smaller congregations in less densely populated areas. Some small churches increasingly employ part-time ministers who are seminary students, retired ministers, or holders of secular jobs. Unpaid pastors serve other churches with meager funds. In addition, some churches employ specially trained members of the laity to conduct nonliturgical functions.

Training and Other Qualifications

Educational requirements for entry into the Protestant ministry vary greatly. Many denominations require, or at least strongly prefer, a bachelor's degree followed by study at a theological seminary. However, some denominations have no formal educational requirements, and others ordain persons having various types of training from Bible colleges or liberal arts colleges. Many denominations now allow women to be ordained, but others do not. Persons considering a career in the ministry should first verify the ministerial requirements with their particular denomination.

In general, each large denomination has its own schools of theology that reflect its particular doctrine, interests, and needs. However, many of these schools are open to students from other denominations. Several interdenominational schools associated with universities give both undergraduate and graduate training covering a wide range of theological points of view.

In 1998-99, the Association of Theological Schools in the United States and Canada accredited 135 Protestant denominational theological schools. These schools admit only students who have received a bachelor's degree or its equivalent from an accredited college. After college graduation, many denominations require a three-year course of professional study in one of these accredited schools, or seminaries, for the degree of Master of Divinity.

The standard curriculum for accredited theological schools consists of four major categories: Biblical studies, history, theology, and practical theology. Courses of a practical nature include pastoral care, preaching, religious education, and administration. Many accredited schools require that students work under the supervision of a faculty member or experienced minister. Some institutions offer Doctor of Ministry degrees to students who have completed additional study—usually two or more years—and served at least two years as a minister. Scholarships and loans often are available for students of theological institutions.

Persons who have denominational qualifications for the ministry usually are ordained after graduation from a seminary or after serving a probationary pastoral period. Denominations that do not require seminary training ordain clergy at various appointed times. Some churches ordain ministers with only a high school education.

Women and men entering the clergy often begin their careers as pastors of small congregations or as assistant pastors in large churches. Pastor positions in large metropolitan areas or in large congregations often require many years of experience.

Job Outlook

Competition is expected to continue for paid Protestant ministers through the year 2008, reflecting slow growth of church membership and the large number of qualified candidates. Graduates of theological schools should have the best prospects. The degree of competition for paid positions will vary among denominations and geographic regions. For example, relatively favorable prospects are expected for ministers in evangelical churches. Competition, however, will be keen for responsible positions serving large urban congregations. Ministers willing to work part time or for small, rural congregations should have better opportunities. Most job openings will stem from the need to replace ministers who retire, die, or leave the ministry.

For newly ordained Protestant ministers who are unable to find parish positions, employment alternatives include working in youth counseling, family relations, and social welfare organizations; teaching in religious educational institutions; or serving as chaplains in the Armed Forces, hospitals, universities, and correctional institutions.

Earnings

Salaries of Protestant clergy vary substantially, depending on experience, denomination, size and wealth of the congregation, and geographic location. For example, some denominations tie a minister's pay to the average pay of the congregation or the community. As a result, ministers serving larger, wealthier congregations often earned significantly higher salaries than those in smaller, less affluent areas or congregations. Ministers with modest salaries sometimes earn additional income from employment in secular occupations.

Sources of Additional Information

Persons who are interested in entering the Protestant ministry should seek the counsel of a minister or church guidance worker. Theological schools can supply information on admission requirements. Prospective ministers also should contact the ordination supervision body of their particular denomination for information on special requirements for ordination.

Psychologists

(O*NET 27108A, 27108C, 27108D, 27108E, 27108G, 27108H, and 27108J)

Significant Points

- One half of psychologists are self-employed—about 5 times the average for professional workers.

- A doctoral degree is usually required for employment as a licensed clinical or counseling psychologist.

- Opportunities for employment in psychology for those with only a bachelor's degree are severely limited.

Nature of the Work

Psychologists study the human mind and human behavior. Research psychologists investigate the physical, cognitive, emotional, or social aspects of human behavior. Psychologists in applied fields provide mental health care in hospitals, clinics, schools, or private settings.

Like other social scientists, psychologists formulate hypotheses and collect data to test their validity. Research methods may vary depending on the topic under study. Psychologists sometimes gather information through controlled laboratory experiments or by administering personality, performance, aptitude, and intelligence tests. Other methods include observation, interviews, questionnaires, clinical studies, and surveys.

Psychologists apply their knowledge to a wide range of endeavors, including health and human services, management, education, law, and sports. In addition to a variety of work settings, psychologists usually specialize in one of a number of different areas. *Clinical psychologists*—who constitute the largest specialty—usually work in counseling centers, independent or group practices, hospitals, or clinics. They help mentally and emotionally disturbed clients adjust to life and may help medical and surgical patients deal with illnesses or injuries. Some work in physical rehabilitation settings, treating patients with spinal cord injuries, chronic pain or illness, stroke, arthritis, and neurologic conditions. Others help people deal with times of personal crisis, such as divorce or the death of a loved one.

Clinical psychologists often interview patients and give diagnostic tests. They may provide individual, family, or group psychotherapy, and design and implement behavior modification programs. Some clinical psychologists collaborate with physicians and other specialists to develop and implement treatment and intervention programs that patients can understand and comply with. Other clinical psychologists work in universities and medical schools, where they train graduate students in the delivery of mental health and behavioral medicine services. Some administer community mental health programs.

Areas of specialization within clinical psychology include health psychology, neuropsychology, and geropsychology. *Health psychologists* promote good health through health maintenance counseling programs designed to help people achieve goals such as to stop smoking or lose weight. *Neuropsychologists* study the relation between the brain and behavior. They often work in stroke and head injury programs. *Geropsychologists* deal with the special problems faced by the elderly. The emergence and growth of these specialties reflects the increasing participation of psychologists in providing direct services to special patient populations.

Counseling psychologists use various techniques, including interviewing and testing, to advise people on how to deal with problems of everyday living. They work in settings such as university counseling centers, hospitals, and individual or group practices.

School psychologists work in elementary and secondary schools or school district offices to resolve students' learning and behavior problems. They collaborate with teachers, parents, and school personnel to improve classroom management strategies or parenting skills, counter substance abuse, work with students with disabilities or gifted and talented students, and improve teaching and learning strategies. They may evaluate the effectiveness of academic programs, behavior management procedures, and other services provided in the school setting.

Industrial-organizational (I/O) psychologists apply psychological principles and research methods to the workplace in the interest of improving productivity and the quality of work life. They also are involved in research on management and marketing problems. They conduct applicant screening, training and development, counseling, and organizational development and analysis. An industrial psychologist might work with management to reorganize the work setting to improve productivity or quality of life in the workplace. They frequently act as consultants, brought in by management in order to solve a particular problem.

Developmental psychologists study the physiological, cognitive, and social development that takes place throughout life. Some specialize in behavior during infancy, childhood, and adolescence, or changes that occur during maturity or old age. They may also study developmental disabilities and their effects. Increasingly, research is developing ways to help elderly people stay as independent as possible.

Social psychologists examine people's interactions with others and with the social environment. They work in organizational consultation, marketing research, systems design, or other applied psychology fields. Prominent areas of study include group behavior, leadership, attitudes, and perception.

Experimental or *research psychologists* work in university and private research centers and in business, nonprofit, and governmental organizations. They study behavior processes with human beings and animals such as rats, monkeys, and pigeons. Prominent areas of study in experimental research include motivation, thinking, attention, learning and memory, sensory and perceptual processes, effects of substance abuse, and genetic and neurological factors affecting behavior.

Working Conditions

A psychologist's specialty and place of employment determine working conditions. Clinical, school, and counseling psychologists in private practice have their own offices and set their own hours. However, they often offer evening and weekend hours to accommodate their clients. Those employed in hospitals, nursing homes, and other health facilities may work shifts including evenings and weekends, while those who work in schools and clinics generally work regular hours.

Psychologists employed as faculty by colleges and universities divide their time between teaching and research and may also have administrative responsibilities. Many have part-time consulting practices. Most psychologists in government and industry have structured schedules.

Increasingly, many work as part of a team and consult with other psychologists and professionals. Many psychologists experience pressures due to deadlines, tight schedules, and overtime work. Their routines may be interrupted frequently. Travel is required to attend conferences or conduct research.

Employment

Psychologists held about 166,000 jobs in 1998. Educational institutions employed about 4 out of 10 salaried psychologists in positions other than teaching, such as counseling, testing, research, and administration. Three out of 10 were employed in health services, primarily in hospitals, mental health clinics, rehabilitation centers, nursing homes, and other health facilities. Government agencies at the Federal, State, and local levels employed about 17 percent. Governments employ psychologists in hospitals, clinics, correctional facilities, and other settings. The Department of Veterans Affairs and the Department of Defense employ a majority of the psychologists working for Federal agencies. Some psychologists work in social service organizations, research organizations, management consulting firms, marketing research firms, and other businesses.

After several years of experience, some psychologists—usually those with doctoral degrees—enter private practice or set up private research or consulting firms. About one half of psychologists are self-employed.

In addition to the jobs described above, many held positions as psychology faculty at colleges and universities and as high school psychology teachers.

Training, Other Qualifications, and Advancement

A doctoral degree is usually required for employment as a licensed clinical or counseling psychologist. Psychologists with a Ph.D. qualify for a wide range of teaching, research, clinical, and counseling positions in universities, elementary and secondary schools, private industry, and government. Psychologists with a Doctor of Psychology (Psy.D.) degree usually work in clinical positions. An Educational Specialist (Ed.S.) degree will qualify an individual to work as a school psychologist. Persons with a master's degree in psychology may work as industrial-organizational psychologists. Others work as psychological assistants under the supervision of doctoral-level psychologists and conduct research or psychological evaluations.

A bachelor's degree in psychology qualifies a person to assist psychologists and other professionals in community mental health centers, vocational rehabilitation offices, and correctional programs. They may work as research or administrative assistants or become sales or management trainees in business. Some work as technicians in related fields such as marketing research. However, without additional academic training, their opportunities in psychology are severely limited.

In the Federal government, candidates having at least 24 semester hours in psychology and one course in statistics qualify for entry-level positions. Because this is one of the few areas in which one can work as a psychologist without an advanced degree, competition for these jobs is keen.

Clinical psychologists usually must have completed the Ph.D. or Psy.D. requirements and served an internship. Vocational and guidance counselors usually need two years of graduate study in counseling and one year of counseling experience. School psychology requires a master's degree followed by a one-year internship.

Most students need at least two years of full-time graduate study to earn a master's degree in psychology. Requirements usually include practical experience in an applied setting and a master's thesis based on an original research project.

A doctoral degree usually requires five to seven years of graduate study. The Ph.D. degree culminates in a dissertation based on original research. Courses in quantitative research methods, which include the use of computer-based analysis, are an integral part of graduate study and are necessary to complete the dissertation. The Psy.D. may be based on practical work and examinations rather than a dissertation. In clinical or counseling psychology, the requirements for the doctoral degree usually include at least a one-year internship.

Competition for admission into graduate programs is keen. Some universities require an undergraduate major in psychology. Others prefer only course work in basic psychology with courses in the biological, physical, and social sciences, statistics, and mathematics.

The American Psychological Association (APA) presently accredits doctoral training programs in clinical, counseling, and school psychology. The National Council for Accreditation of Teacher Education, with the assistance of the National Association of School Psychologists, also is involved in the accreditation of advanced degree programs in school psychology. The APA also accredits institutions that provide internships for doctoral students in school, clinical, and counseling psychology.

Psychologists in independent practice or those who offer any type of patient care (including clinical, counseling, and school psychologists) must meet certification or licensing requirements in all States and the District of Columbia. Licensing laws vary by State and by type of position. Clinical and counseling psychologists usually require a doctorate in psychology, completion of an approved internship, and one to two years of professional experience. In addition, all States require that applicants pass an examination. Most State boards administer a standardized test and many supplement that with additional oral or essay questions. Most States certify those with a master's degree as school psychologists after completion of an internship. Some States require continuing education for license renewal.

Most States require that licensed or certified psychologists limit their practice to areas in which they have developed professional competence through training and experience.

The American Board of Professional Psychology (ABPP) recognizes professional achievement by awarding certification, primarily in clinical psychology, clinical neuropsychology, counseling, forensic, industrial-organizational, and school psychology. Candidates for ABPP certification need a doctorate in psychology, five years of experience, professional endorsements, and a passing grade on an examination.

Aspiring psychologists who are interested in direct patient care must be emotionally stable, mature, and able to deal effectively with people. Sensitivity, compassion, and the ability to lead and inspire others are particularly important qualities for clinical work and counseling. Research psychologists should be able to do detailed work independently and as part of a team. Excellent communications skills are necessary to succeed in research. Patience and perseverance are vital qualities because results from psychological treatment of patients or from research usually take a long time.

Job Outlook

Employment of psychologists is expected to grow about as fast as the average for all occupations through 2008. Employment in health care will grow fastest in outpatient mental health and substance abuse treatment clinics. Numerous job opportunities will also arise in schools, public and private social service agencies, and management consulting services. Companies will use psychologists' expertise in survey design, analysis, and research to provide marketing evaluation and statistical analysis. The increase in employee assistance programs, which offer employees help with personal problems, should also spur job growth.

Opportunities for people holding doctorates from leading universities in areas with an applied emphasis, such as clinical, counseling, health, and educational psychology, should have particularly good prospects. Psychologists with extensive training in quantitative research methods and computer science may have a competitive edge over applicants without this background.

Graduates with a master's degree in psychology qualify for positions in school and industrial-organizational psychology. Graduates of master's degree programs in school psychology should have the best job prospects, as schools are expected to increase student counseling and mental health services. Masters' degree holders with several years of industrial experience can obtain jobs in consulting and marketing research. Other master's degree holders may find jobs as psychological assistants in the community mental health field, which often requires direct supervision by a licensed psychologist. Still others may find jobs involving research and data collection and analysis in universities, government, or private companies.

Very few opportunities directly related to psychology will exist for bachelor's degree holders. Some may find jobs as assistants in rehabilitation centers or in other jobs involving data collection and analysis. Those who meet State certification requirements may become high school psychology teachers.

Earnings

Median annual earnings of salaried psychologists were $48,050 in 1998. The middle 50 percent earned between $36,570 and $70,870 a year. The lowest 10 percent earned less than $27,960, and the highest 10 percent earned more than $88,280 a year. Median annual earnings in the industries employing the largest number of psychologists in 1997 were as follows:

Offices of other health care practitioners	$54,000
Hospitals	49,300
Elementary and secondary schools	47,400
State government, except education and hospitals	41,600
Health and allied services, not elsewhere classified	38,900

The Federal government recognizes education and experience in certifying applicants for entry-level positions. In general, the starting salary for psychologists having a bachelor's degree was about $20,600 in 1999; those with superior academic records could begin at $25,500. Psychologists with a master's degree and one year of experience could start at $31,200. Psychologists having a Ph.D. or Psy.D. degree and one year of internship could start at $37,800, and some individuals with experience could start at $45,200. Beginning salaries were slightly higher in selected areas of the country where the prevailing local pay level was higher. The average annual salary for psychologists in the Federal government was $66,800 in early 1999.

Related Occupations

Psychologists are trained to conduct research and teach, evaluate, counsel, and advise individuals and groups with special needs. Others who do this kind of work include marketing research analysts, advertising and public relations managers, clinical social workers, physicians, sociologists, clergy, special education teachers, and counselors.

Sources of Additional Information

For information on careers, educational requirements, financial assistance, and licensing in all fields of psychology, contact:

- American Psychological Association, Research Office and Education in Psychology and Accreditation Offices, 750 1st St. NE., Washington, DC 20002. Internet: http://www.apa.org

For information on careers, educational requirements, certification, and licensing of school psychologists, contact:

- National Association of School Psychologists, 4030 East West Hwy., Suite 402, Bethesda, MD 20814. Internet: http://www.naspweb.org

Information about State licensing requirements is available from:

- Association of State and Provincial Psychology Boards, P.O. Box 4389, Montgomery, AL 36103-4389. Internet: http://www.asppb.org

Information on obtaining a job with the Federal government may be obtained from the Office of Personnel Management through a telephone-based system. Consult your telephone directory under U.S. Government for a local number or call (912) 757-3000 (TDD 912 744-2299). This number is not toll free, and charges may result. Information also is available from their Internet site: http://www.usajobs.opm.gov.

Public Relations Specialists

(O*NET 34008)

Significant Points

- Employment of public relations specialists is expected to increase faster than average, but keen competition is expected for entry-level jobs.

- Opportunities should be best for college graduates who combine a degree in journalism, public relations, advertising, or other communications-related fields with public relations work experience.

Nature of the Work

An organization's reputation, profitability, and even its continued existence can depend on the degree to which its targeted "publics" support its goals and policies. Public relations specialists serve as advocates for businesses, governments, universities, hospitals, schools, and other organizations, and they build and maintain positive relationships with the public. As managers recognize the growing importance of good public relations to the success of their organizations, they increasingly rely on public relations specialists for advice on strategy and policy of such programs.

Public relations specialists handle organizational functions such as media, community, consumer, and governmental relations; political campaigns; interest-group representation; conflict mediation; or employee and investor relations. However, public relations is not only "telling the organization's story." Understanding the attitudes and concerns of consumers, employees, and various other groups is also a vital part of the job. To improve communications, public relations specialists establish and maintain cooperative relationships with representatives of community, consumer, employee, and public interest groups and those in print and broadcast journalism.

Informing the general public, interest groups, and stockholders of an organization's policies, activities, and accomplishments is an important part of a public relations specialist's job. Their work keeps management aware of public attitudes and concerns of the many groups and organizations with which they must deal.

Public relations specialists prepare press releases and contact people in the media who might print or broadcast their material. Many radio or television special reports, newspaper stories, and magazine articles start at the desks of public relations specialists. Sometimes the subject is an organization and its policies towards its employees or its role in the community. Often the subject is a public issue, such as health, nutrition, energy, or the environment.

Public relations specialists also arrange and conduct programs for contact between organization representatives and the public. For example, they set up speaking engagements and often prepare speeches for company officials. These specialists represent employers at community projects; make film, slide, or other visual presentations at meetings and school assemblies; and plan conventions. In addition, they are responsible for preparing annual reports and writing proposals for various projects.

In government, public relations specialists—who may be called press secretaries, information officers, public affairs specialists, or communications specialists—keep the public informed about the activities of government agencies and officials. For example, public affairs specialists in the Department of Energy keep the public informed about the proposed lease of offshore land for oil exploration. A press secretary for a member of Congress keeps constituents aware of their elected representative's accomplishments.

In large organizations, the key public relations executive, who is often a vice president, may develop overall plans and policies with other executives. In addition, public relations departments employ public relations specialists to write, do research, prepare materials, maintain contacts, and respond to inquiries.

People who handle publicity for an individual or who direct public relations for a small organization may deal with all aspects of the job. They contact people, plan and do research, and prepare material for distribution. They may also handle advertising or sales promotion work to support marketing.

Working Conditions

Some public relations specialists work a standard 35- to 40-hour week, but unpaid overtime is common. Occasionally they have to be at the job or on call around the clock, especially if there is an emergency or crisis. Public relations offices are busy places; work schedules can be irregular and frequently interrupted. Schedules often have to be rearranged to meet deadlines, deliver speeches, attend meetings and community activities, and travel out of town.

Employment

Public relations specialists held about 122,000 jobs in 1998. Almost two-thirds of salaried public relations specialists worked in services industries—management and public relations firms, educational institutions, membership organizations, health care organizations, social service agencies, and advertising agencies, for example. Others worked for manufacturing firms, financial institutions, and government agencies. About 13,000 public relations specialists were self-employed.

Public relations specialists are concentrated in large cities where press services and other communications facilities are readily available, and many businesses and trade associations have their headquarters. Many public relations consulting firms, for example, are in New York, Los Angeles, Chicago, and Washington, DC. There is a trend, however, for public relations jobs to be dispersed throughout the Nation.

Training, Other Qualifications, and Advancement

Although there are no defined standards for entry into a public relations career, a college degree combined with public relations experience, usually gained through an internship, is considered excellent preparation for public relations work. The ability to write and speak well is essential. Many entry-level public relations specialists have a college major in public relations, journalism, advertising, or communications. Some firms seek college graduates who have worked in electronic or print journalism. Other employers seek applicants with demonstrated communications skills and training or experience in a field related to the firm's business—science, engineering, sales, or finance, for example.

In 1998, well over 200 colleges and about 100 graduate schools offered degree programs or special curricula in public relations, usually in a journalism or communications department. In addition, many other colleges offered at least one course in this field. The Accrediting Council on Education in Journalism and Mass Communications is the only agency authorized to accredit schools or departments of public relations. A common public relations sequence includes courses in public relations principles and techniques; public relations management and administration, including organizational development; writing, emphasizing news releases, proposals, annual reports, scripts, speeches, and related items; preparing visual communications, including desktop publishing and computer graphics; and research, emphasizing social science research and survey design and implementation. Courses in advertising, journalism, business administration, political science, psychology, sociology, and creative writing also are helpful, as is familiarity with word processing and other computer applications. Specialties are offered in public relations for business, government, and nonprofit organizations.

Many colleges help students gain part-time internships in public relations that provide valuable experience and training. The Armed Forces can also be an excellent place to gain training and experience. Membership in local chapters of the Public Relations Student Society of America or the International Association of Business Communicators provides an opportunity for students to exchange views with public relations specialists and to make professional contacts that may help them find a job in the field. A portfolio of published articles, television or radio programs, slide presentations, and other work is an asset in finding a job. Writing for a school publication or television or radio station provides valuable experience and material for one's portfolio.

Creativity, initiative, good judgment, and the ability to express thoughts clearly and simply are essential. Decision making, problem solving, and research skills are also important.

People who choose public relations as a career need an outgoing personality, self-confidence, an understanding of human psychology, and an enthusiasm for motivating people. They should be competitive yet flexible, and able to function as part of a team.

Some organizations, particularly those with large public relations staffs, have formal training programs for new employees. In smaller organizations, new employees work under the guidance of experienced staff members. Beginners often maintain files of material about company activities, scan newspapers and magazines for appropriate articles to clip, and assemble information for speeches and pamphlets. They may also answer calls from the press and public, work on invitation lists and details for press conferences, or escort visitors and clients. After gaining experience, they write news releases, speeches, and articles for publication or design and carry out public relations programs. Public relations specialists in smaller firms usually get all-around experience, whereas those in larger firms tend to be more specialized.

The Public Relations Society of America accredits public relations specialists who have at least five years of experience in the field and have passed a comprehensive six-hour examination (five hours written, one hour oral). The International Association of Business Communicators also has an accreditation program for professionals in the communications field, including public relations specialists. Those who meet all the requirements of the program earn the Accredited Business Communicator designation. Candidates must have at least five years of experience in a communication field and pass a written and oral examination. They also must submit a portfolio of work samples demonstrating involvement in a range of communication projects and a thorough understanding of communication planning. Employers consider professional recognition through accreditation a sign of competence in this field, and it may be especially helpful in a competitive job market.

Promotion to supervisory jobs may come as public relations specialists show they can handle more demanding assignments. In public relations firms, a beginner may be hired as a research assistant or account assistant and be promoted to account executive, account supervisor, vice president, and eventually senior vice president. A similar career path is followed in corporate public relations, although the titles may differ. Some experienced public relations specialists start their own consulting firms.

Job Outlook

Keen competition will likely continue for entry-level public relations jobs as the number of qualified applicants is expected to exceed the number of job openings. Opportunities should be best for individuals who combine a college degree in journalism, public relations, advertising, or another communications-related field with relevant work experience. Public relations work experience as an intern is an asset in competing for entry-level jobs. Applicants without the appropriate educational background or work experience will face the toughest obstacles.

Employment of public relations specialists is expected to increase faster than the average for all occupations through 2008. The need for good public relations in an increasingly competitive business environment should spur demand for public relations specialists in organizations of all sizes. Employment in public relations firms should grow as firms hire contractors to provide public relations services rather than support full-time staff. In addition to growth, numerous job opportunities should result from the need to replace public relations specialists who take other jobs or who leave the occupation altogether.

Earnings

Median annual earnings for salaried public relations specialists were $34,550 in 1998. The middle 50 percent earned between $26,430 and $46,330; the lowest 10 percent earned less than $21,050, and the top 10 percent earned more than $71,360. Median annual earnings in the industries employing the largest numbers of public relations specialists in 1997 were:

Management and public relations	$35,100
State government, except education and hospitals	32,100
Colleges and universities	30,600

According to a salary survey conducted for the Public Relations Society of America, the overall median salary in public relations was about $49,100. Salaries in public relations ranged from less than $22,800 to more than $141,400. There was little difference between the median salaries for account executives in public relations firms, corporations, government, health care, and nonprofit organizations; all ranged from over $32,000 to nearly $34,000.

Public relations specialists in the Federal government in nonsupervisory, supervisory, and managerial positions averaged about $56,700 a year in 1999.

Related Occupations

Public relations specialists create favorable attitudes among various organizations, special interest groups, and the public through effective communication. Other workers with similar jobs include fund raisers; lobbyists; advertising, marketing, and promotion managers; and police officers involved in community relations.

Sources of Additional Information

A comprehensive directory of schools offering degree programs or a sequence of study in public relations, a brochure on careers in public relations, and a $5 brochure entitled *Where Shall I go to Study Advertising and Public Relations* are available from:

- Public Relations Society of America, Inc., 33 Irving Place, New York, NY 10003-2376. Internet: http://www.prsa.org

Career information on public relations in hospitals and other health care settings is available from:

- The Society for Health Care Strategy and Market Development, One North Franklin St., 27th Floor, Chicago, IL 60606. Internet: http://www.shsmd.org

For a list of schools with accredited programs in public relations in their journalism departments, send a stamped self-addressed envelope to:

- The Accrediting Council on Education in Journalism and Mass Communications, University of Kansas School of Journalism, Stauffer Flint Hall, Lawrence, KS 66045. Internet: http://www.ukans.edu/~acejmc

For information on accreditation for public relations specialists, contact:

- International Association of Business Communicators, One Hallidie Plaza, Suite 600, San Francisco, CA 94102. Internet: http://www.iabc.com

Rabbis

(O*NET 27502)

Significant Points

- Ordination usually requires completion of a college degree followed by a four- or five-year program at a Jewish seminary.

- Graduates of Jewish seminaries have excellent job prospects, reflecting current unmet needs for rabbis and the need to replace the many rabbis approaching retirement age.

Nature of the Work

Rabbis serve Orthodox, Conservative, Reform, and Reconstructionist Jewish congregations. Regardless of the branch of Judaism they serve or their individual points of view, all rabbis preserve the substance of Jewish religious worship. Congregations differ in the extent to which they follow the traditional form of worship—for example, in the wearing of head coverings, in the use of Hebrew as the language of prayer, and in the use of instrumental music or a choir. Additionally, the format of the worship service and, therefore, the ritual that the rabbi uses may vary even among congregations belonging to the same branch of Judaism.

Rabbis have greater independence in religious expression than other clergy, because of the absence of a formal religious hierarchy in Judaism. Instead, rabbis are responsible directly to the board of trustees of the congregation they serve. Those serving large congregations may spend considerable time in administrative duties, working with their staffs and committees. Large congregations frequently have associate or assistant rabbis, who often serve as educational directors. All rabbis play a role in community relations. For example, many rabbis serve on committees, alongside business and civic leaders in their communities to help find solutions to local problems.

Rabbis also may write for religious and lay publications and teach in theological seminaries, colleges, and universities.

Working Conditions

For information on working conditions, see the earlier description for Clergy.

Employment

Based on information from organizations representing the four major branches of Judaism, there were approximately 1,800 Reform, 1,175 Conservative, 1,800 Orthodox, and 250 Reconstructionist rabbis in 1999. Although the majority served congregations, many rabbis functioned in other settings. Some taught in Jewish studies programs at colleges and universities, and others served as chaplains in hospitals, colleges, or the military. Additionally, some rabbis held positions in one of the many social service or Jewish community agencies.

Although rabbis serve Jewish communities throughout the Nation, they are concentrated in major metropolitan areas with large Jewish populations.

Training and Other Qualifications

To become eligible for ordination as a rabbi, a student must complete a course of study in a seminary. Entrance requirements and the curriculum depend upon the branch of Judaism with which the seminary is associated. Most seminaries require applicants to be college graduates.

Jewish seminaries typically take five years for completion of studies, with an additional preparatory year required for students without sufficient grounding in Hebrew and Jewish studies. In addition to the core academic program, training generally includes fieldwork and internships providing hands-on experience and, in some cases, study in Jerusalem. Seminary graduates are awarded the title Rabbi and earn the Master of Arts in Hebrew Letters degree. After more advanced study, some earn the Doctor of Hebrew Letters degree.

In general, the curricula of Jewish theological seminaries provide students with a comprehensive knowledge of the Bible, the Torah, rabbinic literature, Jewish history, Hebrew, theology, and courses in education, pastoral psychology, and public speaking. Students receive extensive practical training in dealing with social problems in the community. Training for alternatives to the pulpit, such as leadership in community services and religious education, is increasingly stressed. Some seminaries grant advanced academic degrees in such fields as biblical and Talmudic research. All Jewish theological seminaries make scholarships and loans available.

Major rabbinical seminaries include the Jewish Theological Seminary of America, which educates rabbis for the Conservative branch; the Hebrew Union College—Jewish Institute of Religion, which educates rabbis for the Reform branch; and the Reconstructionist Rabbinical College, which educates rabbis in the newest branch of Judaism. About 35 seminaries educate and ordain Orthodox rabbis. Although the number of Orthodox seminaries is relatively high, the number of students attending each seminary is low. The Orthodox movement, as a whole, constitutes only about 10 percent of the American Jewish community. The Rabbi Isaac Elchanan Theological Seminary and the Beth Medrash Govoha Seminary are representative Orthodox seminaries. In all cases, rabbinic training is rigorous. When students have become sufficiently learned in the Torah, the Bible, and other religious texts, they may be ordained with the approval of an authorized rabbi, acting either independently or as a representative of a rabbinical seminary.

Newly ordained rabbis usually begin as spiritual leaders of small congregations, assistants to experienced rabbis, directors of Hillel Foundations on college campuses, teachers in educational institutions, or chaplains in the Armed Forces. As a rule, experienced rabbis fill the pulpits of large well-established Jewish congregations.

Job Outlook

Job opportunities for rabbis are expected to be excellent in all four of the major branches of Judaism through the year 2008, reflecting current unmet needs for rabbis, together with the need to replace the many rabbis approaching retirement age. Rabbis willing to work in small, underserved communities should have particularly good prospects.

Graduates of Orthodox seminaries who seek pulpits should have good opportunities as growth in enrollments slows and as many graduates seek alternatives to the pulpit. Reconstructionist rabbis are expected to have very good employment opportunities as membership expands rapidly. Conservative and Reform rabbis are expected to have excellent job opportunities serving congregations or in other settings because job prospects will be numerous in these two largest Jewish movements.

Earnings

Based on limited information, annual average earnings of rabbis generally ranged from $50,000 to $100,000 in 1998, including benefits. Benefits may include housing, health insurance, and a retirement plan. Income varies widely, depending on the size and financial status of the congregation, as well as denominational branch and geographic location. Rabbis may earn additional income from gifts or fees for officiating at ceremonies such as bar or bat mitzvahs and weddings.

Sources of Additional Information

Persons who are interested in becoming rabbis should discuss with a practicing rabbi their plans for this vocation. Information on the work of rabbis and allied occupations can be obtained from:

- Rabbinical Council of America, 305 7th Ave., New York, NY 10001. (Orthodox) Internet: http://www.rabbis.org
- The Jewish Theological Seminary of America, 3080 Broadway, New York, NY 10027. (Conservative) Internet: http://www.jtsa.edu
- Hebrew Union College-Jewish Institute of Religion, One West 4th St., New York, NY 10012. (Reform) Internet: http://www.huc.edu
- Reconstructionist Rabbinical College, 1299 Church Rd., Wyncote, PA 19095. (Reconstructionist) Internet: http://www.rrc.edu

Radiologic Technologists

(O*NET 32919 and 32921)

Significant Points

- Radiologic technologists with cross training in nuclear medicine technology or other modalities will have the best prospects.

- Sonographers should experience somewhat better job opportunities than other radiologic technologists, as ultrasound becomes an increasingly attractive alternative to radiologic procedures.

Nature of the Work

Perhaps the most familiar use of the x-ray is the diagnosis of broken bones. However, medical uses of radiation go far beyond that. Radiation is used not only to produce images of the interior of the body, but to treat cancer as well. At the same time, the use of imaging techniques that do not involve x-rays, such as ultrasound and magnetic resonance imaging (MRI), is growing rapidly. The term "diagnostic imaging" embraces these procedures as well as the familiar x-ray.

Radiographers produce x-ray films (radiographs) of parts of the human body for use in diagnosing medical problems. They prepare patients for radiologic examinations by explaining the procedure, removing articles such as jewelry (through which x rays cannot pass), and positioning patients so that the parts of the body can be appropriately radiographed. To prevent unnecessary radiation exposure, technologists surround the exposed area with radiation protection devices, such as lead shields, or limit the size of the x-ray beam. Radiographers position radiographic equipment at the correct angle and height over the appropriate area of a patient's body. Using instruments similar to a measuring tape, technologists may measure the thickness of the section to be radiographed and set controls on the machine to produce radiographs of the appropriate density, detail, and contrast. They place the x-ray film under the part of the patient's body to be examined and make the exposure. They then remove the film and develop it.

Experienced radiographers may perform more complex imaging tests. For fluoroscopies, radiographers prepare a solution of contrast medium for the patient to drink, allowing the radiologist (a physician who interprets radiographs) to see soft tissues in the body. Some radiographers, called *CT technologists,* operate computerized tomography scanners to produce cross sectional views of patients. Others operate machines using giant magnets and radio waves rather than radiation to create an image and are called *magnetic resonance imaging (MRI) technologists.*

Sonographers, also known as ultrasonographers, direct non-ionizing, high frequency sound waves into areas of the patient's body; the equipment then collects reflected echoes to form an image. The image is viewed on a screen and may be recorded on videotape or photographed for interpretation and diagnosis by physicians. Sonographers explain the procedure, record additional medical history, select appropriate equipment settings and use various patient positions as necessary. Viewing the screen as the scan takes place, sonographers look for subtle differences between healthy and pathological areas, decide which images to include, and judge if the images are satisfactory for diagnostic purposes. Sonographers may specialize in neurosonography (the brain), vascular (blood flows), echocardiography (the heart), abdominal (the liver, kidneys, spleen, and pancreas), obstetrics/gynecology (the female reproductive system), and ophthalmology (the eye).

Radiologic technologists must follow physicians' orders precisely and conform to regulations concerning use of radiation to protect themselves, their patients, and coworkers from unnecessary exposure.

In addition to preparing patients and operating equipment, radiologic technologists keep patient records and adjust and maintain equipment. They may also prepare work schedules, evaluate equipment purchases, or manage a radiology department.

Working Conditions

Most full-time radiologic technologists work about 40 hours a week; they may have evening, weekend, or on-call hours.

Technologists are on their feet for long periods and may lift or turn disabled patients. They work at diagnostic machines but may also do some procedures at patients' bedsides. Some radiologic technologists travel to patients in large vans equipped with sophisticated diagnostic equipment.

Although potential radiation hazards exist in this occupation, they are minimized by the use of lead aprons, gloves, and other shielding devices, as well as by instruments monitoring radiation exposure. Technologists wear badges measuring radiation levels in the radiation area, and detailed records are kept on their cumulative lifetime dose.

Employment

Radiologic technologists held about 162,000 jobs in 1998. Most technologists were radiographers, while the rest worked as sonographers. About 1 radiologic technologist in 5 worked part time. More than half of jobs for technologists are in hospitals. Most of the rest are in physicians' offices and clinics, including diagnostic imaging centers.

Training, Other Qualifications, and Advancement

Preparation for this profession is offered in hospitals, colleges and universities, vocational-technical institutes, and the Armed Forces. Hospitals, which employ most radiologic technologists, prefer to hire those with formal training.

Formal training is offered in radiography and diagnostic medical sonography (ultrasound). Programs range in length from one to four years and lead to a certificate, associate degree, or bachelor's degree. Two-year associate degree programs are most prevalent.

Some one-year certificate programs are available for experienced radiographers or individuals from other health occupations (such as medical technologists and registered nurses) who want to change fields or specialize in sonography. A bachelor's or master's degree in one of the radiologic technologies is desirable for supervisory, administrative, or teaching positions.

The Joint Review Committee on Education in Radiologic Technology accredits most formal training programs for this field. They accredited 602 radiography programs in 1999. The Joint Review Committee on Education in Diagnostic Medical Sonography accredited 77 programs in sonography in 1998.

Radiography programs require, at a minimum, a high school diploma or the equivalent. High school courses in mathematics, physics, chemistry, and biology are helpful. The programs provide both classroom and clinical instruction in anatomy and physiology, patient care procedures, radiation physics, radiation protection, principles of imaging, medical terminology, positioning of patients, medical ethics, radiobiology, and pathology.

For training programs in diagnostic medical sonography, applicants with a background in science or experience in one of the health professions generally are preferred. Some programs consider applicants with liberal arts backgrounds, however, as well as high school graduates with courses in math and science.

In 1981, Congress passed the Consumer-Patient Radiation Health and Safety Act, which aims to protect the public from the hazards of unnecessary exposure to medical and dental radiation by ensuring operators of radiologic equipment are properly trained. Under the act, the Federal government sets voluntary standards that the States, in turn, may use for accrediting training programs and certifying individuals who engage in medical or dental radiography. Because ultrasound does not use ionizing radiation, sonographers are excluded from this act.

In 1999, 35 States and Puerto Rico licensed radiologic technologists. No State requires sonographers to be licensed. Voluntary registration is offered by the American Registry of Radiologic Technologists (ARRT) in radiography. The American Registry of Diagnostic Medical Sonographers (ARDMS) certifies the competence of sonographers. To be eligible for registration, technologists generally must graduate from an accredited program and pass an examination. Many employers prefer to hire registered radiographers and sonographers.

With experience and additional training, staff technologists may become specialists, performing CT scanning, angiography, and magnetic resonance imaging. Experienced technologists may also be promoted to supervisor, chief radiologic technologist, and—

ultimately—department administrator or director. Depending on the institution, courses or a master's degree in business or health administration may be necessary for the director's position. Some technologists progress by becoming instructors or directors in radiologic technology programs; others take jobs as sales representatives or instructors with equipment manufacturers.

Radiographers must complete 24 hours of continuing education every other year and provide documentation to prove they have complied with these requirements. Sonographers must complete 30 hours of continuing education every three years.

Job Outlook

Employment of radiologic technologists is expected to grow as fast as the average for all occupations through 2008, as the population grows and ages, increasing the demand for diagnostic imaging and therapeutic technology. Although physicians are enthusiastic about the clinical benefits of new technologies, the extent to which they are adopted depends largely on cost and reimbursement considerations. Some promising new technologies may not come into widespread use because they are too expensive and third-party payers may not be willing to pay for their use.

Sonographers should experience somewhat better job opportunities than radiographers. Ultrasound is becoming an increasingly attractive alternative to radiologic procedures. Ultrasound technology is expected to continue to evolve rapidly and spawn many new ultrasound procedures. Furthermore, because ultrasound does not use radiation for imaging, there are few possible side effects.

Radiologic technologists who are educated and credentialed in more than one type of imaging technology, such as radiography and ultrasonography or nuclear medicine, will have better employment opportunities as employers look for new ways to control costs. In hospitals, multi-skilled employees will be the most sought after, as hospitals respond to cost pressures by continuing to merge departments.

Hospitals will remain the principal employer of radiologic technologists. However, employment is expected to grow most rapidly in offices and clinics of physicians, including diagnostic imaging centers. Health facilities such as these are expected to grow very rapidly through 2008 due to the strong shift toward outpatient care, encouraged by third-party payers and made possible by technological advances that permit more procedures to be performed outside the hospital. Some job openings will also arise from the need to replace technologists who leave the occupation.

Earnings

Median annual earnings of radiologic technologists and technicians were $32,880 in 1998. The middle 50 percent earned between $27,560 and $39,420 a year. The lowest 10 percent earned less than $23,650, and the highest 10 percent earned more than $47,610 a year. Median annual earnings in the industries employing the largest number of radiologic technologists and technicians in 1997 were:

Medical and dental laboratories	$34,400
Hospitals	31,600
Offices and clinics of medical doctors	30,800

Related Occupations

Radiologic technologists operate sophisticated equipment to help physicians, dentists, and other health practitioners diagnose and treat patients. Workers in related occupations include radiation dosimetrists, nuclear medicine technologists, cardiovascular technologists and technicians, radiation therapists, perfusionists, respiratory therapists, clinical laboratory technologists, and electroneurodiagnostic technologists.

Sources of Additional Information

For career information, enclose a stamped, self-addressed business size envelope with your request to:

- American Society of Radiologic Technologists, 15000 Central Ave. SE., Albuquerque, NM 87123-3917.
- Society of Diagnostic Medical Sonographers, 12770 Coit Rd., Suite 708, Dallas, TX 75251.
- American Healthcare Radiology Administrators, 111 Boston Post Rd., Suite 105, P.O. Box 334, Sudbury, MA 01776.

For the current list of accredited education programs in radiography, write to:

- Joint Review Committee on Education in Radiologic Technology, 20 N. Wacker Dr., Suite 600, Chicago, IL 60606-2901.

For a current list of accredited education programs in diagnostic medical sonography, write to:

- The Joint Review Committee on Education in Diagnostic Medical Sonography, 7108 S. Alton Way, Building C., Englewood, CO 80112. Internet: http://www.caahep.org/programs/dms-prog.htm

Receptionists

(O*NET 55305)

Significant Points

- Numerous job openings should arise due to employment growth and high turnover.
- A high school diploma or its equivalent is the most common educational requirement.
- Because receptionists deal directly with the public, a professional appearance and pleasant personality are imperative.

Nature of the Work

Receptionists are charged with a responsibility that may have a lasting impact on the success of an organization—making a good first impression. These workers are often the first representatives of an organization a visitor encounters, so they need to be courteous, professional, and helpful. Receptionists answer telephones, route calls, greet visitors, respond to inquiries from the public and provide information about the organization. In addition, receptionists contribute to the security of an organization by helping to monitor the access of visitors.

Whereas some tasks are common to most receptionists, the specific responsibilities of receptionists vary depending upon the type of establishment in which they work. For example, receptionists in hospitals and doctors' offices may gather personal and financial information and direct patients to the proper waiting rooms. In beauty or hair salons, however, they arrange appointments, direct customers to the hairstylist, and may serve as cashier. In factories, large corporations, and government offices, they may provide identification cards and arrange for escorts to take visitors to the proper office. Those working for bus and train companies respond to inquiries about departures, arrivals, stops, and other related matters.

Increasingly, receptionists use multiline telephone systems, personal computers, and fax machines. Despite the widespread use of automated answering systems or voice mail, many receptionists still take messages and inform other employees of visitors' arrivals or cancellation of an appointment. When they are not busy with callers, most receptionists are expected to perform a variety of office duties including opening and sorting mail, collecting and distributing parcels, making fax transmittals and deliveries, updating appointment calendars, preparing travel vouchers, and performing basic bookkeeping, word processing, and filing.

Working Conditions

Most receptionists work in areas that are clean, well lit, and relatively quiet. Most greet customers and visitors and usually work in highly visible areas that are furnished to make a good impression.

Although most receptionists work a standard 40-hour week, some work part time. The work performed by these employees may be repetitive and stressful. For example, many receptionists spend all day answering telephones while performing additional clerical or secretarial tasks. Additional stress is caused by technology that enables management to electronically monitor use of computer systems, tape record telephone calls, or limit the time spent on each call. Prolonged exposure to a video display terminal may lead to eyestrain for the many receptionists who work with computers.

Employment

Receptionists held about 1.3 million jobs in 1998, accounting for more than two-thirds of all information clerk jobs. More than two-thirds of all receptionists worked in services industries, and almost half of these were employed in the health services industry in doctors' and dentists' offices, hospitals, nursing homes, urgent care centers, surgical centers, and clinics. Manufacturing, wholesale and retail trade, government, and real estate industries also employed large numbers of receptionists. About 3 of every 10 receptionists worked part time.

Training, Other Qualifications, and Advancement

Although hiring requirements for receptionists vary from industry to industry, a high school diploma or its equivalent is the most common educational requirement. Increasingly, familiarity or experience with computers and good interpersonal skills is often equally important to employers.

Receptionists deal directly with the public, so a professional appearance and pleasant personality are important. A clear speaking voice and fluency in the English language also are essential because these employees frequently use the telephone or public address systems. Good spelling and computer literacy are often needed, particularly because most work involves considerable computer use.

Receptionists usually receive on-the-job training, which may include procedures for greeting visitors, operating telephone and computer systems, and distributing mail, fax, and parcel deliveries. Some employers look for applicants who already possess certain skills, such as prior computer and word processing experience or previous formal education. Most receptionists continue to receive instruction on new procedures and company policies after their initial training ends.

Advancement for receptionists usually comes about either by transfer to a position with more responsibilities or by promotion to a supervisory position. Most companies fill office and administrative support supervisory and managerial positions by promoting individuals within their organization, so those who acquire additional skills, experience, and training improve their advancement opportunities. A receptionist may advance to a better paying job as a secretary or administrative assistant.

Job Outlook

Employment of receptionists is expected to grow faster than the average for all occupations through 2008. This increase will result from rapid growth in services industries—including physician's offices, law firms, temporary help agencies, and consulting firms—where most receptionists are employed. In addition, high turnover in this large occupation will create numerous openings as receptionists transfer to other occupations or leave the labor force altogether. Opportunities should be best for persons with a wide range of clerical skills and experience.

Technology should have conflicting effects on the demand for receptionists. The increasing use of voice mail and other telephone automation reduces the need for receptionists by allowing one receptionist to perform work that formerly required several receptionists. However, increasing use of technology also has caused a consolidation of clerical responsibilities and growing demand for workers with diverse clerical skills. Because receptionists may perform a wide variety of clerical tasks, they should continue to be in demand. Further, receptionists perform many tasks that are of an interpersonal nature and are not easily automated, ensuring continued demand for their services in a variety of establishments. Receptionists tend to be less subject to layoffs during recessions than other clerical workers because establishments need someone to perform their duties even during economic downturns.

Earnings

Earnings vary widely, but the median annual earnings of receptionists in 1998 were $18,620. In early 1999, the Federal government typically paid salaries ranging from $16,400 to $18,100 a year to beginning receptionists with a high school diploma or six months of experience. The average annual salary for all receptionists employed by the Federal government was about $22,700 in 1999.

Related Occupations

A number of other workers deal with the public, receive and provide information, or direct people to others who can assist them. Among these are dispatchers, security guards, bank tellers, guides, telephone operators, records processing clerks, counter and rental clerks, survey workers, and ushers and lobby attendants.

Sources of Additional Information

State employment offices can provide information on job openings for receptionists.

Records Processing Occupations

Significant Points

- Most jobs require only a high school diploma.

- Numerous job opportunities should arise due to high turnover in this occupation.

- Little or no change is expected in overall employment, reflecting the spread of computers and other office automation as well as organizational restructuring.

Nature of the Work

Without the assistance of workers in records processing occupations, many organizations would be lost. These workers maintain, update, and process a variety of records, ranging from payrolls to information on the shipment of goods or bank statements. They ensure that other workers get paid on time, customers' questions are answered, and records are kept of all transactions. (Additional information about specific records processing occupations appears in separate statements that follow this introductory statement.)

Depending on their specific titles, these workers perform a wide variety of record keeping duties. *Billing clerks and billing machine operators*, for example, prepare bills and invoices. *Bookkeeping, accounting, and auditing clerks* maintain financial data in computer and paper files. *Brokerage clerks* prepare and maintain the records generated when stocks, bonds, and other types of investments are traded. *File clerks* store and retrieve various kinds of office information for use by staff members. *Human resources clerks* maintain employee records. *Library assistants and bookmobile drivers* assist library patrons. *Order clerks* process incoming orders for goods and services. *Payroll and timekeeping clerks* compute wages for payroll records and review employee timecards. *Statement clerks* prepare monthly statements for bank customers. Other records processing clerks include *advertising clerks* (who receive orders for classified advertising for newspapers or magazines, prepare copy according to customer specifications, and verify conformance of published

ads to specifications for billing purposes) and *correspondence clerks* (who reply to customers regarding damage claims, delinquent accounts, incorrect billings, complaints of unsatisfactory service, and requests for merchandise exchanges or returns).

The duties of records processing clerks vary with the size of the firm. In a small business, a bookkeeping clerk may handle all financial records and transactions, as well as payroll and personnel duties. A large firm, on the other hand, may employ specialized accounting, payroll, and human resources clerks. In general, however, clerical staffs in firms of all sizes increasingly perform a broader variety of tasks than in the past. This is especially true for clerical occupations involving accounting work. As the growing use of computers enables bookkeeping, accounting, and auditing clerks to become more productive, these workers may assume billing, payroll, and timekeeping duties.

Another change in these occupations is the growing use of financial software to enter and manipulate data. Computer programs automatically perform calculations on data that were previously calculated manually. Computers also enable clerks to access data within files more quickly than the former method of reviewing stacks of paper. Nevertheless, most workers still keep backup paper records for research, auditing, and reference purposes.

Despite the growing use of automation, interaction with the public and coworkers remains a basic part of the job for many records processing clerks. Payroll clerks, for example, answer questions concerning employee benefits; bookmobile drivers help patients in nursing homes and hospitals select books; and order clerks call customers to verify special mailing instructions.

Working Conditions

With the exception of library assistants and bookmobile drivers, records processing clerks typically are employed in an office environment. Most work alongside other clerical workers, but some records processing clerks work in centralized units away from the front office.

Because the majority of records processing clerks use computers on a daily basis, these workers may experience eye and muscle strain, backaches, headaches, and repetitive motion injuries. Also, clerks who review detailed data may have to sit for extended periods of time. Although the work does not require heavy lifting, file clerks and library assistants spend a lot of time on their feet and frequently stoop, bend, and reach. Finally, bookmobile drivers must maneuver large vehicles in all kinds of traffic and weather conditions and may also be responsible for the maintenance of the bookmobile.

Most records processing clerks work regular business hours. Library assistants may work evenings and weekends, but those employed in school libraries usually work only during the school year. Accounting clerks may work longer hours to meet deadlines at the end of the fiscal year, during tax time, or when monthly and yearly accounting audits are performed. Billing, bookkeeping, and accounting clerks in hotels, restaurants, and stores may work overtime during peak holiday and vacation seasons. Similarly, order clerks in retail establishments typically work overtime during these seasons. Brokerage clerks may also have to work overtime if there is a high volume of activity in the stock or bond market.

Employment

Records processing clerks held more than 3.7 million jobs in 1998. The following table shows employment in individual clerical occupations:

Bookkeeping, accounting, and auditing clerks 2,078,000

Billing clerks and billing machine operators 449,000

Order clerks 362,000

File clerks 272,000

Payroll and timekeeping clerks 172,000

Library assistants and bookmobile drivers 127,000

Human resources clerks 142,000

Brokerage and statement clerks 92,000

Correspondence clerks 25,000

Advertising clerks 14,000

These workers are employed in virtually every industry. The largest number of records processing clerks work for firms providing health, business, and other types of services. Many also work in trade; finance, insurance, and real estate; manufacturing; and government.

Training, Other Qualifications, and Advancement

Employers typically require applicants to have at least a high school diploma or its equivalent. Although many employers prefer to hire records clerks with a higher level of education, it is only required in a few records processing occupations. For example, brokerage firms usually seek college graduates for brokerage clerk jobs, and order clerks in high-technology firms often need to understand scientific and mechanical processes, which may require some college education. Regardless of the type of work, most employers prefer workers who are computer-literate. Knowledge of word processing and spreadsheet software is especially valuable, as are experience working in an office and good interpersonal skills.

Records processing clerks often learn the skills they need in high schools, business schools, and community colleges. Business education programs offered by these institutions typically include courses in typing, word processing, shorthand, business communications, records management, and office systems and procedures. Specialized order clerks in technical positions obtain their training from technical institutes and two- and four-year colleges.

Some entrants into records processing occupations are college graduates with degrees in business, finance, or liberal arts. Although a degree is rarely required, many graduates accept entry-level clerical positions to get into a particular company or to enter the finance or accounting field with the hope of being promoted to professional or managerial positions. Some companies, such as brokerage and accounting firms, have a set plan of advancement that tracks college graduates from entry-level clerical jobs into managerial positions. Workers with college degrees are likely to start at higher salaries and advance more easily than those without degrees.

Once hired, records processing clerks usually receive on-the-job training. Under the guidance of a supervisor or other senior worker, new employees learn company procedures. Some formal classroom training may also be necessary, such as training in specific computer software.

Records processing clerks must be careful, orderly, and detail-oriented in order to avoid making errors and to recognize errors made by others. These workers should also be discreet and trustworthy because they frequently come in contact with confidential material. Additionally, payroll clerks, billing clerks, and bookkeeping, accounting, and auditing clerks should have a strong aptitude for numbers. Because statement clerks have access to confidential financial information, these workers must be bonded. Many bookmobile drivers are now required to have a commercial driver's license.

Records processing clerks usually advance by taking on more duties in the same occupation for higher pay or transferring to a closely related occupation. For example, some order clerks use their experience to move into sales positions. Most companies fill office and administrative support supervisory and managerial positions by promoting individuals from within their organizations, so information clerks who acquire additional skills, experience, and training improve their advancement opportunities. With appropriate experience and education, some clerks may become accountants; personnel specialists; securities, commodities, and financial services sales representatives; or librarians.

Job Outlook

Little or no change is expected in employment of records processing clerks through 2008. Despite continued growth in the volume of business transactions, rising productivity stemming from the spread of office automation, as well as organizational restructuring, will adversely affect demand for records processing clerks. Turnover in this very large occupation, however, places it among those occupations providing the most job openings. As a result, opportunities should be plentiful for full-time, part-time, and seasonal employment, as records processing clerks transfer to other occupations or leave the labor force.

Many record clerk jobs have already become heavily automated. Productivity has increased significantly, as workers use personal computers instead of more time-consuming equipment such as typewriters, adding machines, and calculators. The growing use of bar code readers, point-of-sale terminals, and optical scanners also reduces much of the data entry handled by records processing clerks. Additionally, managers and professionals now do much of their own clerical work, using computers to access, create, and store data directly in their computer systems. The growing use of local area networks is also facilitating electronic data interchange—the sending of data from computer to computer—abolishing the need for clerks to reenter the data. To further eliminate duplicate functions, many large companies are consolidating their clerical operations in a central office where accounting, billing, personnel, and payroll functions are performed for all offices—main and satellite—within the organization.

Despite the spread of automation and organizational restructuring, average or faster-than-average job growth is projected for some records processing clerks, including billing clerks, brokerage clerks, library assistants, and bookmobile drivers.

Earnings

Salaries of records processing clerks vary considerably. The region of the country, size of city, and type and size of establishment all influence salary levels. The level of industry or technical expertise required and the complexity and uniqueness of a clerk's responsibilities may also affect earnings. Median annual earnings of full-time records processing clerks in 1998 are shown in the following table:

Brokerage clerks	$27,920
Payroll and timekeeping clerks	24,560
Human resources clerks	24,360
Bookkeeping, accounting, and auditing clerks	23,190
Billing clerks	22,670
Correspondence clerks	22,270
Order clerks	21,550
Billing machine operators	20,560
Advertising clerks	20,550
Statement clerks	18,640
Library assistants and bookmobile drivers	16,980
File clerks	16,830

In the Federal government, records processing clerks with a high school diploma or clerical experience typically started at $18,400 a year in 1999. Beginning salaries were slightly higher in areas where the prevailing local pay level was higher. The average salary for all human resources clerks employed by the Federal Government was $29,500 in 1999.

Related Occupations

Today, most records processing clerks enter data into a computer system and perform basic analysis of the data. Other clerical workers who enter and manipulate data include bank tellers, statistical clerks, receiving clerks, medical record clerks, hotel and motel clerks, credit clerks, and reservation and transportation ticket agents.

Sources of Additional Information

State employment service offices can provide information about job openings for records processing occupations.

Billing Clerks and Billing Machine Operators

(O*NET 55344 and 56002)

Significant Points

- Most jobs require only a high school diploma.
- Numerous job opportunities should arise due to high turnover in this occupation.

Nature of the Work

Billing clerks keep records, calculate charges, and maintain files of payments made for goods or services. Billing machine operators run machines that generate bills, statements, and invoices.

Billing clerks review purchase orders, bills of lading, sales tickets, hospital records, or charge slips to calculate the total amount due from a customer. Calculating the charges for an individual's hospital stay may require a letter to an insurance company; a clerk computing trucking rates for machine parts may consult a rate book. In accounting, law, consulting, and similar firms, billing clerks calculate client fees based on the actual time required to perform the task. They keep track of the accumulated hours and dollar amounts to charge to each job, the type of job performed for a customer, and the percentage of work completed.

After billing clerks review all necessary information, they compute the charges using calculators or computers. They then prepare itemized statements, bills, or invoices used for billing and record keeping purposes, depending on the organization's needs. In one organization, the clerk might prepare a bill containing the amount due and date and type of service; in another, the clerk would produce a detailed invoice with codes for all goods and services provided. This latter form might list items sold, credit terms, date of shipment or dates services were provided, a salesperson's or doctor's identification if necessary, and the sales total.

After entering all information, *billing machine operators* run off the bill to send to the customer. Computers and specialized billing software allow many clerks to calculate charges and prepare bills in one step. Computer packages prompt clerks to enter data from hand-written forms and manipulate the necessary entries of quantities, labor, and rates to be charged. Billing clerks verify the entry of information and check for errors before the computer prints the bill. After the bills are printed, billing clerks check them again for accuracy.

Working Conditions

Billing clerks and billing machine operators typically are employed in an office environment. Most work alongside other clerical workers, but some work in centralized units away from the front office. Because the majority of billing clerks and billing machine operators use computers on a daily basis, these workers may experience eye and muscle strain, backaches, headaches, and repetitive motion injuries. Also, clerks who review detailed data may have to sit for extended periods of time. Most billing clerks and billing machine operators work regular business hours. Billing clerks in hotels, restaurants, and stores may work overtime during peak holiday and vacation seasons.

Employment

In 1998, billing clerks held about 342,000 jobs, and billing machine operators held about 107,000 jobs. One-third of the billing clerks' jobs were in health services, mostly in physicians' offices. Transportation and wholesale trade industries each accounted for 1 out of 10 jobs. Most of the remaining jobs were found in manufacturing or retail trade.

Wholesale and retail trade establishments provided about one-third of all billing machine operator jobs; service establishments, including health services, provided another third. Of the remaining jobs, most were found in banks and other financial institutions.

Training, Other Qualifications, and Advancement

Employers typically require applicants to have at least a high school diploma or its equivalent. Most employers prefer workers who are computer-literate. Knowledge of word processing and spreadsheet software is especially valuable, as are experience working in an office and good interpersonal skills.

Billing clerks and billing machine operators often learn the skills they need in high schools, business schools, and community colleges. Business education programs offered by these institutions typically include courses in typing, word processing, shorthand, business communications, records management, and office systems and procedures.

Some entrants are college graduates with degrees in business, finance, or liberal arts. Although a degree is rarely required, many graduates accept entry-level clerical positions to get into a particular company or to enter the finance or accounting field with the hope of being promoted to professional or managerial positions. Workers with college degrees are likely to start at higher salaries and advance more easily than those without degrees.

Once hired, billing clerks and billing machine operators usually receive on-the-job training. Under the guidance of a supervisor or other senior worker, new employees learn company procedures. Some formal classroom training may also be necessary, such as training in specific computer software.

Billing clerks and billing machine operators must be careful, orderly, and detail-oriented in order to avoid making errors and to recognize errors made by others. These workers should also be discreet and trustworthy because they frequently come in contact with confidential material. Additionally, clerks should have a strong aptitude for numbers.

Billing clerks and billing machine operators usually advance by taking on more duties in the same occupation for higher pay or transferring to a closely related occupation. Most companies fill office and administrative support supervisory and managerial positions by promoting individuals from within their organizations, so those who acquire additional skills, experience, and training improve their advancement opportunities.

Job Outlook

Job openings for those seeking work as billing clerks or billing machine operators are expected to be numerous through the year 2008. Despite the lack of rapid employment growth, many job openings will occur as workers transfer to other occupations or leave the labor force. Turnover in this occupation is relatively high, which is characteristic of an entry-level occupation requiring only a high school diploma.

Employment of billing clerks is expected to grow about as fast as the average for all occupations through the year 2008. A growing economy and increased demand for billing services will result in more business transactions. Rising worker productivity as computers manage more account information will not keep employment from rising. More complex billing applications will increasingly require workers with greater technical expertise.

Employment of billing machine operators, on the other hand, is expected to decline through the year 2008. More advanced machines and computers will continue to replace billing machines, enabling billing clerks to perform the jobs formerly done by billing machine operators. In some organizations, productivity gains from billing software will increasingly allow accounting clerks to take over the responsibilities of billing clerks and billing machine operators.

Earnings

Salaries of billing clerks and billing machine operators vary considerably. The region of the country, size of city, and type and size of establishment all influence salary levels. The level of industry or technical expertise required and the complexity and uniqueness of responsibilities may also affect earnings. Median annual earnings for those working full time in 1998 were as follows:

Billing clerks $22,670

Billing machine operators 20,560

Related Occupations

Today, most clerks enter data into a computer system and perform basic analysis of the data. Other clerical workers who enter and manipulate data include bank tellers, statistical clerks, receiving clerks, medical records clerks, hotel and motel clerks, credit clerks, and reservation and transportation ticket agents.

Sources of Additional Information

State employment service offices can provide information about job openings for the occupation.

Bookkeeping, Accounting, and Auditing Clerks

(O*NET 49023B, 55338A, and 55338B)

Nature of the Work

Bookkeeping, accounting, and auditing clerks are an organization's financial record keepers. They compute, classify, record, and verify numerical data to develop and maintain financial records.

In small establishments, *bookkeeping clerks* handle all aspects of financial transactions. They record debits and credits, compare current and past balance sheets, summarize details of separate ledgers, and prepare reports for supervisors and managers. They may also prepare bank deposits by compiling data from cashiers, verifying and balancing receipts, and sending cash, checks, or other forms of payment to the bank.

In large offices and accounting departments, *accounting clerks* have more specialized tasks. Their titles often reflect the type of accounting they do, such as accounts payable clerk or accounts receivable clerk. In addition, responsibilities vary by level of experience. Entry-level accounting clerks post details of transactions, total accounts, and compute interest charges. They may also monitor loans and accounts to ensure that payments are up to date.

More advanced accounting clerks may total, balance, and reconcile billing vouchers; ensure completeness and accuracy of data on accounts; and code documents according to company procedures. They post transactions in journals and on computer files and update these files when needed. Senior clerks also review computer printouts against manually maintained journals and make necessary corrections. They may also review invoices and statements to ensure that all information is accurate and complete, and reconcile computer reports with operating reports.

Auditing clerks verify records of transactions posted by other workers. They check figures, postings, and documents for correct entry, mathematical accuracy, and proper codes. They also correct or note errors for accountants or other workers to adjust.

As organizations continue to computerize their financial records, many bookkeeping, accounting, and auditing clerks use specialized accounting software on personal computers. They increasingly post charges to accounts on computer spreadsheets and databases, as manual posting to general ledgers is becoming obsolete. These workers now enter information from receipts or bills into computers, which is then stored either electronically, as computer printouts, or both. Widespread use of computers has also enabled bookkeeping, accounting, and auditing clerks to take on additional responsibilities, such as payroll, timekeeping, and billing.

Employment

Bookkeeping, accounting, and auditing clerks held about 2.1 million jobs in 1998. About 25 percent worked in wholesale and retail trade, and 16 percent were in organizations providing business, health, and social services. Approximately 1 out of 3 of bookkeeping, accounting, and auditing clerks worked part time in 1998.

Job Outlook

Virtually all job openings for bookkeeping, accounting, and auditing clerks through 2008 will stem from replacement needs. Each year, numerous jobs will become available, as these clerks transfer to other occupations or leave the labor force. Although turnover is lower than among other record clerks, the large size of the occupation ensures plentiful job openings, including many opportunities for temporary and part-time work.

Employment of bookkeeping, accounting, and auditing clerks is expected to decline through 2008. Although a growing economy will result in more financial transactions and other activities that require these clerical workers, the continuing spread of office automation will lift worker productivity and contribute to employment decline. In addition, organizations of all sizes will continue to consolidate various record keeping functions, thus reducing the demand for these clerks.

Brokerage Clerks and Statement Clerks

(O*NET 53126 and 53128)

Significant Points

- Some of these jobs require only a high school diploma, while others are considered entry-level positions for which a bachelor's degree is needed.

- Employment of brokerage clerks is expected to increase faster than the average for all occupations.

Nature of the Work

Brokerage clerks perform a number of different jobs with wide ranging responsibilities, but all involve computing and recording data on securities transactions. Brokerage clerks may also contact customers, take orders, and inform clients of changes to their accounts. Some of these jobs are more clerical and require only a high school diploma, while others are considered entry-level positions for which a bachelor's degree is needed. Brokerage clerks, who work in the operations departments of securities firms, on trading floors, and in branch offices, are also called margin clerks, dividend clerks, transfer clerks, and broker's assistants.

The broker's assistant, also called sales assistant, is the most common type of brokerage clerk. These workers typically assist two brokers, for whom they take calls from clients, write up order tickets, process the paperwork for opening and closing accounts, record a client's purchases and sales, and inform clients of changes in their accounts. All brokers' assistants must be knowledgeable about investment products so they can clearly communicate with clients. Those with a "Series 7" license can make recommendations to clients at the instruction of the broker. The Series 7 license is issued to securities and commodities sales representatives by the National Association of Securities Dealers and allows them to provide advice on securities to the public.

Brokerage clerks in the operations areas of securities firms perform many duties to facilitate the sale and purchase of stocks, bonds, commodities, and other kinds of investments. These clerks produce the necessary records of all transactions that occur in their area of the business. Job titles for many of these clerks depend upon the type of work they perform. Purchase-and-sale clerks, for example, match orders to buy with orders to sell. They balance and verify stock trades by comparing the records of the selling firm to those of the buying firm. Dividend clerks ensure timely payments of stock or cash dividends to clients of a particular brokerage firm. Transfer clerks execute customer requests for changes to security registration and examine stock certificates for adherence to banking regulations. Receive-and-deliver clerks facilitate the receipt and delivery of securities among firms and institutions. Margin clerks post accounts and monitor activity in customers' accounts to ensure that clients make payments and stay within legal boundaries concerning stock purchases.

Technology is changing the nature of many of these workers' jobs. A significant and growing number of brokerage clerks use custom-designed software programs to process transactions more quickly. Only a few customized accounts are still handled manually.

Statement clerks assemble, verify, and send bank statements every month. In many banks, statement clerks are called statement operators because they spend much of their workday running sophisticated, high-speed machines. These machines fold computer-printed statements, collate those longer than one page, insert statements and canceled checks into envelopes, and seal and weigh them for postage. Statement clerks load the machine with statements, canceled checks, and envelopes. They then monitor the equipment and correct minor problems. For more serious problems, they call repair personnel.

In banks that do not have such machines, statement clerks perform all operations manually. They may also be responsible for verifying signatures and checking for missing information on checks, placing canceled checks into trays, and retrieving them to send with the statements. In a growing number of banks, only the statement is printed and sent to the account holder. The canceled checks are not returned; this is known as check truncation.

Statement clerks are employed primarily by large banks. In smaller banks, a teller or bookkeeping clerk, who performs other duties during the rest of the month, usually handles the statement clerk's function. Some small banks send their statement information to larger banks for processing, printing, and mailing.

Working Conditions

Brokerage and statement clerks typically are employed in an office environment. Most work alongside other clerical workers, but some records processing clerks work in centralized units away from the front office. Because the majority of clerks use computers on a daily basis, these workers may experience eye and muscle strain, backaches, headaches, and repetitive motion injuries. Also, clerks who review detailed data may have to sit for extended periods of time. Most clerks work regular business hours. Brokerage clerks may have to work overtime if there is a high volume of activity in the stock or bond market.

Employment

Brokerage clerks held about 77,000 jobs in 1998, and statement clerks held about 16,000 jobs. Brokerage clerks work in firms that sell securities and commodities. Banking institutions employed almost all statement clerks.

Training, Other Qualifications, and Advancement

Employers typically require applicants to have at least a high school diploma or its equivalent, and brokerage firms usually seek college graduates for brokerage clerk jobs. Most employers prefer workers who are computer-literate. Knowledge of word processing and spreadsheet software is especially valuable, as are experience working in an office and good interpersonal skills.

Clerks often learn the skills they need in high schools, business schools, and community colleges. Business education programs offered by these institutions typically include courses in typing, word processing, shorthand, business communications, records management, and office systems and procedures.

Some entrants are college graduates with degrees in business, finance, or liberal arts. Many graduates accept entry-level clerical positions to get into a particular company or to enter the finance or accounting field with the hope of being promoted to professional or managerial positions. Some companies, such as brokerage firms, have a set plan of advancement that tracks college graduates from entry-level clerical jobs into managerial positions. Workers with college degrees are likely to start at higher salaries and advance more easily than those without degrees.

Once hired, clerks usually receive on-the-job training. Under the guidance of a supervisor or other senior worker, new employees learn company procedures. Some formal classroom training may also be necessary, such as training in specific computer software.

Clerks must be careful, orderly, and detail-oriented in order to avoid making errors and to recognize errors made by others. These workers should also be discreet and trustworthy because they frequently come in contact with confidential material. Additionally, clerks should have a strong aptitude for numbers. Because statement clerks have access to confidential financial information, these workers must be bonded.

Clerks usually advance by taking on more duties in the same occupation for higher pay or transferring to a closely related occupation. Most companies fill office and administrative support supervisory and managerial positions by promoting individuals from within their organizations, so clerks who acquire additional skills, experience, and training improve their advancement opportunities. With appropriate experience and education, some clerks may become securities, commodities, and financial services sales representatives.

Job Outlook

Employment of brokerage clerks is expected to increase faster than the average for all occupations, while employment of statement clerks should decline. With people increasingly investing in securities, demand for brokerage clerks will climb to meet the needs of processing larger volumes of transactions. Because most back office operations are now computerized, employment growth among brokerage clerks is not expected to keep pace with overall employment growth in the securities and commodities industry; however, brokerage clerks will still be needed to update records, enter changes to customer's accounts, and verify securities transfers.

Broker's assistants will also increase in number along with the number of full-service brokers. Because these clerks spend much of their day answering telephone calls, placing orders, and often running the office, their jobs are not readily subject to automation.

The number of statement clerks is declining rapidly due to increasing technology in the Nation's banks. With the job of producing statements almost completely automated, the mailing of checks and statements is now done mostly by machine. In addition, the further spread of check truncation and the increased use of automated teller machines and other electronic money transfers should result in significantly fewer checks being written and processed.

Earnings

Salaries of clerks vary considerably. The region of the country, size of city, and type and size of establishment all influence salary levels. The level of industry or technical expertise required and the complexity and uniqueness of a clerk's responsibilities may also affect earnings. Median annual earnings of full-time workers in 1998 were as follows:

Brokerage clerks $27,920
Statement clerks 18,640

Related Occupations

Today, most clerks enter data into a computer system and perform basic analysis of the data. Other clerical workers who enter and manipulate data include bank tellers, statistical clerks, receiving clerks, medical records clerks, hotel and motel clerks, credit clerks, and reservation and transportation ticket agents.

Sources of Additional Information

State employment service offices can provide information about job openings for the occupation.

File Clerks

(O*NET 55321)

Nature of the Work

The amount of information generated by organizations continues to grow rapidly. File clerks classify, store, retrieve, and update this information. In many small offices, they often have additional responsibilities, such as data entry, word processing, sorting mail, and operating copying or fax machines. They are employed across the Nation by organizations of all types.

File clerks, also called records, information, or record center clerks, examine incoming material and code it numerically, alphabetically, or by subject matter. They then store forms, letters, receipts, or reports in paper form or enter necessary information into other storage devices. Some clerks operate mechanized files that rotate to bring the needed records to them; others convert documents to films that are then stored on microforms, such as microfilm or microfiche. A growing number of file clerks use imaging systems that scan paper files or film and store the material on optical disks.

In order for records to be useful, they must be up-to-date and accurate. File clerks ensure that new information is added to the files in a timely manner and may get rid of outdated file materials or transfer them to inactive storage. They also check files at regular inter-

vals to make sure that all items are correctly sequenced and placed. Whenever records cannot be found, the file clerk attempts to locate the missing material. As an organization's needs for information change, file clerks also implement changes to the filing system established by supervisory personnel.

When records are requested, file clerks locate them and give them to the borrower. The record may be a sheet of paper stored in a file cabinet or an image on microform. In the first example, the clerk manually retrieves the document and hands or forwards it to the borrower. In the latter example, the clerk retrieves the microform and displays it on a microform reader. If necessary, file clerks make copies of records and distribute them. In addition, they keep track of materials removed from the files to ensure that borrowed files are returned.

Increasingly, file clerks use computerized filing and retrieval systems. These systems use a variety of storage devices, such as a mainframe computer, magnetic tape, CD-ROM, or floppy disk. To retrieve a document in these systems, the clerk enters the document's identification code, obtains the location, and pulls the document. Accessing files in a computer database is much quicker than locating and physically retrieving paper files. Even when files are stored electronically, however, backup paper or electronic copies usually are also kept.

Employment

File clerks held about 272,000 jobs in 1998. Although file clerk jobs are found in nearly every sector of the economy, about 90 percent of these workers are employed in services, government, finance, insurance, and real estate. More than 1 out of every 4 is employed in temporary services firms, and about 1 out of 3 worked part time in 1998.

Job Outlook

Employment of file clerks is expected to grow about as fast as the average for all occupations through 2008. Projected job growth stems from rising demand for file clerks to record and retrieve information in organizations across the economy. This growth will be moderated, however, by productivity gains stemming from office automation and the consolidation of clerical jobs. Nonetheless, job opportunities for file clerks should be plentiful because a large number of workers will be needed to replace workers who leave the occupation each year. High turnover among file clerks reflects the lack of formal training requirements, limited advancement potential, and relatively low pay.

Jobseekers who have typing and other secretarial skills and are familiar with a wide range of office machines, especially personal computers, should have the best job opportunities. File clerks should find many opportunities for temporary or part-time work, especially during peak business periods.

Human Resources Clerks, Except Payroll and Timekeeping

(O*NET 55314)

Nature of the Work

Human resources clerks maintain the personnel records of an organization's employees. These records include information such as name, address, job title, and earnings, benefits such as health and life insurance, and tax withholding. On a daily basis, these clerks record and answer questions about employee absences and supervisory reports on job performance. When an employee receives a promotion or switches health insurance plans, the human resources clerk updates the appropriate form. Human resources clerks may also prepare reports for managers elsewhere within the organization. For example, they might compile a list of employees eligible for an award.

In smaller organizations, some human resources clerks perform a variety of other clerical duties. They answer telephone or letter inquiries from the public, send out announcements of job openings or job examinations, and issue application forms. When credit bureaus and finance companies request confirmation of a person's employment, the human resources clerk provides authorized information from the employee's personnel records. Payroll departments and insurance companies may also be contacted to verify changes to records.

Some human resources clerks are also involved in hiring. They screen job applicants to obtain information such as education and work experience; administer aptitude, personality, and interest tests; explain the organization's employment policies and refer qualified applicants to the employing official; and request references from present or past employers. Also, human resources clerks inform job applicants, by telephone or letter, of their acceptance or rejection for employment.

Other human resources clerks are known as assignment clerks. Their role is to notify a firm's existing employees of position vacancies and to identify and assign qualified applicants. They keep track of vacancies throughout the organization and complete and distribute vacancy advertisement forms. These clerks review applications in response to advertisements and verify information using personnel records. After a selection is made, they notify all the applicants of their acceptance or rejection.

In some job settings, human resources clerks have specific job titles. Identification clerks are responsible for security matters at defense installations. They compile and record personal data about vendors, contractors, and civilian and military personnel and their dependents. Job duties include interviewing applicants; corresponding with law enforcement authorities; and preparing badges, passes, and identification cards.

Employment

Human resources clerks held about 142,000 jobs in 1998. Although these workers are found in most industries, about 1 in every 5 works for a government agency. Colleges and universities, hospitals, department stores, and banks also employ large numbers of human resources clerks.

Job Outlook

Replacement needs will account for most job openings for human resources clerks. Jobs will open up as clerks advance within the personnel department, take jobs unrelated to personnel administration, or leave the labor force.

Little or no change is expected in employment of human resources clerks through the year 2008, largely due to the increased use of computers. The growing use of computers in personnel or human resource departments means that a lot of data entry done by human resources clerks can be eliminated, as employees themselves enter the data and send it to the personnel office. This is most feasible in large organizations with multiple personnel offices. The increasing use of computers and other automated office equipment by managers and professionals in personnel offices also could mean less work for human resources clerks.

Library Assistants and Bookmobile Drivers

(O*NET 53902)

Significant Points

- Most jobs require only a high school diploma.
- Numerous opportunities should arise due to high turnover.

Nature of the Work

Library assistants and bookmobile drivers organize library resources and make them available to users. They assist librarians and, in some cases, library technicians.

Library assistants—sometimes referred to as library media assistants, library aides, or circulation assistants—register patrons so they can borrow materials from the library. They record the borrower's name and address from an application and then issue a library card. Most library assistants enter and update patrons' records using computer databases. At the circulation desk, assistants lend and collect books, periodicals, video tapes, and other materials. When an item is borrowed, assistants stamp the due date on the material and record the patron's identification from his or her library card. They inspect returned materials for damage, check due dates, and compute fines for overdue material. They review records to compile a list of overdue materials and send out notices. They also answer patrons' questions and refer those they cannot answer to a librarian.

Throughout the library, assistants sort returned books, periodicals, and other items and return them to their designated shelves, files, or storage areas. They locate materials to be loaned, either for a patron or another library. Many card catalogues are computerized, so library assistants must be familiar with the computer system. If any materials have been damaged, these workers try to repair them. For example, they use tape or paste to repair torn pages or book covers and other specialized processes to repair more valuable materials.

Some library assistants specialize in helping patrons who have vision problems. Sometimes referred to as library, talking-books, or Braille-and-talking-books clerks, they review the borrower's list of desired reading material. They locate those materials or closely related substitutes from the library collection of large type or Braille volumes, tape cassettes, and open-reel talking books. They complete the paperwork and give or mail the materials to the borrower.

To extend library services to more patrons, many libraries operate bookmobiles. *Bookmobile drivers* take trucks stocked with books to designated sites on a regular schedule. Bookmobiles serve community organizations such as shopping centers, apartment complexes, schools, and nursing homes. They may also be used to extend library service to patrons living in remote areas. Depending on local conditions, drivers may operate a bookmobile alone or may be accompanied by a library technician.

When working alone, the drivers perform many of the same functions as a library assistant in a main or branch library. They answer patrons' questions, receive and check out books, collect fines, maintain the book collection, shelve materials, and occasionally operate audiovisual equipment to show slides or films. They participate and may assist in planning programs sponsored by the library such as reader advisory programs, used book sales, or outreach programs. Bookmobile drivers keep track of their mileage, the materials lent out, and the amount of fines collected. In some areas, they are responsible for maintenance of the vehicle and any photocopiers or other equipment in it. They record statistics on circulation and the number of people visiting the bookmobile. Drivers may also record requests for special items from the main library and arrange for the materials to be mailed or delivered to a patron during the next scheduled visit. Many bookmobiles are equipped with personal computers and CD-ROM systems linked to the main library system; this allows bookmobile drivers to reserve or locate books immediately. Some bookmobiles now offer Internet access to users.

Because bookmobile drivers may be the only link some people have to the library, much of their work is helping the public. They may assist handicapped or elderly patrons to the bookmobile, or shovel snow to assure their safety. They may enter hospitals or nursing homes to deliver books to patrons who are bedridden.

Working Conditions

Because most library assistants use computers on a daily basis, these workers may experience eye and muscle strain, backaches, headaches, and repetitive motion injuries. Also, assistants who review detailed data may have to sit for extended periods of time. Although the work does not require heavy lifting, library assistants spend a lot of time on their feet and frequently stoop, bend, and reach.

Library assistants may work evenings and weekends, but those employed in school libraries usually work only during the school year.

Bookmobile drivers must maneuver large vehicles in all kinds of traffic and weather conditions and may also be responsible for the maintenance of the bookmobile. The schedules of bookmobile drivers depend on the size of the area being served. Some of these workers go out on their routes every day, while others go only on certain days. On these other days, they work at the library. Some also work evenings and weekends to give patrons as much access to the library as possible.

Employment

Library assistants and bookmobile drivers held about 127,000 jobs in 1998. Over one-half of these workers were employed by local government in public libraries; most of the remaining worked in school libraries. Opportunities for flexible schedules are abundant; over one-half of these workers were on part-time schedules.

Training, Other Qualifications, and Advancement

Employers typically require applicants to have at least a high school diploma or its equivalent. Most employers prefer workers who are computer-literate. Knowledge of word processing and spreadsheet software is especially valuable, as are experience working in an office and good interpersonal skills.

Library assistants often learn the skills they need in high schools, business schools, and community colleges. Business education programs offered by these institutions typically include courses in typing, word processing, shorthand, business communications, records management, and office systems and procedures.

Some entrants are college graduates with degrees in liberal arts. Although a degree is rarely required, many graduates accept entry-level positions with the hope of being promoted. Workers with college degrees are likely to start at higher salaries and advance more easily than those without degrees.

Once hired, library assistants and bookmobile drivers usually receive on-the-job training. Under the guidance of a supervisor or other senior worker, new employees learn procedures. Some formal classroom training may also be necessary, such as training in specific computer software. Library assistants and bookmobile drivers must be careful, orderly, and detail-oriented in order to avoid making errors and to recognize errors made by others. Many bookmobile drivers are now required to have a commercial driver's license.

These employees usually advance by taking on more duties in the same occupation for higher pay or transferring to a closely related occupation. Most companies fill supervisory and managerial positions by promoting individuals from within their organizations, so those who acquire additional skills, experience, and training improve their advancement opportunities. With appropriate experience and education, some may become librarians.

Job Outlook

Opportunities should be good for persons interested in jobs as library assistants or bookmobile drivers through 2008. Turnover of these workers is quite high, reflecting the limited investment in training and subsequent weak attachment to this occupation. This work is attractive to retirees, students, and others who want a part-time schedule, and there is a lot of movement into and out of the occupation. Many openings will become available each year to replace workers who transfer to other occupations or leave the labor force. Some positions become available as library assistants move within the organization. Library assistants can be promoted to library technicians and eventually supervisory positions in public service or technical service areas. Advancement opportunities are greater in larger libraries and may be more limited in smaller ones.

Employment is expected to grow about as fast as the average for all occupations through 2008. The vast majority of library assistants and bookmobile drivers work in public or school libraries. Efforts to contain costs in local governments and academic institutions of all types may result in more hiring of library support staff than librarians. Because most are employed by public institutions, library assistants and bookmobile drivers are not directly affected by the ups and downs of the business cycle. Some of these workers may lose their jobs, however, if there are cuts in government budgets.

Earnings

Salaries of library assistants and bookmobile drivers vary. The region of the country, size of city, and type and size of establishment all influence salary levels. Median annual earnings of full-time library assistants and bookmobile drivers in 1998 were $16,980.

Related Occupations

Other clerical workers who enter and manipulate data include bank tellers, statistical clerks, receiving clerks, medical record clerks, hotel and motel clerks, credit clerks, and reservation and transportation ticket agents.

Sources of Additional Information

Information about a career as a library assistant can be obtained from:

- Council on Library/Media Technology, P.O. Box 951, Oxon Hill, MD 20750. Internet: http://library.ucr.edu/COLT

Public libraries and libraries in academic institutions can provide information about job openings for library assistants and bookmobile drivers.

Order Clerks

(O*NET 55323)

Nature of the Work

Order clerks receive and process incoming orders for a wide variety of goods or services, such as spare parts for machines, consumer appliances, gas and electric power connections, film rentals, and articles of clothing. They are sometimes called order-entry clerks, customer service representatives, sales representatives, order processors, or order takers.

Orders for materials, merchandise, or services can come from inside or from outside of an organization. In large companies with many work sites, such as automobile manufacturers, clerks order parts and equipment from the company's warehouses. *Inside order clerks* receive orders from other workers employed by the same company or from salespersons in the field.

Many other order clerks, however, receive orders from outside companies or individuals. Order clerks in wholesale businesses, for instance, receive orders for merchandise from retail establishments that the retailer, in turn, sells to the public. An increasing number of order clerks work for catalogue companies and online retailers, receiving orders from individual customers by either phone, fax, regular mail, or e-mail. Order clerks dealing primarily with the public sometimes are referred to as *outside order clerks*.

Computers provide order clerks with ready access to information such as stock numbers, prices, and inventory. Orders frequently depend on which products are in stock and which products are most appropriate for the customer's needs. Some order clerks, especially those in industrial settings, must be able to give price estimates for entire jobs, not just single parts. Others must be able to take special orders, give expected arrival dates, prepare contracts, and handle complaints.

Many order clerks receive orders directly by telephone, entering the required information as the customer places the order. However, a rapidly increasing number of orders are now received through computer systems, the Internet, faxes, and e-mail. In some cases, these orders are sent directly from the customer's terminal to the order clerk's terminal. Orders received by regular mail are sometimes scanned into a database that's instantly accessible to clerks.

Clerks review orders for completeness and clarity. They may complete missing information or contact the customer for the information. Similarly, clerks contact customers if customers need additional information, such as prices or shipping dates, or if delays in filling the order are anticipated. For orders received by regular mail, clerks extract checks or money orders, sort them, and send them for processing.

After an order has been verified and entered, the customer's final cost is calculated. The clerk then routes the order to the proper department—such as the warehouse—that actually sends out or delivers the item in question.

In organizations with sophisticated computer systems, inventory records are adjusted automatically, as sales are made. In less automated organizations, order clerks may adjust inventory records. Clerks may also notify other departments when inventories are low or when orders would deplete supplies.

Some order clerks must establish priorities in filling orders. For example, an order clerk in a blood bank may receive a request from a hospital for a certain type of blood. The clerk must first find out if the request is routine or an emergency and then take appropriate action.

Employment

Order clerks held about 362,000 jobs in 1998. About one half were in wholesale and retail establishments and about one quarter in manufacturing firms. Most of the remaining jobs for order clerks were in business services.

Job Outlook

Job openings for order clerks should be plentiful through the year 2008 due to sizable replacement needs. Numerous jobs will become available each year to replace order clerks who transfer to other occupations or leave the labor force completely. Many of these openings will be for seasonal work, especially in catalogue companies or online retailers catering to holiday gift buyers.

Employment of order clerks is expected to grow more slowly than the average through the year 2008, as office automation continues to increase worker productivity. As the economy grows, increasingly more orders for goods and services will be placed. Demand for outside order clerks who deal mainly with the public or other businesses should remain fairly strong. The increasing use of online retailing and toll-free numbers that make placing orders easy and convenient will stimulate demand for these workers. However, productivity gains from increased automation will offset some of the growth in demand for outside order clerks, as each clerk is able to handle an increasingly higher volume of orders. In addition, orders placed over the Internet and other computer systems are often entered directly into the computer by the customer; thus, the order clerk is not involved at all in placing the order.

Employment growth of inside clerks will also be constrained by productivity gains due to automation. The spread of electronic data interchange, a system enabling computers to communicate directly with one another, allows orders within establishments to be placed with little human intervention. Besides electronic data interchange, *extranets* and other systems allowing a firm's employees to place orders directly are increasingly common.

Other types of automation will also limit the demand for order clerks. Sophisticated inventory control and automatic billing systems allow companies to track inventory and accounts with much less help from order clerks than in the past. Some companies use automated phone menus accessible with a touch-tone phone to receive orders, and others use answering machines. Developments in voice recognition technology may also further reduce the demand for order clerks.

Payroll and Timekeeping Clerks

(O*NET 55341)

Nature of the Work

Payroll and timekeeping clerks perform a vital function—ensuring that employees are paid on time and that their paychecks are accurate. If inaccuracies arise, such as monetary errors or incorrect amounts of vacation time, these workers research and correct the records. In addition, they may also perform various other clerical tasks.

The fundamental task of *timekeeping clerks* is distributing and collecting timecards each pay period. They review employee work charts, timesheets, and timecards to ensure that information is properly recorded and that records have the signatures of authorizing officials. In companies that bill for the time spent by staff (such as law or accounting firms), timekeeping clerks make sure the hours recorded are charged to the correct job so clients can be properly billed. These clerks also review computer reports listing timecards that cannot be processed because of errors, and they contact the employee or the employee's supervisor to resolve the problem. In addition, timekeeping clerks are responsible for informing managers and other employees of procedural changes in payroll policies.

Payroll clerks, also called payroll technicians, screen timecards for calculating, coding, or other errors. They compute pay by subtracting allotments (including Federal and State taxes, retirement, insurance, and savings) from gross earnings. Increasingly, computers perform these calculations and alert payroll clerks to problems or errors in the data. In small organizations, or for new employees whose records are not yet entered into a computer system, clerks may perform the necessary calculations manually. In some small offices, clerks or other employees in the accounting department process payroll.

Payroll clerks also maintain paper backup files for research and reference. They record changes in employee addresses; close out files when workers retire, resign, or transfer; and advise employees on income tax withholding and other mandatory deductions. They also issue and record adjustments to pay because of previous errors or retroactive increases. Payroll clerks need to follow changes in tax and deduction laws so they are aware of the most recent revisions. Finally, they prepare and mail earnings and tax withholding statements for employees' use in preparing income tax returns.

In small offices, payroll and timekeeping duties are likely to be included in the duties of a general office clerk, secretary, or accounting clerk. However, large organizations employ specialized payroll and timekeeping clerks to perform these functions.

Employment

Payroll and timekeeping clerks held about 172,000 jobs in 1998. About 35 percent of all payroll and timekeeping clerks worked in business, health, education, and social services; another 25 percent worked in manufacturing; and more than 10 percent were in wholesale and retail trade or in government. About 11 percent of all payroll and timekeeping clerks worked part time in 1998.

Job Outlook

Employment of payroll and timekeeping clerks is expected to decline through 2008 due to the continuing automation of payroll and timekeeping functions and the consolidation of clerical jobs. Nevertheless, a number of job openings should arise in coming years, as payroll and timekeeping clerks leave the labor force or transfer to other occupations. Many payroll clerks use this position as a stepping stone to higher-level accounting jobs.

As in many other clerical occupations, new technology will continue to allow many of the tasks formerly handled by payroll and timekeeping clerks to be partially or completely automated. For example, automated timeclocks, which calculate employee hours, allow large organizations to centralize their timekeeping duties in one location. At individual sites, employee hours are increasingly tracked by computer and verified by managers. This information is then compiled and sent to a central office to be processed by payroll clerks, eliminating the need to have payroll clerks at every site. In addition, the growing use of direct deposit eliminates the need to draft paychecks because these funds are automatically transferred each pay period. Furthermore, timekeeping duties are increasingly being distributed to secretaries, general office clerks, or accounting clerks or are being contracted out to organizations that specialize in these services.

Recreational Therapists

(O*NET 32317)

Significant Points

- Employment of recreational therapists is expected to increase, due to expansion in long-term care, physical and psychiatric rehabilitation, and services for people with disabilities.

- Opportunities should generally be best for persons with a bachelor's degree in therapeutic recreation or in recreation with a concentration in therapeutic recreation.

Nature of the Work

Recreational therapists, also referred to as therapeutic recreation specialists, provide treatment services and recreation activities to individuals with disabilities, illnesses, or other disabling conditions. These therapists use a variety of techniques to treat or maintain the physical, mental, and emotional well-being of clients. Treatments may include the use of arts and crafts, animals, sports, games, dance and movement, drama, music, and community outings. Therapists help individuals reduce depression, stress, and anxiety. They also help individuals recover basic motor functioning and reasoning abilities, build confidence, and socialize effectively to enable greater independence, as well as to reduce or eliminate the effects of illness or disability. Additionally, they help integrate people with disabilities into the community by helping them use community resources and recreational activities. Recreational therapists should not be confused with recreation workers, who organize recreational activities primarily for enjoyment.

In acute health care settings, such as hospitals and rehabilitation centers, recreational therapists treat and rehabilitate individuals with specific health conditions, usually in conjunction or collaboration with physicians, nurses, psychologists, social workers, and physical and occupational therapists. In long-term care facilities and residential facilities, recreational therapists use leisure activities—especially structured group programs—to improve and maintain general health and well-being. They may also treat clients and provide interventions to prevent further medical problems and secondary complications related to illness and disabilities.

Recreational therapists assess clients based on information from standardized assessments, observations, medical records, medical staff, family, and clients themselves. They then develop and carry out therapeutic interventions consistent with client needs and interests. For example, clients who are isolated from others or have limited social skills may be encouraged to play games with others, or right-handed persons with right-side paralysis may be instructed to adapt to using their unaffected left side to throw a ball or swing a racket. Recreational therapists may instruct patients in relaxation techniques to reduce stress and tension, stretching and limbering exercises, proper body mechanics for participation in recreation activities, pacing and energy conservation techniques, and individual as well as team activities. Additionally, therapists observe and document patients' participation, reactions, and progress.

Community-based therapeutic recreation specialists may work in park and recreation departments, special education programs for school districts, or programs for older adults and people with disabilities. Included in the latter group are programs and facilities such as assisted living, adult day service centers, and substance abuse rehabilitation centers. In these programs, therapists use interventions to develop specific skills while providing opportunities for exercise, mental stimulation, creativity, and fun. Although most therapists are employed in other areas, those who work in schools help counselors, teachers, and parents address the special needs of students—most importantly, easing the transition into adult life for disabled students.

Working Conditions

Recreational therapists provide services in special activity rooms but also plan activities and prepare documentation in offices. When working with clients during community integration programs, they may travel locally to instruct clients on the accessibility of public transportation and other public areas, such as parks, playgrounds, swimming pools, restaurants, and theaters.

Therapists often lift and carry equipment as well as lead recreational activities. Recreational therapists generally work a 40-hour week that may include some evenings, weekends, and holidays.

Employment

Recreational therapists held about 39,000 jobs in 1998. About 38 percent of salaried jobs for therapists were in hospitals, and 26 percent were in nursing and personal care facilities. Others worked in residential facilities, community mental health centers, adult day care programs, correctional facilities, community programs for people with disabilities, and substance abuse centers. About 1 out of 3 therapists was self-employed, generally contracting with long-term care facilities or community agencies to develop and oversee programs.

Training, Other Qualifications, and Advancement

A bachelor's degree in therapeutic recreation, or in recreation with a concentration in therapeutic recreation, is the usual requirement for entry-level positions. Persons may qualify for paraprofessional positions with an associate degree in therapeutic recreation or a health care related field. An associate degree in recreational therapy; training in art, drama, or music therapy; or qualifying work experience may be sufficient for activity director positions in nursing homes.

Most employers prefer to hire candidates who are certified therapeutic recreation specialists (CTRS). The National Council for Therapeutic Recreation Certification (NCTRC) certifies therapeutic recreation specialists. To become certified, specialists must have a bachelor's degree, pass a written certification examination, and complete an internship of at least 360 hours under the supervision of a certified therapeutic recreation specialist. A few colleges or agencies may require 600 hours of internship.

Approximately 150 programs prepare recreational therapists. Most offer bachelor's degrees, although some offer associate, master's, or doctoral degrees. As of 1998, 43 recreation programs with options in therapeutic recreation were accredited by the National Council on Accreditation.

Recreational therapy programs include courses in assessment, treatment and program planning, intervention design, and evaluation. Students also study human anatomy, physiology, abnormal psychology, medical and psychiatric terminology, characteristics of illnesses and disabilities, professional ethics, and the use of assistive devices and technology.

Recreational therapists should be comfortable working with persons who are ill or have disabilities. Therapists must be patient, tactful, and persuasive when working with people who have a variety of special needs. Ingenuity, a sense of humor, and imagination are needed to adapt activities to individual needs; good physical coordination is necessary to demonstrate or participate in recreational activities.

Therapists may advance to supervisory or administrative positions. Some teach, conduct research, or perform contract consulting work.

Job Outlook

Employment of recreational therapists is expected to grow as fast as the average for all occupations through the year 2008 because of anticipated expansion in long-term care, physical and psychiatric rehabilitation, and services for persons with disabilities. However, the total number of job openings will be relatively low because the occupation is small. Opportunities should be best for persons with a bachelor's degree in therapeutic recreation or in recreation with an option in therapeutic recreation.

Health care facilities will provide a growing number of jobs in hospital-based adult day care and outpatient programs and in units offering short-term mental health and alcohol or drug abuse services. Rehabilitation, home-health care, transitional programs, and psychiatric facilities will provide additional jobs.

The rapidly growing number of older adults is expected to spur job growth for therapeutic recreation specialists and recreational therapy paraprofessionals in assisted living facilities, adult day care programs, and social service agencies. Continued growth is also expected in community residential facilities, as well as day care programs for individuals with disabilities.

Earnings

Median annual earnings of recreational therapists were $27,760 in 1998. The middle 50 percent earned between $21,580 and $35,000 a year. The lowest 10 percent earned less than $16,380, and the highest 10 percent earned more than $42,440 a year. Median annual earnings for recreational therapists in 1997 were $29,700 in hospitals and $21,900 in nursing and personal care facilities.

Related Occupations

Recreational therapists primarily design activities to help people with disabilities lead more fulfilling and independent lives. Other workers who have similar jobs are recreational therapy paraprofessionals, orientation therapists for persons who are blind or have visual impairments, art therapists, drama therapists, dance therapists, music therapists, occupational therapists, physical therapists, and rehabilitation counselors.

Sources of Additional Information

For information on how to order materials describing careers and academic programs in recreational therapy, write to:

- American Therapeutic Recreation Association, P.O. Box 15215, Hattiesburg, MS 39402-5215. Internet: http://www.atra-tr.org
- National Therapeutic Recreation Society, 22377 Belmont Ridge Rd., Ashburn, VA 20148-4501. Internet: http://www.nrpa.org/branches/ntrs.htm

Certification information may be obtained from:

- National Council for Therapeutic Recreation Certification, P.O. Box 479, Thiells, NY 10984-0479.

Recreation Workers

(O*NET 27311)

Significant Points

- The recreation field has an unusually large number of part-time, seasonal, and volunteer jobs.
- Educational requirements range from a high school diploma to a graduate degree.
- Competition will remain keen for full-time career positions; persons with formal training and experience gained in part-time or seasonal recreation jobs should have the best opportunities.

Nature of the Work

People spend much of their leisure time participating in a wide variety of organized recreational activities, such as aerobics, arts and crafts, little league baseball, tennis, camping, and softball. Recreation workers plan, organize, and direct these activities in local playgrounds and recreation areas, parks, community centers, health clubs, religious organizations, camps, theme parks, and most tourist attractions. Increasingly, recreational workers are also found in workplaces, where they organize and direct leisure activities and athletic programs for employees of all ages.

These workers hold a variety of positions at different levels of responsibility. *Recreation leaders*, who are responsible for a recreation program's daily operation, primarily organize and direct participants. They may lead and give instruction in dance, drama, crafts, games, and sports; schedule use of facilities and keep records of equipment use; and ensure recreation facilities and equipment are used properly. Workers who provide instruction and coach teams in specialties such as art, music, drama, swimming, or tennis may be called *activity specialists*.

Recreation supervisors oversee recreation leaders and also plan, organize, and manage recreational activities to meet the needs of a variety of populations. These workers often serve as liaisons between the director of the park or recreation center and the recreation leaders. Recreation supervisors with more specialized responsibilities may also direct special activities or events and oversee a major activity, such as aquatics, gymnastics, or performing arts.

Directors of recreation and parks develop and manage comprehensive recreation programs in parks, playgrounds, and other settings. Directors usually serve as technical advisors to State and local recreation and park commissions and may be responsible for recreation and park budgets.

Camp counselors lead and instruct children and teenagers in outdoor-oriented forms of recreation, such as swimming, hiking, horseback riding, and camping. In addition, counselors provide campers with specialized instruction in activities such as archery, boating, music, drama, gymnastics, tennis, and computers. In resident camps, counselors also provide guidance and supervise daily living and general socialization.

Working Conditions

The work setting for recreation workers may vary from a cruise ship, to a woodland recreational park, to a playground in the center of a large urban community. Regardless of setting, most recreation workers spend much of their time outdoors and may work in a variety of weather conditions. Recreation directors and supervisors, however, typically spend most of their time in an office, planning programs and special events. Because full-time recreation workers spend more time acting as managers than as hands-on activities leaders, they engage in less physical activity. Nevertheless, recreation workers at all levels risk suffering an injury during physical activities.

Most recreation workers put in about 40 hours a week. People entering this field, especially camp counselors, should expect some night and weekend work and irregular hours. About 3 out of 10 work part time, and many jobs are seasonal.

Employment

Recreation workers held about 241,000 jobs in 1998, and many additional workers held summer jobs in this occupation. Of those with year-round jobs as recreation workers, about half worked in park and recreation departments of municipal and county governments. Nearly 1 in 4 worked in membership organizations, such as the Boy or Girl Scouts, the YMCA, and Red Cross, or worked for programs run by social service organizations, including senior centers, adult daycare programs, or residential care facilities like halfway houses, group homes, and institutions for delinquent youth. Another 1 out of 10 worked for nursing and other personal care facilities.

Other employers of recreation workers included commercial recreation establishments, amusement parks, sports and entertainment centers, wilderness and survival enterprises, tourist attractions, vacation excursion companies, hotels and resorts, summer camps, health and athletic clubs, and apartment complexes.

The recreation field has an unusually large number of part-time, seasonal, and volunteer jobs. These jobs include summer camp counselors, lifeguards, craft specialists, and after-school and weekend recreation program leaders. In addition, many teachers and college students accept jobs as recreation workers when school is not in session. The vast majority of volunteers serve as activity leaders at local day-camp programs or in youth organizations, camps, nursing homes, hospitals, senior centers, YMCAs, and other settings. Some volunteers serve on local park and recreation boards and commissions. Volunteer experience, part-time work during school, or a summer job can lead to a full-time career as a recreation worker.

Training, Other Qualifications, and Advancement

Educational requirements for recreation workers range from a high school diploma (or sometimes less for many summer jobs) to graduate degrees for some administrative positions in large public recreation systems. Full-time career professional positions usually require a college degree with a major in parks and recreation or leisure studies, but a bachelor's degree in any liberal arts field may be sufficient for some jobs in the private sector. In industrial recreation, or "employee services" as it is more commonly called, companies prefer to hire those with a bachelor's degree in recreation or leisure studies and a background in business administration.

Specialized training or experience in a particular field, such as art, music, drama, or athletics, is an asset for many jobs. Some jobs also require certification. For example, when teaching or coaching water-related activities, a lifesaving certificate is a prerequisite. Graduates of associate degree programs in parks and recreation, social work, and other human services disciplines also enter some career recreation positions. High school graduates occasionally enter career positions, but this is not common. Some college students work part time as recreation workers while earning degrees.

A bachelor's degree and experience are preferred for most recreation supervisor jobs and required for most higher-level administrator jobs. However, increasing numbers of recreation workers who aspire to administrator positions obtain master's degrees in parks and recreation or related disciplines. Also, many persons in other disciplines, including social work, forestry, and resource management, pursue graduate degrees in recreation.

Programs leading to an associate or bachelor's degree in parks and recreation, leisure studies, or related fields are offered at several hundred colleges and universities. Many also offer master's or doctoral degrees in this field. In 1997, 93 bachelor's degree programs in parks and recreation were accredited by the National Recreation and Park Association (NRPA). Accredited programs provide broad exposure to the history, theory, and practice of park and recreation management. Courses offered include community organization, supervision and administration, recreational needs of special populations (such as older adults or the disabled) and supervised fieldwork. Students may specialize in areas such as therapeutic recreation, park management, outdoor recreation, industrial or commercial recreation, and camp management.

The American Camping Association offers workshops and courses for experienced camp directors at different times and locations throughout the year. Some national youth associations offer training courses for camp directors at the local and regional levels.

Persons planning recreation careers should be outgoing, good at motivating people, and sensitive to the needs of others. Good health and physical fitness are typically required, while activity planning calls for creativity and resourcefulness. Individuals contemplating careers in recreation at the supervisory or administrative level should develop managerial skills. College courses in management, business administration, accounting, and personnel management are likely to be useful.

Certification in the recreation field is offered by the NRPA National Certification Board. The NRPA, along with its State chapters, offers certification as a Certified Leisure Professional (CLP) for those with a college degree in recreation, and as a Certified Leisure Technician (CLT) for those with less than four years of college. Other NRPA certifications include Certified Leisure Provisional Professional (CLPP), Certified Playground Inspector (CPI), and Aquatic Facility Operations (AFO) Certification. Continuing education is necessary to remain certified.

Job Outlook

Competition will remain keen for career positions in recreation, as the number of jobseekers for full-time positions is expected to exceed the number of job openings. Opportunities for staff positions should be best for persons with formal training and experience gained in part-time or seasonal recreation jobs. Those with graduate degrees should have the best opportunities for supervisory or administrative positions.

Prospects are better for those seeking the large number of temporary, seasonal jobs. These positions, which are typically filled by high school or college students, do not generally have formal education requirements and are open to anyone with the desired personal qualities. Employers compete for a share of the vacationing student labor force, and although salaries in recreation are often lower than those in other fields, the nature of the work and the opportunity to work outdoors is attractive to many. Seasonal employment prospects as program directors should be good for applicants with specialized training and certification in an activity like swimming.

Employment of recreation workers is expected to grow about as fast as the average for all occupations through 2008, as growing numbers of people spend more time and money on leisure services. Growth in these jobs will also stem from increased interest in fitness and health and the rising demand for recreational opportunities for older adults in senior centers and retirement communities. In particular, jobs will increase in social services as more recreation workers are needed to develop and lead activity programs in senior centers, halfway houses, children's homes, and daycare programs for people with special needs.

Recreation worker jobs will also continue to increase as more businesses recognize the benefits of recreation programs and other services like wellness programs and elder care. Job growth will also occur in the commercial recreation industry—in amusement parks, athletic clubs, camps, sports clinics, and swimming pools.

Employment of recreation workers in local government (where nearly half of these workers are employed) is expected to grow more slowly than in other industries due to budget constraints. As a result, some local park and recreation departments are expected to do less hiring for permanent full-time positions than in the past. Because resources and priorities for public services differ from one community to another, this sector's share of recreation worker employment will vary widely by region.

Earnings

Median hourly earnings of recreation workers who worked full time in 1998 were $7.93. The middle 50 percent earned between about $6.14 and $10.65, while the top 10 percent earned $14.74 or more. However, earnings of recreation directors and others in supervisory or managerial positions can be substantially higher. Hourly earnings in the industries employing the largest number of recreation workers in 1997 were:

Nursing and personal care facilities	$8.10
Local government, except education and hospitals	8.00
Individual and family services	7.30
Civic and social associations	6.80
Miscellaneous amusement and recreation services	6.20

Most public and private recreation agencies provide full-time recreation workers with typical benefits; part-time workers receive few, if any, benefits.

Related Occupations

Recreation workers must exhibit leadership and sensitivity in dealing with people. Other occupations that require similar personal qualities include recreational therapists, social workers, parole officers, human relations counselors, school counselors, clinical and counseling psychologists, and teachers.

Sources of Additional Information

For information on jobs in recreation, contact employers such as local government departments of parks and recreation, nursing and personal care facilities, and YMCAs.

Ordering information for materials describing careers and academic programs in recreation is available from:

- National Recreation and Park Association, Division of Professional Services, 22377 Belmont Ridge Road, Ashburn, VA 20148-4501. Internet: http://www.nrpa.org

For information on careers in employee services and corporate recreation, contact:

- National Employee Services and Recreation Association, 2211 York Rd., Suite 207, Oakbrook, IL 60521. Internet: http://www.nesra.org

Registered Nurses

(O*NET 32502)

Significant Points

- The largest health care occupation, with more than 2 million jobs.

- One of the 10 occupations projected to have the largest numbers of new jobs.

- Earnings are above average, particularly for advanced practice nurses who have additional education or training.

Nature of the Work

Registered nurses (R.N.s) work to promote health, prevent disease, and help patients cope with illness. They are advocates and health educators for patients, families, and communities. When providing direct patient care, they observe, assess, and record symptoms, reactions, and progress; assist physicians during treatments and examinations; administer medications; and assist in convalescence and rehabilitation. R.N.s also develop and manage nursing care plans; instruct patients and their families in proper care; and help individuals and groups take steps to improve or maintain their health. While State laws govern the tasks R.N.s may perform, it is usually the work setting that determines their day-to-day job duties.

Hospital nurses form the largest group of nurses. Most are staff nurses, who provide bedside nursing care and carry out medical regimens. They may also supervise licensed practical nurses and aides. Hospital nurses usually are assigned to one area such as surgery, maternity, pediatrics, emergency room, intensive care, or treatment of cancer patients. Some may rotate among departments.

Office nurses care for outpatients in physicians' offices, clinics, surgicenters, and emergency medical centers. They prepare patients for and assist with examinations, administer injections and medications, dress wounds and incisions, assist with minor surgery, and maintain records. Some also perform routine laboratory and office work.

Nursing home nurses manage nursing care for residents with conditions ranging from fractures to Alzheimer's disease. Although they usually spend most of their time on administrative and supervisory tasks, R.N.s also assess residents' medical condition, develop treatment plans, supervise licensed practical nurses and nursing aides, and perform difficult procedures such as starting intravenous fluids. They also work in specialty-care departments, such as long-term rehabilitation units for strokes and head injuries.

Home health nurses provide periodic services, prescribed by a physician, to patients at home. After assessing patients' home environments, they care for and instruct patients and their families. Home health nurses care for a broad range of patients, such as those recovering from illnesses and accidents, cancer, and childbirth. They must be able to work independently and may supervise home health aides.

Public health nurses work in government and private agencies and clinics, schools, retirement communities and other community settings. They focus on populations, working with individuals, groups, and families to improve the overall health of communities. They also work as partners with communities to plan and implement programs. Public health nurses instruct individuals, families, and other groups in health education, disease prevention, nutrition, and child care. They arrange for immunizations, blood pressure testing, and other health screening. These nurses also work with community leaders, teachers, parents, and physicians in community health education.

Occupational health or *industrial nurses* provide nursing care at work sites to employees, customers, and others with minor injuries and illnesses. They provide emergency care, prepare accident reports, and arrange for further care if necessary. They also offer health counseling, assist with health examinations and inoculations, and assess work environments to identify potential health or safety problems.

Head nurses or *nurse supervisors* direct nursing activities. They plan work schedules and assign duties to nurses and aides, provide or arrange for training, and visit patients to observe nurses and to ensure that care is proper. They may also ensure records are maintained and equipment and supplies are ordered.

At the advanced level, *nurse practitioners* provide basic primary health care. They diagnose and treat common acute illnesses and injuries. Nurse practitioners can prescribe medications in all States and the District of Columbia. Other advanced practice nurses include *clinical nurse specialists, certified registered nurse anesthetists,* and *certified nurse-midwives.* Advanced practice nurses have met higher educational and clinical practice requirements beyond the basic nursing education and licensing required of all R.N.s.

Working Conditions

Most nurses work in well-lighted, comfortable health care facilities. Home health and public health nurses travel to patients' homes and to schools, community centers, and other sites. Nurses may spend considerable time walking and standing. They need emotional stability to cope with human suffering, emergencies, and other stresses. Because patients in hospitals and nursing homes require 24-hour care, nurses in these institutions may work nights, weekends, and holidays. They may also be on-call; available to work on short notice. Office, occupational health, and public health nurses are more likely to work regular business hours. Almost 1 in 10 R.N.s held more than one job in 1998.

Nursing has its hazards, especially in hospitals, nursing homes, and clinics where nurses may care for individuals with infectious diseases such as hepatitis. Nurses must observe rigid guidelines to guard against these and other dangers such as radiation, chemicals used for sterilization of instruments, and anesthetics. In addition, they are vulnerable to back injury when moving patients, shocks from electrical equipment, and hazards posed by compressed gases.

Employment

As the largest health care occupation, registered nurses held about 2.1 million jobs in 1998. About 3 out of 5 jobs were in hospitals, in inpatient and outpatient departments. Others were mostly in offices and clinics of physicians and other health practitioners, home health care agencies, nursing homes, temporary help agencies, schools, and government agencies. The remainder worked in residential care facilities, social service agencies, religious organizations, research facilities, management and public relations firms, insurance agencies, and private households. About 1 out of 4 R.N.s worked part time.

Training, Other Qualifications, and Advancement

In all States, students must graduate from a nursing program and pass a national licensing examination to obtain a nursing license. Nurses may be licensed in more than one State, either by examination or endorsement of a license issued by another State. Licenses must be periodically renewed. Some States require continuing education for licensure renewal.

In 1998, there were more than 2,200 entry-level R.N. programs. There are three major educational paths to nursing: Associate degree in nursing (A.D.N.), bachelor of science degree in nursing (B.S.N.), and diploma. A.D.N. programs, offered by community and junior colleges, take about two years. About half of all R.N. programs in 1998 were at the A.D.N. level. B.S.N. programs, offered by colleges and universities, take four or five years. About one-fourth of all programs in 1998 offered degrees at the bachelor's level. Diploma programs, given in hospitals, last two to three years. Only a small number of programs, about 4 percent, offer diploma-level degrees. Generally, licensed graduates of any of the three program types qualify for entry-level positions as staff nurses.

There have been attempts to raise the educational requirements for an R.N. license to a bachelor's degree and, possibly, create new job titles. These changes, should they occur, will probably be made State by State, through legislation or regulation. Changes in licensure requirements would not affect currently licensed R.N.s, who would be "grandfathered" in, no matter what their educational preparation. However, individuals considering nursing should carefully weigh the pros and cons of enrolling in a B.S.N. program because their advancement opportunities are broader. In fact, many career paths are open only to nurses with bachelor's or advanced degrees. A bachelor's degree is usually necessary for administrative positions and is a prerequisite for admission to graduate nursing programs in research, consulting, teaching, or a clinical specialization.

Many A.D.N. and diploma-trained nurses enter bachelor's programs to prepare for a broader scope of nursing practice. They can often find a hospital position and then take advantage of tuition reimbursement programs to work toward a B.S.N.

Nursing education includes classroom instruction and supervised clinical experience in hospitals and other health facilities. Students take courses in anatomy, physiology, microbiology, chemistry, nutrition, psychology and other behavioral sciences, and nursing. Coursework also includes liberal arts classes.

Supervised clinical experience is provided in hospital departments such as pediatrics, psychiatry, maternity, and surgery. A growing number of programs include clinical experience in nursing homes, public health departments, home health agencies, and ambulatory clinics.

Nurses should be caring and sympathetic. They must be able to accept responsibility, direct or supervise others, follow orders precisely, and determine when consultation is required.

Experience and good performance can lead to promotion to more responsible positions. Nurses can advance, in management, to assistant head nurse or head nurse. From there, they can advance to assistant director, director, and vice president. Increasingly, management level nursing positions require a graduate degree in nursing or health services administration. They also require leadership, negotiation skills, and good judgment. Graduate programs preparing executive level nurses usually last one to two years.

Within patient care, nurses can advance to clinical nurse specialist, nurse practitioner, certified nurse-midwife, or certified registered nurse anesthetist. These positions require one or two years of graduate education, leading in most instances to a master's degree or a certificate.

Some nurses move into the business side of health care. Their nursing expertise and experience on a health care team equip them to manage ambulatory, acute, home health, and chronic care services. Some are employed by health care corporations in health planning and development, marketing, and quality assurance. Other nurses work as college and university faculty or do research.

Job Outlook

Employment of registered nurses is expected to grow faster than the average for all occupations through 2008 and because the occupation is large, many new jobs will result. There will always be a need for traditional hospital nurses, but a large number of new nurses will be employed in home health, long-term, and ambulatory care.

Faster than average growth will be driven by technological advances in patient care (which permit a greater number of medical problems to be treated) and an increasing emphasis on primary care. In addition, the number of older people, who are much more likely than younger people to need medical care, is projected to grow very rapidly. Many job openings also will result from the need to replace experienced nurses who leave the occupation, especially as the median age of the registered nurse population continues to rise.

Employment in hospitals, the largest sector, is expected to grow more slowly than in other health-care sectors. While the intensity of nursing care is likely to increase, requiring more nurses per patient, the number of inpatients (those who remain overnight) is not likely to increase much. Patients are being released earlier, and more procedures are being done on an outpatient basis, both in and outside hospitals. Most rapid growth is expected in hospitals' outpatient facilities, such as same-day surgery, rehabilitation, and chemotherapy.

Employment in home health care is expected to grow rapidly. This is in response to a growing number of older persons with functional disabilities, consumer preference for care in the home, and technological advances that make it possible to bring increasingly complex treatments into the home. The type of care demanded will require nurses who are able to perform complex procedures.

Employment in nursing homes is expected to grow much faster than average due to increases in the number of people in their eighties and nineties, many of whom will require long-term care. In addition, the financial pressure on hospitals to release patients as soon as possible should produce more nursing home admissions. Growth in units to provide specialized long-term rehabilitation for stroke and head injury patients or to treat Alzheimer's victims will also increase employment.

An increasing proportion of sophisticated procedures that once were performed only in hospitals are being performed in physicians' offices and clinics, including ambulatory surgicenters and emergency medical centers. Accordingly, employment is expected to grow faster than average in these places as health care in general expands.

In evolving integrated health care networks, nurses may rotate among employment settings. Since jobs in traditional hospital nursing positions are no longer the only option, R.N.s will need to be flexible. Opportunities will be good for nurses with advanced education and training, such as nurse practitioners.

Earnings

Median annual earnings of registered nurses were $40,690 in 1998. The middle 50 percent earned between $34,430 and $49,070 a year. The lowest 10 percent earned less than $29,480, and the highest 10 percent earned more than $69,300 a year. Median annual earnings in the industries employing the largest numbers of registered nurses in 1997 were as follows:

Personnel supply services	$43,000
Hospitals	39,900
Home health care services	39,200
Offices and clinics of medical doctors	36,500
Nursing and personal care facilities	36,300

Many employers offer flexible work schedules, child care, educational benefits, and bonuses.

Related Occupations

Workers in other health care occupations with responsibilities and duties related to those of registered nurses are occupational therapists, emergency medical technicians, physical therapists, physician assistants, and respiratory therapists.

Sources of Additional Information

For information on a career as a registered nurse and nursing education, contact:

● National League for Nursing, 61 Broadway, New York, NY 10006. Internet: http://www.nln.org

For a list of B.S.N. and graduate programs, write to:

● American Association of Colleges of Nursing, 1 Dupont Circle NW., Suite 530, Washington, DC 20036. Internet: http://www.aacn.nche.edu

Information on registered nurses is also available from:

● American Nurses Association, 600 Maryland Ave. SW., Washington, DC 20024-2571. Internet: http://www.nursingworld.org

Respiratory Therapists

(O*NET 32302)

Significant Points

● Hospitals will continue to employ more than 9 out of 10 respiratory therapists, but a growing number will work in home health agencies, respiratory therapy clinics, and nursing homes.

● Job opportunities will be best for therapists who work with newborns and infants.

Nature of the Work

Respiratory therapists evaluate, treat, and care for patients with breathing disorders. To evaluate patients, therapists test the capacity of the lungs and analyze oxygen and carbon dioxide concentration. They also measure the patient's potential of hydrogen (pH), which indicates the acidity or alkalinity level of the blood. To measure lung capacity, therapists have patients breathe into an instrument that measures the volume and flow of oxygen during inhalation and exhalation. By comparing the reading with the norm for the patient's age, height, weight, and sex, respiratory therapists can determine whether lung deficiencies exist. To analyze oxygen, carbon dioxide, and pH levels, therapists draw an arterial blood sample, place it in a blood gas analyzer, and relay the results to a physician.

Respiratory therapists treat all types of patients, ranging from premature infants whose lungs are not fully developed, to elderly people whose lungs are diseased. These workers provide temporary relief to patients with chronic asthma or emphysema and emergency care for patients who suffered heart failure or a stroke or are victims of drowning or shock. Respiratory therapists most commonly use oxygen or oxygen mixtures, chest physiotherapy, and aerosol medications. To increase a patient's concentration of oxygen, therapists place an oxygen mask or nasal cannula on a patient and set the oxygen flow at the level prescribed by a physician. Therapists also connect patients who cannot breathe on their own to ventilators that deliver pressurized oxygen into the lungs. They insert a tube into a patient's trachea, or windpipe; connect the tube to the ventilator; and set the rate, volume, and oxygen concentration of the oxygen mixture entering the patient's lungs.

Therapists regularly check on patients and equipment. If the patient appears to be having difficulty, or if the oxygen, carbon dioxide, or pH level of the blood is abnormal, they change the ventilator setting according to the doctor's order or check equipment for mechanical problems. In home care, therapists teach patients and their families to use ventilators and other life support systems. Additionally, they visit several times a month to inspect and clean equipment and ensure its proper use, and they make emergency visits if equipment problems arise.

Respiratory therapists perform chest physiotherapy on patients to remove mucus from their lungs and make it easier for them to breathe. For example, during surgery, anesthesia depresses respiration, so this treatment may be prescribed to help get the patient's lungs back to normal and to prevent congestion. Chest physiotherapy also helps patients suffering from lung diseases, such as cystic fibrosis, that cause mucus to collect in the lungs. In this procedure, therapists place patients in positions to help drain mucus, thump and vibrate patients' rib cages, and instruct them to cough.

Respiratory therapists also administer aerosols—generally liquid medications suspended in a gas that forms a mist which is inhaled—and teach patients how to inhale the aerosol properly to assure its effectiveness.

Therapists are increasingly asked to perform tasks that fall outside their traditional role. Tasks are expanding into cardiopulmonary procedures like electrocardiograms and stress testing, as well as other tasks like drawing blood samples from patients. Therapists also keep records of materials used and charges to patients. Additionally, some teach or supervise other respiratory therapy personnel.

Working Conditions

Respiratory therapists generally work between 35 and 40 hours a week. Because hospitals operate around the clock, therapists may work evenings, nights, or weekends. They spend long periods standing and walking between patients' rooms. In an emergency, therapists work under a great deal of stress.

Because gases used by respiratory therapists are stored under pressure, they are potentially hazardous. However, adherence to safety precautions and regular maintenance and testing of equipment minimize the risk of injury. As with many health occupations, respiratory therapists run a risk of catching infectious diseases, but carefully following proper procedures minimizes this risk.

Employment

Respiratory therapists held about 86,000 jobs in 1998. About 9 out of 10 jobs were in hospital departments of respiratory care, anesthesiology, or pulmonary medicine. Home health agencies, respiratory therapy clinics, and nursing homes accounted for most of the remaining jobs.

Training, Other Qualifications, and Advancement

Formal training is necessary for entry to this field. Training is offered at the post-secondary level by hospitals, medical schools, colleges and universities, trade schools, vocational-technical institutes, and the Armed Forces. Some programs prepare graduates for jobs as registered respiratory therapists (RRT); other, shorter programs lead to jobs as certified respiratory therapists (CRT). According to the Committee on Accreditation for Respiratory Care (CoARC), there were 327 registered respiratory therapist programs and 134 certified respiratory therapist programs in the United States in 1999.

Formal training programs vary in length and in the credential or degree awarded. Most of the CoARC-accredited registered respiratory therapist programs last two years and lead to an associate degree. Some, however, are four-year bachelor's degree programs. Areas of study for respiratory therapy programs include human anatomy and physiology, chemistry, physics, microbiology, and mathematics. Technical courses deal with procedures, equipment, and clinical tests.

More and more therapists receive on-the-job training, allowing them to administer electrocardiograms and stress tests, as well as draw blood samples from patients.

Therapists should be sensitive to patients' physical and psychological needs. Respiratory care workers must pay attention to detail, follow instructions, and work as part of a team. In addition, operating complicated respiratory therapy equipment requires mechanical ability and manual dexterity.

High school students interested in a career in respiratory care should take courses in health, biology, mathematics, chemistry, and physics. Respiratory care involves basic mathematical problem solving and an understanding of chemical and physical principles. For example, respiratory care workers must be able to compute medication dosages and calculate gas concentrations.

More than 40 States license respiratory care personnel. The National Board for Respiratory Care offers voluntary certification and registration to graduates of CoARC-accredited programs. Two credentials are awarded to respiratory therapists who satisfy the requirements: Registered Respiratory Therapist (RRT) and Certified Respiratory Therapist (CRT). All graduates—those from two- and four-year programs in respiratory therapy, as well as those from one-year CRT programs—may take the CRT examination. CRTs who meet education and experience requirements can take a separate examination, leading to the award of the RRT.

Individuals who have completed a four-year program in a nonrespiratory field but have college level courses in anatomy, physiology, chemistry, biology, microbiology, physics, and mathematics can become a CRT after graduating from an accredited one- or two-year program. After they receive two years of clinical experience, they are eligible to take the registry exam to become an RRT.

Most employers require applicants for entry-level or generalist positions to hold the CRT or be eligible to take the certification examination. Supervisory positions and those in intensive care specialties usually require the RRT (or RRT eligibility).

Respiratory therapists advance in clinical practice by moving from care of general to critical patients who have significant problems in other organ systems, such as the heart or kidneys. Respiratory therapists, especially those with four-year degrees, may also advance to supervisory or managerial positions in a respiratory therapy department. Respiratory therapists in home care and equipment rental firms may become branch managers.

Job Outlook

Job opportunities are expected to remain good. Employment of respiratory therapists is expected to increase much faster than the average for all occupations through the year 2008, because of substantial growth of the middle-aged and elderly population, a development that will heighten the incidence of cardiopulmonary disease.

Older Americans suffer most from respiratory ailments and cardiopulmonary diseases such as pneumonia, chronic bronchitis, emphysema, and heart disease. As their numbers increase, the need for respiratory therapists will increase as well. In addition, advances in treating victims of heart attacks, accident victims, and premature infants (many of whom are dependent on a ventilator during part of their treatment) will increase the demand for the services of respiratory care practitioners.

Opportunities are expected to be highly favorable for respiratory therapists with cardiopulmonary care skills and experience working with infants.

Although hospitals will continue to employ the vast majority of therapists, a growing number of therapists can expect to work outside of hospitals in home health agencies, respiratory therapy clinics, and nursing homes.

Earnings

Median annual earnings for respiratory therapists were $34,830 in 1998. The middle 50 percent earned between $30,040 and $39,830 a year. The lowest 10 percent earned less than $25,910, and the highest 10 percent earned more than $46,760 a year.

Related Occupations

Respiratory therapists, under the supervision of a physician, administer respiratory care and life support to patients with heart and lung difficulties. Other workers who care for, treat, or train people to improve their physical condition include dialysis technicians, registered nurses, occupational therapists, physical therapists, and radiation therapists.

Sources of Additional Information

Information concerning a career in respiratory care is available from:

- American Association for Respiratory Care, 11030 Ables Ln., Dallas, TX 75229-4593. Internet: http://www.aarc.org

Information on gaining credentials as a respiratory therapy practitioner can be obtained from:

- The National Board for Respiratory Care, Inc., 8310 Nieman Rd., Lenexa, KS 66214-1579. Internet: http://www.nbrc.org

For the current list of CoARC-accredited educational programs for respiratory therapy occupations, write to:

- Committee on Accreditation for Respiratory Care, 1248 Harwood Rd., Bedford, TX 76021-4244. Internet: http://www.coarc.com

Restaurant and Food Service Managers

(O*NET 15026B)

Significant Points

- Although many experienced food and beverage preparation and service workers are promoted to fill jobs, job opportunities are expected to be best for those with bachelor's or associate degrees in restaurant and institutional food service management.

- Job opportunities should be better for salaried managers than for self-employed managers, as restaurants increasingly affiliate with national chains instead of being independently owned.

Nature of the Work

The daily responsibilities of many restaurant and food service managers can be as complicated as some meals prepared by a fine chef. In addition to the traditional duties of selecting and pricing menu items, using food and other supplies efficiently, and achieving quality in food preparation and service, managers are now responsible for a growing number of administrative and human resource tasks. For example, managers must carefully find and evaluate new ways of recruiting new employees in a tight job market. Once hired, managers must also find creative ways to retain experienced workers.

In most restaurants and institutional food service facilities, the manager is assisted in these duties by one or more assistant managers, depending on the size and operating hours of the establishment. In most large establishments, as well as in many smaller ones, the management team consists of a *general manager*, one or more *assistant managers*, and an *executive chef*. The executive chef is responsible for the operation of the kitchen, while the assistant managers oversee service in the dining room and other areas. In smaller restaurants, the executive chef also may be the general manager, and sometimes an owner. In fast-food restaurants and other food service facilities open for long hours, often 7 days a week, the manager is aided by several assistant managers, each of whom supervises a shift of workers.

One of the most important tasks of restaurant and food service managers is selecting successful menu items. This task varies by establishment because although many restaurants rarely change their menu, others make frequent alterations. Managers or executive chefs select menu items, taking into account the likely number of customers and the past popularity of dishes. Other issues taken into consideration when planning a menu include unserved food left over from prior meals that should not be wasted, the need for variety, and the availability of foods due to changing seasons. Managers or executive chefs analyze the recipes of the dishes to determine food, labor, overhead costs and to assign prices to various dishes. Menus must be developed far enough in advance that supplies can be ordered and received in time.

On a daily basis, managers estimate food consumption, place orders with suppliers, and schedule the delivery of fresh food and beverages. They receive and check the content of deliveries, evaluating the quality of meats, poultry, fish, fruits, vegetables, and baked goods. To ensure good service, managers meet with sales representatives from restaurant suppliers to place orders replenishing stocks of tableware, linens, paper, cleaning supplies, cooking utensils, and furniture and fixtures. They also arrange for equipment maintenance and repairs and coordinate a variety of services such as waste removal and pest control.

The quality of food and services in restaurants depends largely on a manager's ability to interview, hire, and, when necessary, fire employees. This is especially true in tight labor markets, when many managers report difficulty in hiring experienced food and beverage preparation and service workers. Managers may attend career fairs or arrange for newspaper advertising to expand their pool of applicants. Once a new employee is hired, managers explain the establishment's policies and practices and oversee any necessary training. Managers also schedule the work hours of employees, making sure there are enough workers present to cover peak dining periods. If employees are unable to work, managers may have to fill in for them. Some managers regularly help with cooking, clearing of tables, or other tasks.

Another fundamental responsibility of restaurant and food service managers is supervising the kitchen and dining room. For example, managers often oversee all food preparation and cooking, examining the quality and portion sizes to ensure that dishes are prepared and garnished correctly and in a timely manner. They also investigate and resolve customers' complaints about food quality or service. To maintain company and government sanitation standards, they direct the cleaning of the kitchen and dining areas and washing of tableware, kitchen utensils, and equipment. Managers also monitor the actions of their employees and patrons on a continual basis to ensure that health and safety standards and local liquor regulations are obeyed.

In addition to their regular duties, restaurant and food service managers have a variety of administrative responsibilities. Although much of this work is delegated to a bookkeeper in a larger establishment, managers in most smaller establishments, such as fast-food restaurants, must keep records of the hours and wages of employees, prepare the payroll, and fill out paperwork in compliance with licensing laws and reporting requirements of tax, wage and hour, unemployment compensation, and Social Security laws. Managers also maintain records of supply and equipment purchases and ensure that accounts with suppliers are paid on a regular basis. In addition, managers in full-service restaurants record the number, type, and cost of items sold to evaluate and discontinue dishes that may be unpopular or less profitable.

Many managers are able to ease the burden of record keeping and paperwork through the use of computers. Point-of-service (POS) systems are used in many restaurants to increase employee productivity and allow managers to track the sales of specific menu items. Using a POS system, a server keys in the customer's order and the computer immediately sends the order to the kitchen so preparation can begin. The same system totals checks, acts as a cash register and credit card authorizer, and tracks daily sales. To minimize food costs and spoilage, many managers use inventory tracking software to compare the record of daily sales from the POS with a record of present inventory. In some establishments, when supplies needed for the preparation of popular menu items run low, additional inventory can be ordered directly from the supplier using the computer. Computers also allow restaurant and food service managers to more efficiently keep track of employee schedules and pay.

Managers are among the first to arrive in the morning and the last to leave. At the conclusion of each day, or sometimes each shift, managers tally the cash and charge receipts received and balance them against the record of sales. In most cases, they are responsible for depositing the day's receipts at the bank or securing them in a safe place. Finally, managers are responsible for locking up, checking that ovens, grills, and lights are off, and switching on alarm systems.

Working Conditions

Evenings and weekends are popular dining periods, making night and weekend work common among managers. Many managers of institutional food service facilities work more conventional hours because factory and office cafeterias are usually open only on weekdays for breakfast and lunch. Hours for many managers are unpredictable, however, as managers may have to fill in for absent workers on short notice. It is common for restaurant and food service managers to work 50 to 60 hours or more per week.

Managers often experience the pressure of simultaneously coordinating a wide range of activities. When problems occur, it is the responsibility of the manager to resolve them with minimal disruption to customers. The job can be hectic during peak dining hours, and dealing with irate customers or uncooperative employees can be stressful.

Employment

Restaurant and food service managers held about 518,000 jobs in 1998. Most managers are salaried, but about 1 in 6 is self-employed. Most work in restaurants or for contract institutional food service companies, while a smaller number are employed by educational institutions, hospitals, nursing and personal care facilities, and civic, social, and fraternal organizations. Jobs are located throughout the country, with large cities and tourist areas providing more opportunities for full-service dining positions.

Training, Other Qualifications, and Advancement

Most food service management companies and national or regional restaurant chains recruit management trainees from two- and four-year college hospitality management programs. Food service and restaurant chains prefer to hire people with degrees in restaurant and institutional food service management, but they often hire graduates with degrees in other fields who have demonstrated interest and aptitude. Some restaurant and food service manager positions, particularly self-service and fast-food, are filled by promoting experienced food and beverage preparation and service workers. Waiters, waitresses, chefs, and fast-food workers demonstrating potential for handling increased responsibility sometimes advance to assistant manager or management trainee jobs. Executive chefs need extensive experience working as chefs, and general managers need experience as assistant managers.

A bachelor's degree in restaurant and food service management provides a particularly strong preparation for a career in this occupation. In 1998, more than 150 colleges and universities offered four-year programs in restaurant and hotel management or institutional food service management. For those not interested in pursuing a four-year degree, more than 800 community and junior colleges, technical institutes, and other institutions offer programs in these fields leading to an associate degree or other formal certification. Both two- and four-year programs provide instruction in subjects such as nutrition and food planning and preparation, as well as accounting, business law and management, and computer science. Some programs combine classroom and laboratory study with internships that provide on-the-job experience. In addition, many educational institutions offer culinary programs that provide food preparation training. This training can lead to a career as a cook or chef and provide a foundation for advancement to an executive chef position.

Most employers emphasize personal qualities when hiring managers. For example, self-discipline, initiative, and leadership ability are essential. Managers must be able to solve problems and concentrate on details. They need good communication skills to deal with customers and suppliers, as well as to motivate and direct their staff. A neat and clean appearance is a must because they often are in close personal contact with the public. Restaurant and food service management can be demanding, so good health and stamina also are important.

Most restaurant chains and food service management companies have rigorous training programs for management positions. Through a combination of classroom and on-the-job training, trainees receive instruction and gain work experience in all aspects of the operations of a restaurant or institutional food service facility. Topics include food preparation, nutrition, sanitation, security, company policies and procedures, personnel management, record keeping, and preparation of reports. Training on use of the restaurant's computer system is increasingly important as well. Usually after six months or a year, a trainee receives his or her first permanent assignment as an assistant manager.

A measure of professional achievement for restaurant and food service managers is the designation of certified Foodservice Management Professional (FMP). Although not a requirement for employment or advancement in the occupation, voluntary certification provides recognition of professional competence, particularly for managers who acquired their skills largely on the job. The Educational Foundation of the National Restaurant Association awards the FMP designation to managers who achieve a qualifying score on a written examination, complete a series of courses that cover a range of food service management topics, and meet standards of work experience in the field.

Willingness to relocate often is essential for advancement to positions with greater responsibility. Managers typically advance to larger establishments or regional management positions within restaurant chains. Some eventually open their own eating and drinking establishments. Others transfer to hotel management positions because their restaurant management experience provides a good background for food and beverage manager jobs in hotels and resorts.

Job Outlook

Employment of restaurant and food service managers is expected to increase about as fast as the average for all occupations through 2008. In addition to employment growth, the need to replace managers who transfer to other occupations or stop working will create many job openings. Opportunities to fill these openings are expected to be best for those with a bachelor's or associate degree in restaurant and institutional food service management.

Projected employment growth varies by industry. Eating and drinking places will provide the most new jobs as the number of eating and drinking establishments increases along with the population, personal incomes, and leisure time. In addition, manager jobs will increase in eating and drinking places as schools, hospitals, and other businesses contract out more of their food services to institutional food service companies within the eating and drinking industry.

Food service manager jobs still are expected to increase in many of these other industries, but growth will be slowed as contracting out becomes more common. Growth in the elderly population should result in more food service manager jobs in nursing homes and other health-care institutions and in residential-care and assisted-living facilities.

Job opportunities should be better for salaried managers than for self-employed managers. New restaurants are increasingly affiliated with national chains rather than being independently owned and operated. As this trend continues, fewer owners will manage restaurants themselves, and more restaurant managers will be employed by larger companies to run establishments.

Employment in eating and drinking establishments is not very sensitive to changes in economic conditions, so restaurant and food service managers are rarely laid off during hard times. However, competition among restaurants is always intense, and many restaurants do not survive.

Earnings

Median earnings of food service and lodging managers were $26,700 in 1998. The middle 50 percent earned between $19,820 and $34,690. The lowest paid 10 percent earned $14,430 or less, while the highest paid 10 percent earned more than $45,520. Median annual earnings in the industries employing the largest number of food service and lodging managers in 1997 are shown below.

Hotels and motels $28,600

Eating and drinking places 25,000

Elementary and secondary schools 21,300

In addition to typical benefits, most salaried restaurant and food service managers receive free meals and the opportunity for additional training depending on their length of service.

Related Occupations

Restaurant and food service managers direct the activities of businesses, which provide a service to customers. Other managers in service-oriented businesses include hotel managers and assistants, health services administrators, retail store managers, and bank managers.

Sources of Additional Information

Information about a career as a restaurant and food service manager, two- and four-year college programs in restaurant and food service management and certification as a Foodservice Management Professional is available from:

- The Educational Foundation of the National Restaurant Association, Suite 1400, 250 South Wacker Dr., Chicago, IL 60606.

General information on hospitality careers may be obtained from:

- Council on Hotel, Restaurant, and Institutional Education, 1200 17th St. NW., Washington, DC 20036-3097.

Additional information about job opportunities in the field may be obtained from local employers and local offices of the State employment service.

Roman Catholic Priests

(O*NET 27502)

Significant Points

- Preparation generally requires eight years of study beyond high school, usually including a college degree followed by four or more years of theology study at a seminary.

- The shortage of Roman Catholic priests is expected to continue, resulting in a very favorable outlook.

Nature of the Work

Priests in the Catholic Church belong to one of two groups: diocesan or religious. Both types of priests have the same powers, acquired through ordination by a bishop. Differences lie in their way of life, type of work, and the Church authority to which they are responsible. *Diocesan priests* commit their lives to serving the people of a diocese, a church administrative region, and generally work in parishes assigned by the bishop of their diocese. Diocesan priests take oaths of celibacy and obedience. *Religious priests* belong to a religious order, such as the Jesuits, Dominicans, or Franciscans. In addition to the vows taken by diocesan priests, religious priests take a vow of poverty.

Diocesan priests attend to the spiritual, pastoral, moral, and educational needs of the members of their church. A priest's day usually begins with morning meditation and mass and may end with an individual counseling session or an evening visit to a hospital or home. Many priests direct and serve on church committees, work in civic and charitable organizations, and assist in community projects. Some counsel parishioners preparing for marriage or the birth of a child.

Religious priests receive duty assignments from their superiors in their respective religious orders. Some religious priests specialize in teaching, whereas others serve as missionaries in foreign countries, where they may live under difficult and primitive conditions. Other religious priests live a communal life in monasteries, where they devote their lives to prayer, study, and assigned work.

Both religious and diocesan priests hold teaching and administrative posts in Catholic seminaries, colleges and universities, and high schools. Priests attached to religious orders staff many of the Church's institutions of higher education and many high schools, whereas diocesan priests usually are concerned with the parochial schools attached to parish churches and with diocesan high schools. Members of religious orders do much of the missionary work conducted by the Catholic Church in this country and abroad.

Working Conditions

For information on working conditions, see the earlier description for Clergy.

Employment

According to *The Official Catholic Directory*, there were approximately 47,000 priests in 1998; about two-thirds were diocesan priests. There are priests in nearly every city and town and in many rural communities; however, the most work in metropolitan areas, where most Catholics reside.

Training and Other Qualifications

Men exclusively are ordained as priests. Women may serve in church positions that do not require priestly ordination. Preparation for the priesthood generally requires eight years of study beyond high school, usually including a college degree followed by four or more years of theology study at a seminary.

Preparatory study for the priesthood may begin in the first year of high school, at the college level, or in theological seminaries after college graduation. Nine high-school seminaries provided a college preparatory program in 1998. Programs emphasize English grammar, speech, literature, and social studies, as well as religious formation. Latin may be required, and modern languages are encouraged. In Hispanic communities, knowledge of Spanish is mandatory.

Those who begin training for the priesthood in college do so in one of 87 priesthood formation programs offered either through Catholic colleges or universities or in freestanding college seminaries. Preparatory studies usually include training in philosophy, religious studies, and prayer.

Today, most candidates for the priesthood have a four-year degree from an accredited college or university and then attend one of 47 theological seminaries (also called theologates) and earn either the Master of Divinity or the Master of Arts degree. Thirty-five theologates primarily train diocesan priests; the other 12 theologates mostly educate priests for religious orders. (Slight variations in training reflect the differences in their expected duties.) Theology coursework includes sacred scripture; dogmatic, moral, and pastoral theology; homiletics (art of preaching); Church history; liturgy (sacraments); and canon (church) law. Fieldwork experience usually is required.

Young men are never denied entry into seminaries because of lack of funds. In seminaries for diocesan priests, scholarships or loans are available, and contributions of benefactors and the Catholic Church finance those in religious seminaries—who have taken a vow of poverty and are not expected to have personal resources.

Graduate work in theology beyond that required for ordination is also offered at a number of American Catholic universities or at ecclesiastical universities around the world, particularly in Rome. Also, many priests do graduate work in fields unrelated to theology. Priests are encouraged by the Catholic Church to continue their studies, at least informally, after ordination. In recent years, the Church has stressed continuing education for ordained priests in the social sciences, such as sociology and psychology.

A newly ordained diocesan priest usually works as an assistant pastor. Newly ordained priests of religious orders are assigned to the specialized duties for which they have been trained. Depending on the talents, interests, and experience of the individual, many opportunities for additional responsibility exist within the Church.

Job Outlook

The shortage of Roman Catholic priests is expected to continue, resulting in a very favorable job outlook through the year 2008. Many priests will be needed in the years ahead to provide for the spiritual, educational, and social needs of the increasing number of Catholics. In recent years, the number of ordained priests has been insufficient to fill the needs of newly established parishes and other Catholic institutions and to replace priests who retire, die, or leave the priesthood. This situation is likely to continue, as seminary enrollments remain below the levels needed to overcome the current shortfall of priests.

In response to the shortage of priests, permanent deacons and teams of clergy and laity increasingly are performing certain traditional functions within the Catholic Church. The number of ordained deacons has increased five-fold over the past 20 years, and this trend should continue. Throughout most of the country, permanent deacons have been ordained to preach and perform liturgical functions, such as baptisms, marriages, and funerals, and to provide service to the community. Deacons are not authorized to celebrate Mass, nor are they allowed to administer the Sacraments of Reconciliation and the Anointing of the Sick. Teams of clergy and laity undertake some liturgical and nonliturgical functions, such as hospital visits and religious teaching.

Earnings

Diocesan priests' salaries vary from diocese to diocese. According to the National Federation of Priests' Council, low-end cash only salaries averaged $12,936 per year in 1998; high-end salaries averaged $15,483 per year. Average salaries, including in-kind earnings, were $30,713 per year in 1998. In addition to a salary, diocesan priests receive a package of benefits that may include a car allowance, room and board in the parish rectory, health insurance, and a retirement plan.

Diocesan priests who do special work related to the church, such as teaching, usually receive a salary which is less than a lay person in the same position would receive. The difference between the usual salary for these jobs and the salary the priest receives is called "contributed service." In some situations, housing and related expenses may be provided; in other cases, the priest must make his own arrangements. Some priests doing special work receive the same compensation a lay person would receive.

Religious priests take a vow of poverty and are supported by their religious order. Any personal earnings are given to the order. Their vow of poverty is recognized by the Internal Revenue Service, which exempts them from paying Federal income tax.

Sources of Additional Information

Young men interested in entering the priesthood should seek the guidance and counsel of their parish priests and diocesan vocational office. For information regarding the different religious orders and the diocesan priesthood, as well as a list of the seminaries that prepare students for the priesthood, contact the diocesan director of vocations through the office of the local pastor or bishop.

Individuals seeking additional information about careers in the Catholic Ministry should contact their local diocese.

For information on training programs for the Catholic ministry, contact:

- Center for Applied Research in the Apostolate (CARA), Georgetown University, Washington, DC 20057.

School Teachers—
Kindergarten, Elementary, and Secondary

(O*NET 31304, 31305, and 31308)

Significant Points

- Public school teachers must have at least a bachelor's degree, have completed an approved teacher education program, and be licensed.

- Many States offer alternative licensing programs to attract people into teaching, especially for hard-to-fill positions.

- Employment growth for secondary school teachers will be more rapid than for kindergarten and elementary school teachers due to student enrollments, but job outlook will vary by geographic area and subject specialty.

Nature of the Work

Teachers act as facilitators or coaches, using interactive discussions and "hands-on" learning to help students learn and apply concepts in subjects such as science, mathematics, or English. As teachers move away from the traditional repetitive drill approaches and rote memorization, they are using more "props" or "manipulatives" to help children understand abstract concepts, solve problems, and develop critical thought processes. For example, they teach the concepts of numbers or adding and subtracting by playing board games. As children get older, they use more sophisticated materials such as science apparatus, cameras, or computers.

Many classes are becoming less structured, with students working in groups to discuss and solve problems together. Preparing students for the future workforce is the major stimulus generating the changes in education. To be prepared, students must be able to interact with others, adapt to new technology, and logically think through problems. Teachers provide the tools and environment for their students to develop these skills.

Kindergarten and elementary school teachers play a vital role in the development of children. What children learn and experience during their early years can shape their views of themselves and the world and affect later success or failure in school, work, and their personal lives. Kindergarten and elementary school teachers introduce children to numbers, language, science, and social studies. They use games, music, artwork, films, slides, computers, and other tools to teach basic skills.

Most elementary school teachers instruct one class of children in several subjects. In some schools, two or more teachers work as a team and are jointly responsible for a group of students in at least one subject. In other schools, a teacher may teach one special subject—usually music, art, reading, science, arithmetic, or physical education—to a number of classes. A small but growing number of teachers instruct multilevel classrooms, with students at several different learning levels.

Secondary school teachers help students delve more deeply into subjects introduced in elementary school and expose them to more information about the world. Secondary school teachers specialize in a specific subject, such as English, Spanish, mathematics, history, or biology. They teach a variety of related courses—for example, American history, contemporary American problems, and world geography.

Teachers may use films, slides, overhead projectors, and the latest technology in teaching, including computers, telecommunication systems, and video discs. Use of computer resources, such as educational software and the Internet, exposes students to a vast range of experiences and promotes interactive learning. Through the Internet, American students can communicate with students in other countries. Students also use the Internet for individual research projects and information gathering. Computers are used in other classroom activities as well, from helping students solve math problems to learning English as a second language. Teachers may also use computers to record grades and perform other administrative and clerical duties. They must continually update their skills so they can instruct and use the latest technology in the classroom.

Teachers often work with students from varied ethnic, racial, and religious backgrounds. With growing minority populations in many parts of the country, it is important for teachers to establish rapport with a diverse student population. Accordingly, some schools offer training to help teachers enhance their awareness and understanding of different cultures. Teachers may also include multicultural programming in their lesson plans to address the needs of all students, regardless of their cultural backgrounds.

Teachers design classroom presentations to meet student needs and abilities. They also work with students individually. Teachers plan, evaluate, and assign lessons; prepare, administer, and grade tests; listen to oral presentations; and maintain classroom discipline. They observe and evaluate a student's performance and potential, and increasingly are asked to use new assessment methods. For example, teachers may examine a portfolio of a student's artwork or writing to judge the student's overall progress. They then can provide additional assistance in areas where a student needs help. Teachers also grade papers, prepare report cards, and meet with parents and school staff to discuss a student's academic progress or personal problems.

In addition to classroom activities, teachers oversee study halls and homerooms and supervise extracurricular activities. They identify physical or mental problems and refer students to the proper resource or agency for diagnosis and treatment. Secondary school teachers occasionally assist students in choosing courses, colleges, and careers. Teachers also participate in education conferences and workshops.

In recent years, site-based management, which allows teachers and parents to participate actively in management decisions, has gained popularity. In many schools, teachers are increasingly involved in making decisions regarding the budget, personnel, textbook choices, curriculum design, and teaching methods.

Working Conditions

Seeing students develop new skills and gain an appreciation of knowledge and learning can be very rewarding. However, teaching may be frustrating when dealing with unmotivated and disrespectful students. Occasionally, teachers must cope with unruly behavior and violence in the schools. Teachers may experience stress when dealing with large classes, students from disadvantaged or multicultural backgrounds, and heavy workloads.

Teachers are sometimes isolated from their colleagues because they work alone in a classroom of students. However, some schools are allowing teachers to work in teams and with mentors to enhance their professional development.

Including school duties performed outside the classroom, many teachers work more than 40 hours a week. Most teachers work the traditional 10-month school year with a 2-month vacation during the summer. Those on the 10-month schedule may teach in summer sessions, take other jobs, travel, or pursue other personal interests. Many enroll in college courses or workshops to continue their education. Teachers in districts with a year-round schedule typically work 8 weeks, are on vacation for 1 week, and have a 5-week midwinter break.

Most States have tenure laws that prevent teachers from being fired without just cause and due process. Teachers may obtain tenure after they have satisfactorily completed a probationary period of teaching, normally three years. Tenure does not absolutely guarantee a job, but it does provide some security.

Employment

Teachers held about 3.4 million jobs in 1998. Of those, about 1.9 million were kindergarten and elementary school teachers, and 1.4 million were secondary school teachers. Employment is distributed geographically, much the same as the population.

Training, Other Qualifications, and Advancement

All 50 States and the District of Columbia require public school teachers to be licensed. Licensure is not required for teachers in private schools. Usually licensure is granted by the State board of education or a licensure advisory committee. Teachers may be licensed to teach the early childhood grades (usually nursery school through grade 3); the elementary grades (grades 1 through 6 or 8); the middle grades (grades 5 through 8); a secondary education subject area (usually grades 7 through 12); or a special subject, such as reading or music (usually grades K through 12).

Requirements for regular licenses vary by State. However, all States require a bachelor's degree and completion of an approved teacher training program with a prescribed number of subject and education credits as well as supervised practice teaching. About one-third of the States also require technology training as part of the teacher certification process. A number of States require specific minimum grade point averages for teacher licensure. Other States require teachers to obtain a master's degree in education, which involves at least one year of additional coursework beyond the bachelor's degree with a specialization in a particular subject.

Almost all States require applicants for teacher licensure to be tested for competency in basic skills such as reading, writing, teaching, and subject matter proficiency. Most States require continuing education for renewal of the teacher's license. Many States have reciprocity agreements that make it easier for teachers licensed in one State to become licensed in another.

Increasingly, many States are moving towards implementing performance-based standards for licensure, which require passing a rigorous comprehensive teaching examination to obtain a provisional license. Teachers must then demonstrate satisfactory teaching performance over an extended period of time to obtain a full license.

Many States offer alternative teacher licensure programs for people who have bachelor's degrees in the subject they will teach, but lack the necessary education courses required for a regular license. Alternative licensure programs were originally designed to ease teacher

shortages in certain subjects, such as mathematics and science. The programs have expanded to attract other people into teaching, including recent college graduates and mid-career changers. In some programs, individuals begin teaching quickly under provisional licensure. After working under the close supervision of experienced educators for one or two years while taking education courses outside school hours, they receive regular licensure if they have progressed satisfactorily. Under other programs, college graduates who do not meet licensure requirements take only those courses that they lack, and then they become licensed. This may take one or two semesters of full-time study. States may issue emergency licenses to individuals who do not meet requirements for a regular license when schools cannot attract enough qualified teachers to fill positions. Teachers who need licensure may enter programs that grant a master's degree in education, as well as a license.

For several years, the National Board for Professional Teaching Standards has offered voluntary national certification for teachers. To become nationally certified, teachers must prove their aptitude by compiling a portfolio showing their work in the classroom, and by passing a written assessment and evaluation of their teaching knowledge. Currently, teachers may become certified in one of seven areas. These areas are based on the age of the students and, in some cases, subject area. For example, teachers may obtain a certificate for teaching English Language Arts to early adolescents (ages 11-15), or they may become certified as early childhood generalists. All States recognize national certification, and many States and school districts provide special benefits to teachers holding national certification. Benefits typically include higher salaries and reimbursement for continuing education and certification fees. Additionally, many States allow nationally certified teachers to carry a license from one State to another.

The National Council for Accreditation of Teacher Education currently accredits more than 500 teacher education programs across the United States. Generally, four-year colleges require students to wait until their sophomore year before applying for admission to teacher education programs. Traditional education programs for kindergarten and elementary school teachers include courses—designed specifically for those preparing to teach—in mathematics, physical science, social science, music, art, and literature, as well as prescribed professional education courses such as philosophy of education, psychology of learning, and teaching methods. Aspiring secondary school teachers either major in the subject they plan to teach while also taking education courses, or they major in education and take subject courses. Teacher education programs are now required to include classes in the use of computers and other technologies to maintain accreditation. Most programs require students to perform a student teaching internship.

Many States now offer professional development schools, which are partnerships between universities and elementary or secondary schools. Students enter these 1-year programs after completion of their bachelor's degree. Professional development schools merge theory with practice and allow the student to experience a year of teaching first-hand, with professional guidance.

In addition to being knowledgeable in their subject, the ability to communicate, inspire trust and confidence, and motivate students, as well as to understand their educational and emotional needs, is essential for teachers. Teachers must be able to recognize and respond to individual differences in students and employ different teaching methods that will result in higher student achievement. They also should be organized, dependable, patient, and creative. Teachers must also be able to work cooperatively and communicate effectively with other teaching staff, support staff, parents, and other members of the community.

With additional preparation, teachers may move into positions as school librarians, reading specialists, curriculum specialists, or guidance counselors. Teachers may become administrators or supervisors, although the number of these positions is limited and competition can be intense. In some systems, highly qualified, experienced teachers can become senior or mentor teachers, who receive higher pay and additional responsibilities. They guide and assist less experienced teachers while keeping most of their own teaching responsibilities.

Job Outlook

The job market for teachers varies widely by geographic area and by subject specialty. Many inner cities (often characterized by overcrowded conditions and higher-than-average crime and poverty rates) and rural areas (characterized by their remote location and relatively low salaries) have difficulty attracting enough teachers, so job prospects should continue to be better in these areas than in suburban districts. Currently, many school districts have difficulty hiring qualified teachers in some subjects—mathematics, science (especially chemistry and physics), bilingual education, and computer science. Specialties that currently have an abundance of qualified teachers include general elementary education, physical education, and social studies. Teachers who are geographically mobile and who obtain licensure in more than one subject should have a distinct advantage in finding a job. With enrollments of minorities increasing, coupled with a shortage of minority teachers, efforts to recruit minority teachers should intensify. Also, the number of non-English speaking students has grown dramatically, especially in California and Florida, which have large Spanish-speaking student populations, creating demand for bilingual teachers and those who teach English as a second language.

Overall employment of kindergarten, elementary, and secondary school teachers is expected to increase about as fast as the average for all occupations through the year 2008. The expected retirement of a large number of teachers currently in their 40s and 50s should open up many additional jobs. However, projected employment growth varies among individual teaching occupations.

Employment of secondary school teachers is expected to grow faster than the average for all occupations through the year 2008, while average employment growth is projected for kindergarten and elementary school teachers. Assuming relatively little change in average class size, employment growth of teachers depends on population growth rates and corresponding student enrollments. Enrollments of secondary school students are expected to grow throughout most of the projection period. On the other hand, elementary school enrollment is projected to increase until the year 2001 and then decline.

The number of teachers employed is also dependent on State and local expenditures for education. Pressures from taxpayers to limit spending could result in fewer teachers than projected; pressures to spend more to improve the quality of education could increase the teacher workforce.

In anticipation of growing student enrollments at the secondary school level, many States are implementing policies that will encourage more students to become teachers. Some are giving large signing bonuses that are distributed over the teacher's first few years of teaching. Some are expanding State scholarships; issuing loans for moving expenses; and implementing loan-forgiveness programs, allowing education majors with at least a B average to receive State-paid tuition as long as they agree to teach in the State for four years.

The supply of teachers also is expected to increase in response to reports of improved job prospects, more teacher involvement in school policy, and greater public interest in education. In recent years, the total number of bachelor's and master's degrees granted in education has steadily increased. In addition, more teachers will be drawn from a reserve pool of career changers, substitute teachers, and teachers completing alternative certification programs, relocating to different schools, and reentering the workforce.

Earnings

Median annual earnings of kindergarten, elementary, and secondary school teachers ranged from $33,590 to $37,890 in 1998. The lowest 10 percent earned $19,710 to $24,390; the top 10 percent earned $53,720 to $70,030.

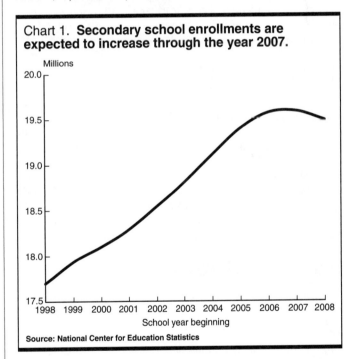

Chart 1. Secondary school enrollments are expected to increase through the year 2007.

Millions

Source: National Center for Education Statistics

According to the American Federation of Teachers, beginning teachers with a bachelor's degree earned an average of $25,700 in the 1997-98 school year. The estimated average salary of all public elementary and secondary school teachers in the 1997-98 school year was $39,300. Private school teachers generally earn less than public school teachers.

In 1998, over half of all public school teachers belonged to unions—mainly the American Federation of Teachers and the National Education Association—that bargain with school systems over wages, hours, and the terms and conditions of employment.

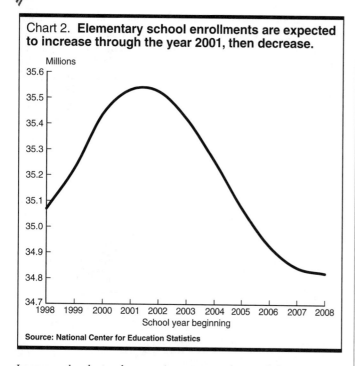

Chart 2. Elementary school enrollments are expected to increase through the year 2001, then decrease.

Millions

Source: National Center for Education Statistics

In some schools, teachers receive extra pay for coaching sports and working with students in extracurricular activities. Some teachers earn extra income during the summer working in the school system or in other jobs.

Related Occupations

Kindergarten, elementary, and secondary school teaching requires a variety of skills and aptitudes, including a talent for working with children; organizational, administrative, and record keeping abilities; research and communication skills; the power to influence, motivate, and train others; patience; and creativity. Workers in other occupations requiring some of these aptitudes include college and university faculty, counselors, education administrators, employment interviewers, librarians, preschool teachers and child-care workers, public relations specialists, sales representatives, social workers, and trainers and employee development specialists.

Sources of Additional Information

Information on licensure or certification requirements and approved teacher training institutions is available from local school systems and State departments of education.

Information on teachers' unions and education-related issues may be obtained from:

- American Federation of Teachers, 555 New Jersey Ave. NW, Washington, DC 20001.
- National Education Association, 1201 16th St. NW, Washington, DC 20036.

A list of institutions with accredited teacher education programs can be obtained from:

- National Council for Accreditation of Teacher Education, 2010 Massachusetts Ave. NW., Suite 500, Washington, DC 20036. Internet: http://www.ncate.org

For information on national teacher certification, contact:

- National Board for Professional Teaching Standards, 26555 Evergreen Rd., Suite 400, Southfield, MI 48076. Internet: http://www.nbpts.org

For information on alternative certification programs, contact:

- ERIC Clearinghouse on Teacher Education, 1307 New York Ave. NW., Washington, DC 20005-4701.

Science Technicians

(O*NET 22599F, 24502A, 24502B, 24502C, 24502D, 24505A, 24505B, 24505C, 24505D, 24505E, 24508A, 24508B, 24511B, 24511E, 24599A, 24599B, 24599C, and 25323)

Significant Points

- Science technicians in production jobs often work in 8-hour shifts around the clock.

- Job opportunities are expected to be very good for qualified graduates of science technician training programs or applied science technology programs who are well trained on equipment used in laboratories and production facilities.

Nature of the Work

Science technicians use the principles and theories of science and mathematics to solve problems in research and development and to help invent and improve products and processes. However, their jobs are more practically oriented than those of scientists. Technicians set up, operate, and maintain laboratory instruments, monitor experiments, make observations, calculate and record results, and often develop conclusions. They must keep detailed logs of all their work-related activities. Those who work in production monitor manufacturing processes and may be involved in ensuring quality by testing products for proper proportions of ingredients and purity or for strength and durability.

As laboratory instrumentation and procedures have become more complex in recent years, the role of science technicians in research and development has expanded. In addition to performing routine tasks, many technicians also develop and adapt laboratory procedures to achieve the best results, interpret data, and devise solutions to problems, under the direction of scientists. Moreover, technicians must master the laboratory equipment, so they can adjust settings when necessary and recognize when equipment is malfunctioning.

The increasing use of robotics to perform many routine tasks has freed technicians to operate more sophisticated laboratory equipment. Science technicians make extensive use of computers, computer-interfaced equipment, robotics, and high-technology industrial applications, such as biological engineering.

Most science technicians specialize, learning skills and working in the same disciplines as scientists. Occupational titles, therefore, tend to follow the same structure as scientists. *Agricultural techni-*

cians work with agricultural scientists in food, fiber, and animal research, production, and processing. Some conduct tests and experiments to improve the yield and quality of crops or to increase the resistance of plants and animals to disease, insects, or other hazards. Other agricultural technicians do animal breeding and nutrition work.

Biological technicians work with biologists studying living organisms. Many assist scientists who conduct medical research—helping to find a cure for cancer or AIDS, for example. Those who work in pharmaceutical companies help develop and manufacture medicinal and pharmaceutical preparations. Those working in the field of microbiology generally work as lab assistants, studying living organisms and infectious agents. Biological technicians also analyze organic substances, such as blood, food, and drugs, and some examine evidence in criminal investigations. Biological technicians working in biotechnology labs use the knowledge and techniques gained from basic research by scientists, including gene splicing and recombinant DNA, and apply these techniques in product development.

Chemical technicians work with chemists and chemical engineers, developing and using chemicals and related products and equipment. Most do research and development, testing, or other laboratory work. For example, they might test packaging for design, integrity of materials, and environmental acceptability; assemble and operate new equipment to develop new products; monitor product quality; or develop new production techniques. Some chemical technicians collect and analyze samples of air and water to monitor pollution levels. Those who focus on basic research might produce compounds through complex organic synthesis. Chemical technicians within chemical plants are also referred to as *process technicians*. They may operate equipment, monitor plant processes, and analyze plant materials.

Environmental technicians perform laboratory and field tests to monitor environmental resources and determine the contaminants and sources of pollution. They may collect samples for testing or be involved in abating, controlling, or remediating sources of environmental pollutants. Some are responsible for waste management operations, control and management of hazardous materials inventory, or general activities involving regulatory compliance. There is a growing emphasis on pollution prevention activities.

Nuclear technicians operate nuclear test and research equipment, monitor radiation, and assist nuclear engineers and physicists in research. Some also operate remote control equipment to manipulate radioactive materials or materials to be exposed to radioactivity.

Petroleum technicians measure and record physical and geologic conditions in oil or gas wells, using instruments lowered into wells or by analysis of the mud from wells. In oil and gas exploration, these technicians collect and examine geological data or test geological samples to determine petroleum and mineral content. Some petroleum technicians, called *scouts*, collect information about oil and gas well drilling operations, geological and geophysical prospecting, and land or lease contracts.

Other science technicians collect weather information or assist oceanographers.

Working Conditions

Science technicians work under a wide variety of conditions. Most work indoors, usually in laboratories, and have regular hours. Some occasionally work irregular hours to monitor experiments that can't be completed during regular working hours. Production technicians often work in 8-hour shifts around the clock. Others, such as agricultural, petroleum, and environmental technicians, perform much of their work outdoors, sometimes in remote locations.

Some science technicians may be exposed to hazards from equipment, chemicals, or toxic materials. Chemical technicians sometimes work with toxic chemicals or radioactive isotopes, nuclear technicians may be exposed to radiation, and biological technicians sometimes work with disease-causing organisms or radioactive agents. However, these working conditions pose little risk if proper safety procedures are followed.

Employment

Science technicians held about 227,000 jobs in 1998. More than 37 percent worked in manufacturing—mostly in the chemical industry—but also in the food processing industry. About 12 percent worked in education services, and another 15 percent worked in research and testing services. In 1998, the Federal government employed about 14,000 science technicians, mostly in the Departments of Defense, Agriculture, and Interior.

Training, Other Qualifications, and Advancement

There are several ways to qualify for a job as a science technician. Many employers prefer applicants who have at least two years of specialized training or an associate degree in applied science or science-related technology. Because employers' preferences vary, however, some science technicians have a bachelor's degree in chemistry or biology or have taken several science and math courses at four-year colleges.

Many technical and community colleges offer associate degrees in a specific technology or a more general education in science and mathematics. A number of two-year associate degree programs are designed to provide easy transfer to a four-year college or university, if desired. Technical institutes usually offer technician training, but they provide less theory and general education than technical or community colleges. The length of programs at technical institutes varies, although one-year certificate programs and two-year associate degree programs are common. Some schools offer cooperative-education or internship programs, allowing students the opportunity to work at a local company or other workplace while attending classes in alternate terms. Participation in such programs can significantly enhance a student's employment prospects.

Persons interested in careers as science technicians should take as many high school science and math courses as possible. Science courses taken beyond high school, in an associate's or bachelor's program, should be laboratory oriented, with an emphasis on bench skills. Because computers and computer-interfaced equipment are often used in research and development laboratories, technicians should have strong computer skills. Communication skills are also important; technicians are often required to report their findings both through speaking and in writing. Additionally, technicians should be able to work well with others because teamwork is common.

Prospective science technicians can acquire good career preparation through two-year formal training programs that combine the teaching of scientific principles and theory with practical hands-on application in a laboratory setting with up-to-date equipment. Graduates of four-year bachelor's degree programs in science who have considerable experience in laboratory-based courses, have completed internships, or held summer jobs in laboratories, are also well qualified for science technician positions and are preferred by some employers. However, those with a bachelor's degree who accept technician jobs generally cannot find employment that uses their advanced academic education.

Technicians usually begin work as trainees in routine positions under the direct supervision of a scientist or a more experienced technician. Job candidates whose training or educational background encompasses extensive hands-on experience with a variety of laboratory equipment, including computers and related equipment, usually require a short period of on-the-job training. As they gain experience, technicians take on more responsibility and carry out assignments under only general supervision, and some eventually become supervisors. However, technicians employed at universities often have their fortunes tied to particular professors; when professors retire or leave, these technicians face uncertain employment prospects.

Job Outlook

Employment of science technicians is expected to increase more slowly than the average for all occupations through the year 2008. Continued growth of scientific and medical research, as well as the development and production of technical products, should stimulate demand for science technicians in all areas. In particular, the growing number of agricultural and medicinal products developed from using biotechnology techniques will increase the need for biological technicians. Employment growth will also be fueled by demand for technicians to help regulate waste products; to collect air, water, and soil samples for measuring levels of pollutants; to monitor compliance with environmental regulations; and to clean up contaminated sites. However, growth will be moderated somewhat by an expected slowdown in overall employment in the chemical industry.

Job opportunities are expected to be very good for qualified graduates of science technician training programs or applied science technology programs, who are well trained on equipment used in industrial and government laboratories and production facilities. As the instrumentation and techniques used in industrial research, development, and production become increasingly more complex, employers are seeking well trained individuals with highly developed technical and communication skills. In addition to opportunities created by growth, many job openings should arise from the need to replace technicians who retire or leave the labor force for other reasons.

Earnings

Median hourly earnings of science technicians were $14.92 in 1998. The middle 50 percent earned between $11.48 and $19.38. The lowest 10 percent earned less than $9.28, and the highest 10 percent earned more than $24.20. Median hourly earnings were $11.20 for chemical technicians and $11.80 for biological and agricultural technicians working in research and testing services in 1997. Chemical technicians working in drug manufacturing earned an hourly median of $15.30 in 1997. Median hourly earnings in the industries employing the largest number of all other science technicians in 1997 were as follows:

Federal government $16.50
State government, except education and hospitals 14.80
Local government, except education and hospitals 14.50
Research and testing services 14.40
Personnel supply services 11.30

In the Federal overnment in 1999, science technicians started at $16,400, $18,400, or $20,600, depending on education and experience. Beginning salaries were slightly higher in selected areas of the country where the prevailing local pay level was higher. The average annual salary for biological science technicians in nonsupervisory, supervisory, and managerial positions employed by the Federal government in early 1999 was $30,300; for mathematical technicians, $41,000; for physical science technicians, $38,200; for geodetic technicians, $48,800; for hydrologic technicians, $36,000; and for meteorologic technicians, $45,200.

Related Occupations

Other technicians who apply scientific principles at a level usually taught in two-year associate degree programs include engineering technicians, broadcast technicians, drafters, and health technologists and technicians. Some of the work of agricultural and biological technicians is related to that in agriculture and forestry occupations.

Sources of Additional Information

For information about a career as a chemical technician, contact:

● American Chemical Society, Education Division, Career Publications, 1155 16th St. NW., Washington, DC 20036. Internet: http://www.acs.org

Secretaries

(O*NET 21999C, 55102, 55105, and 55108)

Significant Points

● Increasing office automation and organizational restructuring will lead to little or no change in overall employment of secretaries.

- Employers increasingly require knowledge of software applications, such as word processing, spreadsheets, and database management.

- Job openings should be plentiful, especially for well-qualified and experienced secretaries, primarily due to the need to replace workers who leave this very large occupation.

Nature of the Work

As technology continues to expand in offices across the Nation, the role of the secretary has greatly evolved. Office automation and organizational restructuring have led secretaries to assume a wide range of new responsibilities once reserved for managerial and professional staff. Many secretaries now provide training and orientation to new staff, conduct research on the Internet, and learn to operate new office technologies. In the midst of these changes, however, their core responsibilities have remained much the same—performing and coordinating an office's administrative activities and ensuring that information is disseminated to staff and clients.

Secretaries are responsible for a variety of administrative and clerical duties necessary to run an organization efficiently. They serve as an information clearinghouse for an office, schedule appointments, provide information to callers, organize and maintain paper and electronic files, manage projects, and produce correspondence. They may also prepare correspondence, handle travel arrangements, and contact clients.

Secretaries are aided in these tasks by a variety of office equipment, such as fax machines, photocopiers, and telephone systems. In addition, secretaries increasingly use personal computers to run spreadsheet, word processing, database management, desktop publishing, and graphics programs—tasks previously handled by managers and other professionals. At the same time, these other workers have assumed many tasks traditionally assigned to secretaries, such as word processing and answering the telephone. Because secretaries are often relieved from dictation and typing, they can support several members of the professional staff. In a number of organizations, secretaries work in teams in order to work flexibly and share their expertise.

Specific job duties vary with experience and titles. Executive secretaries and administrative assistants, for example, perform fewer clerical tasks than lower level secretaries. In addition to greeting visitors, arranging conference calls, and scheduling meetings, they may handle more complex responsibilities such as conducting research, preparing statistical reports, training employees, and supervising other clerical staff.

Some secretaries, such as legal and medical secretaries, perform highly specialized work requiring knowledge of technical terminology and procedures. For instance, legal secretaries prepare correspondence and legal papers such as summonses, complaints, motions, responses, and subpoenas under the supervision of an attorney. They also may review legal journals and assist in other ways with legal research, such as verifying quotes and citations in legal briefs. Medical secretaries transcribe dictation, prepare correspondence, and assist physicians or medical scientists with reports, speeches, articles, and conference proceedings. They also record simple medical histories, arrange for patients to be hospitalized, and order supplies. Most medical secretaries need to be familiar with insurance rules, billing practices, and hospital or laboratory procedures. Other technical secretaries who assist engineers or scientists may prepare correspondence, maintain the technical library, and gather and edit materials for scientific papers.

Working Conditions

Secretaries usually work in offices with other professionals in schools, hospitals, or in legal and medical offices. Their jobs often involve sitting for long periods. If they spend a lot of time typing, particularly at a video display terminal, they may encounter problems of eyestrain, stress, and repetitive motion, such as carpal tunnel syndrome.

Office work can lend itself to alternative or flexible working arrangements, such as part time work. In fact, 1 secretary in 5 works part time, and many others work in temporary positions. A few participate in job sharing arrangements in which two people divide responsibility for a single job. The majority of secretaries, however, are full-time employees who work a standard 40-hour week.

Employment

Secretaries held about 3.2 million jobs in 1998, ranking among the largest occupations in the U.S. economy. The following table shows the distribution of employment by secretarial specialty.

Secretaries, total	3,195,000
Legal secretaries	285,000
Medical secretaries	219,000
Secretaries, except legal and medical	2,691,000

Secretaries are employed in organizations of every type. About 6 out of 10 secretaries are employed in firms providing services, ranging from education and health to legal and business services. Others work for firms engaged in manufacturing, construction, wholesale and retail trade, transportation, and communications. Banks, insurance companies, investment firms, and real estate firms are also important employers, as are Federal, State, and local government agencies.

Training, Other Qualifications, and Advancement

High school graduates who have basic office skills may qualify for entry-level secretarial positions. However, employers increasingly require knowledge of software applications, such as word processing, spreadsheets, and database management. Secretaries should be proficient in keyboarding and good at spelling, punctuation, grammar, and oral communication. Shorthand is necessary for some positions. Because secretaries must be tactful in their dealings with people, employers also look for good interpersonal skills. Discretion, good judgment, organizational ability, and initiative are especially important for higher level secretarial positions.

As office automation continues to evolve, retraining and continuing education will remain an integral part of secretarial jobs.

Changes in the office environment have increased the demand for secretaries who are adaptable and versatile. Secretaries may have to attend classes to learn how to operate new office technologies, such as information storage systems, scanners, the Internet, or new or updated software packages.

Secretaries acquire skills in various ways. Training ranges from high school vocational education programs that teach office skills and keyboarding to one- to two-year programs in office administration offered by business schools, vocational-technical institutes, and community colleges. Many temporary help agencies also provide formal training in computer and office skills. These skills are most often acquired, however, through on-the-job instruction by other employees or by equipment and software vendors. Specialized training programs are available for students planning to become medical or legal secretaries or administrative technology specialists.

Testing and certification for entry-level office skills is available through the Office Proficiency Assessment and Certification program offered by the International Association of Administrative Professionals. As secretaries gain experience, they can earn the Certified Professional Secretary (CPS) designation by meeting certain experience requirements and passing an examination. Similarly, those without experience who want to be certified as a legal support professional may be certified as an Accredited Legal Secretary (ALS) by the Certifying Board of the National Association of Legal Secretaries. This organization also administers an examination to certify a legal secretary with three years of experience as a Professional Legal Secretary (PLS). Legal Secretaries International confers the designation Board Certified Civil Trial Legal Secretary in specialized areas such as litigation, real estate, probate, and corporate law, to those who have five years of law-related experience and pass an examination.

Secretaries generally advance by being promoted to other secretarial positions with more responsibilities. Qualified secretaries who broaden their knowledge of a company's operations and enhance their skills may be promoted to other positions such as senior or executive secretary, clerical supervisor, or office manager. Secretaries with word processing experience can advance to jobs as word processing trainers, supervisors, or managers within their own firms or in a secretarial or word processing service bureau. Secretarial experience can also lead to jobs such as instructor or sales representative with manufacturers of software or computer equipment. With additional training, many legal secretaries become paralegals.

Job Outlook

Job openings should be plentiful, particularly for well-qualified and experienced secretaries, stemming from the need to replace workers who transfer to other occupations or leave this very large occupation for other reasons each year. Overall, however, little or no change is expected in employment of secretaries over the 1998-2008 period.

Projected employment of secretaries will vary by occupational specialty. Rapid growth in the health and legal services industries should lead to average growth for medical and legal secretaries. However, employment of secretaries who do not specialize in legal or medical work (about 7 out of 8) is expected to remain flat. Rapidly growing industries—such as personnel supply, computer and data processing, and management and public relations—will generate new job opportunities.

Growing levels of office automation and organizational restructuring will continue to make secretaries more productive in coming years. Personal computers, electronic mail, scanners, fax machines, and voice message systems will allow secretaries to accomplish more in the same amount of time. The use of automated equipment is also changing the distribution of work in many offices. In some cases, such traditional secretarial duties as typing or keyboarding, filing, copying, and bookkeeping are being assigned to workers in other units or departments. Professionals and managers increasingly do their own word processing and much of their own correspondence rather than submit the work to secretaries and other support staff. Also, in some law offices and physicians' offices, paralegals and medical assistants are assuming some tasks formerly done by secretaries. As other workers assume more of these duties, there is a trend in many offices for professionals and managers to "share" secretaries. The traditional arrangement of one secretary per manager is becoming less prevalent; instead, secretaries increasingly support systems or units. This approach often means secretaries assume added responsibilities and are seen as valuable members of a team, but it also contributes to the decline in employment projected for most secretaries.

Developments in office technology are certain to continue, and they will bring about further changes in the secretary's work environment. However, many secretarial duties are of a personal, interactive nature and, therefore, are not easily automated. Responsibilities such as planning conferences, working with clients, and transmitting staff instructions require tact and communication skills. Because technology cannot substitute for these personal skills, secretaries will continue to play a key role in most organizations.

Earnings

Median annual earnings of secretaries, excluding legal and medical secretaries, were $23,560 in 1998. The middle 50 percent earned between $18,770 and $29,400. The lowest 10 percent earned less than $14,410, and the highest 10 percent earned more than $36,050. Secretaries earn slightly more in urban areas. In 1997, median annual earnings in the industries employing the largest numbers of secretaries, excluding legal and medical secretaries, were:

Local government	$23,900
Hospitals	23,000
Colleges and universities	22,600
Elementary and secondary schools	22,300
Personnel supply services	21,500

In 1998, median annual earnings of legal secretaries were $30,050. Median annual earnings of medical secretaries were $22,390 in 1998; in offices and clinics of medical doctors they earned approximately $22,000 in 1997, and in hospitals, $21,400.

According to the International Association of Administrative Professionals, secretaries averaged $25,500 a year in 1998. Salaries vary a great deal, however, reflecting differences in skill, experience, and level of responsibility. Salaries also vary in different parts of the country; earnings are usually lowest in southern cities, and highest in northern and western cities. In addition, salaries vary by industry; salaries of secretaries tend to be highest in transportation, legal services, and public utilities and lowest in retail trade and finance, insurance, and real estate. Certification in this field usually is rewarded by a higher salary.

The starting salary for inexperienced secretaries in the Federal government was $18,400 a year in 1999. Beginning salaries were slightly higher in selected areas where the prevailing local pay level was higher. All secretaries employed by the Federal government averaged about $30,200 a year in 1999.

Related Occupations

A number of other workers type, record information, and process paperwork. Among them are bookkeepers, receptionists, stenographers, personnel clerks, typists and word processors, paralegals, medical assistants, and medical record technicians. A growing number of secretaries share in managerial and human resource responsibilities. Occupations requiring these skills include office and administrative support supervisor, systems manager, office manager, and human resource specialist.

Sources of Additional Information

For information on the Certified Professional Secretary designation, contact:

- International Association of Administrative Professionals, 10502 NW Ambassador Dr., P.O. Box 20404, Kansas City, MO 64195-0404. Internet: http://www.iaap-hq.org

Information on the Board Certified Civil Trial Legal Secretary designation can be obtained from:

- Legal Secretaries International Inc., 8902 Sunnywood Dr., Houston, TX 77088-3729. Internet: http://www.compassnet.com/legalsec

Information on the Accredited Legal Secretary and Certified Professional Legal Secretary designations is available from:

- National Association of Legal Secretaries, 2448 East 81st St., Suite 3400, Tulsa, OK 74137-4238. Internet: http://www.nals.org

State employment offices provide information about job openings for secretaries.

Social Workers

(O*NET 27305A, 27305B, 27305C, and 27302)

Significant Points

- A bachelor's degree is the minimum requirement for many entry-level jobs, but a master's degree in social work (MSW) or a related field is required for clinical practice and is becoming the norm for many positions.

- Employment is projected to grow much faster than average.

- Competition for jobs is expected to be keen in cities, but opportunities should be good in rural areas.

Nature of the Work

Social work is a profession for those with a strong desire to help people, to make things better, and to make a difference. Social workers help people function the best way they can in their environment, deal with their relationships with others, and solve personal and family problems.

Social workers often see clients who face a life-threatening disease or a social problem. These problems may include inadequate housing, unemployment, lack of job skills, financial distress, serious illness or disability, substance abuse, unwanted pregnancy, or antisocial behavior. Social workers also assist families that have serious domestic conflicts, including those involving child or spousal abuse.

Through direct counseling, social workers help clients identify their concerns, consider effective solutions, and find reliable resources. Social workers typically consult and counsel clients and arrange for services that can help them. Often, they refer clients to specialists in services such as debt counseling, child care or elder care, public assistance, or alcohol or drug rehabilitation. Social workers then follow through with the client to assure that services are helpful and that clients make proper use of the services offered. Social workers may review eligibility requirements, help fill out forms and applications, visit clients on a regular basis, and provide support during crises.

Social workers practice in a variety of settings. In hospitals and psychiatric hospitals, they provide or arrange for a range of support services. In mental health and community centers, social workers provide counseling services on marriage, family, and adoption matters, and they help people through personal or community emergencies, such as dealing with loss or grief or arranging for disaster assistance. In schools, they help children, parents, and teachers cope with problems. In social service agencies, they help people locate basic benefits, such as income assistance, housing, and job training. Social workers also offer counseling to those receiving therapy for addictive or physical disorders in rehabilitation facilities and to people in nursing homes in need of routine living care. In employment settings, they counsel people with personal, family, professional, or financial problems affecting their work performance. Social workers who work in courts and correction facilities evaluate and counsel individuals in the criminal justice system to cope better in society. In private practice, they provide clinical or diagnostic testing services covering a wide range of personal disorders.

Social workers often provide social services in health-related settings that now are governed by managed care organizations. To contain costs, these organizations are emphasizing short-term intervention, ambulatory and community-based care, and greater decentralization of services.

Most social workers specialize in an area of practice. Although some conduct research or are involved in planning or policy development, most social workers prefer an area of practice in which they interact with clients.

Clinical social workers offer psychotherapy or counseling and a range of diagnostic services in public agencies, clinics, and private practice.

Child welfare or family services social workers may counsel children and youths who have difficulty adjusting socially, advise parents on how to care for disabled children, or arrange for homemaker services during a parent's illness. If children have serious problems in school, child welfare workers may consult with parents, teachers, and counselors to identify underlying causes and develop plans for treatment. Some social workers assist single parents, arrange adoptions, and help find foster homes for neglected, abandoned, or abused children. Child welfare workers also work in residential institutions for children and adolescents.

Child or adult protective services social workers investigate reports of abuse and neglect and intervene if necessary. They may initiate legal action to remove children from homes and place them temporarily in an emergency shelter or with a foster family.

Mental health social workers provide services for persons with mental or emotional problems. Such services include individual and group therapy, outreach, crisis intervention, social rehabilitation, and training in skills of everyday living. They may also help plan for supportive services to ease patients' return to the community.

Health care social workers help patients and their families cope with chronic, acute, or terminal illnesses and handle problems that may stand in the way of recovery or rehabilitation. They may organize support groups for families of patients suffering from cancer, AIDS, Alzheimer's disease, or other illnesses. They also advise family caregivers, counsel patients, and help plan for their needs after discharge by arranging for at-home services, ranging from meals-on-wheels to oxygen equipment. Some work on interdisciplinary teams that evaluate certain kinds of patients, geriatric or organ transplant patients, for example.

School social workers diagnose students' problems and arrange needed services, counsel children in trouble, and help integrate disabled students into the general school population. School social workers deal with problems such as student pregnancy, misbehavior in class, and excessive absences. They also advise teachers on how to cope with problem students.

Criminal justice social workers make recommendations to courts, prepare pre-sentencing assessments, and provide services to prison inmates and their families. Probation and parole officers provide similar services to individuals sentenced by a court to parole or probation.

Occupational social workers usually work in a corporation's personnel department or health unit. Through employee assistance programs, they help workers cope with job-related pressures or personal problems that affect the quality of their work. They often offer direct counseling to employees whose performance is hindered by emotional or family problems or substance abuse. They also develop education programs and refer workers to specialized community programs.

Gerontology social workers specialize in services to the aged. They run support groups for family caregivers or for the adult children of aging parents. Also, they advise elderly people or family members about the choices in such areas as housing, transportation, and long-term care; they also coordinate and monitor services.

Social work administrators perform overall management tasks in a hospital, clinic, or other setting that offers social worker services.

Social work planners and policy-makers develop programs to address such issues as child abuse, homelessness, substance abuse, poverty, and violence. These workers research and analyze policies, programs, and regulations. They identify social problems and suggest legislative and other solutions. They may help raise funds or write grants to support these programs.

Working Conditions

Full-time social workers usually work a standard 40-hour week; however, some occasionally work evenings and weekends to meet with clients, attend community meetings, and handle emergencies. Some, particularly in voluntary nonprofit agencies, work part time. Most social workers work in pleasant, clean offices that are well lit and well ventilated. Social workers usually spend most of their time in an office or residential facility, but also may travel locally to visit clients, to meet with service providers, or to attend meetings. Some may use one of several offices within a local area in which to meet with clients. The work, while satisfying, can be emotionally draining. Understaffing and large caseloads add to the pressure in some agencies.

Employment

Social workers held about 604,000 jobs in 1998. About 4 out of 10 jobs were in State, county, or municipal government agencies, primarily in departments of health and human services, mental health, social services, child welfare, housing, education, and corrections. Most private sector jobs were in social service agencies, hospitals, nursing homes, home health agencies, and other health centers or clinics.

Although most social workers are employed in cities or suburbs, some work in rural areas.

Training, Other Qualifications, and Advancement

A bachelor's in social work (BSW) degree is the most common minimum requirement to qualify for a job as a social worker; however, majors in psychology, sociology, and related fields may be sufficient to qualify for some entry-level jobs, especially in small community agencies. Although a bachelor's degree is required for entry into the field, an advanced degree has become the standard for many positions. A master's in social work (MSW) is necessary for positions in health and mental health settings and typically is required for certification for clinical work. Jobs in public agencies also may require an advanced degree, such as a master's in social service policy or administration. Supervisory, administrative, and staff training positions usually require at least an advanced degree. College and university teaching positions and most research appointments normally require a doctorate in social work (DSW or Ph.D).

As of 1999, the Council on Social Work Education accredited more than 400 BSW programs and more than 125 MSW programs. The Group for Advancement of Doctoral Education in Social Work listed

63 doctoral programs for Ph.D.s in social work or DSWs (Doctor of Social Work). BSW programs prepare graduates for direct service positions such as case worker or group worker. They include courses in social work practice, social welfare policies, human behavior and the social environment, social research methods, social work values and ethics, dealing with a culturally diverse clientele, promotion of social and economic justice, and populations-at-risk. Accredited BSW programs require at least 400 hours of supervised field experience.

Master's degree programs prepare graduates for work in their chosen field of concentration and continue to develop their skills to perform clinical assessments, to manage large caseloads, and to explore new ways of drawing upon social services to meet the needs of clients. Master's programs last two years and include 900 hours of supervised field instruction, or internship. A part-time program may take four years. Entry into a master's program does not require a bachelor's in social work, but courses in psychology, biology, sociology, economics, political science, history, social anthropology, urban studies, and social work are recommended. In addition, a second language can be very helpful. Most master's programs offer advanced standing for those with a bachelor's degree from an accredited social work program.

All States and the District of Columbia have licensing, certification, or registration requirements regarding social work practice and the use of professional titles. Although standards for licensing vary by State, a growing number of States are placing greater emphasis on communications skills, professional ethics, and sensitivity for cultural diversity issues. Additionally, the National Association of Social Workers (NASW) offers voluntary credentials. The Academy of Certified Social Workers (ACSW) is granted to all social workers who have met established eligibility criteria. Social workers practicing in school settings may qualify for the School Social Work Specialist (SSWS) credential. Clinical social workers may earn either the Qualified Clinical Social Worker (QCSW) or the advanced credential—Diplomate in Clinical Social Work (DCSW). Social workers holding clinical credentials also may list themselves in the biannual publication of the *NASW Register of Clinical Social Workers*. Credentials are particularly important for those in private practice; some health insurance providers require them for reimbursement.

Social workers should be emotionally mature, objective, and sensitive to people and their problems. They must be able to handle responsibility, work independently, and maintain good working relationships with clients and coworkers. Volunteer or paid jobs as a social work aide offer ways of testing one's interest in this field.

Advancement to supervisor, program manager, assistant director, or executive director of a social service agency or department is possible, but usually requires an advanced degree and related work experience. Other career options for social workers include teaching, research, and consulting. Some also help formulate government policies by analyzing and advocating policy positions in government agencies, in research institutions, and on legislators' staffs.

Some social workers go into private practice. Most private practitioners are clinical social workers who provide psychotherapy, usually paid through health insurance. Private practitioners usually have at least a master's degree and a period of supervised work experience. A network of contacts for referrals also is essential.

Job Outlook

Employment of social workers is expected to increase much faster than the average for all occupations through 2008. The aged population is increasing rapidly, creating greater demand for health and other social services. Social workers also will be needed to help the sizable baby boom generation deal with depression and mental health concerns stemming from mid-life, career, or other personal and professional difficulties. In addition, continuing concern about crime, juvenile delinquency, and services for the mentally ill, the mentally retarded, AIDS patients, and individuals and families in crisis will spur demand for social workers in several areas of specialization. Many job openings will also stem from the need to replace social workers who leave the occupation.

The number of social workers in hospitals and many larger, long-term care facilities will increase in response to the need to ensure that the necessary medical and social services are in place when individuals leave the facility. However, this service need will be shared across several occupations. In an effort to control costs, these facilities increasingly emphasize discharging patients early, applying an interdisciplinary approach to patient care, and employing a broader mix of occupations—including clinical specialists, registered nurses, and health aides—to tend to patient care or client need.

Social worker employment in home health care services is growing, in part because hospitals are releasing patients earlier than in the past. However, the expanding senior population is an even larger factor. Social workers with backgrounds in gerontology are finding work in the growing numbers of assisted living and senior living communities.

Employment of social workers in private social service agencies will grow, but not as rapidly as demand for their services. Agencies increasingly will restructure services and hire more lower-paid human service workers and assistants instead of social workers. Employment in state and local government may grow somewhat in response to increasing needs for public welfare and family services; however, many of these services will be contracted out to private agencies. Additionally, employment levels may fluctuate depending on need and government funding for various social service programs.

Employment of school social workers is expected to grow, due to expanded efforts to respond to rising rates of teen pregnancy and to the adjustment problems of immigrants and children from single-parent families. Moreover, continued emphasis on integrating disabled children into the general school population will lead to more jobs. However, availability of State and local funding will dictate the actual job growth in schools.

Opportunities for social workers in private practice will expand because of the anticipated availability of funding from health insurance and public-sector contracts. Also, with increasing affluence, people will be better able to pay for professional help to deal with personal problems. The growing popularity of employee assistance programs also is expected to spur demand for private practitioners, some of whom provide social work services to corporations on a contractual basis.

Competition for social worker jobs is stronger in cities where demand for services often is highest, training programs for social workers are prevalent, and interest in available positions is strongest. However, opportunities should be good in rural areas, which often find it difficult to attract and retain qualified staff.

Earnings

Median annual earnings of social workers were $30,590 in 1998. The middle 50 percent earned between $24,160 and $39,240. The lowest 10 percent earned less than $19,250, and the top 10 percent earned more than $49,080. Median annual earnings in the industries employing the largest numbers of medical social workers in 1997 were:

Home health care services	$35,800
Offices and clinics of medical doctors	33,700
Offices of other health care practitioners	32,900
State government, except education and hospitals	31,800
Hospitals	31,500

Median annual earnings in the industries employing the largest numbers of social workers, except medical, in 1997 were:

Federal government	$45,300
Elementary and secondary schools	34,100
Local government, except education and hospitals	32,100
Hospitals	31,300
State government, except education and hospitals	30,800

Related Occupations

Through direct counseling or referral to other services, social workers help people solve a range of personal problems. Workers in occupations with similar duties include the clergy, mental health counselors, counseling psychologists, and human services workers and assistants.

Sources of Additional Information

For information about career opportunities in social work, contact:

- National Association of Social Workers, Career Information, 750 First St. NE., Suite 700, Washington, DC 20002-4241.

An annual *Directory of Accredited BSW and MSW Programs* is available for a nominal charge from:

- Council on Social Work Education, 1600 Duke St., Alexandria, VA 22314-3421. Internet: http://www.cswe.org

Information on licensing requirements and testing procedures for each State may be obtained from State licensing authorities or from:

- American Association of State Social Work Boards, 400 South Ridge Parkway, Suite B, Culpeper, VA 22701. Internet: http://www.aasswb.org

Special Education Teachers

(O*NET 31311A, 31311B, and 31311C)

Significant Points

- A bachelor's degree, completion of an approved teacher preparation program, and a license are required to qualify; many States require a master's degree.

- Many States offer alternative licensure programs to attract people into these jobs.

- Job openings arising from rapid employment growth and some job turnover mean excellent job prospects; many school districts report shortages of qualified teachers.

Nature of the Work

Special education teachers work with children and youths who have a variety of disabilities. Most special education teachers instruct students at the elementary, middle, and secondary school level, although some teachers work with infants and toddlers. Special education teachers design and modify instruction to meet a student's special needs. Teachers also work with students who have other special instructional needs, including the gifted and talented.

The various types of disabilities delineated in Federal legislation concerning special education programs include specific learning disabilities, speech or language impairments, mental retardation, emotional disturbance, multiple disabilities, hearing impairments, orthopedic impairments, other health impairments, visual impairments, autism, deaf-blindness, and traumatic brain injury. Students are classified under one of the categories, and special education teachers are prepared to work with specific groups.

Special education teachers use various techniques to promote learning. Depending on the disability, teaching methods can include individualized instruction, problem-solving assignments, and group or individual work. Special education teachers are legally required to help develop an Individualized Education Program (IEP) for each special education student. The IEP sets personalized goals for each student and is tailored to a student's individual learning style and ability. This program includes a transition plan outlining specific steps to prepare special education students for middle school or high school, or in the case of older students, a job or post-secondary study. Teachers review the IEP with the student's parents, school administrators, and often the student's general education teacher. Teachers work closely with parents to inform them of their child's progress and suggest techniques to promote learning at home.

Teachers design curricula, assign work geared toward each student's ability, and grade papers and homework assignments. Special education teachers are involved in a student's behavioral as well as academic development. They help special education students develop emotionally, be comfortable in social situations, and be aware of socially acceptable behavior. Preparing special education students for daily life after graduation is an important aspect of the job. Teachers help students learn routine skills, such as balancing a checkbook, or provide them with career counseling.

As schools become more inclusive, special education teachers and general education teachers increasingly work together in general education classrooms. Special education teachers help general educators adapt curriculum materials and teaching techniques to meet the needs of disabled students. They coordinate the work of teachers, teacher assistants, and themselves to meet the requirements of inclusive special education programs, in addition to teaching special education students. A large part of a special education teacher's job involves interacting with others. They communicate frequently with parents, social workers, school psychologists, occupational and physical therapists, school administrators, and other teachers.

Special education teachers work in a variety of settings. Some have their own classrooms and teach only special education students; others work as special education resource teachers and offer individualized help to students in general education classrooms; and others teach with general education teachers in classes composed of both general and special education students. Some teachers work in a resource room, where special education students work several hours a day, separate from their general education classroom. A significantly smaller proportion of special education teachers works in residential facilities or tutor students in homebound or hospital environments.

Early identification of a child with special needs is another important part of a special education teacher's job. Early intervention is essential in educating these children. Special education teachers who work with infants usually travel to the child's home to work with the child and his or her parents.

Technology is playing an increasingly important role in special education. Special education teachers use specialized equipment such as computers with synthesized speech, interactive educational software programs, and audio tapes.

Working Conditions

Special education teachers enjoy the challenge of working with these students and the opportunity to establish meaningful relationships. Although helping students with disabilities can be highly rewarding, the work can also be emotionally and physically draining. Special education teachers are under considerable stress due to heavy workloads and tedious administrative tasks. They must produce a substantial amount of paperwork documenting each student's progress. Exacerbating this stress is the threat of litigation by students' parents if correct procedures are not followed, or if the parent feels their child is not receiving an adequate education. The physical and emotional demands of the job cause some special education teachers to leave the occupation.

Many schools offer year-round education for special education students, but most special education teachers work the traditional 10-month school year.

Employment

Special education teachers held about 406,000 jobs in 1998. The majority of special education teachers were employed in elementary, middle, and secondary public schools. The rest worked in separate educational facilities—public or private—residential facilities, or in homebound or hospital environments.

Training, Other Qualifications, and Advancement

All 50 States and the District of Columbia require special education teachers to be licensed. Special education licensure varies by State. In many States, special education teachers receive a general education credential to teach kindergarten through grade 12. These teachers train in a specialty, such as learning disabilities or behavioral disorders. Some States offer general special education licenses, others license several different specialties within special education, while others require teachers to first obtain a general education license and then an additional license in special education. State boards of education or a licensure advisory committee usually grant licenses.

All States require a bachelor's degree and completion of an approved teacher preparation program with a prescribed number of subject and education credits and supervised practice teaching. Many States require special education teachers to obtain a master's degree in special education, involving at least one year of additional coursework, including a specialization, beyond the bachelor's degree.

Some States have reciprocity agreements allowing special education teachers to transfer their license from one State to another, but many still require special education teachers to pass licensing requirements for that State. In the future, employers may recognize certification or standards offered by national organization.

Many colleges and universities across the United States offer programs in special education, including undergraduate, master's, and doctoral programs. Special education teachers usually undergo longer periods of training than general education teachers. Most bachelor's degree programs are four-year programs including general and specialized courses in special education. However, an increasing number of institutions require a fifth year or other post-baccalaureate preparation. Courses include educational psychology, legal issues of special education, child growth and development, and knowledge and skills needed for teaching students with disabilities. Some programs require specialization. Others offer generalized special education degrees or study in several specialized areas. The last year of the program is usually spent student teaching in a classroom supervised by a certified teacher.

Alternative and emergency licenses are available in many States, due to the need to fill special education teaching positions. Alternative licenses are designed to bring college graduates and those changing careers into teaching more quickly. Requirements for an alternative license may be less stringent than for a regular license and vary by State. In some programs, individuals begin teaching quickly under a provisional license. They can obtain a regular license by teaching under the supervision of licensed teachers for a period of 1 to 2 years while taking education courses. Emergency licenses are granted when States have difficulty finding licensed special education teachers to fill positions.

Special education teachers must be patient, able to motivate students, understanding of their students' special needs, and accepting of differences in others. Teachers must be creative and apply different types of teaching methods to reach students who are having difficulty. Communication and cooperation are essential traits because special education teachers spend a great deal of time interacting with others, including students, parents, and school faculty and administrators.

Special education teachers can advance to become supervisors or administrators. They may also earn advanced degrees and become instructors in colleges that prepare others for special education teaching. In some school systems, highly experienced teachers can become mentor teachers to less experienced ones; they provide guidance to these teachers while maintaining a light teaching load.

Job Outlook

Employment of special education teachers is expected to increase faster than the average for all occupations through 2008, spurred by continued growth in the number of special education students needing services, legislation emphasizing training and employment for individuals with disabilities, and educational reform. Turnover will lead to additional job openings as special education teachers switch to general education or change careers altogether. Rapid employment growth and job turnover should result in a very favorable job market.

Special education teachers have excellent job prospects, as many school districts report shortages of qualified teachers. Job outlook varies by geographic area and specialty. Positions in rural areas and inner cities are more plentiful than job openings in suburban or wealthy urban areas. In addition, job opportunities may be better in certain specialties—such as speech or language impairments, and learning disabilities—because of large enrollment increases of special education students classified under these disability categories. Legislation encouraging early intervention and special education for infants, toddlers, and preschoolers has created a need for early childhood special education teachers. Special education teachers who are bilingual or have multicultural experience are also needed to work with an increasingly diverse student population.

The number of students requiring special education services has been steadily increasing. This trend is expected to continue because of legislation which expanded the age range of children receiving special education services to include those from birth to age 21; medical advances resulting in more survivors of accidents and illness; the postponement of childbirth by more women, resulting in a greater number of premature births and children born with birth defects; and growth in the general population.

Earnings

Median annual earnings of special education teachers in 1998 were $37,850. The middle 50 percent earned between $30,410 and $48,390. The lowest 10 percent earned less than $25,450; the highest 10 percent earned more than $78,030.

In 1998, about 58 percent of special education teachers belonged to unions—mainly the American Federation of Teachers and the

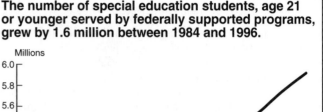

The number of special education students, age 21 or younger served by federally supported programs, grew by 1.6 million between 1984 and 1996.

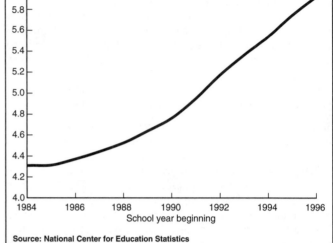

Source: National Center for Education Statistics

National Education Association—that bargain with school systems over wages, hours, and the terms and conditions of employment.

In some schools, teachers receive extra pay for coaching sports and working with students in extracurricular activities. Some teachers earn extra income during the summer by working in the school system or in other jobs.

Related Occupations

Special education teachers work with students who have disabilities and special needs. Other occupations involved with the identification, evaluation, and development of students with disabilities include school psychologists, social workers, speech pathologists, rehabilitation counselors, adapted physical education teachers, special education technology specialists, and occupational, physical, creative arts, and recreational therapists.

Sources of Additional Information

For information on professions related to early intervention and education for children with disabilities, a list of accredited schools, teacher certification, financial aid information, and general information on related personnel issues—including recruitment, retention, and supply of and demand for special education professionals—contact:

● National Clearinghouse for Professions in Special Education, Council for Exceptional Children, 1920 Association Dr., Reston, VA 20191-1589. Internet: http://www.special-ed-careers.org

To learn more about the special education teacher certification and licensing requirements in your State, contact your State's department of education.

Speech-Language Pathologists and Audiologists

(O*NET 32314)

Significant Points

- About half work in schools, and most others are employed by health care facilities.

- A master's degree in speech-language pathology or audiology is the standard credential.

Nature of the Work

Speech-language pathologists assess, treat, and help to prevent speech, language, cognitive, communication, voice, swallowing, fluency, and other related disorders; audiologists identify, assess, and manage auditory, balance, and other neural systems.

Speech-language pathologists work with people who cannot make speech sounds or cannot make them clearly; those with speech rhythm and fluency problems, such as stuttering; people with voice quality problems, such as inappropriate pitch or harsh voice; those with problems understanding and producing language; and those with cognitive communication impairments, such as attention, memory, and problem solving disorders. They may also work with people who have oral motor problems that cause eating and swallowing difficulties.

Speech and language problems can result from hearing loss, brain injury or deterioration, cerebral palsy, stroke, cleft palate, voice pathology, mental retardation, or emotional problems. Problems can be congenital, developmental, or acquired. Speech-language pathologists use written and oral tests, as well as special instruments, to diagnose the nature and extent of impairment and to record and analyze speech, language, and swallowing irregularities. Speech-language pathologists develop an individualized plan of care, tailored to each patient's needs. For individuals with little or no speech capability, speech-language pathologists select augmentative alternative communication methods, including automated devices and sign language, and teach their use. They teach these individuals how to make sounds, improve their voices, or increase their language skills to communicate more effectively. Speech-language pathologists help patients develop, or recover, reliable communication skills so patients can fulfill their educational, vocational, and social roles.

Most speech-language pathologists provide direct clinical services to individuals with communication disorders. In speech and language clinics, they may independently develop and carry out treatment programs. In medical facilities, they may work with physicians, social workers, psychologists, and other therapists to develop and execute treatment plans. Speech-language patholo-

gists in schools develop individual or group programs, counsel parents, and may assist teachers with classroom activities.

Speech-language pathologists keep records on the initial evaluation, progress, and discharge of clients. This helps pinpoint problems, tracks client progress, and justifies the cost of treatment when applying for reimbursement. They counsel individuals and their families concerning communication disorders and how to cope with the stress and misunderstanding that often accompany them. They also work with family members to recognize and change behavior patterns that impede communication and treatment, and they show the family communication-enhancing techniques to use at home.

Some speech-language pathologists conduct research on how people communicate. Others design and develop equipment or techniques for diagnosing and treating speech problems.

Audiologists work with people who have hearing, balance, and related problems. They use audiometers, computers, and other testing devices to measure the loudness at which a person begins to hear sounds, the ability to distinguish between sounds, and the nature and extent of hearing loss. Audiologists interpret these results and may coordinate them with medical, educational, and psychological information to make a diagnosis and determine a course of treatment.

Hearing disorders can result from a variety of causes including trauma at birth, viral infections, genetic disorders, exposure to loud noise, or aging. Treatment may include examining and cleaning the ear canal, fitting and dispensing hearing aids or other assistive devices, and audiologic rehabilitation (including auditory training or instruction in speech or lip reading). Audiologists may recommend, fit, and dispense personal or large area amplification systems, such as hearing aids and alerting devices. Audiologists provide fitting and tuning of cochlear implants and provide the necessary rehabilitation for adjustment to listening with implant amplification systems. They also measure noise levels in workplaces and conduct hearing protection programs in industry, as well as in schools and communities.

Audiologists provide direct clinical services to individuals with hearing or balance disorders. In audiology (hearing) clinics, they may independently develop and carry out treatment programs. Audiologists, in a variety of settings, work as members of interdisciplinary professional teams in planning and implementing service delivery for children and adults, from birth to old age. Similar to speech-language pathologists, audiologists keep records on the initial evaluation, progress, and discharge of clients. These records help pinpoint problems, track client progress, and justify the cost of treatment, when applying for reimbursement.

Audiologists may conduct research on types of and treatment for hearing, balance, and related disorders. Others design and develop equipment or techniques for diagnosing and treating these disorders.

Working Conditions

Speech-language pathologists and audiologists usually work at a desk or table in clean comfortable surroundings. The job is not physically demanding but does require attention to detail and intense concentration. The emotional needs of clients and their families may be demanding. Most full-time speech-language pathologists and audiologists work about 40 hours per week; some work part-time. Those who work on a contract basis may spend a substantial amount of time traveling between facilities.

Employment

Speech-language pathologists and audiologists held about 105,000 jobs in 1998. About one-half provided services in preschools, elementary and secondary schools, or colleges and universities. Others were in offices of speech-language pathologists and audiologists; hospitals; offices of physicians; speech, language, and hearing centers; home health agencies; or other facilities.

Some speech-language pathologists and audiologists are self-employed in private practice. They contract to provide services in schools, physician's offices, hospitals, or nursing homes, or work as consultants to industry. Audiologists are more likely to be employed in independent healthcare offices, while speech-language pathologists are more likely to work in school settings.

Training, Other Qualifications, and Advancement

Of the States that regulate licensing (44 for speech-language pathologists and 49 for audiologists), almost all require a master's degree or equivalent. Other requirements are 300 to 375 hours of supervised clinical experience, a passing score on a national examination, and nine months of postgraduate professional clinical experience. Thirty-six States have continuing education requirements for license renewal. Medicaid, Medicare, and private health insurers generally require a practitioner to be licensed to qualify for reimbursement.

About 235 colleges and universities offer graduate programs in speech-language pathology. Courses cover anatomy and physiology of the areas of the body involved in speech, language, and hearing; the development of normal speech, language, and hearing; the nature of disorders; acoustics; and psychological aspects of communication. Graduate students also learn to evaluate and treat speech, language, and hearing disorders and receive supervised clinical training in communication disorders.

About 115 colleges and universities offer graduate programs in audiology in the United States. Course work includes anatomy; physiology; basic science; math; physics; genetics; normal and abnormal communication development; auditory, balance and neural systems assessment and treatment; audiologic rehabilitation; and ethics.

Speech-language pathologists can acquire the Certificate of Clinical Competence in Speech-Language Pathology (CCC-SLP) offered by the American Speech-Language-Hearing Association, and audiologists can earn the Certificate of Clinical Competence in Audiology (CCC-A). To earn a CCC, a person must have a graduate degree and 375 hours of supervised clinical experience, complete a 36-week postgraduate clinical fellowship, and pass a written examination. According to the American Speech-Language Hearing Association, as of 2007, audiologists will need to have a bachelor's degree and complete 75 hours of credit toward a doctoral degree in

order to seek certification. As of 2012, audiologists will have to earn doctoral degrees in order to be certified.

Speech-language pathologists and audiologists should be able to effectively communicate diagnostic test results, diagnoses, and proposed treatment in a manner easily understood by their clients. They must be able to approach problems objectively and provide support to clients and their families. Because a client's progress may be slow, patience, compassion, and good listening skills are necessary.

Job Outlook

Employment of speech-language pathologists and audiologists is expected to grow much faster than the average for all occupations through the year 2008. Because hearing loss is strongly associated with aging, rapid growth in the population age 55 and over will cause the number of persons with hearing impairment to increase markedly. In addition, baby boomers are now entering middle age, when the possibility of neurological disorders and associated speech, language, and hearing impairments increases. Medical advances are also improving the survival rate of premature infants and trauma and stroke victims, who then need assessment and possible treatment.

Employment growth in health services would be even faster except for Federal legislation imposing limits on reimbursement for therapy services that may continue to adversely affect the job market for therapy providers over the near term. Because of the effects of these provisions, the majority of expected employment growth in health services will occur in the second half of the projection period.

Employment in schools will increase along with growth in elementary and secondary school enrollments, including enrollment of special education students. Federal law guarantees special education and related services to all eligible children with disabilities. Greater awareness of the importance of early identification and diagnosis of speech, language, and hearing disorders will also increase employment.

The number of speech-language pathologists and audiologists in private practice will rise due to the increasing use of contract services by hospitals, schools, and nursing homes. In addition to job openings stemming from employment growth, some openings for speech-language pathologists and audiologists will arise from the need to replace those who leave the occupation.

Earnings

Median annual earnings of speech-language pathologists and audiologists were $43,080 in 1998. The middle 50 percent earned between $34,580 and $55,260 a year. The lowest 10 percent earned less than $27,460 and the highest 10 percent earned more than $80,720 a year. Median annual earnings in the industries employing the largest number of speech-language pathologists and audiologists in 1997 were as follows:

Hospitals $44,800

Offices of other health care practitioners 44,500

Elementary and secondary schools 38,400

According to a 1999 survey by the American Speech-Language-Hearing Association, the median annual salary for full-time certified speech-language pathologists or audiologists who worked 11 or 12 months annually was $44,000. For those who worked 9 or 10 months annually, median annual salaries for speech-language pathologists were $40,000; for audiologists, $42,000.

Related Occupations

Speech-language pathologists specialize in the prevention, diagnosis, and treatment of speech and language problems. Workers in related occupations include occupational therapists, optometrists, physical therapists, psychologists, recreational therapists, and rehabilitation counselors.

Audiologists specialize in the prevention, diagnosis, and treatment of hearing problems. Workers in related occupations include neurologists, neonatologists, acoustical engineers, industrial hygienists, and other rehabilitation professionals.

Sources of Additional Information

State licensing boards can provide information on licensure requirements. State departments of education can supply information on certification requirements for those who wish to work in public schools.

General information on careers in speech-language pathology and audiology is available from:

- American Speech-Language-Hearing Association, 10801 Rockville Pike, Rockville, MD 20852. Internet: http://www.asha.org

Information on a career in audiology is also available from:

- American Academy of Audiology, 8201 Greensboro Dr., Suite 300, McLean, VA 22102.

Surgical Technologists

(O*NET 32928)

Significant Points

- Most educational programs for surgical technologists last approximately one year and result in a certificate.

- Increased demand for surgical technologists is expected as the number of surgical procedures grows.

Nature of the Work

Surgical technologists, also called surgical or operating room technicians, assist in operations under the supervision of surgeons, registered nurses, or other surgical personnel. Before an operation, surgical technologists help set up the operating room with surgical instruments and equipment, sterile linens, and sterile solutions. They assemble, adjust, and check nonsterile equipment to ensure it is working properly. Technologists also prepare patients for surgery by washing, shaving, and disinfecting incision sites. They transport patients to the operating room, help position them on the operating table, and cover them with sterile surgical "drapes." Technologists also observe patients' vital signs, check charts, and help the surgical team scrub and put on gloves, gowns, and masks.

During surgery, technologists pass instruments and other sterile supplies to surgeons and surgeon assistants. They may hold retractors, cut sutures, and help count sponges, needles, supplies, and instruments. Surgical technologists help prepare, care for, and dispose of specimens taken for laboratory analysis and may help apply dressings. Some operate sterilizers, lights, or suction machines, and help operate diagnostic equipment. Technologists may also maintain supplies of fluids, such as plasma and blood.

After an operation, surgical technologists may help transfer patients to the recovery room and clean and restock the operating room.

Working Conditions

Surgical technologists work in clean, well-lighted, cool environments. They must stand for long periods and remain alert during operations. At times they may be exposed to communicable diseases and unpleasant sights, odors, and materials.

Most surgical technologists work a regular 40-hour week, although they may be on call or work nights, weekends, and holidays on a rotating basis.

Employment

Surgical technologists held about 54,000 jobs in 1998. Most are employed by hospitals, mainly in operating and delivery rooms. Others are employed in clinics and surgical centers and in the offices of physicians and dentists who perform outpatient surgery. A few, known as private scrubs, are employed directly by surgeons who have special surgical teams like those for liver transplants.

Training, Other Qualifications, and Advancement

Surgical technologists receive their training in formal programs offered by community and junior colleges, vocational schools, universities, hospitals, and the military. In 1998, the Commission on Accreditation of Allied Health Education Programs (CAAHEP) recognized 165 accredited programs. High school graduation normally is required for admission. Programs last 9 to 24 months and lead to a certificate, diploma, or associate degree. Shorter programs are designed for students who are already licensed practical nurses or military personnel with the appropriate training.

Programs provide classroom education and supervised clinical experience. Students take courses in anatomy, physiology, microbiology, pharmacology, professional ethics, and medical terminology. Other studies cover the care and safety of patients during surgery, aseptic techniques, and surgical procedures. Students also learn to sterilize instruments; prevent and control infection; and handle special drugs, solutions, supplies, and equipment.

Technologists may obtain voluntary professional certification from the Liaison Council on Certification for the Surgical Technologist by graduating from a formal program and passing a national certification examination. They may then use the designation Certified Surgical Technologist, or CST. Continuing education or reexamination is required to maintain certification, which must be renewed every six years. Graduation from a CAAHEP-accredited program will be a prerequisite for certification by March 2000. Most employers prefer to hire certified technologists.

Surgical technologists need manual dexterity to handle instruments quickly. They also must be conscientious, orderly, and emotionally stable to handle the demands of the operating room environment. Technologists must respond quickly and know procedures well to have instruments ready for surgeons without having to be told. They are expected to keep abreast of new developments in the field. Recommended high school courses include health, biology, chemistry, and mathematics.

Technologists advance by specializing in a particular area of surgery, such as neurosurgery or open heart surgery. They may also work as circulating technologists. A circulating technologist is the "unsterile" member of the surgical team who prepares patients; helps with anesthesia; gets, opens, and holds packages for the "sterile" persons during the procedure; interviews the patient before surgery; keeps a written account of the surgical procedure; and answers the surgeon's questions about the patient during the surgery. With additional training, some technologists advance to first assistants, who help with retracting, sponging, suturing, cauterizing bleeders, and closing and treating wounds. Some surgical technologists manage central supply departments in hospitals or take positions with insurance companies, sterile supply services, and operating equipment firms.

Job Outlook

Employment of surgical technologists is expected to grow much faster than the average for all occupations through the year 2008 as the volume of surgery increases. The number of surgical procedures is expected to rise as the population grows and ages. As the "baby boom" generation enters retirement age, the over 50 population will account for a larger portion of the general population. Older people require more surgical procedures. Technological advances, such as fiber optics and laser technology, will also permit new surgical procedures to be performed.

Hospitals will continue to be the primary employer of surgical technologists, although much faster employment growth is expected in offices and clinics of physicians, including ambulatory surgical centers.

Earnings

Median annual earnings of surgical technologists were $25,780 in 1998. The middle 50 percent earned between $22,040 and $30,230 a year. The lowest 10 percent earned less than $18,930, and the highest 10 percent earned more than $35,020 a year.

Related Occupations

Other health occupations requiring approximately one year of training after high school include licensed practical nurses, certified respiratory therapists, medical laboratory assistants, medical assistants, dental assistants, optometric assistants, and physical therapy aides.

Sources of Additional Information

For additional information on a career as a surgical technologist and a list of CAAHEP-accredited programs, contact:

- Association of Surgical Technologists, 7108-C South Alton Way, Englewood, CO 80112. Internet: http://www.ast.org

For information on certification, contact:

- Liaison Council on Certification for the Surgical Technologist, 7790 East Arapahoe Rd., Suite 240, Englewood, CO 80112-1274.

Teacher Assistants

(O*NET 31521 and 53905)

Significant Points

- Almost half of all teacher assistants work part time.
- Educational requirements range from a high school diploma to some college training.
- Employment is expected to grow faster than average due to the need to assist and monitor students, to provide teachers with clerical assistance, and to help teachers meet the education needs of a growing special education population.

Nature of the Work

Teacher assistants, also called teacher aides or instructional aides, provide instructional and clerical support for classroom teachers, allowing teachers more time for lesson planning and teaching. Teacher assistants tutor and assist children in learning class material using the teacher's lesson plans, providing students with individualized attention. Teacher assistants also supervise students in the cafeteria, schoolyard, school discipline center, or on field trips. They record grades, set up equipment, and help prepare materials for instruction.

Large school districts hire some teacher assistants to perform exclusively non-instructional or clerical tasks, such as monitoring nonacademic settings. Playground and lunchroom attendants are examples of such assistants. Most teacher assistants, however, perform a combination of instructional and clerical duties. They generally instruct children, under the direction and guidance of teachers. They work with students individually or in small groups—listening while students read, reviewing or reinforcing class work, or helping them find information for reports. At the secondary school level, teacher assistants often specialize in a certain subject, such as math or science. Teacher assistants often take charge of special projects and prepare equipment or exhibits, such as for a science demonstration. Some assistants work in computer laboratories, helping students using computers and educational software programs.

In addition to instructing, assisting, and supervising students, teacher assistants grade tests and papers, check homework, keep health and attendance records, type, file, and duplicate materials. They also stock supplies, operate audiovisual equipment, and keep classroom equipment in order.

Many teacher assistants work extensively with special education students. Schools are becoming more inclusive, integrating special education students into general education classrooms. As a result, teacher assistants in general education and special education classrooms increasingly assist students with disabilities. Teacher assistants attend to a disabled student's physical needs, including feeding, teaching good grooming habits, or assisting students riding the school bus. They also provide personal attention to students with other special needs, such as those whose families live in poverty, or who speak English as a second language, or who need remedial education. Teacher assistants help assess a student's progress by observing performance and recording relevant data.

Working Conditions

Almost half of all teacher assistants work part time. Most assistants who provide educational instruction work the traditional 9- to 10-month school year, usually in a classroom setting. Teacher assistants work outdoors supervising recess when weather allows, and they spend much of their time standing, walking, or kneeling.

Seeing students develop and gain appreciation of the joy of learning can be very rewarding. However, working closely with students can be both physically and emotionally tiring. Teacher assistants who work with special education students often perform more strenuous tasks, including lifting, as they help students with their daily routine. Those who perform clerical work may tire of administrative duties, such as copying materials or typing.

Employment

Teacher assistants held about 1.2 million jobs in 1998. About 86 percent worked in public and private education, mostly in the elementary grades. A significant number assisted special education teachers in working with disabled children. Most of the others worked in child day care centers and religious organizations.

Training, Other Qualifications, and Advancement

Educational requirements for teacher assistants range from a high school diploma to some college training. Teacher assistants with instructional responsibilities usually require more training than those who do not perform teaching tasks. Increasingly, employers prefer teacher assistants who have some college training. Some teacher assistants are aspiring teachers who are working towards their degrees while gaining experience. Many schools require previous experience in working with children. Schools often require a valid driver's license and perform a background check on applicants.

A number of two-year and community colleges offer associate degree programs that prepare graduates to work as teacher assistants. However, most teacher assistants receive on-the-job training. Those who tutor and review lessons with students must have a thorough understanding of class materials and instructional methods and should be familiar with the organization and operation of a school. Teacher assistants also must know how to operate audiovisual equipment, keep records, and prepare instructional materials, as well as have adequate computer skills.

Teacher assistants should enjoy working with children from a wide range of cultural backgrounds and be able to handle classroom situations with fairness and patience. Teacher assistants also must demonstrate initiative and a willingness to follow a teacher's directions. They must have good writing skills and be able to communicate effectively with students and teachers. Teacher assistants who speak a second language, especially Spanish, are in great demand to communicate with growing numbers of students and parents whose primary language is not English.

About half of all States have established guidelines or minimum educational standards for the hiring and training of teacher assistants, and an increasing number of States are in the process of implementing them. Although requirements vary by State, most require an individual to have at least a high school diploma or general equivalency degree (G.E.D.) or some college training. In States that have not established guidelines or minimum educational standards, local school districts determine hiring requirements.

Advancement for teacher assistants, usually in the form of higher earnings or increased responsibility, comes primarily with experience or additional education. Some school districts provide time away from the job or tuition reimbursement so that teacher assistants can earn their bachelor's degrees and pursue licensed teaching positions. In return for tuition reimbursement, assistants are often required to teach a certain length of time for the school district.

Job Outlook

Employment of teacher assistants is expected to grow faster than the average for all occupations through 2008. Student enrollments are expected to rise, spurring demand for teacher assistants to assist and monitor students and provide teachers with clerical assistance. Teacher assistants will also be required to help teachers meet the educational needs of a growing special education population, particularly as these students are increasingly assimilated into general education classrooms. Education reform and the rising number of students who speak English as a second language will continue to contribute to the demand for teacher assistants. In addition to jobs stemming from employment growth, numerous job openings will arise as workers transfer to other occupations, leave the labor force to assume family responsibilities, return to school, or leave for other reasons—characteristic of occupations that require limited formal education and offer relatively low pay.

The number and size of special education programs are growing in response to increasing enrollments of students with disabilities. Federal legislation mandates appropriate education for all children and emphasizes placing disabled children into regular school settings when possible. Children with special needs require much personal attention, and special education teachers, as well as general education teachers with special education students, rely heavily on teacher assistants. At the secondary school level, teacher assistants work with special education students as job coaches, and help students make the transition from school to work.

School reforms that call for more individual instruction should further enhance employment opportunities for teacher assistants. Schools are hiring more teacher assistants to provide students with the personal instruction and remedial education they need.

Teacher assistant employment is sensitive to changes in State and local expenditures for education. Pressures on education budgets are greater in some States and localities than in others. A number of teacher assistant positions, such as those in Head Start classrooms, are financed through Federal Government programs, which are affected by budget constraints.

Earnings

Median hourly earnings of teacher assistants in 1998 were $7.61. The middle 50 percent earned between $6.08 and $9.51. The lowest 10 percent earned less than $5.61, and the highest 10 percent earned more than $11.27. Median hourly earnings in the industries employing the largest numbers of teacher assistants in 1997 were as follows:

Elementary and secondary schools	$7.30
Colleges and universities	7.10
Individual and family services	7.10
Child day care services	6.50
Local government, except education and hospitals	6.00

About 3 out of 10 teacher aides belonged to unions in 1998—mainly the American Federation of Teachers and the National Education Association—which bargain with school systems over wages, hours, and the terms and conditions of employment.

Related Occupations

Teacher assistants who instruct children have duties similar to those of preschool, elementary, and secondary school teachers and school librarians. However, teacher assistants do not have the same level of responsibility or training. The support activities of teacher assistants and their educational backgrounds are similar to those of child-care workers, family day care providers, library technicians, and library assistants.

Sources of Additional Information

For information on teacher assistants, including training and certification, contact:

● American Federation of Teachers, Paraprofessional and School Related Personnel Division, 555 New Jersey Ave. NW., Washington, DC 20001. Internet: http://www.aft.org/psrp

For information on a career as a teacher assistant, contact:

● National Resource Center for Paraprofessionals in Education and Related Services, 365 5th Ave., New York, NY 10016. Internet: http://web.gc.cuny.edu/dept/case/nrcp

School superintendents and State departments of education can provide details about employment requirements.

Veterinarians

(O*NET 32114A, 32114B, and 32114C)

Significant Points

● Graduation from an accredited college of veterinary medicine and a license to practice are required.

● Competition for admission to veterinary school is keen.

Nature of the Work

Veterinarians play a major role in the health care of pets, livestock, and zoo, sporting, and laboratory animals. Some veterinarians use their skills to protect humans against diseases carried by animals and conduct clinical research on human and animal health problems. Others work in basic research, broadening the scope of fundamental theoretical knowledge, and in applied research, developing new ways to use knowledge.

Most veterinarians perform clinical work in private practices. More than one-half of these veterinarians predominately, or exclusively, treat small animals. Small animal practitioners usually care for companion animals, such as dogs and cats, but also treat birds, reptiles, rabbits, and other animals that can be kept as pets. Some veterinarians work in mixed animal practices where they see pigs, goats, sheep, and some nondomestic animals in addition to companion animals. Veterinarians in clinical practice diagnose animal health problems; vaccinate against diseases, such as distemper and rabies; medicate animals suffering from infections or illnesses; treat and dress wounds; set fractures; perform surgery; and advise owners about animal feeding, behavior, and breeding.

A small number of private practice veterinarians work exclusively with large animals, focusing mostly on horses or cows, but may also care for various kinds of food animals. These veterinarians usually drive to farms or ranches to provide veterinary services for herds or individual animals. Much of this work involves preventive care to maintain the health of the food animals. These veterinarians test for and vaccinate against diseases and consult with farm or ranch owners and managers on animal production, feeding, and housing issues. They also treat and dress wounds, set fractures, and perform surgery—including cesarean sections on birthing animals. Veterinarians also euthanize animals when necessary. Other veterinarians care for zoo, aquarium, or laboratory animals.

Veterinarians who treat animals use medical equipment, such as stethoscopes; surgical instruments; and diagnostic equipment, such as radiographic and ultrasound equipment. Veterinarians working in research use a full range of sophisticated laboratory equipment.

Veterinarians can contribute to human as well as animal health. A number of veterinarians work with physicians and scientists as they research ways to prevent and treat human health problems, such as cancer, AIDS, and alcohol and drug abuse. Some determine the effects of drug therapies, antibiotics, or new surgical techniques by testing them on animals.

Some veterinarians are involved in food safety at various levels. Veterinarians who are livestock inspectors check animals for transmissible diseases, advise owners on treatment, and may quarantine animals. Veterinarians who are meat, poultry, or egg product inspectors examine slaughtering and processing plants, check live animals and carcasses for disease, and enforce government regulations regarding food purity and sanitation.

Working Conditions

Veterinarians often work long hours, with one-third of full-time workers spending 50 or more hours on the job. Those in group practices may take turns being on call for evening, night, or weekend work; and solo practitioners can work extended and weekend hours, responding to emergencies or squeezing in unexpected appointments.

Veterinarians in large animal practice also spend time driving between their office and farms or ranches. They work outdoors in all kinds of weather and have to treat animals or perform surgery under less-than-sanitary conditions. When working with animals that are frightened or in pain, veterinarians risk being bitten, kicked, or scratched.

Veterinarians working in non-clinical areas, such as public health and research, have working conditions similar to those of other professionals in those lines of work. In these cases, veterinarians enjoy clean, well-lit offices or laboratories and spend much of their time dealing with people rather than animals.

Employment

Veterinarians held about 57,000 jobs in 1998. About 30 percent were self-employed in solo or group practices. Most others were employees of another veterinary practice. The Federal government employed about 1,900 civilian veterinarians, chiefly in the U.S. Department of Agriculture, and about 400 military veterinarians in the U.S. Army and U.S. Air Force. Other employers of veterinarians are State and local governments, colleges of veterinary medicine, medical schools, research laboratories, animal food companies, and pharmaceutical companies. A few veterinarians work for zoos; but most veterinarians caring for zoo animals are private practitioners who contract with zoos to provide services, usually on a part-time basis.

Training, Other Qualifications, and Advancement

Prospective veterinarians must graduate from a four-year program at an accredited college of veterinary medicine with a Doctor of Veterinary Medicine (D.V.M. or V.M.D.) degree and obtain a license to practice. There are 27 colleges in 26 States that meet accreditation standards set by the Council on Education of the American Veterinary Medical Association. The prerequisites for admission vary by veterinary medical college. Many of these colleges do not require a bachelor's degree for entrance; but all require a significant

number of credit hours—ranging from 45 to 90 semester hours—at the undergraduate level. However, most of the students admitted have completed an undergraduate program.

Preveterinary courses emphasize the sciences; and veterinary medical colleges typically require classes in organic and inorganic chemistry, physics, biochemistry, general biology, animal biology, animal nutrition, genetics, vertebrate embryology, cellular biology, microbiology, zoology, and systemic physiology. Some programs require calculus; some require only statistics, college algebra and trigonometry, or precalculus; and others require no math at all. Most veterinary medical colleges also require core courses, including some in English or literature, the social sciences, and the humanities.

Most veterinary medical colleges will only consider applicants who have a minimum grade point average (GPA). The required GPA varies by school, from a low of 2.5 to a high of 3.2, based on a maximum GPA of 4.0. However, the average GPA of candidates at most schools is higher than these minimums. Those who receive offers of admission usually have a GPA of 3.0 or better.

In addition to satisfying preveterinary course requirements, applicants must also submit test scores from the Graduate Record Examination (GRE), the Veterinary College Admission Test (VCAT), or the Medical College Admission Test (MCAT), depending on the preference of each college.

Additionally, in the admissions process, veterinary medical colleges weigh heavily a candidate's veterinary and animal experience. Formal experience, such as work with veterinarians or scientists in clinics, agribusiness, research, or in some area of health science, is particularly advantageous. Less formal experience, such as working with animals on a farm or ranch or at a stable or animal shelter, is also helpful. Students must demonstrate ambition and an eagerness to work with animals.

Competition for admission to veterinary school is keen. The number of accredited veterinary colleges has remained at 27 since 1983, whereas the number of applicants has risen. About 1 in 3 applicants was accepted in 1998. Most veterinary medical colleges are public, State-supported institutions and reserve the majority of their openings for in-state residents. Twenty-one States that do not have a veterinary medical college agree to pay a fee or subsidy to help cover the cost of veterinary education for a limited number of their residents at one or more out-of-state colleges. Nonresident students who are admitted under such a contract may have to pay out-of-state tuition, or they may have to repay their State of residency all, or part, of the subsidy provided to the contracting college. Residents of the remaining three States (Connecticut, Maine, and Vermont) and the District of Columbia may apply to any of the 27 veterinary medical colleges as an *at-large* applicant. The number of positions available to at-large applicants is very limited at most schools, making admission difficult.

While in veterinary medical college, students receive additional academic instruction in the basic sciences for the first two years. Later in the program, students are exposed to clinical procedures, such as diagnosing and treating animal diseases and performing surgery. They also do laboratory work in anatomy, biochemistry, medicine, and other scientific subjects. At most veterinary medical colleges, students who plan a career in research can earn both a D.V.M degree and a Doctor of Philosophy (Ph.D.) degree at the same time.

Veterinary graduates who plan to work with specific types of animals or specialize in a clinical area, such as pathology, surgery, radiology, or laboratory animal medicine, usually complete a one-year internship. Interns receive a small salary but usually find that their internship experience leads to a higher beginning salary relative to other starting veterinarians. Veterinarians who seek board certification in a specialty must also complete a two- to three-year residency program that provides intensive training in specialties, such as internal medicine, oncology, radiology, surgery, dermatology, anesthesiology, neurology, cardiology, ophthalmology, and exotic small animal medicine.

All States and the District of Columbia require that veterinarians be licensed before they can practice. The only exemptions are for veterinarians working for some Federal agencies and some State governments. Licensing is controlled by the States and is not strictly uniform, although all States require successful completion of the D.V.M. degree—or equivalent education—and passage of a national board examination. The Educational Commission for Foreign Veterinary Graduates (ECFVG) grants certification to individuals trained outside the U.S. who demonstrate that they meet specified requirements for the English language and clinical proficiency. ECFVG certification fulfills the educational requirement for licensure in all States except Nebraska. Applicants for licensure satisfy the examination requirement by passing the North American Veterinary Licensing Exam (NAVLE), which replaces the National Board Examination (NBE) and the Clinical Competency Test (CCT) as of April 2000. The new NAVLE, administered on computer, takes one day to complete and consists of 360 multiple-choice questions, covering all aspects of veterinary medicine. The NAVLE also includes visual materials designed to test diagnostic skills.

The majority of States also require candidates to pass a State jurisprudence examination covering State laws and regulations. Some States also do additional testing on clinical competency. There are few reciprocal agreements between States, making it difficult for a veterinarian to practice in a different State without first taking another State examination.

Thirty-nine States have continuing education requirements for licensed veterinarians. Requirements differ by State and may involve attending a class or otherwise demonstrating knowledge of recent medical and veterinary advances.

Most veterinarians begin as employees or partners in established practices. Despite the substantial financial investment in equipment, office space, and staff, many veterinarians with experience set up their own practices or purchase established ones.

Newly trained veterinarians can become U.S. government meat and poultry inspectors, disease-control workers, epidemiologists, research assistants, or commissioned officers in the U.S. Public Health Service, U.S. Army, or U.S. Air Force. A State license may be required.

Prospective veterinarians must have good manual dexterity. They should have an affinity for animals and the ability to get along with animal owners. Additionally, they should be able to quickly make decisions in emergencies.

Job Outlook

Employment of veterinarians is expected to grow faster than the average for all occupations through the year 2008. Job openings stemming from the need to replace veterinarians who retire or otherwise leave the labor force will be almost as numerous as new jobs resulting from employment growth over the 1998-2008 period.

Most veterinarians practice in animal hospitals or clinics and care primarily for companion animals. The number of pets is expected to increase more slowly during the projection period than in the previous decade and may moderate growth in the demand for veterinarians who specialize in small animals. One reason for this is that the large baby-boom generation is aging and will probably acquire fewer dogs and cats than earlier. However, as non-necessity income generally increases with age, those who own pets may be more inclined to seek veterinary services. In addition, pet owners are becoming more aware of the availability of advanced care and may increasingly take advantage of nontraditional veterinary services, such as preventive dental care, and may more willingly pay for intensive care than in the past. Finally, new technologies and medical advancements should permit veterinarians to offer better care to animals. Veterinarians who enter small animal practice will probably face competition. Large numbers of new graduates continue to be attracted to small animal medicine because they prefer to deal with pets and to live and work near highly populated areas. However, an oversupply does not necessarily limit the ability of veterinarians to find employment or to set up and maintain a practice in a particular area. Such an oversupply could result in veterinarians taking positions requiring much evening or weekend work to accommodate the extended hours of operation that many practices are offering. Others could take salaried positions in retail stores offering limited veterinary services. Most self-employed veterinarians will probably have to work hard and long to build a sufficient clientele.

The number of jobs for large animal veterinarians is expected to grow slowly, because productivity gains in the agricultural production industry mean demand for fewer veterinarians than before to treat food animals. Nevertheless, job prospects may be better for veterinarians who specialize in farm animals than for small animal practitioners, because most veterinary medical college graduates do not have the desire to work in rural or isolated areas.

Continued support for public health and food safety, disease control programs, and biomedical research on human health problems will contribute to the demand for veterinarians, although such positions are few in number. Also, anticipated budget tightening in the Federal government may lead to low funding levels for some programs, limiting job growth. Veterinarians with training in public health and epidemiology should have the best opportunities for a career in the Federal government.

Earnings

Median annual earnings of veterinarians were $50,950 in 1998. The middle 50 percent earned between $39,580 and $78,670. The lowest 10 percent earned less than $31,320, and the highest 10 percent earned more than $106,370.

Average starting salaries of 1998 veterinary medical college graduates varied by type of practice, as indicated by table 1.

TABLE 1

Average starting salaries of veterinary medical college graduates, 1998

Type of practice

Large animal, exclusive	$37,200
Large animal, predominant	37,500
Mixed animal	35,900
Small animal, exclusive	37,600
Small animal, predominant	36,300
Equine	29,200

SOURCE: American Veterinary Medical Association

New veterinary medical college graduates who enter the Federal government usually start at $37,700. Beginning salaries were slightly higher in selected areas where the prevailing local pay level was higher. The average annual salary for veterinarians in the Federal government in nonsupervisory, supervisory, and managerial positions was $61,600 in 1999.

Related Occupations

Veterinarians prevent, diagnose, and treat diseases, disorders, and injuries in animals. Those who do similar work for humans include chiropractors, dentists, optometrists, physicians, and podiatrists. Veterinarians have extensive training in physical and life sciences, and some do scientific and medical research, closely paralleling occupations such as biological, medical, and animal scientists.

Animal trainers, animal breeders, and veterinary technicians work extensively with animals. Like veterinarians, they must have patience and feel comfortable with animals. However, the level of training required for these occupations is substantially less than that needed by veterinarians.

Sources of Additional Information

For more information on careers in veterinary medicine and a list of U.S. schools and colleges of veterinary medicine, send a letter-size, self-addressed, stamped envelope to:

- American Veterinary Medical Association, 1931 N. Meacham Rd., Suite 100, Schaumburg, IL 60173-4360.

For information on scholarships, grants, and loans, contact the financial aid officer at the veterinary schools to which you wish to apply.

For information on veterinary education, write to:

- Association of American Veterinary Medical Colleges, 1101 Vermont Ave. NW., Suite 710, Washington, DC 20005.

For information on the Federal agencies that employ veterinarians and a list of addresses for each agency, write to:

- National Association of Federal Veterinarians, 1101 Vermont Ave. NW., Suite 710, Washington, DC 20005.

Veterinary Assistants and Nonfarm Animal Caretakers

(O*NET 34058G, 79017A, 79017B, 79017C, 79017D, and 79806)

Significant Points

- Animal lovers get satisfaction in this occupation, but aspects of the work can be unpleasant and physically and emotionally demanding.

- Most animal caretakers are trained on the job, but advancement depends on experience, formal training, and continuing education.

Nature of the Work

Many people like animals. But, as pet owners can attest, taking care of them is hard work. Animal caretakers, sometimes called animal attendants or animal keepers, feed, water, groom, bathe, and exercise animals and clean, disinfect, and repair their cages. They also play with the animals, provide companionship, and observe behavioral changes that could indicate illness or injury.

Boarding kennels, animal shelters, veterinary hospitals and clinics, stables, laboratories, aquariums, and zoological parks all house animals and employ caretakers. Job titles and duties vary by employment setting.

Kennel staff usually care for small companion animals like dogs and cats while their owners are working or traveling out of town. Beginning attendants perform basic tasks, such as cleaning cages and dog runs, filling food and water dishes, and exercising animals. Experienced attendants may provide basic animal health care, as well as bathe animals, trim nails, and attend to other grooming needs. Caretakers who work in kennels may also sell pet food and supplies, assist in obedience training, help with breeding, or prepare animals for shipping.

Animal caretakers who specialize in grooming, or maintaining a pet's—usually a dog's or cat's—appearance are called *groomers*. Some groomers work in kennels, veterinary clinics, animal shelters, or pet supply stores. Others operate their own grooming business. Groomers answer telephones, schedule appointments, discuss with clients their pets' grooming needs, and collect information on the pet's disposition and its veterinarian. Groomers are often the first to notice a medical problem, such as an ear or skin infection, that requires veterinary care.

Grooming the pet involves several steps: An initial brush-out is followed by a first clipping of hair or fur using electric clippers, combs, and grooming shears; the groomer then cuts the nails, cleans the ears, bathes, and blow-dries the animal, and ends with a final clipping and styling.

Animal caretakers in animal shelters perform a variety of duties and work with a wide variety of animals. In addition to attending to the basic needs of the animals, caretakers must also keep records of the animals received and discharged and any tests or treatments done. Some vaccinate newly admitted animals under the direction of a veterinarian or veterinary technician, and euthanize (painlessly put to death) seriously ill, severely injured, or unwanted animals. Caretakers in animal shelters also interact with the public, answering telephone inquiries, screening applicants for animal adoption, or educating visitors on neutering and other animal health issues.

Animal caretakers in stables are called *grooms*. They saddle and unsaddle horses, give them rubdowns, and walk them through a cool-off after a ride. They also feed, groom, and exercise the horses, clean out stalls and replenish bedding, polish saddles, clean and organize the tack (harness, saddle, and bridle) room, and store supplies and feed. Experienced grooms may help train horses.

Animal caretakers in animal hospitals or clinics are called *veterinary assistants*. Veterinarians rely on caretakers to keep a constant eye on the condition of animals under their charge. Caretakers watch as animals recover from surgery, check whether dressings are still on correctly, observe the animals' overall attitude, and notify a doctor if anything seems out of the ordinary. Caretakers clean constantly to maintain sanitary conditions in the hospital.

Laboratory animal caretakers work in research facilities and assist with the care of a wide variety of animals, including mice, rats, sheep, pigs, cattle, dogs, cats, monkeys, birds, fish, and frogs. They feed and water the animals, clean cages and change bedding, and observe the animals for signs of illness, disease, or injury. They may administer medications orally or topically according to instructions; prepare samples for laboratory examination; sterilize laboratory equipment; and record information regarding genealogy, diet, weight, medications, food intake, and clinical signs of pain and distress. They work with scientists, physicians, veterinary technicians, veterinarians, and laboratory technicians.

In zoos, caretakers called *keepers* prepare the diets and clean the enclosures of animals, and sometimes assist in raising them when they are very young. They watch for any signs of illness or injury, monitor eating patterns or any changes in behavior, and record their observations. Keepers also may answer questions and ensure that the visiting public behaves responsibly toward the exhibited animals. Depending on the zoo, keepers may be assigned to work with a broad group of animals such as mammals, birds, or reptiles, or they may work with a limited collection of animals such as primates, large cats, or small mammals.

Working Conditions

People who love animals get satisfaction from working with and helping them. However, some of the work may be unpleasant, as well as physically and emotionally demanding, and sometimes dangerous. Caretakers have to clean animal cages and lift, hold, or restrain animals, risking exposure to bites or scratches. Their work often involves kneeling, crawling, repeated bending, and lifting heavy supplies like bales of hay or bags of feed. Animal caretakers must take precautions when treating animals with germicides or insecticides. The work setting can be noisy.

Animal caretakers who witness abused animals or who assist in the euthanizing of unwanted, aged, or hopelessly injured animals may experience emotional stress. Those working for private humane societies and municipal animal shelters often deal with the public, some of whom might react with hostility to any implication that the owners are neglecting or abusing their pets. Such workers must maintain a calm and professional demeanor while they enforce the laws regarding animal care.

Caretakers may work outdoors in all kinds of weather. Hours are irregular: Animals have to be fed every day, so caretakers often work weekend and holiday shifts. In some animal hospitals, research facilities, and animal shelters, an attendant is on duty 24 hours a day, which means night shifts. Most full-time caretakers work about 40 hours a week; some work 50 hours a week or more. Caretakers of show and sports animals travel to competitions.

Employment

Animal caretakers and veterinary assistants held about 181,000 jobs in 1998. About 45,000 of the total worked as veterinary assistants in veterinary services. The remainder worked primarily in boarding kennels, but also in animal shelters, stables, grooming shops, zoos, and local, State, and Federal agencies. In 1998, more than 1 out of every 4 animal caretakers was self-employed, and more than 1 in 3 worked part time.

Training, Other Qualifications, and Advancement

Most animal caretakers are trained on the job. Employers generally prefer to hire people with some experience with animals. Some training programs are available for specific types of animal caretakers, but formal training is usually not necessary for entry-level positions.

Most pet groomers learn their trade by completing an informal apprenticeship, usually lasting 6 to 10 weeks, under the guidance of an experienced groomer. Prospective groomers may also attend one of the 50 State-licensed grooming schools throughout the country, with programs varying in length from 4 to 18 weeks. The National Dog Groomers Association of America certifies groomers who pass a written examination, with a separate part testing practical skills. Beginning groomers often start by taking on one duty, such as bathing and drying the pet. They eventually assume responsibility for the entire grooming process, from the initial brush-out to the final clipping. Groomers who work in large retail establishments or kennels may, with experience, move into supervisory or managerial positions. Experienced groomers often choose to open their own shops.

Beginning animal caretakers in kennels learn on the job and usually start by cleaning cages and feeding and watering animals. Kennel caretakers may be promoted to kennel supervisor, assistant manager, and manager, and those with enough capital and experience may open up their own kennels. The American Boarding Kennels Association (ABKA) offers a three-stage, home-study program for individuals interested in pet care. The first two study programs address basic and advanced principles of animal care, while the third program focuses on in-depth animal care and good business procedures. Those who complete the third program and pass oral and written examinations administered by the ABKA become Certified Kennel Operators (CKO).

There are no formal educational requirements for animal caretakers in veterinary facilities. They are trained on the job, usually under the guidance of a veterinarian or veterinary technician. They start by performing tasks related to basic animal health care, such as keeping cages and examination areas sanitary. They also help veterinarians prepare for surgery, sterilize surgical equipment, observe recovering animals, and give medications and basic medical treatment under the directions of a veterinarian or veterinary technician. Highly motivated veterinary assistants may become veterinary technicians, with additional training from one of approximately 70 accredited veterinary technology programs.

Employers of entry-level laboratory animal caretakers generally require a high school diploma or General Educational Development (GED) test. A few colleges and vocational schools offer programs in laboratory animal science, which provide training for technician positions, but such training is not strictly necessary. New animal caretakers working in laboratories begin by providing basic care to laboratory animals. With additional training, experience, and certification, they may advance to more technical positions in laboratory animal care, such as research assistant, mid-level technician, or senior-level technologist.

The American Association for Laboratory Animal Science (AALAS) offers certification for three levels of technician competence. Those who wish to become certified as Assistant Laboratory Animal Technicians (ALAT) must satisfy education and experience requirements before taking an examination administered by AALAS. Laboratory Animal Technician and Laboratory Animal Technologist are the second and third levels of certification of the AALAS.

Some zoological parks may require their caretakers to have a bachelor's degree in biology, animal science, or a related field. Most require experience with animals, preferably as a volunteer or paid keeper in a zoo. Zoo keepers may advance to senior keeper, assistant head keeper, head keeper, and assistant curator, but few openings occur, especially for the higher level positions.

Animal caretakers in animal shelters are not required to have any specialized training, but training programs and workshops are increasingly available through the Humane Society of the United States, the American Humane Association, and the National Animal Control Association. Workshop topics include cruelty investigations, appropriate methods of euthanasia for shelter animals, and techniques for preventing problems with wildlife. With experience and additional training, caretakers in animal shelters may become adoption coordinators, animal control officers, emergency rescue drivers, assistant shelter managers, or shelter directors.

Job Outlook

Employment opportunities for animal caretakers and veterinary assistants generally are expected to be good. The outlook for caretakers in zoos, however, is not favorable; jobseekers will face keen competition because of expected slow growth in zoo capacity, low turnover, and the fact that the occupation attracts many candidates.

Employment is expected to grow faster than the average through 2008. The growth of the pet population, which drives employment of animal caretakers in kennels, grooming shops, animal shelters, and veterinary clinics and hospitals, is expected to slow. Nevertheless, pets remain popular and pet owners—including a large number of baby boomers whose disposable income is expected to increase as they age—may increasingly take advantage of grooming services, daily and overnight boarding services, and veterinary services, spurring employment growth for animal caretakers and veterinary assistants. Demand for animal caretakers in animal shelters is expected to remain steady. Communities are increasingly recognizing the connection between animal abuse and abuse toward humans and should continue to commit funds to animal shelters, many of which are working hand-in-hand with social service agencies and law enforcement teams.

Despite growth in demand for animal caretakers, the overwhelming majority of jobs will result from the need to replace workers leaving the field. Many animal caretaker jobs that require little or no training have work schedules that tend to be flexible; therefore, it is ideal for people seeking their first job and for students and others looking for temporary or part-time work. Because turnover is quite high, largely due to the hard physical labor, the overall availability of jobs should be very good. Much of the work of animal caretakers is seasonal, particularly during vacation periods.

Earnings

Median hourly earnings of nonfarm animal caretakers were $7.12 in 1998. The middle 50 percent earned between $5.92 and $8.82. The bottom 10 percent earned less than $5.54, and the top 10 percent earned more than $11.39. Median hourly earnings in the industries employing the largest numbers of nonfarm animal caretakers in 1997 are shown below:

Local government, except education and hospitals	$10.40
Commercial sports	7.60
Animal services, except veterinary	7.10
Membership organizations, not elsewhere classified	6.60
Veterinary services	6.20

Median hourly earnings of veterinary assistants were $7.79 in 1998. The middle 50 percent earned between $6.55 and $9.23. The lowest 10 percent earned less than $5.79, and the top 10 percent earned more than $10.80.

Related Occupations

Others who work extensively with animals include animal breeders, animal trainers, livestock farm workers, ranchers, veterinarians, veterinary technicians and technologists, and wildlife biologists and zoologists.

Sources of Additional Information

For more information on jobs in animal caretaking and control, and the animal shelter and control personnel training program, write to:

- The Humane Society of the United States, 2100 L St. NW., Washington, DC 20037-1598. Internet: http://www.hsus.org
- National Animal Control Association, P.O. Box 480851, Kansas City, MO 64148-0851.

To obtain a listing of State-licensed grooming schools, send a stamped, self-addressed envelope to:

- National Dog Groomers Association of America, Box 101, Clark, PA 16113.

For information on training and certification of kennel staff and owners, contact:

- American Boarding Kennels Association, 4575 Galley Rd., Suite 400A, Colorado Springs, CO 80915. Internet: http://www.abka.com

For information on laboratory animal technicians and certification, contact:

- American Association for Laboratory Animal Science, 9190 Crestwyn Hills Drive, Memphis, TN 38125.

SECTION TWO

THE QUICK JOB SEARCH

Advice on Planning Your Career and Getting a Good Job in Less Time

Features the Complete Text of a Results-Oriented Minibook

While *The Quick Job Search* is short, it covers **all** the major topics needed to explore career options and to conduct an effective job search. The techniques it presents have been proven to reduce the time it takes to find a job and are widely used by job search programs throughout North America.

Major topics include the following:

- ❖ **Skills identification.** Includes checklists and activities to help you identify your key skills—essential for career planning, interviewing, and writing resumes.

- ❖ **Career planning.** Provides activities to help define and research your ideal job.

- ❖ **Results-oriented job seeking skills.** Research-based advice on traditional and nontraditional job search methods, with an emphasis on the two most effective techniques: networking and cold contacts.

- ❖ **Interview skills, resumes, time management, and more.** Specific techniques on answering problem interview questions, writing a superior resume, setting a daily schedule, getting two interviews a day, and many other innovative and useful techniques.

- ❖ **Dealing with job loss.** Practical and upbeat advice on coping with the stress and discouragement of being unemployed.

- ❖ **Handling your finances while out of work.** Brief but helpful tips on conserving cash and stretching your resources.

Beginning on page 254 are sample resumes for some of America's top medical, education and human services jobs. These resumes were written and designed by professional resume writers.

Introduction

I've spent much of the past 20 years of my professional life learning about career planning and job search methods. My original interest was in helping people find jobs in less time, and in helping them find better jobs. While there is a lot of complexity to these tasks, I have also found some elements of simplicity:

1. If you are going to work, you might as well define what it is you really want to do and are good at.

2. If you are looking for a job, you might as well use techniques that will reduce the time it takes to find one—and that help you get a better job than otherwise.

This section covers these topics, along with a few others. While I have written much more detailed works on career planning and job seeking, I present the basics of career planning and job seeking in this minibook. I think that there is enough information here to make a difference for most people, and I hope that it gives you some things to think about, as well as some techniques you have not considered.

About 10 years ago, I decided to write something very short that would cover the most important elements of effective career planning and job seeking. Writing short things is harder for me than writing longer things, since every word has to count. I began by asking myself, "If I only had 30 or so pages, what are the most important things to tell someone?"

The Quick Job Search was the result. While it is a section in this book, it has also been published, in an expanded form, as a book titled *How to Get a Job Now*! It has sold about 300,000 copies in its various forms. I hope you can make good use of this material.

Avoid the Temptation; Do the Activities

I already know that you will resist doing the activities included in *The Quick Job Search*. But trust me, doing them is worthwhile. Those who do them will have a better sense of what they are good at, what they want to do, and how to go about doing it. They are more likely to get more interviews and to present themselves better in those interviews. Is this worth giving up a night of TV? Yes, I think so.

Interestingly enough, you will—after reading *The Quick Job Search* and doing its activities—have spent more time on planning your career than most people. And you will know far more than the average job seeker about how to go about finding a job. While you may want to know more, I hope that this is enough to get you started.

While this minibook will teach you techniques to find a better job in less time, job seeking requires you to act, not just learn. So, in going through this minibook, consider what you can do to put the techniques to work for you. Do the activities. Create a daily plan. Get more interviews. Today, not tomorrow. You see, the sooner and harder you get to work on your job search, the shorter it is likely to be.

Changing Jobs and Careers Is Often Healthy

Most of us were told from an early age that each career move must be up—involving more money, responsibility, and prestige. Yet research indicates people change careers for many other reasons as well.

In a survey conducted by the Gallup Organization for the National Occupational Information Coordinating Committee, 44 percent of the working adults surveyed expected to be in a different job within three years. This is a very high turnover rate.

Logical, ordered careers are found more often with increasing levels of education. For example, while 25 percent of high school dropouts took the only job available, this was true for only 8 percent of those with at least some college.

Many adult developmental psychologists believe occupational change is not only normal but may even be necessary for sound adult growth and development. It is common, even normal, to reconsider occupational roles during your twenties, thirties, and forties—even in the absence of economic pressure to do so.

One viewpoint is that a healthy occupational change allows some previously undeveloped aspect of yourself to emerge. The change may be as natural as from clerk to supervisor, or as drastic as from professional musician to airline pilot. Although risk is always a factor when change is involved, reasonable risks are healthy and can raise self-esteem.

But Not Just Any Job Should Do—Nor Any Job Search

Whether you are seeking similar work in another setting or changing careers, you need a workable plan to find the right job. This section will give you the information you need to help you find a good job quickly.

While the techniques are presented here briefly, they are based on my years of experience in helping people find good jobs (not just any job) and to find jobs in less time. The career decision-making section will help you consider several major issues. The job-seeking skills information has been proven to reduce the time required to find a good job.

Of course, more thorough books have been written on job-seeking techniques, and you may want to look into buying one or more of the better ones to obtain additional information. But, short as this section is, it *does* present the basic skills to find a good job in less time. The techniques work.

The Six Steps for a Quick and Successful Job Search

You can't just read about getting a job. The best way to get a job is to go out and get interviews! And the best way to get interviews is to make a job out of getting a job.

After many years of experience, I have identified just six basic things you need to do that make a big difference in your job search. Each will be covered in this minibook.

The Six Steps for a Quick Job Search

1. Know your skills.
2. Have a clear job objective.
3. Know where and how to look for job leads.
4. Spend at least 25 hours a week looking.
5. Get two interviews a day.
6. Follow up on all contacts.

Identify Your Key Skills

One survey of employers found that 90 percent of the people they interviewed did not present the skills they had to do the job they sought. They could not answer the basic question, "Why should I hire you?"

Knowing your skills is essential to doing well in an interview. This same knowledge is important in deciding what type of job you will enjoy and do well. For these reasons, I consider identifying your skills an essential part of a successful career plan or job search.

The Three Types of Skills

Most people think of "skills" as job-related skills such as using a computer. But we all have other types of skills that are important for success on a job—and that are very important to employers. The triangle below presents skills in three groups, and I think that this is a very useful way to consider skills for our purposes.

The Skills Triad

Let's review these three types of skills and identify those that are most important to you.

Self-Management Skills

Write down three things about yourself that you think make you a good worker.

Your "Good Worker" Traits

1. _____

2. _____

3. _____

The things you just wrote down are among the most important things for an employer to know about you! They have to do with your basic personality—your ability to adapt to a new environment. They are some of the most important things to emphasize in an interview, yet most job seekers don't realize their importance—and don't mention them.

Review the Self-Management Skills Checklist and put a check mark beside any skills you have. The Key Self-Management Skills are skills that employers find particularly important. If one or more of the Key Self-Management Skills apply to you, mentioning them in an interview can help you greatly.

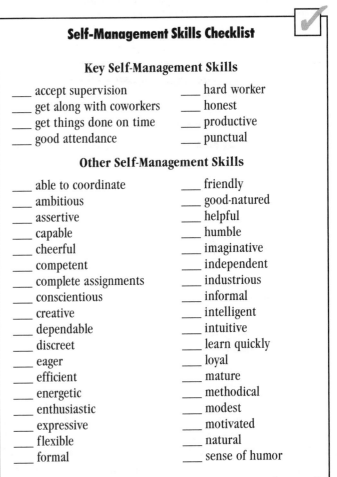

Self-Management Skills Checklist

Key Self-Management Skills

___ accept supervision	___ hard worker
___ get along with coworkers	___ honest
___ get things done on time	___ productive
___ good attendance	___ punctual

Other Self-Management Skills

___ able to coordinate	___ friendly
___ ambitious	___ good-natured
___ assertive	___ helpful
___ capable	___ humble
___ cheerful	___ imaginative
___ competent	___ independent
___ complete assignments	___ industrious
___ conscientious	___ informal
___ creative	___ intelligent
___ dependable	___ intuitive
___ discreet	___ learn quickly
___ eager	___ loyal
___ efficient	___ mature
___ energetic	___ methodical
___ enthusiastic	___ modest
___ expressive	___ motivated
___ flexible	___ natural
___ formal	___ sense of humor

(continued)

(continued)

___ open-minded	___ sincere
___ optimistic	___ solve problems
___ original	___ spontaneous
___ patient	___ steady
___ persistent	___ tactful
___ physically strong	___ take pride in work
___ practice new skills	___ tenacious
___ reliable	___ thrifty
___ resourceful	___ trustworthy
___ responsible	___ versatile
___ self-confident	___ well-organized

Other Self-Management Skills You Have:

_____

_____

_____

After you are done with the list, circle the five skills you feel are most important and list them in the box that follows.

Note: Some people find it helpful to now complete the Essential Job Search Data Worksheet provided later in this section. It organizes skills and accomplishments from previous jobs and other life experiences.

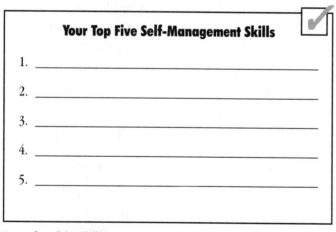

Your Top Five Self-Management Skills ✓

1. _____

2. _____

3. _____

4. _____

5. _____

Transferable Skills

We all have skills that can transfer from one job or career to another. For example, the ability to organize events could be used in a variety of jobs and may be essential for success in certain occupations. Your mission should be to find a job that requires the skills you have and enjoy using.

In the following list, put a check mark beside the skills you have. You may have used them in a previous job or in some nonwork setting.

Transferable Skills Checklist ✓

Key Transferable Skills

___ instruct others	___ negotiate
___ manage money, budget	___ organize/manage
___ manage people	projects
___ meet deadlines	___ public speaking
___ meet the public	___ written communication
	skills

Skills Working with Things

___ assemble things	___ operate tools,
___ build things	machines
___ construct/repair things	___ repair things
___ drive, operate vehicles	___ use complex
___ good with hands	equipment
___ observe/inspect things	___ use computers

Skills Working with Data

___ analyze data	___ evaluate
___ audit records	___ investigate
___ budget	___ keep financial records
___ calculate/compute	___ locate information
___ check for accuracy	___ manage money
___ classify things	___ observe/inspect
___ compare	___ record facts
___ compile	___ research
___ count	___ synthesize
___ detail-oriented	___ take inventory

Skills Working with People

___ administer	___ outgoing
___ advise	___ patient
___ care for	___ perceptive
___ coach	___ persuade
___ confront others	___ pleasant
___ counsel people	___ sensitive
___ demonstrate	___ sociable
___ diplomatic	___ supervise
___ help others	___ tactful
___ instruct	___ tolerant
___ interview people	___ tough
___ kind	___ trusting
___ listen	___ understanding
___ negotiate	

Skills Working with Words, Ideas

___ articulate	___ inventive
___ communicate verbally	___ library research
___ correspond with others	___ logical
___ create new ideas	___ public speaking
___ design	___ remember information
___ edit	___ write clearly
___ ingenious	

Leadership Skills

___ arrange social functions	___ mediate problems
___ competitive	___ motivate people
___ decisive	___ negotiate agreements
___ delegate	___ plan events
___ direct others	___ results-oriented
___ explain things to others	___ risk-taker
___ influence others	___ run meetings
___ initiate new tasks	___ self-confident
___ make decisions	___ self-motivate
___ manage or direct others	___ solve problems

Creative/Artistic Skills

___ artistic	___ expressive
___ dance, body movement	___ perform, act
___ drawing, art	___ present artistic ideas

Other Similar Skills You Have:

_____

_____

_____

_____

_____

_____

_____

When you are finished, identify the five transferable skills you feel are most important for you to use in your next job and list them in the box below.

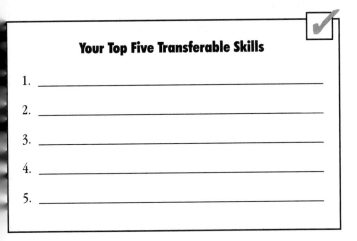

Your Top Five Transferable Skills

1. _____

2. _____

3. _____

4. _____

5. _____

Job-Related Skills

Job content or job-related skills are those you need to do a particular job. A carpenter, for example, needs to know how to use various tools and be familiar with a variety of tasks related to that job.

You may already have a good idea of the type of job that you want. If so, it may be fairly simple for you to identify your job-related skills to emphasize in an interview. But I recommend that you complete at least two other things in this minibook first:

1. Complete the material that helps you define your job objective more clearly. Doing so will help you clarify just what sort of a job you want and allow you to better select those skills that best support it.

2. Complete the Essential Job Search Data Worksheet that appears later (pages 244–246). It will give you lots of specific skills and accomplishments to consider.

Once you have done these two things, come back and complete the box below. Include the job-related skills you have that you would most like to use in your next job.

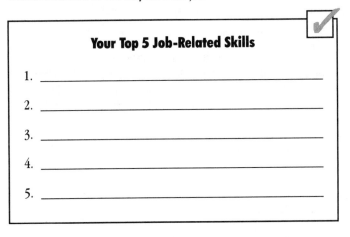

Your Top 5 Job-Related Skills

1. _____

2. _____

3. _____

4. _____

5. _____

Begin by Defining Your Ideal Job (You Can Compromise Later)

Too many people look for a job without having a good idea of exactly what they are looking for. Before you go out looking for "a" job, I suggest that you first define exactly what it is you really want—"the" job. Most people think a job objective is the same as a job title, but it isn't. You need to consider other elements of what makes a job satisfying for you. Then, later, you can decide what that job is called and what industry it might be in.

The Eight Factors to Consider in Defining the Ideal Job for You

Following are eight factors to consider when you define your ideal job. Once you know what you want, your task then becomes finding a job that is as close to your ideal job as you can find.

1. What skills do you want to use?

From the previous skills lists, select the top five skills that you enjoy using and most want to use in your next job.

1. _____

2. _____

3. _____

4. _____

5. _____

2. What type of special knowledge do you have?

Perhaps you know how to fix radios, keep accounting records, or cook food. Write down the things you know about from schooling, training, hobbies, family experiences, and other sources. One or more of them could make you a very special applicant in the right setting.

_____

_____

_____

_____

_____

3. With what types of people do you prefer to work?

Do you like to work with aggressive, hardworking folks, creative personalities, or some other types?

_____

_____

_____

_____

_____

4. What type of work environment do you prefer?

Do you want to work inside, outside, in a quiet place, a busy place, a clean place, or have a window with a nice view? List those things that are important to you.

_____

_____

_____

_____

_____

5. Where do you want your next job to be located— in what city or region?

Near a bus line? Close to a childcare center? If you are open to living and working anywhere, what would your ideal community be like?

_____

_____

_____

_____

_____

6. How much money do you hope to make in your next job?

Many people will take less money if the job is great in other ways—or if they quickly need a job to survive. Think about the minimum you would take as well as what you would eventually like to earn. Your next job will probably pay somewhere in between.

_____

_____

_____

_____

_____

7. How much responsibility are you willing to accept?

Usually, the more money you want to make, the more responsibility you must accept. Do you want to work by yourself, be part of a group, or be in charge? If so, at what level?

_____

_____

_____

_____

_____

_____

_____

8. What things are important or have meaning to you?

Do you have values that you would prefer to include as a basis of the work you do? For example, some people want to work to help others, clean up our environment, build things, make machines work, gain power or prestige, or care for animals or plants. Think about what is important to you and how you might include this in your next job.

_____

_____

_____

_____

_____

_____

Your Ideal Job

Use the points at left and on previous pages to help you define your ideal job. Think about each one and select the points that are most important to you. Don't worry about a job title yet; just focus on the most important things to include from the previous questions to define your ideal job.

My Ideal Job Objective:

_____

_____

_____

_____

_____

_____

_____

_____

_____

_____

Setting a Specific Job Objective

Whether or not you have a good idea of the type of job you want, it is important to know more about various job options.

A very simple but effective way for exploring job alternatives is to go through the table of contents and check those about which you want to learn more. Then read the descriptions to learn more about the jobs that interest you.

If you need help figuring out what type of job to look for, remember that most areas have free or low-cost career counseling and testing services. Contact local government agencies and schools for referrals.

Job Search Methods That Help You Get a Better Job in Less Time

One survey found that 85 percent of all employers don't advertise at all. They hire people they already know, people who find out about the jobs through word of mouth, or people who simply happen to be in the right place at the right time. This is sometimes just luck, but this minibook will teach you ways to increase your "luck" in finding job openings.

Traditional Job Search Methods Are Not Very Effective

Most job seekers don't know how ineffective some traditional job hunting techniques tend to be.

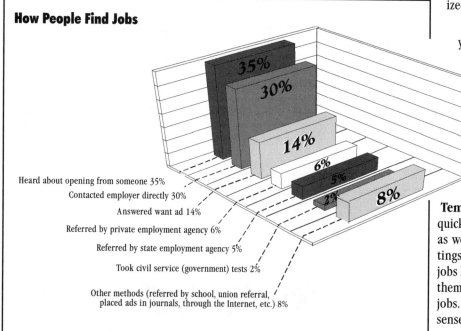

How People Find Jobs

- 35%
- 30%
- 14%
- 6%
- 5%
- 2%
- 8%

Heard about opening from someone 35%
Contacted employer directly 30%
Answered want ad 14%
Referred by private employment agency 6%
Referred by state employment agency 5%
Took civil service (government) tests 2%
Other methods (referred by school, union referral, placed ads in journals, through the Internet, etc.) 8%

The chart above shows that fewer than 15 percent of all job seekers get jobs from reading the want ads. Let's take a quick look at want ads and other traditional job search methods.

Help wanted ads. As you should remember, only about 15 percent of all people get their jobs through the want ads. Everyone who reads the paper knows about these job openings, so competition for advertised jobs is fierce. The Internet also lists many job openings. But like want ads, these lists are viewed by many people. Still, some people do get jobs this way, so go ahead and apply. Just be sure to spend most of your time using more effective methods.

The state employment service. Each state has a network of local offices to administer unemployment compensation and provide job leads and other services. These services are provided without charge to you or employers. Names vary by state, so it may be called "Job Service," "Department of Labor," "Unemployment Office," or another name.

Nationally, only about 5 percent of all job seekers get their jobs here, and these organizations typically know of only one-tenth (or fewer) of the actual job openings in a region. Still, it is worth a weekly visit. If you ask for the same counselor, you might impress the person enough to remember you and refer you for the better openings.

You should also realize that some of the state employment services provide substantial help in the form of job search workshops and other resources. Look into it; the price is right.

Private employment agencies. Studies have found that private agencies work reasonably well for those who use them. But there are cautions to consider. For one thing, these agencies work best for entry-level positions or for those with specialized skills that are in demand.

Private agencies also charge a fee either to you (as high as 20 percent of your annual salary!) or to the employer. Most of them call employers asking if they have any openings, something you could do yourself. Unless you have skills that are in high demand, you may do better on your own—and save money. At the least, you should rely on a private agency as only one of the techniques you use and not depend on them too heavily.

Temporary agencies. These can be a source of quick but temporary jobs to bring in some income as well as give you experience in a variety of settings—something that can help you land full-time jobs later. More and more employers are also using them as a way to evaluate workers for permanent jobs. So consider using these agencies if it makes sense to do so, but make certain that you continue an active search for a full-time job.

Sending out resumes. *One survey found that you would have to mail more than 500 unsolicited resumes to get one interview!* A much better approach is to contact the person who might hire you by phone to set up an interview directly; then send a resume. If you insist on sending out unsolicited resumes, do this on weekends—save your "prime time" for more effective job search techniques.

Filling out applications. Most applications are used to screen you out. Larger organizations may require them, but remember that your task is to get an interview, not fill out an application. If you do complete them, make them neat and error-free, and do not include anything that could get you screened out. If necessary, leave a problematic section blank. It can always be explained after you get an interview.

Personnel departments. Hardly anyone gets hired by interviewers in a personnel department. Their job is to screen you and refer the "best" applicants to the person who would actually supervise you. You may need to cooperate with them, but it is often better to go directly to the person who is most likely to supervise you–even if no job opening exists at the moment. And remember that most organizations don't even have a personnel office; only the larger ones do!

The Two Job Search Methods That Work Best

Two-thirds of all people get their jobs using informal methods. These jobs are often not advertised and are part of the "hidden" job market. How do *you* find them?

There are two basic informal job search methods: networking with people you know (which I call warm contacts), and making direct contacts with an employer (which I call cold contacts). They are both based on the most important job search rule of all.

The Most Important Job Search Rule:
Don't wait until the job is open
before contacting the employer!

Most jobs are filled by someone the employer meets before the job is formally "open." So the trick is to meet people who can hire you before a job is available! Instead of saying, "Do you have any jobs open?" say, "I realize you may not have any openings now, but I would still like to talk to you about the possibility of future openings."

Develop a Network of Contacts in Five Easy Steps

One study found that 40 percent of all people found their jobs through a lead provided by a friend, a relative, or an acquaintance. Developing new contacts is called "networking," and here's how it works:

1. **Make lists of people you know.** Develop a list of anyone with whom you are friendly; then make a separate list of all your relatives. These two lists alone often add up to 25-100 people or more. Next, think of other groups of people with whom you have something in common, such as former co-workers or classmates; members of your social or sports groups; members of your professional association; former employers; and members of your religious group. You may not know many of these people personally, but most will help you if you ask them.

2. **Contact them in a systematic way.** Each of these people is a contact for you. Obviously, some lists and some people on those lists will be more helpful than others, but almost any one of them could help you find a job lead.

3. **Present yourself well.** Begin with your friends and relatives. Call them and tell them you are looking for a job and need their help. Be as clear as possible about what you are looking for and what skills and qualifications you have. Look

at the sample JIST Card and phone script later in this minibook for presentation ideas.

4. **Ask them for leads.** It is possible that they will know of a job opening just right for you. If so, get the details and get right on it! More likely, however, they will not, so here are three questions you should ask.

The Three Magic Networking Questions

1. *Do you know of any openings for a person with my skills?* If the answer is no (which it usually is), then ask:

2. *Do you know of someone else who might know of such an opening?* If your contact does, get that name and ask for another one. If he or she doesn't, ask:

3. *Do you know of anyone who might know of someone else who might?* Another good way to ask this is, "Do you know someone who knows lots of people?" If all else fails, this will usually get you a name.

---

5. **Contact these referrals and ask them the same questions.** For each original contact, you can extend your network of acquaintances by hundreds of people. Eventually, one of these people will hire you or refer you to someone who will! This process is called networking, and it does work if you are persistent.

Contact Employers Directly

It takes more courage, but contacting an employer directly is a very effective job search technique. I call these cold contacts because you don't have an existing connection with these contacts. Following are two basic techniques for making cold contacts.

Use the Yellow Pages to Find Potential Employers

One effective cold contact technique uses the yellow pages. You can begin by looking at the index and asking for each entry, "Would an organization of this kind need a person with my skills?" If the answer is "yes," then that type of organization or business is a possible target. You can also rate "yes" entries based on your interest, giving an A to those that seem very interesting, a B to those you are not sure of, and a C to those that don't seem interesting at all.

Next, select a type of organization that got a "yes" response (such as "hotels") and turn to the section of the yellow pages where they are listed. Then call the organizations listed and ask to speak to the person who is most likely to hire or supervise you. A sample telephone script is included later in this section to give you ideas about what to say.

Drop In Without an Appointment

You can also simply walk in to many potential employers' organizations and ask to speak to the person in charge. This is particularly effective in small businesses, but it works surprisingly well in larger ones too. Remember, you want an interview even if there are no openings now. If your timing is inconvenient, ask for a better time to come back for an interview.

Most Jobs Are with Small Employers

About 70 percent of all people now work in small businesses—those with 250 or fewer employees. While the largest corporations have reduced the number of employees, small businesses have been creating as many as 80 percent of the new jobs. There are many opportunities to obtain training and promotions in smaller organizations, too. Many do not even have a personnel department, so nontraditional job search techniques are particularly effective with them.

JIST Cards—an Effective "Mini Resume"

JIST Cards are a job search tool that gets results. Typed, printed, or even neatly written on a 3-by-5-inch card, a JIST Card contains the essential information most employers want to know. Look at the sample cards below.

JIST Cards are an effective job search tool! Give them to friends and to each of your network contacts. Attach one to your resume. Enclose one in your thank-you notes after an interview. Leave one with employers as a "business card." Use them in many creative ways. Even though they can be typed or even handwritten, it is best to have 100 or more printed so you can put lots of them in circulation. Thousands of job seekers have used them, and they get results!

Sandy Zaremba

Home: (219) 232-7608 **E-Mail:** szaremba@connect.com

Position: General Office/Clerical

Over two years of work experience, plus one year of training in office practices. Type 55 wpm, trained in word processing operations, post general ledger, handle payables, receivables, and most accounting tasks. Responsible for daily deposits averaging $5,000. Good interpersonal skills. Can meet strict deadlines and handle pressure well.

Willing to work any hours.

Organized, honest, reliable, and hardworking.

Chris Vorhees

Home: (602) 253-9678
Leave Message: (602) 257-6643

OBJECTIVE: Electronics—installation, maintenance, and sales

SKILLS: Four years of work experience, plus two years of ad-vanced training in electronics. A.S. degree in Electronics Engineering Technology. Managed a $300,000/yr. business while going to school full time, with grades in the top 25%. Familiar with all major electronic diagnostic and repair equipment. Hands-on experience with medical, consumer, communications, and industrial electronics equipment and applications. Good problem-solving and communication skills. Customer service oriented.

Willing to do what it takes to get the job done.

Use the Phone to Get Job Leads

Once you have created your JIST Card, it is easy to create a telephone contact "script" based on it. Adapt the basic script to call people you know or your yellow pages leads. Select yellow pages index categories that might use a person with your skills and get the numbers of specific organizations in that category. Then ask for the person who is most likely to supervise you and present your phone script.

While it doesn't work every time, most people, with practice, can get one or more interviews in an hour by making these "cold" calls. Here is a phone script based on a JIST Card:

"Hello, my name is Pam Nykanen. I am interested in a position in hotel management. I have four years' experience in sales, catering, and accounting with a 300-room hotel. I also have an associate degree in hotel management plus one year of experience with the Bradey Culinary Institute. During my employment, I helped double revenues from meetings and conferences and increased bar revenues by 46 percent. I have good problem-solving skills and am good with people. I am also well-organized, hardworking, and detail-oriented. When may I come in for an interview?"

While this example assumes you are calling someone you don't know, the script can be easily modified for presentation to warm contacts, including referrals. Using the script for making cold calls takes courage, but it does work for most people.

Make Your Job Search a Full-Time Job

On the average, job seekers spend fewer than 15 hours a week actually looking for work. The average length of unemployment is three or more months, with some people being out of work far longer (older workers and higher earners are two groups who take longer).

Based on many years of experience, I can say that the more time you spend on your job search each week, the less time you are likely to remain unemployed. Of course, using more effective job search methods also helps. Those who follow my advice have proven, over and over, that they get jobs in less than half the average time and they often get better jobs, too. Time management is the key.

Spend at Least 25 Hours a Week Looking for a Job

If you are unemployed and looking for a full-time job, you should look for a job on a full-time basis. It just makes sense to do so, although many do not because of discouragement, lack of good techniques, and lack of structure. Most job seekers have no idea what they are going to do next Thursday—they don't have a plan. The most important thing is to decide how many hours you can commit to your job search, and stay with it. You should spend a minimum of 25 hours a week on hard-core job search activities with no goofing around. Let me walk you through a simple but effective process to help you organize your job search schedule.

Write here how many hours you are willing to spend each week looking for a job: _____

Decide Which Days You Will Look for Work

Answering the questions below requires you to have a schedule and a plan, just as you had when you were working, right?

Which days of the week will you spend looking for a job?

_____

_____

How many hours will you look each day? _____

At what time will you begin and end your job search on each of these days? _____

Create a Specific Daily Schedule

Having a specific daily job search schedule is very important because most job seekers find it hard to stay productive each day. You already know which job search methods are most effective, and you should plan on spending most of your time using those methods. The sample daily schedule that follows has been very effective for people who have used it, and it will give you ideas for your own. Although you are welcome to create your own daily schedule, I urge you to consider one similar to this one. Why? Because it works.

A Daily Schedule That Works

7:00 - 8:00 a.m.	Get up, shower, dress, eat breakfast.
8:00 - 8:15 a.m.	Organize work space; review schedule for interviews or follow-ups; update schedule.
8:15 - 9:00 a.m.	Review old leads for follow-up; develop new leads (want ads, yellow pages, networking lists, etc.).
9:00 - 10:00 a.m.	Make phone calls, set up interviews.
10:00 - 10:15 a.m.	Take a break!
10:15 - 11:00 a.m.	Make more calls.
11:00 - 12:00 p.m.	Make follow-up calls as needed.
12:00 - 1:00 p.m.	Lunch break.
1:00 - 5:00 p.m.	Go on interviews; call cold contacts in the field; research for upcoming interviews at the library and on the Internet.

Do It Now: Get a Planner and Write Down Your Job Search Schedule

This is important: If you are not accustomed to using a daily schedule book or planner, promise yourself that you will get a good one tomorrow. Choose one that allows plenty of space for each day's plan on an hourly basis, plus room for daily "to do" listings. Write in your daily schedule in advance; then add interviews as they come. Get used to carrying it with you and use it!

Redefine What "Counts" As an Interview; Then Get Two a Day

The average job seeker gets about five interviews a month—fewer than two interviews a week. Yet many job seekers using the techniques I suggest routinely get two interviews a day. But to accomplish this, you must redefine what an interview is.

The New Definition of an Interview

An interview is any face-to-face contact with someone who has the authority to hire or supervise a person with your skills—even if the person doesn't have an opening at the time you interview.

With this definition, it is *much* easier to get interviews. You can now interview with all kinds of potential employers, not only those who have job openings. Many job seekers use the yellow pages to get two interviews with just one hour of calls by using the telephone contact script discussed earlier. Others simply drop in on potential employers and get an unscheduled interview. And getting names of others to contact from those you know—networking—is quite effective if you persist.

Getting two interviews a day equals 10 a week and 40 a month. That's 800 percent more interviews than the average job seeker gets. Who do you think will get a job offer quicker? So set out each day to get at least two interviews. It's quite possible to do, now that you know how.

How to Answer Tough Interview Questions

Interviews are where the job search action happens. You have to get them; then you have to do well in them. If you have done your homework, you are getting interviews for jobs that will maximize your skills. That is a good start, but your ability to communicate your skills in the interview makes an enormous difference. This is where, according to employer surveys, most job seekers have problems. They don't effectively communicate the skills they have to do the job, and they answer one or more problem questions poorly.

While thousands of problem interview questions are possible, I have listed just 10 that, if you can answer them well, will prepare you for most interviews.

The Top 10 Problem Questions

1. Why don't you tell me about yourself?

2. Why should I hire you?

3. What are your major strengths?

4. What are your major weaknesses?

5. What sort of pay do you expect to receive?

6. How does your previous experience relate to the jobs we have here?

7. What are your plans for the future?

8. What will your former employer (or references) say about you?

9. Why are you looking for this type of position, and why here?

10. Why don't you tell me about your personal situation?

I don't have the space here to give thorough answers to all of these questions. Instead, let me suggest several techniques that I have developed which you can use to answer almost any interview question.

A Traditional Interview Is Not a Friendly Exchange

Before I present the techniques for answering interview questions, it is important to understand what is going on. In a traditional interview situation, there is a job opening, and you are one of several (or one of a hundred) applicants. In this setting, the employer's task is to eliminate all but one applicant.

Assuming that you got as far as an interview, the interviewer's questions are designed to elicit information that can be used to screen you out. If you are wise, you know that your task is to avoid getting screened out. It's not an open and honest interaction, is it?

This illustrates yet another advantage of nontraditional job search techniques: the ability to talk to an employer before an opening exists. This eliminates the stress of a traditional interview. Employers are not trying to screen you out, and you are not trying to keep them from finding out stuff about you.

Having said that, knowing a technique for answering questions that might be asked in a traditional interview is good preparation for whatever you might run into during your job search.

The Three-Step Process for Answering Interview Questions

I know this might seem too simple, but the Three-Step Process is easy to remember. Its simplicity allows you to evaluate a question and create a good answer. The technique is based on sound principles and has worked for thousands of people, so consider trying it.

Step 1. Understand what is really being asked.

Most questions are really designed to find out about your self-management skills and personality. While they are rarely this blunt, the employer's *real* question is often:

✓ Can I depend on you?

✓ Are you easy to get along with?

✓ Are you a good worker?

✓ Do you have the experience and training to do the job if we hire you?

✓ Are you likely to stay on the job for a reasonable period of time and be productive?

Ultimately, if the employer is not convinced that you will stay and be a good worker, it won't matter if you have the best credentials—he or she won't hire you.

Step 2. Answer the question briefly.

Acknowledge the facts, but...

✓ Present them as an advantage, not a disadvantage.

There are lots of examples in which a specific interview question will encourage you to provide negative information. The classic is the "What are your major weaknesses?" question that I included in my top 10 problem questions list. Obviously, this is a trick question, and many people are just not prepared for it. A good response might be to mention something that is not all that damaging, such as "I have been told that I am a perfectionist, sometimes not delegating as effectively as I might." But your answer is not complete until you continue.

Step 3. Answer the real concern by presenting your related skills.

✓ Base your answer on the key skills that you have identified and that are needed in this job.

✓ Give examples to support your skills statements.

For example, an employer might say to a recent graduate, "We were looking for someone with more experience in this field. Why should we consider you?" Here is one possible answer: "I'm sure there are people who have more experience, but I *do* have more than six years of work experience including three years of advanced training and hands-on experience using the latest methods and techniques. Because my training is recent, I am open to new ideas and am used to working hard and learning quickly."

In the example I presented in Step 2 (about your need to delegate), a good skills statement might be, "I have been working on this problem and have learned to be more willing to let my staff do things, making sure that they have good training and supervision. I've found that their performance improves, and it frees me up to do other things."

Whatever your situation, learn to use it to your advantage. It is essential to communicate your skills during an interview, and the Three-Step Process gives you a technique that can dramatically improve your responses. It works!

Interview Dress and Grooming Rule

If you make a negative first impression, you won't get a second chance to make a good one. So do everything possible to make a good impression.

A Good Rule for Dressing for an Interview

Dress as you think
the boss will dress—*only neater.*

Dress for success! If necessary, get help selecting an interview outfit from someone who dresses well. Pay close attention to your grooming too. Written things like correspondence and resumes must be neat and errorless because they create an impression as well.

Follow Up on All Contacts

People who follow up with potential employers and with others in their network get jobs faster than those who do not.

Four Rules for Effective Follow-Up

1. Send a thank-you note to every person who helps you in your job search.

2. Send the thank-you note within 24 hours after you speak with the person.

3. Enclose JIST Cards with thank-you notes and all other correspondence.

4. Develop a system to keep following up with "good" contacts.

Thank-You Notes Make a Difference

Thank-you notes can be handwritten or typed on quality paper and matching envelopes. Keep them simple, neat, and errorless. Following is a sample:

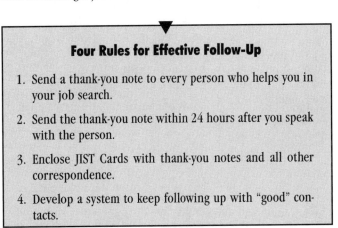

April 16, 20XX

2234 Riverwood Ave.
Philadelphia, PA 17963

Ms. Sandra Kijek
Henderson & Associates, Inc.
1801 Washington Blvd., Suite 1201
Philadelphia, PA 17963

Dear Ms. Kijek:

Thank you for sharing your time with me so generously today. I really appreciated seeing your state-of-the-art computer equipment.

Your advice has already proved helpful. I have an appointment to meet with Mr. Robert Hopper on Friday as you anticipated.

Please consider referring me to others if you think of someone else who might need a person with my skills.

Sincerely,

William Richardson

William Richardson

Use Job Lead Cards to Organize Your Contacts

Use a simple 3-by-5-inch card to keep essential information on each person in your network. Buy a 3-by-5-inch card file box and tabs for each day of the month. File the cards under the date you want to contact the person, and the rest is easy. I've found that staying in touch with a good contact every other week can pay off big. Here's a sample card to give you ideas to create your own:

ORGANIZATION: _Mutual Health Insurance_

CONTACT PERSON: _Anna Tomey_   PHONE: _317-355-0216_

SOURCE OF LEAD: _Aunt Ruth_

NOTES: _4/10 Called. Anna on vacation. Call back 4/15. 4/15 Interview set 4/20 at 1:30. 4/20 Anna showed me around. They use the same computers we used in school! (Friendly people) Sent thank-you note and JIST Card, call back 5/1. 5/1 Second interview 5/8 at 9 a.m.!_

Resumes: Write a Simple One Now and a "Better" One Later

You have already learned that sending out resumes and waiting for responses is not an effective job-seeking technique. However, many employers *will* ask you for them, and they are a useful tool in your job search. If you feel that you need a resume, I suggest that you begin with a simple one that you can complete quickly. I've seen too many people spend weeks working on their resume while they could have been out getting interviews instead. If you want a "better" resume, you can work on it on weekends and evenings. So let's begin with the basics.

Basic Tips to Create a Superior Resume

The following tips make sense for any resume format.

Write it yourself. It's okay to look at other resumes for ideas, but write yours yourself. It will force you to organize your thoughts and background.

Make it errorless. One spelling or grammar error will create a negative impressionist (see what I mean?). Get someone else to review your final draft for any errors. Then review it again because these rascals have a way of slipping in.

Make it look good. Poor copy quality, cheap paper, bad type quality, or anything else that creates a poor physical appearance will turn off employers to even the best resume content. Get professional help with design and printing if necessary. Many resume writers and print shops have desktop publishing services and can do it all for you.

Be brief, be relevant. Many good resumes fit on one page and few justify more than two. Include only the most important points. Use short sentences and action words. If it doesn't relate to and support the job objective, cut it!

Be honest. Don't overstate your qualifications. If you end up getting a job you can't handle, it will not be to your advantage. Most employers will see right through it and not hire you.

Be positive. Emphasize your accomplishments and results. This is no place to be too humble or to display your faults.

Be specific. Instead of saying "I am good with people," say "I supervised four people in the warehouse and increased productivity by 30 percent." Use numbers whenever possible, such as the number of people served, percent of sales increase, or dollars saved.

You should also know that everyone feels he or she is a resume expert. Whatever you do, someone will tell you it is wrong. For this reason, it is important to understand that a resume is a job search tool. You should never delay or slow down your job search because your resume is not "good enough." The best approach is to create a simple and acceptable resume as soon as possible, then use it. As time permits, create a better one if you feel you must.

Chronological Resumes

Most resumes use the chronological format. It is a simple format where the most recent experience is listed first, followed by each previous job. This arrangement works fine for someone with work experience in several similar jobs, but not as well for those with limited experience or for career changers.

Look at the two Judith Jones resumes. Both use the chronological approach, but notice that the second one includes some improvements over her first. The improved resume is clearly better, but either would be acceptable to most employers.

Tips for Writing a Simple Chronological Resume

Here are some tips for writing a basic chronological resume.

Name. Use your formal name rather than a nickname if the formal name sounds more professional.

Address. Be complete. Include your zip code and avoid abbreviations. If moving is a possibility, use the address of a friend or relative or be certain to include a forwarding address.

Telephone number. Employers are most likely to try to reach you by phone, so having a reliable way to be reached is very important. Always include your area code because you never know where your resume might travel. If you don't have an answering machine, get one and make sure you leave it on whenever you are not home. Listen to your message to be sure it presents you in a professional way. Also available are a variety of communication systems: voice

Judith J. Jones

115 South Hawthorne Avenue
Chicago, Illinois 46204
(312) 653-9217 (home)
(312) 272-7608 (message)
E-Mail: jjones@pc.net

JOB OBJECTIVE

Desire a position in the office management or administrative assistant area. Prefer a position requiring responsibility and a variety of tasks.

EDUCATION AND TRAINING

Acme Business College, Chicago, Illinois
Graduate of a one-year business program, 2000

John Adams High School, South Bend, Indiana
Diploma: Business Education

Other: Continuing education classes and workshops in business communication, scheduling systems, and customer relations.

EXPERIENCE

1999-2000 — Returned to school to complete and update my business skills. Learned word processing and new office techniques.

1996-1999 — Claims Processor, Blue Spear Insurance Co., Chicago, Illinois. Handled customer medical claims, filed, miscellaneous clerical duties.

1994-1996 — Sales Clerk, Judy's Boutique, Chicago, Illinois. Responsible for counter sales, display design, and selected tasks.

1992-1994 — Specialist, U.S. Army. Assigned to various stations as a specialist in finance operations. Promoted prior to honorable discharge.

Previous Jobs — Held part-time and summer jobs throughout high school.

PERSONAL

I am reliable, hard working, and good with people.

finish a formal degree or program, list what you did complete. Include any special accomplishments.

Previous experience. The standard approach is to list employer, job title, dates employed, and responsibilities. But there are better ways of presenting your experience. Look over the improved chronological resume for ideas. The improved version emphasizes results, accomplishments, and performance.

Personal data. Neither of the sample resumes has the standard height, weight, or marital status information included on so many resumes. That information is simply not relevant! If you do include some personal data, put it at the bottom and keep it related to the job you want.

References. There is no need to list references. If employers want them, they will ask. If your references are particularly good, it's okay to say so.

Tips for an Improved Chronological Resume

Once you have a simple, errorless, and eye-pleasing resume, get on with your job search. There is no reason to delay! But you may want to create a better one in your spare time (evenings or weekends). If you do, here are some additional tips.

Job objective. Job objectives often limit the types of jobs for which you will be considered. Instead, think of the type of work you want to do and can do well and describe it in more general terms. Instead of writing "Restaurant Manager," write "Managing a small to mid-sized business" if that is what you are qualified to do.

mail, professional answering services, beepers, cell phones, e-mail, etc. If you do provide an alternative phone number or another way to reach you, just make it clear to the caller what to expect.

Job objective. This is optional for a very basic resume but is still important to include. Notice that Judy is keeping her options open with her objective. Writing "Secretary" or "Clerical" might limit her to lower-paying jobs or even prevent her from being considered for jobs she might take.

Education and training. Include any formal training you've had, plus any training that supports the job you seek. If you did not

Education and training. New graduates should emphasize their recent training and education more than those with five years or so of recent and related work experience. Think about any special accomplishments from school and include these if they relate to the job. Did you work full time while in school? Did you do particularly well in work-related classes, get an award, or participate in sports?

Skills and accomplishments. Employers are interested in what you accomplished and did well. Include those things that relate to doing well in the job you seek now. Even "small" things

Sample of an improved chronological resume.

Judith J. Jones

115 South Hawthorne Avenue
Chicago, Illinois 46204
(312) 653-9217 (home)
(312) 272-7608 (message)
E-Mail: jjones@pc.net

JOB OBJECTIVE

Seeking position requiring excellent management and administrative assistant skills in an office environment. Position should require a variety of tasks including typing, word processing, accounting/bookkeeping functions, and customer contact.

EDUCATION AND TRAINING

Acme Business College, Chicago, Illinois.
Completed one-year program in Business and Office Management. Grades in top 30 percent of my class. Courses: word processing, accounting theory and systems, time management, basic supervision, and others.

John Adams High School, South Bend, Indiana.
Graduated with emphasis on business courses.

Other: Continuing education at my own expense (business communications, customer relations, computer applications, other courses).

EXPERIENCE

1999-2000 — Returned to business school to update skills. Advanced course work in accounting and office management. Learned word processing and accounting and spreadsheet software. Gained operating knowledge of computers.

1996-1999 — Claims Processor, Blue Spear Insurance Company, Chicago, Illinois. Handled 50 complex medical insurance claims per day—18 percent above department average. Received two merit raises for performance.

1994-1996 — Assistant Manager, Judy's Boutique, Chicago, Illinois. Managed sales, financial records, inventory, purchasing, correspondence, and related tasks during owner's absence. Supervised four employees. Sales increased 15 percent during my tenure.

1992-1994 — Finance Specialist (E4), U.S. Army. Responsible for the systematic processing of 500 invoices per day from commercial vendors. Trained and supervised eight employees. Devised internal system allowing 15 percent increase in invoices processed with a decrease in personnel.

1988-1992 — Various part-time and summer jobs through high school. Learned to deal with customers, meet deadlines, work hard, and other skills.

SPECIAL SKILLS AND ABILITIES

Type 80 words per minute and can operate most office equipment. Good communication and math skills. Accept supervision, able to supervise others. Excellent attendance record.

Promotions. If you were promoted or got good evaluations, say so. A promotion to a more responsible job can be handled as a separate job if this makes sense.

Problem areas. Employers look for any sign of instability or lack of reliability. It is very expensive to hire and train someone who won't stay or who won't work out. Gaps in employment, jobs held for short periods of time, or a lack of direction in the jobs you've held are all things that employers are concerned about. If you have any legitimate explanation, use it. For example:

"1998–Continued my education at..."

"1999–Traveled extensively throughout the United States."

"1998 to present–Self-employed barn painter and widget maker."

"1997–Had first child, took year off before returning to work."

Use entire years or even seasons of years to avoid displaying a shorter gap you can't explain easily: "Spring 1998–Fall 1999" will not show you as unemployed from October to November, 1998, for example.

Remember that a resume can get you screened out, but it is up to you to get the interview and the job. So, cut out *anything* that is negative in your resume!

count. Maybe your attendance was perfect, you met a tight deadline, did the work of others during vacations, etc. Be specific and include numbers–even if you have to estimate them.

Job titles. Many job titles don't accurately reflect the job you did. For example, your job title may have been "Cashier" but you also opened the store, trained new staff, and covered for the boss on vacations. Perhaps "Head Cashier and Assistant Manager" would be more accurate. Check with your previous employer if you are not sure.

Sample of a simple skills resume.

ALAN ATWOOD
3231 East Harbor Road
Woodland Hills, California 91367
Home: (818) 447-2111   Message: (818) 547-8201

Objective: A responsible position in retail sales

Areas of Accomplishment:

Customer Service
- Communicate well with all age groups.
- Able to interpret customer concerns to help them find the items they want.
- Received 6 Employee of the Month awards in 3 years.

Merchandise Display
- Developed display skills via in-house training and experience.
- Received Outstanding Trainee Award for Christmas toy display.
- Dress mannequins, arrange table displays, and organize sale merchandise.

Stock Control and Marketing
- Maintained and marked stock during department manager's 6-week illness.
- Developed more efficient record-keeping procedures.

Additional Skills
- Operate cash register, IBM-compatible hardware, and calculators.
- Punctual, honest, reliable, and a hard-working self-starter.

Experience:
Harper's Department Store
Woodland Hills, California
1999 to Present

Education:
Central High School
Woodland Hills, California
3.6/4.0 Grade Point Average
Honor Graduate in Distributive Education

Two years of retail sales training in Distributive Education. Also courses in Business Writing, Accounting, and Word Processing.

Skills and Combination Resumes

The functional or "skills" resume emphasizes your most important *skills,* supported by specific examples of how you have used them. This approach allows you to use any part of your life history to support your ability to do the job you seek.

While the skills resume can be very effective, it does require more work to create. And some employers don't like them because they can hide a job seeker's faults (such as job gaps, lack of formal education, or no related work experience) better than a chronological resume.

Still, a skills resume may make sense for you. Look over the sample resumes for ideas. Notice that one resume includes elements of a skills *and* a chronological resume. This is called a "combination" resume–an approach that makes sense if your previous job history or education and training are positive.

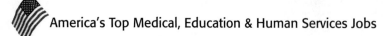

Sample skills resume for someone with substantial experience—but using only one page. Note that no dates are included.

Ann McLaughlin

Career Objective

Challenging position in programming or related areas that would best utilize expertise in the business environment. This position should have many opportunities for an aggressive, dedicated individual with leadership abilities to advance.

Programming Skills

Functional program design relating to business issues including payroll, inventory and database management, sales, marketing, accounting, and loan amortization reports. In conjunction with design would be coding, implementation, debugging, and file maintenance. Familiar with distributed network systems including PCs and Macs.

Areas of Expertise

Interpersonal communication strengths, public relations capabilities, plus innovative problem-solving and analytical talents.

Sales

A total of nine years of experience in sales and sales management. Sold security products to distributors and burglar alarm dealers. Increased company's sales from $16,000 to over $70,000 per month. Creatively organized sales programs and marketing concepts. Trained sales personnel in prospecting techniques while also training service personnel in proper installation of burglar alarms. Result: 90 percent of all new business was generated through referrals from existing customers.

Management

Managed burglar alarm company for four years while increasing profits yearly. Supervised office, sales, and installation personnel. Supervised and delegated work to assistants in accounting functions and inventory control. Worked as assistant credit manager, responsible for over $2 million per month in sales. Handled semiannual inventory of five branch stores totaling millions of dollars and supervised 120 people.

Accounting

Balanced all books and prepared tax forms for burglar alarm company. Eight years of experience in credit and collections, with emphasis on collections. Collection rates were over 98% each year; was able to collect a bad debt in excess of $250,000 deemed "uncollectible" by company.

Education

School of Computer Technology, Pittsburgh, PA
Business Applications Programming/TECH EXEC- 3.97 GPA

Robert Morris College, Pittsburgh, PA
Associate degree in Accounting, Minor in Management

2306 Cincinnati Street, Kingsford, PA 15171
(412) 437-6217
Cell Phone: (412) 464-1273
E-Mail: amclaughlin@enet.com

©2001 • JIST Works • Indianapolis, IN

Sample combination resume emphasizing skills and accomplishments within jobs. Note that each position within a company is listed.

THOMAS P. MARRIN
80 Harrison Avenue
Baldwin L.I., New York 11563
Answering Service: (716) 223-4705
E-Mail: tmarrin@connect.com

OBJECTIVE:

A middle/upper-level management position with responsibilities including problem solving, planning, organizing, and budget management.

EDUCATION:

University of Notre Dame, B.S. in Business Administration. Course emphasis on accounting, supervision, and marketing. Upper 25% of class. Additional training: Advanced training in time management, organizational behavior, and cost control.

MILITARY:

U.S. Army — 2nd Infantry Division, 1990 to 1994, 1st Lieutenant and platoon leader — stationed in Korea and Ft. Knox, Kentucky. Supervised an annual budget of nearly $4 million and equipment valued at over $40 million. Responsible for training, scheduling, and activities of as many as 40 people. Received several commendations. Honorable discharge.

BUSINESS EXPERIENCE:

Wills Express Transit Co., Inc., Mineola, New York

Promoted to Vice President, Corporate Equipment — 1999 to Present
Controlled purchase, maintenance, and disposal of 1100 trailers and 65 company cars with $6.7 million operating and $8.0 million capital expense responsibilities.

- Scheduled trailer purchases, six divisions.
- Operated 2.3% under planned maintenance budget in company's second best profit year while operating revenues declined 2.5%.
- Originated schedule to correlate drivers' needs with available trailers.
- Developed systematic Purchase and Disposal Plan for company car fleet.
- Restructured Company Car Policy, saving 15% on per car cost.

Promoted to Asst. Vice President, Corporate Operations — 1998 to 1999
Coordinated activities of six sections of Corporate Operations with an operating budget over $10 million.

- Directed implementation of zero-base budgeting.
- Developed and prepared Executive Officer Analyses detailing achievable cost-reduction measures. Resulted in cost reduction of over $600,000 in first two years.
- Designed policy and procedure for special equipment leasing program during peak seasons. Cut capital purchases by over $1 million.

Manager of Communications — 1996 to 1998
Directed and managed $1.4 million communication network involving 650 phones, 150 WATS lines, 3 switchboards, 5 employees.

- Installed computerized WATS Control System. Optimized utilization of WATS lines and pinpointed personal abuse. Achieved payback earlier than originally projected.
- Devised procedures that allowed simultaneous 20% increase in WATS calls and a $75,000/year savings.

Hayfield Publishing Company, Hempstead, New York

Communications Administrator — 1994 to 1996

Managed daily operations of a large Communications Center. Reduced costs and improved services.

The Quick Job Search Review

There are a few thoughts I want to emphasize in closing my brief review of job-seeking skills:

1. Approach your job search as if it were a job itself.

2. Get organized and spend at least 25 hours per week actively looking.

3. Follow up on all the leads you generate and send out lots of thank-you notes and JIST Cards.

4. If you want to get a good job quickly, you must get lots o interviews!

5. Pay attention to all the details; then be yourself in the inter view. Remember that employers are people, too. They wil hire someone who they feel will do the job well, be reliable and fit easily into the work environment.

6. When you want the job, tell the employer that you want th job and why. You need to have a good answer to the questio "Why should I hire you?" It's that simple.

Essential Job Search Data Worksheet

Completing this worksheet will help you create your resume, fill out applications, and answer interview questions. Take it with you as a reference as you look for a job. Use an erasable pen or pencil so you can make changes. In all sections, emphasize skills and accomplishments that best support your ability to do the job you want. Use extra sheets as needed.

Key Accomplishments

List three accomplishments that best prove your ability to do well in the kind of job you want.

1. _____

   _____

2. _____

   _____

3. _____

   _____

Education/Training

Name of high school(s); years attended: _____

_____

_____

_____

Subjects related to job objective: _____

_____

_____

_____

_____

Extracurricular activities/Hobbies/Leisure activities:

_____

_____

_____

_____

Accomplishments/Things you did well: _____

_____

_____

_____

Schools you attended after high school; years attended; degrees/certificates earned: _____

_____

_____

_____

_____

Courses related to job objective: _____

_____

_____

_____

Extracurricular activities/Hobbies/Leisure activities:

_____

_____

_____

_____

Accomplishments/Things you did well: _____

_____

_____

_____

_____

Military training, on-the-job, or informal training, such as from a hobby; dates of training; type of certificate earned: _____

_____

_____

_____

_____

Specific things you can do as a result: _____

_____

_____

_____

Work and Volunteer History

List your most recent job first, followed by each previous job. Include military experience and unpaid work here too, if it makes sense to do so. Use additional sheets to cover *all* your significant jobs or unpaid experiences.

Whenever possible, provide numbers to support what you did: number of people served over one or more years, number of transactions processed, percentage of sales increased, total inventory value you were responsible for, payroll of the staff you supervised, total budget you were responsible for, etc. As much as possible, mention results using numbers because they can be impressive in an interview or on a resume.

Job #1 _____

Name of organization: _____

_____

_____

Address: _____

_____

_____

Phone number: _____

_____

Dates employed: _____

Job title(s): _____

_____

_____

Supervisor's name: _____

_____

Details of any raises or promotions: _____

_____

_____

_____

Machinery or equipment you handled: _____

_____

_____

_____

Special skills this job required: _____

_____

_____

_____

List what you accomplished or did well: _____

_____

_____

_____

Job #2 _____

Name of organization: _____

_____

_____

Address: _____

_____

_____

Phone number: _____

_____

Dates employed: _____

Job title(s): _____

_____

Supervisor's name: _____

_____

Details of any raises or promotions: _____

_____

_____

_____

Machinery or equipment you handled: _____

_____

_____

_____

Special skills this job required: _____

_____

_____

_____

List what you accomplished or did well: _____

_____

_____

_____

Job #3 _____

Name of organization: _____

_____

_____

Address: _____

_____

_____

Phone number: _____

_____

Dates employed: _____

Job title(s): _____

_____

_____

Supervisor's name: _____

_____

Details of any raises or promotions: _____

_____

_____

_____

Machinery or equipment you handled: _____

_____

_____

_____

Special skills this job required: _____

_____

_____

_____

List what you accomplished or did well: _____

_____

_____

_____

References

Contact your references and let them know what type of job you want and why you are qualified. Be sure to review what they will say about you. Because some employers will not give out references by phone or in person, have previous employers write a letter of reference for you in advance. If you worry about a bad reference from a previous employer, negotiate what the employer will say about you or get written references from other people you worked with there. When creating your list of references, be sure to include your reference's name and job title, where he or she works, a business address and phone number, and how that person knows you.

The following material is based on content from a book titled Job Strategies for Professionals *written by a team of authors from the U.S. Employment Service.*

Some Tips for Coping with Job Loss

Being out of work is not fun for most people and is devastating to some. It may help you to know that you are not alone in this experience, and I've included some information here on what to expect and some suggestions for getting through it.

Some Problems You May Experience

Here are some feelings and experiences that you may have after losing your job.

✓ **Loss of professional identity.** Most of us identify strongly with our careers, and unemployment can often lead to a loss of self-esteem. Being employed garners respect in the community and in the family. When a job is lost, part of your sense of self may be lost as well.

✓ **Loss of a network.** The loss may be worse when your social life has been strongly linked to the job. Many ongoing "work friendships" are suddenly halted. Old friends and colleagues often don't call because they feel awkward or don't know what to say. Many don't want to be reminded of what could happen to them.

✓ **Emotional unpreparedness.** If you have never before been unemployed, you may not be emotionally prepared for it and devastated when it happens. It is natural and appropriate to feel this way. You might notice that some people you know don't take their job loss as hard as you have taken it. Studies show that those who change jobs frequently, or who are in occupations prone to cyclic unemployment, suffer far less emotional impact after job loss than those who have been steadily employed and who are unprepared for cutbacks.

Adjusting

You can often adjust to job loss by understanding its psychology. There have been a lot of studies done on how to deal with loss. Psychologists have found that people often have an easier time dealing with loss if they know what feelings they might experience during the "grieving process." Grief doesn't usually overwhelm us all at once; it usually is experienced in stages. The stages of loss or grief may include the following:

Shock—you may not be fully aware of what has happened.

Denial—usually comes next; you cannot believe that the loss is true.

Relief—you may feel a burden has lifted and opportunity awaits.

Anger—often follows; you blame (often without cause) those you think might be responsible, including yourself.

Depression—may set in some time later, when you realize the reality of the loss.

Acceptance—the final stage of the process; you come to terms with the loss and get the energy and desire to move beyond

it. The "acceptance" stage is the best place to be when starting a job search, but you might not have the luxury of waiting until this point to begin your search.

Knowing that a normal person will experience some predictable "grieving" reactions can help you deal with your loss in a constructive way. The faster you can begin an active search for a new job, the better off you will be.

Keeping Healthy

Unemployment is a stressful time for most people, and it is important to keep healthy and fit. Try to do the following:

✓ **Eat properly.** How you look and your sense of self-esteem can be affected by your eating habits. It is very easy to snack on junk food when you're home all day. Take time to plan your meals and snacks so they are well-balanced and nutritious. Eating properly will help you maintain the good attitude you need during your job search.

✓ **Exercise.** Include some form of exercise as part of your daily activities. Regular exercise reduces stress and depression and can help you get through those tough days.

✓ **Allow time for fun.** When you're planning your time, be sure to build fun and relaxation into your plans. You are allowed to enjoy life even if you are unemployed. Keep a list of activities or tasks that you want to accomplish such as volunteer work, repairs around the house, or hobbies. When free time occurs, you can refer to the list and have lots of things to do.

Family Issues

Unemployment is a stressful time for the entire family. For them, your unemployment means the loss of income and the fear of an uncertain future, and they are also worried about your happiness. Here are some ways you can interact with your family to get through this tough time.

✓ **Do not attempt to "shoulder" your problems alone.** Be open with family members even though it may be hard. Discussions about your job search and the feelings you have allow your family to work as a group and support one another.

✓ **Talk to your family.** Let them know your plans and activities. Share with them how you will be spending your time.

✓ **Listen to your family.** Find out their concerns and suggestions. Maybe there are ways they can assist you.

✓ **Build family spirit.** You will need a great deal of support from your family in the months ahead, but they will also need yours.

✓ **Seek outside help.** Join a family support group. Many community centers, mental health agencies, and colleges have support groups for the unemployed and their families. These groups can provide a place to let off steam and share frustrations. They can also be a place to get ideas on how to survive this difficult period.

Helping Children

If you have children, realize that they can be deeply affected by a parent's unemployment. It is important for them to know what has happened and how it will affect the family. However, try not to overburden them with the responsibility of too many emotional or financial details.

✓ **Keep an open dialogue with your children.** Letting them know what is really going on is vital. Children have a way of imagining the worst, so the facts can actually be far less devastating than what they envision.

✓ **Make sure your children know it's not anyone's fault.** Children may not understand about job loss and may think that *you* did something wrong to cause it. Or they may feel that somehow *they* are responsible or financially burdensome. They need reassurance in these matters, regardless of their age.

✓ **Children need to feel they are helping.** They want to help, and having them do something like taking a cut in allowance, deferring expensive purchases, or getting an after-school job can make them feel as if they are part of the team.

Some experts suggest that it can be useful to alert school counselors to your unemployment so that they can watch the children for problems at school before they become serious.

Coping with Stress

Here are some coping mechanisms that can help you deal with the stress of being unemployed.

✓ **Write down what seems to be causing the stress.** Identify the "stressors"; then think of possible ways to handle each one. Can some demands be altered, lessened, or postponed? Can you live with any of them just as they are? Are there some that you might be able to deal with more effectively?

✓ **Set priorities.** Deal with the most pressing needs or changes first. You cannot handle everything at once.

✓ **Establish a workable schedule.** When you set a schedule for yourself, make sure it is one that can be achieved. As you perform your tasks, you will feel a sense of control and accomplishment.

✓ **Reduce stress.** Learn relaxation techniques or other stress-reduction techniques. This can be as simple as sitting in a chair, closing your eyes, taking a deep breath and breathing out slowly while imagining all the tension going out with your breath. There are a number of other methods, including listening to relaxation tapes, that may help you cope with stress more effectively.

✓ **Avoid isolation.** Keep in touch with your friends, even former coworkers, if you can do that comfortably. Unemployed people often feel a sense of isolation and loneliness. See your friends, talk with them, socialize with them. You are the same person you were before unemployment. The same goes for the activities that you have enjoyed in the past. Evaluate them. Which can you afford to continue? If you find that your old hobbies or activities can't be part of your new budget, maybe you can substitute new activities that are less costly.

✓ **Join a support group.** No matter how understanding or caring your family or friends might be, they may not be able to understand all that you're going through, and you might be able to find help and understanding at a job-seeking support group.

These groups consist of people who are going through the same experiences and emotions as you. Many groups also share tips on job opportunities, as well as feedback on ways to deal more effectively in the job search process. *The National Business Employment Weekly,* available at major newsstands, lists support groups throughout the country. Local churches, YMCAs, YWCAs, and libraries often list or facilitate support groups.

Forty Plus is a national nonprofit organization and an excellent source of information about clubs around the country and on issues concerning older employees and the job search process. The address is 15 Park Row, New York, NY 10038. The telephone number is (212) 233-6086.

Keeping Your Spirits Up

Here are some ways you can build your self-esteem and avoid depression.

✓ **List your positives.** Make a list of your positive qualities and your successes. This list is always easier to make when you are feeling good about yourself. Perhaps you can enlist the assistance of a close friend or caring relative, or wait for a sunnier moment.

✓ **Replay your positives.** Once you have made this list, replay the positives in your mind frequently. Associate the replay with an activity you do often; for example, you might review the list in your mind every time you go to the refrigerator!

✓ **Use the list before performing difficult tasks.** Review the list when you are feeling down or to give you energy before you attempt some difficult task.

✓ **Recall successes.** Take time every day to recall a success.

✓ **Use realistic standards.** Avoid the trap of evaluating yourself using impossible standards that come from others. You are in a particular phase of your life; don't dwell on what you think society regards as success. Remind yourself that success will again be yours.

✓ **Know your strengths and weaknesses.** What things do you do well? What skills do you have? Do you need to learn new skills? Everyone has limitations. What are yours? Are there certain job duties that are just not right for you and that you might want to avoid? Balance your limitations against your strong skills so that you don't let the negatives eat at your self-esteem. Incorporate this knowledge into your planning.

✓ **Picture success.** Practice visualizing positive results or outcomes and view them in your mind before the event. Play out the scene in your imagination and picture yourself as successful in whatever you're about to attempt.

✓ **Build success.** Make a "to do" list. Include small, achievable tasks. Divide the tasks on your list and make a list for every day so you will have some "successes" daily.

✓ **Surround yourself with positive people.** Socialize with family and friends who are supportive. You want to be around people who will "pick you up," not "knock you down." You know who your fans are. Try to find time to be around them. It can really make you feel good.

✓ **Volunteer.** Give something of yourself to others through volunteer work. Volunteering will help you feel more worthwhile and may actually give you new skills.

Overcoming Depression

Are you depressed? As hard as it is to be out of work, it also can be a new beginning. A new direction may emerge that will change your life in positive ways. This may be a good time to reevaluate your attitudes and outlook.

✓ **Live in the present.** The past is over and you cannot change it. Learn from your mistakes and use that knowledge to plan for the future; then let the past go. Don't dwell on it or relive it over and over. Don't be overpowered by guilt.

✓ **Take responsibility for yourself.** Try not to complain or blame others. Save your energy for activities that result in positive experiences.

✓ **Learn to accept what you cannot change.** However, realize that in most situations, you do have some control. Your reactions and your behavior are in your control and will often influence the outcome of events.

✓ **Keep the job search under your own command.** This will give you a sense of control and prevent you from giving up and waiting for something to happen. Enlist everyone's aid in your job search, but make sure you do most of the work.

✓ **Talk things out with people you trust.** Admit how you feel. For example, if you realize you're angry, find a positive way to vent it, perhaps through exercise.

✓ **Face your fears.** Try to pinpoint them. "Naming the enemy" is the best strategy for relieving the vague feeling of anxiety. By facing what you actually fear, you can see if your fears are realistic or not.

✓ **Think creatively.** Stay flexible, take risks, and don't be afraid of failure. Try not to take rejection personally. Think of it as information that will help you later in your search. Take criticism as a way to learn more about yourself. Keep plugging away at the job search despite those inevitable setbacks. Most importantly, forget magic. What lies ahead is hard work!

Sources of Professional Help

If your depression won't go away or leads you to self-destructive behaviors such as abuse of alcohol or drugs, you may consider asking a professional for help. Many people who have never sought professional assistance before find that in a time of crisis, it really helps to have someone listen and give needed aid. Consult your local mental health clinics, social services agencies, religious organizations, or professional counselors for help for yourself and family members who are affected by your unemployment. Your health insurance may cover some assistance, or, if you do not have insurance, counseling is often available on a "sliding scale" fee, based on income.

Managing Your Finances While Out of Work

As you already know, being unemployed has financial consequences. While the best solution to this is to get a good job in as short a time as possible, you do need to manage your money differently during the time between jobs. Following are some things to think about.

Apply for Benefits Without Delay

Don't be embarrassed to apply for unemployment benefits as soon as possible, even if you're not sure you are eligible. This program is to help you make a transition between jobs, and you helped pay for it by your previous employment. Depending on how long you have worked, you can collect benefits for up to 26 weeks and sometimes even longer. Contact your state labor department or employment security agency for further information. Their addresses and telephone numbers are listed in your phone book.

Prepare Now to Stretch Your Money

Being out of work means lower income and the need to control your expenses. Don't avoid doing this, because the more you plan, the better you can control your finances.

Examine Your Income and Expenses

Create a budget and look for ways to cut expenses. The Monthly Income and Expense Worksheet can help you isolate income and expense categories, but your own budget may be considerably more detailed. I've included two columns for each expense category. Enter in the "Normal" column what you have been spending in that category during the time you were employed. Enter in the "Could Reduce To" column a lower number that you will spend by cutting expenses in that category.

Tips on Conserving Your Cash

While you are unemployed, it is likely that your expenses will exceed your income, and it is essential that you be aggressive in managing your money. Your objective here is very clear: you want to conserve as much cash as possible early on so you can have some for essentials later. Here are some suggestions.

✓ **Begin cutting all nonessential expenses right away.** Don't put this off! There is no way to know how long you will be out of work, and the faster you deal with the financial issues, the better.

✓ **Discuss the situation with other family members.** Ask them to get involved by helping you identify expenses they can cut.

✓ **Look for sources of additional income.** Can you paint houses on weekends? Pick up a temporary job or consulting assignment? Deliver newspapers in the early morning? Can a family member get a job to help out? Any new income will help, and the sooner the better.

✓ **Contact your creditors.** Even if you can make full payments for a while, work out interest-only or reduced-amount payments as soon as possible. When I was unemployed, I went to my creditors right away and asked them to help. They were very cooperative, and most are if you are reasonable with them.

✓ **Register with your local consumer credit counseling organization.** Many areas have free consumer credit counseling organizations that can help you get a handle on your finances and encourage your creditors to cooperate.

✓ **Review your assets.** Make a list of all your assets and their current value. Money in checking, savings, and other accounts is the most available, but you may have additional assets in pension programs, life insurance, and stocks that could be converted to cash if needed. You may also have an extra car that could be sold, equity in your home that could be borrowed against, and other assets that could be sold or used if needed.

✓ **Reduce credit card purchases.** Try to pay for things in cash to save on interest charges and prevent overspending. Be disciplined; you can always use your credit cards later if you are getting desperate for food and other basics.

✓ **Consider cashing in some "luxury" assets.** For example, sell a car or boat you rarely use to generate cash and to save on insurance and maintenance costs.

✓ **Comparison shop** for home/auto/life insurance and other expenses to lower costs.

✓ **Deduct job hunting expenses from your taxes.** Some job hunting expenses may be tax deductible as a "miscellaneous deduction" on your federal income tax return. Keep receipts for employment agency fees, resume expenses, and transportation expenses. If you find work in another city and you must relocate, some moving expenses are tax deductible. Contact an accountant or the IRS for more information.

Monthly Income and Expense Worksheet

Income

Unemployment benefits	_____	Interest/Dividends	_____
Spouse's income	_____	Other income	_____
Severance pay	_____	**TOTALS**	_____

Expenses

	NORMAL	COULD REDUCE TO		NORMAL	COULD REDUCE TO
Mortgage/rent:	_____	_____	**Health insurance:**	_____	_____
maintenance/repairs	_____	_____	medical expenses	_____	_____
Utilities:			dental expenses	_____	_____
electric	_____	_____	**Tuition:**	_____	_____
gas/oil heat	_____	_____	other school costs	_____	_____
water/sewer	_____	_____	**Clothing:**	_____	_____
telephone	_____	_____	**Entertainment:**	_____	_____
Food:	_____	_____	**Taxes:**	_____	_____
restaurants	_____	_____	**Job-hunting costs:**	_____	_____
Car payment:	_____	_____	**Other expenses:**	_____	_____
fuel	_____	_____		_____	_____
maintenance/repairs	_____	_____		_____	_____
insurance	_____	_____		_____	_____
Other loan payments:				_____	_____
_____	_____	_____		_____	_____
_____	_____	_____	**TOTALS**	_____	_____

Review Your Health Coverage

You know that it is dangerous to go without health insurance, but here are some tips.

✓ **You can probably maintain coverage at your own expense.** Under the COBRA law, if you worked for an employer that provided medical coverage and had 20 or more employees, you may continue your health coverage. However, you must tell your former employer within 60 days of leaving the job.

✓ **Contact professional organizations to which you belong.** They may provide group coverage for their members at low rates.

✓ **Speak to an insurance broker.** If necessary, arrange for health coverage on your own or join a local health maintenance organization (HMO).

✓ **Practice preventive medicine.** The best way to save money on medical bills is to stay healthy. Try not to ignore minor ills. If they persist, phone or visit your doctor.

✓ **Investigate local clinics.** Many local clinics provide services based on a sliding scale. These clinics often provide quality health care at affordable prices. In an emergency, most hospitals will provide you with services on a sliding scale, and most areas usually have one or more hospitals funded locally to provide services to those who can't afford them.

Using the Internet for Career Planning and Job Seeking

This brief review assumes you know how to use the Internet, so I won't get into how it works here. If the Internet and World Wide Web are new to you, I recommend a book titled *Cyberspace Job Search Kit* by Mary Nemnich and Fred Jandt. This book covers the basics about how the Internet works, how to get connected, plus a great deal of information on using it for career planning and job seeking.

Some Cautionary Comments

Let me begin by saying that the Internet has its problems as a tool for collecting information or for getting job leads. While the Internet has worked for many in finding job leads, far more users have been disappointed in the results they obtained. The problem is that many users assume that they can simply put their resume in resume databases and that employers will line up to hire them. It sometimes happens, but not often. That is the very same negative experience of people sending out lots of unsolicited resumes to personnel offices, a hopeful approach that has been around since long before computers.

There are two points that I made earlier about job-seeking methods which also apply to using the Internet:

1. It is unwise to rely on just one or two job search methods in conducting your job search.
2. It is essential that you conduct an active rather than a passive approach in your job search.

Just as with sending out lots of unsolicited resumes, simply listing your resume on the Internet is a passive approach that is unlikely to work well for you. Use the Internet in your job search, but plan to use other techniques, including direct contacts with employers.

A Success Story

Now that I have cautioned you regarding its limitations, you should know that the Internet does work very well for some people. To illustrate this, let me share with you a real situation I recently uncovered.

I was doing a series of interviews on jobs for a TV station in a rural area and asked the staff how they got their jobs there. They were all young, and the news anchor had told me that she had only been on the job a few months. It turned out that many of the previous employees had left the station about six months earlier to go to larger markets. That left a remaining recent graduate and new hire in charge but with few staff—and something of an emergency. He had obtained his job by responding to a job posting on a Web site used by broadcasters, so he went ahead and listed on that site all the jobs that were open at his station.

In a few days, new broadcasting graduates from all over the country saw the Internet postings and responded. E-mail went back and forth, and the relatively few willing to come to the station at their expense were invited to interview. Within a few weeks, most of the open positions were filled by young people who had responded on the Internet.

The crises for the TV station ended, and many of those hired told me that they were getting a great opportunity that they did not expect to obtain in any other way. I have to agree. More traditional recruiting methods would have created long delays for the employer and the job seekers. Traditional recruiting would also probably have screened out those with less experience and credentials. These job seekers got these jobs because of their using the Internet. While there were surely people with better credentials, they did not know about or get these jobs.

But note that the ones who got the jobs were those willing to take the chance and travel to the employer at their own expense. They had to be active and take some chances. And they had to be able to make a quick decision to move—something that a young person can more easily do. And they did not simply post their resumes in a resume database somewhere. The winning applicants were proactive in using the Internet to make direct contact with this employer, and then they followed up agressively.

Specific Tips to Increase Your Internet Effectiveness

Here are some things you can do to increase the effectiveness of using the Internet in your job search.

1. **Be as specific as possible in the job you seek.** This is important in using any job search method and even more so in using the Internet. I say this because the Internet is so enor-

mous in its reach that looking for a nonspecific job is simply not an appropriate task. So do your career planning homework and be specific in what you are looking for.

2. **Keep your expectations reasonable.** The people who have the most success on the Internet are those who best understand its limitations. For example, those with technical skills that are in short supply—such as network engineers—will have more employers looking for these skills and more success on the Internet. Keep in mind that many of the advertised jobs are already filled by the time you see them and that thousands of people may apply to those that sound particularly attractive. People do get job leads on the Internet, but be reasonable in your expectations and use a variety of job search methods in addition to the Internet.

3. **Consider your willingness to move.** If you don't want to move, or are willing only to move to certain locations, you should restrict your job search to geographic areas that meet your criteria. Many of the Internet databases allow you to view only those jobs that meet your criteria.

4. **Create a resume that is appropriate for use on the Internet.** With some exceptions, most of the resumes submitted on the Internet end up as simple text files with no graphic elements. Employers can then search a database of resumes for key words or use other searchable criteria. This is why your Internet resume should include a list of key words likely to be used by an employer as search criteria.

5. **Get your resume into the major resume databases used by employers.** Many of the major resume databases allow job seekers to list their resumes for free. Employers are typically charged for advertising their openings or sorting the database for candidates that meet their criteria. Most of these sites are easy to understand and use, and they often provide all sorts of useful information for job seekers.

6. **Seek out relevant sites.** Simply getting your resume listed on several Internet sites is often not enough. Many employers do not use these sites, or they use one but not another. Remember the example that I used earlier—those people found out about TV-related jobs from an Internet site that was run by a trade publication for broadcasters. Many professional associations post job openings on their sites or list other sites that would be of interest to that profession. Check out the resources that are available to people in the industries or occupations that interest you, since many of these resources also have Internet sites.

7. **Find specific employer sites.** Some employers have their own Internet sites that list job openings, allow you to apply online, and even provide access to staff who can answer your questions. While this is mostly used by larger technology-oriented companies, many smaller employers and government agencies have set up their own sites to attract candidates.

8. **Use informal chat rooms or request help.** Many Internet sites have interactive chat rooms or allow you to post a message for others to respond to. If you are not familiar with a chat room, it is a way for you to type responses to what someone else types as you are both online. Many sites also have a place for you to leave a message for others to respond to by sending you e-mail messages. Both of these methods allow you to meet potential employers or others in your field who can provide you with the advice or leads you seek.

9. **Use the listings of large Internet browsers or service providers.** While there are thousands of career-related Internet sites, some are better than others. Many sites provide links to other sites they recommend. Large service providers such as America Online (www.aol.com) and the Microsoft Network (www.msn.com) provide career-related information and job listings on their sites as well as links to other sites. Most of the larger portals provide links to recommended career-related sites and can be quite useful. Some of the larger such sites include Alta Vista (www.altavista.com), Lycos (www.lycos.com), and Yahoo (www.yahoo.com).

10. **Don't get ripped off.** Since the Internet has few regulations, many crooks use it as a way to take money from trusting souls. Remember that anyone can set up a site, even if the person does not provide a legitimate service, so be careful before you pay money for anything on the Internet. A general rule is that if it sounds too good to be true, it probably is. For example, if a site "guarantees" that it will find you a job or charges high fees, I recommend you look elsewhere.

Some Useful Internet Sites

There are hundreds and even thousands of Internet sites that provide information on careers or education, list job openings, or provide other career-related information.

Here are a few sites to get you started:

✓ The Riley Guide at www.rileyguide.com

✓ America's Job Bank at www.ajb.dni.us

✓ CareerPath.com at www.careerpath.com

✓ Monster.com at www.monster.com

✓ JIST at www.jist.com

In Closing

Few people will get a job offer because someone knocks on their door and offers one. The craft of job seeking does involve some luck, but you are far more likely to get lucky if you are out getting interviews. Structure your job search as if it were a full-time job and try not to get discouraged. There are lots of jobs out there, and someone needs what you can do—your job is to find that someone.

I hope this section helps, though you should consider learning more. Career planning and job seeking skills are, I believe, adult survival skills for our new economy. Good luck!

Mike Farr

Sample Resumes for Some of America's Top Medical, Education & Human Services Jobs

I've written many career and job search books, and several resume books are among them. If you've read the preceding *Quick Job Search* content, you know that I believe resumes are an overrated job search tool. Even so, you will probably need one, and you should have a good one.

Unlike some career authors, I do not preach that there is one right way to do a resume. I encourage you to be an individual and to do what you think will work well for you.

But I also know that some resumes are clearly better than others. To help you see examples of particularly good resumes, my editor has selected some from my book *The Quick Resume & Cover Letter Book*.

These resumes present real (but fictionalized) people and have these points in common:

- Each is for an occupation described in this book, although the job title may be a bit different. The resumes are organized alphabetically by occupation.

- Each was written by a professional resume writer who is a member of one or more professional associations, including the Professional Association of Résumé Writers or the National Résumé Writers' Association.

- Each is particularly good in some way. These resumes were selected from among many submitted for my books.

Notes on the resumes point out their features. Beneath each resume is the name of the professional resume writer who wrote it. Many of these folks provide help (for a fee) and welcome your contacting them (though this is not a personal endorsement). Their contact information appears at the end of this section.

I thank the professional resume writers whose resumes are included here. Their efforts bring a richness and diversity of style and design that can't be matched in any other way.

Here are the Web site addresses of the two professional associations. These sites list all association members along with contact information.

- Professional Association of Résumé Writers: www.parw.com

- National Résumé Writers' Association: www.nrwa.com

Biological and Medical Scientists

Writer's comments: The goal was to show Ms. Solent as a competent, problem-solving biologist — even though she had never worked in that field. I did it by documenting her classwork in terms an employer would be drawn to.

Ann Marie Solent

5355 Nora Road ○ Montgomery, Alabama 36100 ○ ℘[334] 555-5555

WHAT I BRING TO EARTHTECH: As an entry-level **water pollution biologist,** help complete the well done environmental studies needed to support your mission.

EDUCATION AND PROFESSIONAL DEVELOPMENT:

○ Bachelor of **Biological Sciences,** major **Environmental Science,** Auburn University, **GPA 3.19, Dean's List,** Dec XX – *Earned taking up to 20 credit hours and working up to 40 hours a week.*

- ○ Carried nearly double the biology class hours required for my major.
- ○ Found and fixed variable that was skewing data supporting study of symbiotic protection strategies in anemones. *Results:* New control group provided reliable baseline.
- ○ Corrected stubborn problem that had produced strong, but unexpected, results in study of scent tracking ability in lizards. *Results:* By eliminating environmental factor I had isolated, study produced results we were looking for.
- ○ Documented unlooked for relationship between sea urchins and arthropods. *Results:* Published biologist accepted my paper without change. Asked to present results in class.
- ○ Pursuing Corps of Engineers Wetland Delineation Certification

COMPUTER LITERACY:

○ Proficient: MiniTab (statistical analysis package)

○ Working knowledge: Windows 95, Internet search tools

Statements support her as hardworking, thorough, and competent

PUBLICATIONS:

Strike-induced Chemosensory Searching in the Colobrid Snakes *Elaphe g. guttata* and *Thamnophis siralis,* with Fred S. Falby, Ph.D., and Susan J. Winters, Ph.D., Ethology, Vol. 89, pp 19 – 28, XX

WORK HISTORY:

○ **Helped with study design, field work and reporting results:**

- ○ Dr. William E. Cooper, Jr., Professor of Biology, Auburn University, Jul XX, Dec XX
- ○ Dr. William Brooks, Professor of Biology, Auburn University, Dec XX, Dec XX

○ **Produced topographical survey maps** and **served as survey crewmember**

- ○ NorTrans, Inc. Montgomery, Alabama, Jul XX – Jan XX
- ○ Jacob Marley & Associates, Mobile, Alabama, Summers of XX and XX

○ Worked my way through school in positions in sales, retail management, equipment repair

Submitted by Don Orlando

Food and Beverage Service Occupations

Writer's comments: This client had the unique opportunity to open and manage a restaurant in a foreign country. Now she was back in the U.S. and ready to work in the food and beverage industry, especially in a position that would capitalize on her international experience.

Melinda E. Pelon

1759 Miller Way	Hudson, OH 44116	330-555-1468

Strong statements of competence as a manager

Profile

➤ Significant experience in food and beverage industry in diverse—including international—settings.
➤ Surprised skeptics by opening and successfully operating two food service properties . . . doubly challenging being a woman *and* an entrepreneur in a foreign country.
➤ A hands-on leader with expertise in building cooperative teams who enjoy their jobs.
➤ Innate understanding of what customers want, with ability to adapt and utilize that knowledge.
➤ Bilingual in English and Italian; conversational knowledge of Spanish and Portuguese.

Highlights of Experience

MANAGEMENT

Good list of specific things she can do

• Managed all aspects of business operations including budgeting, cost control, payroll and accounting functions.
• Monitored and purchased inventory, ensuring sufficient levels to accommodate demands; ordered perishables to maximize freshness and minimize waste.
• Built reputation and recognition of facilities through a variety of marketing efforts.
• Recruited, trained and motivated staff of chef, cooks, front house staff, servers, and bartenders.
• Auditioned and selected musicians to provide live entertainment.
• Delivered personal attention to customers to ensure high level of satisfaction, to generate repeat clientele, and to encourage word of mouth referrals.
• Collaborated with vendors to plan and implement promotions and special events.

BUSINESS START-UP

• Conceptualized and launched successful restaurant frequented by locals and tourists alike.
• Supervised all aspects of property preparation (renovation, selection of equipment, furnishings, decorating) from empty building to efficient, profit-producing operation.
• Developed and opened coffee house-concept property in neighboring community.
• Envisioned and implemented specific decor; searched for and identified local artist to create unique designs for facilities.
• Operated banquet facility (850 capacity) from separate kitchen simultaneously with restaurant.
• Collaborated with chef to create menus and develop dishes.

Professional Experience

HOMETOWN BAR • Hudson, Ohio
Neighborhood lounge catering to long-time clientele.
Manager   xxxx-Present
Bartender   xxxx-xxxx

OLIVE BASKET & BANQUET HALL • Milan, Italy
Unique and intimate atmosphere, specializing in Italian and American cuisine.
Founder/Owner   xxxx-xxxx

Education

OHIO STATE UNIVERSITY • Columbus, OH
Proficiency in English *(certified to teach English abroad)*   xxxx

COE COLLEGE • Akron, OH
Associate Degree - Marketing/Advertising   xxxx

QUALITY TRAVEL SCHOOL • Cleveland, Ohio
Certified Travel Agent   xxxx

References available on request

Submitted by Janet L. Beckstrom

General Managers and Top Executives

This resume was winner of the 1998 PARW Convention Best Résumé Contest — Finance Category.

Writer's Comments: Unemployed for nearly a year, my client had a resume that presented a sketchy employment history. He had mailed over 1,000 resumes with no response. This format showcased his achievements in three areas. He immediately began interviewing and is now happily employed as CFO for a large company.

RAYMOND MONROE
12 Main Street
New York, New York 00000
(555) 555-5555

SENIOR FINANCE EXECUTIVE

Finance & Accounting Management ... **Banking & Cash Management** ... **Budgeting**
Insurance & Risk Management ... **Tax & Regulatory Compliance** ... **Information Systems**

Senior-level executive with extensive finance, administration and public accounting experience in diverse industries including retail/wholesale distribution, financial services and manufacturing. Proven ability to improve operations, impact business growth and maximize profits through achievements in finance management, cost reductions, internal controls, and productivity/efficiency improvements. Strong qualifications in general management, business planning, systems technology design and implementation, and staff development/leadership.

PROFESSIONAL EXPERIENCE

SOUTHINGTON COMPANY • New York, New York • 1991-XXXX
Treasurer/Senior Controller • 1993-XXXX
Corporate Controller • 1991-1993

Chief financial officer appointed to treasurer and Executive Committee member directing $500M international consumer products company. Accountable for strategic planning, development and leadership of entire finance function as well as day-to-day operations management of company's largest domestic division. Recruited, developed and managed team of finance professionals, managers and support staff.

① *Operations Achievements*

Uses numbers to reinforce his results

- **Instrumental in improving operating profits from less than $400K to over $4M, equity from $8.6M to $13.6M and assets from $29.7M to $44.4M.**
- **Boosted market penetration by 27% which increased gross sales 32% through acquisition of 25 operating units as key member of due diligence team.**
- **Initiated strategies to redeploy company resources, resulting in 54% increase in gross margin by partial withdrawal from high-risk/low-margin product lines.**
- **Directed annual plan review process and strengthened accountability by partnering with senior-level department and district managers in all business units.**

Organizes results into three major groups ② *Financial Achievements*

- **Cut receivable write-offs $440K by developing credit policies, instituting aggressive collection strategies and establishing constructive dialogue with delinquent accounts.**
- **Negotiated and structured financing agreements, resulting in basis point reductions, easing/more favorable covenant restrictions and simplification of borrowing process.**
- **Saved over $2M through self-insurance strategy and an estimated $200K annually by positioning company to qualify to self-insure future workers' compensation claims.**
- **Designed executive and management reporting systems and tailored financial and operating reporting system to meet requirements of 100+ business units.**

RAYMOND MONROE • (555) 555-5555 • Page 2

Southington Company continued...

Note how every statement is results-oriented

③ *Technology Achievements*

♦ Turned around organization-wide resistance toward automation and streamlined procedures that significantly improved efficiency while reducing costs.
♦ Championed installation of leading-edge systems technology resolving long-standing profit measurement problems and created infrastructure to support corporate growth.
♦ Implemented automated cash management system in over 100 business unit locations and reduced daily idle cash by 50% ($750K).
♦ Recognized critical need and upgraded automated systems to track long-term assets which had increased from $28M to $48.8M in 5 years.

<u>HAMDEN COMPANY</u> • New York, New York • 1987-1991
Chief Financial Officer

Recruited for 3-year executive assignment to assume key role in building solid management infrastructure and positioning $15M company for its profitable sale in 1991. Directed general accounting, cash management, financial and tax reporting, banking relations, credit and collections, data processing, employee benefits, and administration. Managed and developed staff.

♦ **Converted company to small business corporation saving $450K in taxes over 3-year period.**
♦ **Realized $195K in accumulated tax savings through strategies adopting LIFO inventory method, minimizing taxes on a continual basis.**
♦ **Secured 25% of company's major client base (50% of total sales volume) by leading design, installation and administration of computer-based EDI program.**
♦ **Reduced collection period from 3 weeks to 5 days by initiating new policies and procedures.**

<u>MADISON COMPANY</u> • New York, New York • 1981-1987
Partner

Jointly acquired and managed public accounting firm serving privately held companies (up to $200M in revenues) in wholesale distribution, financial services and manufacturing industries. Concurrent responsibility for practice administration and providing accounting, business and MIS consulting services to corporate clients.

EDUCATION

B.S. in Accounting
New York University • New York, New York

Certified Public Accountant - New York

Submitted by Louise Garver

Home Health and Personal Care Aides

Susan J. Cascade

Each item in the Summary is very important to most employers. Emphasizing these attributes __will__ give Susan an edge over other applicants.

1872 West Main Street
Appleton, Wisconsin 54914
(414) 830-7878

Summary of Attributes

- Excellent communication and interpersonal skills; demonstrate a compassionate and caring approach to patient care and assistance with activities of daily living.
- Enjoy providing care and assisting people to make them comfortable; particularly sensitive to the needs of elderly clients.
- Complete assignments with limited supervision.
- Excellent attendance record; always punctual.
- Accurately record information, paying close attention to details.
- Certified in C.P.R.

Experience

Homecare Specialists, Neenah, Wisconsin   1994-Present
Home Health Aide
- Assist clients in their homes with a variety of duties including meal preparation, daily living tasks, and housekeeping.
- Administer medications and carry out medical treatments as instructed by Registered Nurse.
- Participate in exercise and ambulation programs.

Bethel Home, Oshkosh, Wisconsin   1992-1994
Nursing Assistant
- Provided patient care, monitored and recorded vital signs, maintained patient charts, assisted with daily living skills, and administered range of motion therapy.

Education

Fox Valley Technical College, Appleton, Wisconsin
Certified Nursing Assistant   1992

Additional Training: CPR certified, July 1993

Oshkosh North High School, Oshkosh, Wisconsin; Diploma   1990

Submitted by Kathy Keshemberg

Librarians

Writer's comments: This resume is much improved over the original, with a solid summary, check marks for the strong experience sections, and other changes. Karen got a head librarian job.

Karen A. Librarian
000 Any Street • Anywhere, Michigan 00000 • (000) 000-0000

Summary of Qualifications

Over 10 years of Librarian experience with 8 years at the supervisory level, maintaining a positive working environment. Possess excellent verbal and written communications skills and significant knowledge in reference materials. Conscientious and detail-oriented with ability to plan, organize, and direct library services and programs. Substantial computer experience, including Internet support.

Strong opening

Professional Experience

Any Public Library – Anywhere, Michigan   *XXXX – Present*
Assistant to the Director
- ✓ Supervise, instruct, and schedule 11 staff members, including entire faculty in director's absence
- ✓ Automation Project Manager in regards to interlibrary loans, book status, and budgeting
- ✓ Administer reference and reader advisory services to patrons, provide outreach services to senior center, and schedule various meetings
- ✓ Lead adult book discussions including book selections and conduct library tours
- ✓ Assisted in library expansion, design, and construction (XXXX-XXXX)

Another Public Library – Anywhere, Michigan   *An effective,*   *XXXX – XXXX*
Assistant to the Director, (XXXX – XXXX)   *space-efficient*
- ✓ Supervised, instructed, and scheduled 9 staff members   *format*
- ✓ Maintained microfiche and microfilm storage
- ✓ Handled bookkeeping responsibilities and routine operations of the library

Children's and Young Adult Librarian, (XXXX – XXXX)
- ✓ Selected books, periodicals, and nonprint material for collection development
- ✓ Planned and implemented "Story Time" programs for preschool students, summer reading programs for grade school students, and "Computer Pix" for young adults
- ✓ Updated reference and library materials to exhibit most current information

Another Branch Library – Anywhere, California   *XXXX – XXXX*
Reference Librarian (Temporary)
- ✓ Examined ordered resources for collection development
- ✓ Assisted coworkers and patrons in microfiche operation and computer usage
- ✓ Handled book reservations and answered reference inquiries

Computer Experience
- ✓ Microsoft Word, Excel, and PowerPoint
- ✓ Michigan Occupational Information Systems (MOIS)
- ✓ Data Research Associates (DRA), Intelligent Catalog-Bibliofile, TDD, Magnifiers, RLIN, CLSI, OCLC, GEAC, ERIC Data Base, and Info Track – Magazine Index

Education
Texas Woman's University – Denton, Texas
- • Master of Library Science, XXXX • Bachelor of Library Science, XXXX

Submitted by Maria E. Hebda

Medical Assistants

Writer's comments: This recent graduate's experience was limited. Using a functional format, her history was minimized while her clinical training were stressed.

non-related employment education, certifications, and

She was offered a position on the spot.

MARY ANN BURROWS
123 Randolph Street
City, State 99999
(555) 555-5555

CERTIFIED MEDICAL ASSISTANT

Health care professional with solid qualifications in clinical medical assisting, including performing basic laboratory procedures, assisting with medical/emergency procedures and taking medical histories. Thorough and accurate in completion of insurance forms and patient documentation. Demonstrate a sensitive, caring approach to patient care along with the ability to work cooperatively with all members of the health care team. Excellent interpersonal, organizational, problem solving and communication skills. Computer proficient.

All of this supports what she can do, not her chronological work history

EDUCATIONAL BACKGROUND

Certificate - Medical Assistant Program, Clinical Specialty
Westchester Community College, Valhalla, New York (1997)

Certifications:

Registered Medical Assistant, 1997 (#567834) - American Registry of Medical Assistants
Phlebotomy Technician • EKG Technician • CPR Certified
Level III Collection Services Technician • Psychemedics Sample Collection

CLINICAL and MEDICAL OFFICE SKILLS

Skin/Venipuncture … Specimen Collections (Urinalysis, Hematology & Psychemedics)
Medical Histories … Lab Procedures … Vital Signs … EKGs … Emergency Treatment
Assisting with Physical Examinations … Medical Terminology … Biohazardous Materials Disposal

ACCOMPLISHMENTS

♦ Conducted examinations involving complete patient medical histories, blood pressure readings, urine and blood sample collections, and drug screening for company serving the insurance industry. Frequently assigned to handle difficult clients and recaptured key accounts by ensuring timely service.

♦ Provided ongoing care to private, elderly patients. Took vital signs, administered medications and supplemental nourishment through IV therapy, and assisted patients with activities of daily living.

♦ Performed emergency services rotations at Memorial Hospital, assisting medical team in providing treatment at accidents and other emergency situations.

♦ Taught several courses in Medical Assistant Training Program at Health Education Centers, including anatomy, physiology, medical assisting, EKG, phlebotomy, and medical laboratory testing.

PROFESSIONAL EMPLOYMENT

Paramedical Insurance Examiner • INSURANCE SERVICES, INC., White Plains, New York • 1996-1997
Instructor - Medical Assisting • HEALTH EDUCATION CENTERS, White Plains, New York • 1994-1996

PRIOR EXPERIENCE

Office Manager • SCOPE COMMUNICATIONS, White Plains, New York • 1993-1994
Customer Service Representative • BOWEN CORPORATION, White Plains, New York • 1991-1993

Submitted by Louise Garver

Pharmacists

JACK PATERSON
Licensed in New York and New Jersey
56 83rd Street · Brooklyn, NY 00000
(555) 555-5555

A well-designed format with bold headings, small bullets, and short statements make an attractive, uncrowded resume.

CAREER OBJECTIVE:

Experienced and accomplished professional seeks a position as a staff pharmacist.

DEMONSTRATED STRENGTHS:

DETAIL-ORIENTED · TIME MANAGEMENT · SUPERVISORY SKILLS · COMMUNICATIONS

PROFESSIONAL EXPERIENCE:

GENERAL ISRAEL HOSPITAL   Paramus, New Jersey
Staff Pharmacist   *1992 - Present*
· Supervises two registered pharmacists and two pharmacy technicians.
· Prepares IV solutions, chemotherapy and antibiotics.
· Maintains computer profiles of patients' medications.
· Ensures adequate inventory levels and places orders.
· Fills employee prescriptions.
· Member of the Chemotherapy Committee.
· Develops clinical guidelines for oncology therapies.
· Maintains DUEs for groups of medications used in patient population on assigned units.

HACKENSACK MEDICAL CENTER   Hackensack, New Jersey
Staff Pharmacist   *1987 - 1992*
·· Supervised four technicians and ensured high standards were maintained.
· Prepared IV solutions, chemotherapy and antibiotics.
·· Performed daily functions to ensure smooth operations.

MAIMONIDES MEDICAL CENTER   Brooklyn, New York
Pharmacy Intern   *1987*
· Performed daily functions under the supervision of a licensed pharmacist.
· Filled prescriptions and maintained computerized records.

EDUCATION:

Bachelor of Science in Pharmacy
College of Pharmacy and Health Sciences
Long Island University · Brooklyn, New York (1986)

Bachelor of Science in Biology
Long Island University · Brooklyn, New York

Submitted by Alesia Benedict

PROFESSIONAL MEMBERSHIPS:

NJ Society of Hospital Pharmacists
Society of Toxicology

Physical Therapist Assistants and Aides

ROBIN A. PTA

Since she has relevant training and work experience, Robin uses a chronological resume to best present her move up the career ladder.

910 Yellow Brick Dr. Oz, KS 00000 **(913) 555-5768**

OBJECTIVE:
To contribute my skills and knowledge in Physical Therapy by continuing my career as a Physical Therapist Assistant in a challenging, team-oriented environment.

PROFILE:

Putting key accomplishments up front gets them noticed

- ◆ *Direct Care Provider of the Quarter*
- ◆ *Three-time recipient of the Star Therapist Award by three different facilities.*
- ◆ *Team player experienced with working with other rehabilitative disciplines to incorporate patients' functional activities.*
- ◆ *Highly organized individual with excellent time-management skills and strong work ethics.*

EXPERIENCE:
1993–Present

PHYSICAL THERAPIST ASSISTANT *WIZCARE, INC., LION'S DEN, PA.* Currently work as float between 13 facilities in the Kansas City and surrounding areas. Provide patients with therapeutic exercise, and transfer and mobility training, using modalities such as ultrasound, gait training equipment, and hot and cold packs. Also provide wound care with sharp debridement. Supervise two Restorative Aides.
- ◆ Train as many as 50 staff members at a time on certain rehabilitative aspects of patient care, such as proper body mechanics, proper wheelchair positioning, use of gait belts, and infection control.
- ◆ Teach patients' family members how to assist the patients without hindering independence and self-confidence.
- ◆ Teach patients how to be functional in their living environments and make suggestions for changes in the home to increase independence.
- ◆ Document patients' daily progress for Medicare, insurance and medical records, as well as reassess plans of care and make treatment suggestions with Registered Physical Therapist.

1991–1993

INSTRUCTOR, LIFETIME FITNESS CENTER *HOME COUNTY COMMUNITY COLLEGE, HOME PARK, KS.* Conducted general education seminars on wellness. Developed lesson plans and class materials. Supervised two student employees.
- ◆ Taught approximately 45 people about better wellness, including the importance of fitness and nutrition.
- ◆ Explained and demonstrated the proper use of various pieces of exercise equipment.

1990–1991

PHYSICAL THERAPIST TECHNICIAN *ADVANCED PHYSICAL THERAPY, DOROTHY, IN.* Assisted Physical Therapist with patients before, during and after treatment, using exercise and modalities such as electrical stimulation and hot and cold packs.
- ◆ Implemented patient exercise programs using weight machines, thera-bands and various stretching routines.
- ◆ Instructed pool therapy.

1987–1990

PHYSICAL THERAPIST TECHNICIAN *PHYSICAL MEDICINE ASSOCIATES, SCARECROW, IN.* Gained hands-on training while assisting Physical Therapists. Along with mentioned modalities, also used weights, bicycles, treadmills and whirlpool baths.
- ◆ Assisted with orthotic braces.

EDUCATION:
ASSOCIATES DEGREE IN PHYSICAL THERAPIST ASSISTANT; North Valley Community College; May, 1993.
BACHELOR OF SCIENCE DEGREE IN EXERCISE PHYSIOLOGY; Ball State University; May, 1987.

Submitted by Kristie Cook

Police and Detectives

The summary and recent work experience emphasize Peter's objective to become a police officer.

Peter M. Quinn
7509 Maple Drive
East Haven, Connecticut 06555
(203) 555-5555

Summary

Qualified and certified **Law Enforcement Officer** with two years' experience with the New Haven County Sheriff's Department.

- Graduate of Connecticut Police Officer Training; certified 1994.
- Proven ability to deal effectively with prisoners, establishing respect for authority while treating individuals fairly.
- Thorough, hard working, disciplined, and reliable, with a serious attitude and a career commitment to law enforcement.

Professional Experience

NEW HAVEN COUNTY SHERIFF'S DEPARTMENT   January 1995-Present
Deputy Sheriff/Corrections Officer • County Correctional Facility

Maintain inmate control over 100-plus prisoners in a dormitory-style jail. Supervise inmate behavior and respond to infractions. Count and lead prisoners to meals and recreation. Maintain detailed hourly logs and records of inmate transfers and other activities. Transport felons to higher security jails. Assume responsibility in other areas of the jail on an occasional basis.

- Developed skills in dealing with individuals of all types.
- Gained experience in effectively handling tense situations.
- Consistently achieved excellent performance evaluations.
- Member of Sheriff's Power Lifting Team; hold an American record in bench press.

Other Experience

RYDER'S, New Haven, Connecticut   1994-1995
Doorman/Bouncer

GRANT ASSOCIATES, New Haven, Connecticut   1993-1994
Field Representative

Negotiated and sold the services of a collection firm to business clients such as mortgage companies, doctors and other health care providers.

Education

Completed 6-month **Connecticut Police Officer Training and earned certification** (1994), CONNECTICUT POLICE OFFICERS ACADEMY, Storrs, Connecticut

Enrolled in **Criminal Justice degree program** (1995-Present), QUINNIPIAC COLLEGE

Graduate (1990), NORTH HAVEN HIGH SCHOOL, North Haven, Connecticut
- Member of Wrestling Team

Submitted by Louise Kursmark

Registered Nurses

Rochelle Simonson, RN, BSN, CGRN

10 Cloudell Road
Levittown, NY 11756
(516) 555-5555

The first page presents an image of a very competent, skilled applicant. Her strong credentials on page 2 simply reinforce this.

Statements from others allow you to communicate things you might not say about yourself but that can be very important to employers.

"...Rochelle has always been a very competent person who remains calm in the face of adversity...Her abilities have grown as her responsibilities have grown. She is always pleasant and I would recommend her highly for any position that she is qualified for..."

Garth N. Green, MD
Medical Director
Mid-Suffolk Hospital

"...You are doing an excellent job of caring for the patients entrusted to your care...it is not only the excellent care, but caring manner, compassion and understanding..."

Letter of Commendation
Delia Topping, RN, MA
Vice-president
Nursing Administration

Professional Profile

- Fourteen years experience as nurse and nurse manager in hospital and out-patient settings. Currently employed as assistant head nurse in 14 patient Endoscopy Unit. Certified in Gastroenterology. Licensed in New York State and Florida.

- Recognized for initiative, self-direction and ability to accurately perform multiple tasks. Cool-headed and effective under pressure. Interact well with all levels of staff. Deeply committed to exceptional and compassionate patient care.

Summary of Qualifications

Organized into groups to support her job objective of management

Nursing Management and Administration

- Designed Endoscopy Unit functions; run continuous quality improvement analysis and evaluation. Supervise and schedule 4 to 5 part-time nurses, full-time endoscopy technician and full-time nurses aide. Order all unit supplies and equipment

- As OR director for outpatient cosmetic surgery practice, handled all opening procedures for new practice: set-up operating room and instrumentation; developed policys and procedures; ordered supplies and equipment.

Patient Care and Communication

- Perform all diagnostic and therapeutic endoscopic procedures for up to 14 endoscopy patients a day, working directly with patients and physcians. Experienced in-patient and out-patient OR nurse. Adept at preparing patients for ambulatory surgery; able to do all IVs, meds etc. in one hour for up to 18 pre-surgical patients.

- Treat patients with respect and compassion, using a sense of humor to promote relaxation. Explain all procedures to allay fears and increase comfort levels. Establish a genuine rapport with patients and families. Act as liason between family, patients, and doctors; often consulted for opinion by physcians.

Staff Training and Development

- Train entire endoscopy team and precept new staff members. Directly involved in staff development and evaluation. Give classes on IV insertion

- Developed Endoscopy orientation and competency manuals and exams. Aided in creation of hospital policies for endoscopy unit that are now part of policy and procedure manual.

Rochelle Simonson, RN, BSN, CGRN

page two

Comments from "Customers" are very convincing when used as they are here ↓

"...I wish to make a point as to the excellent nursing staff, in particular, Rochelle S., who carefully went about her work using her notable abilities to work with all the patients in her care while devoting that special attention to each one as an individual..."

Letter of Commendation
Lyndon Smythe
(Patient)

"...writing to tell you of the excellent care I received...Rochelle made a follow-up phone call, during which she made a most constructive suggestion...needless to say, I am pleased with the overall regard for the patient..."

Letter of Commendation
Lauren T. Macalister
(Patient)

Licensure and Certification

- RN: New York State License # 375453-1
- RN: Florida License # 2650712
- Gastroenterology Certification
- IV Therapy Certification
- EKG Certification
- BCLS Certification

Education

B.S. in Nursing
State University of New York at Stony Brook 1984

A.A.S. in Surgical Technology
Nassau Community College, Garden City, NY 1971

Continuing Education

- Conscious Sedation: Nursing Perspectives and Responsibilities
- Clinical Controversies in Conscious Sedation
- AIDS: Legal & Ethical Considerations
- You're in Charge! Now, Create Order Out of Chaos
- The Aging of the Brain, The Aging of the Mind
- Fred Pryor Seminars: How to Supervise People

Career Development

Mid-Suffolk Hospital, Bethpage, NY	**1989 to present**
Assistant Head Nurse	1995 to present
Endoscopy Staff Nurse	1991 to 1995
OR Nurse	1989 to 1991
Cosmetic Surgery Accents, Plainview NY	**1988 to 1989**
OR Director	
North Shore University Hospital, Manhasset, NY	**1986 to 1988**
OR Nurse	
Acting Head Nurse—Ambulatory and Endoscopy	
New York Hospital, New York, NY	**1974 to 1977**
OR Technician	
Terrace Heights Hospital, Jamaica, NY	**1971 to 1974**
OR Technician	

Professional Affiliations

- SGNA Society of Gastroenterology Nurses and Associates
- New York State Nurses Association

Submitted by Deborah Wile Dib

School Teachers—Kindergarten, Elementary, and Secondary

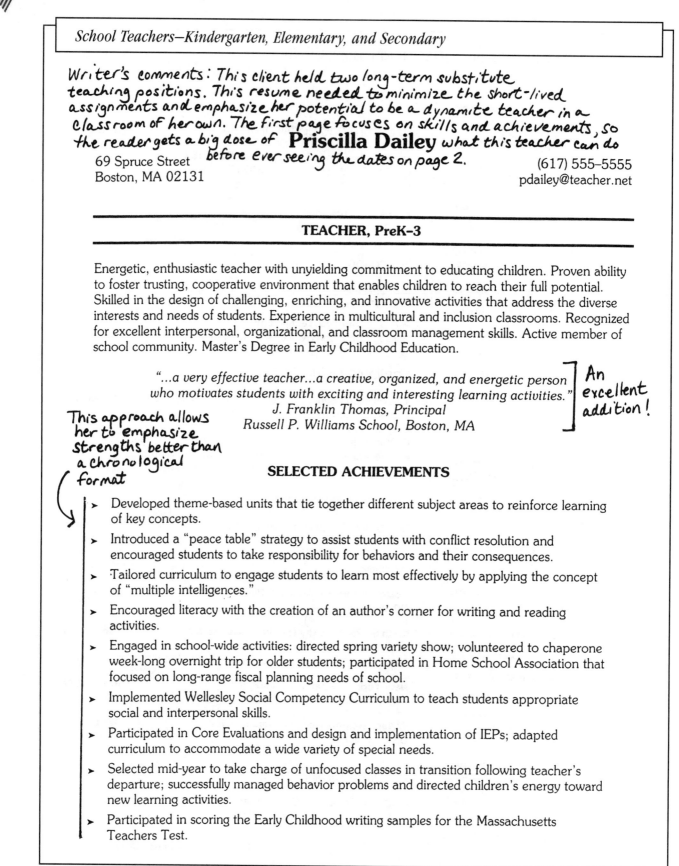

Writer's comments: This client held two long-term substitute teaching positions. This resume needed to minimize the short-lived assignments and emphasize her potential to be a dynamite teacher in a classroom of her own. The first page focuses on skills and achievements, so the reader gets a big dose of **Priscilla Dailey** *what this teacher can do before ever seeing the dates on page 2.*

69 Spruce Street
Boston, MA 02131

(617) 555-5555
pdailey@teacher.net

TEACHER, PreK–3

Energetic, enthusiastic teacher with unyielding commitment to educating children. Proven ability to foster trusting, cooperative environment that enables children to reach their full potential. Skilled in the design of challenging, enriching, and innovative activities that address the diverse interests and needs of students. Experience in multicultural and inclusion classrooms. Recognized for excellent interpersonal, organizational, and classroom management skills. Active member of school community. Master's Degree in Early Childhood Education.

"...a very effective teacher...a creative, organized, and energetic person who motivates students with exciting and interesting learning activities."
J. Franklin Thomas, Principal
Russell P. Williams School, Boston, MA

An excellent addition!

This approach allows her to emphasize strengths better than a chronological format

SELECTED ACHIEVEMENTS

➤ Developed theme-based units that tie together different subject areas to reinforce learning of key concepts.

➤ Introduced a "peace table" strategy to assist students with conflict resolution and encouraged students to take responsibility for behaviors and their consequences.

➤ Tailored curriculum to engage students to learn most effectively by applying the concept of "multiple intelligences."

➤ Encouraged literacy with the creation of an author's corner for writing and reading activities.

➤ Engaged in school-wide activities: directed spring variety show; volunteered to chaperone week-long overnight trip for older students; participated in Home School Association that focused on long-range fiscal planning needs of school.

➤ Implemented Wellesley Social Competency Curriculum to teach students appropriate social and interpersonal skills.

➤ Participated in Core Evaluations and design and implementation of IEPs; adapted curriculum to accommodate a wide variety of special needs.

➤ Selected mid-year to take charge of unfocused classes in transition following teacher's departure; successfully managed behavior problems and directed children's energy toward new learning activities.

➤ Participated in scoring the Early Childhood writing samples for the Massachusetts Teachers Test.

Priscilla Dailey   **Page 2**

Makes the most of her experience

TEACHING EXPERIENCE

Kindergarten Teacher – St. Catherine's School, Roslindale, MA   11/xx–6/xx
Taught full-day class of 20 kindergartners from multicultural backgrounds in private, parochial school. Developed and implemented curriculum in all subject areas, assessed student development, and made recommendations to implement services from outside sources, when necessary. Served as Faculty Representative to Home/School Association.

Kindergarten Teacher – Williams School, Roxbury, MA   1/xx–6/xx
Hired to take charge of full-day kindergarten class during teacher's extended absence. Established order and planned and taught lessons in all subject areas. Maintained ongoing communication with students' families.

Grade 2 Teacher (Clinical Practicum) – Curley School, Hyde Park, MA   9/xx–12/xx
Taught an inclusive, multicultural second grade classroom. Prepared lessons in reading, language arts, math, science, and social studies, using whole group and small group activities and tailoring curriculum to meet individual needs. Implemented objectives identified in IEP's.

Grade 1 Teacher (Provisional Practicum) – Fayerweather School, Cambridge, MA   1/xx–5/xx
Planned and implemented curriculum for reading, language arts, math, social studies, and science for students of varying abilities in multicultural setting.

Substitute Teacher – Boston and Lynn Public Schools   xxxx–xxxx

RELATED EXPERIENCE

Licensed Daycare Provider – Priscilla Dailey Child Care, Boston, MA   xxxx–xxxx
Community Trainer – Catholic Family and Children's Services, Boston, MA   xxxx–xxxx
Residential House Manager – Cambridge Children's Services, Cambridge, MA   xxxx–xxxx

EDUCATION / CERTIFICATION

MS, Early Childhood Education, Lesley College, Cambridge, MA   xxxx
BA, Political Science, Boston University, Boston, MA   xxxx

Certification: Standard, Early Childhood Education (PreK-3)

Submitted by Wendy Gelberg

Contact Information for Resume Contributors

The following professional resume writers contributed resumes to this section:

Alabama

Montgomery

Donald Orlando
The McLean Group
640 South McDonough
Montgomery, AL 36104
Phone: (334) 264-2020
E-mail: Yourcareercoach@aol.com
Member: PARW
Certification: CPRW, JCTC

Connecticut

Broad Brook

Louise Garver
Career Directions
P.O. Box 587
Broad Brook, CT 06016
Phone: (860) 623-9476
Fax: (860) 623-9473
E-mail: CAREERDIRS@aol.com
Web site: www.resumeimpact.com
Member: PARW, NRWA, IACMP, NCDA, ACA
Certification: CPRW, CMP, MA, JCTC

Kansas

Olathe

Kristie Cook
Absolutely Write
913 North Sumac Street
Olathe, KS 66061
Phone: (913) 269-3519
E-mail: Kriscook@absolutely-write.com
Web site: www.absolutely-write.com
Member: PARW
Certification: CPRW, JCTC

Massachusetts

Needham

Wendy Gelberg
Advantage Resume Services
21 Hawthorn Avenue
Needham, MA 02492
Phone: (781) 444-0778
Fax: (781) 444-2778
E-mail: wgelberg@aol.com
Member: NRWA
Certification: CPRW, JCTC

Michigan

Flint

Janet L. Beckstrom
Word Crafter
1717 Montclair Ave.
Flint, MI 48503
Voice/Fax: (800) 351-9818
Voice/Fax: (810) 232-9257
E-mail: wordcrafter@voyager.net
Member: PARW

Trenton

Maria Estela Hebda
Career Solutions, LLC
Trenton, MI 48183
Phone: (734) 676-9170
E-mail: maria@writingresumes.com
Web site: www.writingresumes.com
Member: PARW
Certification: CPRW

New Jersey

Rochelle Park

Alesia Benedict
Career Objectives
151 West Passaic Street
Rochelle Park, NJ 07662
Phone: (800) 206-5353
Fax: (800) 206-5454
E-mail: Careerobj@aol.com
Web site: www.getinterviews.com
Member: PARW
Certification: CPRW, JCTC

New York

Medford

Deborah Wile Dib
Advantage Resumes of New York
77 Buffalo Avenue
Medford, NY 11763
Phone: (631) 475-8513
Fax: (631) 475-8513
E-mail: gethired@advantageresumes.com
Web site: www.advantageresumes.com
Member: NRWA, PARW, AJST, CMI, CPADN
Certification: NCRW, CPRW, IJCTC

Ohio

Cincinnati

Louise Kursmark
Best Impression Career Services, Inc.
9847 Catalpa Woods Court
Cincinnati, OH 45242
Phone: (513) 792-0030
Fax: (513) 792-0961
E-mail: LK@yourbestimpression.com
Web site: www.yourbestimpression.com
Member: NRWA, PARW
Certification: CPRW, JCTC, CCM

Wisconsin

Appleton

Kathy Keshemberg
A Career Advantage
1615 E. Roeland, #3
Appleton, WI 54915
Phone: (920) 731-5167
Fax: (920) 739-6471
E-mail: kathyKC@aol.com
Web site: www.acareeradvantage.com
Member: NRWA
Certification: NCRW

Section Three

Important Trends in Jobs and Industries

I n putting this section together, I had two objectives. The first was to give you a quick review of major labor market trends. My second objective was to provide some information on the many jobs that were not included in this book.

To meet the first objective, I chose two excellent articles originally published in U.S. Department of Labor publications. The first article is "Tomorrow's Jobs: Important Labor Market Trends Through the Year 2008." It provides a superb—and short—review of the major trends that *will* affect your career in the years to come. Read it for ideas on selecting a career path for the long term. The second article is titled "Employment Trends in Major Industries." While you may not have thought much about it, the industry you work in is just as important as your occupational choice. This great article will help you learn about the major trends affecting various industries. Following this article are brief reviews of the three industries that are the focus of this book: health, education, and social services.

To meet the second objective, I included useful data on hundreds of jobs that are not described in this book. You may be working in one of these jobs now, so you may have more than passing interest in their projected growth and other details. Plus, among these many jobs, you may find one or more that interest you enough to consider them further. Many good jobs are not growing quickly, and the one you really want may be among them.

Tomorrow's Jobs: Important Labor Market Trends Through the Year 2008

Comments

This article, with minor changes, comes from the *Occupational Outlook Handbook* and was written by U.S. Department of Labor staff. The material provides a good review of major labor market trends both for occupations and for industries.

Much of this article uses 1998 data, the most recent available at press time. Since labor market trends tend to be fairly predictable, the delay does not affect the material's usefulness.

You may notice that some job titles in this article differ from those used elsewhere in the book. This is not an error. The material that follows uses a different set of occupations than I used in choosing this book's described jobs.

Making informed career decisions requires reliable information about opportunities in the future. Opportunities result from the relationships between the population, labor force, and the demand for goods and services.

Population ultimately limits the size of the labor force—individuals working or looking for work—which constrains how much can be produced. Demand for various goods and services determines employment in the industries providing them. Occupational employment opportunities, in turn, result from skills needed within specific industries. Opportunities for computer engineers and other computer-related occupations, for example, have surged in response to rapid growth in demand for computer services.

Examining the past and projecting changes in these relationships are the foundation of the government's Occupational Outlook Program. This section presents highlights of Bureau of Labor Statistics projections of the labor force and occupational and industry employment that can help guide your career plans.

Population

Population trends affect employment opportunities in a number of ways. Changes in population influence the demand for goods and services. For example, a growing and aging population has increased the demand for health services. Equally important, population changes produce corresponding changes in the size and demographic composition of the labor force.

The U.S. population is expected to increase by 23 million in the 10 years preceding 2008. This growth rate is about the same as during the 1988–98 period but much slower than during the 1978–88 period (chart 1). Continued growth will mean more consumers of goods and services, spurring demand for workers in a wide range of occupations and industries. The effects of population growth in various occupations will differ. The differences are partially accounted for by the age distribution of the future population.

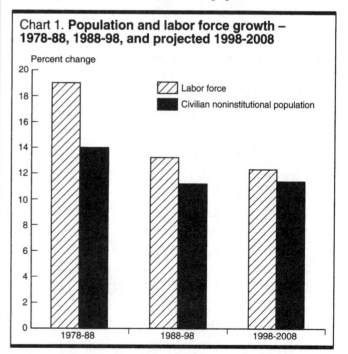

Chart 1. **Population and labor force growth – 1978-88, 1988-98, and projected 1998-2008**

The youth population, ages 16 to 24, is expected to increase as a share of the population for the first time since the 1970s. Overall, the 25-to-54 age group is expected to decrease as a share of the population. Within this group, however, the 45 and over age group will grow as a percent of the population. The 55-and-over age group will grow the fastest, increasing from 26.6 to 30 percent over the 1998–2008 period.

Minorities and immigrants will constitute a larger share of the U.S. population in 2008 than they do today. Substantial increases in the Hispanic, black, and Asian populations are forecasted, reflecting high birth rates as well as a continued flow of immigrants.

Labor Force

Population is the single most important factor in determining the size and composition of the labor force—comprised of people who are either working or looking for work. The civilian labor force is expected to increase by 17 million, or 12 percent, to 154.6 million over the 1998–2008 period. This increase is almost the same as the 13 percent increase during the 1988–98 period but much less than the 19 percent increase during the 1978–88 period.

The U.S. workforce will become more diverse by 2008. White, non-Hispanic persons will make up a decreasing share of the labor force, from 73.9 to 70.7 percent. Hispanics, non-Hispanic blacks, and Asians and other racial groups are projected to comprise an increasing share of the labor force by 2008—10.4 to 12.7 percent, 11.6 to 12.4 percent, and 4.6 to 5.7 percent, respectively (chart 2). However, despite relatively slow growth, white non-Hispanics will have the largest numerical growth in the labor force between 1998 and 2008, reflecting the large size of this group.

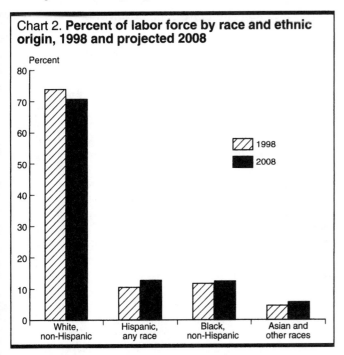

Chart 2. **Percent of labor force by race and ethnic origin, 1998 and projected 2008**

The number of men and women in the labor force will grow, but the number of men will grow at a slower rate than in the past. Between 1998 and 2008, men's share of the labor force is expected to decrease from 53.7 to 52.5 percent while women's share is expected to increase from 46.3 to 47.5 percent.

The youth labor force, ages 16 to 24, is expected to slightly increase its share of the labor force to 16 percent in 2008, growing more rapidly than the overall labor force for the first time in 25 years. The large group of workers 25-to-44 years old, who comprised 51 percent of the labor force in 1998, is projected to decline to 44 percent of the labor force by 2008. Workers 45 and older, on the other hand, are projected to increase from 33 to 40 percent of the labor force between 1998 and 2008, due to the aging baby-boom generation (chart 3).

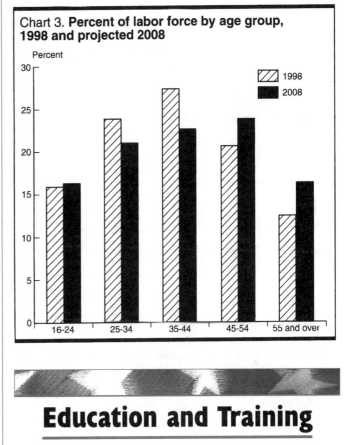

Chart 3. **Percent of labor force by age group, 1998 and projected 2008**

Education and Training

Projected job growth varies widely by education and training requirements. Five out of the six education and training categories projected to have the highest percent change require at least a bachelor's degree (chart 4). These five categories will account for one-third of all employment growth over the 1998-2008 period. Employment in occupations that do not require postsecondary education are projected to grow by about 12 percent while occupations that require at least a bachelor's degree are projected to grow by almost 22 percent, compared to 14 percent for all occupations combined.

Education is essential in getting a high-paying job. In fact, all but a few of the 50 highest-paying occupations require a college degree. However, a number of occupations—for example, blue-collar worker supervisors, electricians, and police patrol officers—do not require a college degree, yet offer higher-than-average earnings.

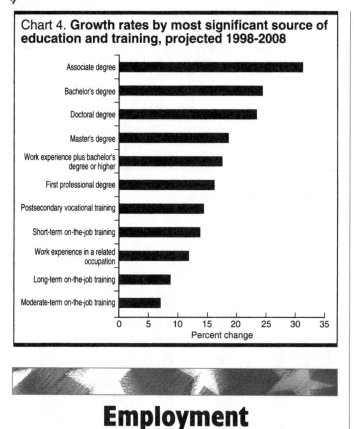

Chart 4. Growth rates by most significant source of education and training, projected 1998-2008

Percent change

- Associate degree
- Bachelor's degree
- Doctoral degree
- Master's degree
- Work experience plus bachelor's degree or higher
- First professional degree
- Postsecondary vocational training
- Short-term on-the-job training
- Work experience in a related occupation
- Long-term on-the-job training
- Moderate-term on-the-job training

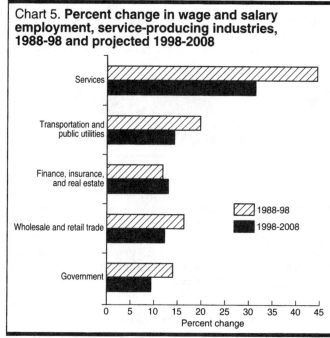

Chart 5. Percent change in wage and salary employment, service-producing industries, 1988-98 and projected 1998-2008

Percent change

- Services
- Transportation and public utilities
- Finance, insurance, and real estate
- Wholesale and retail trade
- Government

☐ 1988-98
■ 1998-2008

Employment

Total employment is expected to increase from 141 million in 1998 to 161 million in 2008, or by 14 percent. The 20 million jobs that will be added by 2008 will not be evenly distributed across major industrial and occupational groups. Changes in consumer demands, technology, and many other factors will contribute to the continually changing employment structure in the U.S. economy.

The following two segments examine projected employment change from both industrial and occupational perspectives. The industrial profile is discussed in terms of primary wage and salary employment; primary employment excludes secondary jobs for those who hold multiple jobs. The exception is agriculture, which includes self-employed and unpaid family workers in addition to salaried workers.

The occupational profile is viewed in terms of total employment—including primary and secondary jobs for wage and salary, self-employed, and unpaid family workers. Of the nearly 141 million jobs in the U.S. economy in 1998, wage and salary workers accounted for over 128 million; self-employed workers accounted for over 12 million; and unpaid family workers accounted for about 200,000. Of the nearly 141 million total jobs, secondary employment accounted for over 2 million. Self-employed workers held 9 out of 10 secondary jobs; wage and salary workers held most of the remainder.

Industry

The long-term shift from goods-producing to service-producing employment is expected to continue (chart 5).

Service-producing industries—including finance, insurance, and real estate; government; services; transportation and public utilities; and wholesale and retail trade—are expected to account for approximately 19.1 million of the 19.5 million new wage and salary jobs generated over the 1998–2008 period. The services and retail trade industry sectors will account for nearly three-fourths of total wage and salary job growth, a continuation of the employment growth pattern of the 1988–98 period.

Services. The largest and fastest-growing major industry group—services—is expected to add 11.8 million new jobs by 2008. Nearly three-fourths of this projected job growth is concentrated in three sectors of services—business, health, and professional and miscellaneous services. Business services—including personnel supply and computer and data processing services, among other detailed industries—will add 4.6 million jobs. Health services—including home health care services and nursing and personal care facilities, among other detailed industries—will add 2.8 million jobs. Professional and miscellaneous services—including management and public relations and research and testing services, among other detailed industries—will add 1.1 million jobs. Employment in computer and data processing services is projected to grow 117 percent between 1998 and 2008, ranking as the fastest-growing industry.

Transportation and public utilities. Overall employment is expected to increase by 674,000 jobs, or 14 percent. Employment in the transportation sector is expected to increase by 16 percent, from 4.3 to 5 million jobs. Air, truck, and local and interurban passenger transportation will account for 32, 30, and 23 percent, respectively, of the job growth in this industry. Employment in communications is expected to grow about as fast as average through 2008, adding about 300,000 new jobs. Employment in utilities is expected to decline by about 4 percent. However, faster-than-average growth is expected in water supply and sanitary services with the creation of about 67,000 jobs.

Finance, insurance, and real estate. Employment is expected to increase by 13 percent—adding 960,000 jobs to the 1998 level of 7.4 million. Demand for financial services is expected to continue. The security and commodity brokers segment of the industry is expected to grow by 40 percent, creating about 255,000 jobs. Nondepository institutions will add 193,000 jobs and have a growth rate of 29 percent, fueled by increased demand for nonbank corporations that offer bank-like services. Continued demand for real estate will create 179,000 new jobs, at a growth rate of about 12 percent. The insurance carriers segment is expected to grow by nearly 10 percent—adding 154,000 jobs.

Wholesale and retail trade. Employment is expected to increase by 7 and 14 percent, respectively, growing from 6.8 to 7.3 million in wholesale trade and from 22.3 to 25.4 million in retail trade. With the addition of 1.3 million jobs, the eating and drinking places segment of the retail industry is projected to have the largest numerical increase in employment.

Government. Between 1998 and 2008, government employment, including public education and public hospitals, is expected to increase by over 9 percent, from 19.8 to 21.7 million jobs. State and local government, particularly education, will drive employment growth. Federal government employment is expected to decline by 165,000 jobs.

Employment in the goods-producing industries has been relatively stagnant since the early 1980s. Overall, this sector is expected to grow by 1.6 percent over the 1998-2008 period. Although employment growth is expected to show little change, projected growth within the sector varies considerably (chart 6).

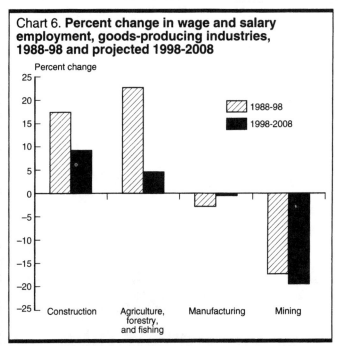

Chart 6. **Percent change in wage and salary employment, goods-producing industries, 1988-98 and projected 1998-2008**

Construction. Construction is expected to increase by 9 percent from 5.9 to 6.5 million. Demand for new housing and an increase in road, bridge, and tunnel construction will account for the bulk of employment growth in this industry.

Agriculture, forestry, and fishing. Overall employment in agriculture, forestry, and fishing is expected to increase by nearly 5 percent from 2.2 to 2.3 million. Strong growth in agricultural services will more than offset an expected continued decline in crops and livestock and livestock products.

Manufacturing. Manufacturing employment is expected to decline by less than 1 percent from the 1998 level of 18.8 million. The projected loss of jobs reflects improved production methods, advances in technology, and increased trade.

Mining. Mining employment is expected to decrease by 19 percent from 590,000 to 475,000. The continued decline is partly due to laborsaving machinery and increased imports.

Occupation

Expansion of the service-producing sector is expected to continue, creating demand for many occupations. However, projected job growth varies among major occupational groups (chart 7).

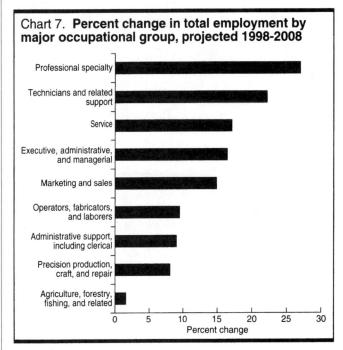

Chart 7. **Percent change in total employment by major occupational group, projected 1998-2008**

Professional specialty. Professional specialty occupations comprise the fastest-growing group. Over the 1998–2008 period, a 27-percent increase in the number of new professional specialty jobs is projected, an increase of 5.3 million. Professional specialty workers perform a wide variety of duties and are employed throughout private industry and government. Computer systems analysts, computer engineers and scientists, special education teachers, and social and recreation workers are among the fastest-growing occupations in this group.

Technicians and related support. Employment of technicians and related support occupations is projected to grow by 22 percent, adding 1.1 million jobs by 2008. Workers in this group provide technical assistance to engineers, scientists, physicians, and other professional specialty workers, and operate and program technical equipment. Over half of the projected employment growth among technicians—about 616,000 jobs—is among health technicians and technologists. Considerable growth is also expected among computer programmers and paralegals and legal assistants.

Service. Employment in service occupations is projected to increase by 3.9 million, or 17 percent, by 2008, the second largest numerical gain among the major occupational groups. Over half of the new jobs are in the rapidly growing services industry division, led by business services, health services, and social services.

Executive, administrative, and managerial. Executive, administrative, and managerial occupations are projected to increase by 16 percent, or 2.4 million, over the 1998–2008 period. Workers in this group establish policies, make plans, determine staffing requirements, and direct the activities of businesses, government agencies, and other organizations. The services industry division is expected to account for half of the job growth, adding 1.2 million jobs. The number of self-employed executive, administrative, and managerial workers is expected to increase by 361,000—more than any other major occupational group—to almost 2.5 million by 2008.

Marketing and sales. Workers in marketing and sales occupations sell goods and services, purchase commodities and property for resale, and stimulate consumer interest. Employment in this group is projected to increase by 15 percent, or 2.3 million, from 1998 to 2008. The services industry division is expected to add the most marketing and sales jobs—719,000— by 2008, followed by an additional 92,000 jobs in the transportation and public utilities industry division.

Operators, fabricators, and laborers. Employment of operators, fabricators, and laborers is expected to increase by 1.8 million workers, or 9.4 percent, from 1998 to 2008. Most new jobs in this group are expected among transportation and material moving machine and vehicle operators; helpers, laborers, and material movers; and hand workers, including assemblers and fabricators, adding 745,000; 626,000; and 290,000 jobs, respectively.

Administrative support, including clerical. The number of workers in administrative support occupations, including clerical, is projected to increase by 9 percent from 1998 to 2008, adding 2.2 million new jobs. With 24.5 million workers, this is the largest major occupational group. Workers perform a wide variety of administrative tasks necessary to keep organizations functioning efficiently. Due mostly to technological change, several large occupations within this group—for example, bookkeeping, accounting, and auditing clerks—are expected to decline. However, other occupations less affected by technological change are expected to increase. These occupations include teacher assistants, adding 375,000 jobs; office and administrative support supervisors and managers, adding 313,000 jobs; receptionists and information clerks, adding 305,000 jobs; and adjusters, investigators, and collectors, adding 302,000 jobs.

Precision production, craft, and repair. Employment in precision production, craft, and repair occupations is projected to grow 8 percent, creating almost 1.3 million new jobs, over

the 1998–2008 period. Mechanics, installers, and repairers are expected to add 588,000 new jobs by 2008; construction trades workers are expected to add 390,000 new jobs; and blue-collar worker supervisors are expected to add 196,000 new jobs.

Agriculture, forestry, fishing, and related. Agriculture, forestry, fishing, and related occupations are projected to grow by only 2 percent, adding 71,000 new jobs. Workers in these occupations cultivate plants, breed and raise livestock, and catch animals. Within this major group, job losses are expected for farmers and farm workers. In contrast, landscaping, groundskeeping, nursery, greenhouse, and lawn service occupations are expected to add 262,000 new jobs by 2008.

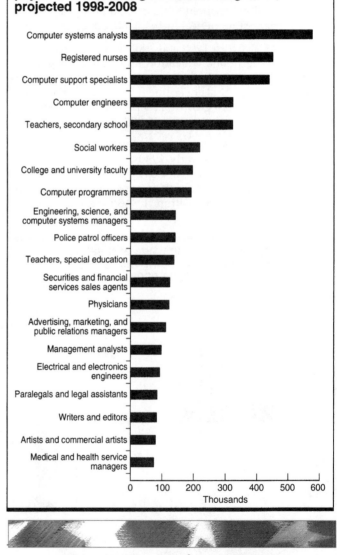

Chart 8. Occupations with fast growth and high pay that have the largest numerical growth, projected 1998-2008

Fast-Growing Jobs

The 20 occupations listed in chart 8 are among those projected to grow fast and produce large numbers of new jobs, in addition to having higher-than-average earnings. Half of these occupations are involved with computer technology, health care, and education. Systems analysts top this list, adding over 577,000 jobs between 1998 and 2008, reflecting high demand for computer services. Among other computer-related occupations, computer support specialists and computer engineers are expected to add 439,000 and 323,000 new jobs, respectively. Similarly, strong demand for health care services will fuel growth among registered nurses, creating 451,000 new jobs. Among education-related occupations, secondary school teachers head the list, adding 322,000 jobs.

Computer-related jobs are expected to grow the fastest over the projection period (chart 9). In fact, these jobs make up the four fastest-growing occupations in the economy. Computer engi-

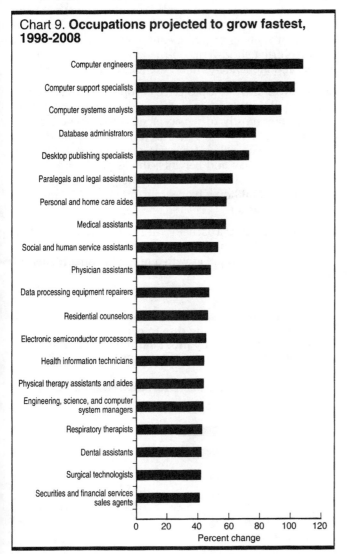

Chart 9. **Occupations projected to grow fastest, 1998-2008**

neers, computer support specialists, computer systems analysts, and database administrators are expected to increase by 108, 102, 94, and 77 percent, respectively. Many other occupations projected to grow the fastest are in health care.

Declining occupational employment stems from declining industry employment, technological advances, organizational changes, and other factors. For example, increased produc-

tivity and farm consolidations are expected to result in a decline of 173,000 farmers over the 1998–2008 period (chart 10). Office automation and the increased use of word processing equipment by professionals and managerial employees will lead to a decline among word processors and typists. Examples of occupations projected to lose jobs along with declining employment in the industries in which they are concentrated include farm workers; sewing machine operators, garment; and child-care workers, private household.

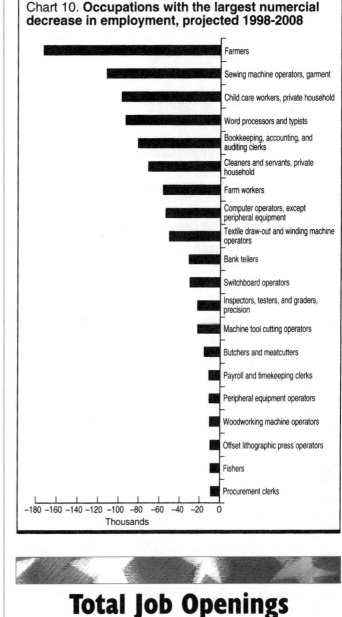

Chart 10. **Occupations with the largest numerical decrease in employment, projected 1998-2008**

Total Job Openings

Job openings stem from both employment growth and replacement needs (chart 11). Replacement needs arise as workers leave occupations. Some transfer to other occupations while others retire, return to school, or quit to assume household responsibilities. Replacement needs are projected to account for 63 percent of the approximately 55 million job openings between 1998 and 2008. Thus, even occupations with slower-than-average growth or little or no change in employment may still offer many job openings.

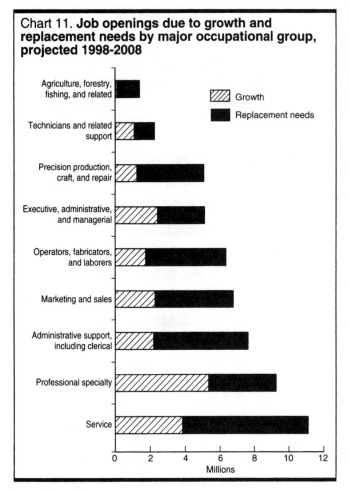

Chart 11. Job openings due to growth and replacement needs by major occupational group, projected 1998-2008

Professional specialty occupations are projected to grow faster and add more jobs than any major occupational group, with 5.3 million new jobs by 2008. Two-thirds of this job growth is expected among teachers, librarians, and counselors; computer, mathematical, and operations research occupations; and health assessment and treating occupations. With 3.9 million job openings due to replacement needs, professional specialty occupations comprise the only major group projected to generate more openings from job growth than from replacement needs.

Due to high replacement needs, service occupations are projected to have the largest number of total job openings, 11.1 million. A large number of replacements are expected to arise as young workers leave food preparation and service occupations. Replacement needs generally are greatest in the largest occupations and in those with relatively low pay or limited training requirements.

Office automation will significantly affect many individual administrative and clerical support occupations. Overall, these occupations are projected to grow more slowly than the average, while some are projected to decline. Administrative

support, including clerical occupations, are projected to create 7.7 million job openings over the 1998–2008 period, ranking third behind service and professional specialty occupations.

Precision production, craft, and repair occupations and operators, fabricators, and laborers are projected to grow more slowly than the average for all occupations through 2008, due mostly to advances in technology and changes in production methods. Replacement needs are projected to account for almost three-fourths of all the job openings in these groups.

Employment in occupations requiring an associate degree is projected to increase 31 percent, faster than any other occupational group categorized by education and training. However, this category only ranks seventh among the 11 education and training categories in terms of total job openings. The largest number of job openings will be among occupations requiring short-term on-the-job training, a bachelor's degree, and moderate-term on-the-job training (chart 12).

Almost two-thirds of the projected job openings over the 1998-2008 period will be in occupations that require on-the-job training, due mostly to replacement needs. These jobs will account for 34.5 million of the projected 55 million total job openings through 2008. However, many of these jobs typically offer low pay and benefits; this is particularly true of jobs requiring only short-term on-the-job training, which account for 24 million job openings, far more than any other occupational group.

Jobs requiring at least a bachelor's degree will account for about 12.7 million job openings through 2008. Most of these openings will result from job growth and usually offer higher pay and benefits.

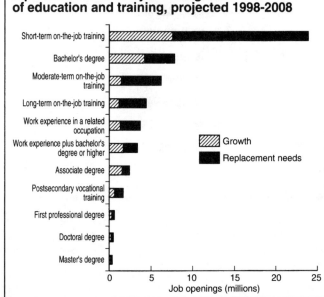

Chart 12. Job openings due to growth and replacement needs by most significant source of education and training, projected 1998-2008

Employment Trends in Major Industries

Comments

While hundreds of specialized industries exist, about 75 percent of all workers are employed in just 42 major ones. The article that follows presents a good overview of trends within industry types and gives important facts to consider in making career plans. At the end of the article, you will find three brief reviews of the industries that are the focus of this book: health, education, and social services. The article and the reviews come, with minor changes, from a book published by the U.S. Department of Labor titled the *Career Guide to Industries,* 2000-2001 edition.

While you may not have thought much about it, the industry you work in will often be as important as the career you choose. For example, some industries pay significantly higher wages. So, if you found your way back to this article, read it over carefully and consider the possibilities.

For more information on a specific industry, look for the *Career Guide to Industries* in your library. A more widely available version of the same book, published by JIST under the same title, is available through bookstores and many libraries. Here are the industries covered in the *Career Guide to Industries:*

Goods-Producing Industries

Agriculture, Mining, and Construction
Agricultural production
Agricultural services
Construction
Mining and quarrying
Oil and gas extraction

Manufacturing
Aerospace manufacturing
Apparel and other textile products
Chemical manufacturing, except drugs
Drug manufacturing
Electronic equipment manufacturing
Food processing
Motor vehicle and equipment manufacturing
Printing and publishing
Steel manufacturing
Textile mill products

Service-Producing Industries

Transportation, Communications, and Public Utilities
Air transportation
Cable and other pay television services
Public utilities
Radio and television broadcasting
Telecommunications
Trucking and warehousing

Wholesale and Retail Trade
Department, clothing, and accessory stores
Eating and drinking places
Grocery stores
Motor vehicle dealers
Wholesale trade

Finance and Insurance
Banking
Insurance
Securities and commodities

Services
Advertising
Amusement and recreation services
Child-care services
Computer and data processing services
Educational services
Health services
Hotels and other lodging places
Management and public relations services
Motion picture production and distribution
Personnel supply services
Social services, except child care

Government
Federal government
State and local government

Overview

The U.S. economy is comprised of industries with diverse characteristics. For each industry covered in the *Career Guide to Industries*, detailed information is provided about specific characteristics: the nature of the industry, working conditions, employment, occupational composition, training and advancement requirements, earnings, and job outlook. This article provides an overview of these characteristics for the economy as a whole.

Nature of the Industry

Industries are defined by the goods and services the industry provides. Because workers in the United States produce such a wide variety of products and services, industries in the U.S. economy range widely, from aerospace manufacturing to motion picture production. Although many of these industries are related, each industry contains a unique combination of occupations, production techniques, and business characteristics. Understanding the nature of the industry is important, because it is this unique combination that determines working conditions, educational requirements, and the job outlook for each industry.

Industries are comprised of many different places of work, called *establishments,* which range from large factories and office complexes employing thousands of workers to small businesses employing only a few workers. Not to be confused with "companies," which are legal entities, establishments are physical locations where people work, such as the branch office of a bank. Establishments that produce similar goods or services are grouped together into *industries*. Industries that produce related types of goods or services are, in turn, grouped together into *major industry divisions*. These are further grouped into the *goods-producing sector* (agriculture, forestry, and fishing; mining; construction; and manufacturing) or the *service-producing sector* (transportation, communications, and public utilities; wholesale and retail trade; finance, insurance, and real estate; services; and government).

Distinctions within industries are also varied. Each industry is comprised of a number of subdivisions, which are determined largely by differences in production processes. An easily recognized example of these distinctions is in the food processing industry, which is made up of subdivisions that produce meat products, preserved fruits and vegetables, bakery items, beverages, and dairy products, among others. Each of these subdivisions requires workers with varying skills and employs unique production techniques. Another example of these distinctions is in public utilities, which employs workers in establishments that provide electricity, sanitary services, water, and natural gas. Working conditions and establishment characteristics often differ widely in each of these smaller subdivisions.

There were nearly 7 million business establishments in the United States in 1997. The average size of these establishments varies widely across industries. Among industry divisions, manufacturing included many industries having among the highest employment per establishment in 1997. For example, the aerospace, motor vehicle, and steel manufacturing industries each averaged 150 or more employees per establishment.

Most establishments in the wholesale and retail trade, finance, and services industries are small, averaging fewer than 20 employees per establishment. Exceptions are the air transportation industry with 62 employees and educational services with 44. In addition, wide differences within industries can exist. Hospitals, for example, employ an average of 716 employees, while doctor's offices employ an average of 9. Similarly, despite an average of 14 employees per establishment for all of retail trade, department stores employ an average of 183 people.

Establishments in the United States are predominantly small; 55 percent of all establishments employed fewer than five workers in 1997. The medium to large establishments, however, employ a greater proportion of all workers. For example, establishments that employed 50 or more workers accounted for only 5 percent of all establishments, yet employed 58 percent of all workers. The large establishments—those with more than 500 workers—accounted for only 0.3 percent of all establishments, but employed 20 percent of all workers. Table 1 presents the percent distribution of employment according to establishment size.

TABLE 1

Percent Distribution of Establishments and Employment in All Industries by Establishment Size, 1997

Establishment Size (Number of Workers)	Establish-ments	Employ-ment
Total	100.0	100.0
1-4	54.5	6.1
5-9	19.6	8.5
10-19	12.4	10.9
20-49	8.3	16.4
50-99	2.8	12.7
100-249	1.7	16.2
250-499	0.4	9.4
500-999	0.2	7.0
1,000 or more	0.1	12.7

Source: Department of Commerce, County Business Patterns, 1997

Establishment size can play a role in the characteristics of each job. Large establishments generally offer workers greater occupational mobility and advancement potential, whereas small establishments may provide their employees with broader experience by requiring them to assume a wider range of responsibilities. Also, small establishments are distributed throughout the nation; every locality has a few small businesses. Large establishments, in contrast, employ more workers and are less common, but they play a much more prominent role in the economies of the areas in which they are located.

Working Conditions

Just as the goods and services of each industry are different, working conditions in industries can vary significantly. In some industries, the work setting is quiet, temperature-controlled, and virtually hazard free. Other industries are characterized by noisy, uncomfortable, and sometimes dangerous work environments. Some industries require long workweeks and shift work; in many industries, standard 35- to 40-hour workweeks are common. Still other industries can be seasonal, requiring long hours during busy periods and abbreviated schedules during slower months. These varying conditions usually are determined by production processes, establishment size, and the physical location of work.

One of the most telling indicators of working conditions is an industry's injury and illness rate. Overexertion, being struck by an object, and falls on the same level were among the most common incidents causing injury or illness. In 1997, approximately 6.1 million nonfatal injuries and illnesses were reported throughout private industry. Among major industry divisions, manufacturing had the highest rate of injury and illness—10.3 cases for every 100 full-time workers—while finance, insurance, and real estate had the lowest rate—2.2 cases. About 6,000 work-related fatalities were reported in 1998; transportation accidents, violent acts, contact with objects and equipment, falls, and exposure to harmful substances or environments were among the most common events resulting in fatal injuries. Table 2 presents industries with the highest and lowest rates of nonfatal injury and illness.

TABLE 2

Nonfatal Injury and Illness Rates of Selected Industries, 1997

Industry	Cases Per 100 Full-Time Employees
All industries	7.1
High rates	
Motor vehicle manufacturing	25.5
Air transportation	16.4
Nursing and personal care facilities	16.2
Food processing	14.5
Trucking and warehousing	10.0

Industry	Cases Per 100 Full-Time Employees
Low rates	
Insurance	1.9
Banking	1.8
Radio and TV broadcasting	1.8
Computer and data processing	0.8
Securities and commodities	0.7

Work schedules are another important reflection of working conditions, and the operational requirements of each industry lead to large differences in hours worked and part-time versus full-time status. The contrast in an average workweek was notable between retail trade and manufacturing—29.1 hours and 41.7 hours, respectively, in 1998. More than 30 percent of workers in retail trade work part time (1 to 34 hours per week), compared to only 5 percent in manufacturing. Table 3 presents industries having relatively high and low percentages of part-time workers.

TABLE 3

Percent of Part-Time Workers in Selected Industries, 1998

Industry	Percent Part Time
All industries	15.9
Many part-time workers	
Apparel and accessory stores	38.6
Eating and drinking places	38.0
Department stores	33.0
Grocery stores	32.5
Child-care services	29.7
Few part-time workers	
Public utilities	3.0
Chemical manufacturing, except drugs	2.9
Textile mill products manufacturing	2.5
Motor vehicle and equipment manufacturing	1.8
Steel manufacturing	1.7

The low proportion of part-time workers in some manufacturing industries often reflects the continuity of the production processes and the specificity of skills. Once begun, it is costly to halt these processes; machinery and materials must be tended and moved continuously. For example, the chemical manufacturing industry produces many different chemical products through controlled chemical reactions. These processes require chemical operators to monitor and adjust the flow of materials into and out of the line of production. Production may continue 24 hours a day, 7 days a week under the watchful eyes of chemical operators who work in shifts.

Retail trade and service industries, on the other hand, have seasonal cycles marked by various events, such as school openings or important holidays, that affect the hours worked.

During busy times of the year, longer hours are common, whereas slack periods lead to cutbacks and shorter workweeks. Jobs in these industries are generally appealing to students and others who desire flexible, part-time schedules.

Employment

The number of wage and salary worker jobs in the United States totaled nearly 128 million in 1998, and it is projected to reach almost 148 million by 2008 (See Table 4). In addition to these workers, the U.S. economy also provided employment for nearly 12 million self-employed workers and about 182,000 unpaid family workers.

As shown in Table 4, employment is not evenly divided among the various industries. The services major industry division is the largest source of employment, with over 47 million workers, followed by wholesale and retail trade and manufacturing major industry divisions.

Among the industries covered in the *Career Guide,* wage and salary employment ranged from 181,000 in cable and other pay television services to 11.2 million in educational services.

Three industries—educational services, health services, and eating and drinking places—together accounted for about 30 million jobs, or nearly a quarter of the nation's employment.

TABLE 4

Wage and Salary Employment in Selected Industries, 1998, and Projected Change, 1998 to 2008

(Employment in thousands)

Industry	1998 Employment	Percent Distribution	2008 Employment	1998-2008 Employment Change	Percent Change
All industries	128,008	100.0	147,543	19,535	15.3
Goods-producing industries	27,506	21.5	27,951	445	1.6
Agriculture, forestry, and fishing	2,159	1.7	2,257	98	4.6
Agricultural services	1,005	0.8	1,251	246	24.5
Agricultural production	1,106	0.9	968	-138	-12.5
Mining	590	0.5	475	-115	-19.4
Oil and gas extraction	339	0.3	283	-56	-16.7
Mining and quarrying	251	0.2	192	-59	-23.2
Construction	5,985	4.7	6,535	550	9.2
Manufacturing	18,772	14.7	18,684	-88	-0.5
Electronics manufacturing	1,564	1.2	1,701	137	8.8
Food processing	1,686	1.3	1,721	35	2.1
Printing and publishing	1,564	1.2	1,545	-19	-1.3
Motor vehicle and equipment manufacturing	990	0.7	940	50	-5.0
Chemicals manufacturing, except drugs	764	0.6	734	-30	-3.9
Apparel and other textile products manufacturing	763	0.6	586	-178	-23.3
Textile mill products manufacturing	598	0.5	501	-97	-16.2
Aerospace manufacturing	524	0.4	656	132	25.2
Drug manufacturing	279	0.2	308	29	10.7
Steel manufacturing	232	0.2	177	-55	-23.7

Industry	1998		2008	1998-2008	
	Employ-ment	Percent Distribution	Employ-ment	Employment Change	Percent Change
Service-producing industries	100,501	78.5	119,590	19,089	19.0
Transportation, communications, and public utilities	6,600	5.2	7,540	940	14.3
Trucking and warehousing................................	1,745	1.4	1,944	199	11.4
Air transportation	1,183	0.9	1,400	217	18.3
Telecommunications	1,042	0.8	1,285	244	23.4
Public utilities	855	0.7	822	-33	-3.8
Radio and television broadcasting	247	0.1	253	6	2.5
Cable and other pay TV services	181	0.1	230	49	27.0
Wholesale and retail trade	29,128	22.8	32,693	3,565	12.2
Eating and drinking places	7,760	6.1	9,082	1,322	17.0
Wholesale trade	6,831	5.3	7,330	499	7.3
Department, clothing, and variety stores	3,872	3.0	4,101	228	5.9
Grocery stores	3,066	2.4	3,240	174	5.7
Motor vehicle dealers	1,145	0.9	1,277	132	11.6
Finance, insurance, and real estate	7,407	5.8	8,367	960	13.0
Insurance..	2,344	1.8	2,576	233	9.9
Banking	2,042	1.6	2,100	58	2.8
Securities and commodities	645	0.5	900	255	39.6
Services	47,528	37.1	60,445	12,917	27.2
Educational services	11,175	8.7	12,885	1,680	15.3
Health services	10,829	8.5	13,614	2,785	25.7
Personnel supply services	3,230	2.5	4,623	1,393	43.1
Social services..	2,039	1.6	2,878	839	41.1
Hotels and other lodging places	1,776	1.4	2,088	312	17.6
Amusement and recreation services	1,601	1.3	2,108	507	31.7
Computer and data processing services.................	1,599	1.2	3,471	1,872	117.1
Management and public relations services	1,034	0.8	1,500	466	45.1
Child-care services	605	0.5	800	196	32.3
Motion picture production and distribution	270	0.2	316	46	16.9
Advertising	268	0.2	323	55	20.5
Government	9,838	7.7	10,545	707	7.2
State and local government	7,152	5.6	7,996	844	11.8
Federal government	1,819	1.4	1,655	-164	-9.0

Although workers of all ages are employed in each industry, certain industries tend to possess workers of distinct age groups. For the reasons mentioned above, retail trade employs a relatively high proportion of younger workers to fill part-time and temporary positions. The manufacturing sector, on the other hand, has a relatively high median age because many jobs in the sector require a number of years to learn and rely on skills that do not easily transfer to other firms. Also, manufacturing employment has been declining, providing fewer opportunities for younger workers to get jobs. As a result, almost one-third of the workers in retail trade were 24 years of age or younger, whereas only 10 percent of workers in manufacturing were 24 or younger. Table 5 contrasts the age distribution of workers in all industries with the distributions in retail trade and manufacturing.

TABLE 5

Percent Distribution of Industry Sector Employment by Age Group, 1998

Age Group	All Industries	Retail Trade	Manu-facturing
Total	100.0	100.0	100.0
16-24	15.0	32.5	9.9
25-54	72.3	56.9	78.2
55 and older	12.7	10.6	11.8

Employment in some industries is concentrated in one region of the country, and job opportunities in these industries should be best in the States in which their establishments are located. Such industries are often located near a source of raw materials upon which the industries rely. For example, oil and gas extraction jobs are concentrated in Texas, Louisiana, and Oklahoma; many textile mill products manufacturing jobs are found in North Carolina, Georgia, and South Carolina; and a significant proportion of motor vehicle and equipment manufacturing jobs are located in Michigan. On the other hand, some industries—such as grocery stores and educational services—have jobs distributed throughout the nation, reflecting population density in different areas.

Occupations in the Industry

As mentioned above, the occupations found in each industry depend on the types of services provided or goods produced. For example, construction companies require skilled trades workers to build and renovate buildings, so these companies employ a large number of carpenters, electricians, plumbers, painters, and sheet metal workers. Other occupations common to the construction sector include construction equipment operators and mechanics, installers, and repairers. Retail trade, on the other hand, displays and sells manufactured goods to consumers, so this sector hires numerous sales clerks and other workers, including nearly 5 out of 6 cashiers. Table 6 shows the major industry divisions and the occupational groups which predominate in the division.

TABLE 6

Industry Divisions and Largest Occupational Concentration, 1998

Industry Division	Largest Occupational Group	Percent of Wage and Salary Jobs
Agriculture, forestry, and fishing	Agriculture and related	78.8
Mining	Precision production	44.0
Construction	Precision production	55.5
Manufacturing	Operators, fabricators, and laborers	45.0
Transportation, communications, and public utilities	Operators, fabricators, and laborers	33.0
Wholesale and retail trade	Marketing and sales	32.7
Finance, insurance, and real estate	Administrative support	44.8
Services	Professional specialty	28.4
Government	Administrative support	26.1

The nation's occupational distribution clearly is influenced by its industrial structure, yet there are many occupations, such as general manager or secretary, which are found in all industries. In fact, some of the largest occupations in the U.S. economy are dispersed across many industries. Because nearly every industry relies on administrative support, for example, this occupational group is the largest in the nation (see Table 7). Other large occupational groups include service occupations, professional specialty workers, and operators, fabricators, and laborers.

TABLE 7

Total Employment in Broad Occupational Groups, 1998 and Projected Change, 1998-2008 (Employment in Thousands)

Occupational Group	1998 Employment	1998-2008 Percent Change
Total, all occupations	140,514	14.4
Executive, administrative, and managerial	14,770	16.4
Professional specialty	19,802	27.0
Technicians and related support	4,949	22.2
Marketing and sales	15,341	14.9
Administrative support, including clerical	24,461	9.0
Services	22,548	17.1
Agriculture, forestry, fishing, and related	4,435	1.6
Precision production, craft, and repair	15,619	8.0
Operators, fabricators, and laborers	18,588	9.4

Training and Advancement

Workers prepare for employment in many ways, but the most fundamental form of job training in the United States is a high school education. Fully 87 percent of the nation's workforce possessed a high school diploma or its equivalent in 1998. As the premium placed on education in today's economy increases, workers are responding by pursuing additional training. In 1998, 28 percent of the nation's workforce had some college or an associate's degree, while an additional 27 percent continued in their studies and attained a bachelor's degree or higher. In addition to these types of formal education, other sources of qualifying training include formal company training, informal on-the-job training, correspondence courses, the Armed Forces, and friends, relatives, and other nonwork-related training.

The unique combination of training required to succeed in each industry is determined largely by the industry's occupational composition. For example, machine operators in manufacturing generally need little formal education after high school, but sometimes complete considerable on-the-job training. These requirements by major industry division are clearly demonstrated in Table 8. Workers with no more than a high school diploma comprised about 67 percent of all workers in agriculture, forestry, and fishing; 65 percent in construction; 55 percent in manufacturing; and 57 percent in wholesale and retail trade. On the other hand, workers who had acquired at least some training at the college level comprised 73 percent of all workers in government; 69 percent in finance, insurance, and real estate; and 63 percent in services. Tables 9 and 10 provide further illustration of how greatly industries vary in their training requirements, which show industries having the highest percentages of college graduates and workers without education beyond high school.

TABLE 8

Percent Distribution of Highest Grade Completed or Degree Received by Industry Division, 1998

Industry Division	Bachelor's Degree or Higher	Some College or Associate Degree	High School Graduate or Equivalent	Less Than 12 Years or No Diploma
Agriculture, forestry, and fishing	13	20	34	33
Mining	24	22	39	15
Construction	10	25	44	21
Manufacturing	21	24	40	15
Transportation, communications, and public utilities	20	33	38	9
Wholesale and retail trade	14	29	37	20
Finance, insurance, and real estate	37	32	27	4
Services	39	24	28	9
Government, public administration	37	36	25	2

TABLE 9

Industries with the Highest Percentage of Workers Who Have a Bachelor's Degree or Higher, 1998

Industry	Percent
Management and public relations services	68.6
Securities and commodities	64.9
Elementary and secondary schools	62.8
Legal services	62.5
Accounting and auditing services	62.3

TABLE 10

Industries with the Highest Percentage of Workers Who Have 12 Years or Less of Schooling or No Diploma, 1998

Industry	Percent
Meat products processing	79.5
Apparel and other finished textile products manufacturing	74.4
Private households	74.4
Lumber and wood products manufacturing	74.2
Services to dwellings and other buildings	73.2
Agricultural production, crops	73.1

Education and training are also important factors in the variety of advancement paths found in different industries. In general, workers who complete additional on-the-job training or education help their chances of being promoted. In much of the manufacturing sector, for example, production workers who receive training in management and computer skills increase their likelihood of being promoted to supervisors. Other factors which may figure prominently in the industries covered in the *Career Guide* include the size of the establishment or company, institutionalized career tracks, and the skills and aptitude of each worker. Each industry has some unique advancement paths, so persons who seek jobs in particular industries should be aware of how these paths may later shape their careers.

Earnings

Like other characteristics, earnings differ from industry to industry, the result of a highly complicated process that relies on a number of factors. For example, earnings may vary due to the occupations in the industry, average hours worked, geographical location, industry profits, union affiliation, and educational requirements. In general, wages are highest in metropolitan areas to compensate for the higher cost of living. And, as would be expected, industries that employ relatively few unskilled minimum-wage or part-time workers tend to have higher earnings.

A good illustration of these differences is shown by the earnings of production and nonsupervisory workers in coal mining, which averaged $858 a week in 1998, and those in eating and drinking places, where the weekly average was $162. These differences are so large because the coal mining industry employs a relatively highly skilled, highly unionized workforce, while eating and drinking places employ many relatively lower skilled, part-time workers, few of whom belong to unions. In addition, many workers in eating and drinking places are able to supplement their low wages with money they receive as tips, which are not included in the industry wages data. Table 11 highlights the industries with the highest and lowest average weekly earnings. Because these data exclude supervisors, they generally are lower than the average earnings for all workers in a given industry.

TABLE 11

Average Weekly Earnings of Nongovernment Production or Nonsupervisory Workers in Selected Industries, 1998

Industry	Earnings
All industries	$442
Industries with high earnings	
Coal mining	858
Railroad transportation	845
Aerospace manufacturing	845
Public utilities	843
Steel manufacturing	822
Computer and data processing services	815
Engineering services	810
Securities and commodities	800
Motion picture production and services	789
Motor vehicle production	780
Industries with low earnings	
Help supply services	330
Nursing and personal care services	318
Apparel and other textile products manufacturing	318
Hotels and other lodging places	279
Grocery stores	276
Amusement and recreation services	258
General merchandise stores	256
Child-care services	237
Apparel and accessory stores	226
Eating and drinking places	162

Employee benefits, once a minor addition to wages and salaries, continue to grow in diversity and cost. In addition to traditional benefits—including paid vacations, life and health insurance, and pensions—many employers now offer various benefits to accommodate the needs of a changing labor force. Such benefits are child care, employee assistance programs that provide counseling for personal problems, and wellness programs that encourage exercise, stress management, and self-improvement. Benefits vary among occupational groups, full- and part-time workers, public and private sector workers, regions, unionized and nonunionized workers, and small and large establishments. Data indicate that full-time workers and those in medium-size and large establishments—those with 100 or more workers—receive better benefits than part-time workers and those in smaller establishments.

Union affiliation may also play a role in earnings and benefits. In 1998, about 15 percent of workers throughout the nation were union members or covered by union contracts. As Table 12 demonstrates, union affiliation of workers varies widely by industry. Over a third of the workers in government and transportation, communications, and public utilities are union members or are covered by union contracts, compared to less than 4 percent in finance, insurance, and real estate and agriculture, forestry, and fishing.

TABLE 12

Percent of Workers Who Are Union Members or Covered by Union Contracts by Industry Division, 1998

Industry Division	Union Members Or Covered by Union Contracts
Total, all industries	15.4
Government, public administration	37.5
Transportation, communications, and public utilities	33.7
Construction	19.8
Manufacturing	16.8
Services	15.4
Mining	13.6
Wholesale and retail trade	5.8
Finance, insurance, and real estate	3.4
Agriculture, forestry, and fishing	2.3

Outlook

Total employment in the United States is projected to increase about 15 percent over the 1998-2008 period. Employment growth, however, is only one source of job openings; the total number of openings provided by any industry depends on its current employment level, its growth rate, and its need to replace workers who leave their jobs. Throughout the economy, in fact, replacement needs will create more job openings than employment growth. Employment size is a major determinant of job openings—larger industries generally provide more openings. The occupational composition of an industry is another factor. Industries with a high concentration of professional, technical, and other jobs that require more formal education—occupations in which workers tend to leave their jobs less frequently—generally have fewer openings resulting from replacement needs. On the other hand, industries with a high concentration of service, laborer, and other jobs that require little formal education and have lower wages generally have more replacement openings because these workers are more likely to leave their occupations.

Employment growth is determined largely by changes in the demand for the goods and services produced by an industry, worker productivity, and foreign competition. Each industry is affected by a different set of variables that impacts the number and composition of jobs that will be available. Even within an industry, employment in different occupations may grow at different rates. For example, changes in technology, production methods, and business practices in an industry might eliminate some jobs, while creating others. Some industries may be growing rapidly overall, yet opportunities for workers in occupations that are adversely affected by technological change could be stagnant. Similarly, employment of some occupations may be declining in the economy as a whole, yet may be increasing in a rapidly growing industry.

As shown in Table 4, employment growth rates over the next decade will vary widely among industries. Employment in goods-producing industries will increase slightly, as growth in construction and agriculture, forestry, and fishing is expected to be offset by declining employment in mining and manufacturing. Growth in construction employment will be driven by new factory construction as existing facilities are modernized; by new school construction, reflecting growth in the school-age population; and by infrastructure improvements, such as road and bridge construction. Overall employment in agriculture, forestry, and fishing will grow more slowly than average, with almost all new jobs occurring in the rapidly growing agricultural services industry—which includes landscaping, farm management, veterinary, soil preparation, and crop services. Employment in mining is expected to decline, due to the spread of labor-saving technology and increasing reliance on foreign sources of energy. Manufacturing employment also will decline slightly, as improvements in production technology and rising imports eliminate many production occupations. Apparel manufacturing is projected to lose about 178,000 jobs over the 1998-2008 period—more than any other manufacturing industry—due primarily to increasing imports. Some manufacturing industries with strong domestic markets and export potential, however, are expected to experience increases in employment. The drug manufacturing and aerospace manufacturing industries are two examples. Sales of drugs are expected to increase with the rise in the population, particularly the elderly, and the availability of new drugs on the market. An increase in air traffic, coupled with the need to replace aging aircraft will generate strong sales for commercial aircraft. Both industries have large export markets.

Growth in overall employment will result primarily from growth in service-producing industries over the 1998-2008 period, almost all of which are expected to witness increasing employment. Rising employment in these industries will be driven by services industries—the largest and fastest growing major industry sector—which is projected to provide more than 2 out of 3 new jobs across the nation. Health, education, and business services will account for almost 9 million of these new jobs. In addition, employment in the nation's fastest growing industry—computer and data processing services—is expected to more than double, adding another 1.8 million jobs. Job growth in the services sector will result from overall population growth, the rise in the elderly and school age population, and the trend toward contracting out for computer, personnel, and other business services.

Wholesale and retail trade is expected to add an additional 3.6 million jobs over the coming decade. Nearly 500,000 of these jobs will arise in wholesale trade, driven mostly by growth in trade and the overall economy. Retail trade is expected to add 3 million jobs over the 1998-2008 period, resulting largely from a greater population and increased personal income levels. Although most retail stores are expected to add employees, nonstore retailers will experience the fastest growth rate—55 percent—as electronic commerce and mail order sales account for an increasing portion of retail sales. Eating and drinking places will have the largest number of openings, over 1.3 million.

Employment in transportation, communications, and public utilities is projected to increase by nearly 940,000 new jobs. The telecommunications industry will have the biggest increase—244,000 jobs. Strong demand for new telecommunications services, such as Internet and wireless communications, will lead to an expansion of the telecommunications infrastructure and provide strong employment growth. Trucking and air transportation are expected to generate over 400,000 jobs. Trucking industry growth will be fueled by growth in the volume of goods that need to be shipped as the economy expands. Air transportation will expand as consumer and business demand increases, reflecting a rising population and increased business activity. Finally, while radio and television broadcasting will show little employment growth due to consolidations in the industry, cable and other pay television companies will increase by 27 percent as they upgrade their systems to deliver a wider array of communication and programming services.

Overall employment growth in finance, insurance, and real estate is expected to be around 13 percent, with close to 1 million jobs added by 2008. Securities and commodities will be the fastest growing industry in this sector, adding over 250,000 jobs. A growing interest in investing and the rising popularity of 401(k) and other pension plans are fueling increases in this industry. In contrast, the largest industry in this sector, banking, will grow by only 2.8 percent, or 58,000 jobs, as technological advances and the increasing use of electronic banking reduce the need for large administrative support staffs. Nondepository institutions—including personal and business credit institutions, as well as mortgage banks—are expected to grow at a rapid rate, and insurance will also expand, increasing by 232,000 jobs.

All 707,000 new government jobs are expected to arise in state and local government, reflecting growth in the population and its demand for public services. In contrast, the federal government is expected to lose more than 160,000 jobs over the 1998-2008 period, as efforts continue to cut costs by contracting out services and giving States more responsibility for administering federally funded programs.

In sum, recent changes in the economy are having far-reaching and complex effects on employment in each of the industries covered in the *Career Guide to Industries*. Jobseekers should be aware of these changes, keeping alert for developments that can affect job opportunities in industries and the variety of occupations which are found in each industry. For more detailed information on specific occupations, consult the 2000-2001 edition of the *Occupational Outlook Handbook*, which provides information on 250 occupations. (Note that both books mentioned above are available from JIST.)

On the following pages are brief reviews titled:

* Health Services

* Educational Services

* Social Services, Except Child-Care

These reviews provide additional information on the three industries which are the focus of this book, and they are from the U.S. Department of Labor's *Career Guide to Industries*, 2000-2001 edition.

Health Services

SIGNIFICANT POINTS

- Health services is one of the largest industries in the country, with about 11.3 million jobs, including the self-employed.

- About 14 percent of all wage and salary jobs created between 1998 and 2008 will be in health services.

- Twelve out of 30 occupations projected to grow the fastest are concentrated in health services.

- Most jobs require less than 4 years of college education.

Nature of the Industry

Combining medical technology and the human touch, the health services industry administers care around the clock, responding to the needs of millions of people—from newborns to the critically ill.

More than 460,000 establishments make up the health services industry; all vary greatly in terms of size, staffing, and organization. Two-thirds of all private health services establishments are offices of physicians or dentists. Although hospitals comprise less than 2 percent of all private health services establishments, they employ nearly 40 percent of all workers (table 1). When government hospitals are included, the proportion rises to almost half the workers in the industry.

TABLE 1

Percent distribution of wage and salary employment and establishments in private health services, 1997

Establishment type	Establish-ments	Employ-ment
Total, health services	100.0	100.0
Hospitals, private	1.6	39.6
Offices of physicians and osteopaths	41.8	18.5
Nursing and personal care facilities	4.3	18.1
Home health care services	3.3	7.3
Offices of dentists	23.8	6.5
Offices of other health practitioners	18.7	4.5
Health and allied services, not elsewhere classified	3.1	3.4
Medical and dental laboratories	3.4	2.0

The health services industry includes small-town physicians with private practices who employ only one medical assistant, as well as busy inner city hospitals that provide thousands of diverse jobs. Over half of all non-hospital health services establishments employ fewer than 5 workers (see chart). On the other hand, almost two-thirds of hospital employees were in establishments with over 1,000 workers (see chart).

The health services industry is made up of the following eight segments:

Hospitals. Hospitals provide complete health care, ranging from diagnostic services to surgery and continuous nursing care. Some hospitals specialize in treatment of the mentally ill, cancer patients, or children. Hospital-based care may be on an inpatient (overnight) or outpatient basis. The mix of workers needed varies, depending on the size, geographic location, goals, philosophy, funding, organization, and management style of the institution. As hospitals work to improve their efficiency, care continues to shift from an inpatient to outpatient basis whenever possible. Many hospitals have also expanded into long-term and home health care services, providing a continuum of care for the communities they serve.

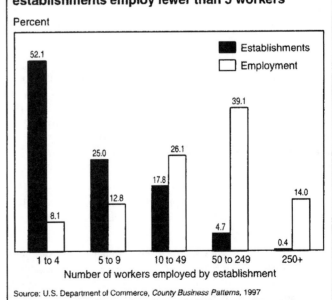

Over half of all non-hospital health services establishments employ fewer than 5 workers

Percent

- Establishments
- Employment

Number of workers employed by establishment	Establishments	Employment
1 to 4	52.1	8.1
5 to 9	25.0	12.8
10 to 49	17.8	26.1
50 to 249	4.7	39.1
250+	0.4	14.0

Source: U.S. Department of Commerce, *County Business Patterns*, 1997

Nursing and personal care facilities. Nursing facilities provide inpatient nursing, rehabilitation, and health-related personal care to those who need continuous health care, but do not require hospital services. Nursing aides provide the vast majority of direct care. Other facilities, such as convalescent homes, help patients who need less assistance. A growing segment within personal care is assisted living facilities. These facilities house the elderly in a home-like, independent setting and provide care appropriate to each resident's level of need.

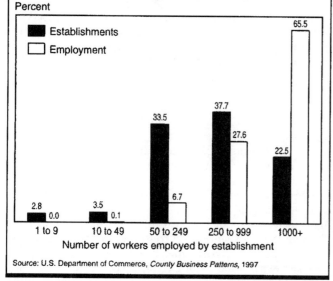

Unlike other segments of the health services industry, almost two-thirds of hospital employees work in establishments with 1,000 or more workers

Percent

■ Establishments
□ Employment

2.8 / 0.0	3.5 / 0.1	33.5 / 6.7	37.7 / 27.6	22.5 / 65.5
1 to 9	10 to 49	50 to 249	250 to 999	1000+

Number of workers employed by establishment

Source: U.S. Department of Commerce, *County Business Patterns*, 1997

Offices and clinics of physicians, including osteopaths. Doctors of medicine and osteopathy practice alone and in groups of practitioners who have the same or different specialties. Group practice has become the recent trend, including clinics, free standing emergency care centers, and ambulatory surgical centers. Physicians are more likely now to work as salaried employees of group medical practices, clinics, or health care networks than in the past.

Home health care services. Skilled nursing or medical care is sometimes provided in the home, under a physician's supervision. Home health care services are provided mainly to the elderly. The development of in-home medical technologies, substantial cost savings, and patients' preference for care in the home have helped make this once small segment of the industry one of the fastest growing in the U.S. economy.

Offices and clinics of dentists. Almost 1 out of every 4 health care establishments is a dentist's office. Most employ only a few workers who provide general or specialized dental care, including dental surgery.

Offices and clinics of other health practitioners. This segment includes offices of chiropractors, optometrists, and podiatrists, as well as occupational and physical therapists, psychologists, audiologists, speech-language pathologists, dietitians, and other miscellaneous health practitioners. Demand for services in this industry is related to the ability of patients to pay, either directly or through health insurance. Hospitals and nursing facilities may contract out for these services. This industry also includes alternative medicine practitioners, such as acupuncturists, hypnotists, and naturopaths. Demand for these services has grown with public awareness of the professions.

Health and allied services, not elsewhere classified. Among the diverse establishments in this group are kidney dialysis centers, outpatient facilities such as drug treatment clinics and rehabilitation centers, and other miscellaneous establishments such as blood banks and providers of childbirth preparation classes.

Medical and dental laboratories. Medical laboratories provide professional analytic or diagnostic services to the medical profession or directly to patients following a physician's prescription. Workers analyze blood, take x rays, or perform other clinical tests. In dental laboratories, workers make dentures, artificial teeth, and orthodontic appliances. Medical and dental laboratories provide the fewest number of jobs in health services.

Technological advances have made many new procedures and methods of diagnosis and treatment possible. For example, information technology continues to improve care and efficiency with devices such as hand held computers that record notes on each patient. Information on vital signs and orders for tests are then transferred to a main database, eliminating paper and reducing record keeping errors. Clinical developments such as organ transplants, less invasive surgical techniques, skin grafts, and gene therapy for cancer treatment continue to increase longevity and improve the quality of life for many Americans, as well as redistribute the demand for health care workers. Advances in medical technology have improved the survival rates of trauma victims and the severely ill, who then need extensive care from therapists and social workers, among other support personnel.

Cost containment in the health care industry is important as shown by the growing emphasis on providing services on an outpatient, ambulatory basis; limiting unnecessary or low priority services; and stressing preventive care that reduces the eventual cost of undiagnosed, untreated medical conditions. Enrollment in managed health care programs— predominantly Health Maintenance Organizations (HMO's), Preferred Provider Organizations (PPO's), and hybrid plans such as Point-of-Service (POS) programs—continues to grow. These prepaid plans provide comprehensive coverage to members and control health insurance costs by emphasizing preventive care. A growing phenomenon in the health services industry is the formation of Integrated Delivery Systems (IDS) where two or more segments of the industry are combined to increase efficiency through the streamlining of primarily financial and managerial functions. According to a 1998 Deloitte & Touche Survey, only 34 percent of surveyed hospitals expect to be stand-alone, independent facilities in 2003, as compared to 58 percent in 1998. These changes will continue to reshape not only the nature of the health services workforce, but also the manner in which health services are provided.

Working Conditions

Nonsupervisory workers in private health services averaged 33.1 hours per week in 1998, compared to 34.6 for all private industry. Hours varied somewhat among the different segments of the industry. Workers in home health care averaged only 29.0 hours per week; those in nursing and personal care facilities worked 32.6 hours; and hospital workers averaged 35.0 hours.

Many workers in the health services industry are on part-time schedules. Part-time workers comprised 15.9 percent of the workforce as a whole in 1998, but accounted for 35.6 percent of workers in offices of dentists and 19.6 percent of those in offices of physicians. Students, parents with young children, dual jobholders, and older workers make up much of the part-time workforce.

Many health services establishments operate around the clock and need staff at all hours. Shift work is common in some occupations, such as registered nurses. Many health service workers hold more than one job; particularly registered nurses, health technologists and technicians, and nursing aides.

In 1997, the incidence rate for occupational injury and illness in hospitals was 10.0 cases per 100 full-time workers, compared to an average of 7.1 for the private sector. Nursing and personal care facilities had a much higher rate, 16.2. Health care workers involved in direct patient care must take precautions to guard against back strain from lifting patients and equipment, exposure to radiation and caustic chemicals, and infectious diseases such as AIDS, tuberculosis, and hepatitis. Home care personnel who make house calls are exposed to the possibility of being injured in highway accidents, all types of overexertion when assisting patients, and falls inside and outside homes. Mechanical lifting devices, found in institutional settings, are seldom available in patients' homes.

Employment

The health services industry provided over 10.8 million wage and salary jobs in 1998. Almost one-half of all health services jobs were in hospitals; another one-third were in either nursing and personal care facilities or offices of physicians. About 92 percent worked in the private sector; the remainder worked in State and local government hospitals.

In addition to wage and salary workers, an estimated 446,000 workers in the industry were self-employed in 1998. Of these, about 70 percent were in offices of physicians, dentists, and other health practitioners. Health services jobs are found throughout the country, but are concentrated in large States, specifically California, New York, Florida, Texas, and Pennsylvania.

Workers in this industry tend to be older than workers in other industries, especially in occupations requiring higher levels of education and training, because they are more likely to stay in such occupations for a number of years.

Occupations in the Industry

Health services firms employ workers in professional specialty and service occupations in about equal numbers. Together,

these two occupational groups cover nearly 3 out of 5 jobs in the industry. The next largest share of jobs is in administrative support occupations, followed by technicians and related support occupations. Executive, administrative, and managerial occupations account for only 6 percent of employment. Other occupations in health services comprise only 1 percent of the total (table 2).

Professional specialty occupations, such as *physicians, registered nurses, social workers*, and *therapists*, mostly require a bachelor's degree in a specialized field or higher education in a specific health field, although registered nurses also enter through associate degree or diploma programs. Respiratory therapists often do not need a bachelor's degree, but this degree or a higher one is the most significant source of training for all other therapist occupations. Professional workers often have high levels of responsibility and complex duties. They may supervise other workers or conduct research, as well as provide services.

Service occupations attract many workers with little or no specialized education or training. This group includes *nursing and psychiatric aides, food preparation and service occupations, janitors and cleaners, dental* and *medical assistants, and personal care and home health aides*. Service workers may advance to higher-level positions or to new occupations, with experience and, in some cases, further education and training.

Technicians and related support occupations include many fast growing health occupations, such as *health information technicians* and *dental hygienists*. These workers may operate technical equipment and assist health practitioners and other professional workers. Graduates of 1- or 2-year training programs often fill these positions; these jobs usually require specific formal training beyond high school, but less than 4 years of college.

Most jobs in health services provide clinical services, but there also are many in occupations with other functions as well. Numerous workers in executive, administrative, and managerial occupations and marketing and administrative support jobs keep organizations running smoothly. Although many *health services managers* have a background in a clinical specialty or training in health services administration, many enter these jobs with a general business education.

Each segment of the health services industry employs a different mix of health-related occupations and other workers.

Hospitals. Hospitals employ workers with all levels of education and training to provide a wider variety of services than other segments of the health services industry. About 1 in 4 hospital workers is a registered nurse. Hospitals also employ many physicians, therapists, and social workers. About 2 in 10 jobs is in a service occupation, such as *nursing aide, psychiatric aide, food preparation and service worker*, or *janitor*. Hospitals also employ large numbers of health technicians, administrative support workers, craft workers, and operatives.

Nursing and personal care facilities. Almost two-thirds of all nursing facility jobs are in service occupations, primarily *nursing aides*. Professional specialty and administrative support occupations are a much smaller percentage of nursing facility employment than for other parts of the health services industry. Federal law requires nursing facilities to have licensed personnel on hand 24 hours a day, and to maintain an appropriate level of care.

TABLE 2

Employment of wage and salary workers in health services by occupation, 1998, and projected change, 1998-2008

(Employment in thousands)

Occupation	1998 Employment		1998-2008 Percent change
	Number	Percent	
All occupations	10,829	100.0	25.7
Professional specialty	3,195	29.5	27.4
Registered nurses	1,734	16.0	21.6
Physicians	412	3.8	35.3
Social workers	157	1.5	47.4
Physical therapists	109	1.0	34.5
Respiratory therapists	84	0.8	43.0
Dentists	80	0.7	18.9
Physician assistants	60	0.6	52.0
Pharmacists	54	0.5	11.5
Occupational therapists	49	0.5	30.3
Computer systems analysts, engineers, and scientists	41	0.4	62.3
Speech-language pathologists and audiologists	39	0.4	37.3
Dietitians and nutritionists	29	0.3	20.1
Service	3,011	27.8	29.7
Nursing aides and psychiatric aides	1,064	9.8	23.8
Personal care and home health aides	368	3.4	74.5
Janitors and cleaners, including maids and housekeeping cleaners	333	3.1	7.3
Medical assistants	246	2.3	58.8
Dental assistants	222	2.1	43.4
Food preparation workers	132	1.2	3.4
Food and beverage service occupations	92	0.9	6.9
Physical therapy assistants and aides	79	0.7	44.7
Guards	41	0.4	-1.7
Pharmacy assistants	34	0.3	11.6
Administrative support	2,030	18.8	18.2
General office clerks	280	2.6	30.1
Receptionists and information clerks	376	3.5	15.2
Medical secretaries	210	1.9	12.5
Office and administrative support supervisors and managers	174	1.6	30.2
Secretaries, except legal and medical	173	1.6	15.9
Billing, cost, and rate clerks	113	1.1	34.7
Bookkeeping, accounting, and auditing clerks	95	0.9	8.8

Occupation	1998 Employment		1998-2008 Percent change
	Number	Percent	
Technicians and related support	1,707	15.8	26.9
Licensed practical nurses	567	5.2	19.2
Clinical laboratory technologists and technicians	277	2.6	17.4
Radiologic technologists and technicians	160	1.5	19.8
Dental hygienists	140	1.3	41.3
Medical records and health information technicians	81	0.8	48.2
Surgical technologists	54	0.5	41.8
Psychiatric technicians	50	0.5	4.3
Emergency medical technicians	35	0.3	37.6
Dispensing opticians	34	0.3	22.8
Executive, administrative, and managerial	597	5.5	27.4
Health services managers	175	1.6	36.1
General managers and top executives	90	0.8	31.3
Precision production, craft, and repair	152	1.4	3.7
Dental lab technicians, precision	34	0.3	-1.8
All other occupations	136	1.3	13.4

Offices and clinics of physicians, including osteopaths. Many of the jobs in offices of physicians are in professional specialty occupations, primarily physicians and registered nurses. Even more jobs, however, are in administrative support occupations, such as *receptionists* and *medical secretaries*, who comprise almost two-fifths of the workers in physicians' offices.

Home health care services. More than half of the jobs in home health care are in service occupations, mostly *personal care* and *home health aides.* Nursing and therapist jobs also account for substantial shares of employment in this industry.

Offices and clinics of dentists. About one-third of the jobs in this segment are in service occupations, mostly *dental assistants.* The typical staffing pattern in dentists' offices consists of one professional with a support staff of *dental hygienists* and *dental assistants.* Larger practices are more likely to employ office managers and administrative support workers, as well as *dental laboratory technicians.*

Offices and clinics of other health practitioners. As in offices of physicians, many jobs are in administrative support occupations. About 1 in 6 jobs in this segment were for physical therapists, occupational therapists, or speech-language pathologists and audiologists.

Medical and dental laboratories. Technician and related support workers account for almost twice the proportion of jobs in this segment as in the total health services industry. These workers are mostly *clinical laboratory technologists and technicians* and *radiologic technologists*. This segment also has the smallest percentage of professional specialty workers of any segment of the health services industry. Many jobs also are in precision production, craft, and repair occupations—most notably, *dental laboratory technicians*.

Health and allied services, not elsewhere classified. This segment employs the highest percentage of professional specialty workers, many of whom are *social workers, social and human services assistants, registered nurses*, and *therapists*.

Training and Advancement

A variety of programs after high school provide specialized training for jobs in health services. Students preparing for health careers can enter programs leading to a certificate or a degree at the associate, baccalaureate, professional, or graduate levels. Two-year programs resulting in certificates or associate degrees are the minimum standard credential for occupations such as *dental hygienist or radiologic technologist*. Most *therapists* and *social workers* have at least a bachelor's degree; *physicians, optometrists*, and *podiatrists* have additional education and training beyond college. Persons considering careers in health care should have a strong desire to help others, genuine concern for the welfare of patients and clients, and an ability to deal with diverse people and stressful situations.

The health services industry provides many job opportunities for people without specialized training beyond high school. In fact, 56 percent of the workers in nursing and personal care facilities have a high school diploma or less, as do 24 percent of the workers in hospitals.

Some health services establishments provide on-the-job or classroom training, as well as continuing education. For example, in all certified nursing facilities, nursing aides must complete a State-approved training and competency evaluation program and participate in at least 12 hours of in-service education annually. Hospitals are more likely than other segments of the industry to have the resources and incentive to provide training programs and advancement opportunities to their employees. In other segments, staffing patterns tend to be more fixed and the variety of positions and advancement opportunities more limited. Larger establishments usually offer a greater range of opportunities.

Some hospitals provide training or tuition assistance in return for a promise to work for a particular length of time in the hospital after graduation. Many nursing facilities have similar programs. Some hospitals have cross-training programs that train their workers—through formal college programs, continuing education, or in-house training—to perform functions outside their specialties.

Health specialists with clinical expertise can advance to department head positions or even higher level management jobs. Health services managers can advance to more responsible positions, all the way up to chief executive officer.

Earnings

Average earnings of nonsupervisory workers in health services are slightly higher than the average for all private industry, with hospital workers earning considerably more than the average, and those in nursing and personal care facilities and home health care services earning considerably less (table 3). Average earnings often are higher in hospitals because their percentage of jobs requiring higher levels of education and training is greater than in other segments. Segments of the industry with lower earnings employ a large number of part-time service workers.

TABLE 3

Average earnings and hours of nonsupervisory workers in private health services by segment of industry, 1998

Industry segment	Earnings Weekly	Earnings Hourly	Weekly hours
Total, private industry	$442	$12.77	34.6
Health services	454	13.72	33.1
Hospitals, private	541	15.46	35.0
Offices of physicians	470	14.28	32.9
Offices of dentists	399	14.15	28.2
Offices of other health practitioners	397	13.13	30.2
Home health care services	334	11.50	29.0
Nursing and personal care facilities	318	9.76	32.6

As in most industries, professionals and managers typically earn more than other workers. Earnings in individual health services occupations vary as widely as their duties, level of education and training, and amount of responsibility (table 4). Some establishments offer tuition reimbursement, paid training, child day care services, and flexible work hours. Health care establishments that must be staffed around the clock to care for patients and handle emergencies often pay premiums for overtime and weekend work, holidays, late shifts, and when on-call. Bonuses and profit-sharing payments also may add to earnings.

Earnings vary not only by type of establishment and occupation, but also by size. Salaries are often higher in larger hospitals and group practices. Geographic location also can affect earnings.

TABLE 4

Median hourly earnings of the largest occupations in health services, 1997

Occupation	Health services	All industries
Registered nurses	$18.84	$18.88
Licensed practical nurses	12.34	12.46
Dental assistants	10.59	10.62

(continues)

Occupation	Health services	All industries
Medical assistants	9.71	9.71
Receptionists and information clerks	9.19	8.69
General office clerks	9.05	9.10
Home health aides	7.94	7.75
Nursing aides, orderlies, and attendants	7.70	7.76
Maids and housekeeping cleaners	7.16	6.74

Unionization is more common in hospitals, although most segments of the health services industry are not heavily unionized. In 1998, 14.9 percent of hospital workers and 10.7 percent of workers in nursing and personal care facilities were members of unions or covered by union contracts, compared to 15.4 percent of all workers in private industry.

Outlook

Employment in the health services industry is projected to increase 26 percent through 2008, compared to an average of 15 percent for all industries (table 5). Employment growth is expected to add about 2.8 million new jobs—14 percent of all wage and salary jobs added to the economy over the 1998-2008 period. Projected rates of employment growth for the various segments of this industry range from 8 percent in hospitals, the largest and slowest growing industry segment, to 80 percent in the much smaller home health care services.

TABLE 5

Employment of wage and salary workers in health services by segment of industry, 1998, and projected change, 1998-2008

(Employment in thousands)

Industry	1998 Employment	1998-2008 Percent change
All industries	128,008	15.3
Health services	10,829	25.7
Hospitals, public and private	4,909	7.7
Nursing and personal care facilities	1,762	25.6
Offices of physicians	1,853	41.2
Home health care services	672	80.5
Offices of dentists	646	29.9
Offices of other health practitioners	450	42.8
Health and allied services, not elsewhere classified	339	64.9
Medical and dental laboratories	199	24.5

Employment in health services will continue to grow for a number of reasons. The elderly population, a group with much greater than average health care needs, will grow faster than the total population between 1998 and 2008, increasing the demand for health services, especially for home health care

and nursing and personal care. As the baby boom generation ages, the incidence of stroke and heart disease will increase. Advances in medical technology will continue to improve the survival rate of severely ill and injured patients, who will then need extensive therapy. New technologies often lower the cost of treatment and diagnosis, but also enable identification and treatment of conditions not previously treatable. In addition, medical group practices and health networks will become larger and more complex, and will need more managerial and support workers.

Employment growth in the hospital segment will be the slowest within the health services industry, as it consolidates to control costs and as clinics and other alternate care sites become more common. Hospitals will provide more outpatient care, rely less on inpatient care, and streamline health care delivery operations. Job opportunities, however, will remain plentiful because hospitals employ a large number of people. The demand for dental care will increase due to population growth, greater retention of natural teeth by the middle-aged and older persons, and greater awareness of the importance of dental care and ability to pay for services. Rapid growth in other health services segments will mainly result from the aging of the population, new medical technologies, and the subsequent increase in demand for all types of health services. Also contributing to industry growth will be the shift from inpatient to less expensive outpatient care, made possible by technological improvements and Americans' increasing awareness and emphasis on all aspects of health. Various combinations of all these factors will assure robust growth in this massive, diverse industry.

The fastest growth is expected for workers in occupations concentrated outside the inpatient hospital sector, such as *medical assistants* and *personal care and home health aides*. Because of cost pressures, many health care facilities will adjust their staffing patterns to lower bottom-line labor costs. Where patient

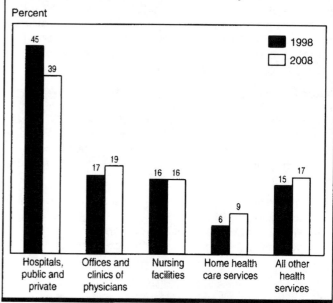

The proportion of health services jobs in public and private hospitals will decrease by 2008

care demands and outside regulations allow, health care facilities will substitute lower-paid providers and cross-train their workforce. Many facilities have cut the number of middle managers, while simultaneously creating new managerial positions as they diversify. Because traditional inpatient hospital positions are no longer the only option for many future health care workers, they must be flexible and forward-looking (chart).

Besides job openings due to employment growth, additional openings will result as workers leave the labor force or transfer to other occupations. Occupations with the most replacement openings are usually large with high turnover due to low pay and status, poor benefits, low training requirements, and a high proportion of young and part-time workers. Many are service occupations, such as nursing aides. Occupations with relatively few replacement openings, on the other hand, are those with high pay and status, lengthy training requirements, and a high proportion of full-time workers, such as physicians.

For some executive, administrative, and managerial occupations, rapid growth will be countered by restructuring to reduce administrative costs and streamline operations. The effects of office automation and other technological changes will slow employment growth in administrative support occupations, but because the employment base is large, replacement needs will still create substantial numbers of job openings. Slower growing service occupations will also have job openings due to replacement needs.

Many of the occupations projected to grow the fastest are concentrated in the health services industry. By 2008, employment in all industries of personal care and home health aides is projected to increase by 58 percent, medical assistants by 58 percent, physician assistants by 48 percent, and health information technicians by 44 percent.

Technological changes, such as increased laboratory automation, will also affect the demand for some occupations. For example, the use of robotics in blood analysis may limit growth of clinical laboratory technologists and technicians, although the nature of health care precludes wholesale productivity gains in many instances.

Although workers at all levels of education and training will continue to be in demand, in many cases it may be easier for job seekers with health-specific training to obtain jobs and advance. Specialized clinical training is a requirement for many jobs in health services and is an asset even for many administrative jobs that do not specifically require it.

Sources of Additional Information

For referrals to hospital human resources departments about local opportunities in health care careers, write to:

- American Hospital Association/American Society for Hospital Human Resources Administrators, One North Franklin, Chicago, IL 60606.

For information on educational programs for allied health occupations from the *Health Professions Education Directory*, contact:

- American Medical Association, 515 North State St., Chicago, IL 60610. Internet: http://www.ama-assn.org

There is also a wealth of information on health careers and job opportunities available on the Internet from schools, associations, and employers.

Educational Services

- With about 1 in 4 Americans enrolled in educational institutions, educational services is one of the largest industries with over 11 million jobs.

- Most managerial and professional specialty positions—which account for more than 6 out of every 10 jobs—require at least a bachelor's degree, and some require a master's or doctoral degree.

- The number of job openings for teachers should increase substantially due to expected increases in enrollments and retirements.

Nature of the Industry

Education is an important part of life. The type and level of education that an individual attains often influences such important aspects of life as occupational choice and earnings potential. Lifelong learning is important to acquire new knowledge and upgrade skills, particularly in this age of rapid technological and economic changes.

Educational services are provided in cities, suburbs, small towns, and rural areas throughout the Nation. The industry includes a variety of institutions that offered academic instruction, technical instruction, and other educational and training services to about 67 million students in 1998. Most students are enrolled in elementary and secondary schools, and institutions of higher learning. Of these, about 86 percent were enrolled in public schools and 14 percent were enrolled in private schools.

School attendance is compulsory, usually until age 16 to 18, in all 50 States and the District of Columbia, so elementary and secondary schools are the most numerous of all educational establishments, making up 37 percent of the educational services industry in 1997. Elementary and secondary schools provide academic courses, ordinarily for kindergarten through grade 12, in public schools, parochial schools, boarding and other private schools, and military academies. Some secondary schools provide a mixture of academic and technical instruction.

Higher education institutions accounted for about 8 percent of all educational establishments in 1997, and provide academic or technical courses or both in colleges, universities, professional schools, community or junior colleges, and technical institutes. Universities offer bachelor's, master's, and doctoral degrees, while colleges generally offer only the bachelor's degree. Professional schools offer graduate degrees in fields such as law, medicine, business administration, and engineering. The undergraduate bachelor's degree typically requires four years of study, while graduate degrees require additional years of study. Community colleges and technical institutes offer associate degrees, certificates, or diplomas, typically involving two years of study or less.

Establishments that make up the remainder of the educational services industry include libraries; vocational schools, such as data processing, business, secretarial, commercial art, practical nursing, and correspondence schools; and institutions providing a variety of specialized training and services, such as student exchange programs, curriculum development, and charm, drama, language, music, reading, modeling, and survival schools.

In recent decades, the Nation has focused attention on the educational system because of the growing importance of producing a trained and educated workforce. Government, private industry, and numerous research organizations have become involved in improving the quality of education. For example, businesses often donate instructional equipment, lend personnel for teaching and mentoring, host work-site visits, and provide job shadowing and internship opportunities. Businesses also collaborate with educators to develop curriculums that will provide students with the skills they need to cope with new technology in the workplace.

Secondary schools, in addition to preparing students for higher education, also prepare the large number of students who do not attend college for the transition from school to work. School-to-work programs integrate academic subjects with vocational classes providing skills specific to an occupation or discipline and teach problem solving, communication, and teamwork skills. Programs providing students with marketable skills include cooperative education, tech-prep, and youth apprenticeship programs. Youth apprenticeship programs, although relatively small in number, provide students with occupational skill training by working under the supervision of a mentor. Tech-prep programs begin in high school and continue through 2 years of postsecondary training, usually leading to an associate degree or certificate. Technical vocational education programs at the community college level have grown as employers have increasingly demanded higher levels of education from their employees. While most vocational programs focus on technical skills training—such as those skills needed in manufacturing, health services, or automotive repair—more programs are offering training for service sector jobs, including financial services, hospitality and culinary jobs, and child care.

Many school districts have enacted reforms in response to declining student test scores, concerns that students would not be prepared to enter the workforce, or other reasons. The methods and goals of school reform vary by locale and the results achieved have been mixed over the years. In recent years, the average number of high school credits earned in mathematics, science, and foreign languages has risen; the high school dropout rate has fallen; and the proportion of women in the labor force with 4 or more years of college has risen. However, many problems remain. American students at the elementary and secondary levels continue to lag behind their peers in some other countries in mathematics and science, and Scholastic Assessment Test scores have risen only marginally. Although the difference in high school graduation rates between blacks and whites has decreased in recent years, graduation rates for Hispanics remain far behind. Social and economic problems continue to affect schools and students—for example, the quality of education in many schools with high minority enrollments and high poverty rates does not measure up to that in schools in other districts. Study of mathematics, science, and foreign languages has increased among high school students, but some employers still complain that many entry-level workers lack the basic writing, math, and computer skills necessary to perform in the workplace. In addition, some school districts are experiencing funding problems under tight government budgets, sometimes forcing them to restrict or eliminate some services.

Working Conditions

In educational institutions with a traditional school year schedule, most workers—including teachers, teacher assistants, library workers, school counselors, cooks, and food preparation workers—work about 10 months a year. Some workers take jobs related to or outside of education during their summer break, and others pursue personal interests. Education administrators, administrative support and clerical workers, and janitors often work the entire year. Night and weekend work is common for adult education teachers, college faculty, and college library workers. Part-time work is common for school busdrivers, adult education teachers, college faculty, teacher assistants, and some library workers. School busdrivers often work a split shift, driving one or two routes in the morning and afternoon; drivers who are assigned field trips, athletic and other extracurricular activities, or midday kindergarten routes work additional hours during or after school.

Seeing students develop and enjoy learning can be very rewarding for teachers. Dealing with unmotivated students, however, requires patience and understanding. College faculty and adult education teachers instruct older students, who tend to be highly motivated. These instructors generally do not encounter the behavioral and social problems sometimes found when teaching younger kindergarten, elementary, and secondary school students. Many teachers spend significant time outside of school preparing for class, doing administrative tasks, conducting research, writing articles and books, and pursuing advanced degrees.

Library workers who work at video display terminals for extended periods may experience headaches, eyestrain, or musculoskeletal strain. In general, however, educational services is a relatively safe industry. There were 2.9 cases of

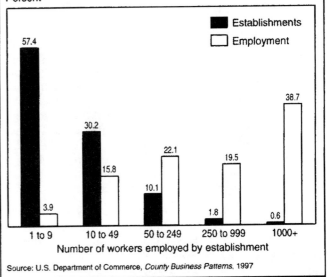

About 4 out of 5 workers were in educational services establishments with 50 or more workers in 1997

Source: U.S. Department of Commerce, *County Business Patterns*, 1997

occupational injury and illness per 100 full-time workers in private educational establishments in 1997, compared with 7.1 in all industries combined.

Employment

Educational services was the largest industry in the economy in 1998, providing jobs for nearly 11.2 million workers—about 11 million wage and salary workers, and 155,000 self-employed workers. About 57 percent of private educational establishments had 1 to 9 workers. However, 4 out of 5 jobs were in private establishments with 50 or more workers (chart).

Employees in educational services were older than average, with 42 percent over age 45, compared to 34 percent of employees in all industries combined (table 1).

TABLE 1

Percent distribution of employment in educational services by age group, 1998

Age group	Educational services	All industries
Total	100.0	100.0
16-24	10.4	14.9
25-34	19.6	23.9
35-44	25.6	27.5
45-54	29.2	21.0
55-64	12.6	9.8
65 and older	0.3	2.9

Occupations in the Industry

Workers in this industry take part in all aspects of education, from teaching and counseling students to driving school buses and serving cafeteria lunches. Although most occupations are professional, the industry employs many administrative support, managerial, service, and other workers (table 2).

Teachers account for almost half of all workers in the educational services industry. Their duties depend on the age group and subject they teach and on the type of institution in which they work. Teachers should have a sincere interest in helping students and the ability to inspire respect, trust, and confidence. Strong speaking and writing skills, inquiring and analytical minds, and a desire to pursue and disseminate knowledge are vital for teachers. (*Preschool workers*, who nurture and teach children younger than 5 years old, are discussed in the *Career Guide* statement on child-care services.)

Kindergarten and *elementary school teachers* play a critical role in the early development of children. They usually instruct one class in a variety of subjects, introducing the children to mathematics, language, science, and social studies. They use games, artwork, music, computers, and other tools to teach basic skills. Kindergarten and elementary teachers also may supervise extracurricular activities after school.

TABLE 2

Employment of wage and salary workers in educational services by occupation, 1998 and projected change, 1998-2008

(Employment in thousands)

Occupation	1998 Employment Number	Percent	1998-2008 Percent change
All occupations	11,175	100.0	15.3
Professional specialty	6,133	54.9	17.7
Teachers, elementary school	1,677	15.0	11.5
Teachers, secondary school	1,425	12.8	22.6
College and university faculty	863	7.7	22.6
Teachers, special education	402	3.6	33.7
Adult and vocational education teachers	268	2.4	14.1
Teachers, preschool and kindergarten	226	2.0	11.5
Instructors and coaches, sports and physical training	138	1.2	11.5
Counselors	129	1.2	22.6
Health assessment and treating occupations	127	1.1	36.9
Librarians, professional	98	0.9	0.3
Administrative support, including clerical	2,210	19.8	19.9
Teacher assistants	1,026	9.2	33.7
Secretaries	459	4.1	10.9
General office clerks	209	1.9	12.5

Occupation	1998 Employment Number	Percent	1998-2008 Percent change
Records processing occupations	164	1.5	9.3
Service	1,238	11.1	.4
Janitors and cleaners, including maids and housekeeping cleaners	489	4.4	0.3
Cooks, institution or cafeteria	178	1.6	-10.8
Food preparation workers	170	1.5	0.3
Executive, administrative, and managerial	742	6.6	11.5
Education administrators	367	3.3	11.5
Management support occupations	140	1.3	15.1
Operators, fabricators, and laborers	367	3.3	9.8
Bus drivers, school	318	2.8	11.5
Precision production, craft, and repair	226	2.0	15.7
Maintenance repairers, general utility	99	0.9	21.5
Technicians and related support	74	1.6	10.9
All other occupations	85	0.8	9.7

Secondary school teachers help students delve more deeply into subjects introduced in elementary school. Secondary school teachers specialize in a specific subject, such as English, Spanish, mathematics, history, or biology. They also may help students deal with academic problems and choose courses, colleges, and careers.

Special education teachers work with students—from toddlers to those in their early 20s—who have a variety of disabilities. Most special education teachers are found at the elementary, middle, and secondary school level. Special education teachers design and modify instruction to meet a student's special needs. These teachers also work with students who have other special instructional needs, including those who are gifted and talented.

College and *university faculty* generally are organized into departments or divisions, based on subject or field. Faculty teach and advise college students and perform a significant part of our Nation's research. They also consult with government, business, nonprofit, and community organizations. They prepare lectures, exercises, and laboratory experiments; grade exams and papers; and advise and work with students individually. Faculty keep abreast of developments in their field by reading current literature, talking with colleagues, and participating in professional conferences. They also do their own research to expand knowledge in their field, often publishing their findings in scholarly journals, books, and electronic media.

Adult education teachers work mainly in four areas—adult vocational-technical education, adult remedial education, adult continuing education, and prebaccalaureate training. Adult education teachers in vocational-technical education provide instruction for occupations that do not require a college degree, such as welder, cosmetologist, or dental hygienist. These teachers may also help people update their job skills or adapt to technological advances. Adult remedial education teachers provide instruction in basic education courses for school dropouts. Adult education teachers in junior or community colleges prepare students for a 4-year degree program, teaching classes for credit that can be applied towards that degree. Other adult education teachers teach courses that students take for personal enrichment, such as cooking or dancing.

Education administrators provide vision, direction, leadership, and day-to-day management of educational activities in schools, colleges and universities, businesses, correctional institutions, museums, and job training and community service organizations. They set educational standards and goals and aid in establishing the policies and procedures to carry them out. They develop academic programs; monitor students' educational progress; hire, train, motivate, and evaluate teachers and other staff; manage guidance and other student services; administer recordkeeping; prepare budgets; and handle relations with staff, parents, current and prospective students, employers, and the community.

School and college counselors—who work at the elementary, middle, secondary, and postsecondary school levels—help students evaluate their abilities, talents, and interests so that the student can develop realistic academic and career options. They also help students understand and deal with their social, behavioral, and personal problems. Secondary school counselors use interviews, counseling sessions, tests, or other methods when advising and evaluating students. They advise on college majors, admission requirements, entrance exams, and on trade, technical school, and apprenticeship programs. Elementary school counselors do more social and personal counseling and less vocational and academic counseling than secondary school counselors. School counselors work with students individually, in small groups, or with entire classes.

Librarians assist people in finding information and using it effectively in their scholastic, personal, and professional pursuits. They manage staff and develop and direct information programs and systems for the public as well as oversee the selection and organization of library materials. Librarians may supervise *library technicians*—who help librarians acquire, prepare, and organize material; direct library users to standard references; and retrieve information from computer data bases—and *library assistants* and *bookmobile drivers*—who check out and receive library materials, collect overdue fines, and shelve materials.

Teacher assistants, also called teacher aides or instructional aides, provide instructional and clerical support for classroom teachers, allowing teachers more time for lesson planning and teaching. Teacher assistants tutor and assist children in learning class material using the teacher's lesson plans, providing students with individualized attention. Assistants also aid and supervise students in the cafeteria, schoolyard, school discipline center, or on field trips. They record grades, set up equipment, and prepare materials for instruction.

School busdrivers transport students to and from school and related events.

The educational services industry employs many other workers who are found in a wide range of industries. For example, *secretaries, general office clerks*, and other *administrative support* and *clerical workers* account for about 1 out of 10 jobs in educational services.

Many State and local school systems are engaged in efforts to restructure the learning environment. This is resulting in increased responsibilities, and the need for additional skills, among some occupations in the educational services industry. For example, teachers are more involved in developing curricula and multiple instructional approaches in the classroom, including the use of computers and other technologies. Teachers also are more involved in matters outside the classroom, such as management of the school budget and parent and community relations. Similarly, principals are assuming more responsibility for management of their schools, taking less direction from higher-level education administrators such as school superintendents. In addition, principals are taking a more active role in working with the community. In response to the growing number of dual-income and single parent families and teenage parents, principals are setting up before- and after-school child-care programs and family research centers. They also are establishing programs to combat the increase in crime, drug and alcohol abuse, and violence.

Training and Advancement

The educational services industry employs some of the most highly educated workers in the labor force. College and university faculty generally need a doctoral degree for full-time, tenure-track employment, but sometimes can teach with a master's degree, particularly at 2-year colleges. Most faculty members are hired as instructors or assistant professors and may advance to associate professor and full professor. Some faculty advance to administrative and managerial positions, such as department chairperson, dean, or president.

Elementary and secondary school teachers must have a bachelor's degree and complete an approved teaching training program, with a prescribed number of subject and education credits and supervised practice teaching. All States require public school teachers to be licensed; licensure requirements vary by State. Many States offer alternate licensure programs for people who have bachelor's degrees in the subject they will teach, but lack the necessary education courses required for a regular license. Alternative licensure programs were originally designed to ease teacher shortages in certain subjects, such as math and science. However, the programs have expanded to attract other people into teaching, including recent college graduates and mid-career changers. With additional education or certification, teachers may become school librarians, reading specialists, curriculum specialists, or guidance counselors. Some teachers advance to administrative or supervisory positions—such as department chairperson, assistant principal, or principal—but the number of these jobs is limited. In some school systems, highly qualified, experienced elementary and secondary school teachers can become senior or mentor teachers, with higher pay and additional responsibilities.

Adult education teachers normally need work or other experience in their field—and a license or certificate when required by the field—for full professional status. Most States and the District of Columbia require adult education teachers to have a bachelor's degree and some States also require teacher certification.

School counselors generally need a master's degree in a counseling specialty or a related field. All States require school counselors to hold State school counseling certification; however, certification varies from State to State. Some States require public school counselors to have both counseling and teaching certificates. Depending on the State, a master's degree in counseling and 2 to 5 years of teaching experience may be required for a counseling certificate. Experienced school counselors may advance to a larger school; become directors or supervisors of counseling, guidance, or student personnel services; or, with further graduate education, become counseling psychologists or school administrators.

Training requirements for education administrators depend on where they work. Principals, assistant principals, and school administrators usually have held a teaching or related job before entering administration, and they generally need a master's or doctoral degree in education administration or educational supervision, as well as State teacher certification. Academic deans usually have a doctorate in their specialty. Education administrators may advance up an administrative ladder or transfer to larger schools or school systems. They also may become superintendent of a school system or president of an educational institution.

Training requirements for teacher assistants range from a high school diploma to some college training. Districts that assign teaching responsibilities to teacher assistants usually have higher training requirements than those that do not. Teacher assistants who obtain a bachelor's degree, usually in education, may become certified teachers.

Librarians normally need a master's degree in library science. Many States require school librarians to be licensed as teachers and have courses in library science. Experienced librarians may advance to administrative positions, such as department head, library director, or chief information officer. Training requirements for library technicians range from a high school diploma to specialized postsecondary training; a high school diploma is sufficient for library assistants. Library workers can advance—from assistant, to technician, to librarian—with experience and the required formal education. School busdrivers, who need a commercial driver's license, have limited opportunities for advancement; some become supervisors or dispatchers.

Earnings

Earnings of occupations concentrated in the educational services industry—education administrators, teachers, counselors, and librarians—are significantly higher than the average for all occupations, reflecting their older age and higher level of educational attainment. Among teachers, earnings increase with higher educational attainment and more years of service. College and university faculty earn the most, followed by secondary and elementary school teachers. Educational services employees who work the traditional school year can earn additional money during the summer in jobs related to or outside of education. Earnings in selected occupations in educational services appear in table 3.

TABLE 3

Median hourly earnings of the largest occupations in educational services, 1997

Occupation	Educational services	All industries
Education administrators	$29.12	$28.02
Teachers, special education	17.63	—
Teachers, secondary school	17.61	—
Teachers, elementary school	16.81	—
Secretaries, except legal and medical	10.76	11.00
Janitors and cleaners, except maid and housekeeping cleaners	9.16	7.44
General office clerks	9.10	9.10
Bus drivers, school	8.58	8.80
Teacher aides, paraprofessional	7.51	7.51

Almost 50 percent of workers in the educational services industry—the largest number being in elementary and secondary schools—are union members or are covered by union contracts, compared to only 15.4 percent of workers in all industries combined. The American Federation of Teachers and the National Education Association are the largest unions representing teachers and other school personnel.

Outlook

Employment in the educational services industry is projected to increase by 15 percent over the 1998-2008 period, the same as the rate of growth projected for all industries combined. In addition to employment growth, the need to replace experienced workers who find jobs in other industries or stop working will create many job openings. Due to the large size of this industry, the number of jobs arising from replacement needs is particularly significant. On the other hand, the number of individuals competing for kindergarten, elementary, and secondary school teaching positions also may increase in response to alternate certification programs, increased salaries, and greater teacher involvement in school policies and programs. Prestigious occupations such as education administrators and college faculty will continue to attract a large number of applicants for available positions.

Several important factors will shape the outlook for the industry. Enrollment growth at the secondary and postsecondary level over the 1998-2008 period should spur employment growth in educational services. At the postsecondary level, in addition to growth in domestic enrollment, enrollment of foreign students has been growing rapidly. Enrollment of special education students has been rising significantly over the last 20 years, and growth is expected to continue. In addition, teacher retirements are projected to create many new job openings in the industry.

Concerns that the future workforce may not meet employers' needs are leading educational institutions and employers to work together in developing programs to train students for jobs of the future. Initiatives include enhanced programs in reading, writing, and mathematics; emphasis on skills traditionally required only of managers, such as communications, decision making, and problem solving; and increased focus on technical and computer skills. Such emphasis on marketable skills should increase the importance of postsecondary education, and could spur employment growth in the educational services industry.

Projected employment growth varies by occupation. The number of special education teachers is expected to grow the fastest, spurred by growing enrollment of special education students, increased emphasis on inclusion of disabled students into general education classrooms, and the effort to reach students with problems at a young age. The number of teacher assistants also will grow much faster than average as many assist special education teachers; as school reforms call for more individual attention to students; and as the number of students who speak English as a second language rises.

Occupations expected to grow faster than average include secondary school teachers, college and university faculty, and counselors. Average growth is projected for school bus drivers, sports and physical fitness instructors and coaches, adult education teachers, elementary school teachers, and preschool and kindergarten teachers. Little or no growth is expected for librarians. Projected growth reflects demographic changes, enrollment increases, government legislation affecting education, expanded responsibilities of workers, and efforts to improve the quality of education.

Despite an expected increase in education expenditures, budget constraints at all levels of government may place restrictions on educational services, particularly in light of the rapidly escalating cost of college tuition and special education and other services. Cuts in funding could affect student services—such as school busing, educational materials, and extracurricular activities—and employment of administrative, instructional, and support staff. Budget considerations also will affect attempts to expand school programs, such as increasing the number of counselors and teacher assistants in elementary schools.

Sources of Additional Information

Information on unions and education-related issues can be obtained from:

- American Federation of Teachers, 555 New Jersey Ave. NW., Washington, DC 20001.

- National Education Association, 1201 16th St. NW., Washington, DC 20036.

Social Services, Except Child-Care

SIGNIFICANT POINTS

- Social services, except child-care, ranks among the fastest growing industries.

- About 2 out of 3 jobs are in professional, technical, and service occupations.

- Human service workers and assistants—the ninth fastest growing occupation—are concentrated in social services.

- Average earnings are low because of the large number of part-time and low-paying service jobs.

Nature of the Industry

Careers in social services appeal to persons with a strong desire to make lives better and easier for others. Workers in this industry usually are good communicators and enjoy interacting with people. Social services workers assist the homeless, housebound, and infirm to cope with circumstances of daily living; counsel troubled and emotionally disturbed individuals; train or retrain the unemployed or underemployed; care for the elderly, and physically and mentally disabled; help the needy obtain financial assistance; and solicit contributions for various social services organizations. About 102,000 establishments in the private sector provided social services in 1998. Thousands of other establishments, mainly in State and local government, provided many additional social services. For information about government social services, see the *Career Guide* statements on Federal Government, and State and local government, excluding education and hospitals.

Social services contain four segments—individual and family services, residential care, job training and vocational rehabilitation services, and miscellaneous social services.

Individual and family social services establishments provide counseling and welfare services including refugee, disaster, and temporary relief services. Government offices distribute welfare aid, rent supplements, and food stamps. Some agencies provide adult day care, home-delivered meals, and home health and personal care services. Other services concentrate on children, such as big brother and sister organizations, youth centers, and adoption services. Workers in crisis centers may focus on individual, marriage, child, or family counseling.

Residential care facilities provide around-the-clock social and personal care to children, the elderly, and others who have limited ability to care for themselves. Workers care for residents of alcohol and drug rehabilitation centers, group homes, and halfway houses. Nursing and medical care, however, is not the main focus of establishments providing residential care, as it is in nursing or personal care facilities.

Job training and related services establishments train the unemployed, underemployed, disabled, and others with job market disadvantages. Vocational specialists and counselors work with clients to overcome deficient education, job skills, or experience. Often industrial psychologists or career counselors will assess the job skills of a client and, working with both the employer and the client, decide whether the client would be better served by taking additional job training, by being placed in a different job with his or her current skills, or by restructuring the job to accommodate any skill deficiency.

Miscellaneous social services include many different kinds of establishments, such as advocacy groups, antipoverty boards, community development groups, and health and welfare councils. Many miscellaneous social services organizations are concerned with community improvement and social change. They may solicit contributions, administer appropriations, and allocate funds among other agencies engaged in social welfare services.

Working Conditions

Some social services establishments—such as residential care facilities—operate around the clock. Thus evening, weekend, and holiday work is not uncommon. Some establishments may be understaffed, resulting in large caseloads for each worker. Jobs in voluntary, nonprofit agencies often are part time.

Some workers spend a substantial amount of time traveling within the local area. For example, home health and personal care aides routinely visit clients in their homes; social workers and human service workers and assistants also may make home visits. In 1997, the incidence rate for occupational injury and illness in social services varied by industry sector. Compared to the rate of 7.1 per 100 full-time workers for the entire private sector, residential care and job training and related services had higher rates—9.9 and 9.7, respectively. On the other hand, individual and family services and miscellaneous social services had lower than average rates—4.7 and 3.8, respectively.

Employment

Social services provided about 2 million nongovernment wage and salary jobs in 1998. Almost half were in individual and miscellaneous social services (table 1). An estimated 52,000 self-employed persons also worked in the industry.

TABLE 1

Employment of nongovernment wage and salary workers in social services by detailed industry, 1998

Occupation	1998 Employment Number	1998 Employment Percent	1998-2008 Percent change
Total	11,175	100.0	15.3
Individual and miscellaneous social services	923	45.3	32.5
Residential care	747	36.6	56.8
Job training and related services	369	18.1	31.0

In 1997, about 65 percent of social services establishments employed fewer than 10 workers; however, larger establishments accounted for most jobs (chart).

Social services workers are somewhat older than workers in other industries (table 2). About 39 percent were 45 years old or older, compared to 34 percent of all workers. Jobs in social services are concentrated in large States with heavily populated urban areas, such as New York and California.

TABLE 2

Percent distribution of employment in social services by age group, 1998

Age group	Social services	All industries
Total	100.0	100.0
16-24	12.2	14.9
25-34	24.3	23.9
35-44	24.8	27.5
45-54	21.8	21.0
55-64	11.9	9.8
65 and older	5.1	2.9

Occupations in the Industry

More than one-third of nongovernment social service jobs are in professional and technical occupations (table 3). *Social workers* counsel and assess the needs of clients, refer them to the appropriate sources of help, and monitor their progress. They may specialize in child welfare and family services, mental health, medical social work, school social work, community organization activities, or clinical social work. *Human service workers and assistants* serve in a variety of social and human

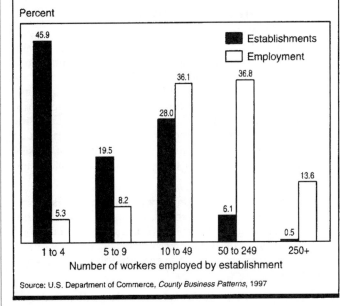

Few social services establishments employ more than 50 workers

Percent

Legend: ■ Establishments □ Employment

Number of workers employed by establishment	Establishments	Employment
1 to 4	45.9	5.3
5 to 9	19.5	8.2
10 to 49	28.0	36.1
50 to 249	6.1	36.8
250+	0.5	13.6

Source: U.S. Department of Commerce, *County Business Patterns*, 1997

service delivery settings. Job titles and duties of these workers vary, but they include social service assistant, case management aide, social work assistant, residential counselor, alcoholism or drug abuse counselor, mental health aide, child abuse worker, community outreach worker, and gerontology aide. *Counselors* help people evaluate their interests and abilities and advise and assist them with personal and social problems.

About 3 out of 10 nongovernment jobs in social services are in service occupations. *Residential counselors* develop and coordinate non-medical activities for residents of long-term care and treatment facilities, such as assisted-living housing for the elderly. The social services industry employs over 4 out of 5 residential counselors. *Home health and personal care aides* help elderly, disabled, and ill persons live in their own homes instead of an institution. Although some are employed by public or private agencies, many are self-employed. Persons in *food preparation and service occupations* serve residents at social services institutions. *Nursing and psychiatric aides* help care for physically or mentally ill, injured, disabled, or infirm individuals.

As in most industries, administrative support workers—secretaries and bookkeepers, for example—as well as executives and managers account for many jobs. However, social services employ a much smaller percentage of precision production, craft, and repair, and of marketing and sales jobs, than the economy as a whole.

Certain occupations are more heavily concentrated in some segments of the industry than in others. Individual and miscellaneous social services, for example, employ the greatest numbers of social workers, human service workers and assistants, and home health and personal care aides. Job training and vocational rehabilitation services provide the most jobs for adult education teachers. Nursing and psychiatric aides and food preparation and service workers work mainly in the residential care segment of the industry.

Training and Advancement

Some occupations in social services have very specific entrance requirements. These include most of the professional specialty occupations. Those requiring specific clinical training, such as clinical social workers and psychologists also require appropriate State licensure or certification. Nevertheless, people with a limited background in social services or little education beyond high school can find a job in the industry. Nursing aides and home health and personal care aides are two such occupations. Many establishments provide on-the-job or classroom training, especially for those with limited background or training.

Many employers prefer human service workers and assistants with some related work experience or college courses in human services, social work, or one of the social or behavioral sciences. Other employers prefer a 4-year college degree. A number of employers provide in-service training, such as seminars and workshops.

Entry-level jobs for social workers require a bachelor's degree in social work or in an undergraduate major such as psychology or sociology. However, most agencies require a master's degree in social work or a closely related field. Public agencies and private practice clinics that offer clinical or consultative services require an advanced degree in clinical social work; supervisory, administrative, and staff training positions usually require at least a master's degree.

TABLE 3

Employment of nongovernment wage and salary workers in social services by occupation, 1998 and projected change, 1998-2008

(Employment in thousands)

Occupation	1998 Employment Number	Percent	1998-2008 Percent change
All occupations	2,039	100.0	41.1
Professional specialty	684	33.6	49.7
Social workers	156	7.6	37.6
Residential counselors	154	7.5	54.1
Human service workers and assistants	130	6.4	73.4
Adult and vocational education teachers	49	2.4	43.6
Registered nurses	31	1.5	41
Counselors	28	1.4	43.9
Recreation workers	25	1.2	31.9
Teachers, preschool	22	1.1	36.4
Service	620	30.4	41.8
Home health and personal care aides	246	12.1	46
Nursing aides and psychiatric aides	109	5.4	44.4

Occupation	1998 Employment Number	Percent	1998-2008 Percent change
Janitors and cleaners, including maids and housekeeping cleaners	63	3.1	31.3
Child care workers	51	2.5	54.7
Cooks, institution or cafeteria	28	1.4	37.0
Food preparation workers	23	1.1	26.6
Administrative support, including clerical	252	12.3	26.6
Secretaries	50	2.5	12.3
General office clerks	40	2.0	39.1
Receptionists and information clerks	30	1.5	41.1
Teacher assistants	28	1.4	39.1
Office and administrative support supervisors and managers	27	1.3	34.6
Bookkeeping, accounting, and auditing clerks	26	1.3	14.9
Executive, administrative, and managerial	251	12.3	35.8
General managers and top executives	81	4.0	37.9
Management support occupations	46	2.3	38.2
Administrative services managers	20	1.0	33.0
Operators, fabricators, and laborers	91	4.5	30.1
Motor vehicle operators	37	1.8	32.2
Hand workers, including assemblers and fabricators	30	1.5	32.3
Technicians and related support	58	2.9	45.4
Licensed practical and licensed vocational nurses	24	1.2	42.3
Precision production, craft, and repair	47	2.3	35.8
Maintenance repairers, general utility	21	1.0	35.9
Marketing and sales	27	1.3	31.5
All other occupations	10	0.5	40.6

Volunteering with a student, religious, or charitable organization is a good way for persons to test their interest in social services, and may provide an advantage when applying for jobs in this industry.

Advancement paths vary. For example, some home health and personal care aides get additional training and become licensed practical nurses. Formal education—usually a bachelor's or master's degree in counseling, rehabilitation, social work, or a related field—almost always is necessary for human service workers and assistants to advance. Social workers can advance to supervisor, program manager, assistant director, or executive director of an agency or department. They also may enter private practice and provide psychotherapeutic counseling and other services on a contract basis. Private practice for social workers depends on the affordability of services, including the availability of funding from third parties.

Earnings

Earnings in selected occupations in the four components of the social services, except child care, industry in 1997 appear in table 4. As in most industries, professionals and managers—whose salaries reflect higher education levels, broader experience, and greater responsibility—commonly earn more than other workers in social services.

TABLE 4

Median hourly earnings of the largest occupations in social services, except child care, 1997

Occupation	Individual and family services	Job training and related services	Residential care	Social services, not elsewhere classified	All industries
General managers and top executives	$19.08	$22.11	$18.55	$22.69	$26.05
Social workers, except medical and psychiatric ...	12.13	11.37	12.05	12.03	14.01
Secretaries, except legal and medical	9.39	9.51	9.64	10.27	11.00
Human services workers	9.45	8.60	8.12	9.72	9.89
Social workers, medical and psychiatric	13.09	—	12.32	—	14.72
Residential counselors	8.41	8.73	8.63	—	8.57
Nursing aides, orderlies, and attendants	7.17	—	7.20	—	7.76
Home health aides	7.17	—	7.23	—	7.75
Personal and home care aides	6.99	7.29	7.20	—	6.96
Child care workers	6.98	—	7.55	—	6.48

About 10.9 percent of workers in the social services industry were union members or were covered by union contracts in 1998, compared to about 15.4 percent of workers throughout private industry.

Outlook

Job opportunities in social services should be numerous through the year 2008. The number of nongovernment wage and salary jobs is expected to increase 41 percent, compared to only 15 percent for all industries combined. Expected growth rates for the various segments of the industry range from 31 percent in job training and vocational rehabilitation services to 57 percent in residential care over the 1998-2008 period (table 1). In addition to employment growth, many job openings will stem from the need to replace workers who transfer to other occupations or stop working. The greatest number of job openings should arise in large occupations with easy entry, relatively low pay, and high turnover, such as home health and personal care aides.

The expected rapid growth is due to expanding services for the elderly, the mentally and physically disabled, and families in crisis. Older people comprise a rapidly expanding segment of the population and are more likely to need social services than younger age groups. A continuing influx of foreign-born nationals to this country will spur demand for social services, such as relocation, financial, and job training assistance. Businesses are implementing more employee counseling programs. Programs also are increasing for child protective services and special groups, such as adults who were abused as children. The growing emphasis on providing home care services rather than more costly nursing home or hospital care, and on earlier and better integration of the disabled into society also will contribute to employment growth in the social services industry.

Some of the fastest growing occupations in the Nation are concentrated in social services. The number of home health and personal care aides within social services is projected to grow 46 percent by 2008, and human service workers and assistants, 73 percent, compared to the industry average of 41 percent.

Sources of Additional Information

For additional information about careers in social work, write to:

- National Association of Social Workers, 750 First St. NE., Suite 700, Washington, DC 20002.

For information on programs and careers in human services, contact:

- Council for Standards in Human Services Education, Northern Essex Community College, 100 Elliott Way, Haverhill, MA 01830

State employment service offices may also be able to provide information on job opportunities in social services.

Details on 500 Major Jobs:
Earnings, Projected Growth, Education Required, Unemployment Rates, and Other Details

Selected Occupational Data, 1998 and Projected 2008

Every other year, the Bureau of Labor Statistics updates data on current and projected employment, employment change, self-employment, annual average job openings, and other characteristics for all national industry-occupation matrix occupations to ensure that the information is current.

The following table displays this data for 1998 and for projected 2008. Also presented are quartile rankings designating the relative magnitude of data for each detailed occupation. As a result, you can obtain specific data about several variables for any occupation and can use the rankings to determine how information for a specific occupation compares with that for other occupations.

Comments

The table that follows provides a comprehensive picture of over 500 major jobs and makes it easier to compare the attributes of different occupations. The jobs are organized into clusters of related jobs, which helps you quickly identify occupations of interest.

In addition to statistics on employment and employment changes, growth rates, job openings, and self-employed workers, the table includes rankings from very low to very high for a number of variables. It also identifies the most significant source of education or training for each occupation.

The text that follows is from the U.S. Department of Labor and further explains the elements used in the table.

Data Presented

Information about each variable's data source and potential use is presented below. The Occupational Employment Statistics (OES) survey and the Current Population Survey (CPS) provide almost all the employment data used in developing the 1998-2008 projections. These surveys also are the source of the other statistical information contained in the table.

Occupational data from the OES survey are not entirely comparable with those from the CPS because of differences in occupational classification systems, and differences in concepts and methods used in the two surveys. Information about worker characteristics that is based on CPS data is applied to industry-occupation matrix occupations based on judgments identifying the most comparable CPS occupations. Comparisons were excluded if they were based on CPS occupations with fewer than 50,000 workers in 1998 or on other occupations for which the data appeared unreliable; data for CPS proxy occupations were substituted. Where possible, larger, closely related CPS occupations were chosen as proxies. For example, data for purchasing agents and buyers, not elsewhere classified, were used to represent purchasing agents and buyers of farm products. When a detailed occupation could not be identified, a summary occupational group was used. For example, data about all therapists were substituted for those about inhalation therapists.

Rankings for data categories identify the relative magnitude of variables in terms of the distribution of employment. For example, to rank the projected percent change in employment, 1998 employment and projected 1998-2008 percent change in employment data were assembled for each occupation. Each occupation's employment as a percent of 1998 total employment was calculated. The occupations were sorted by employment change in descending order and the cumulative percent of 1998 employment for each was determined. Occupations within the group accounting for less than 25 percent of total employment are designated "vh" for a very high growth rate. Similarly, occupations sorted by descending order of employment change accounting for 25 to 50 percent of employment are "h" (high); 50 to 75 percent, "l" (low); and 75 to 100 percent, "vl" (very low). Occupations were sorted by other data elements, and rankings were determined in the same manner.

Employment, 1998 and 2008. (Source: Bureau of Labor Statistics, national industry-occupation matrixes for 1998 and 2008.) Employment information is a useful starting point for assessing opportunities, because large occupations usually have more openings than small ones, regardless of growth or replacement rates. The data include jobs in all industries.

Employment change, 1998-2008, numeric. (Source: Bureau of Labor Statistics, national industry-occupation matrixes for 1998 and 2008.) Information on numerical change provides an absolute measure of projected job gains or losses.

Employment change, 1998-2008, percent. (Source: Bureau of Labor Statistics, national industry-occupation matrixes for 1998 and 2008.) The percent change in employment measures the rate of change. A rapidly growing occupation usually indicates favorable prospects for employment. Moreover, the high demand for workers in a rapidly growing occupation improves their chances for advancement and mobility. A modest employment growth in a large occupation can result in many more job openings than rapidly growing employment growth in a small occupation.

Percent self-employed, 1998. (Source: Bureau of Labor Statistics, national industry-occupation matrixes for 1998 and 2008.) Individuals who are interested in creating and managing their own business may find it important to know the percentage of self-employed workers. This percentage is calculated from CPS data about unincorporated, self-employed persons in their primary or secondary job who are included in industry-occupation matrix employment data. Unincorporated, self-employed persons work for earnings or fees in their own business and, unlike self-employed persons in businesses that are incorporated, do not receive a wage or salary.

Job openings due to growth plus total replacement needs, 1998-2008. (Source: Bureau of Labor Statistics, *Occupational Projections and Training Data*, 2000-01 Edition.) These data provide the broadest measure of opportunities and identify the total number of additional employees needed annually in an occupation. Growth is calculated using data on increases in occupational employment from national industry-occupation matrixes for 1998-2008. These replacements refer to all job openings, regardless of experience level, and reflect the normal movements in the labor force. If employment declines, job openings due to growth are zero. Total replacement needs are calculated from 1995-96 CPS data. Data from CPS proxy occupations are used to estimate replacement needs for some matrix occupations.

Job openings due to growth plus net replacement needs, 1998-2008. (Source: Bureau of Labor Statistics, *Occupational Projections and Training Data*, 2000-01 Edition.) These data estimate the number of new workers needed annually in an occupation and, if training is required, measure minimum training needs. Growth is calculated using data on increases in occupational employment from national industry-occupation matrixes for 1998-2008. If employment declines, job openings due to growth are zero. These net replacement job openings typically are due to experienced workers leaving the occupation or the labor force. Net replacement needs are calculated from CPS data. Data from CPS proxy occupations estimate replacement needs for some matrix occupations.

Median annual earnings, 1998. (Source: 1998 Occupational Employment Statistics survey, with some exceptions. OES data are not available for government chief executives and legislators. OES data also are not available for private household workers; farm operators and managers; captains and other officers, fishing vessels. Estimates developed from 1998 Current Population Survey annual average data for wage and salary employees provide information for child care workers, private household; and cleaners and servants, private household.) The table uses median annual earnings of workers to compare earnings among different occupations.

Unemployment rate. (Source: Average of 1996-98 Current Population Survey data.) Some occupations are more susceptible to factors that result in unemployment: seasonality, fluctuations in economic conditions, and individual business failures. A high unemployment rate indicates that individuals in that occupation are more likely to become unemployed than are those in occupations with a low rate. Data from CPS proxy occupations are used to estimate unemployment rates for some matrix occupations.

Percent part-time. (Source: Average of 1996-98 Current Population Survey data.) Persons who prefer part-time work may want to know the proportion of employees who work fewer than 35 hours per week. Data from CPS proxy occupations are used to estimate the proportion of part-time workers for some matrix occupations.

Most significant source of education or training. (Source: Bureau of Labor Statistics.) Occupations are classified into 1 of 11 categories that describe the education or training needed by most workers to become fully qualified. The categories are first professional degree, doctoral degree, master's degree, work experience in an occupation requiring a bachelor's or higher degree, bachelor's degree, associate degree, postsecondary vocational training, work experience in a related occupation, long-term on-the-job training, moderate-term on-the-job training, and short-term on-the-job training. The following are definitions of these categories:

Occupations that require a first professional degree. The first professional degree is the minimum preparation required for entry into several professions, including law, medicine, dentistry, and the clergy. Completion of this academic program usually requires at least 2 years of full-time academic study beyond a bachelor's degree.

Occupations that generally require a doctoral degree. The doctoral degree also can be easily related to specific occupations. It normally requires at least 3 years of full-time academic work beyond the bachelor's degree.

Occupations that generally require a master's degree. Completion of a master's degree program usually requires 1 or 2 years of full-time study beyond the bachelor's degree.

Occupations that generally require work experience in an occupation requiring a bachelor's or higher degree. Most occupations in this category are managerial occupations that require experience in a related nonmanagerial occupation. Jobs in these occupations usually are filled with experienced staff who are promoted into a managerial position, such as engineers who advance to engineering manager. It is very difficult to become a judge without first working as a lawyer, or to become a personnel, training, or labor relations manager without first gaining experience as a specialist in one of these fields.

Occupations that generally require a bachelor's degree. This is a degree program requiring at least 4 but not more than 5 years of full-time academic work after high school. The bachelor's degree is considered the minimum requirement for most professional occupations, such as mechanical engineer, pharmacist, recreational therapist, and landscape architect.

Occupations that generally require an associate degree. Completion of this degree program usually requires at least 2 years of full-time academic work after high school. Most occupations in this category are health related, such as registered nurse, respiratory therapist, and radiologic technologist. Also included are science and mathematics technicians and paralegals.

Occupations that generally require completion of vocational training provided in postsecondary vocational schools. Workers normally qualify for jobs by completing vocational training programs or by taking job-related college courses that do not result in a degree. Some programs take less than a year to complete and lead to a certificate or diploma. Others last longer than a year, but less than 4 years. Occupations in this category include some that require only the completion of a training program (such as a travel agent) and those that require individuals to pass a licensing exam after completion of the program before they can work (such as barber and cosmetologist).

Occupations that generally require skills developed through work experience in a related occupation. Jobs in this category require skills and experience gained in another occupation; the category also includes occupations in which skills may be developed from hobbies or other activities besides current or past employment or from service in the Armed Forces. Among these

occupations are cost estimators, who generally need prior work experience in one of the construction trades; police detectives, who are selected based on their experience as police patrol officers; and lawn service managers, who may be hired based on their experience as groundskeepers.

Long-term on-the-job training. This category includes occupations that usually require more than 12 months of on-the-job training or combined work experience and formal classroom instruction before workers develop the skills needed for average job performance. Among these are such occupations as electrician, bricklayer, and machinist that normally require formal or informal apprenticeships lasting up to 4 years. Long-term on-the-job training also includes intensive occupation-specific, employer-sponsored programs that workers must successfully complete before they can begin work. These include fire and police academies and schools for air traffic controllers and flight attendants. In other occupations—insurance sales and securities sales, for example—trainees take formal courses, often provided at the job site, to prepare for the required licensing exams. Individuals undergoing training usually are considered employed in the occupation. This group of occupations also includes musicians, athletes, actors, and other entertainers—occupations that require natural ability that must be developed over several years.

Moderate-term on-the-job training. Workers can achieve average job performance after 1 to 12 months of combined job experience and informal training, which can include observing experienced workers. Individuals undergoing training normally are considered employed in the occupation. This type of training is found among occupations such as dental assistants, drywall installers and finishers, operating engineers, and machine operators. The training involves trainees watching experienced workers and asking questions. Trainees are given progressively more difficult assignments as they demonstrate their mastery of lower level skills.

Short-term on-the-job training. Included are occupations like cashier, bank teller, messenger, highway maintenance worker, and veterinary assistant. In these occupations, workers usually can achieve average job performance in just a few days or weeks by working with and observing experienced employees and by asking questions.

Using Ranked Information

The table consolidates 1998 and 2008 projected employment data and also provides comparisons of occupational data. It ranks information about current and projected employment, projected job openings, earnings, unemployment rates, and the proportion of part-time workers. Except for the unemployment and part-time categories, a high rating indicates a favorable assessment. A high rating for the unemployment rate is considered undesirable. Unemployment rates in construction occupations, however, are inflated by the nature of the industry and distort comparisons. Construction workers typically incur periods of unemployment after completing a project and before starting work on a new project.

The rating for the part-time category also should not be used routinely in assessing the desirability of employment because the assessment depends on the perspective of the user. For example, high school students may consider a large proportion of part-time work desirable because they normally prefer not to work full time. A recent college graduate or anyone seeking full-time employment may reach the opposite conclusion.

The data in the table have many potential uses. At times, users may want to know how a particular occupation—cashiers, for example—compares with others. The "vh" (very high) rankings in the table for the increase in the number of jobs and for both categories of job openings point out that many jobs are available, certainly a favorable rating. The "vl" (very low) ranking for earnings and "vh" (very high) for unemployment, however, are unfavorable in comparison with other occupations, and these characteristics detract from the desirability of employment in the occupation. The table also shows that cashiers require only short-term on-the-job training.

Some readers might wish to identify occupations with favorable characteristics that jobseekers can pursue through a specific type of training. For example, a student might be interested in a technical occupation but not care to obtain a four-year college degree. In another instance, a planner might wish to ensure that training programs provided by junior colleges in the area are consistent with the needs of the national labor market. To obtain appropriate information, both the student and the planner could examine information for occupations placed in the associate degree educational or training category.

Although the table contains a great deal of information useful for career guidance, information about occupation comparisons should be used as an aid, not a sole source of information for making career choices. After using the table to identify occupations with favorable prospects, individuals should obtain additional information from other sources such as the *Occupational Outlook Handbook*, the *Occupational Outlook Quarterly,* and local sources, if available. Consideration should be given to individual aptitudes and preferences, and alternative sources of training available in the local area should be investigated. An electronic version of the table is available on the Internet at ftp://146.142.4.23/pub/special.requests/ep/OPTDData/.

Occupational employment and job openings data, 1998-2008, and worker characteristics, 1998

(Numbers in thousands)

1998 Matrix Occupation	Employment		Employment change, 1998-2008				Per-cent self-emp-loyed, 1998	Annual average job openings due to growth and total replacement needs, 1998-2008	
	1998	2008	Numeric		Percent				
			Number	Rank	Number	Rank		Number	Rank
Total, all occupations	140,514	160,795	20,281	-	14.4	-	8.7	28,351	-
Executive, administrative, and managerial occupations	14,770	17,196	2,426	-	16.4	-	14.3	2,090	-
Managerial and administrative occupations	10,139	11,823	1,684	-	16.6	-	16.2	1,402	-
Administrative services managers	364	430	66	L	18.1	H	.0	47	L
Advertising, marketing, promotions, public relations, and sales managers	485	597	112	L	23.0	VH	2.5	89	L
Communication, transportation, and utilities operations managers	196	234	38	L	19.3	VH	.0	25	VL
Construction managers	270	308	38	L	14.0	L	16.6	33	VL
Education administrators	447	505	58	L	13.0	L	8.7	60	L
Engineering, natural science, and computer and information systems managers	326	468	142	H	43.5	VH	.0	54	L
Financial managers	693	791	97	L	14.0	L	.8	78	L
Food service and lodging managers[1]	595	691	97	L	16.3	H	35.0	139	L
Funeral directors and morticians[1]	28	32	4	VL	16.1	H	8.8	4	VL
General managers and top executives	3,362	3,913	551	VH	16.4	H	.0	421	VH
Government chief executives and legislators[1]	80	82	2	VL	2.8	VL	.0	6	VL
Human resources managers	230	274	45	L	19.4	VH	.5	33	VL
Industrial production managers	208	207	-2	VL	-.9	VL	.0	21	VL
Medical and health services managers	222	297	74	L	33.3	VH	6.3	31	VL
Postmasters and mail superintendents[1]	26	27	1	VL	3.0	VL	.0	3	VL
Property, real estate, and community association managers[1] ...	315	359	43	L	13.7	L	47.6	48	L
Purchasing managers	176	188	13	VL	7.1	VL	.1	25	VL
All other managers and administrators[1]	2,114	2,420	305	VH	14.4	H	54.9	284	H
Management support occupations	4,631	5,374	743	-	16.0	-	10.3	688	-
Accountants and auditors	1,080	1,202	122	L	11.3	L	13.2	130	L
Assessors and real estate appraisers	70	78	8	-	11.3	-	18.1	9	-
Assessors	22	25	3	VL	11.8	L	.0	2	VL
Real estate appraisers	48	53	5	VL	11.2	L	26.6	6	VL
Budget analysts	59	67	8	VL	13.7	L	.0	10	VL
Buyers and purchasing agents	371	396	25	-	6.7	-	6.4	79	-
Purchasing agents and buyers, farm[1]	29	30	1	VL	5.0	VL	13.0	5	VL
Purchasing agents, except wholesale, retail, and farm products	224	248	24	L	10.8	L	1.2	42	VL
Wholesale and retail buyers, except farm products	118	118	0	VL	-.4	VL	14.6	31	VL
Construction and building inspectors	68	79	11	VL	15.7	H	6.0	4	VL
Cost estimators	152	171	20	VL	13.0	L	.0	28	VL
Credit analysts	42	50	8	VL	19.9	VH	.0	7	VL
Employment interviewers, private or public employment service	66	74	8	VL	12.9	L	.0	14	VL
Human resources, training, and labor relations specialists	367	433	66	L	17.9	H	3.9	83	L
Inspectors and compliance officers, except construction	176	195	19	VL	10.5	L	3.0	20	VL
Insurance claims adjusters, appraisers, examiners, and investigators	239	284	45	-	18.0	-	4.7	21	-
Insurance claims adjusters, examiners, and investigators	229	272	43	-	18.7	-	4.9	20	-
Claims examiners, property and casualty insurance	49	55	6	VL	12.5	L	.0	4	VL
Insurance adjusters, examiners, and investigators	180	217	37	L	20.4	VH	6.2	16	VL
Insurance appraisers, auto damage	10	12	2	VL	16.0	H	.0	1	VL
Insurance underwriters	97	100	3	VL	2.7	VL	1.1	4	VL
Loan counselors and officers	227	276	48	L	21.2	VH	.0	40	VL
Management analysts[1]	344	442	98	L	28.4	VH	53.5	24	VL
Tax examiners, collectors, and revenue agents	62	66	3	VL	5.4	VL	.0	5	VL
Tax preparers	79	95	15	VL	19.3	VH	33.1	14	VL
All other management support workers[1]	1,130	1,366	236	H	20.9	VH	4.4	199	H

[1] One or more Current Population Survey (CPS) proxy occupations are used to estimate CPS based data.
[2] Current Population Survey data are used to estimate median weekly earnings ranking.
[3] Bachelor's degree or higher.

NOTE: Rankings are based on employment in all detailed occupations in the National Industry-Occupation Matrix. For details, see "Data presented" section of text. Codes for describing the ranked variables are: VH = Very high, H = High, L = Low, VL = Very low, n. a. = Data not available. A dash indicates data are not applicable.

Occupational employment and job openings data, 1998-2008, and worker characteristics, 1998

(Numbers in thousands)

Annual average job openings due to growth and net replacement needs, 1998-2008		Median annual earnings		Ranking of:		Most significant source of education or training	1998 Matrix Occupation
Number	Rank	Dollars	Rank	Unemploy-ment rate	Per-cent part-time		
5,462	-	-	-	-	-	-	**Total, all occupations**
511	-	-	-	-	-	-	**Executive, administrative, and managerial occupations**
348	-	-	-	-	-	-	Managerial and administrative occupations
13	L	44,370	VH	VL	L	Work experience plus degree[3]	Administrative services managers
18	L	57,300	VH	L	VL	Work experience plus degree[3]	Advertising, marketing, promotions, public relations, and sales managers
7	VL	52,810	VH	VL	L	Work experience plus degree[3]	Communication, transportation, and utilities operations managers
9	VL	47,610	VH	VL	L	Bachelor's degree	Construction managers
17	L	60,400	VH	VL	H	Work experience plus degree[3]	Education administrators
20	L	75,330	VH	VL	L	Work experience plus degree[3]	Engineering, natural science, and computer and information systems managers
21	L	55,070	VH	VL	VL	Work experience plus degree[3]	Financial managers
20	L	26,700	H	L	H	Related work experience	Food service and lodging managers[1]
1	VL	35,040	VH	VL	L	Associate degree	Funeral directors and morticians[1]
114	VH	55,890	VH	VL	L	Work experience plus degree[3]	General managers and top executives
2	VL	n.a.	-	VL	L	Work experience plus degree[3]	Government chief executives and legislators[1]
10	VL	49,010	VH	L	VL	Work experience plus degree[3]	Human resources managers
4	VL	56,320	VH	VL	L	Bachelor's degree	Industrial production managers
11	L	48,870	VH	L	H	Work experience plus degree[3]	Medical and health services managers
1	VL	44,730	VH	VL	L	Related work experience	Postmasters and mail superintendents[1]
9	VL	29,930	H	L	H	Bachelor's degree	Property, real estate, and community association managers[1]
5	VL	41,830	VH	VL	VL	Work experience plus degree[3]	Purchasing managers
68	H	49,300	VH	VL	L	Work experience plus degree[3]	All other managers and administrators[1]
162	-	-	-	-	-	-	Management support occupations
29	L	37,860	VH	VL	L	Bachelor's degree	Accountants and auditors
2	-	-	-	-	-	-	Assessors and real estate appraisers
1	VL	29,830	H	VL	L	Bachelor's degree	Assessors
2	VL	40,290	VH	VL	H	Bachelor's degree	Real estate appraisers
2	VL	44,950	VH	VL	L	Bachelor's degree	Budget analysts
12	-	-	-	-	-	-	Buyers and purchasing agents
1	VL	32,070	H	L	L	Bachelor's degree	Purchasing agents and buyers, farm[1]
8	VL	38,040	VH	L	L	Bachelor's degree	Purchasing agents, except wholesale, retail, and farm products
3	VL	31,560	H	L	H	Bachelor's degree	Wholesale and retail buyers, except farm products
3	VL	37,540	VH	L	L	Related work experience	Construction and building inspectors
4	VL	40,590	VH	L	H	Bachelor's degree	Cost estimators
2	VL	35,590	VH	VL	L	Bachelor's degree	Credit analysts
3	VL	29,800	H	L	L	Bachelor's degree	Employment interviewers, private or public employment service
16	L	37,710	VH	L	L	Bachelor's degree	Human resources, training, and labor relations specialists
5	VL	36,820	VH	VL	VL	Related work experience	Inspectors and compliance officers, except construction
8	-	-	-	-	-	-	Insurance claims adjusters, appraisers, examiners, and investigators
8	-	-	-	-	-	-	Insurance claims adjusters, examiners, and investigators
1	VL	40,110	VH	VL	L	Bachelor's degree	Claims examiners, property and casualty insurance
7	VL	38,290	VH	VL	L	Long-term on-the-job	Insurance adjusters, examiners, and investigators
0	VL	40,000	VH	VL	L	Long-term on-the-job	Insurance appraisers, auto damage
3	VL	38,710	VH	L	H	Bachelor's degree	Insurance underwriters
10	VL	35,340	VH	VL	L	Bachelor's degree	Loan counselors and officers
12	L	49,470	VH	L	H	Work experience plus degree[3]	Management analysts[1]
2	VL	39,540	VH	VL	VL	Bachelor's degree	Tax examiners, collectors, and revenue agents
3	VL	27,960	H	VL	L	Moderate-term on-the-job	Tax preparers
46	H	37,860	VH	VL	L	Bachelor's degree	All other management support workers[1]

[1] One or more Current Population Survey (CPS) proxy occupations are used to estimate CPS based data.

[2] Current Population Survey data are used to estimate median weekly earnings ranking.

[3] Bachelor's degree or higher.

NOTE: Rankings are based on employment in all detailed occupations in the National Industry-Occupation Matrix. For details, see "Data presented" section of text. Codes for describing the ranked variables are: VH = Very high, H = High, L = Low, VL = Very low, n. a. = Data not available. A dash indicates data are not applicable.

Occupational employment and job openings data, 1998-2008, and worker characteristics, 1998

(Numbers in thousands)

1998 Matrix Occupation	Employment 1998	Employment 2008	Numeric Number	Numeric Rank	Percent Number	Percent Rank	Percent self-employed, 1998	Annual average job openings due to growth and total replacement needs, 1998-2008 Number	Rank
Professional specialty occupations	19,802	25,145	5,343	-	26.9	-	9.9	2,799	-
Engineers	1,462	1,752	290	-	19.8	-	3.4	133	-
Aerospace engineers	53	58	5	VL	8.8	L	.8	2	VL
Chemical engineers[1]	48	53	5	VL	9.5	L	2.3	4	VL
Civil engineers	195	236	41	L	20.9	VH	6.1	21	VL
Electrical and electronics engineers	357	450	93	L	25.9	VH	4.4	30	VL
Industrial engineers, except safety engineers	126	142	16	VL	12.8	L	2.6	13	VL
Materials engineers	20	21	2	VL	9.0	L	3.7	2	VL
Mechanical engineers	220	256	36	L	16.4	H	2.0	9	VL
Mining engineers, including mine safety engineers[1]	4	4	-1	VL	-12.6	VL	.0	0	VL
Nuclear engineers[1]	12	12	1	VL	5.8	VL	.0	1	VL
Petroleum engineers[1]	12	12	0	VL	-3.6	VL	15.0	1	VL
All other engineers[1]	415	509	94	L	22.6	VH	2.6	51	L
Architects and surveyors	163	185	23	-	13.8	-	25.1	17	-
Architects, except landscape and naval	99	118	19	VL	18.9	H	29.9	8	VL
Landscape architects	22	25	3	VL	14.5	H	40.7	2	VL
Surveyors, cartographers, and photogrammetrists[1]	41	42	1	VL	1.4	VL	5.4	7	VL
Life scientists	173	219	45	-	26.2	-	4.4	19	-
Agricultural and food scientists[1]	21	24	2	VL	10.9	L	17.4	2	VL
Biological scientists	81	109	28	L	35.0	VH	.9	10	VL
Conservation scientists and foresters[1]	39	46	7	VL	17.9	H	5.5	3	VL
Medical scientists	31	39	8	VL	24.6	VH	3.4	3	VL
All other life scientists	1	1	0	VL	16.5	H	.0	0	VL
Computer, mathematical, and operations research occupations	1,653	3,182	1,529	-	92.4	-	7.1	404	-
Actuaries[1]	16	17	1	VL	7.1	VL	14.2	2	VL
Computer systems analysts, engineers, and scientists	1,530	3,052	1,522	-	99.4	-	7.4	395	-
Computer engineers and scientists	914	1,858	944	-	103.3	-	4.7	241	-
Computer engineers	299	622	323	VH	107.9	VH	10.8	81	L
Computer support specialists	429	869	439	VH	102.3	VH	.0	113	L
Database administrators	87	155	67	L	77.2	VH	.0	19	VL
All other computer scientists	97	212	115	L	117.5	VH	11.0	28	VL
Systems analysts	617	1,194	577	VH	93.6	VH	11.5	154	L
Statisticians[1]	17	17	0	VL	2.3	VL	5.4	2	VL
Mathematicians and all other mathematical scientists[1]	14	13	-1	VL	-5.5	VL	.0	1	VL
Operations research analysts	76	83	7	VL	8.7	L	.7	5	VL
Physical scientists	200	229	29	-	14.6	-	4.0	17	-
Atmospheric scientists[1]	8	10	1	VL	14.6	H	.0	1	VL
Chemists	96	110	13	VL	13.9	L	1.6	8	VL
Geologists, geophysicists, and oceanographers[1]	44	51	7	VL	15.5	H	13.3	4	VL
Physicists and astronomers[1]	18	18	0	VL	2.2	VL	1.6	1	VL
All other physical scientists[1]	33	41	8	VL	22.7	VH	1.0	3	VL
Religious workers	304	356	53	-	17.2	-	1.2	32	-
Clergy	149	169	20	VL	13.4	L	.0	14	VL
Directors, religious activities and education[1]	112	140	28	L	25.1	VH	.0	13	VL
All other religious workers[1]	43	48	5	VL	10.7	L	8.7	4	VL
Social scientists	321	365	44	-	13.7	-	33.1	45	-
Economists and marketing research analysts	70	83	13	VL	18.4	H	25.7	12	VL
Psychologists	166	185	19	VL	11.4	L	49.8	21	VL
Urban and regional planners[1]	35	41	6	VL	17.4	H	.0	5	VL
All other social scientists[1]	50	56	6	VL	12.7	L	10.9	7	VL
Social and recreation workers	1,303	1,797	494	-	37.8	-	1.3	265	-
Recreation workers	241	287	46	L	19.2	H	.3	44	L
Residential counselors	190	278	88	L	46.3	VH	.0	28	VL
Social and human service assistants	268	410	141	H	52.7	VH	.0	92	L
Social workers	604	822	218	H	36.1	VH	2.6	103	L
Lawyers and judicial workers	752	871	119	-	15.8	-	32.4	41	-

[1] One or more Current Population Survey (CPS) proxy occupations are used to estimate CPS based data.
[2] Current Population Survey data are used to estimate median weekly earnings ranking.
[3] Bachelor's degree or higher.

NOTE: Rankings are based on employment in all detailed occupations in the National Industry-Occupation Matrix. For details, see "Data presented" section of text. Codes for describing the ranked variables are: VH = Very high, H = High, L = Low, VL = Very low, n. a. = Data not available. A dash indicates data are not applicable.

Occupational employment and job openings data, 1998-2008, and worker characteristics, 1998

(Numbers in thousands)

Annual average job openings due to growth and net replacement needs, 1998-2008		Median annual earnings		Ranking of:		Most significant source of education or training	1998 Matrix Occupation
Number	Rank	Dollars	Rank	Unemployment rate	Percent part-time		
915	-	-	-	-	-	-	**Professional specialty occupations**
61	-	-	-	-	-	-	Engineers
1	VL	66,950	VH	VL	VL	Bachelor's degree	Aerospace engineers
2	VL	64,760	VH	VL	VL	Bachelor's degree	Chemical engineers[1]
8	VL	53,450	VH	VL	VL	Bachelor's degree	Civil engineers
17	L	62,260	VH	VL	VL	Bachelor's degree	Electrical and electronics engineers
3	VL	52,610	VH	VL	VL	Bachelor's degree	Industrial engineers, except safety engineers
1	VL	57,970	VH	VL	VL	Bachelor's degree	Materials engineers
8	VL	53,290	VH	VL	VL	Bachelor's degree	Mechanical engineers
0	VL	56,090	VH	VL	VL	Bachelor's degree	Mining engineers, including mine safety engineers[1]
0	VL	71,310	VH	VL	VL	Bachelor's degree	Nuclear engineers[1]
0	VL	74,260	VH	VL	VL	Bachelor's degree	Petroleum engineers[1]
21	L	61,060	VH	VL	VL	Bachelor's degree	All other engineers[1]
5	-	-	-	-	-	-	Architects and surveyors
3	VL	47,710	VH	VL	L	Bachelor's degree	Architects, except landscape and naval
1	VL	37,930	VH	VL	L	Bachelor's degree	Landscape architects
1	VL	37,640	VH	L	L	Bachelor's degree	Surveyors, cartographers, and photogrammetrists[1]
9	-	-	-	-	-	-	Life scientists
1	VL	42,340	VH	VL	L	Bachelor's degree	Agricultural and food scientists[1]
5	VL	46,140	VH	VL	L	Doctoral degree	Biological scientists
2	VL	42,750	VH	VL	L	Bachelor's degree	Conservation scientists and foresters[1]
2	VL	50,410	VH	VL	L	Doctoral degree	Medical scientists
0	VL	41,320	VH	VL	L	Doctoral degree	All other life scientists
166	-	-	-	-	-	-	Computer, mathematical, and operations research occupations
0	VL	65,560	VH	VL	L	Bachelor's degree	Actuaries[1]
163	-	-	-	-	-	-	Computer systems analysts, engineers, and scientists
101	-	-	-	-	-	-	Computer engineers and scientists
34	H	61,910	VH	VL	L	Bachelor's degree	Computer engineers
47	H	37,120	VH	VL	L	Associate degree	Computer support specialists
8	VL	47,980	VH	VL	L	Bachelor's degree	Database administrators
12	L	46,670	VH	VL	L	Bachelor's degree	All other computer scientists
62	H	52,180	VH	VL	L	Bachelor's degree	Systems analysts
0	VL	48,540	VH	VL	L	Master's degree	Statisticians[1]
0	VL	49,120	VH	VL	L	Master's degree	Mathematicians and all other mathematical scientists[1]
3	VL	49,070	VH	VL	VL	Master's degree	Operations research analysts
8	-	-	-	-	-	-	Physical scientists
0	VL	54,430	VH	VL	L	Bachelor's degree	Atmospheric scientists[1]
3	VL	46,220	VH	VL	L	Bachelor's degree	Chemists
2	VL	53,890	VH	VL	L	Bachelor's degree	Geologists, geophysicists, and oceanographers[1]
1	VL	73,240	VH	VL	L	Doctoral degree	Physicists and astronomers[1]
2	VL	48,990	VH	VL	L	Bachelor's degree	All other physical scientists[1]
11	-	-	-	-	-	-	Religious workers
5	VL	28,890	H	VL	H	First professional degree	Clergy
5	VL	25,040	H	L	H	Bachelor's degree	Directors, religious activities and education[1]
1	VL	18,440	L	L	H	Bachelor's degree	All other religious workers[1]
11	-	-	-	-	-	-	Social scientists
3	VL	48,330	VH	VL	H	Bachelor's degree	Economists and marketing research analysts
5	VL	48,050	VH	VL	VH	Master's degree	Psychologists
1	VL	42,860	VH	VL	H	Master's degree	Urban and regional planners[1]
2	VL	38,990	VH	VL	H	Master's degree	All other social scientists[1]
75	-	-	-	-	-	-	Social and recreation workers
11	L	16,500	VL	L	H	Bachelor's degree	Recreation workers
13	L	18,840	L	VL	H	Bachelor's degree	Residential counselors
21	L	21,360	L	L	VH	Moderate-term on-the-job	Social and human service assistants
30	L	30,590	H	L	H	Bachelor's degree	Social workers
20	-	-	-	-	-	-	Lawyers and judicial workers

[1] One or more Current Population Survey (CPS) proxy occupations are used to estimate CPS based data.
[2] Current Population Survey data are used to estimate median weekly earnings ranking.
[3] Bachelor's degree or higher.

NOTE: Rankings are based on employment in all detailed occupations in the National Industry-Occupation Matrix. For details, see "Data presented" section of text. Codes for describing the ranked variables are: VH = Very high, H = High, L = Low, VL = Very low, n. a. = Data not available. A dash indicates data are not applicable.

Occupational employment and job openings data, 1998-2008, and worker characteristics, 1998

(Numbers in thousands)

1998 Matrix Occupation	Employment		Employment change, 1998-2008				Per- cent self- emp- loyed, 1998	Annual average job openings due to growth and total replacement needs, 1998-2008	
			Numeric		Percent				
	1998	2008	Number	Rank	Number	Rank		Number	Rank
Judges, magistrates, and other judicial workers[1]	71	73	2	VL	2.9	VL	.0	3	VL
Lawyers	681	798	117	L	17.2	H	35.8	38	VL
Teachers, librarians, and counselors	6,939	8,248	1,309	-	18.8	-	3.5	1,043	-
Teachers, preschool and kindergarten	529	645	116	-	21.9	-	1.0	61	-
Teachers, preschool	346	437	92	L	26.5	VH	1.5	42	VL
Teachers, kindergarten	184	208	25	L	13.4	L	.0	19	VL
Teachers, elementary school	1,754	1,959	205	H	11.7	L	.0	204	H
Teachers, secondary school	1,426	1,749	322	VH	22.6	VH	.0	134	L
Teachers, special education	406	543	137	H	33.8	VH	.0	37	VL
College and university faculty[1]	865	1,061	195	H	22.6	VH	.0	139	L
Other teachers and instructors	956	1,139	183	-	19.1	-	19.1	259	-
Farm and home management advisors	10	10	0	VL	-2.2	VL	.0	2	VL
Instructors and coaches, sports and physical training	359	460	102	L	28.4	VH	16.5	104	L
Adult and vocational education teachers	588	669	81	-	13.0	-	21.1	153	-
Instructors, adult (nonvocational) education	168	203	35	L	20.9	VH	20.5	46	L
Teachers and instructors, vocational education and training	420	466	46	L	11.0	L	21.3	106	L
All other teachers and instructors[1]	644	739	95	L	14.7	H	8.3	155	L
Librarians, archivists, curators, and related workers	175	186	10	-	5.8	-	.4	29	-
Archivists, curators, museum technicians, and conservators[1]	23	26	3	VL	12.6	L	3.1	4	VL
Librarians	152	159	7	VL	4.8	VL	.0	25	VL
Counselors	182	228	46	L	25.0	VH	.9	21	VL
Health diagnosing occupations	892	1,049	157	-	17.6	-	27.5	42	-
Chiropractors[1]	46	57	11	VL	22.8	VH	64.3	3	VL
Dentists	160	165	5	VL	3.1	VL	48.5	2	VL
Optometrists[1]	38	42	4	VL	10.6	L	33.6	2	VL
Physicians	577	699	122	L	21.2	VH	17.6	33	VL
Podiatrists[1]	14	15	1	VL	10.5	L	47.2	1	VL
Veterinarians[1]	57	71	14	VL	24.7	VH	29.9	3	VL
Health assessment and treating occupations	2,860	3,531	671	-	23.4	-	2.5	258	-
Dietitians and nutritionists	54	64	10	VL	19.1	H	10.4	8	VL
Pharmacists	185	199	14	VL	7.3	VL	3.9	6	VL
Physician assistants[1]	66	98	32	L	48.0	VH	.0	6	VL
Registered nurses	2,079	2,530	451	VH	21.7	VH	1.0	195	H
Therapists	476	640	164	-	34.5	-	8.1	42	-
Occupational therapists[1]	73	98	25	L	34.2	VH	10.6	6	VL
Physical therapists[1]	120	161	41	L	34.0	VH	5.3	11	VL
Radiation therapists[1]	12	14	2	VL	16.7	H	.0	1	VL
Recreational therapists[1]	39	44	5	VL	13.4	L	31.3	2	VL
Respiratory therapists[1]	86	123	37	L	42.6	VH	.9	9	VL
Speech-language pathologists and audiologists[1]	105	145	40	L	38.5	VH	10.3	10	VL
All other therapists[1]	40	54	14	VL	35.7	VH	2.3	4	VL
Writers, artists, and entertainers	1,996	2,409	413	-	20.0	-	39.6	352	-
Actors, directors, and producers[1]	160	198	38	L	23.8	VH	28.4	31	VL
Announcers	60	58	-3	VL	-4.3	VL	19.9	13	VL
Artists and commercial artists	308	388	79	L	25.7	VH	57.5	59	L
Athletes, coaches, umpires, and related workers	52	66	14	VL	27.9	VH	30.0	19	VL
Dancers and choreographers[1]	29	33	4	VL	13.6	L	30.8	5	VL
Designers	423	532	110	-	25.9	-	40.6	72	-
Designers, except interior designers	335	426	91	L	27.1	VH	44.0	58	L
Interior designers	53	68	15	VL	27.2	VH	44.9	9	VL
Merchandise displayers and window dressers	34	38	4	VL	12.7	L	.0	5	VL
Musicians, singers, and related workers	273	314	41	L	14.8	H	43.6	45	L
News analysts, reporters, and correspondents	67	68	2	VL	2.8	VL	7.1	8	VL
Photographers and camera operators	161	176	15	-	9.2	-	54.6	22	-
Camera operators, television, motion picture, video	11	15	3	VL	29.0	VH	8.1	2	VL
Photographers	149	161	12	VL	7.7	VL	58.1	20	VL

[1] One or more Current Population Survey (CPS) proxy occupations are used to estimate CPS based data.

[2] Current Population Survey data are used to estimate median weekly earnings ranking.

[3] Bachelor's degree or higher.

NOTE: Rankings are based on employment in all detailed occupations in the National Industry-Occupation Matrix. For details, see "Data presented" section of text. Codes for describing the ranked variables are: VH = Very high, H = High, L = Low, VL = Very low, n. a. = Data not available. A dash indicates data are not applicable.

Occupational employment and job openings data, 1998-2008, and worker characteristics, 1998

(Numbers in thousands)

Annual average job openings due to growth and net replacement needs, 1998-2008		Median annual earnings		Ranking of:		Most significant source of education or training	1998 Matrix Occupation
Number	Rank	Dollars	Rank	Unemployment rate	Percent part-time		
1	VL	35,630	VH	VL	L	Work experience plus degree[3]	Judges, magistrates, and other judicial workers[1]
19	L	78,170	VH	VL	L	First professional degree	Lawyers
283	-	-	-	-	-	-	Teachers, librarians, and counselors
23	-	-	-	-	-	-	Teachers, preschool and kindergarten
17	L	17,310	L	L	VH	Bachelor's degree	Teachers, preschool
6	VL	33,590	H	L	VH	Bachelor's degree	Teachers, kindergarten
61	H	36,110	VH	VL	H	Bachelor's degree	Teachers, elementary school
78	H	37,890	VH	VL	H	Bachelor's degree	Teachers, secondary school
17	L	37,850	VH	VL	H	Bachelor's degree	Teachers, special education
44	H	46,630	VH	L	VH	Doctoral degree	College and university faculty[1]
28	-	-	-	-	-	-	Other teachers and instructors
0	VL	37,200	VH	L	VH	Bachelor's degree	Farm and home management advisors
14	L	22,230	L	L	VH	Moderate-term on-the-job	Instructors and coaches, sports and physical training
14	-	-	-	-	-	-	Adult and vocational education teachers
5	VL	24,800	H	L	VH	Related work experience	Instructors, adult (nonvocational) education
9	VL	34,430	H	L	VH	Related work experience	Teachers and instructors, vocational education and training
18	L	27,180	H	L	VH	Bachelor's degree	All other teachers and instructors[1]
6	-	-	-	-	-	-	Librarians, archivists, curators, and related workers
1	VL	31,750	H	VL	VH	Master's degree	Archivists, curators, museum technicians, and conservators[1]
5	VL	38,470	VH	VL	VH	Master's degree	Librarians
9	VL	38,650	VH	VL	H	Master's degree	Counselors
31	-	-	-	-	-	-	Health diagnosing occupations
2	VL	63,930	VH	VL	H	First professional degree	Chiropractors[1]
4	VL	110,160	VH	VL	VH	First professional degree	Dentists
1	VL	68,500	VH	VL	H	First professional degree	Optometrists[1]
21	L	124,000	VH	VL	L	First professional degree	Physicians
0	VL	79,530	VH	VL	H	First professional degree	Podiatrists[1]
3	VL	50,950	VH	VL	H	First professional degree	Veterinarians[1]
116	-	-	-	-	-	-	Health assessment and treating occupations
2	VL	35,020	VH	L	VH	Bachelor's degree	Dietitians and nutritionists
6	VL	66,220	VH	VL	H	First professional degree	Pharmacists
4	VL	47,090	VH	VL	VH	Bachelor's degree	Physician assistants[1]
79	VH	40,690	VH	VL	VH	Associate degree	Registered nurses
24	-	-	-	-	-	-	Therapists
4	VL	48,230	VH	VL	VH	Bachelor's degree	Occupational therapists[1]
6	VL	56,600	VH	VL	VH	Master's degree	Physical therapists[1]
0	VL	39,640	VH	VL	VH	Associate degree	Radiation therapists[1]
1	VL	27,760	H	VL	VH	Bachelor's degree	Recreational therapists[1]
5	VL	34,830	H	VL	VH	Associate degree	Respiratory therapists[1]
6	VL	43,080	VH	VL	VH	Master's degree	Speech-language pathologists and audiologists[1]
2	VL	30,270	H	VL	VH	Bachelor's degree	All other therapists[1]
83	-	-	-	-	-	-	Writers, artists, and entertainers
7	VL	27,400	H	H	VH	Long-term on-the-job	Actors, directors, and producers[1]
1	VL	17,930	L	H	VH	Moderate-term on-the-job	Announcers
14	L	31,690	H	H	VH	Work experience plus degree[3]	Artists and commercial artists
3	VL	22,210	L	H	VH	Long-term on-the-job	Athletes, coaches, umpires, and related workers
1	VL	21,430	L	H	VH	Postsecondary vocational	Dancers and choreographers[1]
17	-	-	-	-	-	-	Designers
14	L	29,200	H	L	H	Bachelor's degree	Designers, except interior designers
2	VL	31,760	H	L	H	Bachelor's degree	Interior designers
1	VL	18,180	L	L	H	Moderate-term on-the-job	Merchandise displayers and window dressers
9	VL	30,020	H	H	VH	Long-term on-the-job	Musicians, singers, and related workers
2	VL	26,470	H	L	H	Bachelor's degree	News analysts, reporters, and correspondents
4	-	-	-	-	-	-	Photographers and camera operators
0	VL	21,530	L	H	VH	Moderate-term on-the-job	Camera operators, television, motion picture, video
3	VL	20,940	L	H	VH	Postsecondary vocational	Photographers

[1] One or more Current Population Survey (CPS) proxy occupations are used to estimate CPS based data.
[2] Current Population Survey data are used to estimate median weekly earnings ranking.
[3] Bachelor's degree or higher.

NOTE: Rankings are based on employment in all detailed occupations in the National Industry-Occupation Matrix. For details, see "Data presented" section of text. Codes for describing the ranked variables are: VH = Very high, H = High, L = Low, VL = Very low, n. a. = Data not available. A dash indicates data are not applicable.

Occupational employment and job openings data, 1998-2008, and worker characteristics, 1998
(Numbers in thousands)

1998 Matrix Occupation	Employment		Employment change, 1998-2008				Per-cent self-emp-loyed, 1998	Annual average job openings due to growth and total replacement needs, 1998-2008	
			Numeric		Percent				
	1998	2008	Number	Rank	Number	Rank		Number	Rank
Public relations specialists	122	152	30	L	24.6	VH	10.4	25	VL
Writers and editors, including technical writers	341	424	83	L	24.4	VH	39.8	53	L
All other professional workers[1]	785	952	166	H	21.2	VH	1.3	136	L
Technicians and related support occupations	**4,949**	**6,048**	**1,098**	-	**22.1**	-	**2.1**	**575**	-
Health technicians and technologists	2,447	3,063	616	-	25.1	-	1.1	257	-
Cardiovascular technologists and technicians[1]	21	29	8	VL	39.4	VH	.0	3	VL
Clinical laboratory technologists and technicians	313	366	53	L	17.0	H	.2	20	VL
Dental hygienists	143	201	58	L	40.5	VH	.6	15	VL
EKG technicians[1]	12	10	-3	VL	-23.1	VL	.0	1	VL
Electroneurodiagnostic technologists[1]	5	6	0	VL	5.9	VL	.0	1	VL
Emergency medical technicians and paramedics[1]	150	197	47	L	31.6	VH	.0	23	VL
Licensed practical and licensed vocational nurses	692	828	136	H	19.7	VH	.3	43	L
Medical records and health information technicians[1]	92	133	41	L	43.9	VH	.7	11	VL
Nuclear medicine technologists	14	16	2	VL	11.6	L	.0	1	VL
Opticians, dispensing	71	81	10	VL	13.8	L	7.3	6	VL
Pharmacy technicians[1]	109	126	17	VL	15.7	H	.0	14	VL
Psychiatric technicians	66	73	7	VL	10.9	L	.0	15	VL
Radiologic technologists and technicians	162	194	32	L	20.1	VH	.4	11	VL
Surgical technologists[1]	54	77	23	L	41.8	VH	.0	9	VL
Veterinary technologists and technicians[1]	32	37	5	VL	16.2	H	.0	3	VL
All other health professionals and paraprofessionals[1]	510	688	178	H	35.0	VH	3.4	80	L
Engineering and science technicians and technologists	1,351	1,525	175	-	12.9	-	2.5	175	-
Engineering technicians	771	897	126	-	16.3	-	1.1	114	-
Electrical and electronic technicians and technologists	335	391	56	L	16.8	H	1.7	43	VL
All other engineering technicians and technologists	437	506	70	L	15.9	H	.6	71	L
Drafters	283	301	18	VL	6.4	VL	6.2	30	VL
Science and mathematics technicians[1]	227	243	16	VL	7.0	VL	1.3	17	VL
Surveying and mapping technicians	69	84	15	VL	21.8	VH	6.6	15	VL
Technicians, except health and engineering and science	1,152	1,460	308	-	26.7	-	3.8	142	-
Aircraft pilots and flight engineers	94	99	6	VL	5.9	VL	2.0	5	VL
Air traffic controllers[1]	30	30	1	VL	2.3	VL	.0	2	VL
Broadcast and sound technicians[1]	37	39	2	VL	6.0	VL	5.9	3	VL
Computer programmers	648	839	191	H	29.5	VH	4.8	75	L
Legal assistants and technicians, except clerical	252	346	94	-	37.4	-	3.2	47	-
Paralegals and legal assistants	136	220	84	L	62.0	VH	2.5	34	VL
Title examiners, abstractors, and searchers	30	29	0	VL	-.6	VL	11.1	4	VL
All other legal assistants, including law clerks	86	96	10	VL	11.6	L	1.7	9	VL
Library technicians[1]	72	85	13	VL	18.2	H	.0	9	VL
All other technicians[1]	20	21	1	VL	4.1	VL	1.9	2	VL
Marketing and sales occupations	**15,341**	**17,627**	**2,287**	-	**14.9**	-	**13.4**	**4,285**	-
Cashiers	3,198	3,754	556	VH	17.4	H	.8	1,290	VH
Counter and rental clerks	469	577	108	L	23.1	VH	3.3	199	H
Insurance sales agents	387	396	9	VL	2.2	VL	29.4	39	VL
Marketing and sales worker supervisors	2,584	2,847	263	H	10.2	L	33.9	411	H
Models, demonstrators, and product promoters	92	121	30	L	32.3	VH	6.1	28	VL
Parts salespersons	300	303	4	VL	1.2	VL	.7	35	VL
Real estate agents and brokers	347	382	34	-	9.8	-	70.5	46	-
Brokers, real estate	63	71	8	VL	13.5	L	65.1	9	VL
Sales agents, real estate	285	310	26	L	9.0	L	71.6	37	VL
Retail salespersons	4,056	4,620	563	VH	13.9	L	4.0	1,305	VH
Sales engineers	79	92	12	VL	15.7	H	1.2	3	VL
Securities, commodities, and financial services sales agents	303	427	124	L	41.0	VH	25.7	61	L
Travel agents[1]	138	163	25	L	18.4	H	12.5	17	VL
All other sales and related workers[1]	3,388	3,945	558	VH	16.5	H	15.0	865	VH

[1] One or more Current Population Survey (CPS) proxy occupations are used to estimate CPS based data.
[2] Current Population Survey data are used to estimate median weekly earnings ranking.
[3] Bachelor's degree or higher.

NOTE: Rankings are based on employment in all detailed occupations in the National Industry-Occupation Matrix. For details, see "Data presented" section of text. Codes for describing the ranked variables are: VH = Very high, H = High, L = Low, VL = Very low, n. a. = Data not available. A dash indicates data are not applicable.

Occupational employment and job openings data, 1998-2008, and worker characteristics, 1998

(Numbers in thousands)

Annual average job openings due to growth and net replacement needs, 1998-2008		Median annual earnings		Ranking of:		Most significant source of education or training	1998 Matrix Occupation
Number	Rank	Dollars	Rank	Unem-ploy-ment rate	Per-cent part-time		
6	VL	34,550	H	L	H	Bachelor's degree	Public relations specialists
17	L	36,480	VH	L	H	Bachelor's degree	Writers and editors, including technical writers
36	H	36,730	VH	L	H	Bachelor's degree	All other professional workers[1]
220	-	-	-	-	-	-	**Technicians and related support occupations**
112	-	-	-	-	-	-	Health technicians and technologists
1	VL	35,770	VH	L	VH	Associate degree	Cardiovascular technologists and technicians[1]
9	VL	32,440	H	L	H	Bachelor's degree	Clinical laboratory technologists and technicians
9	VL	45,890	VH	L	VH	Associate degree	Dental hygienists
0	VL	24,360	H	L	VH	Moderate-term on-the-job	EKG technicians[1]
0	VL	32,070	H	L	VH	Moderate-term on-the-job	Electroneurodiagnostic technologists[1]
8	VL	20,290	L	L	VH	Postsecondary vocational	Emergency medical technicians and paramedics[1]
28	L	26,940	H	L	VH	Postsecondary vocational	Licensed practical and licensed vocational nurses
6	VL	20,590	L	L	VH	Associate degree	Medical records and health information technicians[1]
0	VL	39,610	VH	VL	VH	Associate degree	Nuclear medicine technologists
2	VL	22,440	L	VL	H	Moderate-term on-the-job	Opticians, dispensing
4	VL	17,770	L	L	VH	Moderate-term on-the-job	Pharmacy technicians[1]
2	VL	20,890	L	H	VH	Postsecondary vocational	Psychiatric technicians
5	VL	32,880	H	VL	VH	Associate degree	Radiologic technologists and technicians[1]
4	VL	25,780	H	L	VH	Postsecondary vocational	Surgical technologists[1]
1	VL	19,870	L	L	H	Associate degree	Veterinary technologists and technicians[1]
30	L	26,940	H	L	VH	Associate degree	All other health professionals and paraprofessionals[1]
48	-	-	-	-	-	-	Engineering and science technicians and technologists
30	-	-	-	-	-	-	Engineering technicians
12	L	35,970	VH	L	L	Associate degree	Electrical and electronic technicians and technologists
18	L	37,310	VH	L	H	Associate degree	All other engineering technicians and technologists
9	VL	32,370	H	L	L	Postsecondary vocational	Drafters
7	VL	31,030	H	L	H	Associate degree	Science and mathematics technicians[1]
3	VL	25,940	H	L	L	Moderate-term on-the-job	Surveying and mapping technicians
59	-	-	-	-	-	-	Technicians, except health and engineering and science
3	VL	91,750	VH	VL	H	Bachelor's degree	Aircraft pilots and flight engineers
1	VL	64,880	VH	L	H	Long-term on-the-job	Air traffic controllers[1]
1	VL	25,270	H	L	H	Postsecondary vocational	Broadcast and sound technicians[1]
39	H	47,550	VH	VL	L	Bachelor's degree	Computer programmers
12	-	-	-	-	-	-	Legal assistants and technicians, except clerical
10	VL	32,760	H	L	H	Associate degree	Paralegals and legal assistants
0	VL	26,850	H	L	H	Moderate-term on-the-job	Title examiners, abstractors, and searchers
2	VL	29,520	H	VL	H	Associate degree	All other legal assistants, including law clerks
3	VL	21,730	L	L	H	Short-term on-the-job	Library technicians[1]
1	VL	27,200	H	L	H	Moderate-term on-the-job	All other technicians[1]
681	-	-	-	-	-	-	**Marketing and sales occupations**
195	VH	13,690	VL	VH	VH	Short-term on-the-job	Cashiers
31	L	14,510	VL	VH	VH	Short-term on-the-job	Counter and rental clerks
10	VL	34,370	H	VL	H	Bachelor's degree	Insurance sales agents
60	H	29,570	H	VL	L	Related work experience	Marketing and sales worker supervisors
5	VL	16,940	L	VH	VH	Moderate-term on-the-job	Models, demonstrators, and product promoters
9	VL	22,730	L	L	H	Moderate-term on-the-job	Parts salespersons
10	-	-	-	-	-	-	Real estate agents and brokers
2	VL	45,640	VH	VL	H	Related work experience	Brokers, real estate
8	VL	28,020	H	VL	H	Postsecondary vocational	Sales agents, real estate
194	VH	15,830	VL	H	VH	Short-term on-the-job	Retail salespersons
3	VL	54,600	VH	VL	VL	Bachelor's degree	Sales engineers
15	L	48,090	VH	VL	L	Bachelor's degree	Securities, commodities, and financial services sales agents
5	VL	23,010	L	L	H	Postsecondary vocational	Travel agents[1]
144	VH	31,140	H	H	VH	Moderate-term on-the-job	All other sales and related workers[1]

[1] One or more Current Population Survey (CPS) proxy occupations are used to estimate CPS based data.
[2] Current Population Survey data are used to estimate median weekly earnings ranking.
[3] Bachelor's degree or higher.

NOTE: Rankings are based on employment in all detailed occupations in the National Industry-Occupation Matrix. For details, see "Data presented" section of text. Codes for describing the ranked variables are: VH = Very high, H = High, L = Low, VL = Very low, n. a. = Data not available. A dash indicates data are not applicable.

Occupational employment and job openings data, 1998-2008, and worker characteristics, 1998

(Numbers in thousands)

1998 Matrix Occupation	Employment		Employment change, 1998-2008				Per-cent self-emp-loyed, 1998	Annual average job openings due to growth and total replacement needs, 1998-2008	
			Numeric		Percent				
	1998	2008	Number	Rank	Number	Rank		Number	Rank
Administrative support occupations, including clerical	24,461	26,659	2,198	-	8.9	-	1.8	4,986	-
Adjusters, investigators, and collectors	1,237	1,540	302	-	24.4	-	.2	292	-
Adjustment clerks	479	642	163	H	34.0	VH	.0	142	L
Bill and account collectors	311	420	110	L	35.3	VH	.6	106	L
Insurance claims, examining and policy processing clerks	339	377	38	-	11.2	-	.0	48	-
Insurance claims clerks	160	183	23	L	14.5	H	.0	13	VL
Insurance examining clerks	10	11	2	VL	17.3	H	.0	2	VL
Insurance policy processing clerks	170	183	13	VL	7.9	VL	.0	33	VL
Welfare eligibility workers and interviewers	109	100	-8	VL	-7.6	VL	.0	2	VL
Communications equipment operators	297	252	-46	-	-15.0	-	.2	64	-
Telephone operators	261	220	-41	-	-15.6	-	.2	57	-
Central office operators	23	19	-4	VL	-16.6	VL	.0	5	VL
Directory assistance operators	23	16	-7	VL	-31.1	VL	.0	5	VL
Switchboard operators	214	185	-30	VL	-13.9	VL	.2	47	L
All other communications equipment operators[1]	36	32	-5	VL	-13.6	VL	.0	8	VL
Computer operators	251	187	-64	-	-25.5	-	2.0	32	-
Peripheral equipment operators[1]	27	17	-10	VL	-37.6	VL	.0	3	VL
Computer operators, except peripheral equipment	224	170	-54	VL	-24.1	VL	2.2	29	VL
Information clerks	1,910	2,296	386	-	20.2	-	1.3	549	-
Hotel, motel, and resort desk clerks	159	180	21	L	13.5	L	.8	60	L
Interviewing clerks, except personnel and social welfare	128	158	30	L	23.3	VH	.4	44	L
New accounts clerks, banking	111	127	16	VL	14.7	H	.0	36	VL
Receptionists and information clerks	1,293	1,599	305	H	23.6	VH	1.8	387	H
Reservation and transportation ticket agents and travel clerks[1]	219	232	13	VL	6.0	VL	.0	23	VL
Mail clerks and messengers	247	270	23	-	9.1	-	4.2	62	-
Couriers and messengers	120	130	11	VL	8.8	L	7.6	35	VL
Mail clerks, except mail machine operators and postal service	128	140	12	VL	9.5	L	.9	26	VL
Postal clerks and mail carriers	405	434	30	-	7.3	-	.0	12	-
Postal mail carriers	332	357	25	L	7.4	VL	.0	7	VL
Postal service clerks	73	78	5	VL	6.8	VL	.0	5	VL
Material recording, scheduling, dispatching, and distributing occupations	4,183	4,382	199	-	4.7	-	.2	876	-
Dispatchers	248	278	30	-	12.1	-	1.2	48	-
Dispatchers, except police, fire, and ambulance	163	186	23	L	14.4	H	1.8	32	VL
Dispatchers, police, fire, and ambulance	85	92	7	VL	8.0	VL	.0	16	VL
Meter readers, utilities[1]	50	51	0	VL	.4	VL	.0	11	VL
Procurement clerks	58	49	-9	VL	-14.8	VL	.1	10	VL
Production, planning, and expediting clerks	248	249	1	VL	.4	VL	1.0	62	VL
Shipping, receiving, and traffic clerks	1,000	1,031	31	L	3.1	VL	.2	243	H
Stock clerks and order fillers	2,331	2,462	131	H	5.6	VL	.1	442	VH
Weighers, measurers, checkers, and samplers, recordkeeping[1]	51	51	1	VL	1.5	VL	.4	12	VL
All other material recording, scheduling, and distribution workers[1]	196	210	13	VL	6.8	VL	.0	48	L
Records processing occupations	3,731	3,775	44	-	1.1	-	6.0	670	-
Advertising clerks[1]	14	14	1	VL	4.4	VL	.0	2	VL
Brokerage clerks	77	98	22	L	28.4	VH	.0	18	VL
Correspondence clerks[1]	25	28	3	VL	12.2	L	.0	4	VL
File clerks	272	298	26	L	9.6	L	1.2	117	L
Financial records processing occupations	2,698	2,653	-44	-	-1.6	-	8.1	415	-
Billing, cost, and rate clerks	342	392	50	L	14.6	H	1.1	63	L
Billing and posting clerks and machine operators[1]	107	104	-3	VL	-2.6	VL	3.0	11	VL
Bookkeeping, accounting, and auditing clerks	2,078	1,997	-81	VL	-3.9	VL	10.1	325	H
Payroll and timekeeping clerks	172	161	-11	VL	-6.2	VL	.9	15	VL
Library assistants and bookmobile drivers	127	148	21	L	16.5	H	.0	36	VL

[1] One or more Current Population Survey (CPS) proxy occupations are used to estimate CPS based data.
[2] Current Population Survey data are used to estimate median weekly earnings ranking.
[3] Bachelor's degree or higher.

NOTE: Rankings are based on employment in all detailed occupations in the National Industry-Occupation Matrix. For details, see "Data presented" section of text. Codes for describing the ranked variables are: VH = Very high, H = High, L = Low, VL = Very low, n. a. = Data not available. A dash indicates data are not applicable.

Occupational employment and job openings data, 1998-2008, and worker characteristics, 1998

(Numbers in thousands)

Annual average job openings due to growth and net replacement needs, 1998-2008		Median annual earnings		Ranking of:		Most significant source of education or training	1998 Matrix Occupation
Number	Rank	Dollars	Rank	Unemployment rate	Percent part-time		
746	-	-	-	-	-	-	**Administrative support occupations, including clerical**
50	-	-	-	-	-	-	Adjusters, investigators, and collectors
19	L	22,040	L	L	H	Short-term on-the-job	Adjustment clerks
19	L	22,540	L	H	H	Short-term on-the-job	Bill and account collectors
9	-	-	-	-	-	-	Insurance claims, examining and policy processing clerks
5	VL	24,010	H	VL	L	Moderate-term on-the-job	Insurance claims clerks
0	VL	23,750	H	L	H	Moderate-term on-the-job	Insurance examining clerks
4	VL	23,960	H	L	H	Moderate-term on-the-job	Insurance policy processing clerks
2	VL	33,100	H	L	L	Moderate-term on-the-job	Welfare eligibility workers and interviewers
6	-	-	-	-	-	-	Communications equipment operators
6	-	-	-	-	-	-	Telephone operators
1	VL	26,220	H	H	VH	Moderate-term on-the-job	Central office operators
1	VL	30,530	H	H	VH	Moderate-term on-the-job	Directory assistance operators
5	VL	18,220	L	VH	VH	Short-term on-the-job	Switchboard operators
1	VL	26,400	H	H	VH	Moderate-term on-the-job	All other communications equipment operators[1]
4	-	-	-	-	-	-	Computer operators
0	VL	22,860	L	L	H	Moderate-term on-the-job	Peripheral equipment operators[1]
3	VL	25,030	H	L	H	Moderate-term on-the-job	Computer operators, except peripheral equipment
82	-	-	-	-	-	-	Information clerks
8	VL	15,160	VL	H	VH	Short-term on-the-job	Hotel, motel, and resort desk clerks
7	VL	18,540	L	VH	VH	Short-term on-the-job	Interviewing clerks, except personnel and social welfare
5	VL	21,340	L	VH	VH	Related work experience	New accounts clerks, banking
55	H	18,620	L	H	VH	Short-term on-the-job	Receptionists and information clerks
6	VL	22,120	L	L	H	Short-term on-the-job	Reservation and transportation ticket agents and travel clerks[1]
8	-	-	-	-	-	-	Mail clerks and messengers
4	VL	16,680	VL	H	VH	Short-term on-the-job	Couriers and messengers
4	VL	17,660	L	VH	H	Short-term on-the-job	Mail clerks, except mail machine operators and postal service
13	-	-	-	-	-	-	Postal clerks and mail carriers
12	L	34,840	VH	VL	L	Short-term on-the-job	Postal mail carriers
2	VL	35,100	VH	L	L	Short-term on-the-job	Postal service clerks
90	-	-	-	-	-	-	Material recording, scheduling, dispatching, and distributing occupations
7	-	-	-	-	-	-	Dispatchers
5	VL	26,370	H	L	L	Moderate-term on-the-job	Dispatchers, except police, fire, and ambulance
2	VL	23,670	H	L	L	Moderate-term on-the-job	Dispatchers, police, fire, and ambulance
1	VL	25,380	H	H	H	Short-term on-the-job	Meter readers, utilities[1]
1	VL	22,630	L	H	H	Short-term on-the-job	Procurement clerks
3	VL	29,270	H	L	VH	Short-term on-the-job	Production, planning, and expediting clerks
20	L	22,500	L	H	H	Short-term on-the-job	Shipping, receiving, and traffic clerks
50	H	16,520	VL	H	H	Short-term on-the-job	Stock clerks and order fillers
1	VL	22,310	L	VH	H	Short-term on-the-job	Weighers, measurers, checkers, and samplers, recordkeeping[1]
6	VL	21,070	L	H	H	Short-term on-the-job	All other material recording, scheduling, and distribution workers[1]
94	-	-	-	-	-	-	Records processing occupations
0	VL	20,550	L	L	H	Short-term on-the-job	Advertising clerks[1]
3	VL	27,920	H	L	H	Moderate-term on-the-job	Brokerage clerks
1	VL	22,270	L	L	H	Short-term on-the-job	Correspondence clerks[1]
12	L	16,830	L	VH	VH	Short-term on-the-job	File clerks
56	-	-	-	-	-	-	Financial records processing occupations
12	L	22,670	L	L	H	Short-term on-the-job	Billing, cost, and rate clerks
2	VL	20,560	L	L	H	Short-term on-the-job	Billing and posting clerks and machine operators[1]
39	H	23,190	L	L	VH	Moderate-term on-the-job	Bookkeeping, accounting, and auditing clerks
3	VL	24,560	H	L	H	Short-term on-the-job	Payroll and timekeeping clerks
8	VL	16,980	L	H	VH	Short-term on-the-job	Library assistants and bookmobile drivers

[1] One or more Current Population Survey (CPS) proxy occupations are used to estimate CPS based data.
[2] Current Population Survey data are used to estimate median weekly earnings ranking.
[3] Bachelor's degree or higher.

NOTE: Rankings are based on employment in all detailed occupations in the National Industry-Occupation Matrix. For details, see "Data presented" section of text. Codes for describing the ranked variables are: VH = Very high, H = High, L = Low, VL = Very low, n. a. = Data not available. A dash indicates data are not applicable.

Occupational employment and job openings data, 1998-2008, and worker characteristics, 1998

Table 2. Occupational employment and job openings data, 1998-2008, and worker characterisitcs, 1998 — Continued

(Numbers in thousands)

1998 Matrix Occupation	Employment		Employment change, 1998-2008				Per-cent self-emp-loyed, 1998	Annual average job openings due to growth and total replacement needs, 1998-2008	
			Numeric		Percent				
	1998	2008	Number	Rank	Number	Rank		Number	Rank
Order clerks	362	378	17	VL	4.6	VL	.5	57	L
Human resources assistants, except payroll and timekeeping[1]	142	145	3	VL	2.0	VL	.0	22	VL
Statement clerks	16	12	-3	VL	-22.3	VL	10.2	3	VL
Secretaries, stenographers, and typists	3,764	3,744	-19	-	-.5	-	3.0	518	-
Court reporters, medical transcriptionists, and stenographers[1]	110	121	11	VL	9.7	L	31.4	16	VL
Secretaries	3,195	3,258	63	-	1.9	-	1.8	436	-
Legal secretaries	285	322	37	L	13.0	L	.2	44	L
Medical secretaries	219	246	26	L	12.0	L	1.6	34	VL
Secretaries, except legal and medical	2,690	2,691	0	VL	.0	VL	1.9	358	H
Word processors and typists	459	365	-93	VL	-20.4	VL	4.9	65	L
Other clerical and administrative support workers	8,436	9,780	1,344	-	15.9	-	.6	1,931	-
Bank tellers	560	529	-31	VL	-5.5	VL	.0	107	L
Court, municipal, and license clerks	100	112	12	-	11.6	-	.0	26	-
Court clerks	51	57	6	VL	10.8	L	.0	13	VL
License clerks	24	27	3	VL	13.1	L	.0	6	VL
Municipal clerks	25	28	3	VL	11.9	L	.0	7	VL
Credit and loan authorizers, checkers, and clerks	254	271	17	-	6.7	-	.0	63	-
Credit authorizers	17	15	-2	VL	-10.7	VL	.0	4	VL
Credit checkers	41	42	1	VL	1.5	VL	.0	9	VL
Loan and credit clerks	179	200	21	L	11.8	L	.0	47	L
Loan interviewers	16	14	-3	VL	-17.0	VL	.0	4	VL
Data entry keyers	435	474	39	L	9.0	L	2.1	107	L
Duplicating, mail, and other office machine operators[1]	197	201	4	VL	1.9	VL	.2	43	L
Office and administrative support supervisors and managers	1,611	1,924	313	VH	19.4	VH	.1	238	H
Office clerks, general	3,021	3,484	463	VH	15.3	H	.3	745	VH
Proofreaders and copy markers[1]	41	34	-7	VL	-17.1	VL	3.1	9	VL
Statistical clerks	72	69	-3	VL	-4.5	VL	.1	5	VL
Teacher assistants	1,192	1,567	375	VH	31.5	VH	.2	344	H
All other clerical and administrative support workers	953	1,116	162	H	17.0	H	3.1	243	H
Service occupations	22,548	26,401	3,853	-	17.0	-	5.7	6,720	-
Cleaning and building service occupations, except private household	3,623	4,031	408	-	11.2	-	5.0	822	-
Institutional cleaning supervisors	87	97	9	VL	10.5	L	1.8	9	VL
Janitors and cleaners, including maids and housekeeping cleaners	3,184	3,549	365	VH	11.5	L	4.8	736	VH
Pest control workers[1]	52	65	13	VL	25.4	VH	9.0	8	VL
All other cleaning and building service workers[1]	300	320	20	VL	6.7	VL	8.1	68	L
Food preparation and service occupations	8,735	9,831	1,096	-	12.5	-	.9	3,392	-
Chefs, cooks, and other kitchen workers	3,306	3,748	442	-	13.3	-	1.7	1,201	-
Cooks, except short order	1,373	1,560	187	-	13.6	-	3.6	443	-
Bakers, bread and pastry	171	200	28	L	16.6	H	5.2	57	L
Cooks, institution or cafeteria	418	431	12	VL	2.9	VL	.0	124	L
Cooks, restaurant	783	929	146	H	18.7	H	5.1	263	H
Cooks, short order and fast food	677	801	124	H	18.4	H	1.0	226	H
Food preparation workers[1]	1,256	1,387	131	H	10.4	L	.0	529	VH
Food and beverage service occupations	5,150	5,778	628	-	12.0	-	.4	2,081	-
Bartenders	404	412	8	VL	1.9	VL	1.5	86	L
Dining room and cafeteria attendants and bar helpers	405	422	16	VL	4.0	VL	.6	182	H
Food counter, fountain, and related workers[1]	2,025	2,272	247	H	12.2	L	.1	945	VH
Hosts and hostesses, restaurant, lounge, or coffee shop	297	351	54	L	18.2	H	1.1	111	L
Waiters and waitresses	2,019	2,322	303	H	15.0	H	.4	758	VH
All other food preparation and service workers	280	306	26	L	9.4	L	.8	110	L
Health service occupations	2,309	2,984	676	-	29.2	-	1.8	547	-
Ambulance drivers and attendants, except EMTs	19	26	7	VL	35.0	VH	.0	4	VL
Dental assistants	229	325	97	L	42.2	VH	.0	56	L

[1] One or more Current Population Survey (CPS) proxy occupations are used to estimate CPS based data.
[2] Current Population Survey data are used to estimate median weekly earnings ranking.

NOTE: Rankings are based on employment in all detailed occupations in the National Industry-Occupation Matrix. For details, see "Data presented" section of text. Codes for describing the ranked variables are: VH = Very high, H = High, L = Low, VL = Very low, n. a. = Data not available. A dash

Occupational employment and job openings data, 1998-2008, and worker characteristics, 1998

(Numbers in thousands)

Annual average job openings due to growth and net replacement needs, 1998-2008		Median annual earnings		Ranking of:		Most significant source of education or training	1998 Matrix Occupation
Number	Rank	Dollars	Rank	Unemployment rate	Percent part-time		
10	L	21,550	L	L	H	Short-term on-the-job	Order clerks
3	VL	24,360	H	L	H	Short-term on-the-job	Human resources assistants, except payroll and timekeeping[1]
0	VL	18,640	L	L	H	Short-term on-the-job	Statement clerks
70	-	-	-	-	-	-	Secretaries, stenographers, and typists
3	VL	25,430	H	L	VH	Postsecondary vocational	Court reporters, medical transcriptionists, and stenographers[1]
58	-	-	-	-	-	-	Secretaries
8	VL	30,050	H	L	VH	Postsecondary vocational	Legal secretaries
6	VL	22,390	L	L	VH	Postsecondary vocational	Medical secretaries
44	H	23,560	H	L	VH	Moderate-term on-the-job	Secretaries, except legal and medical
9	VL	22,590	L	H	VH	Moderate-term on-the-job	Word processors and typists
329	-	-	-	-	-	-	Other clerical and administrative support workers
24	L	17,200	L	L	VH	Short-term on-the-job	Bank tellers
3	-	-	-	-	-	-	Court, municipal, and license clerks
1	VL	22,960	L	L	H	Short-term on-the-job	Court clerks
1	VL	22,900	L	L	H	Short-term on-the-job	License clerks
1	VL	22,810	L	L	H	Short-term on-the-job	Municipal clerks
5	-	-	-	-	-	-	Credit and loan authorizers, checkers, and clerks
0	VL	22,990	L	L	H	Short-term on-the-job	Credit authorizers
0	VL	21,550	L	L	H	Short-term on-the-job	Credit checkers
4	VL	22,580	L	L	H	Short-term on-the-job	Loan and credit clerks
0	VL	23,190	L	L	H	Short-term on-the-job	Loan interviewers
7	VL	19,190	L	H	VH	Moderate-term on-the-job	Data entry keyers
6	VL	20,370	L	H	VH	Short-term on-the-job	Duplicating, mail, and other office machine operators[1]
68	H	31,090	H	VL	VL	Related work experience	Office and administrative support supervisors and managers
130	VH	19,580	L	H	VH	Short-term on-the-job	Office clerks, general
1	VL	18,620	L	H	VH	Short-term on-the-job	Proofreaders and copy markers[1]
1	VL	23,380	L	L	H	Moderate-term on-the-job	Statistical clerks
51	H	15,830	VL	H	VH	Short-term on-the-job	Teacher assistants
33	L	23,520	L	L	H	Short-term on-the-job	All other clerical and administrative support workers
1,111	-	-	-	-	-	-	**Service occupations**
116	-	-	-	-	-	-	Cleaning and building service occupations, except private household
3	VL	19,600	L	L	L	Related work experience	Institutional cleaning supervisors
103	VH	15,340	VL	VH	VH	Short-term on-the-job	Janitors and cleaners, including maids and housekeeping cleaners
2	VL	22,490	L	VH	VH	Moderate-term on-the-job	Pest control workers[1]
8	VL	17,910	L	VH	VH	Short-term on-the-job	All other cleaning and building service workers[1]
516	-	-	-	-	-	-	Food preparation and service occupations
167	-	-	-	-	-	-	Chefs, cooks, and other kitchen workers
55	-	-	-	-	-	-	Cooks, except short order
7	VL	16,990	L	VH	VH	Moderate-term on-the-job	Bakers, bread and pastry
12	L	16,090	VL	VH	VH	Long-term on-the-job	Cooks, institution or cafeteria
35	H	16,250	VL	VH	VH	Long-term on-the-job	Cooks, restaurant
30	L	12,720	VL	VH	VH	Short-term on-the-job	Cooks, short order and fast food
82	VH	13,710	VL	VH	VH	Short-term on-the-job	Food preparation workers[1]
336	-	-	-	-	-	-	Food and beverage service occupations
18	L	13,000	VL	H	VH	Short-term on-the-job	Bartenders
14	L	12,550	VL	VH	VH	Short-term on-the-job	Dining room and cafeteria attendants and bar helpers
148	VH	12,600	VL	VH	VH	Short-term on-the-job	Food counter, fountain, and related workers[1]
14	L	13,410	VL	H	VH	Short-term on-the-job	Hosts and hostesses, restaurant, lounge, or coffee shop
142	VH	12,170	VL	VH	VH	Short-term on-the-job	Waiters and waitresses
13	L	14,560	VL	VH	VH	Short-term on-the-job	All other food preparation and service workers
106	-	-	-	-	-	-	Health service occupations
1	VL	16,970	L	L	VH	Short-term on-the-job	Ambulance drivers and attendants, except EMTs
13	L	22,640	L	L	VH	Moderate-term on-the-job	Dental assistants

[1] One or more Current Population Survey (CPS) proxy occupations are used to estimate CPS based data.
[2] Current Population Survey data are used to estimate median weekly earnings ranking.
[3] Bachelor's degree or higher.

NOTE: Rankings are based on employment in all detailed occupations in the National Industry-Occupation Matrix. For details, see "Data presented" section of text. Codes for describing the ranked variables are: VH = Very high, H = High, L = Low, VL = Very low, n. a. = Data not available. A dash indicates data are not applicable.

Occupational employment and job openings data, 1998-2008, and worker characteristics, 1998

(Numbers in thousands)

1998 Matrix Occupation	Employment		Employment change, 1998-2008				Per-cent self-emp-loyed, 1998	Annual average job openings due to growth and total replacement needs, 1998-2008	
			Numeric		Percent				
	1998	2008	Number	Rank	Number	Rank		Number	Rank
Medical assistants[1]	252	398	146	H	57.8	VH	.0	49	L
Nursing and psychiatric aides	1,461	1,794	332	-	22.7	-	2.9	371	-
Nursing aides, orderlies, and attendants	1,367	1,692	325	VH	23.8	VH	3.1	350	H
Psychiatric aides	95	102	7	VL	7.7	VL	.0	21	VL
Occupational therapy assistants and aides[1]	19	26	7	VL	39.8	VH	.0	3	VL
Pharmacy aides[1]	61	71	10	VL	15.9	H	.0	9	VL
Physical therapy assistants and aides	82	118	36	L	43.7	VH	.0	14	VL
All other health service workers	185	226	41	L	22.3	VH	.0	36	VL
Personal service occupations	2,934	3,828	894	-	30.4	-	28.9	835	-
Amusement and recreation attendants	337	439	102	L	30.2	VH	.8	142	L
Baggage porters and bellhops[1]	40	45	5	VL	13.7	L	.0	10	VL
Child care workers	905	1,141	236	H	26.1	VH	54.6	329	H
Barbers, cosmetologists, and related workers	723	796	73	-	10.0	-	46.6	84	-
Barbers	54	50	-4	VL	-7.3	VL	76.7	2	VL
Hairdressers, hairstylists, and cosmetologists	605	667	62	L	10.2	L	45.4	73	L
Manicurists	49	62	13	VL	26.0	VH	42.3	7	VL
Shampooers	15	17	2	VL	14.5	H	.0	2	VL
Flight attendants	99	129	30	L	30.1	VH	1.5	5	VL
Personal care and home health aides[1]	746	1,179	433	VH	58.1	VH	1.9	250	H
Ushers, lobby attendants, and ticket takers[1]	84	99	15	VL	17.6	H	.0	23	VL
Private household workers	928	751	-178	-	-19.1	-	.0	280	-
Child care workers, private household[2]	306	209	-97	VL	-31.7	VL	.0	115	L
Cleaners and servants, private household[1,2]	600	530	-71	VL	-11.8	VL	.0	157	L
Cooks, private household[1,2]	5	2	-2	VL	-51.3	VL	.0	1	VL
Housekeepers and butlers[1,2]	17	10	-7	VL	-42.4	VL	.0	4	VL
Protective service occupations	2,769	3,486	717	-	25.8	-	.9	465	-
Fire fighting occupations	314	334	20	-	6.4	-	.7	20	-
Firefighters	239	251	11	VL	4.7	VL	.0	10	VL
Fire fighting and prevention supervisors[1]	60	66	6	VL	10.7	L	.5	9	VL
Fire inspection occupations[1]	15	17	2	VL	17.2	H	12.9	1	VL
Law enforcement occupations	1,147	1,501	354	-	30.8	-	.0	143	-
Correctional officers	383	532	148	H	38.7	VH	.0	65	L
Police and detectives	727	929	202	-	27.7	-	.0	77	-
Detectives and criminal investigators	79	96	17	VL	21.0	VH	.0	8	VL
Police and detective supervisors	111	124	13	VL	12.0	L	.0	14	VL
Police patrol officers	446	586	141	H	31.6	VH	.0	52	L
Sheriffs and deputy sheriffs	91	123	31	L	34.2	VH	.0	3	VL
Other law enforcement occupations	37	40	3	VL	9.4	L	.0	1	VL
Other protective service workers	1,308	1,651	343	-	26.1	-	1.8	304	-
Crossing guards[1]	54	57	2	VL	4.0	VL	.0	10	VL
Guards	1,027	1,321	294	H	28.6	VH	.2	257	H
Private detectives and investigators	61	76	15	VL	24.3	VH	34.8	15	VL
All other protective service workers	166	198	32	L	19.0	H	.0	23	VL
All other service workers[1]	1,249	1,490	241	H	19.3	H	8.6	319	H
Agriculture, forestry, fishing, and related occupations	4,435	4,506	71	-	1.0	-	38.3	767	-
Farm operators and managers	1,483	1,309	-174	-	-11.7	-	88.4	145	-
Farmers[2]	1,308	1,135	-173	VL	-13.2	VL	99.5	133	L
Farm managers[2]	175	174	-1	VL	-.8	VL	5.3	11	VL
Farm workers	851	794	-57	VL	-6.6	VL	3.0	157	L
Fishers and fishing vessel operators	51	40	-11	-	-21.7	-	58.3	10	-
Captains and other officers, fishing vessels[1,2]	11	9	-2	VL	-18.6	VL	41.1	2	VL
Fishers[1,2]	40	31	-9	VL	-22.7	VL	63.2	8	VL
Forestry, conservation, and logging occupations	120	116	-4	-	-3.1	-	27.8	18	-
Forest and conservation workers[1]	33	33	0	VL	.7	VL	9.7	5	VL
Timber cutting and logging occupations	87	83	-4	-	-4.5	-	34.6	13	-

[1] One or more Current Population Survey (CPS) proxy occupations are used to estimate CPS based data.
[2] Current Population Survey data are used to estimate median weekly earnings ranking.
[3] Bachelor's degree or higher.

NOTE: Rankings are based on employment in all detailed occupations in the National Industry-Occupation Matrix. For details, see "Data presented" section of text. Codes for describing the ranked variables are: VH = Very high, H = High, L = Low, VL = Very low, n. a. = Data not available. A dash indicates data are not applicable.

Occupational employment and job openings data, 1998-2008, and worker characteristics, 1998

(Numbers in thousands)

Annual average job openings due to growth and net replacement needs, 1998-2008		Median annual earnings		Ranking of:		Most significant source of education or training	1998 Matrix Occupation
Number	Rank	Dollars	Rank	Unemployment rate	Percent part-time		
21	L	20,680	L	L	VH	Moderate-term on-the-job	Medical assistants[1]
54	-	-	-	-	-		Nursing and psychiatric aides
52	H	16,620	VL	H	VH	Short-term on-the-job	Nursing aides, orderlies, and attendants
2	VL	22,170	L	H	VH	Short-term on-the-job	Psychiatric aides
1	VL	28,690	H	L	VH	Associate degree	Occupational therapy assistants and aides[1]
2	VL	18,480	L	L	VH	Short-term on-the-job	Pharmacy aides
6	VL	21,870	L	L	VH	Associate degree	Physical therapy assistants and aides
8	VL	19,160	L	L	VH	Short-term on-the-job	All other health service workers
141	-	-	-	-	-	-	Personal service occupations
16	L	12,860	VL	VH	VH	Short-term on-the-job	Amusement and recreation attendants
1	VL	13,340	VL	H	VH	Short-term on-the-job	Baggage porters and bellhops[1]
32	L	13,760	VL	H	VH	Short-term on-the-job	Child care workers
26	-	-	-	-	-		Barbers, cosmetologists, and related workers
2	VL	18,470	L	L	VH	Postsecondary vocational	Barbers
22	L	15,150	VL	L	VH	Postsecondary vocational	Hairdressers, hairstylists, and cosmetologists
3	VL	13,490	VL	L	VH	Postsecondary vocational	Manicurists
1	VL	12,570	VL	L	VH	Short-term on-the-job	Shampooers
5	VL	37,800	VH	VL	VH	Long-term on-the-job	Flight attendants
57	H	15,760	VL	H	VH	Short-term on-the-job	Personal care and home health aides[1]
3	VL	12,480	VL	VH	VH	Short-term on-the-job	Ushers, lobby attendants, and ticket takers[1]
28	-	-	-	-	-		Private household workers
14	L	10,733	VL	VH	VH	Short-term on-the-job	Child care workers, private household[2]
13	L	14,435	VL	VH	VH	Short-term on-the-job	Cleaners and servants, private household[1,2]
0	VL	n.a.	-	VH	VH	Moderate-term on-the-job	Cooks, private household[1,2]
0	VL	n.a.	-	VH	VH	Moderate-term on-the-job	Housekeepers and butlers[1,2]
149	-	-	-	-	-	-	Protective service occupations
10	-	-	-	-	-		Fire fighting occupations
7	VL	31,170	H	VL	VL	Long-term on-the-job	Firefighters
3	VL	44,830	VH	VL	VL	Related work experience	Fire fighting and prevention supervisors[1]
1	VL	40,040	VH	L	VL	Related work experience	Fire inspection occupations[1]
64	-	-	-	-	-		Law enforcement occupations
25	L	28,540	H	VL	VL	Long-term on-the-job	Correctional officers
38	-	-	-	-	-		Police and detectives
4	VL	46,180	VH	VL	VL	Related work experience	Detectives and criminal investigators
5	VL	48,700	VH	VL	VL	Related work experience	Police and detective supervisors
26	L	37,710	VH	VL	VL	Long-term on-the-job	Police patrol officers
4	VL	28,270	H	VL	VL	Long-term on-the-job	Sheriffs and deputy sheriffs
1	VL	28,830	H	VL	L	Long-term on-the-job	Other law enforcement occupations
74	-	-	-	-	-		Other protective service workers
2	VL	14,940	VL	VH	VH	Short-term on-the-job	Crossing guards[1]
55	H	16,240	VL	VH	H	Short-term on-the-job	Guards
3	VL	21,020	L	VH	H	Related work experience	Private detectives and investigators
15	L	17,470	L	VH	VH	Short-term on-the-job	All other protective service workers
55	H	20,360	L	H	VH	Related work experience	All other service workers[1]
136	-	-	-	-	-	-	**Agriculture, forestry, fishing, and related occupations**
23	-	-	-	-	-		Farm operators and managers
20	L	n.a.	-	VL	H	Long-term on-the-job	Farmers[2]
3	VL	n.a.	-	VL	H	Work experience plus degree[3]	Farm managers[2]
26	L	12,570	VL	VH	H	Short-term on-the-job	Farm workers
1	-	-	-	-	-		Fishers and fishing vessel operators
0	VL	n.a.	-	VH	L	Related work experience	Captains and other officers, fishing vessels[1,2]
1	VL	n.a.	-	VH	L	Short-term on-the-job	Fishers[1,2]
3	-	-	-	-	-		Forestry, conservation, and logging occupations
1	VL	23,140	L	VH	L	Short-term on-the-job	Forest and conservation workers[1]
2	-	-	-	-	-		Timber cutting and logging occupations

[1] One or more Current Population Survey (CPS) proxy occupations are used to estimate CPS based data.

[2] Current Population Survey data are used to estimate median weekly earnings ranking.

[3] Bachelor's degree or higher.

NOTE: Rankings are based on employment in all detailed occupations in the National Industry-Occupation Matrix. For details, see "Data presented" section of text. Codes for describing the ranked variables are: VH = Very high, H = High, L = Low, VL = Very low, n. a. = Data not available. A dash indicates data are not applicable.

Occupational employment and job openings data, 1998-2008, and worker characteristics, 1998

(Numbers in thousands)

1998 Matrix Occupation	Employment		Employment change, 1998-2008				Per-cent self-emp-loyed, 1998	Annual average job openings due to growth and total replacement needs, 1998-2008	
			Numeric		Percent				
	1998	2008	Number	Rank	Number	Rank		Number	Rank
Fallers and buckers	18	16	-2	VL	-11.5	VL	37.5	2	VL
Logging equipment operators	56	55	-1	VL	-2.0	VL	37.2	8	VL
All other timber cutting and related logging workers	13	12	-1	VL	-6.0	VL	19.2	2	VL
Landscaping, groundskeeping, nursery, greenhouse, and lawn service occupations	1,285	1,548	262	-	20.4	-	19.0	310	-
Laborers, landscaping and groundskeeping[1]	1,130	1,364	234	H	20.7	VH	16.1	283	H
Lawn service managers[1]	86	104	17	VL	20.0	VH	71.1	10	VL
Nursery and greenhouse managers[1]	5	6	1	VL	15.1	H	19.5	1	VL
Pruners	45	50	5	VL	12.1	L	.0	11	VL
Sprayers/applicators	19	23	4	VL	23.6	VH	.0	5	VL
Supervisors, farming, forestry, and agricultural related occupations[1]	92	97	6	VL	6.2	VL	13.9	12	VL
Veterinary assistants and nonfarm animal caretakers	181	223	42	-	23.0	-	19.4	58	-
Animal caretakers, except farm	137	166	30	L	21.6	VH	25.7	43	L
Veterinary assistants	45	57	12	VL	28.0	VH	.0	15	VL
All other agricultural, forestry, fishing, and related workers[1]	373	379	6	VL	1.7	VL	1.7	71	L
Precision production, craft, and repair occupations	15,619	16,871	1,252	-	8.0	-	12.1	2,118	-
Blue-collar worker supervisors[1]	2,198	2,394	196	H	8.9	L	10.4	216	H
Construction trades	4,628	5,018	390	-	8.4	-	21.3	762	-
Boilermakers[1]	18	19	0	VL	1.6	VL	6.6	.2	VL
Bricklayers, blockmasons, and stonemasons[1]	157	176	19	VL	12.3	L	27.6	30	VL
Carpenters	1,071	1,145	74	L	6.9	VL	32.1	236	H
Carpet, floor, and tile installers and finishers	138	147	8	-	6.0	-	53.2	21	-
Carpet installers	85	88	3	VL	3.6	VL	64.0	11	VL
Hard tile setters[1]	29	31	3	VL	8.7	L	39.0	5	VL
All other carpet, floor, and tile installers and finishers	25	28	3	VL	11.0	L	33.0	4	VL
Ceiling tile installers and acoustical carpenters	16	17	1	VL	8.9	L	.0	3	VL
Concrete finishers, cement masons, and terrazzo workers	139	148	9	VL	6.1	VL	5.0	14	VL
Construction equipment operators	321	346	25	-	7.0	-	6.3	39	-
Grader, bulldozer, and scraper operators	122	129	7	VL	5.7	VL	6.5	6	VL
Operating engineers	126	135	10	VL	7.9	VL	8.7	20	VL
Paving, surfacing, and tamping equipment operators[1]	74	82	8	VL	10.6	L	2.0	14	VL
Drywall installers and finishers	163	175	12	VL	7.5	VL	25.6	33	VL
Electricians	656	724	68	L	10.3	L	10.5	93	L
Elevator installers and repairers	30	33	4	VL	12.2	L	1.1	5	VL
Glaziers[1]	44	46	2	VL	3.9	VL	12.9	8	VL
Hazardous materials removal workers	38	45	7	VL	19.3	VH	.0	5	VL
Highway maintenance workers	155	173	17	VL	11.1	L	.0	21	VL
Insulation workers	67	72	5	VL	7.5	VL	4.1	7	VL
Painters and paperhangers	476	517	41	L	8.6	L	43.7	87	L
Pipelayers and pipelaying fitters	57	60	3	VL	4.9	VL	11.0	7	VL
Plasterers and stucco masons[1]	40	47	7	VL	17.1	H	16.9	8	VL
Plumbers, pipefitters, and steamfitters	426	449	22	L	5.3	VL	19.5	58	L
Roofers	158	177	19	VL	12.0	L	31.9	29	VL
Sheet metal workers and duct installers[1]	230	262	32	L	14.1	H	2.2	23	VL
Structural and reinforcing metal workers	81	87	6	VL	8.0	VL	1.9	14	VL
All other construction trades workers[1]	146	155	8	VL	5.7	VL	11.0	18	VL
Extractive and related workers, including blasters	244	255	11	-	4.4	-	1.7	19	-
Oil and gas extraction occupations	69	63	-6	-	-9.0	-	.0	4	-
Roustabouts, oil and gas[1]	30	23	-6	VL	-21.1	VL	.0	2	VL
All other oil and gas extraction occupations[1]	40	40	0	VL	.0	VL	.0	2	VL
Mining, quarrying, and tunneling occupations[1]	23	18	-4	VL	-19.1	VL	2.2	1	VL
All other extraction and related workers[1]	152	173	21	L	14.1	H	2.4	14	VL
Mechanics, installers, and repairers	5,176	5,763	588	-	11.3	-	8.8	690	-

[1] One or more Current Population Survey (CPS) proxy occupations are used to estimate CPS based data.
[2] Current Population Survey data are used to estimate median weekly earnings ranking.
[3] Bachelor's degree or higher.

NOTE: Rankings are based on employment in all detailed occupations in the National Industry-Occupation Matrix. For details, see "Data presented" section of text. Codes for describing the ranked variables are: VH = Very high, H = High, L = Low, VL = Very low, n. a. = Data not available. A dash indicates data are not applicable.

Occupational employment and job openings data, 1998-2008, and worker characteristics, 1998
(Numbers in thousands)

Annual average job openings due to growth and net replacement needs, 1998-2008		Median annual earnings		Ranking of:		Most significant source of education or training	1998 Matrix Occupation
Number	Rank	Dollars	Rank	Unemploy-ment rate	Per-cent part-time		
0	VL	23,510	L	VH	L	Short-term on-the-job	Fallers and buckers
1	VL	23,150	L	VH	L	Moderate-term on-the-job	Logging equipment operators
0	VL	24,230	H	VH	L	Short-term on-the-job	All other timber cutting and related logging workers
63	-	-	-	-	-	-	Landscaping, groundskeeping, nursery, greenhouse, and lawn service occupations
57	H	17,140	L	VH	H	Short-term on-the-job	Laborers, landscaping and groundskeeping[1]
2	VL	25,420	H	VL	H	Related work experience	Lawn service managers[1]
0	VL	25,360	H	VL	H	Related work experience	Nursery and greenhouse managers[1]
2	VL	22,070	L	VH	H	Short-term on-the-job	Pruners
1	VL	21,650	L	VH	H	Moderate-term on-the-job	Sprayers/applicators
2	VL	24,560	H	VL	H	Related work experience	Supervisors, farming, forestry, and agricutural related occupations[1]
7	-	-	-	-	-	-	Veterinary assistants and nonfarm animal caretakers
5	VL	14,820	VL	H	VH	Short-term on-the-job	Animal caretakers, except farm
2	VL	16,200	VL	H	VH	Short-term on-the-job	Veterinary assistants
11	L	15,760	VL	VH	H	Short-term on-the-job	All other agricultural, forestry, fishing, and related workers[1]
505	-	-	-	-	-	-	**Precision production, craft, and repair occupations**
80	VH	37,180	VH	L	VL	Related work experience	Blue-collar worker supervisors[1]
143	-	-	-	-	-	-	Construction trades
0	VL	38,380	VH	L	VL	Long-term on-the-job	Boilermakers[1]
5	VL	35,200	VH	VH	L	Long-term on-the-job	Bricklayers, blockmasons, and stonemasons[1]
36	H	28,740	H	VH	L	Long-term on-the-job	Carpenters
4	-	-	-	-	-	-	Carpet, floor, and tile installers and finishers
2	VL	26,480	H	H	H	Moderate-term on-the-job	Carpet installers
1	VL	33,810	H	VH	L	Long-term on-the-job	Hard tile setters[1]
1	VL	25,840	H	VH	L	Moderate-term on-the-job	All other carpet, floor, and tile installers and finishers
1	VL	31,750	H	VH	L	Moderate-term on-the-job	Ceiling tile installers and acoustical carpenters
3	VL	25,770	H	VH	L	Long-term on-the-job	Concrete finishers, cement masons, and terrazzo workers
8	-	-	-	-	-	-	Construction equipment operators
2	VL	26,920	H	VH	VL	Moderate-term on-the-job	Grader, bulldozer, and scraper operators
3	VL	35,260	VH	VH	VL	Moderate-term on-the-job	Operating engineers
3	VL	24,510	H	VH	L	Moderate-term on-the-job	Paving, surfacing, and tamping equipment operators[1]
3	VL	29,920	H	VH	L	Moderate-term on-the-job	Drywall installers and finishers
20	L	35,310	VH	L	VL	Long-term on-the-job	Electricians
1	VL	47,860	VH	L	L	Long-term on-the-job	Elevator installers and repairers
1	VL	26,410	H	VH	L	Long-term on-the-job	Glaziers[1]
2	VL	27,620	H	VH	L	Moderate-term on-the-job	Hazardous materials removal workers
5	VL	24,490	H	VH	L	Short-term on-the-job	Highway maintenance workers
3	VL	25,490	H	VH	L	Moderate-term on-the-job	Insulation workers
16	L	25,110	H	VH	L	Moderate-term on-the-job	Painters and paperhangers
2	VL	25,690	H	VH	L	Moderate-term on-the-job	Pipelayers and pipelaying fitters
2	VL	29,390	H	VH	L	Long-term on-the-job	Plasterers and stucco masons[1]
8	VL	34,670	H	H	VL	Long-term on-the-job	Plumbers, pipefitters, and steamfitters
7	VL	25,340	H	VH	H	Moderate-term on-the-job	Roofers
9	VL	28,030	H	H	VL	Moderate-term on-the-job	Sheet metal workers and duct installers[1]
3	VL	32,880	H	VH	L	Long-term on-the-job	Structural and reinforcing metal workers
4	VL	25,390	H	VH	L	Moderate-term on-the-job	All other construction trades workers[1]
8	-	-	-	-	-	-	Extractive and related workers, including blasters
2	-	-	-	-	-	-	Oil and gas extraction occupations
1	VL	19,780	L	H	VL	Short-term on-the-job	Roustabouts, oil and gas[1]
1	VL	25,540	H	H	VL	Moderate-term on-the-job	All other oil and gas extraction occupations[1]
1	VL	32,660	H	H	VL	Long-term on-the-job	Mining, quarrying, and tunneling occupations[1]
6	VL	27,270	H	H	VL	Moderate-term on-the-job	All other extraction and related workers[1]
184	-	-	-	-	-	-	Mechanics, installers, and repairers

[1] One or more Current Population Survey (CPS) proxy occupations are used to estimate CPS based data.
[2] Current Population Survey data are used to estimate median weekly earnings ranking.
[3] Bachelor's degree or higher.

NOTE: Rankings are based on employment in all detailed occupations in the National Industry-Occupation Matrix. For details, see "Data presented" section of text. Codes for describing the ranked variables are: VH = Very high, H = High, L = Low, VL = Very low, n. a. = Data not available. A dash indicates data are not applicable.

Occupational employment and job openings data, 1998-2008, and worker characteristics, 1998

(Numbers in thousands)

1998 Matrix Occupation	Employment		Employment change, 1998-2008				Per-cent self-emp-loyed, 1998	Annual average job openings due to growth and total replacement needs, 1998-2008	
			Numeric		Percent				
	1998	2008	Number	Rank	Number	Rank		Number	Rank
Electrical and electronic equipment mechanics, installers, and repairers	409	472	63	-	15.3	-	8.5	52	-
Computer, automated teller, and office machine repairers	138	184	46	-	33.7	-	11.6	22	-
Data processing equipment repairers	79	117	37	L	47.0	VH	17.9	20	VL
Office machine and cash register servicers	58	67	9	VL	15.6	H	3.2	3	VL
Telecommunications equipment mechanics, installers, and repairers	125	138	13	-	10.0	-	1.3	13	-
Radio mechanics	7	7	0	VL	-1.4	VL	.0	1	VL
Telephone equipment installers and repairers	69	75	6	-	8.8	-	2.4	6	-
Central office and PBX installers and repairers[1]	44	59	14	VL	32.3	VH	3.8	5	VL
Station installers and repairers, telephone[1]	24	16	-8	VL	-33.8	VL	.0	1	VL
All other telecommunications equipment mechanics, installers, and repairers[1]	49	56	7	VL	13.3	L	.0	6	VL
Miscellaneous electrical and electronic equipment mechanics, installers, and repairers	146	150	4	-	2.6	-	11.7	17	-
Electronic home entertainment equipment repairers	36	31	-4	VL	-11.9	VL	21.3	4	VL
Electronics repairers, commercial and industrial equipment	72	81	9	VL	12.7	L	10.6	10	VL
All other electrical and electronic equipment mechanics, installers, and repairers	39	38	-1	VL	-2.4	VL	4.7	3	VL
Machinery mechanics, installers, and repairers	1,850	1,967	117	-	6.3	-	3.8	222	-
Industrial machinery mechanics[1]	535	559	24	L	4.4	VL	3.4	37	VL
Maintenance repairers, general utility	1,232	1,327	95	L	7.7	VL	4.2	181	H
Millwrights	82	81	-2	VL	-1.9	VL	.1	5	VL
Vehicle and mobile equipment mechanics and repairers	1,612	1,828	216	-	13.4	-	15.7	219	-
Aircraft mechanics and service technicians[1]	133	147	14	VL	10.4	L	.4	11	VL
Automotive body and related repairers	227	263	36	L	15.8	H	16.0	33	VL
Automotive mechanics and service technicians[1]	790	922	132	H	16.7	H	22.2	119	L
Bus and truck mechanics and diesel engine specialists	255	280	25	L	9.8	L	5.8	22	VL
Farm equipment mechanics[1]	49	47	-3	VL	-5.2	VL	10.6	8	VL
Mobile heavy equipment mechanics	106	116	10	VL	9.3	L	5.0	19	VL
Motorcycle, boat, and small engine mechanics	52	54	2	-	4.7	-	30.5	8	-
Motorcycle mechanics[1]	14	14	1	VL	3.9	VL	30.4	2	VL
Small engine mechanics[1]	38	40	2	VL	5.0	VL	30.5	6	VL
Other mechanics, installers, and repairers	1,305	1,496	191	-	14.6	-	7.6	197	-
Bicycle repairers	11	13	2	VL	22.6	VH	24.5	2	VL
Camera and photographic equipment repairers[1]	9	10	1	VL	8.2	VL	63.9	1	VL
Coin, vending, and amusement machine servicers and repairers	27	31	4	VL	15.6	H	.0	4	VL
Heating, air conditioning, and refrigeration mechanics and installers	286	334	48	L	16.9	H	15.0	30	VL
Home appliance and power tool repairers[1]	51	54	3	VL	5.6	VL	15.0	8	VL
Line installers and repairers	279	335	56	-	19.9	-	.7	24	-
Electrical powerline installers and repairers	99	100	1	VL	1.1	VL	1.4	6	VL
Telephone and cable TV line installers and repairers[1]	180	235	55	L	30.3	VH	.3	18	VL
Locksmiths and safe repairers[1]	27	30	3	VL	10.0	L	32.2	5	VL
Medical equipment repairers	11	12	1	VL	13.5	L	.0	2	VL
Musical instrument repairers and tuners[1]	13	13	1	VL	6.5	VL	64.1	2	VL
Precision instrument repairers[1]	33	32	-1	VL	-4.0	VL	8.4	5	VL
Riggers	11	11	0	VL	.5	VL	.0	2	VL
Tire repairers and changers	83	92	9	VL	10.4	L	3.1	26	VL
Watch repairers[1]	8	8	0	VL	-4.2	VL	63.7	1	VL
All other mechanics, installers, and repairers[1]	455	520	65	L	14.3	H	2.3	85	L
Production occupations, precision	2,971	3,010	39	-	1.3	-	6.9	395	-
Assemblers, precision	422	442	20	-	4.6	-	.8	68	-
Aircraft assemblers, precision[1]	17	20	3	VL	19.3	VH	.0	2	VL
Electrical and electronic equipment assemblers, precision	201	213	12	VL	6.0	VL	1.7	39	VL

[1] One or more Current Population Survey (CPS) proxy occupations are used to estimate CPS based data.
[2] Current Population Survey data are used to estimate median weekly earnings ranking.
[3] Bachelor's degree or higher.

NOTE: Rankings are based on employment in all detailed occupations in the National Industry-Occupation Matrix. For details, see "Data presented" section of text. Codes for describing the ranked variables are: VH = Very high, H = High, L = Low, VL = Very low, n. a. = Data not available. A dash indicates data are not applicable.

Occupational employment and job openings data, 1998-2008, and worker characteristics, 1998

(Numbers in thousands)

Annual average job openings due to growth and net replacement needs, 1998-2008		Median annual earnings		Ranking of:		Most significant source of education or training	1998 Matrix Occupation
Number	Rank	Dollars	Rank	Unemploy-ment rate	Per-cent part-time		
18	-	-	-	-	-	-	Electrical and electronic equipment mechanics, installers, and repairers
7	-	-	-	-	-	-	Computer, automated teller, and office machine repairers
5	VL	29,340	H	L	L	Postsecondary vocational	Data processing equipment repairers
2	VL	27,830	H	H	L	Long-term on-the-job	Office machine and cash register servicers
6	-	-	-	-	-	-	Telecommunications equipment mechanics, installers, and repairers
0	VL	30,590	H	L	L	Postsecondary vocational	Radio mechanics
4	-	-	-	-	-	-	Telephone equipment installers and repairers
3	VL	43,680	VH	VL	VL	Postsecondary vocational	Central office and PBX installers and repairers[1]
1	VL	39,630	VH	VL	VL	Postsecondary vocational	Station installers and repairers, telephone[1]
2	VL	42,850	VH	L	L	Postsecondary vocational	All other telecommunications equipment mechanics, installers, and repairers[1]
5	-	-	-	-	-	-	Miscellaneous electrical and electronic equipment mechanics, installers, and repairers
1	VL	23,540	L	L	L	Postsecondary vocational	Electronic home entertainment equipment repairers
3	VL	35,590	VH	L	L	Postsecondary vocational	Electronics repairers, commercial and industrial equipment
1	VL	31,300	H	L	VL	Postsecondary vocational	All other electrical and electronic equipment mechanics, installers, and repairers
54	-	-	-	-	-	-	Machinery mechanics, installers, and repairers
14	L	31,850	H	L	VL	Long-term on-the-job	Industrial machinery mechanics[1]
37	H	23,290	L	L	L	Long-term on-the-job	Maintenance repairers, general utility
2	VL	36,940	VH	VH	VL	Long-term on-the-job	Millwrights
62	-	-	-	-	-	-	Vehicle and mobile equipment mechanics and repairers
4	VL	38,060	VH	VL	VL	Postsecondary vocational	Aircraft mechanics and service technicians[1]
10	VL	27,400	H	H	L	Long-term on-the-job	Automotive body and related repairers
33	L	27,360	H	H	L	Postsecondary vocational	Automotive mechanics and service technicians[1]
8	VL	29,340	H	L	VL	Long-term on-the-job	Bus and truck mechanics and diesel engine specialists
1	VL	22,750	L	L	VL	Long-term on-the-job	Farm equipment mechanics[1]
4	VL	31,520	H	L	VL	Long-term on-the-job	Mobile heavy equipment mechanics
2	-	-	-	-	-	-	Motorcycle, boat, and small engine mechanics
0	VL	23,440	L	L	VL	Long-term on-the-job	Motorcycle mechanics[1]
1	VL	21,580	L	L	VL	Long-term on-the-job	Small engine mechanics[1]
51	-	-	-	-	-	-	Other mechanics, installers, and repairers
0	VL	15,700	VL	L	L	Moderate-term on-the-job	Bicycle repairers
0	VL	28,320	H	L	L	Moderate-term on-the-job	Camera and photographic equipment repairers[1]
1	VL	23,260	L	L	L	Long-term on-the-job	Coin, vending, and amusement machine servicers and repairers
10	VL	29,160	H	L	VL	Long-term on-the-job	Heating, air conditioning, and refrigeration mechanics and installers
2	VL	26,010	H	L	L	Long-term on-the-job	Home appliance and power tool repairers[1]
14	-	-	-	-	-	-	Line installers and repairers
2	VL	42,600	VH	VL	VL	Long-term on-the-job	Electrical powerline installers and repairers
11	L	32,750	H	VL	VL	Long-term on-the-job	Telephone and cable TV line installers and repairers[1]
1	VL	24,890	H	L	L	Moderate-term on-the-job	Locksmiths and safe repairers[1]
0	VL	34,190	H	L	L	Long-term on-the-job	Medical equipment repairers
0	VL	23,010	L	L	L	Long-term on-the-job	Musical instrument repairers and tuners[1]
1	VL	39,580	VH	L	L	Long-term on-the-job	Precision instrument repairers[1]
0	VL	31,770	H	L	L	Long-term on-the-job	Riggers
5	VL	16,810	VL	VH	VH	Short-term on-the-job	Tire repairers and changers
0	VL	24,590	H	L	L	Long-term on-the-job	Watch repairers[1]
16	L	29,240	H	L	L	Long-term on-the-job	All other mechanics, installers, and repairers[1]
74	-	-	-	-	-	-	Production occupations, precision
12	-	-	-	-	-	-	Assemblers, precision
1	VL	38,400	VH	L	VL	Related work experience	Aircraft assemblers, precision[1]
6	VL	21,740	L	VH	VL	Related work experience	Electrical and electronic equipment assemblers, precision

[1] One or more Current Population Survey (CPS) proxy occupations are used to estimate CPS based data.

[2] Current Population Survey data are used to estimate median weekly earnings ranking.

[3] Bachelor's degree or higher.

NOTE: Rankings are based on employment in all detailed occupations in the National Industry-Occupation Matrix. For details, see "Data presented" section of text. Codes for describing the ranked variables are: VH = Very high, H = High, L = Low, VL = Very low, n. a. = Data not available. A dash indicates data are not applicable.

Occupational employment and job openings data, 1998-2008, and worker characteristics, 1998
(Numbers in thousands)

1998 Matrix Occupation	Employment		Employment change, 1998-2008				Per-cent self-emp-loyed, 1998	Annual average job openings due to growth and total replacement needs, 1998-2008	
			Numeric		Percent				
	1998	2008	Number	Rank	Number	Rank		Number	Rank
Electromechanical equipment assemblers, precision	50	52	3	VL	5.7	VL	.0	10	VL
Fitters, structural metal, precision[1]	17	15	-2	VL	-13.0	VL	.0	2	VL
Machine builders and other precision machine assemblers[1]	74	76	1	VL	1.7	VL	.0	9	VL
All other precision assemblers[1]	64	66	2	VL	3.7	VL	.0	8	VL
Food workers, precision	310	303	-7	-	-2.3	-	7.9	36	-
Bakers, manufacturing	55	60	5	VL	8.5	L	28.8	11	VL
Butchers and meatcutters	216	201	-15	VL	-7.1	VL	3.3	18	VL
All other precision food and tobacco workers[1]	39	42	3	VL	8.5	L	3.5	7	VL
Inspectors, testers, and graders, precision	689	667	-22	VL	-3.2	VL	.6	96	L
Metal workers, precision[1]	707	734	27	-	3.7	-	4.4	74	-
Jewelers and precious stone and metal workers[1]	30	28	-2	VL	-6.0	VL	32.1	3	VL
Machinists	426	452	26	L	6.2	VL	2.5	42	VL
Numerical control machine tool programmers	8	9	1	VL	6.1	VL	.0	1	VL
Shipfitters[1]	9	8	0	VL	-4.5	VL	.0	1	VL
Tool and die makers	138	136	-2	VL	-1.5	VL	1.1	15	VL
All other precision metal workers[1]	97	101	4	VL	4.0	VL	9.8	11	VL
Printing workers, precision	138	137	-1	-	-1.0	-	4.0	24	-
Bookbinders[1]	7	6	-1	VL	-15.2	VL	5.2	1	VL
Prepress printing workers, precision	115	114	0	-	-.4	-	4.6	20	-
Camera operators[1]	9	6	-3	VL	-31.4	VL	.0	1	VL
Compositors and typesetters, precision[1]	14	11	-3	VL	-18.9	VL	38.2	2	VL
Desktop publishing specialists[1]	26	44	19	VL	72.6	VH	.0	8	VL
Film strippers, printing[1]	23	15	-8	VL	-33.0	VL	.0	3	VL
Job printers	17	18	1	VL	4.3	VL	.0	3	VL
Paste-up workers[1]	9	4	-5	VL	-51.2	VL	.0	1	VL
Photoengravers[1]	3	1	-1	VL	-51.5	VL	.0	0	VL
Platemakers[1]	15	14	-1	VL	-5.2	VL	.0	2	VL
All other printing workers, precision[1]	17	17	0	VL	.2	VL	.0	3	VL
Textile, apparel, and furnishings workers, precision	234	226	-8	-	-3.3	-	31.3	23	-
Custom tailors and sewers	74	67	-6	VL	-8.4	VL	56.5	6	VL
Patternmakers and layout workers, fabric and apparel[1]	16	15	-1	VL	-3.8	VL	.0	1	VL
Shoe and leather workers and repairers, precision[1]	23	19	-4	VL	-17.6	VL	24.3	2	VL
Upholsterers[1]	66	67	1	VL	.9	VL	36.2	5	VL
All other precision textile, apparel, and furnishings workers[1]	55	58	2	VL	4.4	VL	3.7	9	VL
Woodworkers, precision	229	236	7	-	2.8	-	15.1	35	-
Cabinetmakers and bench carpenters	123	129	6	VL	5.2	VL	18.9	20	VL
Furniture finishers[1]	38	38	0	VL	-1.0	VL	27.1	5	VL
Wood machinists	40	41	1	VL	3.2	VL	.0	6	VL
All other precision woodworkers[1]	27	27	-1	VL	-2.5	VL	3.2	4	VL
Other precision workers	242	266	25	-	10.2	-	12.2	38	-
Dental laboratory technicians, precision	44	44	0	VL	1.0	VL	20.1	3	VL
Ophthalmic laboratory technicians	23	24	1	VL	4.7	VL	.0	2	VL
Photographic process workers, precision	18	19	1	VL	7.0	VL	51.2	4	VL
All other precision workers	157	179	22	L	14.0	L	7.3	29	VL
Plant and system occupations	403	431	28	-	6.0	-	.7	35	-
Chemical plant and system operators[1]	43	48	5	VL	11.0	L	.0	3	VL
Electric power generating plant operators, distributors, and dispatchers	45	44	-1	-	-1.5	-	.0	3	-
Power distributors and dispatchers[1]	14	12	-2	VL	-12.2	VL	.0	1	VL
Power generating and reactor plant operators[1]	31	32	1	VL	3.1	VL	.0	2	VL
Gas and petroleum plant and system occupations[1]	38	33	-5	VL	-12.6	VL	.0	2	VL
Stationary engineers	31	29	-2	VL	-5.7	VL	3.8	2	VL
Water and liquid waste treatment plant and system operators	98	112	14	VL	14.2	H	.0	13	VL
All other plant and system operators[1]	148	164	16	VL	11.1	L	1.2	12	VL

[1] One or more Current Population Survey (CPS) proxy occupations are used to estimate CPS based data.
[2] Current Population Survey data are used to estimate median weekly earnings ranking.
[3] Bachelor's degree or higher.

NOTE: Rankings are based on employment in all detailed occupations in the National Industry-Occupation Matrix. For details, see "Data presented" section of text. Codes for describing the ranked variables are: VH = Very high, H = High, L = Low, VL = Very low, n. a. = Data not available. A dash indicates data are not applicable.

Occupational employment and job openings data, 1998-2008, and worker characteristics, 1998

(Numbers in thousands)

Annual average job openings due to growth and net replacement needs, 1998-2008		Median annual earnings		Ranking of:		Most significant source of education or training	1998 Matrix Occupation
Number	Rank	Dollars	Rank	Unemployment rate	Percent part-time		
1	VL	23,250	L	VH	VL	Related work experience	Electromechanical equipment assemblers, precision
0	VL	26,180	H	L	VL	Related work experience	Fitters, structural metal, precision[1]
2	VL	29,250	H	L	VL	Related work experience	Machine builders and other precision machine assemblers[1]
2	VL	22,110	L	L	VL	Related work experience	All other precision assemblers[1]
8	-	-	-	-	-	-	Food workers, precision
1	VL	22,030	L	H	VH	Moderate-term on-the-job	Bakers, manufacturing
5	VL	20,420	L	H	L	Long-term on-the-job	Butchers and meatcutters
2	VL	22,400	L	H	H	Long-term on-the-job	All other precision food and tobacco workers[1]
15	L	23,470	L	H	L	Related work experience	Inspectors, testers, and graders, precision
18	-	-	-	-	-	-	Metal workers, precision[1]
1	VL	23,820	H	L	VL	Postsecondary vocational	Jewelers and precious stone and metal workers[1]
11	L	28,860	H	L	VL	Long-term on-the-job	Machinists
0	VL	40,490	VH	L	H	Related work experience	Numerical control machine tool programmers
0	VL	28,840	H	L	VL	Long-term on-the-job	Shipfitters[1]
3	VL	37,250	VH	VL	VL	Long-term on-the-job	Tool and die makers
3	VL	26,300	H	L	VL	Long-term on-the-job	All other precision metal workers[1]
4	-	-	-	-	-	-	Printing workers, precision
0	VL	20,690	L	H	L	Moderate-term on-the-job	Bookbinders[1]
4	-	-	-	-	-	-	Prepress printing workers, precision
0	VL	24,370	H	L	L	Long-term on-the-job	Camera operators[1]
0	VL	22,560	L	L	L	Long-term on-the-job	Compositors and typesetters, precision[1]
2	VL	29,130	H	L	L	Long-term on-the-job	Desktop publishing specialists[1]
0	VL	32,300	H	L	L	Long-term on-the-job	Film strippers, printing[1]
0	VL	24,100	H	L	L	Long-term on-the-job	Job printers
0	VL	19,830	L	L	L	Long-term on-the-job	Paste-up workers[1]
0	VL	28,430	H	L	L	Long-term on-the-job	Photoengravers[1]
0	VL	28,600	H	L	L	Long-term on-the-job	Platemakers[1]
0	VL	30,420	H	L	L	Long-term on-the-job	All other printing workers, precision[1]
5	-	-	-	-	-	-	Textile, apparel, and furnishings workers, precision
1	VL	18,630	L	H	VH	Related work experience	Custom tailors and sewers
0	VL	21,580	L	H	H	Long-term on-the-job	Patternmakers and layout workers, fabric and apparel[1]
0	VL	16,610	VL	H	H	Long-term on-the-job	Shoe and leather workers and repairers, precision[1]
1	VL	22,050	L	L	H	Long-term on-the-job	Upholsterers[1]
1	VL	16,790	VL	VH	VH	Long-term on-the-job	All other precision textile, apparel, and furnishings workers[1]
4	-	-	-	-	-	-	Woodworkers, precision
2	VL	22,390	L	L	L	Long-term on-the-job	Cabinetmakers and bench carpenters
1	VL	19,880	L	L	L	Long-term on-the-job	Furniture finishers[1]
1	VL	19,980	L	L	L	Long-term on-the-job	Wood machinists
1	VL	22,430	L	L	L	Long-term on-the-job	All other precision woodworkers[1]
8	-	-	-	-	-	-	Other precision workers
1	VL	25,660	H	VL	H	Long-term on-the-job	Dental laboratory technicians, precision
0	VL	19,530	L	VL	H	Long-term on-the-job	Ophthalmic laboratory technicians
1	VL	21,620	L	H	VH	Moderate-term on-the-job	Photographic process workers, precision
6	VL	22,720	L	H	L	Long-term on-the-job	All other precision workers
15	-	-	-	-	-	-	Plant and system occupations
2	VL	39,030	VH	VL	VL	Long-term on-the-job	Chemical plant and system operators[1]
2	-	-	-	-	-	-	Electric power generating plant operators, distributors, and dispatchers
0	VL	45,690	VH	VL	VL	Long-term on-the-job	Power distributors and dispatchers[1]
1	VL	44,840	VH	VL	VL	Long-term on-the-job	Power generating and reactor plant operators[1]
1	VL	43,820	VH	VL	VL	Long-term on-the-job	Gas and petroleum plant and system occupations[1]
1	VL	38,270	VH	VL	VL	Long-term on-the-job	Stationary engineers
4	VL	29,660	H	VL	VL	Long-term on-the-job	Water and liquid waste treatment plant and system operators
6	VL	22,580	L	VL	VL	Long-term on-the-job	All other plant and system operators[1]

[1] One or more Current Population Survey (CPS) proxy occupations are used to estimate CPS based data.

[2] Current Population Survey data are used to estimate median weekly earnings ranking.

[3] Bachelor's degree or higher.

NOTE: Rankings are based on employment in all detailed occupations in the National Industry-Occupation Matrix. For details, see "Data presented" section of text. Codes for describing the ranked variables are: VH = Very high, H = High, L = Low, VL = Very low, n. a. = Data not available. A dash indicates data are not applicable.

Occupational employment and job openings data, 1998-2008, and worker characteristics, 1998

(Numbers in thousands)

1998 Matrix Occupation	Employment		Employment change, 1998-2008				Per-cent self-emp-loyed, 1998	Annual average job openings due to growth and total replacement needs, 1998-2008	
			Numeric		Percent				
	1998	2008	Number	Rank	Number	Rank		Number	Rank
Operators, fabricators, and laborers	18,588	20,341	1,753	-	9.4	-	3.4	3,941	-
Machine setters, set-up operators, operators, and tenders	5,139	5,230	91	-	1.7	-	1.8	812	-
Numerical control machine tool operators and tenders, metal and plastic[1]	88	108	20	VL	22.6	VH	.0	19	VL
Combination machine tool setters, set-up operators, operators, and tenders, metal and plastic[1]	107	122	15	VL	13.8	L	.0	21	VL
Machine tool cut and form setters, operators, and tenders, metal and plastic	726	690	-36	-	-4.9	-	.7	83	-
Drilling and boring machine tool setters and set-up operators, metal and plastic[1]	42	34	-8	VL	-18.3	VL	.0	7	VL
Grinding, lapping, and buffing machine tool setters and set-up operators, metal and plastic	75	68	-7	VL	-9.6	VL	4.6	4	VL
Lathe and turning machine tool setters and set-up operators, metal and plastic[1]	72	66	-6	VL	-8.4	VL	.0	12	VL
Machine forming operators and tenders, metal and plastic	163	157	-6	VL	-3.9	VL	.0	16	VL
Machine tool cutting operators and tenders, metal and plastic	109	88	-22	VL	-19.9	VL	.0	6	VL
Punching machine setters and set-up operators, metal and plastic	47	44	-4	VL	-7.5	VL	.2	6	VL
All other machine tool setters, set-up operators, metal and plastic[1]	218	235	17	VL	7.7	VL	.6	34	VL
Metal fabricating machine setters, operators, and related workers	167	178	10	-	6.1	-	.0	22	-
Metal fabricators, structural metal products[1]	46	49	3	VL	7.5	VL	.0	9	VL
Soldering and brazing machine operators and tenders[1]	12	13	1	VL	8.2	VL	.0	2	VL
Welding machine setters, operators, and tenders	110	116	6	VL	5.4	VL	.0	11	VL
Metal and plastic processing machine setters, operators, and related workers	478	528	50	-	10.5	-	.0	55	-
Electrolytic plating machine setters, set-up operators, operators, and tenders, metal and plastic[1]	45	49	4	VL	9.6	L	.0	5	VL
Foundry mold assembly and shake out workers	9	10	0	VL	2.5	VL	.0	1	VL
Furnace operators and tenders[1]	23	22	-1	VL	-5.0	VL	.0	2	VL
Heat treating, annealing, and tempering machine operators and tenders, metal and plastic[1]	23	22	-1	VL	-4.1	VL	.0	2	VL
Metal molding machine setters, set-up operators, operators, and tenders	58	63	5	VL	9.0	L	.0	6	VL
Plastic molding machine setters, set-up operators, operators, and tenders	171	196	25	L	14.7	H	.0	21	VL
All other metal and plastic machine setters, operators, and related workers[1]	148	166	18	VL	11.9	L	.0	17	VL
Printing, binding, and related workers	406	410	4	-	1.0	-	2.1	64	-
Bindery machine operators and set-up operators[1]	90	100	10	VL	11.5	L	.0	16	VL
Prepress printing workers, production	20	11	-9	-	-44.7	-	.0	3	-
Photoengraving and lithographic machine operators and tenders[1]	7	6	-1	VL	-15.0	VL	.0	1	VL
Typesetting and composing machine operators and tenders[1]	13	5	-8	VL	-59.8	VL	.0	2	VL
Printing press operators	225	225	0	-	.1	-	3.8	33	-
Letterpress operators	10	8	-2	VL	-18.2	VL	.0	1	VL
Offset lithographic press operators	63	54	-9	VL	-14.7	VL	4.5	8	VL
Printing press machine setters, operators and tenders	142	154	12	VL	8.3	VL	4.1	22	VL
All other printing press setters and set-up operators	10	9	0	VL	-4.5	VL	.0	1	VL
Screen printing machine setters and set-up operators	28	29	1	VL	3.0	VL	.0	4	VL
All other printing, binding, and related workers[1]	43	45	2	VL	4.1	VL	.0	7	VL
Textile and related setters, operators, and related workers	851	687	-164	-	-19.2	-	2.5	108	-
Extruding and forming machine operators and tenders, synthetic or glass fibers[1]	33	35	3	VL	7.9	VL	.0	6	VL
Pressing machine operators and tenders, textile, garment, and related materials	69	66	-3	VL	-4.0	VL	.0	10	VL
Sewing machine operators, garment	369	257	-112	VL	-30.3	VL	3.6	42	VL

[1] One or more Current Population Survey (CPS) proxy occupations are used to estimate CPS based data.
[2] Current Population Survey data are used to estimate median weekly earnings ranking.
[3] Bachelor's degree or higher.

NOTE: Rankings are based on employment in all detailed occupations in the National Industry-Occupation Matrix. For details, see "Data presented" section of text. Codes for describing the ranked variables are: VH = Very high, H = High, L = Low, VL = Very low, n. a. = Data not available. A dash indicates data are not applicable.

Occupational employment and job openings data, 1998-2008, and worker characteristics, 1998

(Numbers in thousands)

Annual average job openings due to growth and net replacement needs, 1998-2008		Median annual earnings		Ranking of:		Most significant source of education or training	1998 Matrix Occupation
Number	Rank	Dollars	Rank	Unemployment rate	Percent part-time		
637	-	-	-	-	-	-	**Operators, fabricators, and laborers**
146	-	-	-	-	-	-	Machine setters, set-up operators, operators, and tenders
4	VL	27,110	H	H	VL	Moderate-term on-the-job	Numerical control machine tool operators and tenders, metal and plastic[1]
4	VL	23,860	H	H	VL	Moderate-term on-the-job	Combination machine tool setters, set-up operators, operators, and tenders, metal and plastic[1]
19	-	-	-	-	-	-	Machine tool cut and form setters, operators, and tenders, metal and plastic
1	VL	25,630	H	H	VL	Moderate-term on-the-job	Drilling and boring machine tool setters and set-up operators, metal and plastic[1]
2	VL	24,740	H	H	VL	Moderate-term on-the-job	Grinding, lapping, and buffing machine tool setters and set-up operators, metal and plastic
2	VL	28,250	H	H	VL	Moderate-term on-the-job	Lathe and turning machine tool setters and set-up operators, metal and plastic[1]
4	VL	20,170	L	H	VL	Moderate-term on-the-job	Machine forming operators and tenders, metal and plastic
3	VL	24,510	H	H	VL	Moderate-term on-the-job	Machine tool cutting operators and tenders, metal and plastic
1	VL	23,270	L	VH	VL	Moderate-term on-the-job	Punching machine setters and set-up operators, metal and plastic
7	VL	25,020	H	H	VL	Moderate-term on-the-job	All other machine tool setters, set-up operators, metal and plastic[1]
5	-	-	-	-	-	-	Metal fabricating machine setters, operators, and related workers
1	VL	24,070	H	H	VL	Moderate-term on-the-job	Metal fabricators, structural metal products[1]
0	VL	20,950	L	VH	L	Moderate-term on-the-job	Soldering and brazing machine operators and tenders[1]
3	VL	25,010	H	H	VL	Moderate-term on-the-job	Welding machine setters, operators, and tenders
17	-	-	-	-	-	-	Metal and plastic processing machine setters, operators, and related workers
2	VL	21,210	L	VH	VL	Moderate-term on-the-job	Electrolytic plating machine setters, set-up operators, operators, and tenders, metal and plastic[1]
0	VL	21,910	L	H	VL	Moderate-term on-the-job	Foundry mold assembly and shake out workers
0	VL	25,870	H	H	VL	Moderate-term on-the-job	Furnace operators and tenders[1]
1	VL	25,160	H	VH	VL	Moderate-term on-the-job	Heat treating, annealing, and tempering machine operators and tenders, metal and plastic[1]
2	VL	24,870	H	H	VL	Moderate-term on-the-job	Metal molding machine setters, set-up operators, operators, and tenders
7	VL	18,580	L	H	VL	Moderate-term on-the-job	Plastic molding machine setters, set-up operators, operators, and tenders
5	VL	22,780	L	VH	VL	Moderate-term on-the-job	All other metal and plastic machine setters, operators, and related workers[1]
11	-	-	-	-	-	-	Printing, binding, and related workers
3	VL	20,610	L	L	L	Moderate-term on-the-job	Bindery machine operators and set-up operators[1]
0	-	-	-	-	-	-	Prepress printing workers, production
0	VL	23,960	H	L	L	Moderate-term on-the-job	Photoengraving and lithographic machine operators and tenders[1]
0	VL	23,050	L	L	L	Moderate-term on-the-job	Typesetting and composing machine operators and tenders[1]
6	-	-	-	-	-	-	Printing press operators
0	VL	28,620	H	L	VL	Moderate-term on-the-job	Letterpress operators
1	VL	31,000	H	L	VL	Moderate-term on-the-job	Offset lithographic press operators
4	VL	26,030	H	L	VL	Moderate-term on-the-job	Printing press machine setters, operators and tenders
0	VL	27,720	H	L	L	Moderate-term on-the-job	All other printing press setters and set-up operators
1	VL	18,880	L	L	L	Moderate-term on-the-job	Screen printing machine setters and set-up operators
1	VL	22,950	L	L	L	Moderate-term on-the-job	All other printing, binding, and related workers[1]
13	-	-	-	-	-	-	Textile and related setters, operators, and related workers
1	VL	27,940	H	VH	L	Moderate-term on-the-job	Extruding and forming machine operators and tenders, synthetic or glass fibers[1]
1	VL	15,150	VL	VH	VH	Moderate-term on-the-job	Pressing machine operators and tenders, textile, garment, and related materials
5	VL	14,740	VL	VH	L	Moderate-term on-the-job	Sewing machine operators, garment

[1] One or more Current Population Survey (CPS) proxy occupations are used to estimate CPS based data.
[2] Current Population Survey data are used to estimate median weekly earnings ranking.
[3] Bachelor's degree or higher.

NOTE: Rankings are based on employment in all detailed occupations in the National Industry-Occupation Matrix. For details, see "Data presented" section of text. Codes for describing the ranked variables are: VH = Very high, H = High, L = Low, VL = Very low, n. a. = Data not available. A dash indicates data are not applicable.

Occupational employment and job openings data, 1998-2008, and worker characteristics, 1998

(Numbers in thousands)

1998 Matrix Occupation	Employment		Employment change, 1998-2008				Per-cent self-emp-loyed, 1998	Annual average job openings due to growth and total replacement needs, 1998-2008	
	1998	2008	Numeric		Percent			Number	Rank
			Number	Rank	Number	Rank			
Sewing machine operators, non-garment	137	140	3	VL	2.5	VL	3.8	19	VL
Textile bleaching and dyeing machine operators and tenders[1]	24	22	-2	VL	-9.0	VL	3.2	4	VL
Textile draw-out and winding machine operators and tenders[1]	192	141	-50	VL	-26.3	VL	.9	23	VL
Textile machine setters and set-up operators	28	26	-3	VL	-9.6	VL	.0	4	VL
Woodworking machine setters, operators, and other related workers	143	130	-14	-	-9.4	-	5.6	45	-
Head sawyers and sawing machine operators and tenders, setters and set-up operators	64	61	-4	VL	-5.7	VL	2.0	24	VL
Woodworking machine operators and tenders, setters and set-up operators[1]	79	69	-10	VL	-12.5	VL	8.5	21	VL
Other machine setters, set-up operators, operators, and tenders	2,172	2,377	205	-	9.4	-	2.3	396	-
Boiler operators and tenders, low pressure	16	14	-2	VL	-11.0	VL	.0	1	VL
Cement and gluing machine operators and tenders[1]	32	27	-5	VL	-15.6	VL	.0	5	VL
Chemical equipment controllers, operators and tenders[1]	100	111	11	VL	11.4	L	.0	20	VL
Cooking and roasting machine operators and tenders, food and tobacco[1]	31	28	-3	VL	-8.5	VL	1.6	4	VL
Crushing, grinding, mixing, and blending machine operators and tenders	150	154	4	VL	2.8	VL	1.6	27	VL
Cutting and slicing machine setters, operators and tenders	96	102	6	VL	6.4	VL	2.5	18	VL
Dairy processing equipment operators, including setters[1]	15	12	-3	VL	-20.4	VL	6.8	2	VL
Electronic semiconductor processors	63	92	29	L	45.2	VH	.0	11	VL
Extruding and forming machine setters, operators and tenders[1]	126	132	6	VL	5.0	VL	.0	23	VL
Furnace, kiln, oven, drier, or kettle operators and tenders[1]	25	24	-1	VL	-5.6	VL	.0	2	VL
Laundry and dry-cleaning machine operators and tenders, except pressing	167	184	16	VL	9.8	L	14.7	38	VL
Motion picture projectionists[1]	9	7	-2	VL	-21.8	VL	6.4	1	VL
Packaging and filling machine operators and tenders	377	425	49	L	12.9	L	.0	88	L
Painting and coating machine operators	171	186	15	-	8.7	-	5.5	35	-
Coating, painting, and spraying machine operators, tenders, setters, and set-up operators	129	140	11	VL	8.7	L	2.3	26	VL
Painters, transportation equipment	42	46	4	VL	9.0	L	15.4	9	VL
Paper goods machine setters and set-up operators[1]	62	59	-3	VL	-4.1	VL	.0	9	VL
Photographic processing machine operators and tenders	46	41	-5	VL	-11.4	VL	.0	10	VL
Separating, filtering, clarifying, precipitating, and still machine operators and tenders[1]	28	26	-2	VL	-7.2	VL	.0	5	VL
Shoe sewing machine operators and tenders[1]	7	4	-2	VL	-35.8	VL	.0	1	VL
Tire building machine operators	18	17	0	VL	-1.4	VL	.0	2	VL
All other machine operators, tenders, setters, and set-up operators[1]	635	732	97	L	15.2	H	1.4	92	L
Hand workers, including assemblers and fabricators	3,092	3,382	290	-	9.3	-	3.6	636	-
Cannery workers	50	44	-6	VL	-12.0	VL	.0	10	VL
Coil winders, tapers, and finishers	22	22	1	VL	2.5	VL	.0	5	VL
Cutters and trimmers, hand[1]	42	39	-4	VL	-8.3	VL	1.2	7	VL
Electrical and electronic assemblers	246	265	19	VL	7.7	VL	.0	59	L
Grinders and polishers, hand	81	84	3	VL	4.3	VL	.0	13	VL
Machine assemblers	67	71	4	VL	5.5	VL	.0	16	VL
Meat, poultry, and fish cutters and trimmers, hand[1]	143	178	35	L	24.2	VH	.0	33	VL
Painting, coating, and decorating workers, hand[1]	39	46	7	VL	17.7	H	18.4	9	VL
Pressers, hand	13	12	-2	VL	-11.4	VL	.0	2	VL
Sewers, hand	10	8	-1	VL	-14.8	VL	.0	1	VL
Solderers and brazers[1]	35	40	5	VL	14.4	H	.0	8	VL
Welders and cutters	368	398	31	L	8.3	L	5.2	38	VL
All other assemblers, fabricators, and hand workers[1]	1,976	2,175	198	H	10.0	L	4.2	437	VH

[1] One or more Current Population Survey (CPS) proxy occupations are used to estimate CPS based data.
[2] Current Population Survey data are used to estimate median weekly earnings ranking.
[3] Bachelor's degree or higher.

NOTE: Rankings are based on employment in all detailed occupations in the National Industry-Occupation Matrix. For details, see "Data presented" section of text. Codes for describing the ranked variables are: VH = Very high, H = High, L = Low, VL = Very low, n. a. = Data not available. A dash indicates data are not applicable.

Occupational employment and job openings data, 1998-2008, and worker characteristics, 1998

(Numbers in thousands)

Annual average job openings due to growth and net replacement needs, 1998-2008		Median annual earnings		Ranking of:		Most significant source of education or training	1998 Matrix Occupation
Number	Rank	Dollars	Rank	Unemployment rate	Percent part-time		
2	VL	16,990	L	VH	H	Moderate-term on-the-job	Sewing machine operators, non-garment
0	VL	19,350	L	VH	L	Moderate-term on-the-job	Textile bleaching and dyeing machine operators and tenders[1]
3	VL	19,480	L	VH	H	Moderate-term on-the-job	Textile draw-out and winding machine operators and tenders[1]
0	VL	21,620	L	VH	H	Moderate-term on-the-job	Textile machine setters and set-up operators
4	-	-	-	-	-	-	Woodworking machine setters, operators, and other related workers
2	VL	19,490	L	VH	L	Moderate-term on-the-job	Head sawyers and sawing machine operators and tenders, setters and set-up operators
2	VL	19,260	L	VH	L	Moderate-term on-the-job	Woodworking machine operators and tenders, setters and set-up operators[1]
69	-	-	-	-	-	-	Other machine setters, set-up operators, operators, and tenders
0	VL	30,320	H	VL	VL	Moderate-term on-the-job	Boiler operators and tenders, low pressure
1	VL	20,720	L	H	L	Moderate-term on-the-job	Cement and gluing machine operators and tenders[1]
4	VL	32,180	H	VL	VL	Moderate-term on-the-job	Chemical equipment controllers, operators and tenders[1]
1	VL	21,710	L	H	VL	Moderate-term on-the-job	Cooking and roasting machine operators and tenders, food and tobacco[1]
4	VL	23,350	L	H	L	Moderate-term on-the-job	Crushing, grinding, mixing, and blending machine operators and tenders
3	VL	21,680	L	H	L	Moderate-term on-the-job	Cutting and slicing machine setters, operators and tenders
0	VL	25,800	H	VL	VL	Moderate-term on-the-job	Dairy processing equipment operators, including setters[1]
4	VL	24,810	H	H	VL	Moderate-term on-the-job	Electronic semiconductor processors
4	VL	23,180	L	H	L	Moderate-term on-the-job	Extruding and forming machine setters, operators and tenders[1]
0	VL	25,110	H	H	VL	Moderate-term on-the-job	Furnace, kiln, oven, drier, or kettle operators and tenders[1]
6	VL	14,670	VL	VH	VH	Moderate-term on-the-job	Laundry and dry-cleaning machine operators and tenders, except pressing
0	VL	15,420	VL	H	L	Short-term on-the-job	Motion picture projectionists[1]
15	L	20,060	L	VH	L	Moderate-term on-the-job	Packaging and filling machine operators and tenders
5	-	-	-	-	-	-	Painting and coating machine operators
4	VL	21,820	L	VH	VL	Moderate-term on-the-job	Coating, painting, and spraying machine operators, tenders, setters, and set-up operators
1	VL	29,120	H	VH	VL	Moderate-term on-the-job	Painters, transportation equipment
1	VL	25,990	H	H	VL	Moderate-term on-the-job	Paper goods machine setters and set-up operators[1]
2	VL	17,810	L	H	VH	Short-term on-the-job	Photographic processing machine operators and tenders
1	VL	29,600	H	VL	VL	Moderate-term on-the-job	Separating, filtering, clarifying, precipitating, and still machine operators and tenders[1]
0	VL	16,230	VL	VH	VL	Moderate-term on-the-job	Shoe sewing machine operators and tenders[1]
0	VL	36,430	VH	H	VL	Moderate-term on-the-job	Tire building machine operators
19	L	22,170	L	H	VL	Moderate-term on-the-job	All other machine operators, tenders, setters, and set-up operators[1]
97	-	-	-	-	-	-	Hand workers, including assemblers and fabricators
1	VL	15,720	VL	VH	L	Short-term on-the-job	Cannery workers
0	VL	18,660	L	VH	L	Short-term on-the-job	Coil winders, tapers, and finishers
1	VL	17,130	L	VH	L	Short-term on-the-job	Cutters and trimmers, hand[1]
6	VL	18,800	L	VH	L	Short-term on-the-job	Electrical and electronic assemblers
3	VL	20,450	L	VH	L	Short-term on-the-job	Grinders and polishers, hand
2	VL	22,640	L	VH	L	Short-term on-the-job	Machine assemblers
7	VL	16,270	VL	VH	L	Short-term on-the-job	Meat, poultry, and fish cutters and trimmers, hand[1]
2	VL	19,060	L	VH	L	Short-term on-the-job	Painting, coating, and decorating workers, hand[1]
0	VL	14,750	VL	VH	L	Short-term on-the-job	Pressers, hand
0	VL	15,520	VL	H	VH	Short-term on-the-job	Sewers, hand
1	VL	17,610	L	VH	L	Short-term on-the-job	Solderers and brazers[1]
12	L	25,810	H	H	VL	Long-term on-the-job	Welders and cutters
61	H	18,770	L	VH	L	Short-term on-the-job	All other assemblers, fabricators, and hand workers[1]

[1] One or more Current Population Survey (CPS) proxy occupations are used to estimate CPS based data.

[2] Current Population Survey data are used to estimate median weekly earnings ranking.

[3] Bachelor's degree or higher.

NOTE: Rankings are based on employment in all detailed occupations in the National Industry-Occupation Matrix. For details, see "Data presented" section of text. Codes for describing the ranked variables are: VH = Very high, H = High, L = Low, VL = Very low, n. a. = Data not available. A dash indicates data are not applicable.

Occupational employment and job openings data, 1998-2008, and worker characteristics, 1998
(Numbers in thousands)

| 1998 Matrix Occupation | Employment | | Employment change, 1998-2008 | | | | Per-cent self-emp-loyed, 1998 | Annual average job openings due to growth and total replacement needs, 1998-2008 | |
| | | | Numeric | | Percent | | | | |
	1998	2008	Number	Rank	Number	Rank		Number	Rank
Transportation and material moving machine and vehicle operators	5,215	5,960	745	-	14.2	-	6.8	866	-
Motor vehicle operators	4,084	4,723	639	-	15.6	-	8.1	685	-
Bus drivers	638	747	108	-	1.0	-	1.1	95	-
Bus drivers, transit and intercity	203	235	32	L	15.8	H	3.3	30	VL
Bus drivers, school	435	511	76	L	17.6	H	.0	65	L
Taxi drivers and chauffeurs	132	158	26	L	20.0	VH	34.4	27	VL
Truck drivers	3,274	3,782	507	-	15.4	-	8.6	557	-
Driver/sales workers	305	319	14	VL	4.7	VL	4.5	23	VL
Truck drivers light and heavy	2,970	3,463	493	VH	16.6	H	9.0	535	VH
All other motor vehicle operators[1]	40	37	-3	VL	-8.5	VL	.0	6	VL
Rail transportation workers	85	75	-10	-	-11.0	-	.0	5	-
Locomotive engineers[1]	33	35	2	VL	4.8	VL	.0	2	VL
Railroad brake, signal, and switch operators[1]	14	7	-7	VL	-47.8	VL	.0	1	VL
Railroad conductors and yardmasters[1]	25	24	-2	VL	-6.7	VL	.0	2	VL
Subway and streetcar operators[1]	3	4	0	VL	7.1	VL	.0	0	VL
All other rail transportation workers[1]	8	5	-3	VL	-35.6	VL	.0	0	VL
Water transportation and related workers	56	58	3	-	4.7	-	5.5	11	-
Able seamen, ordinary seamen, and marine oilers[1]	23	24	1	VL	5.1	VL	.6	4	VL
Captains and pilots, water vessels[1]	19	19	1	VL	3.0	VL	15.7	4	VL
Mates, ship, boat, and barge[1]	8	9	1	VL	7.9	VL	.0	2	VL
Ship engineers[1]	6	7	0	VL	4.3	VL	.0	1	VL
Material moving equipment operators	808	883	74	-	9.0	-	2.2	131	-
Crane and tower operators	49	49	0	VL	.5	VL	.0	6	VL
Excavation and loading machine operators[1]	106	122	16	VL	15.3	H	14.4	6	VL
Hoist and winch operators[1]	11	11	1	VL	6.0	VL	6.1	2	VL
Industrial truck and tractor operators	415	454	38	L	9.2	L	.2	81	L
All other material moving equipment operators	228	247	19	VL	8.3	L	.4	36	VL
All other transportation and material moving equipment operators[1]	183	222	39	L	21.5	VH	.0	35	VL
Helpers, laborers, and material movers, hand	5,142	5,768	626	-	12.1	-	1.4	1,636	-
Cleaners of vehicles and equipment	288	360	72	L	25.0	VH	8.2	117	L
Freight, stock, and material movers, hand[1]	822	834	12	VL	1.5	VL	1.7	307	H
Hand packers and packagers	984	1,197	213	H	21.7	VH	.8	249	H
Helpers, construction trades	576	618	42	L	7.3	VL	.4	167	L
Machine feeders and offbearers	213	211	-2	VL	-.9	VL	.0	40	VL
Parking lot attendants[1]	86	113	27	L	31.2	VH	.0	18	VL
Refuse and recyclable material collectors[1]	99	103	4	VL	3.9	VL	1.7	39	VL
Service station attendants	141	139	-2	VL	-1.2	VL	3.0	40	VL
All other helpers, laborers, and material movers, hand[1]	1,934	2,194	260	H	13.4	L	.9	654	VH

[1] One or more Current Population Survey (CPS) proxy occupations are used to estimate CPS based data.
[2] Current Population Survey data are used to estimate median weekly earnings ranking.
[3] Bachelor's degree or higher.

NOTE: Rankings are based on employment in all detailed occupations in the National Industry-Occupation Matrix. For details, see "Data presented" section of text. Codes for describing the ranked variables are: VH = Very high, H = High, L = Low, VL = Very low, n. a. = Data not available. A dash indicates data are not applicable.

Occupational employment and job openings data, 1998-2008, and worker characteristics, 1998

(Numbers in thousands)

Annual average job openings due to growth and net replacement needs, 1998-2008		Median annual earnings		Ranking of:		Most significant source of education or training	1998 Matrix Occupation
Number	Rank	Dollars	Rank	Unemployment rate	Percent part-time		
161	-	-	-	-	-	-	Transportation and material moving machine and vehicle operators
127	-	-	-	-	-	-	Motor vehicle operators
22	-	-	-	-	-	-	Bus drivers
7	VL	24,380	H	L	VH	Moderate-term on-the-job	Bus drivers, transit and intercity
15	L	18,820	L	L	VH	Short-term on-the-job	Bus drivers, school
5	VL	15,550	VL	H	H	Short-term on-the-job	Taxi drivers and chauffeurs
99	-	-	-	-	-	-	Truck drivers
7	VL	19,330	L	VL	L	Short-term on-the-job	Driver/sales workers
92	VH	24,260	H	H	L	Short-term on-the-job	Truck drivers light and heavy
1	VL	18,330	L	H	H	Short-term on-the-job	All other motor vehicle operators[1]
3	-	-	-	-	-	-	Rail transportation workers
1	VL	39,800	VH	VL	VL	Related work experience	Locomotive engineers[1]
0	VL	36,550	VH	VL	VL	Related work experience	Railroad brake, signal, and switch operators[1]
1	VL	38,500	VH	VL	VL	Related work experience	Railroad conductors and yardmasters[1]
0	VL	43,330	VH	VL	VL	Moderate-term on-the-job	Subway and streetcar operators[1]
0	VL	35,600	VH	VL	VL	Moderate-term on-the-job	All other rail transportation workers[1]
2	-	-	-	-	-	-	Water transportation and related workers
1	VL	23,700	H	L	VL	Short-term on-the-job	Able seamen, ordinary seamen, and marine oilers[1]
1	VL	41,210	VH	L	VL	Related work experience	Captains and pilots, water vessels[1]
0	VL	29,310	H	L	VL	Related work experience	Mates, ship, boat, and barge[1]
0	VL	40,150	VH	L	VL	Related work experience	Ship engineers[1]
21	-	-	-	-	-	-	Material moving equipment operators
1	VL	30,510	H	H	VL	Moderate-term on-the-job	Crane and tower operators
4	VL	27,090	H	H	VL	Moderate-term on-the-job	Excavation and loading machine operators[1]
0	VL	28,030	H	VH	VL	Moderate-term on-the-job	Hoist and winch operators[1]
9	VL	23,360	L	H	VL	Short-term on-the-job	Industrial truck and tractor operators
7	VL	23,970	H	VH	L	Moderate-term on-the-job	All other material moving equipment operators
7	VL	24,120	H	H	H	Moderate-term on-the-job	All other transportation and material moving equipment operators[1]
234	-	-	-	-	-	-	Helpers, laborers, and material movers, hand
16	L	14,540	VL	VH	VH	Short-term on-the-job	Cleaners of vehicles and equipment
31	L	18,460	L	VH	VH	Short-term on-the-job	Freight, stock, and material movers, hand[1]
46	H	14,550	VL	VH	H	Short-term on-the-job	Hand packers and packagers
31	L	19,510	L	VH	H	Short-term on-the-job	Helpers, construction trades
6	VL	18,810	L	VH	H	Short-term on-the-job	Machine feeders and offbearers
4	VL	13,920	VL	H	H	Short-term on-the-job	Parking lot attendants[1]
4	VL	21,860	L	VH	H	Short-term on-the-job	Refuse and recyclable material collectors[1]
6	VL	14,350	VL	VH	VH	Short-term on-the-job	Service station attendants
89	VH	17,920	L	VH	H	Short-term on-the-job	All other helpers, laborers, and material movers, hand[1]

[1] One or more Current Population Survey (CPS) proxy occupations are used to estimate CPS based data.

[2] Current Population Survey data are used to estimate median weekly earnings ranking.

[3] Bachelor's degree or higher.

NOTE: Rankings are based on employment in all detailed occupations in the National Industry-Occupation Matrix. For details, see "Data presented" section of text. Codes for describing the ranked variables are: VH = Very high, H = High, L = Low, VL = Very low, n. a. = Data not available. A dash indicates data are not applicable.

252 Major Jobs, Sorted by Percent of Projected Growth

Comments

America's Top Medical, Education & Human Services Jobs is part of JIST's America's Top Jobs series. I update the books in this series every two years in response to new data from the U.S. Department of Labor. The DOL provides data on 252 major occupations that account for about 90 percent of the American workforce.

I created the following list by sorting these 252 occupations in descending order by their percent of projected growth through 2008. I thought you would find this list interesting. It is the basis for *America's Fastest Growing Jobs*, another book in the America's Top Jobs series.

If you are interested in a job that is not described in this book, you can find a description for it in one of the other books in the America's Top Jobs series, which are referenced on page ii. Descriptions for all the jobs can be found in the *Occupational Outlook Handbook*, which is published by the U.S. Department of Labor. You can order the America's Top Jobs books or the *Occupational Outlook Handbook* from a bookstore or from JIST. You can also find them in your local library.

252 Major Jobs, in Order of Projected Percent Growth

Order of Projected Percent Growth	Occupation	Percent Growth in Employment, 1998-2008	Employment 1998	Numerical Change in Employment, 1998-2008
1	Computer systems analysts, engineers, and scientists	99	1,530,000	1,522,000
2	Paralegals	62	136,000	84,000
3	Medical assistants	58	252,000	146,000
4	Home health and personal care aides	58	746,000	433,000
5	Human service workers and assistants	53	268,000	141,000
6	Services sales representatives	51	841,000	429,000
7	Physician assistants	48	66,000	32,000
8	Electronic semiconductor processors	45	63,000	29,000
9	Health information technicians	44	92,000	41,000
10	Physical therapist assistants and aides	44	82,000	36,000
11	Engineering, natural science, and computer and information systems managers	43	326,000	142,000
12	Respiratory therapists	43	86,000	37,000
13	Surgical technologists	42	54,000	23,000
14	Dental assistants	42	229,000	97,000
15	Dental hygienists	41	143,000	58,000
16	Securities, commodities, and financial services sales representatives	41	303,000	124,000
17	Occupational therapy assistant and aides	40	19,000	7,400

©2001 • JIST Works • Indianapolis, IN

Order of Projected Percent Growth	Occupation	Percent Growth in Employment, 1998-2008	Employment 1998	Numerical Change in Employment, 1998-2008
18	Correctional officers	39	383,000	148,000
19	Speech-language pathologists and audiologists	38	105,000	40,000
20	Social workers	36	604,000	218,000
21	Special education teachers	34	406,000	137,000
22	Occupational therapists	34	73,000	25,000
23	Physical therapists	34	120,000	41,000
24	Computer, automated teller, and office machine repairers	34	138,000	46,000
25	Health services managers	33	222,000	74,000
26	Biological and medical scientists	32	112,000	36,000
27	Emergency medical technicians and paramedics	32	150,000	47,000
28	Demonstrators, product promoters, and models	32	92,000	30,000
29	Teacher assistants	31	1,192,000	375,000
30	Computer programmers	30	648,000	191,000
31	Flight attendants	30	99,000	30,000
32	Guards	29	1,027,000	294,000
33	Management analysts	28	344,000	98,000
34	Instructors and coaches, sports and physical training	28	359,000	102,000
35	Police and detectives	27	764,000	205,000
36	Electrical and electronics engineers	26	357,000	93,000
37	Designers	26	423,000	110,000
38	Visual artists	26	308,000	79,000
39	Preschool teachers and child-care workers	26	1,250,000	328,000
40	Sheet metal workers and duct installers	26	122,000	32,000
41	Counselors	25	182,000	46,000
42	Veterinarians	25	57,000	14,000
43	Pest controllers	25	52,000	13,000
44	Public relations specialists	24	122,000	30,000
45	Writers and editors, including technical writers	24	341,000	83,000
46	Actors, directors, and producers	24	160,000	38,000
47	Adjusters, investigators, and collectors	24	1,466,000	345,000
48	Receptionists	24	1,293,000	305,000
49	Private detectives and investigators	24	61,000	15,000
50	Advertising, marketing, and public relations managers	23	485,000	112,000
51	College and university faculty	23	865,000	195,000
52	Chiropractors	23	46,000	11,000
53	Counter and rental clerks	23	469,000	108,000
54	Nursing and psychiatric aides	23	1,461,000	332,000
55	Veterinary assistants and nonfarm animal caretakers	23	181,000	42,000
56	Registered nurses	22	2,079,000	451,000
57	Loan officers and counselors	21	227,000	48,000
58	Civil engineers	21	195,000	41,000
59	Physicians	21	577,000	122,000

Order of Projected Percent Growth	Occupation	Percent Growth in Employment, 1998-2008	Employment 1998	Numerical Change in Employment, 1998-2008
60	Engineers	20	1,462,000	290,000
61	Licensed practical nurses	20	692,000	136,000
62	Radiologic technologists	20	162,000	32,000
63	Information clerks	20	1,910,000	386,000
64	Brokerage clerks and statement clerks	20	92,000	18,000
65	Landscaping, groundskeeping, nursery, greenhouse, and lawn service occupations	20	1,285,000	262,000
66	Line installers and repairers	20	279,000	56,000
67	Taxi drivers and chauffeurs	20	132,000	26,000
68	Architects, except landscape and naval	19	99,000	19,000
69	Recreation workers	19	241,000	46,000
70	Dietitians and nutritionists	19	54,000	10,000
71	Interviewing and new accounts clerks	19	239,000	46,000
72	Office and administrative support supervisors and managers	19	1,611,000	313,000
73	Hazardous materials removal workers	19	38,000	7,300
74	Administrative services and facility managers	18	364,000	66,000
75	Human resources, training, and labor relations specialists and managers	18	597,000	110,000
76	Restaurant and food service managers	18	518,000	92,000
77	Conservation scientists and foresters	18	39,000	7,000
78	Economists and marketing research analysts	18	70,000	13,000
79	Library technicians	18	72,000	13,000
80	Travel agents	18	138,000	25,000
81	Urban and regional planners	17	35,000	6,100
82	Clinical laboratory technologists and technicians	17	313,000	53,000
83	Cashiers	17	3,198,000	556,000
84	Automotive mechanics and service technicians	17	790,000	132,000
85	Heating, air-conditioning, and refrigeration mechanics and installers	17	286,000	48,000
86	Plasterers and stucco masons	17	40,000	6,900
87	Busdrivers	17	638,000	108,000
88	Construction and building inspectors	16	68,000	11,000
89	Funeral directors and morticians	16	28,000	4,400
90	General managers and top executives	16	3,362,000	551,000
91	Mechanical engineers	16	220,000	36,000
92	Engineering technicians	16	771,000	126,000
93	Geologists, geophysicists, and oceanographers	16	44,000	6,800
94	Lawyers and judicial workers	16	752,000	119,000
95	School teachers—kindergarten, elementary, and secondary	16	3,364,000	552,000
96	Cardiovascular technologists and technicians	16	33,000	5,300
97	Pharmacy technicians and assistants	16	170,000	27,000
98	Library assistants and bookmobile drivers	16	127,000	21,000
99	Automotive body repairers	16	227,000	36,000

Order of Projected Percent Growth	Occupation	Percent Growth in Employment, 1998-2008	Employment 1998	Numerical Change in Employment, 1998-2008
100	Coin, vending, and amusement machine servicers and repairers	16	27,000	4,200
101	Landscape architects	15	22,000	3,200
102	Atmospheric scientists	15	8,400	1,200
103	Musicians, singers, and related workers	15	273,000	41,000
104	Office clerks, general	15	3,021,000	463,000
105	Truckdrivers	15	3,274,000	507,000
106	Budget analysts	14	59,000	8,100
107	Construction managers	14	270,000	38,000
108	Financial managers	14	693,000	97,000
109	Property, real estate, and community association managers	14	315,000	43,000
110	Surveyors, cartographers, photogrammetrists, and surveying technicians	14	110,000	16,000
111	Chemists	14	96,000	13,000
112	Adult and vocational education teachers	14	588,000	81,000
113	Opticians, dispensing	14	71,000	9,800
114	Dancers and choreographers	14	29,000	3,900
115	Water and wastewater treatment plant operators	14	98,000	14,000
116	Cost estimators	13	152,000	20,000
117	Education administrators	13	447,000	58,000
118	Employment interviewers, private or public employment service	13	66,000	8,500
119	Industrial engineers, except safety engineers	13	126,000	16,000
120	Social scientists, other	13	50,000	6,400
121	Archivists, curators, museum technicians, and conservators	13	23,000	2,900
122	Recreational therapists	13	39,000	5,200
123	Hotel, motel, and resort desk clerks	13	159,000	21,000
124	Chefs, cooks, and other kitchen workers	13	3,306,000	442,000
125	Electronics repairers, commercial and industrial equipment	13	72,000	9,100
126	Nuclear medicine technologists	12	14,000	1,600
127	Retail salespersons	12	4,582,000	565,000
128	Dispatchers	12	248,000	30,000
129	Food and beverage service occupations	12	5,429,000	655,000
130	Bricklayers and stonemasons	12	157,000	19,000
131	Elevator installers and repairers	12	30,000	3,600
132	Roofers	12	158,000	19,000
133	Handlers, equipment cleaners, helpers, and laborers ...	12	5,142,000	626,000
134	Accountants and auditors	11	1,080,000	122,000
135	Inspectors and compliance officers, except construction	11	176,000	19,000
136	Agricultural and food scientists	11	21,000	2,300
137	Psychologists	11	166,000	19,000
138	Optometrists	11	38,000	4,000

Order of Projected Percent Growth	Occupation	Percent Growth in Employment, 1998-2008	Employment 1998	Numerical Change in Employment, 1998-2008
139	Podiatrists	11	14,000	1,500
140	Billing clerks and billing machine operators	11	449,000	47,000
141	Janitors and cleaners and institutional cleaning supervisors	11	3,271,000	374,000
142	Chemical engineers	10	48,000	4,600
143	Real estate agents and brokers	10	347,000	34,000
144	Court reporters, medical transcriptionists, and stenographers	10	110,000	11,000
145	File clerks	10	272,000	26,000
146	Barbers, cosmetologists, and related workers	10	723,000	73,000
147	Telecommunications equipment mechanics, installers, and repairers	10	125,000	13,000
148	Aircraft mechanics and service technicians	10	133,000	14,000
149	Diesel mechanics and service technicians	10	255,000	25,000
150	Electricians	10	656,000	68,000
151	Bindery workers	10	96,000	9,300
152	Aerospace engineers	9	53,000	4,600
153	Materials engineers	9	20,000	1,800
154	Operations research analysts	9	76,000	6,700
155	Photographers and camera operators	9	161,000	15,000
156	Mail clerks and messengers	9	247,000	23,000
157	Mobile heavy equipment mechanics	9	106,000	9,900
158	Painters and paperhangers	9	476,000	41,000
159	Blue-collar worker supervisors	9	2,198,000	196,000
160	Painting and coating machine operators	9	171,000	15,000
161	Material moving equipment operators	9	808,000	74,000
162	Retail sales worker supervisors and managers	8	1,675,000	134,000
163	Maintenance mechanics, general utility	8	1,232,000	95,000
164	Construction equipment operators	8	321,000	25,000
165	Structural and reinforcing metal workers	8	87,000	7,300
166	Welders, cutters, and welding machine operators	8	477,000	37,000
167	Purchasing managers, buyers, and purchasing agents	7	547,000	38,000
168	Actuaries	7	16,000	1,100
169	Science technicians	7	227,000	16,000
170	Pharmacists	7	185,000	14,000
171	Loan clerks and credit authorizers, checkers, and clerks	7	254,000	17,000
172	Carpenters	7	1,086,000	76,000
173	Drywall installers and finishers	7	163,000	12,000
174	Insulation workers	7	67,000	5,000
175	Hotel managers and assistants	6	76,000	4,500
176	Aircraft pilots and flight engineers	6	94,000	5,500
177	Nuclear engineers	6	12,000	700
178	Drafters	6	283,000	18,000
179	Electroneurodiagnostic technologists	6	5,400	300

Order of Projected Percent Growth	Occupation	Percent Growth in Employment, 1998-2008	Employment 1998	Numerical Change in Employment, 1998-2008
180	Broadcast and sound technicians	6	37,000	2,200
181	Reservation and transportation ticket agents and travel clerks	6	219,000	13,000
182	Stock clerks	6	2,331,000	131,000
183	Fire fighting occupations	6	314,000	20,000
184	Home appliance and power tool repairers	6	51,000	2,800
185	Musical instrument repairers and tuners	6	13,000	800
186	Carpet, floor, and tile installers and finishers	6	138,000	8,300
187	Cement masons, concrete finishers, and terrazzo workers	6	139,000	8,500
188	Machinists and numerical control machine tool programmers	6	434,000	27,000
189	Librarians	5	152,000	7,300
190	Material recording, scheduling, dispatching, and distributing occupations	5	3,957,000	203,000
191	Shipping, receiving, and traffic clerks	5	774,000	36,000
192	Order clerks	5	362,000	17,000
193	Motorcycle, boat, and small-engine mechanics	5	52,000	2,500
194	Plumbers, pipefitters, and steamfitters	5	426,000	22,000
195	Precision assemblers	5	422,000	20,000
196	Butchers and meat, poultry, and fish cutters	5	359,000	19,000
197	Ophthalmic laboratory technicians	5	23,000	1,100
198	Water transportation occupations	5	56,000	2,600
199	Postal clerks and mail carriers	4	631,000	25,000
200	Industrial machinery repairers	4	535,000	24,000
201	Glaziers	4	44,000	1,700
202	Government chief executives and legislators	3	80,000	2,200
203	Insurance underwriters	3	97,000	2,600
204	Dentists	3	160,000	5,000
205	News analysts, reporters, and correspondents	3	67,000	1,900
206	Manufacturers' and wholesale sales representatives ...	3	1,525,000	44,000
207	Metalworking and plastics-working machine operators	3	1,509,000	53,000
208	Air traffic controllers	2	30,000	700
209	Statisticians	2	17,000	400
210	Physicists and astronomers	2	18,000	400
211	Insurance sales agents	2	387,000	8,500
212	Human resources clerks, except payroll and timekeeping	2	142,000	2,900
213	Secretaries	2	3,195,000	63,000
214	Boilermakers	2	18,000	300
215	Records processing occupations	1	3,731,000	44,000
216	Upholsterers	1	66,000	600
217	Dental laboratory technicians	1	44,000	400
218	Printing press operators	0	253,000	1,200

Order of Projected Percent Growth	Occupation	Percent Growth in Employment, 1998-2008	Employment 1998	Numerical Change in Employment, 1998-2008
219	Industrial production managers	-1	208,000	-1,800
220	Millwrights	-2	82,000	-1,500
221	Tool and die makers	-2	138,000	-2,100
222	Electric power generating plant operators and power distributors and dispatchers	-2	45,000	-700
223	Woodworking	-2	372,000	-6,900
224	Forestry, conservation, and logging	-3	120,000	-3,800
225	Inspectors, testers, and graders	-3	689,000	-22,000
226	Petroleum engineers	-4	12,000	-400
227	Announcers	-4	60,000	-2,600
228	Bookkeeping, accounting, and auditing clerks	-4	2,078,000	-81,000
229	Mathematicians	-5	14,000	-800
230	Bank tellers	-5	560,000	-31,000
231	Farm equipment mechanics	-5	49,000	-2,600
232	Payroll and timekeeping clerks	-6	172,000	-11,000
233	Word processors, typists, and data entry keyers	-6	894,000	-54,000
234	Jewelers and precious stone and metal workers	-6	30,000	-1,800
235	Stationary engineers	-6	31,000	-1,800
236	Prepress workers	-6	152,000	-9,400
237	Photographic process workers	-6	63,000	-4,000
238	Rail transportation occupations	-11	85,000	-9,600
239	Farmers and farm managers	-12	1,483,000	-174,000
240	Electronic home entertainment equipment repairers	-12	36,000	-4,300
241	Mining engineers, including mine safety engineers	-13	4,400	-600
242	Communications equipment operators	-15	297,000	-46,000
243	Apparel workers	-17	729,000	-124,000
244	Shoe and leather workers and repairers	-18	23,000	-4,000
245	Private household workers	-19	928,000	-178,000
246	Textile machinery operators	-19	277,000	-53,000
247	Fishers and fishing vessel operators	-22	51,000	-11,000
248	Computer operators	-26	251,000	-64,000
249	Job opportunities in the Armed Forces	(1)	1,238,000	(1)
250	Protestant ministers	(2)	400,000	(2)
251	Rabbis	(2)	5,000	(2)
252	Roman Catholic priests	(2)	47,000	(2)

(1) Projections not available from the Bureau of Labor Statistics
(2) Estimates not available

Here Are Just Some of Our Products!

JIST publishes hundreds of books, videos, software products, and other items. Some of our best-selling career and educational reference books are presented here, followed by an order form. You can also order these books through any bookstore or Internet bookseller's site.

Check out JIST's Web site at www.jist.com for tables of contents and free chapters on these and other products.

Guide for Occupational Exploration, Third Edition

J. Michael Farr; LaVerne L. Ludden, Ed.D., and Laurence Shatkin, Ph.D.

The first major revision since the *GOE* was released in 1979 by the U.S. Department of Labor! It still uses the same approach of exploration based on major interest areas but is updated to reflect the many changes in our labor market. The new *GOE* also uses the recently released O*NET database of occupational information developed by the U.S. Department of Labor. An essential career reference!

ISBN 1-56370-636-9 / Order Code LP-J6369 / **$39.95** Softcover
ISBN 1-56370-826-4 / Order Code LP-J8264 / **$49.95** Hardcover

Occupational Outlook Handbook, 2000-2001 Edition

U.S. Department of Labor

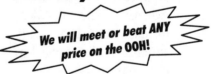

We will meet or beat ANY price on the OOH!

The *Occupational Outlook Handbook* is the most widely used career exploration resource. This is a quality reprint of the government's *OOH*, only at a less-expensive price. It describes 250 jobs–jobs held by almost 90 percent of the U.S. workforce–making it ideal for students, counselors, teachers, librarians, and job seekers. Job descriptions cover the nature of the work, working conditions, training, job outlook, and earnings. Well-written narrative with many charts and photos. New edition every two years.

ISBN 1-56370-676-8 / Order Code LP-J6768 / **$18.95** Softcover
ISBN 1-56370-677-6 / Order Code LP-J6776 / **$22.95** Hardcover

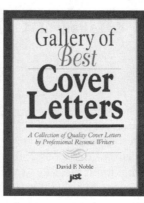

The Federal Resume Guidebook, Second Edition

Kathryn Kraemer Troutman

This resource leads you through the complexities of analyzing job announcements, writing federal resumes for both human and scanner "eyes," and packaging a resume to meet both federal and vacancy announcement criteria. Includes many helpful tips and examples.

ISBN 1-56370-545-1 / Order Code LP-J5451
$21.95

Career Success Is Color-Blind, Second Edition

Overcoming Prejudice and Eliminating Barriers in the Workplace

Ollie Stevenson

A veteran career counselor explains the basic rules of the "Business Mindset" that govern career success in America today. These guidelines have been used effectively by thousands of people to set career paths, move forward, and gain satisfaction at work.

ISBN 1-56370-733-0 / Order Code LP-J7330
$16.95

Quick Internet Guide to Career and Education Information, 2001 Edition

Anne Wolfinger

The author has researched thousands of career, job search, and education sites on the Web and includes only the very best places for solid information and advice. Saves you hours of time and frustration!

ISBN 1-56370-807-8 / Order Code LP-J8078
$16.95

Job Search Handbook for People with Disabilities

Daniel J. Ryan, Ph.D.

This book shows you how to prepare yourself for the overall job search. It helps you to best represent yourself to potential employers and to reassure them that you are a capable worker. Also covers employment laws and how they affect you.

ISBN 1-56370-665-2 / Order Code LP-J6652
$16.95

Young Person's Occupational Outlook Handbook, Third Edition

Compiled by JIST Editors from U.S. government data

Based on the *Occupational Outlook Handbook*, this text is ideal for helping young people explore careers. This book covers 250 jobs–each on one page–held by 85 percent of the workforce. It clusters job descriptions, making it easy to explore job options based on interest. It also makes direct connections between school subjects and the skills needed for jobs.

ISBN 1-56370-731-4 / Order Code LP-J7314
$19.95

The College Majors Handbook

The Actual Jobs, Earnings, and Trends for Graduates of 60 College Majors

Neeta P. Fogg, Paul E. Harrington, and Thomas F. Harrington

Faced with the college decision? This book details what actually happened to more than 15,000 under-graduates from 60 college majors. This is the only college planning guide with the perspective of what actually happened to college undergraduates. It identifies jobs in which the graduates now work and their earnings on those jobs.

ISBN 1-56370-518-4 / Order Code LP-J5184
$24.95

The Kids' College Almanac, Second Edition

A first Look at College

Barbara C. Greenfeld and Robert A. Weinstein

Selected by the New York Public Library as one of the best books for teens and preteens, it provides helpful information about going to college and encourages career and educational planning.

ISBN 1-56370-730-6 / Order Code LP-J7306
$16.95

Health-Care Careers for the 21st Century

Saul Wischnitzer, Ph.D., and Edith Wischnitzer

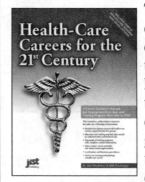

This three-in-one book is a career guidance manual, job description overview, and training program directory. It provides detailed descriptions of over 80 health-care careers, organized into five groups. It lists thousands of training programs with complete contact information. And it offers career guidance on everything from self-assessment to the interview process. Sample resumes and cover letters are included.

ISBN 1-56370-667-9 / Order Code LP-J6679
$24.95

JIST Ordering Information

JIST specializes in publishing the very best results-oriented career and self-directed job search material. Since 1981 we have been a leading publisher in career assessment devices, books, videos, and software. We continue to strive to make our materials the best there are, so that people can stay abreast of what's happening in the labor market, and so they can clarify and articulate their skills and experiences for themselves as well as for prospective employers. **Our products are widely available through your local bookstores, wholesalers, and distributors.**

The World Wide Web

For more occupational or book information, get online and see our Web site at **www.jist.com**. Advance information about new products, services, and training events is continually updated.

Quantity Discounts Available!

Quantity discounts are available for businesses, schools, and other organizations.

The JIST Guarantee

We want you to be happy with everything you buy from JIST. If you aren't satisfied with a product, return it to us within 30 days of purchase along with the reason for the return. Please include a copy of the packing list or invoice to guarantee quick credit to your order.

How to Order

For your convenience, the last page of this book contains an order form.

24-Hour Consumer Order Line:
Call toll free 1-800-648-JIST
Please have your credit card (VISA, MC, or AMEX) information ready!

Mail your order to:

JIST Publishing, Inc.
8902 Otis Avenue
Indianapolis, IN 46216-1033
Fax: Toll free 1-800-JIST-FAX

JIST Order and Catalog Request Form

Purchase Order #: _____ (Required by some organizations)

Billing Information

Organization Name: _____

Accounting Contact: _____

Street Address: _____

_____

_____

City, State, Zip: _____

Phone Number: ( ) _____

Please copy this form if you need more lines for your order.

**Phone: 1-800-648-JIST
Fax: 1-800-JIST-FAX
World Wide Web Address:
http://www.jist.com**

Shipping Information with Street Address (If Different from Above)

Organization Name: _____

Contact: _____

Street Address: (We *cannot* ship to P.O. boxes) _____

_____

_____

City, State, Zip: _____

Phone Number: ( ) _____

Credit Card Purchases: VISA_____ MC_____ AMEX_____

Card Number: _____

Exp. Date: _____

Name As on Card: _____

Signature: _____

Quantity	Order Code	Product Title	Unit Price	Total
	———	**Free JIST Catalog**	**Free**	———
			Subtotal	
			+5% Sales Tax *Indiana Residents*	
			+Shipping / Handling / Ins. (See left)	
			TOTAL	

jist ®
Publishing

**8902 Otis Avenue
Indianapolis, IN 46216**

Shipping / Handling / Insurance Fees

In the continental U.S. add 7% of subtotal:
- Minimum amount charged = $4.00
- Maximum amount charged = $100.00
- FREE shipping and handling on any prepaid orders over $40.00

Above pricing is for regular ground shipment only. For rush or special delivery, call JIST Customer Service at 1-800-648-JIST for the correct shipping fee.

Outside the continental U.S. call JIST Customer Service at 1-800-648-JIST for an estimate of these fees.

Payment in U.S. funds only!

JIST thanks you for your orde